MENTAL ILLNESSES AND TREATMENTS

SCHIZOPHRENIA RESEARCH

RECENT ADVANCES

MENTAL ILLNESSES AND TREATMENTS

Additional books in this series can be found on Nova's website under the Series tab.

Additional e-books in this series can be found on Nova's website under the e-book tab.

MENTAL ILLNESSES AND TREATMENTS

SCHIZOPHRENIA RESEARCH

RECENT ADVANCES

TOMIKI SUMIYOSHI
EDITOR

NOVINKA
New York

Library of Congress Cataloging-in-Publication Data

Schizophrenia research : recent advances / Tomiki Sumiyoshi, editor.
viii, 398 pages : illustrations (some color) ; 27 cm.
Includes bibliographical references and index.
ISBN: 978-1-62808-703-1 (softcover)
1. Schizophrenia. I. Sumiyoshi, Tomiki.
RC514 .S336375 2012
616.89/8

2012472142

Published by Nova Science Publishers, Inc. † New York

CONTENTS

PREFACE

Schizophrenia is a relatively common disease whose lifetime prevalence in general population is reported to be about 1%. From the perspective of public health, the illness has been associated with serious consequences, as indexed by the disability-adjusted life year. Besides psychotic symptoms, schizophrenia is characterized by disturbances of cognitive function, which is considered to largely determine outcome of patients. The neural and genetic substrates underlying its pathophysiology have not been fully demarcated, posing a challenge for the development of breakthrough therapeutics.

This edited book, "Schizophrenia Research: Recent Advances," provides the key information about the latest endeavor to solve these difficulties characterizing this enigmatic disease.

Social and physical well-being of patients should be facilitated by a range of perspectives, including symptoms and underlying mechanisms, as well as attitudes of caregivers toward treatment. *Chapter 1* by Shoji Tanaka proposes a neural circuit model that integrates anatomical and neurochemical substrates responsible for the generation of psychotic symptoms. Jitsuki Sawamura, Shigeru Morishita, and Jun Ishigooka, in *Chapter 2*, discuss some concerns on a frequently used measure of psychotic symptoms, and seek to improve the rating method in order to better evaluate outcome. In *Chapter 3*, Anna Galuppi, Maria Cristina Turola, and Paola Mazzoni report the importance of social cognition and quality of life based on data from a sizable number of patients at a mental health facility in the community. A meta-analysis of natural-mortality in schizophrenia is conducted by Carmen Bouza, Teresa López-Cuadrado, Zuleika Saz-Parkinson, Raimundo Alcázar Alcázar, and José María Amate Blanco, as described in *Chapter 4*. Setsuko Hanzawa, Kayomi Yatabe, Goro Tanaka, and Yoshibumi Nakane in *Chapter 5* investigate the beliefs of psychiatric nurses about the treatability of schizophrenia, and suggest the need for an educational program to enhance their ability to support patients. (*Section I: Phenomenology, epidemiology, and conceptual issues*).

Progress is eminent also in the pursuit of the etiology, intermediate phenotypes, and biomarkers of schizophrenia, by means of a variety of research modalities. In *Chapter 6*, Gianluca Serafini, Maurizio Pompili, Marco Innamorati, Gloria Giordano, Roberto Tatarelli, and Paolo Girardi provide a review of this issue in relation to early intervention of psychosis. Specifically, the brain imaging study by Xiaobo Li and Lynn E. Delisi (*Chapter 7*) demonstrate abnormalities in the white matter regions governing language-processing both in patients with schizophrenia and genetically high-risk people. Regarding cognitive endophenotypes, Jamie K. Opper, Patrick Monnier, and Deana Davalos provide a review of visual processing deficits in schizophrenia, a potential new target for intervention (*Chapter 8*). Emotional disturbances are addressed in *Chapter 9* by Roelie J. Hempel, Hugo G. van Steenis, Nico J.M. van Beveren, Christian H. Roder, and Joke H.M. Tulen, suggesting a specific focus on sexual needs and expectations of patients. *Chapters 10 and 11* address a role for the aberrant immune system in the gene-environment epigenetic interplay that has been suggested to underline the pathogenesis of schizophrenia. Thus, Aren Khoyetsyan, Anna Boyajyan, and Roksana Zakharyan report an association of the illness with dysregulation of the inflammation/autoimmune system, based on altered activities of the complement cascade, cytokines network, and so on. (*Section II: Neuropsychobiological insights*)

The search for novel therapeutics, with the feedback from basic science, should be directed toward the enhancement of social function, both in pharmacological and non-pharmacological paradigms. *Chapter 12* by Alessandro De Risio emphasizes the importance of social cognition as a mediator for improving long-term outcome in patients treated with antipsychotic drugs. Tereza Nekovarova, Ales Stuchlik, Karel Vales, Lukas Rambousek, and Tomiki Sumiyoshi, *in Chapter 13,* introduce new methods to effectively evaluate impaired spatial perception in rodent models of schizophrenia for the discovery of novel cognition enhancers. Much attention is paid to the role for serotonin (5-HT) receptor subtypes in the development of novel compounds to gain cognitive benefits, as discussed by Yukihiro Ohno, Ayata Tatara, Saki Shimizu, and Masashi Sasa in *Chapter 14*. Specifically, Adrian Newman-Tancredi and Paul R. Albert provide a view that stimulation of $5\text{-}HT_{1A}$ receptors constitutes promising personalized pharmacotherapies for negative and cognitive symptoms, based on pharmacogenetics studies on these receptors (*Chapter 15*). For the treatment of negative symptoms resistant to existing antipsychotics, Radovan Prikryl, Libor Ustohal, and Hana Prikrylova-Kucerova in *Chapter 16* proposes repetitive transcranial magnetic stimulation as a potential augmentation tool. (*Section III: Strategies for novel therapeutics*)

When the editorial process of this book was launched, East Japan had been hit by the great earthquake. Due to its geographical location, my country is prone to suffer from periodic relapses of the natural disaster. Schizophrenia may occur in subjects with certain vulnerability, but they can be rescued through collaborative support by dedicated neighbors. It is just like our continued efforts can overcome the difficulties in the affected areas in Tohoku.

Tomiki Sumiyoshi,
Editor,
Toyama, Japan

SECTION I

PHENOMENOLOGY, EPIDEMIOLOGY AND CONCEPTUAL ISSUES

In: Schizophrenia Research: Recent Advances
Editor: Tomiki Sumiyoshi
ISBN: 978-1-62808-703-1

Chapter 1

A MODEL-BASED APPROACH TO SCHIZOPHRENIA RESEARCH

Shoji Tanaka*

Department of Information and Communication Sciences,
Sophia University, Tokyo, Japan

ABSTRACT

There is an increasing demand for the integration of clinical and pre-clinical data to construct useful models for understanding mental illnesses. This chapter proposes a system model as a "platform" into which experimental data can be incorporated. This model consists primarily of two modules: a neural circuit model, which contains the dorsolateral prefrontal cortex (DLPFC) and the striatum with dopaminergic innervations, and a receptor binding model. The circuit model of the DLPFC is consistent with previous computational model developed by the author. The receptor binding model can incorporate the results from receptor imaging studies. A stability analysis with the third module (a control system model) suggests that hypodopaminergic transmission in the DLPFC causes instability of the dynamics of the DLPFC circuit. This instability is due to the switch from a stable, *negative* feedback scheme to an unstable, *positive* feedback scheme in the mesocortical dopaminergic system. By contrast, increasing the dopamine (DA) level in the DLPFC increases the stability of the DLPFC circuit. This model predicts that an increase in the DA level in the DLPFC would reduce the large variability of DLPFC activation that has frequently been observed in patients with schizophrenia. This output would be a novel way to test the DA hypothesis of schizophrenia (the hypodopaminergia of the DLPFC). By using the binding potential data of striatal DA D2 receptors, the system model also predicts that patients with lower DLPFC activity will have a better clinical response to treatment with antipsychotic medication. Further analyses of available experimental data within this framework would make this model more practical in investigating schizophrenia and other psychiatric diseases.

---

* Shoji Tanaka, PhD; Department of Information and Communication Sciences; Sophia University; 7-1 Kioicho, Chiyoda-ku, Tokyo 102-8554, Japan; Phone: +81-3-3238-3331; Fax: +81-3-3238-3321; E-mail: tanaka-s@sophia.ac.jp.

Keywords: Cognitive; computational model; dynamics; neuroimaging; positron emission tomography

INTRODUCTION

There is an increasing demand for the integration of clinical and pre-clinical data to construct useful models of mental illnesses. However, it is apparent that simply building a large database of many experimental studies is not useful. A platform into which experimental data from multiple studies can be incorporated is needed. A circuitry-based system model is one of the candidates for such a platform because virtually all mental illnesses can be regarded as diseases with abnormalities in the dynamics and architecture of the neural circuits of the brain. Mental functions emerge as a collective interaction among numerous neurons, and this interaction is constrained by neurocircuitry. The abnormalities in the neurocircuitry of patients with mental illnesses could be partly attributable to genetic factors. Neurochemical disturbances may also underlie the abnormalities in circuit dynamics. Brain dysfunction is a consequence of such abnormalities. Therefore, research on mental illnesses requires a neural circuit perspective [1,2,3,4]. This chapter will propose a system model that is based on the circuitry of the brain.

The dopamine (DA) hypothesis has long been the cornerstone of research on schizophrenia; however, it has not yet provided a satisfactory explanation for the pathogenesis of schizophrenia [5,6,7]. One of the reasons for this uncertainty is that there has been little convincing evidence for the consequences of DA dysfunction [7]. A neural circuit perspective may be useful in finding the missing link. Recently, it has been proposed that a circuit perspective of schizophrenia could account for experimental observations that lack clear explanations [8]. This proposal is based on computational studies of the abnormalities in the dorsolateral prefrontal cortex (DLPFC) circuit of patients with schizophrenia. The computational studies showed that the stability of the DLPFC circuit depended on the DA level in the DLPFC. Under hypodopaminergic conditions in the DLPFC, the circuit loses its stability and DLPFC activity fluctuates greatly. One consequence of this instability, for example, would be high test-retest variability of functional magnetic resonance imaging (fMRI) data. This variability has been observed in patients with schizophrenia in brain regions associated with cognition (the DLPFC, the intraparietal sulcus, and the insula) but not in other regions, such as motor and premotor cortical areas [9]. A large fluctuation of symptoms of schizophrenia during the course of the disease would also result from this type of circuit instability [4]. A system model with a circuit perspective links abnormal brain activity with neurochemical disturbances. This chapter will illustrate the usefulness of this model.

Receptor imaging by positron emission tomography (PET) or single-photon emission computed tomography (SPECT) has emerged as a useful tool for investigating neurochemical abnormalities in the brains of patients with psychiatric diseases. Extensive effort has been spent investigating dopaminergic dysregulation in the brains of patients with schizophrenia. Several, but not all, studies have detected increased DA levels in the striatum of patients with schizophrenia [10,11]. Abnormalities in D1 receptor availability have not been detected in the striatum of patients with schizophrenia [12,13,14]. Receptor imaging studies have observed alterations in D1 receptor availability in the DLPFCs of patients [12,14]. PET studies using levodopa (L-DOPA) or fluorodopa (F-DOPA) have suggested that DA synthesis is elevated within the striatum as well as in the medial PFC in patients with schizophrenia, although there is less consistency in the latter finding [15,16,17,18,19,20]. Studies of dopamine transporter (DAT) binding in the striatum have found no difference between schizophrenia patients and healthy controls [21,22,23,24,25], but other studies have reported a decrease in striatal DAT binding in patients [26,27]. Interestingly, a later study reported a significant correlation between DAT and D2 receptor binding potentials (BPs) in patients and an inverse correlation between DAT and D2 receptor BPs and the extent of positive symptoms [28]. Although some findings are inconsistent, these receptor imaging studies can provide useful information on the parameters of the system model. Fortunately, practical radioligand pharmacokinetic models are available [29,30]. Therefore, the system model will be able to incorporate a receptor binding model.

METHODS

Framework of the System Model

The framework of the system model is illustrated in Figure 1. The core of this model is a neural circuit model, which is based on the neurocircuitry of the brain and can simulate the dynamics of a part of the brain system. The circuit model is combined with a receptor binding model to incorporate receptor imaging data. Both models will be used to analyze the relationship between dysregulated regional activities and neurochemical disturbances. A control system model, the third module, will be used to analyze the dynamics of the circuit model. The results from these modules will then be associated with macroscopic brain functions, such as cognitive performance, and with symptoms of psychiatric diseases.

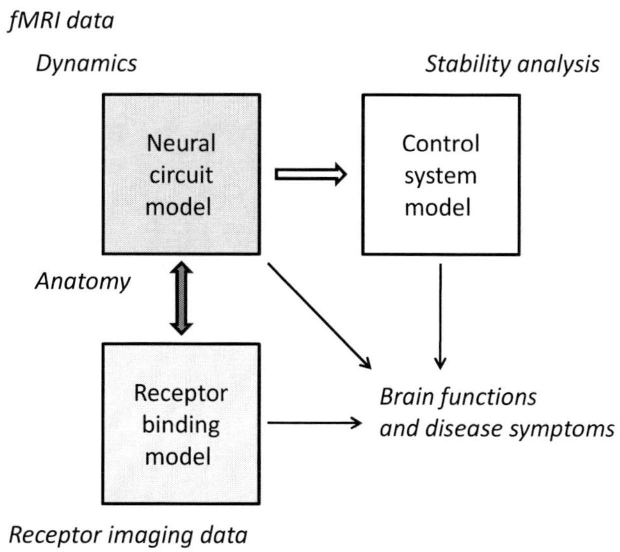

Figure 1. The framework of the system model proposed in this chapter.

Dorsolateral Prefrontal Cortex

A schematic diagram of the model of the DLPFC with dopaminergic innervation is shown in Figure 2. Pyramidal neurons in the DLPFC send axons to DA neurons, and the mesocortical dopaminergic system innervates the DLPFC. The closed-loop circuitry has been confirmed anatomically and physiologically in rodents [31,32,33]. In primates, cortical projection to midbrain DA neurons might be polysynaptic [34]. The DLPFC could, therefore, influence the activity of midbrain DA neurons. DA released from the DA neurons modulates the activity of DLPFC neurons. The closed-loop circuitry plays a critical role in the regulation of DLPFC activity and DA release in the DLPFC [8,35].

For the circuit model of the DLPFC, we introduce here the state variables: the population activity of the pyramidal neurons x_p and the population activity of the interneurons x_n. These variables obey the following differential equations:

$$\begin{aligned} \frac{dx_p}{dt} &= -\frac{x_p}{\tau_p} + W_{pp}(z) f(x_p) - W_{np} f(x_n) + I_{cue} \\ \frac{dx_n}{dt} &= -\frac{x_n}{\tau_n(z)} + W_{pn}(z) f(x_p) - W_{nn} f(x_n) \end{aligned} \quad (1)$$

where τ_p and τ_n are the time constants of the pyramidal neurons and the interneurons, respectively, W_{ij} $(i, j = p, n)$ is the synaptic efficacy of the projection from population i to j, I_{cue} is the transient external input that mimics the cue input for working memory formation [8], and $f(x)$ is the activation function, which is given by

$$f(x) = \begin{cases} \tanh(x) & x \geq 0 \\ 0 & x < 0 \end{cases} \quad (2)$$

This activation function is assumed to be common to both populations of neurons. The parameters that are functions of z are subject to dopaminergic modulation via D1 receptors, where z is the D1 receptor activation level. The activation of D1 receptors affects the conductance of ion channels, such as N-methyl-D-aspartic acid (NMDA), α-amino-3-hydroxyl-5-methyl-4-isoxazole-propionate (AMPA), and potassium, thereby changing the efficacy of glutamatergic signal transmission, W_{pp} and W_{pn}, and the time constant of the interneurons, τ_n [8]. These are described by

$$\begin{aligned} W_{pp}(z) &= W_{pp}(0)(1 + az) \\ W_{pn}(z) &= W_{pn}(0)(1 + bz) \\ \tau_n(z) &= \tau_n(0)(1 + cz) \end{aligned} \quad (3)$$

where a, b and c are constants.

The DLPFC influences the activity of the DA neurons in the midbrain. The dynamics of the dopaminergic system obey the following set of equations [8]:

$$\frac{dx_d}{dt} = -\frac{x_d}{\tau_d} + W_{pd} f(x_p) + I_{phasic} + I_{tonic}$$
$$\frac{dy_p}{dt} = -\frac{y_p}{\tau_y} + W_{dy} f(x_d) \tag{4}$$

where x_d is the population activity of the DA neurons, τ_d is the time constant of the DA neurons, W_{pd} is the strength of the projection from the DLPFC to the DA neurons, I_{phasic} and I_{tonic} are the phasic and tonic inputs to the DA neurons, y_p is the DA release in the DLPFC, τ_y is the time constant of the DA release, and W_{dy} is the DA releasability, which refers to the efficiency of the DA release from the DA neurons.

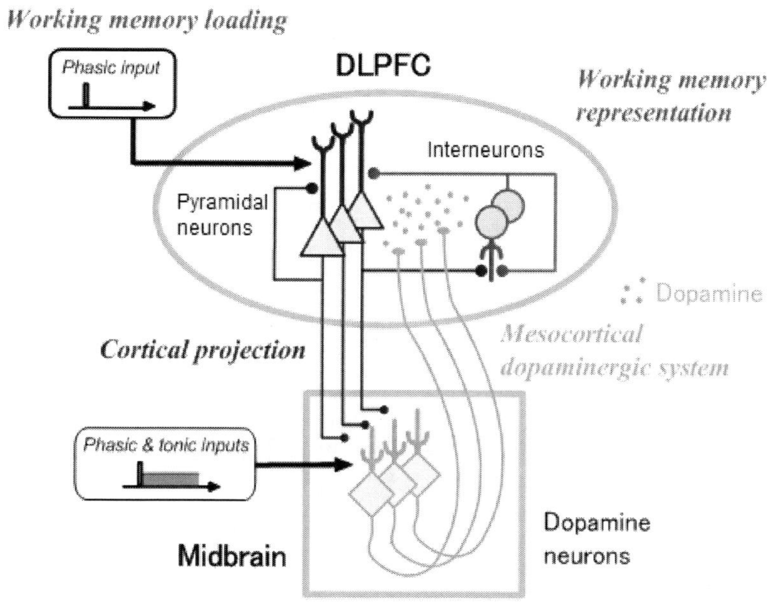

Figure 2. A schematic diagram of the model. The DLPFC contains pyramidal neurons and GABAergic interneurons, which are reciprocally connected and also have self-innervations. Pyramidal neurons in the DLPFC send axons to midbrain DA neurons, and the mesocortical dopaminergic system innervates the DLPFC. In the DLPFC, DA modulates the activities of both populations of neurons via D1 receptors. The phasic input to the pyramidal neurons (I_{cue} in Equation 1) triggers the dynamics of the circuit. The phasic and tonic inputs to the DA neurons ($I_{phasic} + I_{tonic}$ in Equation 4) evoke the activity of the DA neurons, and the subsequent DA release, which mimics that observed experimentally [67]. Note, however, that it is the glutamatergic input through the cortical projection that regulates the DA release from the axon terminals in this closed-loop circuit model.

Prefrontostriatal System

Neural Circuit Model

The model prefrontostriatal system consists of the following three brain regions: the PFC, the striatum, and the substantia nigra (SN) (Figure 3). The PFC projects to the striatum, and the striatum projects to the SN. The nigrostriatal dopaminergic system innervates the striatum. The dynamics of the population activities of the striatum and the SN and the DA release in the striatum are given by

$$\frac{dx_s}{dt} = -\frac{x_s}{\tau_s} + W_{ps} f(x_p)$$
$$\frac{dx_d}{dt} = -\frac{x_d}{\tau_d} - W_{sd} f(x_s) + I_{phasic} + I_{tonic} \quad (5)$$
$$\frac{dy_s}{dt} = -\frac{y_s}{\tau_y} + W_{dy} f(x_d)$$

where x_s is the population activity of the striatal neurons, τ_s is the time constant of the striatal neurons, W_{ps} is the synaptic efficacy of the prefrontostriatal projection, W_{sd} is the synaptic efficacy of the projection from the striatum to the SN, and y_s is the DA release in the striatum.

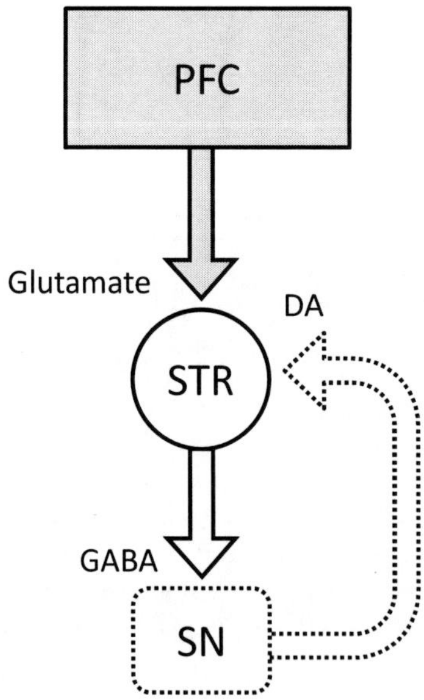

Figure 3. Diagram of the prefrontostriatal system. The prefrontostriatal projection is glutamatergic and the projection from the striatum (STR) to the substantia nigra (SN) is GABAergic. The DA neurons in the SN innervate the STR.

Receptor Binding

The BP of D2 receptors is given by [36]

$$BP = \frac{B_{\max}}{K_d\left(1+\frac{[DA]}{K_{DA}}\right)} \tag{6}$$

where $B_{\max}$ is the density of D2 receptors, K_d is the dissociation constant of a radiotracer at D2 receptors, $[DA]$ is the free DA concentration in the synapse, and K_{DA} is the dissociation constant of DA at D2 receptors. The occupancy of D2 receptors by DA is given by

$$P = \frac{[DA]}{K_{DA}+[DA]} \tag{7}$$

RESULTS

Equilibrium State of the DLPFC Circuit

Using Equations 1-4, one can simulate the dynamics of the DLPFC circuit with dopaminergic modulation. One example [8] showed the state transitions of the DLPFC circuit to a stable fixed point, indicating stability under normal conditions. Under hypodopaminergic conditions, however, the DLPFC circuit loses its stability. The dynamics of the DLPFC circuit, therefore, qualitatively change with the DA level in the DLPFC. Figure 4 illustrates how the circuit dynamics change with DA releasability. The inverted-U shaped curve is represented by a parabola in Figure 4. This curve is actually determined by the steady-state condition of Equation 1, which is

$$\begin{aligned} x_p &= \tau_p[W_{pp}(z)f(x_p) - W_{np}f(x_n)] \\ x_n &= \tau_n(z)[W_{pn}(z)f(x_p) - W_{nn}f(x_n)] \end{aligned} \tag{8}$$

The above equations are rewritten as

$$\begin{aligned} x_p &= \tau_p[W_{pp}(z)f(x_p) - W_{np}f[\tau_n(z)\{[W_{pn}(z) - \frac{W_{nn}}{W_{np}}W_{pp}(z)]f(x_p) + \frac{W_{nn}}{\tau_p W_{np}}x_p\}]] \\ x_n &= \tau_n(z)[W_{pn}(z)f[\tau_p\{\frac{W_{pp}(z)}{\tau_n(z)W_{pn}}x_n + [\frac{W_{nn}}{W_{pn}}W_{pp}(z) - W_{np}]f(x_n)\}] - W_{nn}f(x_n)] \end{aligned} \tag{9}$$

From Equation 4, the steady-state of the dopaminergic system is given by

$$x_d = \tau_d [W_{pd} f(x_p) + I_{tonic}]$$
$$y_p = \tau_y W_{dy} f(x_d) \qquad (10)$$

The D1 receptor activation depends on the DA release; i.e., $z = z_{\max} f(y_p)$, where $z_{\max}$ is a constant. Because the DA release is related to the population activity of the pyramidal neurons by Equation 10, the D1 receptor activation is then related to the population activity of the pyramidal neurons by

$$z = z_{\max} f[\tau_y W_{dy} f\{\tau_d [W_{pd} f(x_p) + I_{tonic}]\}] \qquad (11)$$

This $x_p - z$ relationship is actually represented by a slightly bending curve. In Figure 4, it is drawn simply by the following straight line: $x_p = a(z - z_0)$, which is a linear approximation of Equation 11. The prefronto-mesoprefrontal system is in equilibrium when both of the steady-state conditions are satisfied. This state is given by the point where the inverted-U shaped curve for the DLPFC and the straight line for the DA system intersect. The point is called a "fixed point". In the figure, small circles and triangles are fixed points. However, only the right ones in each pair are stable; the left ones are always unstable (Figure 4). Unless the DLPFC is extremely hypodopaminergic, the inverted-U shaped curve and the straight line for the DA system intersect, and the system operates around the stable fixed point (a circle on the inverted-U shaped curve). A disturbance applied to this system could change the state of the system only transiently and the state would return to its fixed point because it is stable; that is, the system works as a regulator. This characteristic means that DLPFC activity and the DA level in the DLPFC are automatically maintained at certain levels. By contrast, there is no fixed point but the origin under extremely hypodopaminergic conditions, which means that the DLPFC can no longer maintain its activity.

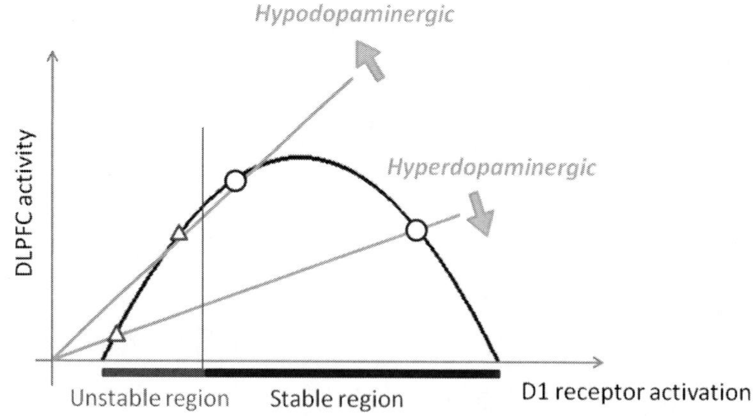

Figure 4. Two pairs of fixed points on the inverted-U shaped curve for hypodopaminergic and hyperdopaminergic conditions. The right fixed point of each pair (circle) is always a stable fixed point, whereas the left one (triangle) is always an unstable fixed point. A set of the unstable fixed points defines the unstable region.

Control System Model

The stability of the DLPFC circuit can be analyzed by a conventional mathematical method [37]. In this section, we will use an alternative method to illustrate how the system becomes unstable under hypodopaminergic conditions. To do this, we introduce a control system model (Figure 5A). In this model, the dynamical characteristic of the DLPFC is represented simply by a first-order transfer function, $G(s) = 1/(s + 1)$, where s is the Laplace variable [38]. The feedback loop represents the mesocortical dopaminergic system. The feedback gain, K, represents the DA action, which varies with the DA level in the DLPFC. Due to the nonlinear interactions of DA with glutamate as well as with gamma-aminobutyric acid (GABA) in the circuit, which produce the inverted-U shaped characteristic, the feedback gain, K, is positive in the left half of the inverted-U shaped curve and is negative in the right half [8]. Here, we assume that K is proportional to the gradient of the curve. This assumption means that, if the inverted-U shaped curve has the form of $y = 1-(x-1)^2$ ($0 \le x \le 2$, with the peak at x = 1), the feedback gain is given by $K = dy/dx = -2(x-1)$ ($K > 0$ for $0 \le x \le 1$). According to control theory [38], the transfer function of the whole system (the DLPFC and the mesocortical dopaminergic system) is given by

$$T(s) = \frac{G(s)}{1-KG(s)} = \frac{1}{s+1-K} \tag{12}$$

This transfer function takes DA action into account, so that it contains the feedback gain K.

Stability Analysis

From Equation 12, the characteristic equation of this system is given by $s+1-K=0$. This equation has the solution of $s = K-1$, which is the characteristic root and is also called the pole of this system. The condition of this system being stable is $s < 0$, which gives $K < 1$. This system works as a *negative* feedback control system when the feedback gain is negative (in the region filled with light blue in Figure 5B). An increase in DLPFC activity increases the population activity of the DA neurons, thereby increasing the DA release in the DLPFC. This release decreases the neuronal activity of the DLPFC because the feedback gain is negative. At the tip of the inverted-U shaped curve, the negative feedback gain becomes zero. The feedback gain becomes positive in the hypodopaminergic region (i.e., the left half of the inverted-U shaped curve) and, thus, turns into a *positive* feedback system. Interestingly, however, the positive feedback system is stable when $0 < K < 1$, and the stability limit is given by $K = 1$. The unstable region, where $K > 1$, lies to the left of this critical point (i.e., the region filled with magenta in Figure 5B). In classical control theory [38], stability is associated with the location of the pole of the system ($s = K-1$) on the s plane (Figure 5C).

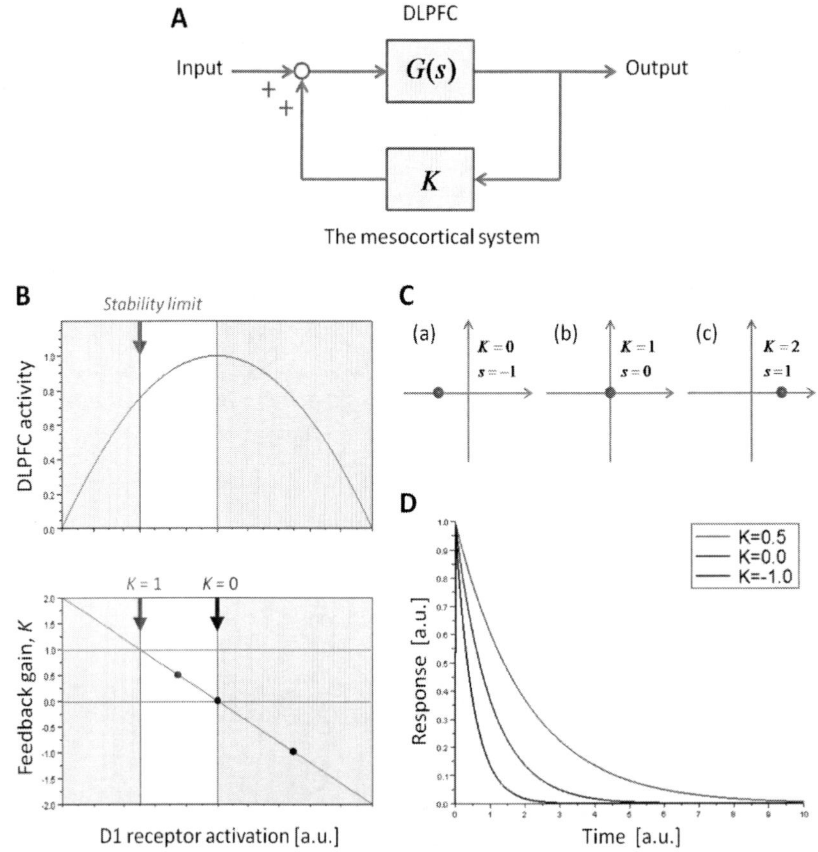

Figure 5. Control system analysis. A: Block diagram of a simple closed-loop or feedback control system, which explains how DA regulates the dynamics of the DLPFC circuit. The transfer function, G(s), represents the dynamical characteristic of the DLPFC circuit. The feedback loop represents the mesocortical dopaminergic system, and the feedback gain, *K*, represents the DA action in the DLPFC. When the feedback gain is negative ($K < 0$), this system works as a negative feedback control system. B: The relationship between the inverted-U shaped curve and the feedback gain. The stability limit is given by $K = 1$. C: Pole placement in the complex plane (the s plane) with different *K* values. (a) When the pole of the system is located in the left half, the system is stable. (b) When the pole is located on the imaginary axis (the *y* axis), the system is marginally stable. (c) When the pole is located in the right half, the system is unstable. D: Impulse responses of this system (red: $K = 0.5$, blue: $K = 0$, black: $K = -1.0$).

Processing Speed

Prolonged reaction times have been consistently observed in patients with schizophrenia [9,39,40,41]. Figure 6 compares the reaction times between patients and healthy controls in a choice reaction time task [9]. In the control system model, the time constant of the DLPFC circuit with the mesocortical dopaminergic system is given by $\tau = 1/(1-K)$ from Equation 12. The time constant determines the response time of the circuit to an input, so it would be a measure of reaction time or processing speed. Interestingly, the time constant is an increasing function of *K* as long as $K < 1$. Figure 5D shows the impulse responses of this system with different feedback gains (K = -1.0, 0, 0.5). The time constants are τ = 0.5, 1.0, and 2.0 [a.u.], respectively. Because K decreases with DA level, the time constant becomes shorter as the DA level is increased, suggesting that reaction time is a monotonically decreasing function of the DA level. In the unstable region, where $K > 1$, the circuit would no longer be able to process incoming information properly.

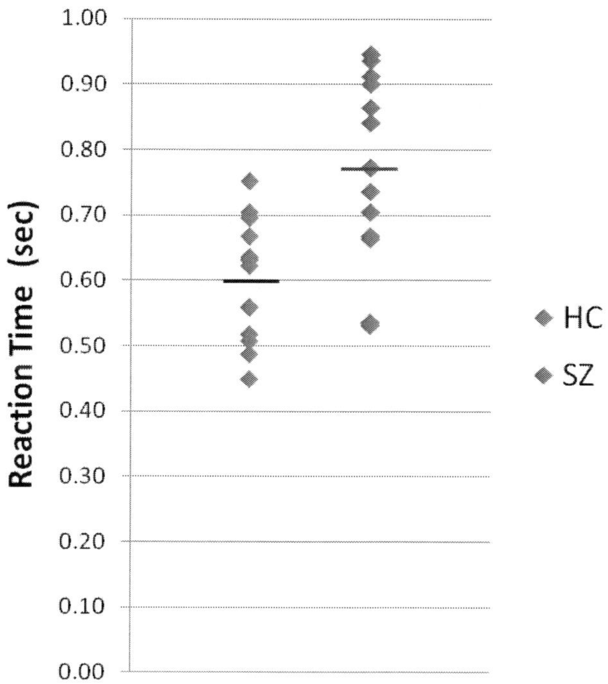

Figure 6. Reaction times in a choice reaction time task (HC: 0.60 ± 0.09 sec, SZ: 0.77 ± 0.14 sec, $p < 0.001$). Reproduced from [9].

Cognitive Performance

In contrast to the activity of the DLPFC, cognitive performance consistently declines under hypodopaminergic conditions. Figure 7 shows the 3-back task performance of healthy subjects and schizophrenia patients versus the DLPFC D1 receptor BP, which has been reproduced from a study [12]. The data were fitted to the second-order polynomial: $y = -0.25x^2 + 0.38x + 0.66\ (R^2 = 0.41)$. In this case, y is the adjusted hit rate (AHR) in the 3-back task and x is the BP of D1 receptors in the DLPFC. We thus obtained the regression model: $AHR = 0.80 - 0.25(BP - 0.75)^2$. A small change in the BP, ΔBP, leads to a change in the cognitive performance AHR as $\Delta AHR = -0.5(BP - 0.75)\Delta BP$. Because the BPs of patients with schizophrenia are larger than 1.0, this regression model gives $\Delta AHR / \Delta BP$ < 0. This relationship means that D1 agonists, which cause ΔBP to be < 0, improve the task performance in patients with schizophrenia (because ΔAHR > 0). By contrast, D1 antagonists (causing $\Delta BP > 0$) would decrease the task performance in patients (because $\Delta AHR < 0$).

Prefrontostriatal System

The dynamics of the nigrostriatal dopaminergic system are likely to differ from those of the mesocortical system. The former seems to be an intrinsically negative feedback system because of GABAergic projection neurons in the striatum. The negative feedback system is essentially stable, so that, from an engineering point of view, it is suited for the regulation of DA release in the striatum. Unlike the DLPFC, the striatum does not seem to have complex nonlinear interactions [42]; the striatal DA level would be controlled by the inputs from other brain regions, such as the PFC. This suggests that appropriate levels of input can normally maintain the DA level. In other words, once the input strength varies, the striatal DA level can easily deviate from the normal level.

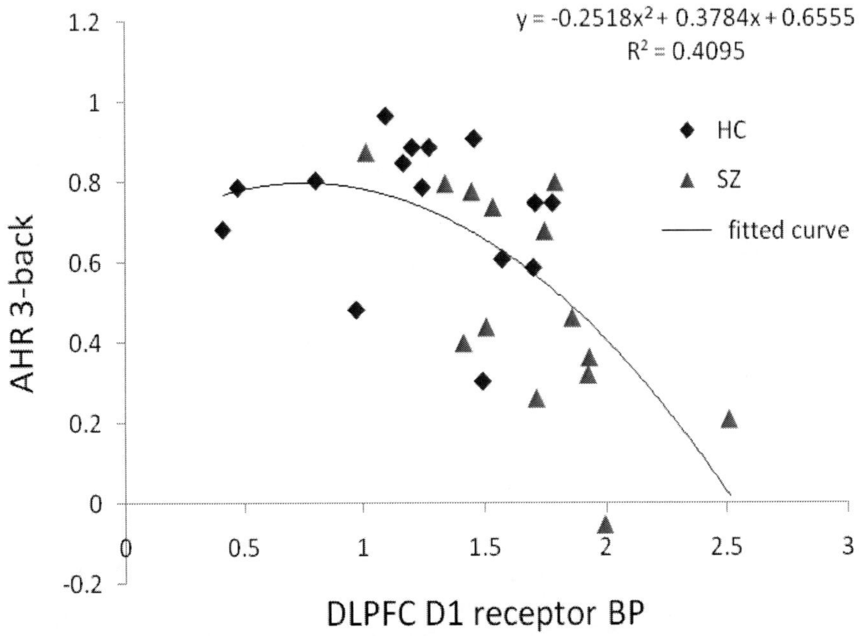

Figure 7. Relationship between the 3-back task performance (AHR: adjusted hit rate) and [^{11}C]NNC112 BP in the DLPFC. Reproduced from Figure 7 of [12]. The data are fitted to the regression curve: $AHR = 0.80 - 0.25(BP - 0.75)^2 \quad (R^2 = 0.41)$. This curve has the peak at $BP = 0.75$. All of the BPs of the patients were > 1.0, whereas the BPs of the controls were distributed across $BP = 0.75$. Note that the BP is higher when the synaptic concentration of DA is lower.

Equilibrium State of the Prefrontostriatal System

From Equation 5, the equilibrium state of the prefrontostriatal system with dopaminergic innervation is given by

$$\frac{x_s}{\tau_s} = W_{ps} f(x_p)$$

$$\frac{x_d}{\tau_d} = I_{tonic} - W_{sd} f(x_s) \tag{13}$$

$$\frac{y_s}{\tau_y} = W_{dy} f(x_d)$$

Using the linear approximation of the activation function $f(x) \approx x$ and introducing new variables: $X_p \equiv \tau_s \tau_d \tau_y W_{ps} W_{sd} W_{dy} x_p / K_{DA}$, $X_s \equiv \tau_d \tau_y W_{sd} W_{dy} x_s / K_{DA}$, $X_d \equiv \tau_y W_{dy} x_d / K_{DA}$, $I_d \equiv \tau_d \tau_y W_{dy} I_{tonic} / K_{DA}$, and $Y \equiv y_s / K_{DA}$, we rewrite the above equations as

$$X_s = X_p$$
$$X_d = I_d - X_s \tag{14}$$
$$Y = X_d$$

The variables have the physiological constraint that all of them are positive ($X_p, X_s, X_d, Y > 0$). From the above equations, we obtain the relationship between the normalized DA release in the striatum, *Y*, and the normalized PFC activity, X_p, as

$$Y = 1 - X_p \tag{15}$$

where we assumed $I_d = 1$ for simplicity. This equation shows a simple reciprocal relationship between striatal DA release and PFC activity. The above equations do not take into account the effects of D2 receptor activation on the state variables. The analysis of these effects has been reported in a separate article [43].

Receptor Occupancy

Equations 6 and 7 give the expressions that relate the relative change in the BP, $\Delta BP / BP$, with the change in the synaptic DA concentration, ΔY, and with the change in the DA occupancy, ΔP, as

$$\frac{\Delta BP}{BP} = -\frac{\Delta Y}{1+Y} = -(1+Y)\Delta P \tag{16}$$

where $Y \equiv [DA]/K_{DA}$ is the baseline synaptic DA concentration normalized by the dissociation constant. The change in the synaptic DA concentration and the change in the DA occupancy are then estimated using the above equation when the baseline synaptic DA concentration is known. In receptor imaging studies, the baseline synaptic DA concentration is provided by DA depletion experiments.

Alpha-methyl-p-tyrosine (AMPT), a competitive and reversible inhibitor of tyrosine hydroxylase, significantly reduces the concentration of endogenous DA [10,36]. Comparing the BPs, given by Equation 6, before and after the administration of AMPT, we have

$$\frac{BP_{AMPT}}{BP} = \frac{1+Y}{1+Y_{AMPT}} = \frac{1+Y}{1+\alpha Y} \tag{17}$$

where BP_{AMPT} is the BP after AMPT, BP is the BP before AMPT, $Y_{AMPT} \equiv \alpha Y$ $(\alpha < 1)$ is the normalized DA concentration after AMPT, and α is the rate of residual DA after AMPT. Equation 17 is rewritten as

$$Y = \frac{\dfrac{BP_{AMPT}}{BP} - 1}{1 - \alpha \dfrac{BP_{AMPT}}{BP}} \tag{18}$$

In the above equations, we assumed that the D2 receptor density, $B_{\max}$, did not change upon acute administration of AMPT. This assumption has been confirmed in rats [36] but not in humans. In patients with schizophrenia, however, there is no reason for the receptor density, $B_{\max}$, to be the same as that of healthy controls. Therefore, we distinguish the receptor density of patients with schizophrenia (SZ) from that of healthy controls (HC) using $B_{\max,SZ}$ and $B_{\max,HC}$, respectively. Similarly, the synaptic DA concentration differs between patients and healthy controls. The ratio of the BP of patients to that of healthy controls is then given by

$$\frac{BP_{SZ}}{BP_{HC}} = \frac{B_{\max,SZ}}{B_{\max,HC}} \frac{1+Y_{HC}}{1+Y_{SZ}} \tag{19}$$

for both before and after AMPT, where $Y_{HC} \equiv [DA]_{HC}/K_{DA}$ and $Y_{SZ} \equiv [DA]_{SZ}/K_{DA}$. The dissociation constant of DA, K_{DA}, is also assumed to be unchanged in schizophrenia patients. The baseline D2 occupancies in healthy subjects and patients with schizophrenia are thus estimated from the PET/SPECT imaging results (Table 1).

Table 1. Baseline D2 receptor occupancies and B_{max} ratios, if available, in the striatum as estimated from receptor imaging studies with DA depletion

DA depletion	D2 occupancy		B_{max} ratio	Radiotracer	Study
	HC	SZ			
0.30	13%	23%	1.17	[^{123}I]IBZM	SPECT [10]
0.30	13%	18%	1.09	[^{11}C]raclopride	PET [63]
0.30	29%	-	-	[^{123}I]IBZM	SPECT [36]
0.29	13%	-	-	[^{18}F]fallypride	PET [64]
0.29	22%	-	-	[^{11}C]raclopride	PET [65]
0.30	-	39%	-	[^{123}I]IBZM	SPECT [66]

We used the values of DA depletion from the literature, if available, or otherwise assumed values to be 0.30, which corresponds to the depletion of 70% of the DA. The B_{max} ratio is defined by the ratio of the B_{max} of the patient group to that of the healthy controls.

Amphetamine Challenge

Acute administration of amphetamine increases DA release. Receptor imaging studies have measured the effect of amphetamine administration on the BP of D2 receptors in the striatum [44,45,46,47,48]; these results are summarized in Table 2. From Equation 16, we have the relationship between the relative change in the BP as a result of amphetamine administration, $\Delta BP / BP$, and the normalized synaptic concentrations of DA before and after amphetamine, Y and Y', respectively, as

$$\frac{\Delta BP}{BP} = \frac{Y - Y'}{1 + Y'} \tag{20}$$

Using the results from the only study that has performed both DA depletion and amphetamine administration [45], we estimated the free synaptic concentrations of DA and the D2 receptor occupancies in the striatum before and after amphetamine administration for both healthy controls and patients with schizophrenia (Table 3).

Table 2. Percent changes in the BP of striatal D2 receptors after amphetamine challenge

ΔBP/BP		Amphetamine	Radiotracer	Study
HC	SZ			
-7.1%	-13.8%	0.3 mg/kg i.v.	[^{123}I]IBZM	SPECT [44]
-10%	-18%	0.3 mg/kg i.v.	[^{123}I]IBZM	SPECT [45]
-15.5%	-22.3%	0.2 mg/kg i.v.	[^{11}C]raclopride	PET [48]
-7.6%	-19.5%	0.3 mg/kg i.v.	[^{123}I]IBZM	SPECT [46]
-7.5%	-17.1%	0.3 mg/kg i.v.	[^{123}I]IBZM	SPECT [47]

Table 3. Free synaptic concentrations of DA and D2 receptor occupancies by DA in the striatum before and after amphetamine challenge

	Baseline		Post amphetamine	
	$[DA]/K_{DA}$	Occupancy	$[DA]/K_{DA}$	Occupancy
HC	0.141	12%	0.224	18%
SZ	0.288	22%	0.554	36%

The estimation is based on the published data [45].

Prediction of Clinical Outcome

Equations 15 and 18 give the relationship between the normalized DLPFC activity, X_p, and the change in the striatal D2 receptor BP due to AMPT administration, ΔBP, as

$$X_p = \frac{(1-\alpha)-(1+\alpha)\dfrac{\Delta BP}{BP}}{(1-\alpha)-\alpha\dfrac{\Delta BP}{BP}} \tag{21}$$

where $\Delta BP \equiv BP_{AMPT} - BP$. We apply this equation to a six-week antipsychotic medication trial of inpatients with schizophrenia (n = 14) [10]. The drugs used were olanzapine (n = 8), risperidone (n = 2), quetiapine (n = 2), clozapine (n = 1), and haloperidol (n = 1); benzodiazepine medications were added as needed.

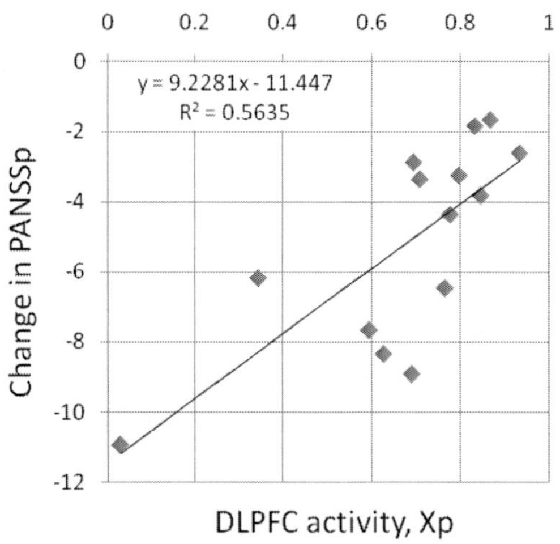

Figure 8. A prediction of the outcome of subchronic (6 weeks) antipsychotic treatment. PANSSp: the PANSS subscale for positive symptoms. This prediction was made by transforming the data [10] using Equation 21 in this model, where $\alpha = 0.30$. Note the negative values of the change in PANSSp to indicate improvement.

AMPT-induced increases in the D2 receptor BP were measured before treatment, and Positive and Negative Syndrome Scale (PANSS) scores were measured one week and six weeks after treatment. The increase in the D2 receptor BP caused by the acute administration of AMPT to the patients had a significant positive correlation with the improvement of positive symptoms after six weeks of antipsychotic treatment ($R^2 = 0.58$, $p = 0.0015$). Changes in negative symptoms were not statistically significant. Equation 21 transforms the data [10] into the relationship between the improvement of positive symptoms and the DLPFC activity, as shown in Figure 8. The regression model thus obtained is ΔPANSSp = $9.23 X_p - 11.4$ ($R^2 = 0.56$, $p = 0.002$), where ΔPANSSp is the change in the PANSS subscale for positive symptoms. This model suggests that patients with lower DLPFC activity tend to have greater improvement of positive symptoms following subchronic antipsychotic treatment.

Discussion

The interaction of the DA system with other neurotransmitter systems is an important issue. Although this chapter has not analyzed this interaction, there have been attempts to analyze it. For example, the complex interaction between DA and glutamate in the PFC was illustrated by computer simulation with a neural circuit model [49]. In this study, DA acts via D1 receptors in the PFC, which changes the conductance of AMPA- and NMDA-type receptor channels as well as the conductance of calcium-dependent potassium channels and the leak conductance. The synergistic interactions among ionic currents generated by glutamatergic, GABAergic, and dopaminergic transmissions produced the inverted-U shaped characteristic of PFC activity. The administration of a DA releaser into the PFC had a variable influence on the level of DA release, depending on the state of the neural circuit. When D1 receptors were upregulated, the administration did not increase DA release. Recently, a consequence of reduced GABAergic inhibition in the PFC [50,51,52] was investigated computationally [53]. This study extended the computer simulation of the PFC circuit from the inverted-U shaped region to the hyperdopaminergic region. The computer simulation predicts the existence of the "H mode" or hyperactivity of the PFC, and that the probability of transition to the H mode increases under hypoGABAergic conditions.

The analysis of the dynamics of the DLPFC circuit suggests important features. First, the prefrontal-mesoprefrontal circuit forms a "regulator" of the DA release in the DLPFC as well as the activity of the DLPFC. This function is due to the stability of the dynamics, which is produced intrinsically by the interactions among the glutamatergic, GABAergic, and dopaminergic neurotransmissions. The DLPFC loses its stability under hypodopaminergic conditions. The instability of the DLPFC circuit means that the state of the circuit can change significantly even with a weak fluctuation of input. A consequence of this circuit instability is that the stability of the PFC circuit increases with the DA level in the DLPFC. This hypothesis is testable. By increasing the DA release in the DLPFC, one would expect a decrease in test-retest variability of DLPFC activity, which was unusually high in patients with schizophrenia [9]. So far, receptor imaging studies have not reached agreement on how dopaminergic neurotransmission in the DLPFC is altered [12,54]. Therefore, this chapter proposes an observation of the variability in DLPFC activity as an alternative way to test the DA hypothesis of schizophrenia (the hypodopaminergia of the DLPFC).

Cognitive functions appear to consistently decline under hypodopaminergic conditions. A PET study using the D1 receptor antagonist radioligand [^{11}C]NNC112 showed that the BP in the DLPFC was significantly higher in untreated patients with schizophrenia than healthy controls and that only the BPs of the patients had a significant negative correlation with 3-back task performance [12]. Pioneering studies with nonhuman primates have demonstrated the importance of D1 receptors in working memory [55,56,57]. These studies led to the current development of novel antipsychotics targeting D1 receptors [58,59,60]. Given that the DLPFC circuit has complex nonlinear dynamics, the circuitry-based system model approach that incorporates imaging studies is expected to facilitate the development of novel drugs.

In neuroscience and psychiatry, control system models would be able to relate brain machinery as well as its abnormalities to macroscopic brain functions and symptoms of diseases. The structure of the control system model in this chapter is simpler than the circuit models. The simplicity enables theoretical analyses of the dynamics without detailed computer simulation, which is why control system models have long been used in control engineering. In this chapter, we used the control system model to investigate the relationship between neurochemical dysregulation and abnormality in the dynamics. Besides the instability, this model predicts that the time constant of the system is a monotonically decreasing function of DA level in the DLPFC. The time constant might be a factor that determines the reaction time. If this is the case, it would be interesting to hypothesize that the reaction times of schizophrenia patients are longer than healthy controls because the cortical DA levels are lower in patients. This approach could be used as another test of the DA hypothesis.

The prefrontostriatal system would be stable by itself because of the GABAergic innervation of the DA neurons. This inhibitory projection would link the striatal hyperdopaminergia with hypofrontality in patients with schizophrenia. Although the results of functional imaging studies seem inconsistent, a meta-analysis indicated that schizophrenia patients did demonstrate hypofrontality [61]. This reciprocal relationship has been confirmed in neuroimaging studies [16]. There is also a possibility that glutamatergic input from the PFC to the striatum is suppressed by DA [62]. If the D2 receptors at the terminal of the glutamatergic projection are hyperactivated, the release of DA would be further increased in the striatum. Acute administration of amphetamine elevates the DA release in the striatum. Receptor imaging studies have consistently reported that the elevation of striatal DA release was significantly higher in patients with schizophrenia compared with healthy subjects [44,45,46,47,48]. It appears that the receptor binding model satisfactorily estimates unobserved variables. When combined with the circuit model, it predicts that patients with lower DLPFC activity will have a better response to antipsychotic medication. Further analyses of experimental data with this framework will elucidate many other aspects of schizophrenia and other psychiatric diseases.

The integration of a neural circuit model and a receptor binding model is possible, as shown in this chapter, but this approach is still in its infancy. More data are needed to elaborate the model. Studies that combine fMRI and receptor imaging would be particularly interesting. Precise information on the circuitry of the brain is important to increase the reliability of the model. With future elaboration, this model could provide researchers with insights into the interpretation of experimental results and the understanding of disease mechanisms. It would also be useful for the evaluation of medication effects because antipsychotics and other psychotropic drugs modify circuit dynamics in relevant brain regions. A major advantage of this model-based approach is that the model does not have any *a priori* assumptions on the abnormalities of the patients' brains. Instead, observed data provide *a posteriori* constraints on the model. The constraints depend on the available experimental data, but this approach would be able to reduce a risk of making erroneous assumptions. Furthermore, because the model in this chapter is universal and not designed specifically for schizophrenia, it can also be applied to other psychiatric disease. More work is yet to be done on this model to establish a useful platform for this kind of integrative approach in psychiatry.

Acknowledgment

The author acknowledges discussion with Dr. Anissa Abi-Dargham at Columbia University when preparing the manuscript of this chapter.

Financial Disclosure

This work was supported by a grant from the Human Informatics Research Center, Sophia University. The funder had no role in study design, data collection and analysis, decision to publish, or preparation of the manuscript.

Disclosure/Conflict of Interest

The author declares that the research was conducted in the absence of any commercial or financial relationships that could be construed as a potential conflict of interest.

References

[1] Akil H, Brenner S, Kandel E, Kendler KS, King M-C, et al. (2010) The Future of Psychiatric Research: Genomes and Neural Circuits. *Science*. 327: 1580-1581. PMID: 20339051.

[2] Hyman SE (2000) Mental illness: genetically complex disorders of neural circuitry and neural communication. *Neuron*. 28: 321-323. PMID: 11144341.

[3] Haber SN, Rauch SL (2010) Neurocircuitry: a window into the networks underlying neuropsychiatric disease. *Neuropsychopharmacology*. 35: 1-3. PMID: 20010702.

[4] Eisenberg DP, Berman KF (2010) Executive function, neural circuitry, and genetic mechanisms in schizophrenia. *Neuropsychopharmacology*. 35: 258-277. PMID: 19693005.

[5] Kahn RS, Davis KL (2000) New developments in dopamine and schizophrenia. *Psychopharmacology: The Fourth Generation of Progress*

[6] Davis KL, Kahn RS, Ko G, Davidson M (1991) Dopamine in schizophrenia: a review and reconceptualization. *Am. J. Psychiatry.* 148(11): 1474-1486. PMID: 1681750.

[7] Howes OD, Kapur S (2009) The dopamine hypothesis of schizophrenia: version III -- the final common pathway. *Schizophr. Bull.* 35: 549-562. PMID: 19325164.

[8] Tanaka S (2006) Dopaminergic control of working memory and its relevance to schizophrenia: a circuit dynamics perspective. *Neuroscience.* 139: 153-171. PMID: 16324800.

[9] Manoach DS, Halpern EF, Kramer TS, Chang Y, Goff DC, et al. (2001) Test-retest reliability of a functional MRI working memory paradigm in normal and schizophrenic subjects. *Am. J. Psychiatry.* 158(6): 955-958. PMID: 11384907.

[10] Abi-Dargham A, Rodenhiser J, Printz D, Zea-Ponce Y, Gil R, et al. (2000) Increased baseline occupancy of D2 receptors by dopamine in schizophrenia. *Proc. Natl. Acad. Sci. U.S.A.* 97: 8104-8109. [comments in Seeman and Kapur (2000) Proc. Natl. Acad. Sci. U.S.A., PMID: 10884398] PMID: 10884434.

[11] Weinberger DR, Laruelle M (2002) Neurochemical and neuropharmacological imaging in schizophrenia. In: Davis KL, Charney D, Coyle JT, Nemeroff C, editors. *Neuropsychopharmacology: The Fifth Generation of Progress.* Philadelphia: Lippincott Williams Wilkins. pp. 833-855.

[12] Abi-Dargham A, Mawlawi O, Lombardo I, Gil R, Martinez D, et al. (2002) Prefrontal dopamine D1 receptors and working memory in schizophrenia. *J. Neurosci.* 22: 3708-3719. PMID: 11978847.

[13] arlsson P, Farde L, Halldin C, Sedvall G (2002) PET study of D1 dopamine receptor binding in neuroleptic-naive patients with schizophrenia. *Am. J. Psychiatry.*159(5): 761-767. PMID: 11986129.

[14] Okubo Y, Suhara T, Suzuki K, Kobayashi K, Inoue O, et al. (1997) Decreased prefrontal dopamine D1 receptors in schizophrenia revealed by PET. *Nature.* 385: 634-636. PMID: 9024661.

[15] Lindström LH, Gefvert O, Hagberg G, Lundberg T, Bergström M, Hartvig P, Långström B (1999) Increased dopamine synthesis rate in medial prefrontal cortex and striatum in schizophrenia indicated by L-(-11C) DOPA and PET. *Biol. Psychiatry.* 46(5): 681-688. PMID: 10472420.

[16] Meyer-Lindenberg A, Miletich RS, Kohn PD, Esposito G, Carson RE, et al. (2002) Reduced prefrontal activity predicts exaggerated striatal dopaminergic function in schizophrenia. *Nat. Neurosci.* 5(3): 267-271. PMID: 11865311.

[17] McGowan S, Lawrence AD, Sales T, Quested D, Grasby P (2004) Presynaptic dopaminergic dysfunction in schizophrenia: a positron emission tomographic [18F]fluorodopa study. *Arch. Gen. Psychiatry.* 61: 134 - 142. PMID: 14757589.

[18] Howes OD, Montgomery AJ, Asselin M-C, Murray RM, Valli I, et al. (2009) Elevated striatal dopamine function linked to prodromal signs of schizophrenia. *Arch. Gen. Psychiatry.* 66: 13-20. PMID: 19124684.

[19] Kumakura Y, Cumming P, Vernaleken I, Buchholz H-G, Siessmeier T, et al. (2007) Elevated [18F]fluorodopamine turnover in brain of patients with schizophrenia: an [18F]fluorodopa/positron emission tomography study. *J. Neurosci.* 27: 8080-8087. PMID: 17652599.

[20] Nozaki S, Kato M, Takano H, Ito H, Takahashi H, et al. (2009) Regional dopamine synthesis in patients with schizophrenia using L-[[beta]-11C]DOPA PET. *Schizophrenia Research.* 108(1-3): 78-84. PMID: 19056247.

[21] Laakso A, Vilkman H, Alakare B, Haaparanta M, Bergman J, et al. (2000) Striatal dopamine transporter binding in neuroleptic-naive patients with schizophrenia studied with positron emission tomography. *Am. J. Psychiatry.* 157: 269-271. PMID: 10671399.

[22] Schmitt G, Frodl T, Dresel S, la Fougère C, Bottlender R, et al. (2006) Striatal dopamine transporter availability is associated with the productive psychotic state in first episode, drug–naive schizophrenic patients. European Archives of Psychiatry and Clinical Neuroscience 256: 115-121. PMID: 16284713.

[23] Laruelle M, Abi-Dargham A, van Dyck C, Gil R, D'Souza DC, Krystal J, Seibyl J, Baldwin R, Innis R (2000) Dopamine and serotonin transporters in patients with schizophrenia: an imaging study with [123I]-CIT. *Biol. Psychiatry.* 47: 371-379. PMID: 10704949.

[24] Lavalaye J, Linszen DH, Booij J, Dingemans PMAJ, Reneman L, et al. (2001) Dopamine transporter density in young patients with schizophrenia assessed with [123]FP-CIT SPECT. *Schizophrenia Research.* 47: 59-67. PMID: 11163545.

[25] Yoder KK, Hutchins GD, Morris ED, Brashear A, Wang C, et al. (2004) Dopamine transporter density in schizophrenic subjects with and without tardive dyskinesia. *Schizophrenia Research.* 71: 371-375. PMID: 15474908.

[26] Mateos J, Lomeña F, Parellada E, Font M, Fernandez E, et al. (2005) Decreased striatal dopamine transporter binding assessed with [123I] FP-CIT in first-episode schizophrenic patients with and without short-term antipsychotic-induced parkinsonism. *Psychopharmacology.* (Berl) 181: 401-406. PMID: 15830229.

[27] Mateos J, Lomeña F, Parellada E, Mireia F, Fernandez-Egea E, et al. (2007) Lower striatal dopamine transporter binding in neuroleptic-naive schizophrenic patients is not related to antipsychotic treatment but it suggests an illness trait. *Psychopharmacology.* 191: 805-811. PMID: 17019564.

[28] Schmitt GJE, Fougère Cl, Dresel S, Frodl T, Hahn K, et al. (2008) Dual-isotope SPECT imaging of striatal dopamine: First episode, drug naïve schizophrenic patients. *Schizophrenia Research.* 101: 133-141. PMID: 18083348.

[29] Innis RB, Cunningham VJ, Delforge J, Fujita M, Gjedde A, et al. (2007) Consensus nomenclature for in vivo imaging of reversibly binding radioligands. *J. Cereb. Blood Flow Metab.* 27: 1533-1539. PMID: 17519979.

[30] Slifstein M, Laruelle M (2001) Models and methods for derivation of in vivo neuroreceptor parameters with PET and SPECT reversible radiotracers. *Nuclear Medicine and Biology.* 28(5): 595-608. PMID: 11516703.

[31] Tzschentke TM (2001) Pharmacology and behavioral pharmacology of the mesocortical dopamine system. *Progress in Neurobiology*. 63(3): 241-320. PMID: 11115727.

[32] Sesack SR, Carr DB (2002) Selective prefrontal cortex inputs to dopamine cells: implications for schizophrenia. *Physiology & Behavior.* 77(4-5): 513-517. PMID: 12526992.

[33] Sesack SR, Carr DB, Omelchenko N, Pinto A (2003) Anatomical substrates for glutamate-dopamine interactions: evidence for specificity of connections and

extrasynaptic actions. Annals of the New York Academy of Sciences. 1003: 36-52. PMID: 14684434.
[34] Frankle WG, Laruelle M, Haber SN (2006) Prefrontal cortical projections to the midbrain in primates: evidence for a sparse connection. *Neuropsychopharmacology.* 31: 1627-1636. PMID: 16395309.
[35] Yamashita K, Tanaka S (2003) Circuit properties of the cortico-mesocortical system. *Neurocomputing.* 52-54: 969-975.
[36] Laruelle M, D'Souza CD, Baldwin RM, Abi-Dargham A, Kanes SJ, et al. (1997) Imaging D2 Receptor Occupancy by Endogenous Dopamine in Humans. *Neuropsychopharmacology.* 17: 162-174. PMID: 9272483.
[37] Khalil HK (2000) Nonlinear systems, third edition. Upper Saddle River, NJ: Prentice-Hall.
[38] Phillips CL, Harbor RD (1996) Feedback control systems, 3/e. Upper Saddle River, NJ.: Prentice-Hall.
[39] Fuller R, Jahanshahi M (1999) Impairment of willed actions and use of advance information for movement preparation in schizophrenia. *J. Neurol. Neurosurg. Psychiatry.* 66: 502-509. PMID: 10201424.
[40] Luck SJ, Gold JM (2008) The Translation of Cognitive Paradigms for Patient Research. *Schizophr. Bull.* 34: 629-644. PMID: 18487226.
[41] Krieger S, Lis S, Janik H, Cetin T, Gallhofer B, et al. (2005) Executive function and cognitive subprocesses in first-episode, drug-naive schizophrenia: an analysis of N-back performance. *Am. J. Psychiatry.* 162(6): 1206-1208. Erratum in: *Am. J. Psychiatry.* 2005 Aug;1162(1208):1559. PMID: 15930072.
[42] Tepper JM, Koos T, Wilson CJ (2004) GABAergic microcircuits in the neostriatum. *Trends Neurosci.* 27(11): 662-669. [erratum: 027 (2004) 0701] PMID: 15474166.
[43] Tanaka S (2010) Model-based parametric study of frontostriatal abnormalities in schizophrenia patients. BMC Psychiatry 10: 17. [Erratum in: *BMC Psychiatry.* 10:93]. PMID: 20187970.
[44] Abi-Dargham A, Gil R, Krystal J, Baldwin RM, Seibyl JP, et al. (1998) Increased striatal dopamine transmission in schizophrenia: confirmation in a second cohort. *Am. J. Psychiatry.* 155: 761-767. PMID: 9619147.
[45] Abi-Dargham A, van de Giessen E, Slifstein M, Kegeles LS, Laruelle M (2009) Baseline and Amphetamine-Stimulated Dopamine Activity Are Related in Drug-Naive Schizophrenic Subjects. *Biological Psychiatry.* 65: 1091-1093. PMID: 19167701.
[46] Laruelle M, Abi-Dargham A, Dyck CHv, Gil R, D'Souza CD, et al. (1996) Single photon emission computerized tomography imaging of amphetamine-induced dopamine release in drug-free schizophrenic subjects. *Proc. Natl. Acad. Sci. U. S. A.* 93: 9235-9240. PMID: 8799184.
[47] Laruelle M, Abi-Dargham A, Gil R, Kegeles L, Innis R (1999) Increased dopamine transmission in schizophrenia: relationship to illness phases. *Biological Psychiatry.* 46: 56-72. PMID: 10394474.
[48] Breier A, Su T-P, Saunders R, Carson RE, Kolachana BS, et al. (1997) Schizophrenia is associated with elevated amphetamine-induced synaptic dopamine concentrations: Evidence from a novel positron emission tomography method. *Proc. Natl. Acad. Sci. U. S. A.* 94: 2569-2574. PMID: 9122236.

[49] Tanaka S (2005) State-dependent alteration of dopamine and glutamate transmission in the prefrontal cortex by psychostimulants. *Neurocomputing*. 65-66: 587-594.

[50] Benes FM, Berretta S (2001) GABAergic interneurons: implications for understanding schizophrenia and bipolar disorder. *Neuropsychopharmacology*. 25: 1-27. Review. PMID: 11377916.

[51] Lewis DA, Gonzalez-Burgos G (2006) Pathophysiologically based treatment interventions in schizophrenia. *Nature Medicine*. 12: 1016-1022. PMID: 16960576.

[52] Reynolds GP, Zhang ZJ, Beasley CL (2001) Neurochemical correlates of cortical GABAergic deficits in schizophrenia: selective losses of calcium binding protein immunoreactivity. *Brain Res. Bull.* 55(5): 579-584. PMID: 11576754.

[53] Tanaka S (2008) Dysfunctional GABAergic inhibition in the prefrontal cortex leading to "psychotic" hyperactivation. *BMC Neuroscience*. 9: 41. PMID: 18439259.

[54] Kosaka J, Takahashi H, Ito H, Takano A, Fujimura Y, et al. (2010) Decreased binding of [11C]NNC112 and [11C]SCH23390 in patients with chronic schizophrenia. *Life Sciences*. 86: 814-818. PMID: 20361984.

[55] Arnsten AFT, Cai JX, Murphy BL, Goldman-Rakic PS (1994) Dopamine D1 receptor mechanisms in the cognitive performance of young adult and aged monkeys. *Psychopharmacology*. (Berl) 116: 143-151. PMID: 7862943.

[56] Goldman-Rakic PS, Muly EC, Williams GV (2000) D1 receptors in prefrontal cells and circuits. *Brain Research Review*. 31(2-3): 295-301. PMID: 10719156.

[57] Goldman-Rakic PS, Castner SA, Svensson TH, Siever LJ, Williams GV (2004) Targeting the dopamine D1 receptor in schizophrenia: insights for cognitive dysfunction. *Psychopharmacology*. (Berl) 174: 3-16. PMID: 15118803.

[58] George MS, Molnar CE, Grenesko EL, Anderson B, Mu Q, et al. (2007) A single 20 mg dose of dihydrexidine (DAR-0100), a full dopamine D1 agonist, is safe and tolerated in patients with schizophrenia. *Schizophrenia Research*. 93: 42-50. PMID: 17467956.

[59] Mu Q, Johnson K, Morgan PS, Grenesko EL, Molnar CE, et al. (2007) A single 20 mg dose of the full D1 dopamine agonist dihydrexidine (DAR-0100) increases prefrontal perfusion in schizophrenia. *Schizophrenia Research*. 94: 332-341. PMID: 17596915.

[60] Slifstein M, Suckow RF, Javitch JA, Cooper T, Lieberman J, et al. (2010) Characterization of in vivo pharmacokinetic properties of the dopamine D1 receptor agonist DAR-0100A in nonhuman primates using PET with [lsqb]11C[rsqb] NNC112 and [lsqb]11C[rsqb] raclopride. *J. Cereb. Blood Flow Metab:* PMID: 20571519.

[61] Hill K, Mann L, Laws KR, Stephenson CME, Nimmo-Smith I, et al. (2004) Hypofrontality in schizophrenia: a meta-analysis of functional imaging studies. *Acta Psychiatrica Scandinavica*. 110: 243-256. PMID: 15352925.

[62] Bamford NS, Robinson S, Palmiter RD, Joyce JA, Moore C, et al. (2004) Dopamine modulates release from corticostriatal terminals. *J. Neurosci.* 24(43): 9541-9552. PMID: 15509741.

[63] Kegeles LS, Abi-Dargham A, Frankle WG, Gil R, Cooper TB, et al. (2010) Increased Synaptic Dopamine Function in Associative Regions of the Striatum in Schizophrenia. *Arch. Gen. Psychiatry*. 67: 231-239. PMID: 20194823.

[64] Riccardi P, Baldwin R, Salomon R, Anderson S, Ansari MS, et al. (2008) Estimation of Baseline Dopamine D2 Receptor Occupancy in Striatum and Extrastriatal Regions in

Humans with Positron Emission Tomography with [18F] Fallypride. *Biological psychiatry*. 63: 241-244. PMID: 17586476.

[65] Verhoeff NP, Kapur S, Hussey D, Lee M, Christensen B, et al. (2001) A simple method to measure baseline occupancy of neostriatal dopamine D2 receptors by dopamine in vivo in healthy subjects. *Neuropsychopharmacology*. 25(2): 213-223. PMID: 11425505.

[66] Voruganti L, Slomka P, Zabel P, Costa G, So A, et al. (2001) Subjective effects of AMPT-induced dopamine depletion in schizophrenia: correlation between dysphoric responses and striatal D2 binding ratios on SPECT imaging. N*europsychopharmacology*. 25: 642-650. PMID: 11682247.

[67] Grace AA (1995) The tonic/phasic model of dopamine system regulation: Its relevance for understanding how stimulant abuse can alter basal ganglia function. *Drug and Alcohol Dependence*. 37: 111-129. PMID: 7758401.

In: Schizophrenia Research: Recent Advances
Editor: Tomiki Sumiyoshi

ISBN: 978-1-62808-703-1

Chapter 2

How the Degree of the Linearity of the Brief Psychiatric Rating Scale Could Be Measured and Improved: A Retrospective Analysis

Jitsuki Sawamura[1†], Shigeru Morishita[2††] and Jun Ishigooka[1#]

[1] Department of Psychiatry, Tokyo Women's Medical University, Tokyo, Japan
[2] Depression Prevention Medical Center,
Kyoto Jujo Rehabilitation Hospital, Kyoto, Japan

Abstract

Introduction: Although the Brief Psychiatric Rating Scale (BPRS) is widely used for evaluating patients with schizophrenia, it has limited value in estimating the clinical weight of individual symptoms. The aim of this study was 4-fold: 1) to investigate the relationship of the BPRS to the Clinical Global Impression-Schizophrenia scale (CGI-SCH), 2) to express this relationship in mathematical form, 3) to seek significant symptoms, and 4) to consider a possible modified BPRS subscale.

Methods: We evaluated 150 schizophrenia patients using the BPRS and the CGI-SCH, then examined the scatter plot distribution of the two scales and expressed it in a mathematical equation. Next, backward stepwise regression was performed to select BPRS items that were highly associated with the CGI-SCH. Multivariate regression was conducted to allocate marks to individual items, proportional to their respective magnitudes. We assessed the influence of modifications to the BPRS in terms of Pearson's r correlation coefficient and r-squared to evaluate the relationship between the two scales. Utilizing symptom weighting, we assumed a possible BPRS subscale.

Results: By plotting the scores for the two scales, a logarithmic curve was obtained. By performing a logarithmic transformation of the BPRS total score, the curve was modified to a linear distribution, described by [CGI-SCH] = 3.1051 × ln[18-item BPRS]

---

† Corresponding author: Tel: +81-3-3353-8111; Fax: +81-3-3351-8979; jsawamura@psy.twmu.ac.jp.
†† s.morishita69@mopera.net.
# ishigoj@psy.twmu.ac.jp.

– 6.7705 ($p < 0.001$). Pearson's r for the relationship between the scales was 0.7926 and r-squared was 0.7560 (both $p < 0.001$). Pearson's r between the ln[18-item BPRS] and the CGI-SCH was 0.8304 ($p < 0.001$). Applying backward stepwise regression using small sets of items, eight symptoms were positively correlated with the CGI-SCH ($p < 0.005$) and the subset gave Pearson's r of 0.8185 and r-squared of 0.7198. Further selection at the multivariate regression yielded Pearson's r of 0.8315 and r-squared of 0.7036. Then, modification of point allocation provided Pearson's r of 0.8339 and r-squared of 0.7036 (all these $p < 0.001$). A possible modified BPRS subscale, "the modified seven-item BPRS", was designed.

Conclusions: Within the limits of our data, a logarithmic relationship was assumed between the two scales, and not only individual items of the BPRS but also their weightings were considered important for a linear relationship and improvement of the BPRS for evaluating schizophrenia.

INTRODUCTION

Schizophrenia is a serious mental disorder characterized by a number of symptoms. To evaluate the effects of treatment for schizophrenia, it is important to assign quantitative values to the symptoms. Many rating scales have been used to evaluate various symptomatic domains in schizophrenia [1]. This has led to confusion regarding the suitability of the different scales available, not only in relation to evaluation and treatment of the disease but also in research and clinical studies of the effects of medication. Currently, consensus is lacking about which rating scales are appropriate to evaluate schizophrenia. Evaluation scales that are relevant, quick, user-friendly, graduated at equal intervals and with high linearity are needed to facilitate measurement-based treatment of schizophrenia. The Brief Psychiatric Rating Scale (BPRS) [2] is one of the standard instruments used most frequently in daily practice for evaluating the severity of schizophrenia. Also popular are the Clinical Global Impression-Schizophrenia scale (CGI-SCH) [3], the Positive and Negative Syndrome Scale (PANSS) [4], the Scale for Assessment of Positive Symptoms (SAPS) [5] and the Scale for Assessment of Negative Symptoms (SANS) [6]. Although the BPRS includes 18 items and the allocation of marks is defined clearly, as all items have the same range of marks (i.e., 1–7), it is not unusual to find that scores for the BPRS differ widely from those for the CGI-SCH.

Ideally, scores from one scale could be mapped directly onto the other, making it possible to compare individuals evaluated with one scale or the other. We decided to investigate this divergence analytically, looking at the clinical weight of respective symptoms (the relative magnitudes of symptoms in schizophrenia) and the issue of scale nonlinearity. In the present study, we investigated whether there was a linear relationship between the scores of the two scales, to observe whether linearity of the BPRS to the CGI-SCH could be influenced by changing point allocation of the BPRS through devising an example of a possible modified BPRS subscale.

The aim of the present study is 4-fold: 1) to investigate the linearity of the BPRS in relation to its items and mark allocation by examining the reasons for the incongruity between BPRS scores and clinicians' impressions of symptom severity in schizophrenic patients; 2) to determine a mathematical expression that represents the relationship between the BPRS and the CGI-SCH more precisely; 3) to seek which symptoms are important from a clinical standpoint; and 4) if possible, to construct an example of a possible modified BPRS subscale that is expected to have improved correlation with the CGI-SCH scores compared with the full BPRS within the limitations of the data obtained in this trial. It must be noted that this article is a revision of our previous version [7].

METHODS

Participants

This was a retrospective study of outpatients and inpatients treated at the Tokyo Women's Medical University, Miyazaki Hospital and Depression Prevention Medical Center, Kyoto Jujo Rehabilitation Hospital, Japan, who met the DSM-IV-TR [8] criteria for schizophrenia. A total of 150 patients (74 males, 76 females) with a mean age of 44.5 years (range, 17–83) were included in this study. Fifty patients were suffering their first episode of schizophrenia or attending for initial treatment (Group A) and 100 were randomly selected during either the acute or chronic phase of schizophrenia (Group B). The study involved a retrospective chart review and was approved by the ethics committee of our institution.

Reserch Design

All patients were evaluated and rated from their medical records using the BPRS and the CGI-SCH during the same session, but at initial consultation for Group A and at a random treatment session for Group B. In this study, we utilized the CGI-SCH as a scale that substituted for the evaluation made by the patients' psychiatrists under the tentative assumption that the CGI-SCH had perfect linearity and that it represented the precise clinical global impression of the treating psychiatrists.

If the linearity of the BPRS to the CGI-SCH was not initially apparent, we aimed to derive a mathematical equation to represent more precisely the relationship between the scales, clarifying which symptoms were important in evaluating schizophrenia and how we could improve the correlation between the BPRS and the CGI-SCH. Two experienced psychiatrists shared their evaluations, and the scores for the BPRS and the CGI-SCH were presented graphically, making it possible to examine whether the two demonstrated a linear relationship. At this stage, we examined the distribution on the scatter plot of the two scales and expressed the relationship in a precise mathematical equation. Next, backward stepwise regression was performed, with the CGI-SCH as a dependent variable and with all 18 items of the BPRS as independent variables. An F-value of less than 2.000 was used to identify variables for removal. In addition, backward stepwise regression with the same F-value condition was performed using three small sets of variables based on derived scores. These independent variable groups were: positive symptoms (conceptual disorganization, grandiosity, hostility, suspiciousness, hallucinations, and excitement); negative symptoms (emotional withdrawal and blunted affect); and general psychopathological symptoms (somatic concern, anxiety, guilt, tension, bizarre behavior, depressed mood, motor retardation, uncooperativeness, unusual thought content, and disorientation) with reference to three domains of the PANSS. Variables showing a positive association with the CGI-SCH were derived from these three domains, and multivariate regression analysis was performed using the selected items as independent variables and the CGI-SCH as a dependent variable. By convention in stepwise regression, even if p values exceed 0.05, it is permissible to adopt the variables if those symptoms are judged as clinically important, as long as the p values do not exceed 0.20.

However, we selected the variables positively associated with the CGI-SCH within the condition that p values were less than 0.05. In the stepwise and multivariate regression analyses, we often obtained variables inversely associated with the CGI-SCH. In this study, we adopted a way to remove them. Furthermore, utilizing the results of multivariate regression, we allocated marks in proportion to the magnitude of the multiple regression coefficient of each variable so that each symptom was allocated different marks proportional to the positive multiple regression coefficient.

With regard to linearity, we then examined the distribution on the scatter plot of the BPRS and the CGI-SCH scores. We obtained the Pearson's r coefficient as an indication of the degree of linearity of the relationship between the two scales, r-squared being one of values used to estimate how much the fit of model shrinks (by observing how r-squared decreased) before and after exclusion of the various items and modification of the mark allocation. Furthermore, we examined whether the selection of specific items and/or changing the distribution of the marks enhanced the correlation of the BPRS with the CGI-SCH and how much the r-squared decreased.

On the basis of the results, we constructed an example of a possible modified BPRS subscale, "the modified seven-item BPRS", which would be expected to have a higher correlation with the CGI-SCH within the limitations of the applicability for our data at this stage. We used SPSS for Windows, version 14 [9] for the stepwise regression analysis, Stata Release 10.0 [10] for the multivariate regression analysis, and Microsoft Excel 2003 [11] for plotting the graph.

RESULTS

Figure 1 shows the relationship between the 18-item BPRS score and the CGI-SCH score. Pearson's r coefficient for the relationship between the 18-item BPRS and the CGI-SCH was 0.7926 ($p < 0.001$) and r-squared (that of multivariate regression using the full item of BPRS) was 0.7560. Although there was a rough correlation, a curve with an upper convexity was obtained and the straight-line relationship that had been thought to exist between the two scales was not apparent.

Because the shape of the curve was similar to a logarithmic curve, we performed a natural logarithmic transformation of the 18-item BPRS total score. The curve was then modified to an almost linear distribution, which was described by the equation [CGI-SCH] = 3.1051 × ln[18-item BPRS] – 6.7705 ($p < 0.001$; Figure 2). Pearson's r between the ln[18-item BPRS] and the CGI-SCH was 0.8304 ($p < 0.001$).

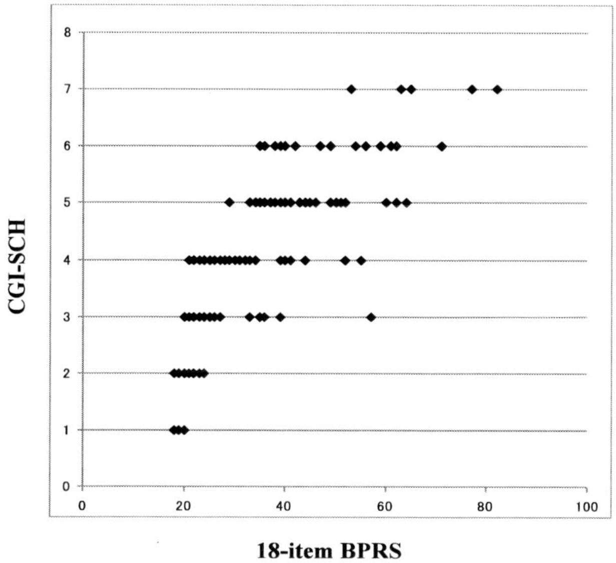

Figure 1. Scatter plot of the 18-item BPRS total score and the CGI-SCH score.

An upper convexity curve similar to a logarithmic curve was evident and a linear relationship was not apparent. The range of the 18-item BPRS is 18–126, and that of the CGI-SCH is 1–7.

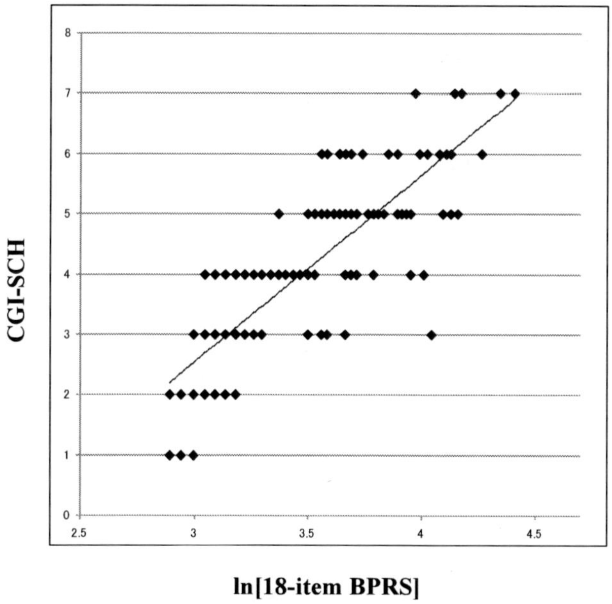

$$[\text{CGI-SCH}] = 3.1051 \times \ln[\text{18-item BPRS}] - 6.7705 \ (p < 0.001)$$

Figure 2. Scatter plot of the natural logarithm of the 18-item BPRS total score and the CGI-SCH score.

After performing a natural logarithmic transformation on the 18-item BPRS score, the approximately logarithmic curve was modified to an almost linear distribution and the increase in the natural logarithm of the 18-item BPRS total score was almost proportional to the increase in the CGI-SCH score.

The results of the backward stepwise analysis for correlation are shown in Table 1 ($p < 0.001$). According to the results of other backward stepwise regressions for the variables divided into three groups, eight items were selected ($p < 0.001$; Table 2). 'Conceptual disorganization' ($p < 0.001$), 'hostility' ($p < 0.001$), 'hallucinations' ($p < 0.001$), 'emotional withdrawal' ($p < 0.001$), 'anxiety' ($p < 0.001$), 'motor retardation' ($p < 0.001$), 'uncooperativeness' ($p = 0.004$), and 'unusual thought content' ($p < 0.001$) were significantly correlated with the CGI-SCH.

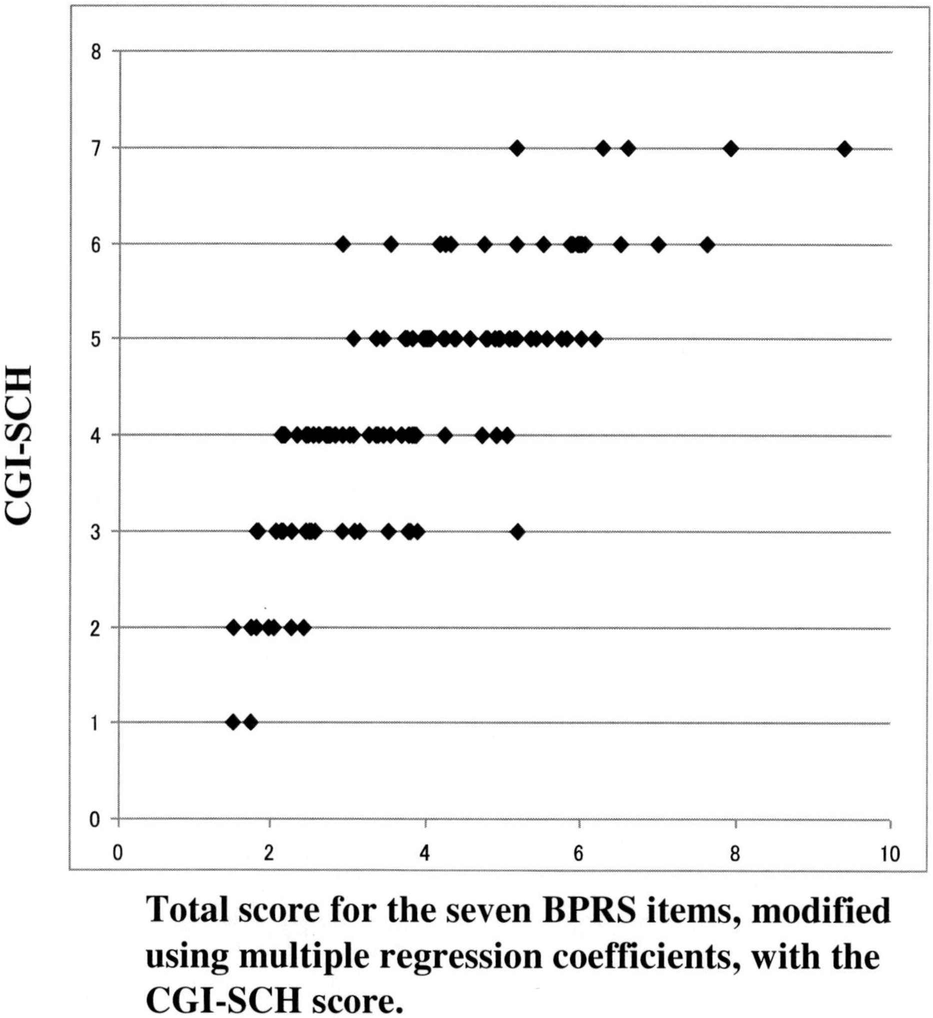

Figure 3. Scatter plot of the seven-item total score, modified using multiple regression coefficients, and the CGI-SCH score.

The score for each of the seven items was multiplied by the multiple regression coefficient for each respective symptom. The range of the total score for the seven BPRS items modified using multiple regression coefficients was 1.497–10.479, and that for CGI-SCH was 1–7. The sum of the regression coefficients for the seven variables positively associated with the CGI-SCH score was 1.497.

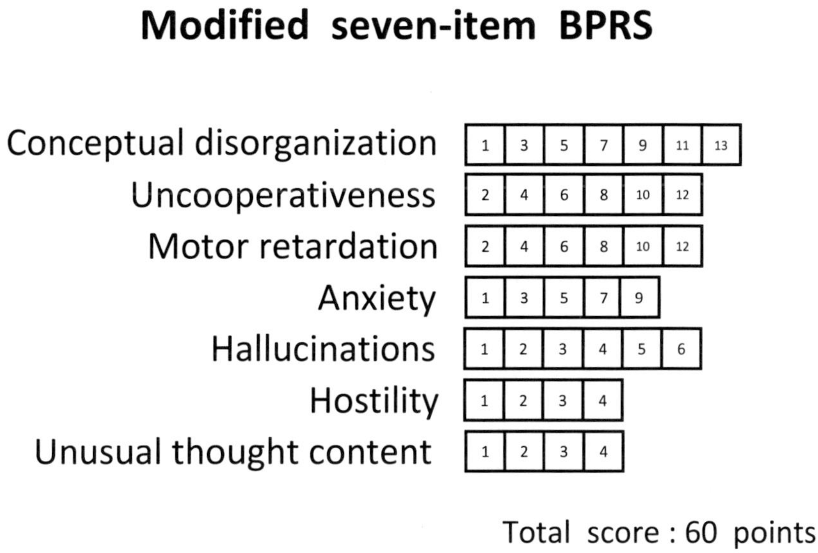

Figure 4. An example of a possible modified BPRS subscale.

Marks for each item were obtained by multiplying the respective regression coefficients for the seven selected items by 40.

The selection of the above eight variables from the 18-item BPRS gave Pearson's r of 0.8185 and r-squared of 0.7198. Using these eight items as independent variables that were expected to be important for the correlation between the BPRS and the CGI-SCH, multivariate regression analysis was performed (Table 3). After further selection of the seven variables from the above eight variables at the multivariate regression, "the seven-item BPRS" was obtained that comprised these positively associated seven items. Pearson's r for the relationship between "the seven-item BPRS" and the CGI-SCH was 0.8315 and r-squared was 0.7036 ($p < 0.001$). Furthermore, because we were able to consider the weights of the multiple regression coefficient as the clinical weights, the standard deviation of each variable was assumed to be almost the same, and by allocating marks to each respective item of "the seven-item BPRS" in proportion to the magnitude of the multiple regression coefficient, Pearson's r was increased further to 0.8339 (between "the modified seven-item BPRS" and the CGI-SCH; $p < 0.001$; Figure 3) and r-squared did not change (0.7036). As a result, the distribution on the scatter plot of the two scales changed from that shown in Figure 1 to that shown in Figure 3, yielding a more linear relationship between "the modified seven-item BPRS" and the CGI-SCH than was the case between the 18-item BPRS and the CGI-SCH. Pearson's r was increased after the series of manipulations, and r-squared decreased by slow degrees, although statistical significance was not apparent for this change. By multiplying each multiple regression coefficient by 40, we composed an example of a possible modified BPRS subscale: "the modified seven-item BPRS" (of tentative meaning, given the limits of our data at this stage) (Figure 4).

Table 1. Results of stepwise regression 1

Variable	Unstandardized β	Standard Error	Standardized β	t	p-Value	95% Confidence Interval
Somatic concern	-0.253525**	0.078032	-0.171	-3.249	0.001	-0.407828 – -0.099222
Anxiety	0.413167†	0.082008	0.411	5.038	0.000	0.251002 – 0.575332
Emotional withdrawal	-0.351087**	0.106518	-0.324	-3.296	0.001	-0.561719 – -0.140454
Conceptual disorganization	0.358483†	0.069136	0.353	5.185	0.000	0.221771 – 0.495195
Grandiosity	-0.189250*	0.088471	-0.099	-2.139	0.034	-0.364195 – -0.014304
Hostility	0.166995	0.104009	0.140	1.606	0.111	-0.038676 – 0.372666
Suspiciousness	-0.152787	0.091570	-0.164	-1.669	0.097	-0.333861 – 0.028287
Hallucinations	0.162475**	0.057716	0.204	2.815	0.006	0.048346 – 0.276605
Motor retardation	0.258352**	0.090433	0.190	2.857	0.005	0.079527 – 0.437178
Uncooperativeness	0.262802*	0.109879	0.239	2.392	0.018	0.045524 – 0.480081
Unusual thought content	0.147787*	0.073080	0.162	2.022	0.045	0.003277 – 0.292296
Blunted affect	0.139060	0.079696	0.095	1.745	0.083	-0.018534 – 0.296652
Constant	1.138607	0.256029		4.447	0.000	0.632328 – 1.644886

*$p < 0.05$, **$p < 0.01$, †$p < 0.001$ Data for schizophrenic patients (n = 150)

Results of backward stepwise regression using the full set of variables of the BPRS. Eight items of the BPRS as independent variables were positively associated with the CGI-SCH score as a dependent variable, and four items were inversely associated with the CGI-SCH score. F-value < 2.000 was the criterion for removal ($p < 0.001$). R-squared was 0.7524 (p value of analysis of variance was less than 0.001). Unstandardized β, standardized β, and the p value are also shown.

Table 2. Results of stepwise regression 2

Positive symptoms (conceptual disorganization, grandiosity, hostility, suspiciousness, hallucinations and excitement)

Variable	Unstandardized β	Standard Error	Standardized β	t	p-Value	95% Confidence Interval
Conceptual disorganization	0.419673†	0.062355	0.414	6.730	0.000	0.296437 – 0.542909
Hostility	0.247835†	0.066360	0.208	3.735	0.000	0.116685 – 0.378984
Hallucinations	0.288605†	0.047700	0.363	6.050	0.000	0.194333 – 0.382877
Constant	1.586381	0.163776		9.686	0.000	1.262703 – 1.910059

Negative symptoms
(emotional withdrawal and blunted affect)

Variable	Unstandardized β	Standard Error	Standardized β	t	p-Value	95% Confidence Interval
Emotional withdrawal	0.668840†	0.069960	0.618	9.560	0.000	0.530592 – 0.807089
Constant	2.624571	0.167903		15.631	0.000	2.292775 – 2.956368

General psychopathological symptoms (somatic concern, anxiety, guilt, tension, bizarre behavior, depressed mood, motor retardation, uncooperativeness, unusual thought content and disorientation)

Variable	Unstandardized β	Standard Error	Standardized β	t	p-Value	95% Confidence Interval
Somatic concern	-0.220833**	0.082965	-0.149	-2.662	0.009	-0.384830 – -0.056837
Anxiety	0.251795†	0.0667485	0.250	3.772	0.000	0.119856 – 0.383734
Motor retardation	0.303597†	0.078253	0.224	3.880	0.000	0.148916 – 0.458278
Uncooperativeness	0.223711**	0.076051	0.204	2.942	0.004	0.073381 – 0.374041
Unusual thought content	0.350995†	0.062647	0.386	5.603	0.000	0.227160 – 0.474829
Disorientation	0.244946	0.168480	0.076	1.454	0.148	-0.088087 – 0.577979
Constant	1.430263	0.234066		6.111	0.000	0.967587 – 1.892939

*$p < 0.05$, **$p < 0.01$, †$p < 0.001$ Data for schizophrenic patients ($n = 150$).

Results of backward stepwise regression using small sets of variables based on the three domains of the PANSS (positive symptoms, negative symptoms and general psychopathological symptoms). Within positive symptoms, ‘conceptual disorganization’, ‘hostility’ and ‘hallucinations’ were significantly and positively associated with the CGI-SCH score ($p < 0.001$); within negative symptoms: ‘emotional withdrawal’ ($p < 0.001$); within general psychopathological symptoms: ‘anxiety’, ‘motor retardation’, ‘uncooperativeness’, and ‘unusual thought content’ were significantly and positively associated with the CGI-SCH score ($p < 0.005$), and ‘somatic concern’ was inversely associated with the CGI-SCH score ($p < 0.01$). F-value < 2.000 as a criterion for removal, multiple regression coefficient, and the p value are shown. R-squared was 0.6661 (positive symptoms), 0.3818 (negative symptoms) and 0.6716 (general psychopathological symptoms); all p values of respective analyses of variance were less than 0.001.

DISCUSSION

The BPRS is one of the most frequently used instruments for evaluating the psychopathology of patients with schizophrenia. Although its psychometric properties in terms of reliability, validity and sensitivity have been extensively examined [12], patients are evaluated by clinicians with different observer ratings using different criteria. On the other hand, assessment with the CGI-SCH is based on a score of 1–7, making it simple and relevant. The CGI-SCH may be as sensitive as the BPRS in detecting efficacy differences between antipsychotic drugs [13], but it is necessary that treatment response be interpreted in the context of patient characteristics [14]. However, patients with different characteristics but with similar scores are often treated similarly in clinical trials. Therefore, training is required for performing a standardized evaluation [15]. Other user-friendly assessments include the Revised Global Outcome Assessment of Life in Schizophrenia (Revised GOALS) [16], the Investigator's Assessment Questionnaire (IAQ) [17] and the Targeted Inventory on Problems in Schizophrenia (TIP-Sz) [18], although they have some limitations in terms of methodology. We also believe that other important aspects of illness management should be supplemented with appropriate subjective scales as necessary [19]. Nonetheless, there is no consensus among clinicians regarding the most suitable scale. To address this perplexing issue, more advanced investigations are necessary to devise rating scales using some form of statistical method.

Leaving aside the debate over whether psychopathological severity or state can be expressed in evaluation scales such as the BPRS or the CGI-SCH and accepting the need and utility of such instruments, we focused here on improving the BPRS scale. We examined whether the more detailed assessment afforded by its items and individual point allocations could be made proportional to the simpler and more global CGI-SCH scale.

Many previous attempts have been made to evaluate the adequacy of the BPRS from the viewpoint of which items should be selected because of their relevance. However, no study has approached this issue by addressing how the degree of linearity of the BPRS could be measured and improved by modifying not only its constituent items but also their weighting, using stepwise regression and multivariate regression analysis. In the present study, we first examined whether the BPRS and the CGI-SCH showed a mutual linear relationship. By plotting the BPRS scores and the CGI-SCH scores in the form of a graph, we compared their respective distributions. The scatter plot of the 18-item BPRS and the CGI-SCH yielded a curve with upper convexity, thus demonstrating that the relationship between the two scales was not linear (see Figure 1). Because the shape of the curve had upper convexity similar to a logarithmic curve, we performed a natural logarithmic transformation on the 18-item BPRS score. Then, we were able to obtain a possibly more precise equation as a logarithmic form shown in Figure 2. From this result, we presumed that there was a possibility that an increase in the logarithm of the total score for all symptoms might be roughly proportional to the global increase in symptom severity observed clinically in schizophrenic patients. We recognize, however, that the results have applicability to only this trial at this stage. Interestingly, because Pearson's r between the ln[18-item BPRS] and the CGI-SCH was 0.8304 ($p < 0.001$) (higher than that between the original BPRS and the CGI-SCH of 0.7926), this might imply the possible existence of the more linear relationship between the log-transformed BPRS and the CGI-SCH than that between the non-log-transformed BPRS and the CGI-SCH. We inferred that the logarithmic relationship between the single score scale, the CGI-SCH, and the plural score scale, the BPRS, might be an important tool in our determination of the severity of illness (e.g., there might be a possibility that a clinicians' impression of the severity of a certain disease is approximately proportional not to the simple sum of respective severity of symptoms but to the logarithm of this sum). We then investigated whether modifying the constituent items and/or allocation of marks could affect the linearity of the BPRS, at least, within this trial itself, looking at the correlation of the BPRS with the CGI-SCH in terms of Pearson's r and r-squared, which express one of the degrees of the fit between the two scales. To evaluate the clinical severity of schizophrenia, we substituted the CGI-SCH score for the clinical impression.

Partly because the values of Pearson's r were slightly higher between "the seven-item BPRS" (constructed by selection of specific items) and the CGI-SCH than between the 18-item BPRS and the CGI-SCH without considerable decreases of r-squared, the shape of the scatter plot between the two scales became more linear than that before the selection. We inferred that there was a possibility that the selection of these 7 items from the full 18 items is related to the linearity of the BPRS. The clinical weights might be related to the heightened values of Pearson's r between "the modified seven-item BPRS" (constructed by changing the allocation of marks) and the CGI-SCH, as the shape of the scatter plot between the two scales became more linear than before. We presumed that there was a possibility that the weighting was also associated with the linearity of the BPRS.

Furthermore, by assigning different weights to each item proportional to the respective regression coefficients, we were able to compose a possible modified BPRS subscale, "the modified seven-item BPRS", by assuming that the magnitude of each regression coefficient represented the respective clinical weight of each item. This scale is only an example of a possible modified BPRS subscale that we are able to construct within our data, decreasing the number of items from 18 to 7.

Historically, a widely used algorithm employing a stepwise method was first proposed by Efroymson [20], and supplementary articles were later reported by Hocking [21] and others. In the field of psychiatry, stepwise methods have been used for predicting the quality of life of schizophrenic patients by reference to schizophrenia symptoms [22], for estimating predictive values of neurocognition in schizophrenic patients [23], and for estimation of the relationship between executive functions and positive symptoms in schizophrenia [24].

However, some problems with stepwise and multivariate regression analysis have been reported. To compare the relative magnitudes of variables, the partial regression coefficients are often normalized using their respective standard deviations. However, the predictor variable is at least partially redundant with other predictors and the regression coefficient is influenced by the range of the predictor variable [25]. In addition, the relative importance of predictor variables is a tenuous concept, and comparison of the importance of predictors is not always the best approach in multiple regression. As the individual items of the BPRS had the same range of marks (1–7), we considered that there would not be crucial differences in the sizes of standard deviations for predictor variables in this study. With this assumption, we considered that, for practical purposes, the magnitudes of the standardized and unstandardized βs might be regarded as almost equivalent. For these reasons, we utilized the magnitude of the unstandardized βs (multiple regression coefficients) to modify the distribution of marks of the BPRS and to design a tentative BPRS subscale. If supplemented with this adjustment, the scatter plot representing the relationship between "the modified seven-item BPRS" and the

CGI-SCH showed a distribution proportional to the scatter plot connecting the score of "the seven-item BPRS" multiplied by the unstandardized βs (multiple regression coefficients) for each item and the score of the CGI-SCH. This is because both have almost the same significance on the graph. Additional improvements in fit may be possible.

The limitations of the present study should be noted. The first was the use of the CGI-SCH as a scale that substituted for the evaluation made by the patients' psychiatrists. There is no evidence that the CGI-SCH has perfect linearity; this was merely an assumption to allow modification of the BPRS under a determinate condition. For the CGI-SCH, only a certain degree of reliability has been reported [3, 13, 14]. Nonetheless, we thought that this kind of simplification was unavoidable and the trade-off necessary, even if this assumption would sacrifice rigor to some extent in exchange for examining the degree of an abstract value such as 'linearity.'

Second, there is no evidence supporting the assumption that the BPRS score and the CGI-SCH score obtained retrospectively by coding of the symptoms reported in the clinical chart would be comparable to the data obtained from trained BPRS raters monitored for inter-rater reliability and performing standardized interviews to probe for presence and severity of a complete list of symptoms. The quality of the clinical chart is notoriously variable, so there may exist errors and distortions from missing symptoms and from falsely rating symptoms as absent when reviewing a chart, because of the failure of the clinician to mention them in the chart, which would have been detected in a structured, face-to-face interview. To our knowledge, Mullins et al. reported the utility of the Brief Psychiatric Rating Scale for Children (BPRS-C) for transcribing narrative medical records into a standard quantitative form in which the medical records were the primary sources of information and the inter-rater reliabilities were adequate in most major domains of psychopathology, the one notable exception being symptoms in the anxiety domain [26]. The 0.7926 value of Pearson's r might be to some extent considered high. However, we presume that this was because the study was retrospective. Therefore, some items of the BPRS might not have been marked, thus minimizing the distribution of the BPRS score. In effect, the results of this paper may be applicable only within our own data at this stage (including the derived stepwise regression, multivariate regression and, particularly, "the modified seven-item BPRS") and there is no guarantee that the results would be comparable to prospective research. From this standpoint, our report might be regarded as an experimental case study. Nonetheless, the validity of our model can be tested to some degree theoretically by using even fictional data sets, because the theme intended to be examined in this study is only whether increasing the magnitudes of independent variables of significance (e.g., symptom scores of the BPRS) that are positively associated with the dependent variable (e.g., the CGI-SCH score) could heighten the degree of the correlation (e.g., Pearson's r) of two data sets, such as the BPRS and the CGI-SCH, and/or could reduce the number of variables (symptoms) while keeping the same degree of correlation between them. At any rate, prospectively randomized trials are needed in future studies.

Third, however, through the manipulations employed here, the degree of change in Pearson's r was rather ambiguous. The increases appear slight (as a total, from 0.7926 to 0.8339; particularly, in the final manipulation, from 0.8315 to 0.8339). Moreover, it is considerably uncertain whether statistical significance exists. From another viewpoint, despite the fact that the scale was simplified, and in particular, the number of items decreased, the degree of correlation (Pearson's r) stayed at the same level or increased just slightly.

Although this might indicate that a simplified subscale might be valuable in comparison with the full scale, and it might be useful to clinicians for shortening time of rating, the reproducibility of items and point allocation is quite uncertain in this model. We believe that a study of this theme in the future is desirable.

Fourth, as for r-squared, in general, the more variables we exclude from the model, the more r-squared tends to decrease. The selection of the subset for which the decrease of r-squared is smallest is preferred so that the loss of model fit would be minimal. The r-squared of our data ranged from about 0.70–0.75. The size of these numbers is not low, but they may not be sufficiently high even with the moderate degree of decrease. For example, 0.7560 for the full item BPRS; 0.7524 for the results of stepwise regression using the full items of BPRS; 0.7198 for the selected eight items from stepwise regression using three small sets; and 0.7036 for the selected seven items from multivariate regression (all p values of respective analysis of variance were less than 0.001). This means that the selection of items might have caused shrinkage of the model.

Fifth, the selection of items and modification of point allocation may have contributed some artifacts of multicollinearity. There are likely to be intercorrelations among the data. In this study, variables that were inversely correlated with the CGI-SCH score, indicating that the more severe the BPRS item, the lower the CGI-SCH score (a phenomenon which was a departure from the clinicians' experiences), were simply excluded from the model in an ad hoc procedure. This ignored the fact that the selection of the other predictors from among the list of candidates depended on the presence of the excluded variable. Additional unknown and complicated factors are predicted to exist as well, for example, that both inpatients and outpatients were evaluated by the CGI-SCH, and that the results might have been negatively influenced by differences in cognitive ability [27]. The treatment of negative coefficients is a crucial weakness of our model.

Sixth, it is also problematic that the intercepts of the regression lines of the stepwise and multivariate regressions were ignored, whose presence and/or absence might yield biases for the results. Other than this, despite the fact that we could have utilized the visual analogue scale, which ranges from 0 to 10, for the scores that we substituted for the clinical impression, we chose instead the ordinal CGI-SCH scores, which range ordinarily from 1 to 7 (taking '0' as "not assessed"), to express the clinicians' global impression of illness with schizophrenic patients. S. Stevens proposed a 'ratio scale' on which four arithmetic operations could be possible [28]. As the '0' of the BPRS and of the CGI-SCH means "not assessed", these might produce differences from the ordinal meaning of '0' (none) of the 'ratio scale'. If so, the difference between the definitions of '0' might cause a distortion for the BPRS and the CGI-SCH. As we commented previously, the possible absence of linearity and the equal increments between each point of the CGI-SCH are serious problems that could not be ignored. In addition, the individual scores of the BPRS should ideally correspond to a visual analogue scale whose respective score ranges of 0-7 or 0-10 would have a more adequate degree of linearity than the CGI-SCH. If this condition were met, the BPRS would become one of the more linear evaluating scales.

Seventh, we consider that our model is only applicable for a pair of scales where one is a single score scale (e.g., the CGI-SCH) and the other is a plural score scale (e.g., the BPRS). The condition that those two scales are intended for the same state of illness and are in positive relationship intrinsically, at least roughly, is presumed necessary. Otherwise, if the two are in an inverse relationship, for instance, as is the case between the CGI-SCH and the

Global Assessment of Functioning (GAF) [8], the method we discussed might be expected to produce nothing.

Eighth, above all, the results are not likely to be reproducible. If we performed the same procedure on new data, it is very likely that different symptoms would be selected, and different point allocations would probably be assigned to individual items. We infer that a possible way to remedy this problem, even if partially, might be to perform a number of prospective trials in line with our method, and then summarize and calculate an average on items and point allocation. If these scales are composed as a summary, they might be less problematic than that of our trials. However, even in such scales, there would still be no assurance that they would have a greater degree of reproducibility. Therefore, the extent to which the results of this paper could be applicable may be quite limited: at the extreme, only within our present data. For this reason, future studies are necessary.

Ninth, this problem may be insoluble in principle. This approach to optimizing many parameters (variables) so that a certain value would be maximized might not always be able to provide the ideal magnitudes for the other values. The challenge of the setting of this study is to find the optimized value of individual symptoms whose severities were recognized independently when they were rated. This kind of problem may suffer from the restrictions of 'the three-body problem (many-body problem)', which has been investigated historically in the physical world [29, 30]. That the three-body problem may be insoluble has been discussed and demonstrated impressively by Naganuma, although this unique textbook is published only in Japanese at present [31]. At any rate, if the solution of these kinds of problems, in which many values should be determined ideally at the same instant under the condition that a certain parameter (e.g., Pearson's r) would take the maximum value, is impossible in principle, the regions we are able to approach might then be quite limited.

The true aim of this manipulation was not always to determine the best subset and/or point allocation, but to consider a specific example of a possible modified scale. Therefore, "the modified seven-item BPRS" is merely a tentative idea at this stage, to propose a new viewpoint of the importance of point allocation in the BPRS. Needless to say, the present study has many limitations, and is thus only a first step from which further studies may learn. We believe that improving evaluation scales to make them more linear could minimize distortions in evaluation for severity of illness, including over- and under-diagnosis and estimations for efficiency and effect in clinical research. We anticipate that our present results will serve as a useful reference for clinicians attempting to devise an evaluation scale, and that further research will focus on the optimal number of items, the fittest items for selection, and the allocation of marks in rigorous methodology to maximize the linearity of the BPRS.

Conclusion

Within the limits of our data, although there was a rough correlation, the linear relationship that had been thought to exist between the 18-item BPRS and the CGI-SCH was not apparent. Also, a roughly logarithmic relationship was assumed between the two scales. In addition, not only specific items but also their weightings were considered to be important in the realization of a linear relationship between the BPRS and the CGI-SCH and in the further improvement of the BPRS as a diagnostic scale.

Competing Interests

The authors declare that they have no competing interests.

Authors' Contributions

JS performed the evaluation of the patients and the statistical analysis, and wrote the manuscript. SM also performed the evaluation of the patients and revised the manuscript. JI was responsible for checking the methodology of the study and evaluating the results of the statistical analysis. In addition, all authors read and approved the final version of the manuscript.

Acknowledgments

The authors wish to acknowledge Katsuji Nishimura, Takao Kanai, Ken Inada and Kaoru Sakamoto for providing us with very useful advice in this study.

References

[1] Lindenmayer JP, Harvey PD, Khan A, Kirkpatrick B. Schizophrenia: Measurements of psychopathology. *Psychiatr. Clin. North Am. 2007;30:339-63.*

[2] Overall JE, Gorham DR. The Brief Psychiatric Rating Scale. *Psychol. Rep.* 1962;10:799-812.

[3] Haro JM, Kamath SA, Ochoa S, et al., SOHO Study Group. The Clinical Global Impression-Schizophrenia Scale: a simple instrument to measure the diversity of symptoms present in schizophrenia. *Acta Psychiatr. Scand.* 2003;Suppl 416:16-23.

[4] Kay SR, Fiszbein A, Opler LA. The Positive and Negative Syndrome Scale (PANSS) for schizophrenia. *Schizophr. Bull.* 1987;13:261-76.

[5] Andreasen, NC. Scale for the Assessment of Positive Symptoms (SAPS). Iowa City: University of Iowa, 1984.

[6] Andreasen NC. Scale for the Assessment of Negative Symptoms (SANS). Iowa City: University of Iowa, 1983.

[7] Sawamura J, Morishita S, Ishigooka J. Is there a linear relationship between the Brief Psychiatric Rating Scale and the Clinical Global Impression-Schizophrenia scale? A retrospective analysis. *BMC Psychiatry.* 2010;10:105.

[8] American Psychiatric Association. Diagnostic and Statistical Manual of Mental Disorders. 4th ed, Text Revision. New York: American Psychiatric Publishing, 2000.

[9] SPSS Inc. SPSS for Windows Version 14. Chicago, IL: SPSS Inc, 2007.

[10] Stata Corporation, 2007. Stata user's guide. Release 10.0. College Station, Texas: Stata Corporation, 2007.

[11] Microsoft Corporation. Microsoft Excel 2003. Redmond, Wa.: Microsoft Corp., 2003.

[12] Hedlund JL, Vieweg BW. The Brief Psychiatric Rating Scale (BPRS): a comprehensive review. *J. Oper. Psychiatry.* 1980;11:48-65.
[13] Leucht S, Engel R. The relative sensitivity of the Clinical Global Impressions Scale and the Brief Psychiatric Rating Scale in antipsychotic drug trials. *Neuropsychopharmacol.* 2006;31:406-12.
[14] Leucht S, Kane JM, Kissling W, Hamann J, Etschel E, Engel R. Clinical implications of Brief Psychiatric Rating Scale scores. *Br. J. Psychiatry.* 2005;187:366-71.
[15] *Müller* MJ, Rossbach W, Dannigkeit P, *Müller*-Siecheneder F, Szegedi A, Wetzel H. Evaluation of standardized rater training for the Positive and Negative Syndrome Scale (PANSS). *Schizophr. Res.* 1998;32:151-60.
[16] Naber D, Vita A. Tools for measuring clinical effectiveness. *Eur. Neuropsychopharmacol.* 2004; 14(Suppl 4):S435-44.
[17] Tandon R, Devellis RF, Han J, et al., IAQ Validation Study Group. Validation of the Investigator's Assessment Questionnaire, a new clinical tool for relative assessment of response to antipsychotics in patients with schizophrenia and schizoaffective disorder. *Psychiatry Res.* 2005;136:211-21.
[18] Suzuki T, Uchida H, Nomura K, et al. Novel rating scales for schizophrenia-Targeted Inventory on Problems in Schizophrenia (TIP-Sz) and Functional Assessment for Comprehensive Treatment of Schizophrenia (FACT-Sz). *Schizophr. Res.* 2008;106:328-36.
[19] Burlingame GM, Dunn TW, Chen S, et al. Selection of outcome assessment instruments for inpatients with severe and persistent mental illness. *Psychiatr. Serv.* 2005;56:444-51.
[20] Efroymson MA. Multiple regression analysis. In: Ralston A, Wilf HS, eds. *Mathematical Methods for Digital Computers.* New York: Wiley, 1960:191-203.
[21] Hocking RR. The analysis and selection of variables in linear regression. *Biometrics.* 1976;32:1-49.
[22] Bow-Thomas CC, Velligan DI, Miller AL. Predicting quality of life from symptomatology in schizophrenia at exacerbation and stabilization. *Psychiatr. Res.* 1999;86:131-42.
[23] Milev P. Predictive values of neurocognition and negative symptoms on functional outcome in schizophrenia: a longitudinal first-episode study with 7-year follow-up. *Am. J. Psychiatry.* 2005;162:495-506.
[24] Guillem F, Rinaldi M, Pampoulova T, Stip E. The complex relationships between executive functions and positive symptoms in schizophrenia. *Psychol. Med. 2008*;38:853-60.
[25] Judd CM, McClelland GH, Ryan CS. Data analysis: A model comparison approach. 2nd ed. New York: Routledge/Taylor and Francis, 2009.
[26] Mullins D, Pfefferbaum B, Schultz H, Overall JE. Brief Psychiatric Raying Scale for Children: Quantitative scoring of the medical records. *Psychiatr. Res.* 1985;19:43-9.
[27] Brekke JS, Kohrt B, Green MF. Neuropsychological functioning as a moderator of the relationship between psychosocial functioning and the subjective experience of self and life in schizophrenia. *Schizophr. Bull.* 2001;27:697-708.
[28] Stevens SS. On the Theory of Scales of Measurement. *Science,* New Series 1964;103:677-80.

[29] Aarseth SJ, Zare K. A regularization of the three-body problem. *Celestial Mechanics.* 1974;10:185-205.

[30] Marchal C, Yoshida J, Yi-Sui S. Three-body problem. *Celestial Mechanics.* 1984;34:65-93.

[31] Naganuma S. A method for the intuitive comprehension of physical mathematics. Second Edition. Tokyo: Tsusho Sangyo Kenkyusha, 2000:183-246.

Reviewed by Ken Inada, Department of Psychiatry, Tokyo Women's Medical University, Tokyo, Japan

In: Schizophrenia Research: Recent Advances
Editor: Tomiki Sumiyoshi
ISBN: 978-1-62808-703-1

Chapter 3

Quality of Life and Personal and Social Functioning: New Targets in Schizophrenia Treatment

***Anna Galuppi*[1], *Maria Cristina Turola*[2] *and Paola Mazzoni*[2]**
[1] Section of Child Neurology and Psychiatry,
Children's Hospital A. Meyer – University of Florence, Italy
[2] Mental Health Department, Local Health Agency, Ferrara, Italy

Abstract

In classical reports, schizophrenia is represented as a chronic, worsening, serious disease, with poor outcomes. The complex set of symptoms, apparently so far from common experience, evoked fear and detachment, and led to alienation from civil society and reclusion in Asylums.

Much has changed in recent decades, and the current integrated model of outpatient care allows to observe the disease course in vivo, without the artifacts of institutionalization. The complete application of the Psychiatric Reform Law of 1978 in the province of Ferrara, Italy, and in its district of Copparo, provides an observation period of over thirty years; in addition, the presence of cases registers and, since the eighties, of computerized data base, allows us to follow the path of each patient over time

In Copparo Community Mental Health Center, professionals carried out a research, sought to assess the extent and typology of schizophrenia in real life in the area, studying retrospectively the course of all patients (n =201) treated in the 1979-2008 period (mean observation time 11.9 ±7.9), and evaluating, in 2009, the outcomes in terms of symptoms, personal and social functioning and quality of life.

The hospitalization index (mean 19,8 per person/year ±45.6) and the number of outpatient consultations (27.3 ppy ±49.6), draw a picture of schizophrenia much less serious than "historic" : a disease with wide course variability , which needs only of short time hospitalizations for acute crisis, or rehabilitative residential programs in most complex cases, and usually can be treated in outpatient centers.

Furthermore, outcomes have undergone a profound change: symptomatic remission is nowadays a realistic goal (87 % of cases asymptomatic or had light symptoms), while personal and social functioning is in many cases more problematic (55.7 % of cases have marked or severe difficulties), persisting working and relational difficulties, partly related to enduring stigma. The percentage of subjects with disruptive or aggressive behavior is very low (9 %)

Perceived quality of life is not negative; rather, schizophrenia cases showed, on WHOQol-bref environmental and physical dimensions, higher scores than average of National Italian WHOQol healthy subjects group.

Cases' quality of life assessment by professional is currently in progress, using Qol-P, and we would ask relatives for the same evaluation, in order to make a comparison of the three assessments.

The research provided professionals for a useful feedback on their work, a better definition of treatment programs and critical areas; also, enabled them to identify cases with good or excellent outcome, often underestimated under the influence of urgent serious cases. Furthermore, this study allows to underline, with users, their personal progresses, and provide correct and documented information to new cases, their families and local agency, so fighting prejudice and stigma.

INTRODUCTION

In classical reports, schizophrenia is represented as a chronic, worsening, serious disease, with poor outcomes. The complex set of symptoms, apparently so far from common experience, evoked fear and detachment, and led to alienation from civil society and reclusion in Asylums.

Much has changed in recent decades: drug therapies have been discovered, effective on evident symptoms; in many countries an integrated model of outpatient care is advancing; psycho-education and other psychotherapies are currently used; psychiatric rehabilitation and disability prevention are common concepts; therapies' side effects are kept to the minimum [1]. So, nowadays it is possible to observe the schizophrenia disease course in real life, without the artifacts of institutionalization; the intervention aim gradually shifted from sedation to symptom remission and to the maintenance of remission, increasing the value of personal and social functioning and quality of life.

In parallel, in the scientific literature began to appear first non-negative outcomes, then the concept of remission [2,3], finally the focus on patient' subjective aspects and quality of life [4]. WHO estimates that about 20% of cases have continuous symptoms with increasing disability, 35% show alternating remissions and relapsing, 45% had recovered after one or more morbid episodes [5]. Andreasen defines "the Rule of Thirds": one third of cases improve, one third deteriorates and the other third is placed in intermediate conditions [6].

In 2005, the International Group for Remission sets precise criteria to define clinical remission [2].

Schizophrenia is an extremely heterogeneous illness with many possible variables influencing psychopathology and disability [1,6]. Lasalvia et al. considers the course of schizophrenia as dynamic and evolving, with frequent opportunities for change [7].

Currently, the concept of outcomes includes different dimensions, such as clinical symptoms, personal and social functioning, and quality of life [4].

Quality of life (QoL) may be defined as a person's sense of wellbeing and satisfaction with his/her life circumstances, as well as a person's health status and access to resources and opportunities [8]. Factors influencing QoL in schizophrenia and other severe mental illnesses are various and not well known: studies have identified a number of influential factors, such as social support, unmet needs and medication side effects [5], but there are variation among studies, partially due to differences in the definition and measurement of QoL [5,10]. Some definitions refer to it as a multidimensional set of components consisting of a person's satisfaction with life as a whole, or general wellbeing; observable social and material wellbeing, or objective QoL; satisfaction with social and material wellbeing, or subjective QoL; health and functional status, or health-related QoL. Clarifying the relationship between psychiatric symptoms, global functioning and QoL can represent an important step both in elucidating factors affecting Qol for individuals and in orienting future treatment development efforts [4].

In Italy, the Psychiatric Reform Law of 1978 closed Psychiatric Hospitals and established a Community Based model care, with a major function in psychiatric care placed in the Community Mental Health Centre (CMHC) that provide psychiatric integrated interventions in different settings, mostly in outpatients clinics, and patients' own homes [13].

In the province of Ferrara, Emilia Romagna, Northern Italy, and in its district of Copparo, the reform was completely applied since 1978, providing an observation period of over thirty years; in addition, the presence of cases registers and, since the eighties, of computerized data base, allows us to follow the path of each patient over time.

In recent years, a period of organizational crisis and cuts in public budgets occurred: professionals, overworked, are often asked to pay more attention to the bureaucracy that therapeutic efficiency. They, who are facing users, increasingly in emergencies, are in danger of losing sight of the main objective of their work, health care, and were demoralizing, having always in the mind the most severe cases. The impression of all was to carry out a useless work, a never-ending task. The research was born from the need to look at the past, understand characteristics and needs of users, to better planning of interventions, but also to restore value and meaning to their work, and to find motivations. Community Mental Health Center handles all types of psychiatric disorders: anxiety disorders and depression are the most frequent, but is schizophrenia which commits more to travel time, number of interventions and needs for hospitalization. So, it was natural to choose schizophrenia syndrome as target of research and all professionals, doctors and nurses together, carried out a study, sought to assess the extent and typology of schizophrenia in real life in that area, and the subjective Quality of Life of users.

Since the creation of the Department of Mental Health and the implementation of the psychiatric services after the 1978 reform in the Emilia-Romagna Region [13], community mental health centers have played a central role in delivering integrated care for patients with schizophrenia and their families.

Copparo Center is the health facility to which 37.803 inhabitants refer to, 19678 females and 18125 males; 4051 are under 18 and 10526 are over 65. Population is spread over 6 municipalities and mainly works in agricultural, commercial and industrial activities, in a flat countryside, well-supplied with facilities.

The Center is made up by an outpatient department and a day-hospital, both open eight hours a day on working days; it provides medical examinations and home consulting, drug therapies whenever needed, group therapies, individual and group rehabilitations activities, meetings with family members. Compulsory psychiatric hospitalizations for acute illnesses are made by the Psychiatric Unit of Ferrara Hospital, which is 18 km far, while voluntary hospitalizations for severe illnesses use both Ferrara and Lagosanto Hospital Units, 30 km far. Both units provide 15 beds, for the whole district, with a caseload of 351463 inhabitants.

Rehabilitating residential programs, with projects from 1 to 3 months, are made in specific district facilities. There are three residences, providing 50 beds.

In the area do not exist private clinics for psychiatric disorders

The Copparo Centre staff is composed by 6 psychiatric nurses, 2 psychiatrists, 1 psychologist and 1 social worker. The Centre deals with any sort of psychiatric illness, from reactive forms to psychoses, and supplies consulting at the local hospital and cooperates with family doctors and with the Drug Abuse Service. All subjects, even non-residents, have the right to receive free assistance, paying simply a money contribution. Subjects with a low income or with severe illnesses don't pay the money contribution: schizophrenic subjects have totally free assistance.

METHODS

The first step of the research was to select all users of the Centre who received a diagnosis of schizophrenia in the period 1979-2008, using as source of data the computerized database of Local Health Unit.

The second step was to verify the correctness of the diagnosis, that is, its correspondence to the ICD10 criteria. Professionals reviewed their cases and responded to an interview conducted by psychiatrists outside the team. In currently untreated cases, the medical records were reviewed.

The third step was to choice the parameters available and relevant in courses study: age at first consultation; number and length of admissions for acute crisis and for rehabilitation programs; day center programs; number of consultations in CMHC per year.

The individual course variability made it difficult to compare different cases: this problem was overcome by calculating some "Indexes":

THI Total Hospitalization Index = average number of hospitalisation days per year

AHI Acute Hospitalization Index = average number of acute hospitalisation days per year

RRI Residential rehabilitation Index = average number of residentilal rehabilitation days per year

HCUI Health Center Utilization Index = average number of CMHC consultations or interventions per year

The indices represent the annual time that any person spent in hospital or in rehabilitation residence, and HCUI is an index of utilization of outpatient services. The indices provide a measure of the individual disease severity and also of Service workload.

The fourth step was to decide the measurement instruments for symptoms level, personal and social functioning, and Quality of life, in subjects who were treated in CMHC in the year 2008.

The World Health Organization Quality of Life Assessment Instrument (WHOQoL-Bref) was used to assess the patients' quality of life. The WHOQoL-BREF includes 26 items measuring the following domains: physical health, psychological health, social relationships, and environment. Two further items evaluate the individual's overall perception of quality of life and the individual's overall perception of their health. Domain scores are scaled in a positive direction (i.e., higher scores correspond to better quality of life). The average score of items within each domain is used to calculate the domain score. Mean scores are then multiplied by 4 in order to make domain scores comparable with the scores used in the WHOQOL-100. Where more than 20% of data is missing from an assessment, the assessment should be discarded. Where an item is missing, the average of other items in the domain is substituted. Where more than two items are missing from the domain, the domain score should not be calculated (with the exception of domain 3, where the domain should only be calculated if < 1 item is missing) [16].

The WHOQol-Bref questionnaires were handed to users when they came for a scheduled check-up in CMHC, were self–administered by the respondents and collected in the same day.

The VADO Personal and Social Functioning Scale (FPS), which is a modified version of the Social and Occupational Functioning Assessment Scale (SOFAS) [15], was used to assess the patients' level of functioning in four main areas: work and/or socially useful activities; family, personal and social relationships; self-care; aggressive and destructive behaviors. Suicide risk is considered in the score only as much as suicidal ruminations may interfere with social-functioning. The FPS requires a brief and simple training, which is described in the VADO manual [16]. An evaluation is assessed according to the following levels: absent, slight, evident, marked, and severe. The evaluation is then turned into a score from 0 to 100 (higher scores correspond to better functioning) according to VADO guide instructions.

In the present study, a young psychiatrist in training collected information on single cases from referent professionals and filled out semi-structured schedules. Separate evaluations of the schedules were carried out by two psychiatrists with training in the administration of the scale.

The Italian version of Brief Psychiatric Rating Scale (BPRS), in its 24-item 4.0 version [17,18] was used to assess psychiatric symptoms. Each item is rated on a scale from 1 = no symptom to 7 = extremely severe symptom; the range score is 24-168. The scale provides measures in four areas: anxiety and depression, positive symptoms, negative symptoms, mania and hostility.

BPRS data were collected from referent psychiatrist and nurses.

Statistical analysis was carried out using the SPSS 12.0 and Winstat for Excel statistic system.

Statistical procedure included: descriptive statistics, frequencies distribution, Pearson r Test, significance (p) test with level of significance set at 0.05.

RESULTS

Sample and Courses Analysis

205 subjects who had received a schizophrenia diagnosis were selected from the Local Health Unit database; 201 of them, with confirmed diagnosis according to the ICD10 criteria,

were included in the study: 113 males and 88 females. Observation mean time was 11.9 years, standard deviation 7.9, without gender difference.

Mean age at the first consultation was 33.7 years ± 13.7 in males, 40.1 ± 14.2 in females (statistically significant difference, P-value Kruskal-Wallis < 0.0001). Age distribution at the first consultation is represented in Figure 1.

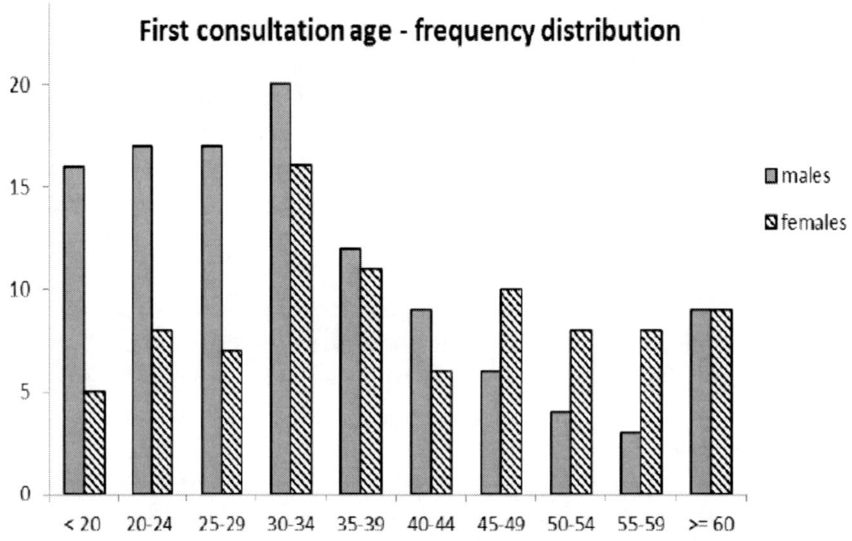

Figure 1. First consultation age in males and females: frequency distribution.

We found a few cases who had first consultation in old age: they were cases yet diagnosed and treated elsewhere, who recently went to live in the area.

Table 1 shows means and standard deviations of outcomes parameters: total admissions' number and length, acute crisis admissions' number and length, rehabilitation residential programs' number and length, and three indexes: THI, AHI, RRI. The table shows the total and gender-disaggregated data.

All parameters of admission have a small negative correlation with the age at first consultation (Pearson test r = - 0.2).

41 cases (20.4 %) never had hospitalization, whilst 30 cases (14.9 %), 6 females and 24 males, have a THI > 30 days/year. Of a total of 1060 admissions, 157 (18.3%) were compulsory admissions due to acute crises; their average length was 11.3 days.

35 subjects attended day-center programs of varying duration (average 6.7 months); some of them have participated several times, so we had a total of 54 day-center programs.

Outcomes Analysis

During the period 1979-2008 67 cases (33 %) were discharged, 5 (2.5 %) have moved elsewhere, 22 (10.9 %) are dead: one by suicide, one, who had a dual diagnosis, by overdose, the others twenty are dead by natural causes.

107 cases (53.2 %) were in treatment on December 2008. The study was proposed to all them, but 3 refused, so we had a sample of 104 users: 62 males and 42 females. The mean age

at the first consultation was 33.3 years ± 13.6, and the average observation time is 13.4 years ± 7.4; the present mean age is 47.0 years ± 13.5.

32 cases are working, 6 are retired, 4 are looking for a work, 62 (59.6 %) receive a disability check; 89 (85.6 %) live at home, the other in protected shared flat or small communities within the city or close to it. 40 (38.5 %) have a partner, 64 (61.5 %) are singles. All of them follow individual treatment programs, almost all currently are taking antipsychotic drugs, typical (21.1 %) or atypical (76.9 %) ; in 28 cases the treatment uses depot antipsychotics.

In this group, the mean age at the first consultation is 30.9 ± 11.7 in males, 38.1 ± in females: significantly (p = 0.0001) younger than total sample; the differences between males and females are similar to those of the general sample.

Descriptive statistic of course parameters in this group are represented in Table 2.

Table 1. Outcome parameters:
Total sample and gender-disaggregated data

	Total sample N= 201		Males N = 113		Females N = 88	
	average	Standard deviation	average	Standard deviation	average	Standard deviation
Total number of admissions	5.3	9.3	5.6	9.06	4.4	9.5
Total length of admissions (days) **	213.1	596.1	239.6	597.8	179.4	596.1
Number of admission for acute crises **	4.3	7.4	4.6	7.4	3.8	6.8
Length of admissions for acute crisis (days) **	72.2	132.6	87.2	155.7	53.5	92.5
Number of rehabilitation/ residential programs	1.0	3.2	0.9	2.2	1.05	4.25
Length of rehabilitation/ residential programs (days)	140.9	541.5	152.3	535.9	125.9	552.1
THI **	19.8	45.6	19.2	36.8	13.4	45.1
AHI **	7.3	12.8	9.5	15.8	4.5	6.3
RRI	9.4	36.5	9.8	30.1	8.9	43.4

** the gender difference in these parameters is statistically significant, p value < 0.0001 at Kruskall-Wallis test.

All parameters are higher than the overall sample, in particular: the total number of admissions, the time spent in conditions of hospitalization (an average of 80 days more per capita), the duration of the rehabilitation/residential programs (60 days more per person), the THI (4.5 days more per person per year), the RRI (5 days more per person per year)

The HCUI, namely the average number of intervention/consultation per person per year is 41.3 ± 56.1, 51.8 ± 64.3 in males and 27.0 ± 38.8 in females.

Table 2. Patients in treatment at 2008: course parameters

	Total		Males		Females	
	mean	S.D.	mean	S.D.	mean	S.D.
Total admission number	6.3	9.4	6.5	7.6	6.1	11.6
Total admissions length (days)	288.1	693.6	304.6	665.8	265.5	735.1
Acute crisis admissions number	4.8	6.4	5.1	5.5	4.4	7.4
Acute crisis admissions length (days)	84.8	118.3	97.0	123.6	68.2	109.6
Rehabilitation/residential admissions number	1.5	3.9	1.4	2.5	1.6	5.2
Rehabilitation/residential admissions length (days)	203.2	649.1	207.6	626.8	197.3	683.9
THI	22.3	48.1	24.8	41.8	18.9	55.8
AHI	8.4	13.1	10.9	16.1	4.9	6.2
RRI	14	44.2	13.9	35.6	14.0	54.0
HCUI	41.3	56.1	51.8	64.3	27.0	38.8

Symptoms and Functioning

Symptoms are evaluated using the BPRS 24 items scale: the data are represented in Table 3.

Table 3. Descriptive statistics of BPRS score: total and subscales

	Total sample		Males		Females	
	Mean	S.D.	Mean	S.D.	Mean	S.D.
BPRS scale total score	**47.8**	**18.9**	**50.4**	**18.9**	**44.0**	**18.2**
Anxiety depression subscale	12.9	5.9	13.4	6.6	12.2	4.8
Positive Symptoms subscale	10.4	5.6	11.1	5.6	9.3	5.5
Negative Symptoms subscale	13.7	7.6	14.0	7.9	13.2	7.0
Mania subscale	10.4	5.4	11.2	5.2	9.2	5.4

The average score in total BPRS scale corresponds to very mild symptoms in females and mild symptoms in males; the majority of subjects (more than 80%) is asymptomatic or shows mild symptoms in BPRS and its subscales; only a small percentage of cases, no more than 5%, has severe symptoms. This distribution is represented in Figure 2.

The frequency distribution of BPRS subscales is represented in Figure 3. Even in the subscales, the majority of individuals is asymptomatic or show only mild symptoms.

In our cases in treatment, social and personal functioning, evaluated using FPS scale, shows evident difficulties, mostly in the work and relationships areas (mean value 2.0, namely evident problems), whilst in the bother/aggressiveness area the mean value is between 0 – absent and 1 –mild difficulties. On a scale 0-100, the overall functioning average is 52.0 ± 22.6 in males and 60.1 ± 23.4 in females (the difference is statistically significant, $p < 0.0001$). The descriptive statistics of FPS total and subscales score are represented in Table 4. The frequency distributions in males and females are represented in Figure 4 and Figure 5.

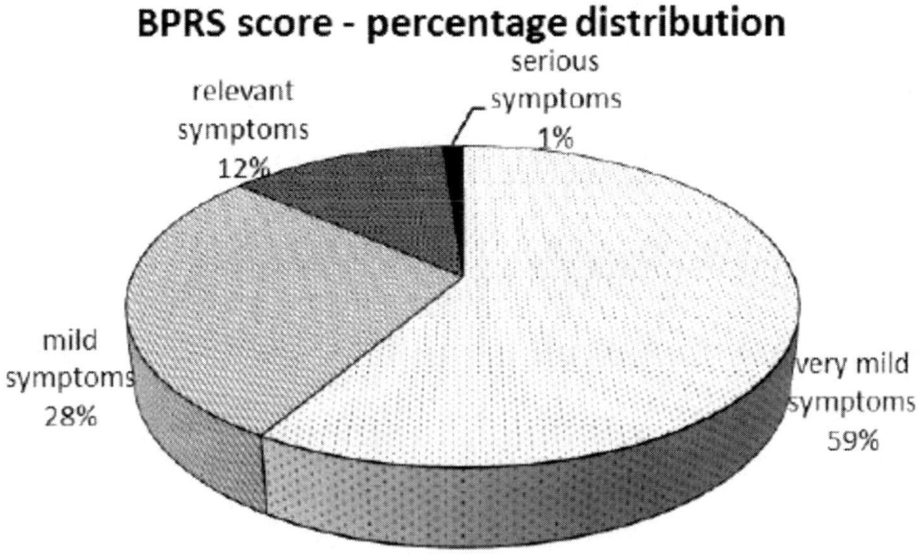

Figure 2. Graphic of percentage distribution in total BPRS score.

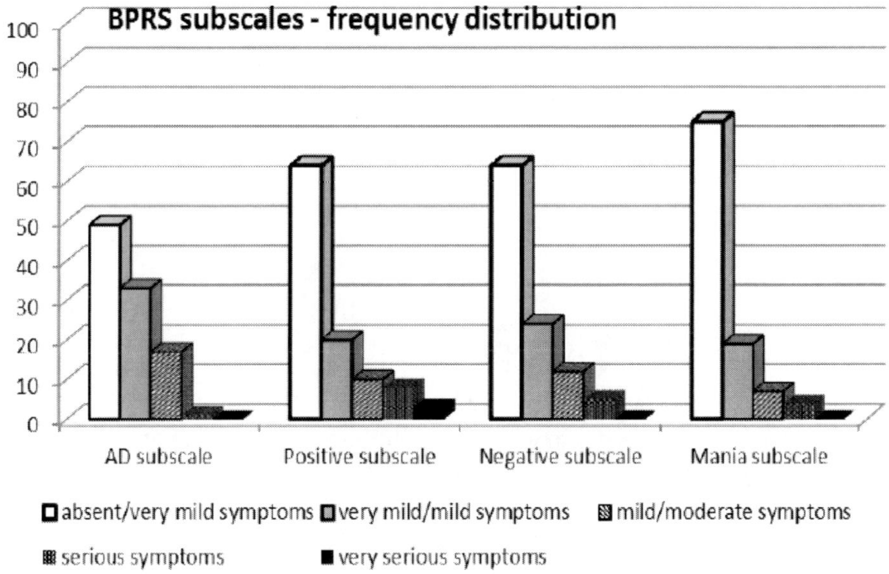

Figure 3. Frequency distribution of BPR subscales.

Table 4. Descriptive statistics of FPS score: total and subscales

	Total sample		Males		Females	
	Mean	S.D.	Mean	S.D.	Mean	S.D.
FPS scale total score	**55.2**	**23.2**	**52.0**	**22.6**	**60.1**	**23.4**
Work/social utility	2.0	1.6	2.0	1.6	1.9	1.5
Personal/ social relationships	2.0	1.3	2.0	1.3	1.9	1.4
Self-care	1.6	1.3	1.8	1.4	1.3	1.2
Bother/aggressiveness	0.7	1.3	0.9	1.4	0.4	0.9

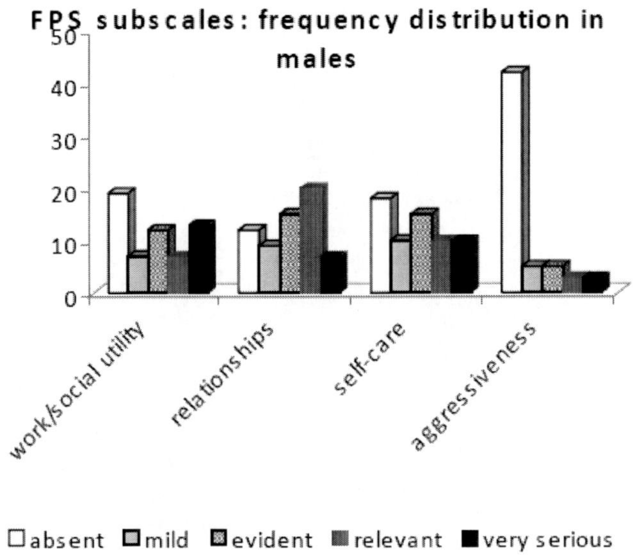

Figure 4. Frequency distribution of FPS subscales in males.

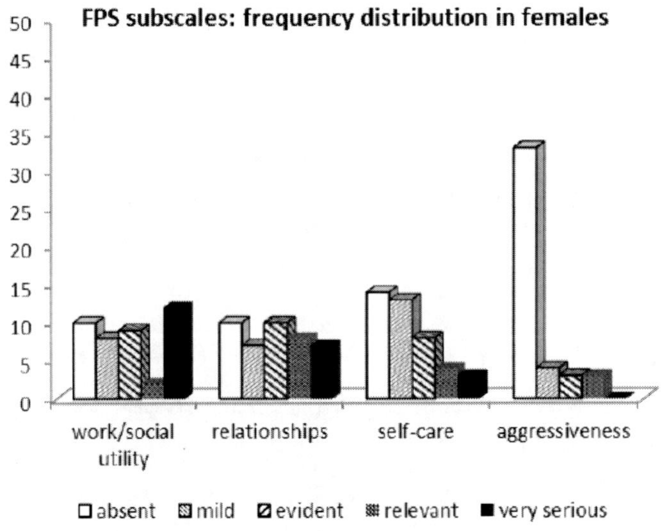

Figure 5. Frequency distribution of FPS subscales in females.

Quality of Life

101 subjects, 60 males and 41 females, completed the WHOQoL-bref questionnaire.

General QoL (item Q1) was judged “neither poor nor good”: total sample mean score is 3.2 (males 3.3, females 3.1); in subjects aged <45 years the mean score is 3.2 both in men and women; in subjects aged = 45 years, the mean score is 3.4 in men and 1.9 in women.

On General Health (item Q2) the mean opinion is “neither satisfied nor dissatisfied”: total sample mean score is 3.1 (males 3.3, females 2.9); in subjects < 45 years the mean score is

3.2 in men and 3.3 in women, in cases aged = 45 years the mean score is 3.4 in men and 2.6 in women.

Frequency distribution of score is represented in Figure 3.

Figure 3. Frequency distribution of WHOQoL items Q1 and Q2 in males and females.

Domain 1 – Physical Health and Well-Being

People generally claim: to be free from pain (Q3 mean reverse score = 3.9), to be free of dependence on drugs and treatment (Q4 mean reverse score 3.2), having enough energy for everyday life (Q10 mean score 3.05), to be able to get around (Q15 mean score 3.8) , to sleep well (Q16 mean score 3.6) , to be satisfied with ability to perform daily living activities (Q17 mean score 3.3).

All these items are located between the answer 3 = "neither satisfied nor dissatisfied" and the answer 4 = "satisfied". Only the item Q18: "How satisfied are you with your capacity for work?" has a lower score (mean 2.45), between "dissatisfied" and "neither/nor"; in this item 4 cases don't answer.

The mean score of Domain1 is 22.8 ± 5.2 (males 23.03, females 22.04), corresponding to 13 on a scale 4-20 and 56 on a scale 0-100.

Domain 2 – Psychological Health and Well-Being

Happiness and enjoyment of life and feeling of life as meaningful are not so good (Q5 mean score 2.4, Q6 reverse mean score 2.7); difficulties on concentration are experienced in moderate amount (Q7 mean score 3.0); our subjects say to accept their bodily appearance from "a little" to "moderately" (Q11 mean score 2.8) ; the self-satisfaction is rather poor (Q19 mean score 2.7), whilst they affirm to have seldom negative feeling, such as blue mood, despair, anxiety, depression (Q26 reverse score 3.9).

The mean score of Domain 2 is 17.8 ± 3.2 (males 18.05, females 16.1), corresponding to 12 on a scale 4-20 and 50 on a scale 0-100.

Domain 3 – Social Relations

In this area, all items show more dissatisfaction: personal relationships (Q20 mean score 2.8), sex life (Q21 mean score 2.1), and support from friends (Q22 mean score 2.4).

The mean score of Domain 3 is 7.2 ± 2.9 (males 7.5, females 6.9), corresponding to 9 on a scale 4-20 and 31 on a scale 0-100.

Domain 4 – Environment

People affirm to have not enough money to meet their needs (Q12 mean score 2.5) and little opportunity for leisure activities (Q14 mean score 2.6); physical environment is perceived as not too much healthy (Q9 mean score 2.7); subjects think to be almost moderately safe in their daily life (Q8 mean score 2.9) and are neither dissatisfied nor satisfied with the conditions of their living place (Q23 mean score 2.9). They think to have available information in their daily life (Q13 mean score 3.6, between moderately and mostly) and they are enough satisfied with their access to health services (Q24 mean score 3.8) and with their transport (Q25 mean score 3.8).

The mean score of Domain4 is 24.4±5.6 (males 25.4, females 23.7), corresponding to 12 on a scale 4-20 and 50 on a scale 0-100.

Mean transformed scores of WHOQol domains are reported in Figure 4.

Figure 4. WHOQoL domain mean scores, converted to transformed scores, in males and females, < 45 years and = 45 years.

Compared to national Italian WHOQoL validation group, our sample shows a much lower level of satisfaction in social relationships and a lower degree of satisfaction in the psychological domain, but a little more satisfaction in the physical and environmental domains.

Correlations

The study of correlations between the course and outcome variables, using the Pearson test, shows some interesting results.

The age at first contact has a negative correlation ($r = -0.34$) with the period spent in hospital for acute symptoms, but only a weak correlation with BPRS total score ($r = -18$) and FPS total score ($r = 0.14$). The early onset does not necessarily determine the outcome.

How much symptoms and functioning are interconnected? BPRS total score and FPS total score are negatively correlated ($r = -0.58$) and the level of symptoms is particularly correlated with the subscales of aggressiveness ($r = 0.66$) and self-care ($r = 0.57$) of the FPS. Between the BPRS subscales, is the negative symptoms subscales that results negatively related to total FPS score ($r = -0.65$, $p < 0.0005$) and all its subscales, with r range between 0.44 for the A subscale to 0.69 for the C subscale. Higher level of symptoms, particularly negative symptoms, corresponds to a global minor functioning: self-care and bother/aggressiveness are the more problematic areas.

The subjective quality of life is negatively correlated to patient's age at present time: older subjects have lower WHOQoL scores in general ($r = -0.35$, $p < 0.0005$), in the Domain 1 – health satisfaction ($r = -0.35$, $p < 0.0005$) and, to a lesser extent, in the Domain 2 – psychological health satisfaction ($r = - 12$, $p < 0.05$).

The disease length shows a low negative correlation with the health satisfaction ($r = -0.18$, $p < 0.05$).

The subjective quality of life is related to personal and social functioning. Global functioning – FPS total score is related to WhoQoL Domain 1 ($r = 0.57$, $p < 0.0005$), domain 4 ($r = 0.43$, $p < 0.0005$) and Domain 3 ($r = 0.37$, $p < 0.005$): higher functioning means higher health and environment satisfaction, and also social relationships satisfaction.

The WHOQol domain 1 is negatively correlated to FPS subscale A ($r = - 0.54$, $p < 0.0005$), subscale B ($r = - 0.46$, $p < 0.0005$) and subscale C ($r = - 0.45$, $p < 0.0005$): problems in work, social relationships and self-care correspond to lower health satisfaction.

The WhoQol Domain 4 – environmental satisfaction is negatively correlated to FPS subscale B – social relationships ($r = - 0.35$, $p < 0.05$).

Quality of life is to some extent affected by the level of symptoms: the individual overall perception of QoL-Q1 is negatively correlated with BPRS anxiety-depression scale ($r = -0.32$, $p < 0.05$) and with BPRS positive symptoms scale ($r = - 0.17$, $p < 0.05$).

The Domain 1 shows negative correlations with BPRS negative symptoms subscale ($r = -0.29$, $p < 0.05$), the Domain 2 is negatively correlated with the anxiety-depression BPRS subscale ($r = - 0.28$, $p< 0.05$) and the Domain 4 shows a low negative correlation with BPRS negative symptoms subscale.

The social relations Domain 3, shows a low negative correlation with the BPRS anxiety-depression subscale ($r = - 0.15$, $p < 0.05$) and the BPRS positive symptoms subscale ($r = -0.15$, $p < 0.05$).

Data Analysis

One of the more evident findings of this work is the statistically significant difference, in course and outcome, between males and females, namely:

a) the number of cases diagnosed with schizophrenia in the Copparo area is higher in males than in females; but in the population of the area the male/female ratio is less than 1 as early as the age group 15-20, and decreases more more with increasing age.
b) males have the first consultation (T0), at an earlier age, on average 7 years earlier. This finding agrees with studies reported in the international literature [1]
c) males have a higher number of admissions, especially for acute crises, and a longer hospitalization' length; on average, they spend in the hospital 6 days more per person per year, compared to females.
d) males require almost twice the number of interventions in Community Mental Health Centre: 51.8 versus 27 per person per year.
e) in the study of outcomes, males are more symptomatic than females (mean BPRS score 50.4 vs. 44.0) and this gap is present in all BPRS subscales.
f) males show a lower level of personal and social functioning, with average FPS score of 52.0 vs. 60.1 , on a scale from 0 - worst functioning to 100 - best functioning . The level of difficulties is higher in all areas, especially in self-care (mean score 1.8 vs. 1.3) and bother/aggressiveness (mean score 0.9 vs. 0.4).

The research highlights encouraging results. The disease is treated for most of the time at home, and the need for hospitalization is lower than expected: about 20 days per person each year, and just over one week each year for acute symptoms. The compulsory admissions are less than 1/5 of the total: this means that they are not used as a primary system for the resolution of crisis, but only as a last possible strategy when all others have failed.

The CMHC is committed about three times a month for each subject.

Most patients (87%) are asymptomatic or show a low level of psychopathological symptoms.

The personal and social functioning, however, is quite poor, with evident difficulties, mainly in the area of work and in relationships; contrary to current opinion, however, the area of the disturbance/aggressiveness is the least problematic: nearly 80% of subject has no such problems, or they have very mild. It should be point up that, in this evaluation, it was considered the entire observation time of each subject, an average of nearly 12 years. The correlation between negative symptoms and level of functioning should be detailed for its implications for therapeutic and rehabilitative programs.

The early onset appears to influence only slightly the course and outcome of the disease, and the long duration of illness does not necessarily result in high rates of hospitalization, or poor outcomes, but it do affects the quality of life.

If all the indexes of course and outcome are worse in males than in females, it is curious that males declare greater satisfaction for their lives; the difference reflects the age, as women over 45 years are more dissatisfied both generally and in different domains.

Our subjects with schizophrenia show no negative levels of satisfaction or dissatisfaction with various aspects of QoL: they declare more problems in social relationships (personal relationships, sex life, support from friends), in the availability of money and in the opportunity of leisure activities. They are quite satisfied with their access to health services and transport.

Patients more symptomatic or less functioning declare lower quality of life: this means that they are aware of their difficulties, and this too would be subject to a specific clinical work.

CONCLUSION

The observation of schizophrenia syndrome in natural conditions, for a long time, allows to highlight aspects impossible to detect in the trials: the great variability of the course, the existence of prolonged remissions, the state often marked by relapses and remissions and the persistence of potential for improvement even after many years of illness.

In our study, the disease results treatable mainly at home, and the prognosis is good from the standpoint of symptoms, with a high percentage of cases asymptomatic or mildly symptomatic. Instead, much remains to be done to prevent and minimize difficulties in personal and social functioning, but the main problems are the difficulties in work and relationships, not aggression or disturbance.

Perceived Quality of Life is not negative; rather, schizophrenia cases showed, on WHOQoL-bref environmental and physical domains, higher scores than the average of National Italian WHOQoL healthy subjects group. This results are very interesting for us, so we are working on WHOQoL retest in cases and on evaluation, using QoL-P [19], of their QoL by professionals; we would ask to relatives for the same evaluation, in order to make a comparison.

The research provided professionals for a useful feedback on their work and allowed to better define critical areas and treatment programs; but it enabled them to highlight the cases with good or excellent outcome, often underestimated, under the influence of urgent serious cases. Furthermore, this study allows to underline, with users, their personal progresses, and provide a correct and documented information to new cases and their families.

We think that it is important to consider each individual case as a unique person, evaluating many different aspects: personal characteristics, history of illness, symptoms, premorbid and current functioning, capacities and potential resources, family and social environment, support networks, compliance and any other possible factor.

It is also very important to contrast prejudice and stigma, both socially and in health care systems, because schizophrenia is a disease that can be studied and understood, it can be approached and treated, respecting the dignity of persons and allowing them a quite satisfying quality of life.

REFERENCES

[1] Jobe HT. Long-term outcome of patients with schizophrenia: a review. *Can. J. Psychiatry*. 2005;50:892–900

[2] Andreasen NC. Standardized remission criteria in schizophrenia. *Acta Psychiatr. Scand.* 2006 Feb;113(2):81.

[3] Andreasen NC, Carpenter WT Jr, Kane JM, Lasser RA, Marder SR, Weinberger DR. Remission in schizophrenia: proposed criteria and rationale for consensus. Am. J. Psychiatry. 2005 Mar;162(3):441-9.

[4] Eack SM, Newhill CE. Psychiatric Symptoms and Quality of Life in Schizophrenia: A Meta-Analysis. *Schizophrenia Bullettin.* 2007;33(5):1225–1237.

[5] WHO-World Health Organisation. Course and outcome of schizofrenia. http://www.who.int/mental_health/management/schizophrenia

[6] WHO-World Health Organization. *Schizophrenia and public health.* Geneva. 1998.

[7] Lasalvia A, Ruggeri M Assessing the outcome of community-based psychiatric care: building a feedback loop from 'real world' health services research into clinical practice. *Acta Psychiatr. Scand. Suppl.* 2007;437:6-15.

[8] Lehman AF. In: Quality of Life in Mental Disorders. Katschnig H, Freeman H, Sartorius N, editor. New York, NY: Wiley; 1997. *Instruments for measuring quality of life in mental illnesses;* pp. 79–94.

[9] Lambert M, Naber D. Current issues in schizophrenia: overview of patient acceptability, functioning capacity and quality of life. *CNS Drugs.* 2004;18:5–17.

[10] McNary SW, Lehman AF, O'Gardy KE. Measuring subjective life satisfaction in persons with severe and persistent mental illness: a measurement quality and structural model analysis. *Psychol. Assess. 1*997;9:503–307.

[11] Ritsner M. Predicting changes in domain-specific quality of life of schizophrenia patients. *J. Nerv. Ment. Dis.* 2003;191:287–294.

[12] Becker T, Leese M, Krumm S, Ruggeri M, Vazquez-Barquero JL. Needs and quality of life among patients with schizophrenia in five European centres: what is the impact of global functioning scores. *Soc. Psychiatry Psychiatr. Epidemiol.* 2005;40:628–634

[13] Garaci E. Thirty years after the reform of the Italian Law on mental health: time for celebrating, evaluating, moving forward. *Ann. Ist. Super Sanita.* 2009;45(1):3–4

[14] WHO. WHOQOL-BREF. Introduction, administration, scoring and generic version of the assessment. *Field Trial Version. Programme in mental health world health organisation.* Geneva. 1996.

[15] Morosini P, Magliano L, Brambilla L, Ugolini S, Pioli R. Development, reliability and acceptability of a new version of the DSM IV Social and Occupational Functioning Assessment Scale (SOFAS) to assess routine social functioning. *Acta Psychiatr. Scand.* 2000;101:323–329.

[16] Morosini P, Magliano L, Brambilla L. V.A.D.O. Valutazione di Abilità e Definizione di Obiettivi. Trento: Edizioni Erickson. 1998.

[17] Ventura J, Lukoff D, Nuechterlein KH, Liberman RP, Green M, Shaner A. Appendix 1: Brief Psychiatric Rating Scale (BPRS) Expanded Version (4.0) scales, anchor points and administration manual. *International Journal of Methods in Psychiatric Research.* 1993;3:227–243.

[18] Morosini P, Roncone R, Impallomeni M, Casacchia M. Presentazione dell'adattamento italiano della Brief Psychiatric Rating Scale, versione 4.0 ampliata (BPRS 4.0) *Rivista di riabilitazione psichiatrica e psicosociale.* 1994;3(94):195–198.

[19] Ruggeri M, Placentino A, Sebastiani G, Spagnolo A, Rossi G, Rucci P Quality of life-proxy (QoL-P) *Epidemiol. Psichiatr .Soc.* 2002;11(4):284-97.

In: Schizophrenia Research: Recent Advances
Editor: Tomiki Sumiyoshi

ISBN: 978-1-62808-703-1

Chapter 4

NATURAL-MORTALITY IN SCHIZOPHRENIA: AN UPDATED META-ANALYSIS

Carmen Bouza[1*], Teresa López-Cuadrado[2], Zuleika Saz-Parkinson[1], Raimundo Alcázar Alcázar[1] and José María Amate Blanco[1]

[1] Health Technology Assesment Agency. Instituto de Salud Carlos III. Ministry of Science and Innovation. Madrid, Spain

[2] National Epidemiology Center. Carlos III. Instituto de Salud Carlos III. Ministry of Science and Innovation. Madrid, Spain

ABSTRACT

Introduction: Physical health represents a challenge in Schizophrenia. We aimed to update the aggregate risk of natural-mortality among individuals with schizophrenia versus the general population and to quantify the excess mortality associated with common physical disorders.

Method: Systematic review and meta-analysis of longitudinal cohort studies published up to March 2009.

Results: 34 studies met the inclusion criteria. Patients with schizophrenia had a risk ratio of natural-mortality of 1.89 (95% CI: 1.86, 1.93) vis-à-vis the general population. This risk is high across the sexes and has increased in recent years. Pooled estimates show a significantly higher risk of mortality for respiratory, endocrine, digestive, cardiovascular and neoplastic disorders, with gender-related differences in some cases. Excess mortality, however, varied considerably among the specific disorders.

Conclusion: Schizophrenia associates with an increasing risk of natural mortality. It is essential that monitoring and control of common physical disorders be urgently incorporated into standard management of these patients.

Keywords: Schizophrenia, mortality, meta-analysis

* Corresponding author: Carmen Bouza, MD, PhD. Sinesio Delgado 4, 28029 Madrid, Spain. Tel: +34 91 822 2018; Fax: +34 91 387 7841. e-mail: cbouza@isciii.es.

Introduction

The aim of this chapter is to carry out an update, using meta-analytical techniques, of previous studies which have attempted to study the aggregate risk of natural-mortality among individuals with schizophrenia as compared to that of the general population, and quantify the excess mortality associated with common physical-disorders.

Schizophrenia is not only one of the most severe health problems world-wide [1-3], but also a life shortening illness [4, 5]. As a number of authors have pointed out as far back as the first part of the 20th century [4, 5], life expectancy of patients with schizophrenia is lower than that of the general population, with the ensuing excess mortality being attributable to both natural and unnatural causes [4-6].

At present, excess mortality among patients with schizophrenia is fundamentally ascribed to unnatural causes, and to suicide in particular [7-9], and recent publications report a gradual decrease in mortality due to natural causes [6, 9]. However, the impact of physical disorders on this population's mortality and the excess mortality associated with specific physical disorders are topics that have seldom been targeted for systematic analysis in the literature. Accordingly, the publications by Brown [7]) and Harris & Barraclough [8], which include primary studies published up to1996 and 1995, respectively, are still the references for mortality due to natural causes in this population.

In the wake of these chief analyses, a considerable number of individual studies have examined the risk of natural mortality and different physical disorders in patients with schizophrenia. Yet, the methodology of some of these studies, their occasionally small sample sizes, lack of the necessary power to identify significant differences in the results and inconsistency of results, render it difficult to ascertain excess mortality with accuracy, or establish whether or not certain disorders, such as cancer, pose a higher risk of mortality to schizophrenic patients than they do to the general population.

This situation, coupled with the evident changes in health care and therapy that have come about in medical practice in general and management of schizophrenic patients in particular, call for an updated quantification of the risk of natural mortality in this population.

Methods

Studies were identified through a systematic search in Medline up to March 2009. To ensure the greatest sensitivity and specificity possible, the strategy used included the terms "schizophrenia" [Mesh] and "mortality" [Mesh] without any language restrictions. We also searched bibliographies of retrieved studies and contacted content experts to identify additional studies [10].

Inclusion and Exclusion Criteria

Studies were required to [5,11]: 1) be longitudinal cohort studies reporting all-cause, natural-cause or specific physical-cause mortality; 2) be conducted on patients with formal diagnosis of schizophrenia; 3) cover more than 50 patients and report more than 5 observed deaths; 4) have a suitable comparison group; and, 5) include the number of observed and expected deaths, or contain sufficient details to allow these figures to be calculated. We excluded studies that specifically explored the efficacy of antipsychotic drugs or conducted intercomparisons of antipsychotic drugs.

Study Selection

Two reviewers independently screened studies for inclusion, retrieved potentially relevant studies, and decided on study eligibility. Disagreements between the reviewers were settled by discussion of the respective study data.

Data Extraction and Quality Assessment

We used a standardized form to abstract data on outcomes of interest, namely all-cause mortality, natural mortality and cause specific mortality. Additionally, the following information categories were also extracted: a) information on study design, initial year of data-collection, target country, duration of follow-up and year of publication; and b) details on both the study population -containing age, sex, degree of institutionalisation, and use or non-use of psychotropic drugs- and comparator group.

Validated recommendations [12] were used to assess the quality of studies. We attempted to contact authors to request additional data and clarify methods and data if necessary.

Data Analysis

To obtain a global measure of risk (Risk Ratio) of mortality among schizophrenia-sufferers versus the reference population, we used a Mantel-Haenszel fixed-effects meta-analysis [13]. The I^2 statistic was used to measure inconsistency across studies (14,15) with suggested thresholds for low (25%-49%), moderate (50%-74%), and high (≥75%) values, and meta-regression to explore potential reasons of statistical heterogeneity (15). In accordance with some recent literature, we have not used funnel plots to examine the possibility of publication bias, given the limitations and potential misleading results of these graphs [16].

As the primary outcome in this Chapter was mortality due to natural causes, we performed several analyses to examine the influence of a number of factors. The factors were defined after a first review of the literature [5, 6] and included: a) population characteristics, such as gender, age and socio-economic data; b) health-care and therapeutic factors such as treatment setting (inpatient versus outpatient status) and use of antipsychotics; c) geographic factors, i.e., continent of study; and c) methodological factors, such as the study's methodological quality, date of publication, sample size, inclusion of incident or prevalent cases, initial date of data-collection (before vs. in or after 1980) and duration of follow-up (under 10 years or 10 years and over).

Excess mortality was calculated using the following formula: (observed number of deaths - expected number of deaths) x100/expected number of deaths. All analyses were performed using SE Stata 9 computer software (StataCorp LP Texas USA 1984-2005).

RESULTS

The bibliographic search yielded 772 references. Manual search and contact made with experts did not yield any additional results that would also meet the inclusion criteria, other than the ones obtained with the bibliographic search. After excluding publications without abstract, reviews, editorials and duplications, 34 primary studies [4, 17-49] were selected.

Study Characteristics

Studies furnished data on 127,370 patients with schizophrenia, among whom there were 31,760 deaths. Their fundamental characteristics, results and quality are summarised in Table 1. On two occasions (Joukama and Allebeck studies), the same patients seemed to be included in more than one study. These patients were quantified once for the purpose of calculating the total number of cases included; yet the publications, rather than being identical, were complementary in terms of data analyzed, and we therefore chose not to eliminate them but to incorporate them in a unified manner. Thirty-one studies reported all-cause mortality, 21 natural-cause mortality and 19 studies specific physical-cause mortality in schizophrenic subjects versus a reference group. Study sample size varied considerably across the studies, as did study duration and, though they contained data from 17 countries, over two thirds corresponded to European countries. The studies analysed mortality among cases with diagnosis of schizophrenia versus the general population, whether national or local, and generally expressed the results as a standardised mortality rate or risk ratio adjusted for age and sex. Most were based on information drawn from extensive databases, namely, health organizations records, mental health departments, psychiatric case registers and hospital registers. Only a few analysed patients basically treated in a community setting or incident cases of schizophrenia. The criteria used for diagnosis of schizophrenia varied among studies, though the great majority used the International Classification of Diseases (ICD) system in its different versions and updates. Likewise, the ICD format was used for coding physical diseases in almost all studies that reported natural-cause mortality. As Table 1 shows, patients were over 15 years of age at the commencement of the inclusion period and just over half of cases were males. However, the great majority of studies made no reference whatsoever to the treatment received and, particularly, to treatment with antipsychotics.

1. All-Cause Mortality

Of the studies located, 31 reported all-cause mortality in patients with schizophrenia versus a reference group (Table 1). However, after reading them all, only 27 [4, 17, 19-22, 26, 27, 29, 31, 44, 46-49] furnished sufficient data to be combined using meta-analytical techniques. As shown in Table 2, meta-analysis of these 27 studies, including 125,933 subjects, indicated that patients with schizophrenia registered a risk ratio of all-cause death more than double that of the general population. Sensitivity analysis showed that exclusion of the data relating to Anderson's and Ciompi's studies, in which diagnosis of schizophrenia differed from that used by the remaining studies (Table 1), led to no significant changes in the global estimator.

Table 1. Summary of characteristics and principal results of studies

Author/year of publication/ country	Duration	Design	Data source	Diagnosis	No. patients	Age (years)	Sex (% male)	NL	T/N/S	All-cause mortality estimate* (95% CI)	Natural-mortality estimate* (95% CI)	Quality
Kurihara 2006# Indonesia	1990-01	P	Hospital registry	DSMIII	59	27.1±7.7	63%	NR	T	5.98 (3.4,10.5)	NR	1b
Joukama 2006, 2001 Finland	1978-94	P	National registry	PSE-9, ICD-8	99	≥ 30	46%	Yes 79	TNS	2.84 (2.06-3.9)	2.80 (2-3.93)	1b
Heila 2005# Finland	1980-96	R	National hospital registry	ICD-8, 9,10	58761	NR	NA	NR	TNS	2.59 (2.5-2.6)	2.24	2b
Enger 2004 USA	1995-99	P	Health organisation registry	ICD-9	1920	15-64 M:38±14	43%	Yes	TNS	4.41 (2.9-7.9)	2.69 (1.4-5.1)	1b
Morgan 2003 Ireland	1992-99	P	Regional health registry	DSMIII-R	72	57±15	56%	92%	T	2.06 (1.4-2.8)	NR	1b
Politi 2002 Italy	1978-94	P	Regional hospital registry	ICD-9	655	>15	45%	NR	T	3.11 (2.7-3.6)	NR	1b
Babidge 2001 Australia	1988-91	P	Mental department registry	ICD-10	506	39±12	90%	NR	T	3.3 (2.2-4.9)	NR	1b
Bralet 2000 France	1991-99	P	Regional identification	RDC	150	Mean 39±10	58%	Yes	T	2.5 (NR)	NR	1b
Brown 2000# England	1981-94	P	Regional hospital registry	ICD-9	370	16-65	58	NR	TNS	2.98 (2.4-3.7)	2.32 (1.76-3.)	1b
Lawrence 2000 Australia	1982-95	R	Mental department registry	ICD-8 ICD-9	496	NR	50%	NR	S	NR	NR	2b
Osby 2000# Sweden	1973-95	R	Regional health registry	ICD-8, -9	7784	≥15	50%	NR	TNS	2.6 (2.5-2.7)	1.93 (1.83-2.0)	2b
Casadebaig 1999 France	1993-96	P	Public-sector psychiatry registry	ICD-10	3470	18-64	64%	NR	TNS	4.5 (3.8-5.4)	2.5 (1.9-3.2)	1b

Table 1. (Continued)

Author/year of publication/ country	Duration	Design	Data source	Diagnosis	No. patients	Age (years)	Sex (% male)	NL	T/N/S	All-cause mortality estimate* (95% CI)	Natural-mortality estimate* (95% CI)	Quality
Salazar-Fraile 1998 Spain	1986-93	P	Psychiatric case registry	ICD-9	186	>15	NR	NR	TS	1,5 (0.94-2.6)	NR	1b
Ringbäck-Weitoft 1998 Sweden	1986-90	R	Regional health registry	ICD-8	2632	16-74	NR	NR	TN	3.1 (2.7-3.55)	2.56 (2.2-2.97)	2b
Hansen 1997# Norway	1980-92	P	Regional hospital registry	ICD-9	672	≥15	60%	NR	T	3.14 (2.5-3.9)	NR	1b
Baxter 1996 England	1969-85	P¿	Psychiatric case registry	ICD-8, -9	1398	15-85	NR	NR	T	1.59 (1.4-1.7)	NR	1b
Chen 1996 Taiwan	1987-93	P	National psychiatric registry	ICD-9	10039	15-80	71%	NR	TN	2.88 (2.7-3.0)	2.68 (2.5-2.8)	1b
Prior 1996 England	1974-85	P	Psychiatric case registry	ICD-8, -9	745	15-89	44%	NR	TNS	1.48 (1.2-1.8)	1.32 (1.0-1.7)	1b
Amaddeo 1995 Italy	1982-91	P	Psychiatric case registry	ICD-9	262	>14	NA	NR	T	1.76 (1.1-2.6)	NR	1b
Saku 1995 Japan	1948-85	P	Hospital registry	DSMIII-R	2268	0-85	63%	NR	TNS	2.68 (2.4-2.4)	1.48 (1.3-1.7)	1b
Mortensen # 1993 Denmark	1970-87	P	Psychiatric case registry	ICD-8	9156	≥15	62%	NR	TNS	3.45 (3.2-3.7)	1.37 (1.2-1.5)	1b
Anderson 1991 England	1975 -89	P	Regional psychiatric case registry	NR	532	≥15	55%	NR	TS	2.50 (1.9-3.2)	NR	1b
Newman 1991 Canada	1976-85	R	Mental health system registry	ICD-8,-9	3623	Mean 37.3	56%	NR	TNS	2.6 (2.3-2.9)	1.66 (1.4-1.9)	2b
Lesage 1990 Italy	1979-86	P	Psychiatric case registry	ICD-9 PSE	61	6.5% >65 y	51%	NR	T	3.6 (1.9-6.3)	NR	1b
Mortensen 1990 Denmark	1957-86	P	Psychiatric case registry	ICD-8	6152	≥15	48%	85%	TNS	1.2 (1.16-1.2)	1.15 (1.1-1.18)	1b

Author/year of publication/ country	Duration	Design	Data source	Diagnosis	No. patients	Age (years)	Sex (% male)	NL	T/N/S	All-cause mortality estimate* (95% CI)	Natural-mortality estimate* (95% CI)	Quality
Allebeck 1989,1986 Sweden	1971-81	R	Regional hospital registry	ICD-8	1190	0-≥80	48%	NR	TNS	2.77 (2.46-3.1)	1.8 (1.56-2.14)	2b
Zilber 1989 Israel	1978-83	P	Psychiatric case registry	ICD-9	9178	>10	NR	NR	TNS	2.07 (1.9-2.2)	~2	1b
Black 1988 USA	1972-81	R	Hospital registry	ICD-9	891	NR	54%	NR	TNS	2.53 (1.8-3.4)	1.55 (0.9-2.3)	2b
Herrman 1983 England	1971-82	P	Psychiatric case registry	ICD-8	592	≥ 15	50%	NR	TNS	1.93 (1.4-2.5)	1.64 (1.1-2.29)	1b
Tsuang 1980 USA	1934-74	R	Hospital registry	ICD-8	200	NR	NR	NR	TNS	1.97 (1.5-2.5)	1.8 (1.39-2.3)	1b
Weiner 1977 USA	1962-72	R	Mental health registry	ICD-8	1689	Mean ~40	NR	NR	T	1.9 (1.6-2.15)	NR	2b
Ciompi 1976 Switzerland	---1962	NR	Hospital registry	Bleuler's criteria	1562	<65	42	No	T	1.73 (1.6-1.8)	NR	2b

incident cases or furnish data of first admission.

NR: not reported.

Design: P: prospective. R: retrospective.

DSMIII/DSMIII-R: Diagnostic and Statistical Manual of Mental Disorders, 3rd edition, revised; American Psychiatric Association 1987. ICD 8,9,10: International Classification of Diseases version 8, 9, 10 respectively. PSE: Present State Examination, 9th edition.

Age: at commencement of inclusion or selection criterion.

NL: treatment with neuroleptics.

T N S: Analysis of total (all-cause), natural or specific physical-cause mortality respectively.

*All studies reported adjustments for covariables, among others, age and sex.

Quality of studies: all based on reference (12).

This increased risk remained present, albeit with a somewhat lower estimator, after separate analyses of studies that reported data by gender, with the aggregate risk proving slightly higher among males.

Table 2. All-cause mortality. Results of Meta-analysis

	No. studies	Patients	I^2	Risk ratio (95% CI)*
Both sexes	27	125,933	99 %	2.17 (2.13, 2.21)
Men	19	28,841	98.2 %	1.87 (1.81, 1.93)
Women	18	20,800	96.3 %	1.68 (1.63,1.74)

*All based on fixed effects meta-analysis.

2. Natural-Cause Mortality

Of the studies located, 21 reported natural mortality. These studies included a total of 119,824 patients. All the studies displayed a rise in observed versus expected mortality. Nevertheless, due to disparity in the way in which the outcome variable was expressed and failure to publish the data needed for its calculation, only 17 studies [4, 19, 20, 26, 27, 29, 31, 34, 35, 37, 38, 40, 42-44, 46, 47] could be combined with meta-analytical techniques. These studies covered 118,971 patients, and aggregate analysis indicates (Figure 1) that these subjects registered a risk of death due to natural causes 89% higher than that of the general population (95%CI: 86%-93%).

As shown in Table 3, this risk is high across the sexes proving somewhat higher in males. Additionally, our results indicate that the risk of natural mortality had risen in recent years, a finding borne out by analyses performed by initial year of inclusion (pre- or post-1980) and year of publication (pre- or post-1997) (Table 3). Similarly, this risk was clearly higher in studies that analysed incident rather than prevalent cases. When studies were compared by reference to time of follow-up, the estimator obtained in those with a follow-up of less than ten years after inclusion, was also higher than that in studies with a more prolonged follow-up. Moreover, joint analysis of the studies that included subjects basically treated in a community setting displayed a risk of natural-cause mortality clearly higher than that observed in studies that included institutionalised patients or those of both types. It should be borne in mind, however, that the number of subjects in the former group was relatively low. In terms of gender, the analysis showed a higher aggregate risk in studies that reported data independently for men than in those that did so for women. Insofar as possible geographical differences were concerned, the analysis indicated a higher risk in the 3 studies conducted in Asia.

Additionally, in an attempt to analyse whether the change in risk of natural mortality over time was due to an increase in observed deaths or a reduction in expected deaths, the studies were stratified into several categories. From Figure 2 it will be observed that recent years witnessed an increase in observed deaths in subjects with schizophrenia, along with a reduction in expected mortality based on estimated mortality in the general population. This difference results in an increasing disparity in mortality rate between patients with schizophrenia and the general population.

Finally, multivariate meta-regression analysis shows (Table 4) that the heterogeneity across studies was attributable to a number of factors, including patient inclusion date, duration of follow-up, degree of institutionalisation, continent of study, and the study's methodological quality.

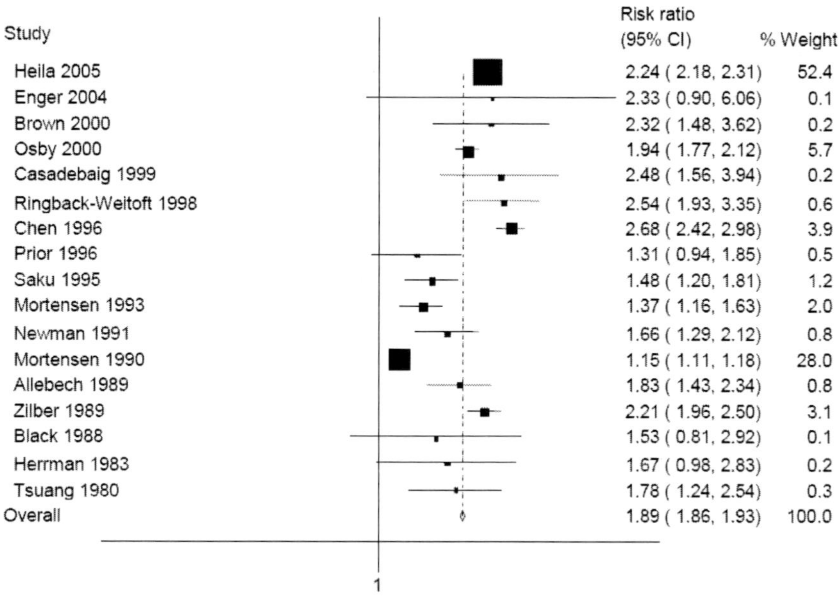

Figure 1. Mortality due to natural causes. Meta-analysis results.

Table 3. Mortality due to natural causes. Meta-analysis results

	No. studies	Patients	I^2	Risk ratio (95% CI)*
Gender				
Male	11	26,008	96.9%	1.49 (1.43, 1.55)
Female	11	17,041	92.8%	1.39 (1.34, 1.45)
Initial year inclusion				
<1980	11	41,779	96.1%	1.38 (1.34, 1.42)
≥1980	6	77,192	55.4%	2.27 (2.22, 2.34)
Follow-up duration				
< 10 years	7	31,753	63.8%	2.39 (2.22,2.56)
≥ 10 years	10	87,218	99.2%	1.85 (1.81, 1.89)
Geographic area				
Europe	10	90,852	99.2%	1.86 (1.82, 1.90)
North America	4	6,634	0.0%	1.70 (1.40, 2.06)
Asia	3	21,485	92.5	2.32 (2.16, 2.50)
First admission				
Yes	3	75,701	94.9%	2.19 (2.13, 2.24)
Not available	14	43,270	97%	1.46 (1.41, 1.50)
Degree of institutionalisation				
Institutionalised	11	108,251	99.2%	1.89 (1.86, 1.94)
Ambulatory-Community	2	2,290	0%	2.32 (1.55, 3.48)
Both	4	9,828	36.5%	1.67 (1.40, 1.98)
Year of publication				
<1997	11	44,034	96.9%	1.43 (1.38, 1.47)
≥1997	6	74,937	53.9%	2.22 (2.16, 2.28)

*All based on fixed effects meta-analysis.

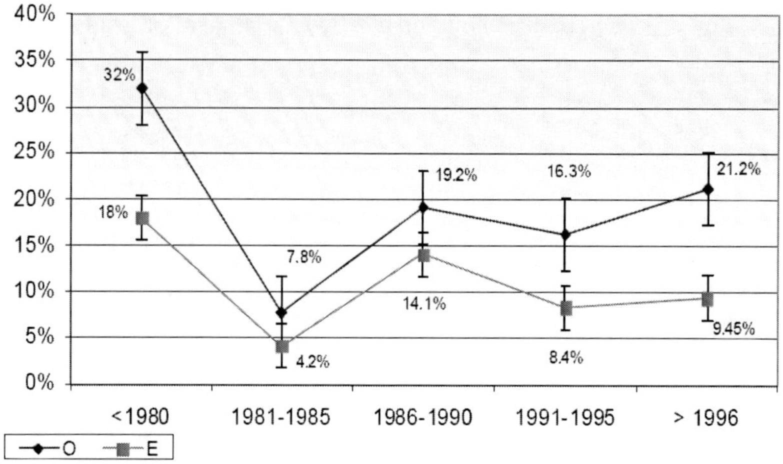

Figure 2. Natural mortality: comparative time trends in observed and expected deaths in studies included in the meta-analysis.

Table 4. Meta-regression analysis

Variable (no. of studies)*	Univariate	Multivariate	
	P-value	Coefficient (95% CI)	*P*-value
Initial year of inclusion (≥1980 vs. <1980) (n=17)	0.001	0.048 (0.04, 0.057)	0.000
Duration of follow-up (years) (n=17)	0.012	0.02 (0.007, 0.031)	0.002
Degree of institutionalisation (n=17) (Institutionalisation vs. rest)	0.92	0.34 (0.16, 0.51)	0.000
Continent (Europe vs. rest of world) (n =17)	0.753	-0.52 (-0.63, -0.41)	0.000
Methodological quality - level of evidence (high vs. low quality) (n=17)	0.636	0.22 (0.13, 0.32)	0.000
Year of publication (n=17)	0.056	0.01 (-0.01, 0.04)	0.244
Sample size (n=17)	0.369	4.58 (-2.37, 3.28)	0.750

*No. of studies in analysis.

Table 5. Summary of specific physical causes of mortality: Results of meta-analysis

Disorder	No. of studies with reported outcomes	No. subjects	I^2	Risk Ratio (95% CI)*
Cancer				
Both sexes	15	104,912	89%	1.38 (1.32, 1.45)
Men	10	17,707	0 %	0.88 (0.79, 0.98)
Women	10	14,406	0 %	1.17 (1.06, 1.29)
Cardiovascular				
Both sexes	16	106,832	95.8%	1.66 (1.60, 1.73)
Men	8	10,616	82.6%	1.29 (1.19, 1.39)
Women	8	10,073	85.3%	1.29 (1.19, 1.4)
-Ischaemic heart disease				
Both sexes	4	63,508	24.1%	2.11 (2.0 .2,22)
Men	3	2,710	0%	1.42 (0.86, 2.34)
Women	3	2,037	0%	2.14 (1.14, 4.03)

Disorder	No. of studies with reported outcomes	No. subjects	I2	Risk Ratio (95% CI)*
Respiratory				
Both sexes	11	94,111	70%	3.1 (2.87, 3.36)
Men	8	16,935	11.5%	2.3 (1.94, 2.73)
Women	8	13,755	0%	2.56 (2.15, 3.05)
Digestive				
Both sexes	8	31,288	0%	1.91 (1.61, 2.27)
Men	7	16,638	0%	2.12 (1.66, 2.72)
Women	7	13,460	0%	1.67 (1.3, 2.14)
Endocrine				
Both sexes	6	18,705	0%	2.36 (1.44, 3.89)
Men	4	7,697	0%	2.38 (1.13, 5.01)
Women	4	6,348	0%	2.16 (1.02, 4.6)
Neurological				
Both sexes	5	16,437	0%	1.73 (0.92, 3.27)
Men	3	6,264	0%	2.16 (0.83, 5.7)
Women	2	5,356	0%	1 (0.32, 3.1)
Cerebrovascular				
Both sexes	8	31,297	81.8%	0.87 (0.77, 0.97)
Men	7	16,686	30.7%	0.82 (0.68, 0.98)
Women	7	13,421	77.7%	0.89 (0.76, 1.03)
Urogenital				
Both sexes	5	27,905	0%	1.66 (1.33, 2.09)
Men	4	14,665	0%	1.84 (1.34, 2.53)
Women	4	12,050	0%	1.36 (0.96, 1.92)
Infectious diseases				
Both sexes	6	24,243	77.5%	10.44 (7.35,14.83)
Men	2	6,197	0%	4 (1.50, 10.65)
Women	3	7,624	1.7%	3.43 (1.97, 5.99)
HIV- AIDS infection				
Both sexes	1	3,470	NA	3.3 (1.2, 7.3)

*All based on fixed effects meta-analysis. NA: not applicable.

Excess Mortality due to Natural Causes in Both Sexes

Meta-analysis of 17 studies, which furnished data on all-cause and natural-cause mortality among 118,971 subjects, indicated that, overall, deaths due to natural causes constituted 76.4% of all-cause deaths. Moreover, natural mortality accounted for 66.2% of excess all-cause deaths in the population analysed. It should be borne in mind here that this is only an approximate calculation because, for analysis purposes, all studies that furnished data on all-cause but not on natural-cause mortality had to be excluded.

3. Natural Mortality: Specific Disorders

Nineteen studies estimated cause-specific risk of death in schizophrenic subjects versus a reference group. Table 5 sets out the results of the meta-analysis for each of the physical disorders analysed.

Concerning excess mortality due to specific disorders, the studies reported 14,488 observed deaths, whereas expected deaths based on general population estimates for the selfsame processes totalled 8,509. This represents 5,979 excess deaths or, expressed in percentage terms, a 70% excess over expected mortality.

Table 6 shows the difference between observed deaths among schizophrenia patients and expected deaths among the corresponding comparison population, for each specific disorder.

The data are listed in descending order according to the percentage which the excess deaths represent in each case.

Table 6. Excess mortality by specific physical diseases

Disease	No. patients	Observed deaths (OD)	Expected deaths (ED)	Excess mortality* (%)
Infectious	24,243	355	34	944%
Respiratory	94,111	2588	833	210%
Endocrine	18,705	52	22	136%
Digestive	31,288	367	192	91%
Neurological	16,437	26	15	73%
Cardiovascular	106,832	6676	4013	66%
Urogenital	27,907	186	112	66%
Cancer	104,912	3703	2673	38%
Stroke	31,297	535	615	-6.7%

* All based on the formula: (OD-ED) x 100/ED.

Discussion

This updated meta-analysis expands existing data on risk of death due to natural causes in schizophrenia and provides new important findings.

First, the results from the research carried out for this chapter show that the risk of natural mortality in schizophrenia is almost twofold that of the general population and that this risk has risen considerably in recent years. Our data show that patients with schizophrenia had a 89% (95% CI: 86%, 93%) higher risk of natural-mortality than does the general population. In addition, data show that natural mortality represents 76.4% of all-cause deaths in schizophrenia and accounts for 66.2% of the excess mortality. These figures are substantially higher than those observed in Brown's 1997 meta-analysis [7]. In this analysis, which covered 66,161 subjects, Brown concluded that 59% of excess mortality among patients with schizophrenia was due to natural causes, and that such patients registered a standardised natural mortality rate of 1.34 vis-à-vis the general population (95% CI:1.31-1.37). The same applies to data obtained by Harris & Barraclough in 1998 (8); after analysing 35,815 schizophrenic subjects, they reported a natural-cause mortality rate of 1.37 (95% CI: 1.34-1.41).

The discrepancy between these results and those obtained by us could be due to methodological differences (and the use of different methods of analysis in particular) or the selection criteria applied [10, 13, 15]. We nevertheless feel that the essential difference lies in the inclusion in our analysis of publications subsequent to 1995 [8] and 1996 [7], the designated end dates of the respective authors' search strategies. This augmented body of evidence enabled us not only to analyse a very much greater number of patients than have previous published studies, thus increasing the accuracy of the pooled estimate, but also to determine that the risk of natural death has risen recently.

Hence, the results presented in this chapter indicate that, whilst the value of the pooled risk obtained in the studies published prior to 1997 was 1.43 (95% CI: 1.38, 1.47), close to the figures obtained by Brown and Harris [7, 8], the risk of mortality yielded by studies subsequent to this date is 2.22 (95% CI: 2.16, 2.28). In view of the considerable degree of consistency among the studies in this latter group and the increase in the number of patients covered, we feel that the risk of mortality observed in our study can be regarded as being more in line with reality. Furthermore, if the increased risk of mortality observed in the most recently published studies is coupled with the finding that the pooled risk is higher in studies undertaken in the last two decades (initial year of inclusion $\geq$ 1980) than in those undertaken previously, it can be concluded that, in contrast to the generally held view [6, 9], there has been a considerable rise in natural mortality in schizophrenia in recent years.

Although the specific characteristics of our study render it impossible for the factors responsible for excess natural mortality to be accurately identified, our results suggest that this rise is linked to changes made in the care of patients with schizophrenia. Hence, the higher risk observed in groups treated exclusively in a community setting, may well be linked to the deinstitutionalisation that has taken place in most Western countries over recent decades [50, 51]. Nevertheless, a statement of this type would have to be ratified by comprehensive analysis of diverse aspects of variability and uncertainty, since the real context in which care has been administered in some primary studies cannot be easily established, and regional differences do undoubtedly exist both in the availability of mental services and admission criteria, as well as in health-care practice management.

Similarly, the absence of information on treatment received, prevents the influence that such drugs may have on the excess natural mortality of schizophrenic patients from being quantitatively analysed, despite the acknowledged influence of antipsychotics at a somatic level [52, 53].

The results presented in this chapter also show that the rise in risk of natural mortality is due, not only to an increase in natural mortality among schizophrenic subjects, but also to the effect of a reduction in expected mortality, based on estimated mortality in the general population. There can be no doubt that the magnitude of excess mortality among subjects with mental disorders is strongly influenced by general population mortality rates [54]. In this regard, our data thus suggest that, as a group, patients with schizophrenia are not benefiting from the improvements in health care experienced by the general population in recent decades [55-58].

Additionally, though the dearth of information in the original papers bars analysis of the distribution of age of death in the schizophrenic population and possible differences between age groups, our results indicate that risk of natural mortality is more elevated in the first decade of follow-up. This finding, in line with other studies [59, 60], suggests an important premature loss of potential years of life in such patients and reminds us that physical health represents a dramatic challenge to the population with schizophrenia.

In keeping with that observation, there would seem to be a higher risk of mortality in the group of patients with first diagnosis of schizophrenia than in studies which include patients at any stage of disease progression, or which do not clearly specify that incident cases are involved. It should be stressed here that, though our results coincide with the findings reported by other authors [7, 58], only a small number of studies analyse first-diagnosis cohorts longitudinally, and these display a notable degree of heterogeneity.

Finally, concerning specific physical causes of mortality the results of this research show that, except for neurological and cerebrovascular disorders, schizophrenic patients, as a group, face a risk of mortality due to the processes analysed, that is significantly higher than that faced by the appropriate general population.

One of the most relevant findings of our research is the elevated excess mortality due to respiratory diseases, which, in view of the unquestionable relationship between such diseases and modifiable risk factors, such as smoking, calls for a compelling specific approach [52,59,60]. The same can be said regarding digestive and endocrine disorders in that the elevated risk of mortality due to these processes found in our research may well be linked to the high incidence and prevalence rates of diseases such as diabetes or metabolic syndrome [52,53,60] and to well-known lifestyles and risk behaviours in the population with schizophrenia [61-63].

Insofar as cardiovascular disorders are concerned, it should be noted that, albeit responsible for the greatest number of observed deaths in the population with schizophrenia (Table 6), these disorders register an excess mortality which is appreciably lower than that of above-mentioned diseases. When both sexes are analysed, the overall risk of mortality is 66% higher in the schizophrenic than in the general population, though an appreciable degree of inter-study heterogeneity is observable. In contrast, and with far greater consistency, analysis of data on mortality due to ischaemic heart disease indicates a rate of risk that doubles the expected rate in the general population. In this connection, it is important to stress the discrepancy in the results with regard to gender, which indicate that it is schizophrenic women, rather than men, who register a significantly increased risk of death. This finding comes in sharp contrast to the results of Brown and Harris [7,8], which report a higher-than-expected risk in men as opposed to women.

We feel that infectious disorders call for an altogether more cautious discussion because, though these register the highest excess mortality by far, it should be stressed that this is due to the exceptionally high rates reported by Zilber [43] and Tsuang [47]. However, their studies' demographic, health care and epidemiological contexts may differ substantially from those generally found nowadays, in which certain infectious processes should no longer constitute an important cause of mortality among schizophrenia sufferers. A further point to be regarded as especially important is the lack of information on mortality due to HIV infection, the prevalence of which is undeniably high in this population [62] and which constitutes a highly relevant topic from both the individual and public health points of view.

Lastly, special mention must be made to cancer mortality, since this is a controversial topic owing to the contradictory nature of the results published in the literature. After conducting an aggregate analysis of the results of 15 primary studies covering over 100,000 patients of both sexes, the results of our research show that risk of cancer-related death is significantly higher in schizophrenic subjects than in the general population. Yet, the panorama changes when a separate analysis is conducted on studies which report their results broken down by gender and which, despite involving fewer patients, furnish greater data consistency. In this case, our results point to a higher-than-expected risk solely in schizophrenic women, while in men, the risk is significantly lower than that of the general population, a finding in line with previously published results [8].

It is evident that a study such as ours does not allow for clarification as to whether the pattern of natural mortality is intrinsic to the disease itself or might be explained by the combination of unhealthy lifestyle-related factors, unidentified physical comorbidities, scant adherence to treatment of medical diseases, type of treatment or care provided, etc., [5, 55, 64, 65]. Our results cannot establish relationships of causality, yet they do nevertheless indicate that common processes, similar to those at work in the general population, cause an excess of mortality in this population. Accordingly, the impact of such disorders could be reduced by implementation of evidence-based monitoring and treatment systems, which may, however, have to be inserted into health-care guidelines tailored to the features of schizophrenic patients and characterised by a closer working relationship between mental health and primary/specialised-care professionals.

Potential Limitations of this Research

We recognise there are some limitations to the research carried out in order to elaborate this chapter. An inherent difficulty in assessing observational studies is the fact that a good proportion of these studies do not describe the quality, comprehensiveness and validation of the information which they include and upon which the validity of their data relies. Hence, a limitation in some registry-based studies is validation of clinical diagnoses, since only in recent decades has there been rigorous standardisation and generalised application of diagnostic criteria for schizophrenia [4]. It should nevertheless be pointed out that the use of hospital discharge registries has been validated, with these displaying a high degree of sensitivity and specificity for classification of patients with psychotic diseases [66, 67] when more homogeneous criteria are applied, as occurs with most of the studies that use the ICD system. Depending on the study period, different ICD versions may have been applied, yet in no case were there any substantial differences in the criteria used to diagnose the disease [27].

Further uncertainties inherent in the primary studies located stem from material limitations in the information about critical aspects, such as presentation of methods and results, epidemiological representativeness, and adjustment for potentially relevant factors, such as the demographic, socio-economic, ethnic, geographical, health-care and therapeutic characteristics of the study population [68], all of which limits precise identification of possible biases. Thus, on a purely demographic and health-care basis, mention should be made of the source of the studies analysed, since, though these reflect data corresponding to 17 countries, the setting was mostly European and, more specifically, Scandinavian. Accordingly, the transcultural value of the findings should be viewed with caution.

Similarly, the existence of selection biases cannot be ruled out concerning time of progression and severity of mental disease, given the sparse information furnished in this respect by the authors. It is thus possible that, at the time of their inclusion in the study, subjects might have already overcome or survived the period of highest mortality risk, or that the studies might include patients at different points in the disease, thereby making for a lack of homogeneity.

Additionally, we regard two particular limitations as being of special relevance. In the first place, there is the absence of information on antipsychotic treatment received, which prevents the influence that such drugs may have on the excess natural mortality of schizophrenic patients from being quantitatively analysed. In the second place, there is the fact that practically all the studies fail to report the age distribution of the study subjects and their age at death, thereby making it impossible to conduct an in-depth analysis of potential years of life lost.

Another concern regards the risk for publication bias given that our research is entirely dependent on published literature [69]. Nevertheless, we feel that any such bias would necessarily have been minimized by the scope of and systematic strategy used in the search of literature and are confident that the majority of the research conducted in this field was successfully identified (10,70,71). We have also tried to reduce the possible impact of publication bias using the fixed-model effect to combine the results of individual studies in the meta-analysis. This procedure has the advantage of reducing bias impact, as less weight is given to smaller studies which are associated with a greater risk of publication bias [72]. We also endeavour to reduce such bias by having the studies separately analyzed by two independent reviewers and using defined criteria for the purposes of study inclusion and analysis [70, 71]. Conversely, in line with recent reports indicating that publication bias cannot be ruled out safely in the meta-analysis by means of funnel-plots, [16, 69] we decided not to use them in our work.

Also, sight must not be lost of the inevitable methodological limitation of any research based on sample or population data, namely, that group variables (risk of death, its causes or related factors) may differ from those for the individual, thus constituting the so-called phenomenon of the "ecological fallacy" [73].

Finally, without ignoring the importance of any of the above considerations, we nevertheless consider that longitudinal cohort studies of good methodological quality continue to be critical to assess mortality in schizophrenia. When such studies are well conducted, with an adequate follow-up and proper description of results, they provide realistic information on the situation of this vulnerable population [4-6, 11, 71, 74].

ACKNOWLEDGMENTS

This research has been undertaken by the Spanish National R+D+I Programme (Grant number PI06/90571). The authors thank Michael Benedict for assistance with the English translation of the manuscript.

REFERENCES

[1] WHO. The global burden of disease. Cambridge, Mass: Harvard University Press 1997.

[2] Goldner Em, Hsu L, Waraich P, Somers Jm. Prevalence and incidence of schizophrenic disorders: a systematic review of the literature. *Can. J. Psychiatry.* 2002;47: 833-843.

[3] Rice Dp. The economic impact of schizophrenia. *J. Clin. Psychiatry.* 1999;60 (Suppl.1):4-6.

[4] Allebeck P. Schizophrenia: a life-shortening disease. *Schizophr. Bull.* 1989;15:81-89

[5] Simpson Jc. Mortality studies in schizophrenia. In Tsuang MT, Simpson JC, eds. Handbook of Schizophrenia volume 3: nosology, epidemiology and genetics of schizophrenia. Amsterdam: Elsevier Science Ltd 1988:245-274.

[6] Simpson Jc, Tsuang Mt. Mortality among patients with schizophrenia. *Schizophr. Bull.* 1996;22:485-499.

[7] Brown S. Excess mortality of schizophrenia. A meta-analysis. *Br. J. Psychiatry.* 1997;171:502-508.

[8] HArris Ec, Barraclough B. Excess mortality of mental disorder. *Br. J. Psychiatry.* 1998;173:11-53.

[9] Neeleman J. A continuum of premature death. Meta-analysis of competing mortality in the psychosocially vulnerable. *Int. J. Epidemiol.* 2001;30:154-162.

[10] Royle P, Waugh N. Literature searching for clinical and cost-effectiveness studies used in health technology assessments reports carried out for the National Institute for Clinical Excellence appraisal system. *Health Technol. Assess.* 2003;7(34) iii, ix-x,1-51.

[11] Lipper S, Werman Ds. Schizophrenia and intercurrent physical illness: a critical review of the literature. *Compr. Psychiatry.* 1977;18:11-22.

[12] Oxford Centre For Evidence-Based Medicine Levels Of Evidence 2001 http://www.cebm.net/downloads/Oxford_EBM_Levels_5.rtf

[13] Sterne Ja. Meta-analysis in STATATM . Chapter 18 pps 347-369. En Egger M, Davey Smith G, Altman DG eds. Systematic reviews in Health Care: Meta-Analysis in Context. 2nd edition. *BMJ books.* Blackwell Publishing. London 2001. ISBN:0-7279-1488-X.

[14] Higgins Jpt, Thompson Sg, Deeks Jj, Altman Dg. Measuring inconsistency in metaanalyses. *Br. Med. J.* 2003; 327:557-60.

[15] Higgins J, Thompson S, Deeks J, Altman D. Statistical heterogeneity in systematic reviews of clinical trials: a critical appraisal of guidelines and practice. *J. Health Serv. Res. Policy.* 2002; 7:51-61.

[16] Tang J, Liu Jl. Misleading funnel plot for detection of bias in meta-analysis. *J. Clin. Epidemiol.* 2000;53:477–484.

[17] Kurihara T, Kato M, Kashima H, Takebayashi T, Reverger R, I Gusti Ray Tirta. Excess mortality of schizophrenia in the developing country of Bali. *Schizophr. Res.* 2006;83:103-105.

[18] Joukamaa M, Heliövaara M, Knekt P, Aromaa A, Raitasalo R, Lehtinen V. Schizophrenia, neuroleptic medication and mortality. *Br. J. Psychiatry.* 2006;188:122-127.

[19] Heila H, Haukka J, Suvisaari J, Lonnqvist J. Mortality among patients with schizophrenia and reduced psychiatric hospital care. *Psychol. Med.* 2005;35:725-732.

[20] Enger C, Weatherby L, Reynolds Rf, Glasser Db, Walker Am. Serious cardiovascular events and mortality among patients with schizophrenia. *J. Nerv. Ment. Dis.* 2004;192:19-27.

[21] Morgan Mg, Scully Pj, Youssef Ha, Kinsella A, Owens Jm., Waddington Jl. Prospective analysis of premature mortality in schizophrenia in relation to health service engagement: a 7.5-year study within an epidemiologically complete, homogeneous population in rural Ireland. *Psychiatry Res.* 2003;117:127-135.

[22] Politi P, Piccinelli M, Klersy C et al. Mortality in psychiatric patients 5 to 21 years after hospital admission in Italy. *Psychol. Med.* 2002;32:227-237.

[23] Babidge Nc, Buhrich N, Butler T. Mortality among homeless people with schizophrenia in Sydney, Australia: a 10-year follow-up. *Acta Psychiatr. Scand.* 2001;103:105-110.

[24] Joukamaa M, Heliövaara M, Knekt P, Aromaa A, Raitasalo R, Lehtinen V. Mental disorders and cause-specific mortality. *Br. J. Psychiatry.* 2001;179:498-502.

[25] Bralet Mc, Yon V, Loas G, Noisette C. Cause of mortality in schizophrenic patients: prospective study of years of a cohort of 150 chronic schizophrenic patients. *Encephale.* 2000;26:32-41.

[26] Brown S, Inskip H, Barraclough B. Causes of the excess mortality of schizophrenia. *Br. J. Psychiatry.* 2000;177:212-217.

[27] Osby U, Correia N, Brandt L, Ekbom A, Sparén P. Mortality and causes of death in schizophrenia in Stockholm County, Sweden. *Schizophr. Res.* 2000;45:21-28.

[28] Lawrence D, Holman Cdj, Jablensky Av, Threlfall Tj, Fuller Sa. Excess cancer mortality in Western Australian psychiatric patients due to high case fatality rates. *Acta Psychiatr. Scand.* 2000;101:382-388.

[29] Casadebaig F, Philippe A. Mortality among schizophrenic patients.3 years follow-up of a cohort. *Encephale.* 1999;25:329-337.

[30] Salazar-Fraile J, Gómez-Beneyto M, Pérez-Hoyos S, Hurtado-Navarro I. Mortality among psychiatric patients referred to the mental health services in Valencia. *Soc. Psychiatry Psychiatr. Epidemiol.* 1998;33:224-229.

[31] Ringbäck-Weitoft G, Gullberg A, Rosén M. Avoidable mortality among psychiatric patients. *Soc. Psychiatry Psychiatr. Epidemiol.* 1998;33:430-437.

[32] Hansen V, Arnesen E, Jacobsen Bk. Total mortality in people admitted to a psychiatric hospital. *Br. J. Psychiatry.* 1997;170:186-190.

[33] BAXTER DN. The mortality experience of individuals on the Salford Psychiatric Case Register. All-cause mortality. *Br. J. Psychiatry.* 1996;168:772-779.

[34] Chen Wj, Huang Yj, Yeh Ll, Rin H, Hwu Hg. Excess mortality of psychiatric inpatients in Taiwan. *Psychiatry Res.* 1996;62:239-250.

[35] Prior P, Hassall C, Cross Kw. Causes of death associated with psychiatric illness. *J. Public Health Med.* 1996;18:381-389.

[36] Amaddeo F, Bisoffi G, Bonizzato P, Micciolo R, Tansella M. Mortality among patients with psychiatric illness a ten-year case register study in an area with a community-based system of care. *Br. J. Psychiatry.* 1995;166:783-788.

[37] Saku M, Tokudome S, Ikeda M et al. Mortality in psychiatric patients, with a specific focus on cancer mortality associated with schizophrenia. *Int. J. Epidemiol.* 1995;24:366-372.

[38] Mortensen Pb, Juel K. Mortality and causes of death in first admitted schizophrenic patients. *Br. J. Psychiatry.* 1993;163:183-189.

[39] Anderson C, Connelly J, Eve C, Johnstone Ec, Owens Gc. Disabilities and circumstances of schizophrenic patients- a follow up study: Cause of Death. *Br. J. Psychiatry.* 1991;159 (suppl.13):30-33.

[40] Newman Sc, Bland Rc. Mortality in a cohort of patients with schizophrenia: a record linkage study. *Can. J. Psychiatry.* 1991;36:239-245.

[41] Lesage Al, Trapani V, Tansella M. Excess mortality by natural causes of Italian schizophrenia patients. *Eur. Arch. Psychiatry Neurol. Sci.* 1990;239:361-365.

[42] Mortensen Pb, Juel K. Mortality and causes of death in schizophrenic patients in Denmark. *Acta Psychiatr. Scand.* 1990; 81:372-377.

[43] Zilber N, Schufman N, Lerner Y. Mortality among psychiatric patients- the groups at risk. *Acta Psychiatr. Scand.* 1989;79:248-256.

[44] Black Dw. Mortality in schizophrenia: The Iowa record-linkage study. *Psychosomatics.* 1988; 29:55-60.

[45] Allebeck P, Wistedt B. Mortality in Schizophrenia. *Arch. Gen. Psychiatry.* 1986;43:650-653.

[46] Herrman He, Baldwin Ja, Christie D. A record-linkage study of mortality and general hospital discharge in patients diagnosed as schizophrenic. *Psychol. Med.* 1983;13:581-593.

[47] Tsuang Mt, Woolson Rf, Fleming Ja. Causes of death in Schizophrenia and Manic-Depression. *Br. J. Psychiatry.* 1980;136:239-242.

[48] Weiner Bp, Marvit Rc. Schizophrenia in Hawaii: analysis of cohort mortality risk in a multi-ethnic population. *Br. J. Psychiatry.* 1977;131:497-503.

[49] Ciompi L, Medvecka J. [Comparative study of long-term mortality in the mentally ill]. *Schweiz Arch. Neurol. Neurochir. Psychiatr.* 1976;118:111-135.

[50] Osby U, Correia N, Brandt L, Ekbom A, Sparén P. Time trends in schizophrenia mortality in Stockholm County, Sweden: cohort study. *Br. Med. J.* 2000;321:483-484.

[51] Hansen V, Jacobsen Bk, Arnesen E. Cause-specific mortality in psychiatric patients after deinstitutionalization. *Br. J. Psychiatry.* 2001;179:438-443.

[52] Mitchell Aj, Malone D. Physical health and Schizophrenia. *Curr. Opin. Psychiatry.* 2006;19:432-437.

[53] Cohn Ta, Sernyak Mj. Metabolic monitoring for patients treated with antipsychotic medications. *Can. J. Psychiatry.* 2006;51:492-501.

[54] Harrison G, Hopper K, Craig T et al. Recovery from psychotic illness: a 15– and 25-year international follow-up study. *Br. J. Psychiatry.* 2001;178:506-17.

[55] Druss Bg, Bradford Wd, Rosenheck Ra et al. Quality of medical care and excess mortality in older patients with mental disorders. *Arch. Gen. Psychiatry.* 2001; 58:565-572.

[56] Cradock-O'leary J, Young As, Yano Em et al. Use of general medical services by VA patients with psychiatric disorders. *Psychiatr. Serv.* 2002; 53:874-878.

[57] Dombrovski A, Rosenstock J. Bridging general medicine and psychiatry: providing general medical and preventive care for the severely mentally ill. *Curr. Opin. Psychiatry.* 2004;17: 523-529.

[58] Munk-Jørgensen P, Mortensen P. Incidence and other aspects of the epidemiology of schizophrenia in Denmark 1971-87. *Br. J. Psychiatry.* 1992;161:489-495.

[59] Lambert Tj, Velakoulis D, Pantelis C. Medical comorbidity in schizophrenia. *Med. J. Aust.* 2003;178 (suppl.):67-70.

[60] Marder Sr, Essock Sm, Miller Al et al. Physical health monitoring of patients with schizophrenia. *Am. J. Psychiatry.* 2004;161:1334-1349.

[61] Regier Da, Farmer Me, Rae Ds et al. Comorbidity of mental disorders with alcohol and drug abuse: results from the Epidemiologic Catchment Area (ECA) study. *JAMA.* 1990; 264:2511-2518.

[62] Cantwell R. Substance use and schizophrenia: effects on symptoms, social functioning and service use. *Br. J. Psychiatry.* 2003;182:324-329.

[63] Rosenberg Sd, Goodman La, Osher Fc et al: Prevalence of HIV, hepatitis B, and hepatitis C in people with severe mental illness. *Am. J. Public Health.* 2001;91:31–37.

[64] Jeste Dv, Gladsjo Ja, Lindamer La, Lacro Jp. Medical comorbidity in schizophrenia. *Schizophr. Bull.* 1996;22:413-430.

[65] Brown S, Birtwistle J, Roe L Et al.. The unhealthy lifestyle of people with schizophrenia. *Psychol. Med.* 1999; 29: 697-701.

[66] Nazareth I, King M, Haines A et al.. Accuracy of diagnosis of psychosis on general practice computer system. *Br. Med. J.* 1993; 307: 32-34.

[67] Byrne N, Regan C, Howard L. Administrative registers in psychiatric research: a systematic review of validity studies. *Acta Psychiatr. Scand.* 2005; 112: 409-414.

[68] Kuller Lh. The use of existing databases in morbidity and mortality studies. *Am. J. Public Health.* 1995; 85:1198-1200.

[69] Song F, Eastwood Aj, Gibody S, Duley L, Sutton Aj. Publication and related biases. *Health Technol. Assess.* 2000,4:1-105.

[70] Ferguson D, Laupacis A,Salmi Lr, Mcalister Fa, Huet C. What should be included in meta-analysis?: an exploration of methodological issues. Int *J. Technol. Assess. Health Care.* 2000;16:1109-1119.

[71] Dickersin K. Systematic reviews in epidemiology: why are we so far behind? *Int. J. Epidemiol.* 2002,31:6-12.

[72] Greenland S. Invited commentary: A critical look at some popular meta-analytic methods. *Am. J. Epidemiol.* 1994;140:290-296.

[73] Lau J, Ioannidis Jp, Schmid Ch. Quantitative synthesis in systematic reviews. *Ann. Intern. Med.* 1997;127:820-826.

[74] Atkins D, Fink K, Slutsky J. Better Information for Better Health Care: The Evidence-based Practice Center Program and the Agency for Healthcare Research and Quality. *Ann. Intern. Med.* 2005,142:1035-1041.

In: Schizophrenia Research: Recent Advances
Editor: Tomiki Sumiyoshi
ISBN: 978-1-62808-703-1

Chapter 5

PSYCHIATRIC NURSES' BELIEFS ABOUT THE TREATABILITY OF SCHIZOPHRENIA IN JAPAN

***Setsuko Hanzawa*[1], *Kayomi Yatabe*[1], *Goro Tanaka*[2] *and Yoshibumi Nakane*[3]**

[1] School of Nursing, Jichi Medical University, Japan
[2] Graduate School of Biomedical Sciences, Nagasaki University, Japan
[3] Health Management Center Nagasaki
Atomic Bomb Casualty Council, Japan

ABSTRACT

In Japan, there are many advanced mental health inpatient facilities but limited professional mental health care in the community. We investigated the beliefs of psychiatric nurses about the treatability of schizophrenia and the difficulty of community living, as well as investigating their psychiatric nursing experiences. The subjects included 108 psychiatric nurses who were employed in psychiatric hospitals. Beliefs about the difficulty of community living were evaluated using a Difficulty of Community Living Scale (DCLS) with a vignette that described chronic schizophrenia. The understanding of mental illness was evaluated using the 'Mental Illness and Disorder Understanding Scale' (MIDUS). Analysis of the results revealed the following: (1) the "Treatability of mental illness" MIDUS subscale (TMI-MIDUS) was not associated with socio-demographic characteristics of psychiatric nurses, (2) the TMI-MIDUS was associated with some inpatient and outpatient nursing experiences and beliefs about the "Resources for community living" DCLS subscale, (3) the "Social recognition of illness" MIDUS subscale, the "Resources for community life" DCLS subscale, and the "Participation in the discharge planning conference for inpatients" subscale were significantly associated with the TMI-MIDUS. Our findings suggest the need for an educational program for psychiatric nurses to enable them to effectively coordinate support for patients who transition from hospital facilities to community living settings with a multi-professional team approach in Japan.

INTRODUCTION

In Japan, the number of psychiatric beds has not decreased in the past 20 years [1]. There are many advanced mental health inpatient facilities and a long-term hospitalisation system; however, there is little outreach treatment provided by mental health professionals. Even for emergency situations, access to a psychiatric treatment team is limited. In 1998, the Psychiatric Welfare Workers' Act was enacted, and the main psychiatric hospitals proceeded to discharge patients who had been hospitalised long-term. Nevertheless, in 2010, the number of inpatients is still high, and there has been limited progress in psychiatric outreach services; even with a clearly written public policy, the situation continues in Japan. We recommend that you add some brief information on why these patients were discharged (and, perhaps, what the effect was).

After 1950, the Mental Hygiene Law allowed involuntary hospitalisation, which requires family consent in lieu of that of the patient. Furthermore, family caregivers were obligated to do the following: (1) protect the family member with a mental disorder, ensure treatment and protect his or her proprietary interests; (2) cooperate with the physician to ensure that the person with a mental disorder is correctly diagnosed; and (3) comply with the physician's instructions to ensure medical care for the mentally ill individual [2]. Therefore, for many years, family members of a person with a mental disorder experienced guilt related to "involuntary hospitalisation" and the member with the mental illness often blamed the family for giving consent. Therefore, psychiatric hospitalisation can lead to complex family relationships in Japan, especially during the acute delusional stage of schizophrenia, when the patient has little insight into the seriousness of the illness.

A long period of hospitalisation for a schizophrenia patient might help to balance the caregiver's burden because it is likely that the caregiver has sacrificed much of his or her own life to provide care. Helping an ill family member and sacrificing to give care is a common social and cultural value. In fact, 80% to 90% of schizophrenia patients in Japan live with their families [3]. Asian American and Latino patients have been shown to be considerably more likely than white patients to live with family members and to receive family support. Ethnocultural differences and living with the family may explain treatment intensity disparities and whether patients describe themselves as being dependent on family support [4].

It has been reported that people from Asian communities are unwilling to access help from mainstream services because of their beliefs as well as stigma and shame are key factors that influence this reluctance [5]. Furthermore, although the Japanese family caregiver experiences a great burden, both patients and family caregivers have been reported to have a strong desire to restrict the care to the family circle [3]. Few outreach treatment services are available, including home-visit nurses and assertive community service programs; therefore, family caregivers must struggle with psychiatric treatment options.

If schizophrenia patients have multiple mental or physical health issues that have created many problems for the family prior to hospitalisation, they might be hospitalised for a long time; therefore, interventions for long-term inpatients are targeted at coping with hospital life.

In fact, there are a large number of psychiatric nurses in Japan compared to other WHO regions. Japan has 59 psychiatric nurses per 100,000 population (see Figure 1); however, Japan has a larger number of psychiatric beds (29/10,000) than each WHO region (under 10

/10,000) [1] (see Figure 2). In Japan, most psychiatric nurses are employed in hospitals and care for inpatients. Few psychiatric nurses are employed as part of an outreach team that assists outpatients and family caregivers.

One might question why these nurses are only involved with inpatients and do not work with service providers in community settings. Taiwan is an East Asian country that has adopted the concept of community mental health, an idea of case management for longitudinal care that is grounded in psychiatric treatment [6]. Several cultural and social issues drive the rehabilitation process in China and India, including the use of traditional medicine and healers, an emphasis on family involvement, stigma, gender inequality, and a lack of resources [7].

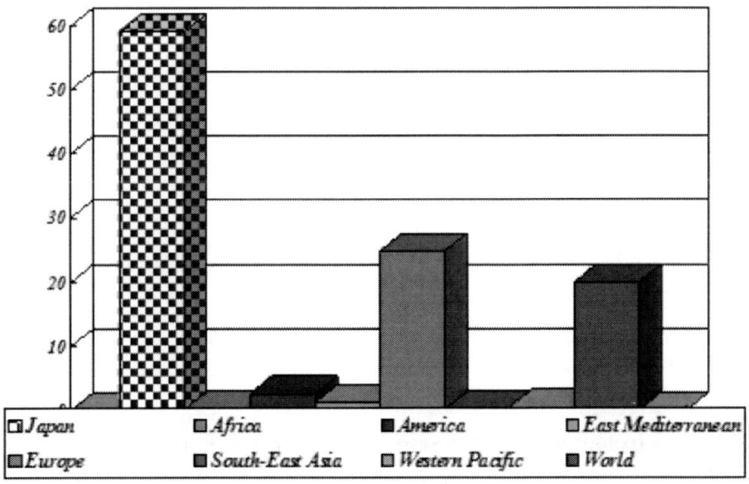

Mental Health Atlas 2005, WHO, 2005.

Figure 1. Numbers of total psychiatric nurses in Japan compared with each WHO region (per 100,000 population).

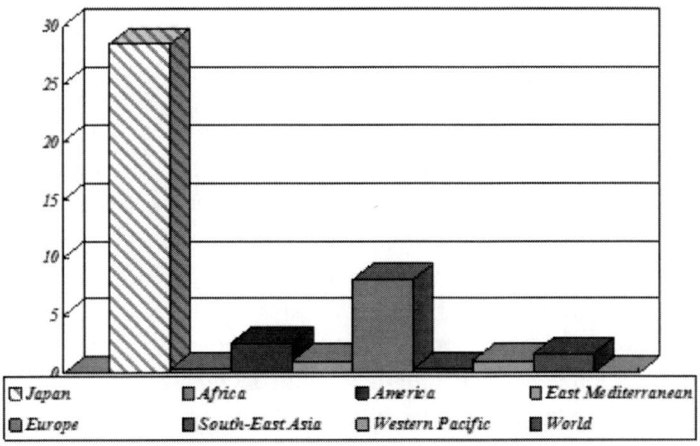

Mental Health Atlas 2005, WHO, 2005.

Figure 2. Numbers of total psychiatric beds in Japan compared with each WHO region (per 10,000 population).

In Japan, there are few public health centres that could offer personal case management according to the Taiwanese model, and there is a need to establish a relationship between psychiatric hospitals and resources for community living. For example, outpatient nurses, home-visiting nurses, outpatient physicians, and hospital social workers need to be included in and informed about facilitating the continuity of care. However, little is known about the concept of case management for longitudinal intervention and outcomes. We are especially interested in engaging psychiatric nurses who work in psychiatric wards to facilitate the connection between resources for community living and the psychiatric treatment team approach. Furthermore, little is known about nurses' understanding of the resources available to individuals with schizophrenia who live in community settings and the relationship between their knowledge of these resources and their understanding of mental illness.

The purpose of this chapter was to investigate the psychiatric nurses' beliefs about the treatability of schizophrenia and the difficulty of community living, as well as their experiences with inpatient or outpatient care. We hypothesised that psychiatric nurses with greater knowledge of the resources for patients who transition back into the community might have a better understanding of how to help schizophrenia patients and their families.

METHODS

The subjects included 108 psychiatric nurses employed in psychiatric hospitals in Japan who gave informed consent to participate. Before conducting the survey, all subjects received a written explanation about the purpose of the study.

The participating psychiatric nurses completed a questionnaire composed of three parts, including socio-demographic features, the Difficulty of Community Living Scale (DCLS), and the Mental Illness and Disorder Understanding Scale (MIDUS). Socio-demographic items included the age and gender of the nurse, whether the participant was a registered nurse (RN) or a licensed practical nurse (LPN), and the total years of employment at a psychiatric hospital.

Difficulty of Community Living Scale (DCLS)

The 12-item Difficulty of Community Living Scale (DCLS) was used to rate psychiatric nurses' understanding about the difficulties that a patient might experience [8]. A vignette was presented about a male patient with chronic schizophrenia who was living in the community. The vignette was based on the International Classification of Diseases, Tenth Revision (ICD-10) [9] (see Appendix). This self-administered scale consisted of three subscales: "Beliefs about the most appropriate form of hospitalisation" (i.e., "People with a problem like John's cannot be cared for by family members who have no experience as healthcare professionals"), "Resources for living in the community" (i.e., "When people with a problem like John's live alone in the community, outpatient physicians can be depended on"), and "Social disadvantages of living in the community" (i.e., "Family members caring for people with a problem like John's will sacrifice their lifestyles").

The DCLS uses a 5-point Likert scale (1=strongly agree, 2=agree, 3=neither agree nor disagree, 4=disagree, and 5=strongly disagree); lower scores indicate a belief in greater difficulties in living in the community for the person in the schizophrenia vignette.

Cronbach's alpha coefficient was used to test the content validity of the subscales. This coefficient has been shown to range from 0.69 to 0.75 in Japan for the following subscales: (a) "Beliefs about the most appropriate form of hospitalisation", 0.75; (b) "Resources for living in the community", 0.73; and (c) "Social disadvantages of community living", 0.69 [8].

Mental Illness and Disorder Understanding Scale (MIDUS)

The 15-item Mental Illness and Disorder Understanding Scale (MIDUS) was used to rate the psychiatric nurses' degree of understanding of mental illness and disorders. This self-administered scale consists of three subscales: "Treatability of mental illness" (i.e., "Delayed treatment worsens the prognosis of mental illness" and "Living environment has an influence on recovery from illness"), "Efficacy of medication" (i.e., "Medication improves brain function"), and "Social recognition of illness" (i.e., "People with mental disorders can live in the community if they receive appropriate support"). The MIDUS uses a 5-point Likert scale (0=strongly agree, 1=tend to agree, 2=neither agree nor disagree, 3=tend to disagree, 4=strongly disagree); lower scores indicate better understanding of mental illness and disorders.

Cronbach's alpha coefficient, which was used to test the content validity of the subscales, ranged from 0.62 to 0.74 for the following subscales: (a) "Treatability of mental illness", 0.74; (b) "Efficacy of medication", 0.73; and (c) "Social recognition of illness", 0.62 [10].

Statistical Analyses

The resources for living in the community (RLC) subscale of the DCLS for patients with schizophrenia compares different socio-demographic characteristics using a t test (for comparisons between 2 groups) and analysis of variance (for comparisons between 3 or more groups). The relationship between the RLC subscale and other factors was analysed using multiple regression analysis. The RLC subscale was used as the dependent variable after deriving Spearman's rank-order correlation coefficients. SPSS 18.0 for Windows (SPSS Inc, Chicago, IL, USA) was used for all statistical analyses. The level of statistical significance was set at <5%.

RESULTS

Socio-Demographic Characteristics

The socio-demographic characteristics of the subjects were evaluated in the study. The mean age of the subjects was 48.0 years (SD=12.0), and the age range was 20 to 71 years. There were 83 (76.9%) women, 65 (60.2%) RNs and 41 (38.0%) LPNs. The total years of employment in psychiatric hospitals was 0 to 3 years for 6 nurses (5.6%), 3 to 10 years for 35 nurses (32.4%), 10 to 20 years for 41 nurses (38.0%), and >20 years for 24 nurses (22.2%) out of the total 108 nurses, of whom 79 (73.1%) were staff nurses. The current place of employment of the psychiatric nurses included the following: 18 (16.7%) were in acute treatment wards, 17 (15.7%) were in general treatment wards, 53 (49.1%) were in recuperation wards, and 18 (16.7%) were in the psychiatry department for outpatients. A significant correlation between the "Treatability of mental illness" of the MIDUS scores and the socio-demographic characteristics was not observed for the subjects.

Evaluation of MIDUS and DCLS Scores

The results of the MIDUS and the distribution of response scores for each item are shown in Table 1. For the MIDUS, Cronbach's alpha was moderately high at 0.73. The mean total score for the MIDUS was 12.71 (SD=6.53), that for "Treatability of mental illness" of the MIDUS subscale was 2.37 (SD=2.35), that for "Efficacy of medication" was 7.41 (SD=3.54), and that for "Social recognition of illness" was 2.93 (SD=2.70).

Table 1. Mean and standard deviation for MIDUS

		Mean	SD
Mental Illness and Disorder Understanding Scale; MIDUS†		12.71	6.53
1st factor: Treatability of mental illness		2.37	2.35
5	Mental illness requires early treatment	0.09	0.32
12	Mental illness is treatable	0.77	0.92
15	Delayed treatment worsens the prognosis of mental illness	0.44	0.74
10	Living environment has an influence on recovery from illness	0.25	0.64
14	Misunderstanding of mental illnesses makes it difficult for people with mental disorder to participate in society	0.31	0.66
7	Rehabilitation is effective in improving mental disorder	0.51	0.74
2nd factor: Efficacy of medication		7.41	3.54
6	Treatment requires medication	1.09	1.10
2	Medication improves brain function	1.94	1.09
9	Medication is effective in improving symptoms	0.76	0.89
13	Continuous administration of medication dose not lead to intoxication or addiction	2.19	1.21
8	Mental illness is a brain disease	1.42	1.29
3rd factor: Social recognition of illness		2.93	2.70
1	Mental illnesses (depression, schizophrenia etc) are very common	0.67	1.04
11	Anybody can suffer from mental illness	0.35	0.71
4	Mental illness is a medical condition like other illnesses	1.30	1.42
3	People with mental disorders can live in the community, if they receive appropriate support	0.65	0.85

† MIDUS uses a 5-point Likert scale (0=strongly agree, 1=tend to agree, 2=neither agree nor disagree, 3=tend to disagree, 4=strongly disagree). Lower scores indicate better understanding.

Table 2. Correlation between MIDUS and DCLS

		MIDUS				DCLS					
		2		3		4		5		6	
		r	*P*	*r*	*P*	*r*	*P*	*r*	*P*	*r*	*P*
MIDUS†	1. Treatability of mental illness	0.345	0.001	0.452	0.001	-0.088	0.367	-0.438	0.001	-0.186	0.054
	2. Efficacy of medication	—	—	0.382	0.001	-0.093	0.339	-0.236	0.014	-0.049	0.615
	3. Social recognition of illness			—	—	-0.273	0.004	-0.266	0.005	-0.177	0.068
DCLS‡	4. Preference for hospitalization					—	—	-0.088	0.362	0.423	0.001
	5. Resources for living in the community							—	—	0.001	0.991
	6. Social disadvantage of community living									—	—

† MIDUS uses a 5-point Likert scale (0=strongly agree, 1=tend to agree, 2=neither agree nor disagree, 3=tend to disagree, 4=strongly disagree). Lower scores indicate better understanding.

‡ DCLS uses a 5-point Likert scale (1=strongly agree, 2=agree, 3=neither agree nor disagree, 4=disagree, 5=strongly disagree). Lower scores indicate greater difficulties in living in the community for the person in the schizophrenia vignette.

Table 3. Comparison of mean and standard deviation for various parameters, including MIDUS

			n	%	"Treatability of mental illness" of MIDUS†			
Nursing experiences					Mean	SD	*t*	*P*
1	Participate in the conference about discharge plan for inpatients	yes	78	72.2	1.99	1.96	2.177	0.036
		no	30	27.8	3.27	2.98		
2	Experiences about hearing of community living of outpatinet actually from care staff in the community	yes	69	63.9	2.13	2.26	1.254	0.213
		no	39	36.1	2.72	2.48		
3	Going out for training of community living for inpatients	yes	57	52.8	2.04	2.18	1.448	0.151
		no	51	47.2	2.69	2.49		
4	Experiences about visiting day care center for outpatinet actually	yes	54	50.0	2.06	1.93	1.183	0.240
		no	51	47.2	2.61	2.76		
5	Experiences to observe life training facilities for outpatient actually	yes	50	46.3	1.78	1.84	2.325	0.022
		no	55	50.9	2.82	2.69		

Table 3. (Continued)

			n	**%**	**"Treatability of mental illness" of MIDUS†**			
Nursing experiences					Mean	SD	*t*	*P*
6	Home visiting nursing for outpatients	yes	29	26.9	1.41	2.11	2.628	0.010
		no	78	72.2	2.72	2.34		
7	Home visiting nursing for inpatients	yes	27	25.0	1.30	1.73	3.258	0.002
		no	81	75.0	2.69	2.43		

† MIDUS uses a 5-point Likert scale (0=strongly agree, 1=tend to agree, 2=neither agree nor disagree, 3=tend to disagree, 4=strongly disagree). Lower scores indicate better understanding.

Cronbach's alpha for the DCLS was moderately high at 0.70. The mean total score for the DCLS was 35.55 (SD=4.98), that for "Beliefs about the most appropriate form of hospitalisation" of the DCLS subscale was 15.72 (SD=3.21), that for "Resources for living in the community" was 11.66 (SD=2.58), and that for "Social disadvantages of community living" was 8.17 (SD=1.97).

Factors Related to the "Treatability of mental Illness" of the MIDUS

The relationship between the MIDUS and the DCLS subscales is shown in Table 2. Significant correlations were observed between the "Treatability of mental illness" of the MIDUS subscale and the "Efficacy of medication" ($r=0.345$, $P<0.001$) or "Social recognition of illness" of the MIDUS subscale ($r=0.452$, $P<0.001$) and "Resources for community living" of the DCLS subscale ($r=-0.438$, $P<0.001$).

Comparison between Nursing Experiences and the MIDUS Subscale

The results of the comparison analysis for various parameters of nursing experiences with the MIDUS subscale are summarised in Table 3. Overall, 27 (25.0%) and 29 (26.9%) subjects were home-visit nurses for inpatients and outpatients, respectively, and 78 (72.2%) participated in the discharge plan conference for inpatients. Fifty (46.3%) nurses just saw life training facilities for outpatients (see Figure 3-5). These variables had a significant impact on the mean score for "Treatability of mental illness" of the MIDUS subscale ($P<0.05$).

Multiple Regression Analysis Using "Treatability of Mental Illness" of the MIDUS Subscale as the Dependent Variable

Results of the multiple regression analysis are summarised in Table 4. Multiple regression analysis was performed using variables that were significantly associated with "Treatability of mental illness" of the MIDUS subscale. The independent variables were "Efficacy of medication" and "Social recognition of illness" of the MIDUS subscale, "Resources for community living" of the DCLS subscale, "home-visit nursing for inpatients", "home-visit nursing for outpatients", "participation in the discharge planning conference for inpatients", and "observation of life training facilities for outpatients"; the dependent variable was "Treatability of mental illness" of the MIDUS subscale. The scores of "Social recognition of illness" of the MIDUS subscale ($\beta=0.390$, $P<0.001$), "Resources for community living" of the DCLS subscale ($\beta=-0.301$, $P<0.001$), and "participation in the discharge planning conference for inpatients" ($\beta=0.177$, $P<0.05$) were significantly associated with "Treatability of mental illness" of the MIDUS subscale.

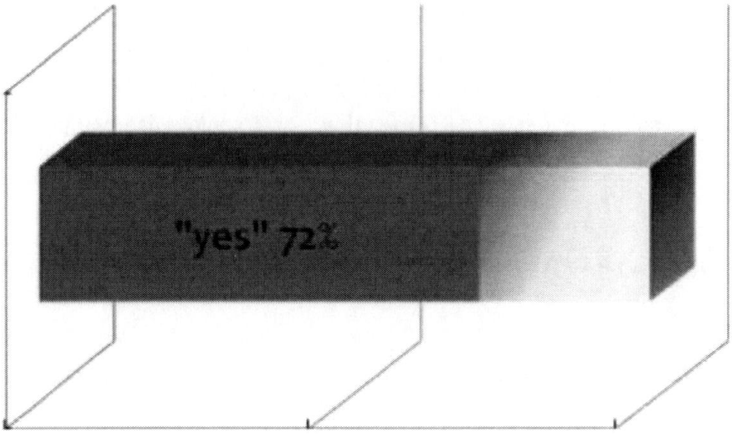

Figure 3. "Have you ever experienced to **participate** in the conference about discharge planning for inpatients?".

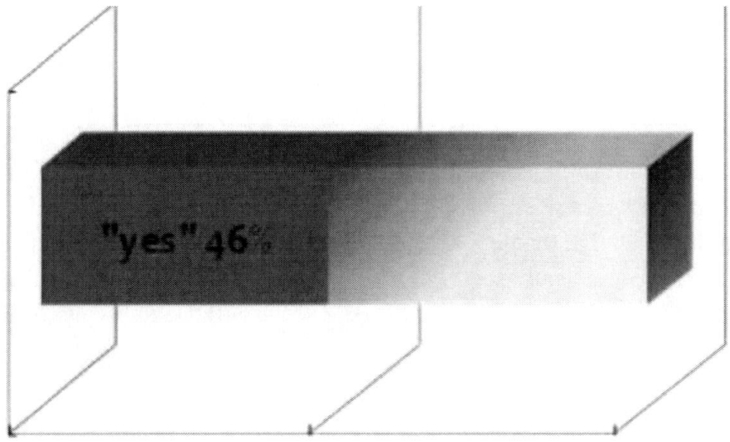

Figure 4. "Have you ever experienced about **observation training** facilities for outpatient **actually**?".

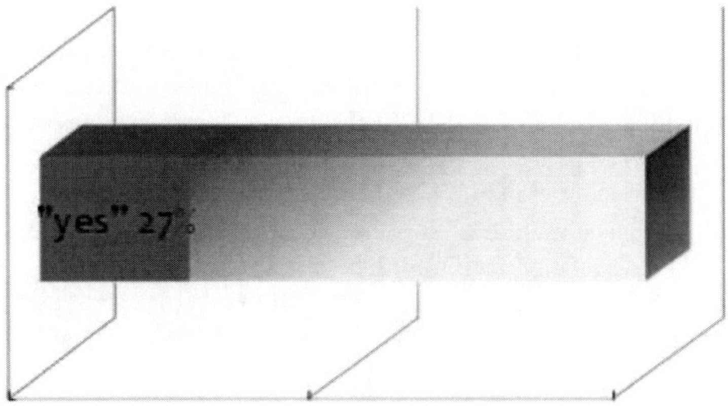

Figure 5. "Have you ever experienced about **home visiting nursing** for outpatient?".

Table 4. Multiple regression for "Treatability of mental illness" of MIDUS as a dependent variable

Independent variable		β	t	P	R^2
"Treatability of mental illness" of MIDUS†					
Step1	"Social recognition of illness" of MIDUS	0.487	5.624	0.000	0.237
Step2	"Social recognition of illness" of MIDUS	0.415	4.951	0.000	0.327
	"Resources for living in the community" of DCLS‡	-0.309	-3.687	0.000	
Step3	"Social recognition of illness" of MIDUS	0.390	4.693	0.000	0.358
	"Resources for living in the community" of DCLS‡	-0.301	-3.652	0.000	
	Participate in the conference about discharge plan for inpatients§	0.177	2.180	0.032	

*P<0.05, **P<0.01, ***P<0.001 (Spearman)

† MIDUS uses a 5-point Likert scale, with lower scores indicating better understanding.

‡ DCLS uses a 5-point Likert scale , with lower scores indicating greater difficulty living in the community.

§ "participate in the conference about discharge plan for inpatients"; yes=1 or no=2.

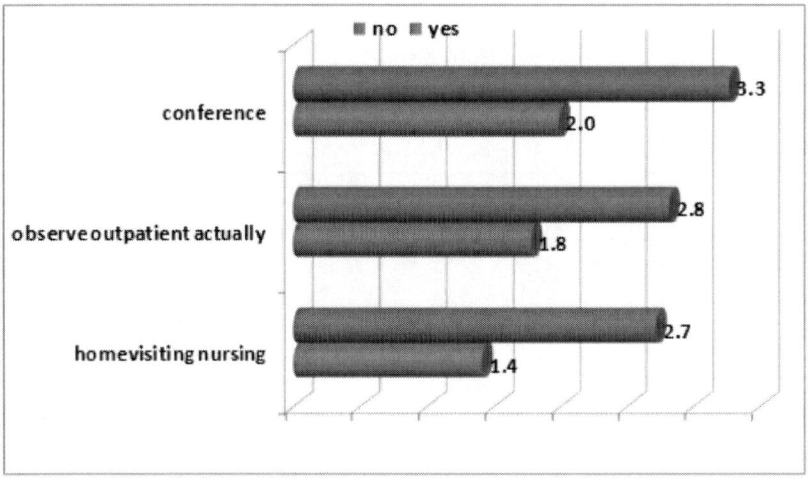

Figure 6. "Treatability of mental illness" with nursing experiences (not treatability as large numer of score).

Discussion

We examined the relationship between psychiatric nurses' knowledge about resources for persons with schizophrenia who are living in the community and their understanding of how to help patients with mental illness, especially with regards to "Treatability of mental illness". The results revealed that "Social recognition of illness" "Resources for community living" and "participation in the discharge planning conference for inpatients" were significant predictors for "Treatability of mental illness", according to the MIDUS.

In our previous research with a sample of Japanese psychiatric nurses, RN or LPN status and gender were significant predictors for "Beliefs about the most appropriate form of hospitalisation". However, in the present study, these factors were not as significant for predicting the "Treatability of mental illness". This finding demonstrates a possible difference between "Beliefs about the most appropriate form of hospitalisation" and knowledge about the "Treatability of mental illness" among psychiatric nurses employed in psychiatric hospitals. We did not attempt to investigate the correlation between these factors. It was evident that Japanese psychiatric nurses do not believe that inpatient treatment and hospitalisation of schizophrenia patients are necessarily the most appropriate options to improve mental disorders. They believed that limited social recognition of mental illness, social disadvantages, and the lack of resources in community life. In the past decade, there has been a substantial increase in research on stigmatising beliefs and attitudes among mental health professionals. People with mental illness often report encountering negative attitudes among mental health staff about their prognosis, which is associated in part with physician bias [11]. For example, in an Italian sample, responses of the general public differed from responses given by mental health professionals and patients' relatives regarding the effectiveness of psychological treatments, patients' unpredictability, and whether patients should be admitted to asylums. Mental health professionals were advised to be aware of their own attitudes towards people with schizophrenia because professionals can influence the beliefs of lay people and the general social acceptance of these patients [12]. In a study in Turkey, the majority of nurses stated that schizophrenia is caused by social problems and cannot be completely cured and that schizophrenic patients are aggressive. This research highlighted the need for nurses to avoid stigmatising patients and to promote a therapeutic environment, particularly on the wards [13].

Health professionals rate long-term outcomes more negatively than does the general public, and the public is more optimistic about the long-term prognosis after treatment than health professionals [14][15]. In a South Australian study, health professionals were generally more pessimistic about the chances of recovery than the general public, and psychiatrists were even less optimistic than nurses [15]. A recent study in Japan revealed that psychiatric nurses were more pessimistic about schizophrenia patients' outcome than psychiatrists [16]. Some patients do recover quickly and are rapidly discharged from care; however, over time, many Japanese psychiatric nurses who are employed in hospitals may base their opinions on caring for patients who do not fully recover. Their clinical experience is filled with patients who continue to live in the psychiatric hospital as "psychiatric patients" seemingly permanent, who rarely experience a meaningful life in the community. We found that when nurses had the opportunity to participate in discharge planning for inpatients, this experience was one of the significant predictors for beliefs about the "Treatability of mental illness".

In Japan, there is little psychiatric care for the majority of the population, and the only services available are in mental hospitals or psychiatric clinics. These services are usually centralised, but they are not readily used because of the stigma associated with psychiatric treatment and the patients' lack of insight. In addition, there are limited psychiatric outreach services, so patients with mental illness and family caregivers often seek help only as a last resort. Furthermore, in Japan, as in most East Asian countries, there is a widespread belief that the most appropriate form of care is the family. This deeply dependant relationship between patients and families is due to a Confucian idea of obligation that is common in East Asian countries, and family caregivers may have difficulties sharing this familial obligation and responsibility with professional psychiatric nurses [3].

Studies have shown that nurses who work in psychiatric departments experience severe psychological trauma when exposed to patients' verbal abuse or violence [17]. This type of experience may be one of the reasons that psychiatric nurses have the greatest level of biased perceptions among medical workers. Nurses tend to have the closest contact with inpatients on psychiatric wards; this association makes them easy targets for patients' verbal abuse or violence [17][18]. This finding may explain why psychiatric nurses have difficulty taking care of a relative with mental illness [8].

Negative attitudes towards individuals with mental illness among psychiatric nurses and family caregivers have been identified as an obstacle for recovering from illness and fully participating in society. Japanese society must break this vicious cycle so that patients can be discharged and live successfully as members of the community. To support patients in the community, mental health staff must be available to give care on an outpatient basis.

In conclusion, the availability of resources had significant and independent effects on psychiatric nurses' beliefs about the treatability of mental illness. These resources included outpatient nurses, physicians, and hospital social workers who could assist individuals with schizophrenia to successfully live in the community in Japan. The present findings suggest that effective educational programs are needed for psychiatric nurses to effectively coordinate support for patient transition from hospital facilities to community settings. Furthermore, care-management skills using the multi-professional team approach must be emphasised in Japan. Japan's vast network of inpatient treatment facilities and the limited number of community support programs must be considered in the context of the overall society. The social and cultural values that are attached to the East Asian Confucian idea of family obligation and responsibility as well as the beliefs about the treatability of mental illness must be incorporated into the care of patients with chronic schizophrenia.

We recruited psychiatric nurses who were employed at two psychiatric hospitals in Japan. Although our target population was not representative of the general population, the study findings may be useful for identifying underlying factors related to psychiatric nurses' beliefs about the recovery of schizophrenia inpatients and the development of effective educational programs. In future studies, it will be necessary to compare the factors that influence beliefs about the treatability of mental illness for inpatient and outpatients among psychiatric nurses. In addition, these findings should be compared to those from other East Asian countries that have smaller numbers of psychiatric beds. We plan to address these issues in future studies.

Acknowledgments

The authors deeply appreciate the cooperation of the participants of the research project in Japan.

Appendix: Chronic Schizophrenia Vignette

John is 44 years old. He lives in a boarding house in an industrial area. He has not worked for years. He wears the same clothes regardless of the weather and has let his hair grow long and untidy. He is always on his own and is often seen sitting in the park talking to himself. At times, he stands and moves his hands as if to communicate to someone in the nearby trees. He rarely drinks alcohol. He speaks carefully, using uncommon and sometimes made-up words. He is polite but avoids talking with other people. At times, he accuses shopkeepers of giving information about him to other people. He has asked his landlord to put extra locks on his door and to remove the television set from his room. He says spies are trying to keep him under observation because he has secret information about international computer systems that control people through television transmitters. His landlord complains that John will not let him clean his apartment, which is becoming increasingly dirty and is filled with glass objects. John says he is using these glass objects "to receive messages from space".

References

[1] World Health Organization, *Mental Health Atlas-2005,* Geneva (2005).
[2] Law Related to Mental Health and Welfare of the Person with Mental Disorder, Tokyo (2006).
[3] S. Hanzawa, J. K. Bae, and H. Tanaka, *Psychiatry Clin. Neurosci.* 64, 377 (2010).

[4] L. R. Snowden, *Cult. Med. Psychiatry* 31, 389 (2007).
[5] D. Wynaden, R. Chapman, and O. Angelica, *Int. J. Ment. Health Nurs.* 14, 88 (2005).
[6] F. Noda and T. Sasaki, *Jpn. J. Clin. Psychiatry* 20, 665 (in Japanese) (1991).
[7] L. Higgins, P. Dey-Ghatak, G. Davey, *Int. J. Ment. Health Nurs.* 16, 22 (2007).
[8] S. Hanzawa, S. Sato, and K. Yatabe, *Jpn. Bull Soc. Psychiatry,* 19, 187 (in Japanese) (2010).
[9] World Health Organization, *The ICD-10 Classification of Mental and Behavioral Disorders: Diagnostic Criteria for Research.* World Health Organization, Geneva (1993).
[10] G. Tanaka, *Int. J. Sociology* 12, 95 (2003).
[11] G. Thornicroft, D. Rose, and A. Kassam, *Int. Rev. Psychiatry* 19, 113 (2007).
[12] L. Magliano, A. Fiorillo, and C. D. Rosa, *Can. J. Psychiatry* 49, 322 (2004).
[13] K. Kukulu, and G. Ergun, *J. Psychiatr. Ment. Health Nurs.* 14, 302 (2007).
[14] A. F. Jorm, A. E. Korten, and P. A. Jacomb, *Aust. N Z. J. Psychiatry* 33, 77 (1999).
[15] M. Hugo, *J. Psychiatr. Ment. Health Nurs.* 8, 419 (2001).
[16] S. Hanzawa, Y. Nakane, K. Yoshioka, and H. Nakane, *Seishin Igaku (Clin Psychiatry)* 51, 541 (in Japanese) (2009).
[17] M. Inoue, K. Tsukano, and M. Muraoka, *Psychiatry Clin. Neurosci.*60, 29 (2006).
[18] W. C. Chen, C. J. Huang, and J. S. Hwang, *Qual. Life Res.* 19, 1155 (2010).

SECTION II

NEUROPSYCHOBIOLOGICAL INSIGHTS

In: Schizophrenia Research: Recent Advances
Editor: Tomiki Sumiyoshi
ISBN: 978-1-62808-703-1

Chapter 6

CURRENT NEUROBIOLOGICAL RESEARCH IN EARLY ONSET SCHIZOPHRENIA

Gianluca Serafini*[1*]*, Maurizio Pompili*[1,2]*, Marco Innamorati*[1]*,
***Gloria Giordano*[1]*, Roberto Tatarelli*[1] *and Paolo Girardi*[1]**
[1]Department of Neurosciences, Mental Health and Sensory Organs,Sant'Andrea Hospital,
Suicide Prevention Center, "Sapienza" University of Rome, Rome, Italy
[2] McLean Hospital, Harvard Medical School, US

ABSTRACT

Schizophrenia is an invalidating disorder usually with an onset during adolescence or young adulthood and tending to persist throughout life. Both cognitive and emotional dysfunctions may be found in schizophrenic patients determining severe psychosocial impairment. The present chapter aimed to provide a critical overview about early onset schizophrenia and new neurobiological advances in this field of research. The recognition of a biological vulnerability contributing to the development of the illness using genetic and clinical at-risk approach with the latter targeting at the identification of prodromal symptoms and behaviours is crucial. The paradigm of early intervention is focused on the early identification of people considered as at risk mental state (ARMS) and of subjects with ultra high risk criteria (UHR) to develop the illness. Also, the chapter focused on recent neurobiological advances in detecting possible markers of vulnerability resulting from findings of neuroimaging and genetic studies in early onset schizophrenia samples. Both structural and functional neuroimaging studies have demonstrated the presence of some brain abnormalities in early onset schizophrenia subjects; however, whether their appearance and their differential location can be considered predictive of poor outcome and more frequent transition to psychosis in specific subgroups of patients is still a matter of debate. Most studies were limited by the absence of longitudinal studies assessing neuroprogression due to small samples and less short or infrequent follow-up periods. Finally, this chapter presents an update about psychopharmacological treatment in early onset schizophrenia.

---

* E-mail address: gianluca.serafini@uniroma1.it.

Keywords: Early onset schizophrenia; UHR criteria; ARMS; neuroimaging; prevention

INTRODUCTION

Schizophrenia affects nearly 1% of the general population [1] ranking ninth among all global burden of disability and having high societal costs [2-5]. It is a disabling mental disorder characterized by the presence of delusions and hallucinations as well as negative symptoms (social withdrawal, flat affect, anhedonia) and cognitive dysfunctions [6]. Schizophrenia typically arises in the third decade of life; childhood-onset is almost rare whereas considerable prevalence rates occurred during adolescence, particularly between 13 and 18 years of age [7]. According to the DSM-IV-TR, the diagnostic criteria for schizophrenia are two or more of the following, each present for a significant portion of time during six-months period: delusions, hallucinations, disorganized speech (e.g., frequent derailment or incoherence), grossly disorganized or catatonic behaviour and negative symptoms (e.g., flat affect, alogia, or avolition). However, new criteria and a list of disorders have been proposed by the DSM-V task force for the diagnostic category "Schizophrenia Spectrum and Other Psychotic Disorders" (for more details see Table 1).

Both cognitive and emotional dysfunction are major phenotypic characteristics in schizophrenia and other psychotic disorders [8]. The existence of cognitive dysfunction in schizophrenia has been initially conceptualized by Kraepelin [9] when describing "dementia praecox". Dementia praecox refers, in his opinion, to a chronic deteriorating psychotic disorder characterized by rapid cognitive disintegration, usually beginning in early adolescence. Kraepelin postulated that a chronic metabolic autointoxication, perhaps arising from the sex glands, eventually caused chemical brain damage leading to the symptoms of dementia praecox. Actually, we know that the presence of cognitive dysfunction is associated with a relevant psychosocial impairment and severe difficulties in one or more major areas of individual functioning; however, a relevant impairment in emotional functioning is also recognized as one of the key characteristic of this complex disorder [8, 10]. For instance, flat affect and a severe reduction in emotional expressiveness have been evident in schizophrenic subjects and presumably related to impaired ability to perceive and decode emotions in facial expressions [11-12].

Psychiatric comorbidities are common among patients with schizophrenia [13]; above all substance abuse [14], anxiety and depressive disorders [15-16]. Among anxiety disorders, it has been estimated a prevalence of 15% for panic disorder [17], 29% for post-traumatic stress disorder [18] and 23% for obsessive-compulsive disorder [17]. Researchers showed that comorbid depression occurs in 50% of patients, and approximately 47% of patients have a lifetime diagnosis of comorbid substance abuse [13].

The mean life expectancy of people with schizophrenia is approximately 12 to 15 years less compared to the general population, due to the increased medical problems and a higher suicide rate (about 5%) [19]. Suicide is a relevant cause of death among patients with schizophrenia and research [20] has indicated that at least 5–13% of schizophrenic patients die by suicide. Schizophrenic subjects who are more likely to commit suicide are typically young, male, white and never married, having a good premorbid functioning, post-psychotic depression and often with a history of substance abuse and suicide attempts [21].

Table 1. DSM-V criteria for Schizophrenia Spectrum and Other Psychotic Disorders

B 00 Schizophrenia	A. Characteristic symptoms: Two (or more) of the following, each present for a significant portion of time during a 1-month period (or less if successfully treated). At least one of these should include 1-3 1. Delusions 2. Hallucinations 3. Disorganized speech 4. Grossly abnormal psychomotor behavior, such as catatonia 5. Negative symptoms, i.e., restricted affect or avolition/asociality B. Social/occupational dysfunction: For a significant portion of the time since the onset of the disturbance, one or more major areas of functioning such as work, interpersonal relations, or self-care are markedly below the level achieved prior to the onset (or when the onset is in childhood or adolescence, failure to achieve expected level of interpersonal, academic, or occupational achievement). C. Duration: Continuous signs of the disturbance persist for at least 6 months. This 6-month period must include at least 1 month of symptoms (or less if successfully treated) that meet Criterion A (i.e., active-phase symptoms) and may include periods of prodromal or residual symptoms. During these prodromal or residual periods, the signs of the disturbance may be manifested by only negative symptoms or two or more symptoms listed in Criterion A present in an attenuated form (e.g., odd beliefs, unusual perceptual experiences). D. Schizoaffective and Mood Disorder exclusion: Schizoaffective Disorder and Mood Disorder With Psychotic Features have been ruled out because either (1) no Major Depressive or Manic Episodes have occurred concurrently with the activephase symptoms; or (2) if mood episodes have occurred during active-phase symptoms, their total duration has been brief relative to the duration of the active and residual periods. E. Substance/general medical condition exclusion: The disturbance is not due to the direct physiological effects of a substance (e.g., a drug of abuse, a medication) or a general medical condition. F. Relationship to a Pervasive Developmental Disorder: If there is a history of Autistic Disorder or another Pervasive Developmental Disorder or other communication disorder of childhood onset, the additional diagnosis of Schizophrenia is made only if prominent delusions or hallucinations are also present for at least a month (or less if successfully treated). Schizophrenia Subtypes The work group is recommending that these subtypes not be included in DSM-5. Classification of Longitudinal Course for Schizophrenia The course specifiers are to be worked on and potential change is not reflected in the current documents

Table 1. (Continued)

B 01 Schizotypal Personality Disorder	The essential features of a personality disorder are impairments in personality (self and interpersonal) functioning and the presence of pathological personality traits. To diagnose schizotypal personality disorder, the following criteria must be met: A. Significant impairments in personality functioning manifest by: 1. Impairments in self functioning (a or b): a. Identity: Confused boundaries between self and others; distorted self-concept; emotional expression often not congruent with context or internal experience. b. Self-direction: Unrealistic or incoherent goals; no clear set of internal standards. AND 2. Impairments in interpersonal functioning (a or b): a. Empathy: Pronounced difficulty understanding impact of own behaviors on others; frequent misinterpretations of others' motivations and behaviors. b. Intimacy: Marked impairments in developing close relationships, associated with mistrust and anxiety. B. Pathological personality traits in the following domains: 1. Psychoticism, characterized by: a. Eccentricity: Odd, unusual, or bizarre behavior or appearance; saying unusual or inappropriate things. b. Cognitive and perceptual dysregulation: Odd or unusual thought processes; vague, circumstantial, metaphorical, over-elaborate, or stereotyped thought or speech; odd sensations in various sensory modalities. c. Unusual beliefs and experiences: Thought content and views of reality that are viewed by others as bizarre or idiosyncratic; unusual experiences of reality. 2. Detachment, characterized by: a. Restricted affectivity: Little reaction to emotionally arousing situations; constricted emotional experience and expression; indifference or coldness. b. Withdrawal: Preference for being alone to being with others; reticence in social situations; avoidance of social contacts and activity; lack of initiation of social contact. 3. Negative Affectivity, characterized by: a. Suspiciousness: Expectations of – and heightened sensitivity to – signs of interpersonal ill-intent or harm; doubts about loyalty and fidelity of others; feelings of persecution. C. The impairments in personality functioning and the individual's personality trait expression are relatively stable across time and consistent across situations.

	D. The impairments in personality functioning and the individual's personality trait expression are not better understood as normative for the individual's developmental stage or socio-cultural environment. E. The impairments in personality functioning and the individual's personality trait expression are not solely due to the direct physiological effects of a substance (e.g., a drug of abuse, medication) or a general medical condition (e.g., severe head trauma).
B 02 Schizophreniform Disorder	Schizophreniform Disorder A. Criteria A, D, and E of Schizophrenia are met. B. An episode of the disorder (including prodromal, active, and residual phases) lasts at least 1 month but less than 6 months. (When the diagnosis must be made without waiting for recovery, it should be qualified as "Provisional.") Specify if: Without Good Prognostic Features With Good Prognostic Features: as evidenced by two (or more) of the following: (1) onset of prominent psychotic symptoms within 4 weeks of the first noticeable change in usual behavior or functioning (2) confusion or perplexity at the height of the psychotic episode (3) good premorbid social and occupational functioning (4) absence of blunted or flat affect
B 03 Brief Psychotic Disorder	Brief Psychotic Disorder A. Presence of one (or more) of the following symptoms: (1) delusions (2) hallucinations (3) disorganized speech (e.g., frequent derailment or incoherence) (4) grossly disorganized or catatonic behavior Note: Do not include a symptom if it is a culturally sanctioned response pattern. B. Duration of an episode of the disturbance is at least 1 day but less than 1 month, with eventual full return to premorbid level of functioning. C. The disturbance is not better accounted for by a Mood Disorder With Psychotic Features, Schizoaffective Disorder, or Schizophrenia and is not due to the direct physiological effects of a substance (e.g., a drug of abuse, a medication) or a general medical condition. Specify if: With Marked Stressor(s) (brief reactive psychosis): if symptoms occur shortly after and apparently in response to events that, singly or together, would be markedly stressful to almost anyone in similar circumstances in the person's culture Without Marked Stressor(s): if psychotic symptoms do not occur shortly after, or are not apparently in response to events that, singly or together, would be markedly stressful to almost anyone in similar circumstances in the person's culture With Postpartum Onset: if onset within 4 weeks postpartum

Table 1. (Continued)

B 04 Delusional Disorder	Delusional Disorder A. Delusions of at least 1 month's duration. B. Criterion A for Schizophrenia has never been met. Note: Tactile and olfactory hallucinations may be present in Delusional Disorder if they are related to the delusional theme. C. Apart from the impact of the delusion(s) or its ramifications, functioning is not markedly impaired and behavior is not obviously odd or bizarre. D. If mood episodes have occurred concurrently with delusions, their total duration has been brief relative to the duration of the delusional periods. E. The disturbance is not better accounted for by another mental disorder such as body dysmorphic disorder or obsessive compulsive disorder. F. The disturbance is not due to the direct physiological effects of a substance (e.g., a drug of abuse, a medication) or a general medical condition. Specify type (the following types are assigned based on the predominant delusional theme): Erotomanic Type: delusions that another person, usually of higher status, is in love with the individual Grandiose Type: delusions of inflated worth, power, knowledge, identity, or special relationship to a deity or famous person Jealous Type: delusions that the individual's sexual partner is unfaithful Persecutory Type: delusions that the person (or someone to whom the person is close) is being malevolently treated in some way Somatic Type: delusions that the person has some general medical condition Mixed Type: delusions characteristic of more than one of the above types but no one theme predominates Unspecified Type Specify if delusions are bizarre
B 05 Schizoaffective Disorder	Schizoaffective Disorder A. An uninterrupted period of illness during which, at some time, Criterion A symptoms of schizophrenia are present and there is eaither a major depressive episode or a manic episode. B. During the lifetime duration of the illness, delusions and/or hallucinations are present for at least two weeks in the absence of a major mood episode (depressive or manic). C. A major mood episode is present for the majority (> 50%) of the total duration of the illness. (Note periods of successfully treated mood symptoms count towards the cumulative duration of the major mood episode). D. Disturbance is not due to direct physiological effects of a substance (e.g. a drug of abuse, a medication) or a general medical condition.

B 06 Attenuated Psychosis Syndrome	Attenuated Psychosis Syndrome The work group is recommending that this be included in DSM-5 but is still examining the evidence as to whether inclusion is merited in the main manual or in an Appendix for Further Research. As such, the work group strongly encourages feedback regarding this disorder. All six of the following: a) Characteristic symptoms: at least one of the following in attenuated form with intact reality testing, but of sufficient severity and/or frequency that it is not discounted or ignored; (i) delusions (ii) hallucinations (iii) disorganized speech b) Frequency/Currency: symptoms meeting criterion A must be present in the past month and occur at an average frequency of at least once per week in past month c) Progression: symptoms meeting criterion A must have begun in or significantly worsened in the past year; d) Distress/Disability/Treatment Seeking: symptoms meeting criterion A are sufficiently distressing and disabling to the patient and/or parent/guardian to lead them to seek help e) Symtpoms meeting criterion A are not better explained by any DSM-5 diagnosis, including substance-related disorder. f) Clinical criteria for any DSM-V psychotic disorder have never been met
B 07-14 Substance-Induced Psychotic Disorder	The work group is finalizing their criteria for this disorder.
B 15 Psychotic Disorder Associated with a Known General Medical Condition	Psychotic Disorder Associated with a Known General Medical Condition A. Prominent hallucinations or delusions. B. There is evidence from the history, physical examination, or laboratory findings that the disturbance is the direct physiological consequence of a general medical condition. C. The disturbance is not better accounted for by another mental disorder. D. The disturbance does not occur exclusively during the course of a delirium.

Table 1. (Continued)

B 16 Catatonic Disorder Associated with a Known General Medical Condition	Catatonic Disorder Associated with a Known General Medical Condition A. The clinical picture is dominated by at least three of the following: 1. Catalepsy 2. Waxy flexibility 3. Stupor 4. Agitation 5. Mutism 6. Negativism 7. Posturing 8. Mannerisms 9. Stereotypies 10. Grimacing 11. Echolalia 12. Echopraxia B. There is evidence from the history, physical examination, or laboratory findings that the disturbance is the direct physiological consequence of a general medical condition C. The disturbance is not better accountedfor by another mental disorder (e.g., a Manic episode) Coding Note: Include the name of the general medical condition on Axis 1, eg. 293.89 Cataonic disorder due to hepatice encephalopathy; also code the general medical condition on Axis III
B 17 Other Specified Psychotic Disorder	No revisions are being recommended for this disorder at the current time.
B 18 Unspecified Psychotic Disorder	The work group has not yet proposed criteria for this disorder.
B 19 Unspecified Catatonic Disorder	The work group has not yet proposed criteria for this disorder.

Source: available at: www.dsm5.org/ProposedRevision/Pages/SchizophreniaSpectrumandOtherPsychoticDisorders.aspx, accessed on July 27, 2011

Hopelessness, social isolation, frequent hospitalizations, deteriorating health after a high level of premorbid functioning, recent loss or rejection, limited external support and family stress or instability are all risk factors for suicide in patients with schizophrenia [21].

Although multiple recent advances have been performed, the etiology of this complex disorder remains still relatively unknown. It has been postulated that a combination of genetic and environmental factors play a relevant role in the development of schizophrenia. Research is now proposing new methodological advances including neurobehavioural, electrophysiology, animal paradigms, genomics, cellular molecular and, above all, neuroimaging techniques.

Neuroimaging studies [22-24] have clearly indicated that schizophrenia is associated with both white matter (WM) and grey matter (GM) neuroanatomical abnormalities. A recent meta-analytic study [25] revealed, although findings are presumably biased by schizophrenic samples with poor prognosis, an overlapping of both GM and WM structural abnormalities in schizophrenia, characterized by bilateral anterior cortical, limbic and subcortical GM and WM changes in regions connecting these structures within and between hemispheres.

Considering this background, this chapter aimed to provide a detailed overview about early onset schizophrenia and new neurobiological research critically discussing their significance in order to better understand the pathophysiology of this complex disorder.

METHODS

In order to provide a new and timely review chapter about schizophrenia and new research we performed a careful MedLine, Excerpta Medica, PsycLit, PsycInfo and Index Medicus search to identify all papers and book chapters in English for the period between 1980 to 2011. The following search terms were used: "Schizophrenia" OR "Psychotic disorders" OR "Psychotic symptoms" AND "Prodrome" OR "At risk mental state" OR "ARMS" OR "Psychotic onset" OR "Early onset schizophrenia" AND "New research" OR "Current investigations" OR "Neurobiological aspects" OR "Neuroimaging techniques" AND "Psychopharmacological treatment" AND "Prevention". Textbooks on psychiatry were also consulted. We included only those articles that added an original contribution to the literature. Approximately 100 contributions met our inclusion criteria and were considered for the inclusion in the present review. We excluded studies that reported data indirectly related to schizophrenia but not clear about follow-up times, methodology, statistical analysis, diagnostic criteria and sample of patients recruited.

The Paradigm of Early Intervention: Early Recognition of ARMS Subjects and Development of UHR Criteria

Current standpoints on the pathophysiology of schizophrenia have directed growing attention to the recognition of the biological vulnerability contributing to the development of the illness. The most important research paradigms to identify this vulnerability are the genetic and the clinical at-risk approach [26], with the latter targeting at the identification of prodromal symptoms and behaviours [27]. ARMS subjects have an increased vulnerability for developing psychosis and this higher biological risk is associated with the onset of "prodromal" symptoms. ARMS is defined by "duration of time, starting with the onset of decline at the baseline level of functioning and ending with the transition to first-episode psychosis" [28]. ARMS can be considered as a period in wich morbidity is progressively accumulated and finally ends in first episode psychosis (FEP) [27, 29]. Several studies suggested that approximately 35% of ARMS subjects develop psychosis within 12 months [30-32]. However, recently Ruhrmann et al. [33] investigated two hundred forty-five help-seeking patients in a putatively prodromal state of psychosis according to either the UHR criteria or the basic symptoms, particularly cognitive disturbances, and reported in a prospective, multicenter, naturalistic study that after 18-months of follow-up the incidence rate for transition to psychosis was less than 20% (specifically, 19%).

Also, basic symptoms (BS) initially developed by Gerd Huber in 1960 and first analyzed in the Bonn Scale for the Assessment of Basic Symptoms (BSABS) are, together with the UHR criteria, another of the major focus of current research in early detection of helpseeking patients at short-term risk to develop psychosis. BS are subtle, subjective, subclinical symptoms expressing in several mental domains and not usually recognized in measurements of positive symptoms [34-35]. BS can appear more or less continuously between 2 months and 35 years prior to their progression to first psychotic symptoms and they were found pre-psychotically in 37% of patients before transiting to a first episode in the Bonn long-term study [36]. Klosterkötter et al. [37], in the prospective Cologne Early Recognition Study, found that 8% of patients with at least one cognitive-perceptive BS at baseline developed schizophrenia after 9.6 years of follow-up. Another study allowed to identify that the presence of a BS criterion (based on 9 cognitive disturbances) was associated with a transition rate to psychosis of 23.9% after 12 months and 46.3% after 24 months, respectively [38]. The authors postulated that the presence of these 9 cognitive disturbances combined with the UHR criteria may significantly improve the prediction of transition to psychosis. EPOS study was designed in the effort to develop a clinical model aiming to maximize the prediction of psychosis with sufficient sensitivity and specificity and differentiate both magnitude and time of the individual risk of transition to psychosis [39].

The recognition of early psychosis based on an adequate assessment of those individuals at higher risk of developing psychosis is critical for clinicians; early interventions represent a well established goal in clinical practice within the psychiatric health care system. Risk evaluation is mainly based on the clinical occurrence of BS, prodromal symptoms, self-limiting or attenuated psychotic symptoms as well as a family history of psychosis associated with deterioration in social functioning [40-41].

Recent Advances and Research in Early Onset Schizophrenia

Although several studies have documented the presence of different neuroanatomical abnormalities in ARMS subjects [42-49], little is known about the biological meaning and the exact time of onset of these alterations. One of the most relevant question is whether their appearance and their differential location can be considered predictive of poor outcome and more frequent transition to psychosis in specific subgroups of patients. Several structural and functional imaging studies have been conducted to understand this controversial point.

Using a magnetic resonance imaging (MRI) and a region of interest analysis, Phillips et al. [50] have reported that left and right hippocampal volumes of 60 UHR subjects developing a psychotic episode (identified through state and trait criteria) were smaller than those of controls (139 subjects with no mental illness) but not smaller than those of patients with FEP. They found that the left hippocampal volume of the UHR subjects who developed a psychotic disorder was larger than that of the UHR-non-psychotic subgroup and the FEP group but no differences were reported between the UHR-psychotic subjects and the normal group. Also, the right hippocampus of the UHR-non-psychotic group was significantly smaller than that of controls but not different to that of FEP group. In addition, a larger left hippocampal volume of the UHR subjects at intake was associated with the development of acute psychosis rather than a smaller left hippocampal volume. The authors, although stating that selection factors associated with the UHR individuals have presumably created a bias in their findings, suggested that alternatively a process of dynamic central nervous system change may occur during the onset phase of schizophrenia and related disorders rather than earlier in life, as postulated in the neurodevelopmental model.

In a voxel-based analysis of MRI data, Pantelis et al. [51] conducted a first cross-sectional comparison between 23 subjects with prodromal signs of psychosis who had later (after 12 months of follow-up) developed psychosis and 52 subjects who did not, and a second longitudinal comparison between 10 UHR individuals who had developed psychosis and 11 UHR individuals who did not. They found that in the first cross-sectional comparison those UHR subjects who later became psychotic had smaller inferior frontal, cingulate, superior temporal, and hippocampal volumes than those who did not. They also reported in the second longitudinal comparison that individuals who had developed psychosis showed a reduction in GM of the left parahippocampal, fusiform, orbitofrontal and cerebellar cortices, and the cingulate gyri compared to those who had not developed psychosis whose longitudinal changes remained restricted to the cerebellum. Therefore, in their opinion, those UHR subjects had who later developed psychosis showed more brain abnormalities compared to those UHR subjects who did not.

Borgwardt et al. [22] investigated 35 ARMS individuals of which 20 developed schizophrenia after two years of follow up, 25 FEP patients and 22 healthy controls using a 1.5T MRI scanner and found that ARMS subjects showed volumetric deficits which were similar to those observed in FEP subjects. Specifically, the ARMS group had smaller GM volumes in the left insula, adjacent parts of the superior temporal gyrus and in a midline region including the posterior cingulate gyrus and the precuneus. There were also found smaller volumes in the left parahippocampal gyrus, hippocampus, amygdala, a region spanning the right insula and superior temporal gyrus, and the posterior aspect of the cerebellar hemispheres bilaterally. The authors concluded that those volumetric differences (less GM in the right insula, inferior frontal and superior temporal gyrus) within the ARMS group may predict the subsequent onset of schizophrenia in a specific subgroup of individuals at particular high risk.

Also, several functional imaging studies have contributed to recent advances in early recognition of ARMS and early schizophrenia onset subjects. A functional cross-sectional imaging study [52] conducted in fifty-two individuals (10 UHR; 15 early and 11 chronic schizophrenics; 16 controls) reported that ARMS subjects displayed significantly smaller differential activation between task-relevant and task-irrelevant stimuli in the frontal regions relative to controls; Additionally, the authors found a trend toward early group in terms of lower frontostriatal activation associated with target stimuli. They suggested that in this sample prefrontal function started to decline before the onset of clinically defined illness and could represent in UHR subjects a significant vulnerability marker in assessing the risk for developing psychotic disorders.

Longitudinal MRI studies on both ARMS subjects and relatives of patients with schizophrenia have indicated that transition to psychosis was associated with a progressive reduction in medial temporal volume [51, 53]. Velakoulis et al. [54], in a cross-sectional comparison between 386 patient groups (89 with chronic schizophrenia, 162 with FEP, 135 UHR subjects of whom 39 subsequently developed a psychotic illness) and 87 controls, found that patients with chronic schizophrenia showed bilateral hippocampal volume reduction and patients with FEP but not schizophreniform psychosis showed left hippocampal volume reduction. The remaining first-episode subgroup had normal hippocampal volumes compared to controls. Amygdala volume enlargement was identified only in FEP patients with non-schizophrenic psychosis because UHR patients had normal baseline hippocampal and amygdala volumes regardless of subsequent developing or not of a psychotic illness.

Benetti et al. [48] conducted a fMRI study investigating prefrontal-hippocampal interactions in 10 FEP patients, 16 ARMS subjects and 14 healthy controls during a delayed matching to sample task. They showed that during the task, FEP patients revealed considerably increased activation in the inferior frontal gyrus bilaterally relative to both controls and ARMS individuals. There was not important difference in activation between ARMS individuals and healthy controls in this region. Therefore, they suggested that this finding may represent a marker of increased vulnerability to psychosis, not attributable to chronic illness or type of treatment.

Functional imaging studies investigating working memory in individuals with psychosis have repeatedly reported both reduced and increased engagement of neuronal resources within the prefrontal cortex [55-57].

Glhan et al. [57] performed functional brain images in 11 schizophrenic patients and 12 healthy control subjects matched for age, sex, handedness, and parental education and found that when task demands required explicit manipulation of information held in memory, controls more significantly activated right dorsolateral prefrontal cortex (Brodmann areas 45 and 46) compared to schizophrenic patients. The authors concluded that physiological abnormalities in the dorsolateral prefrontal cortex contribute differentially to patients difficulties in maintaining spatial information across a brief delay as well as in manipulating the maintained representation. The reduced activation of dorsolateral prefrontal cortex is presumably associated with working memory dysfunction and lower behavioural performance [58-59] in schizophrenic subjects.

Recently, Koutsouleris et al. [44], using voxel-based morphometry in 40 ARMS and 30 matched healthy control individuals found that ARMS subjects were specifically impaired in their Trail-Making Test-B performance versus controls and brain-cognition associations involving the insular cortices were observed in controls but not in ARMS individuals. Conversely, Trail-Making Test-B correlations in the ventromedial prefrontal cortex, the cerebellum, the fronto-callosal WM were detected in ARMS subjects but not in the control group. They suggested that executive dysfunctions may be presumably present in ARMS subjects before the onset of prodromal symptoms and may be subserved by structurally altered networks of interconnected cortical and subcortical brain regions according to the disconnectivity hypothesis of schizophrenia.

Also, many different brain abnormalities have been found in schizophrenic subjects. A reduction in left superior temporal gyrus and insular volume are well-known findings in both structural and functional imaging studies conducted in schizophrenic individuals [54, 60-71]. Several structural and functional imaging studies have documented more prominent brain abnormalities in the anterior cingulate cortex and cingulate gyrus rather than in posterior cingulate cortex and the medial temporal lobe in schizophrenic subjects [23-24, 72]. Hippocampal volume and medial temporal lobe alterations are also commonly been reported [54, 73-77].

Other brain abnormalities have been described both in patients with chronic schizophrenia and in nonpsychotic relatives of schizophrenic subjects. Patients with schizophrenia and non-psychotic relatives of schizophrenic subjects had significantly smaller right parahippocampal anterior volumes than controls [54, 67]. Reduced volume and differential activation in the cerebellum and the precuneus have been frequently reported [23-24, 78-81]. Also, non-psychotic relatives [51, 53, 82], co-twins of patients with schizophrenia [83-85] and individuals with a schizotypical personality [86-87] showed reduced regional GM volumes compared to controls.

However, further longitudinal studies including larger sample of subjects are needed in order to identify whether some brain abnormalities may represent specific vulnerability markers of poor outcome in subjects displaying BS and for prodromal symptoms who later develop psychosis.

Pathophysiology of Schizophrenia: the Contribution of Neuroimaging and Genetic Studies

According to the neurodevelopmental model postulated by Weinberger [88], relevant neural changes appeared early during development of adolescent schizophrenic brain although not specific histopathological abnormalities may be found in schizophrenic subjects, particularly in regions such as the limbic system, diencephalon and prefrontal cortex. Based on this conceptualization, the appearance of psychotic symptoms is associated with early not specific developmental "neurotoxic" brain changes particularly located in the dorsolateral prefrontal cortex and limbic system.

Both neuropathological structural [89] and functional [90] imaging studies suggestedthe presence of localized anatomical and functional brain abnormalities in the prefrontal cortex and hippocampus of schizophrenic subjects [91-95]. Moreover, cognitive schizophrenic models suggested that altered interactions between these two brain regions might explain most of psychotic symptoms and cognitive deficits [93, 96]. More specifically, Meyer-Lindenber and colleagues [94] reported a regionally specific alteration in the functional coupling between the dorsolateral prefrontal cortex and hippocampal formation during a working memory task [94], and reduced functional connectivity between medial prefrontal cortex and hippocampi has been described in patients studied in the resting state [95].

These volumetric reductions in both prefrontal cortex and hippocampus resulted associated with increased cell packing density, but not with changes in neuronal number; therefore, it is possible that they could be related to decreased amounts of cortical neuropil (including axon terminals, dendrites and dendritic spines, glial processes occupying inter-neuronal spaces) [97]. Several lines of evidence support this assumption. First, post-mortem studies have found modifications in specific cortical molecular markers postulating that both neuronal and/or axonal integrity are compromised [98-99] as well as the number of synapses [100] were reduced in schizophrenia. Additionally, the complexity of dendritic branching, total dendritic length, and dendritic spine density of pyramidal neurons have been found to be reduced in prefrontal cortex of patients with schizophrenia [101-102].

Neuroimaging studies have also provided evidence of damaged connectivity in schizophrenia. Functional studies have shown abnormalities in the activation of the dorsolateral prefrontal cortex, medial temporal lobe, hippocampus, anterior cingulate cortex, striatum, and thalamus [103] associated with impaired working memory [104]. Diffusion tensor imaging (DTI) studies exploring the directionality of water diffusion in the brain estimate the organization and coherence of WM fiber tracts. These tracts serve as anatomical connections between proximal and distant brain regions able to create functional networks. Studies using DTI documented relevant abnormalities in WM tracts already present in the early stages of schizophrenia, even in neuroleptic-naïve patients [105]. Although the pattern of abnormalities is not totally consistent across studies, the most affected WM tracts are the frontotemporal, frontoparietal, and temporo-occipital connections [105] providing evidence of damaged connectivity in schizophrenia.

Also, genetic factors have been recognized in the pathophysiology of schizophrenia by many family and twin studies. One of the most relevant twin study has been conducted in 1956 by Kallman and Roth [106] who demonstrated a monozygotic concordance rate of 88.2% and a dizygotic concordance rate of 22.9%, implicating that early-onset schizophrenia is associated with greater genetic charge than late-onset schizophrenia [107]. However, investigating this genetic component associated to schizophrenia may be very complex because multiple genes located in different chromosomes interacting at multiple levels (with each other and whit different environmental variables) were involved in the pathogenesis of the illness [108]. Despite recent advances in identifying genetic factors implicated in schizophrenia development, the molecular mechanisms underlying its pathogenesis remain quite unclear. Recent research [108] suggested that duplications and/or deletions known as copy number variations, significantly contributing to physiological genetic heterogeneity, were also strongly involved in increasing the genetic risk to develop schizophrenia. Linkage and association studies have implicated several loci in the genome that seem to include genes involving in the risk for developing schizophrenia [109].

Most linkage and association studies of childhood onset schizophrenia have reported associations with several susceptibility genes also involved in adult-onset schizophrenia. These genes included d-amino acid oxidase inhibitor (or G72) [110], neuregulin-1 [111], dysbindin (DTNBP1) [112] and GAD1 [113].

Also, the association between schizophrenia and chromosomal abnormalities has giving relevant opportunities to identify susceptibility genes underlying the illness. Velocardiofacial syndrome is a rare genetic disorder caused by microdeletions and associated with haploinsufficiency of genes at 22q11. Earlier linkage findings on schizophrenia are reported near this region [114] and adults with 22q11 deletions have a high prevalence of psychiatric disorders, especially schizophrenia [115]. Recently, 3,5% of childhood onset subjects carrying a 22q11 deletion was found [116] and an association between 22q11 and progressive GM loss during childhood/adolescence in patients before the onset of psychotic symptoms was reported. The authors concluded that 22q11 deletions may be considered as a significant endophenotype in early onset schizophrenia associated with the onset of several cognitive and behavioural symtoms [117]. Also, Burgess et al. [118] reported in another study the existence of an association between males with childhood onset schizophrenia and excess of CAG/CTG trinucleotide expansions.

Finally, although the recent advances achieved by genetic and neuroimaging studies, further additional investigations are required to more deeply investigate both genetic and molecular aspects underlying schizophrenia and related psychotic disorders in order to develop novel predictive models and therapeutic strategies.

Psychopharmacological Treatment of Schizophrenia

Although many pharmacological options are actually available, the treatment of schizophrenia remained quite challenging and only partial benefits as well as suboptimal outcomes are still frequent in schizophrenic patients. Evidence-based research suggests the importance of a combined approach including not only the treatment of acute symptoms but also the long-term management aiming at preventing relapses after patients have experienced an improvement in acute symptoms [119]. Although acute response to pharmacological treatment and clinical remission may be reported, safety and tolerability of modern treatments as well as the achievement of functional recovery remained unmet needs in clinical practice. The promise of improved efficacy and tolerability of the atypical or second-generation antipsychotics (SGAs) compared with the typical or first-generation antipsychotics (FGAs) remains actually only partially fulfilled. Although most of controlled clinical trials and existing literature have indicated similar levels of efficacy between SGAs and FGAs [120-121], there are also conflicting findings surrounding this issue [120-124].

Additionally, altough consensus grows around the need to treat specific symptom domains of schizophrenia, such as negative and cognitive symptoms, available medications have showed evident shortcomings. Negative symptoms and suicidal behaviour may commonly occur in first-episode schizophrenic patients; every effort should be made by clinicians to treat and minimise these symptoms [125].

Actually, there are no treatments with proven efficacy for primary negative symptoms and suicidal behaviour [126], particularly, none of the modern SGA medications are recognized as effective in treating cognitive dysfunctions. Negative symptoms increase the burden for family members, and contribute to poor long-term treatment outcomes in patients with schizophrenia. Also, cognitive symptoms are considered by some authors [127] the core feature of schizophrenia and other psychotic disorders, negatively impacting on functional outcome. It should be not surprising that the great variation in schizophrenia symptoms, treatment response and functional outcome may be the result of cognitive dysfunctions. Among neurocognitive deficits, verbal memory dysfunctions seem to be one of the most common [128-129].

Also, another relevant limitation concerns metabolic side effects related to modern medications. As serious risks of mortality and impaired psychosocial functioning resulted associated with poor control of schizophrenic symptoms, for many years treatment efficacy has remained the primary concern for clinicians prescribing atypical antipsychotics. In recent years, safety and tolerability profiles of SGAs have received increasing attention in clinical practice. Nasrallah and Newcomer [130] provided a comprehensive review about the association between atypical antipsychotics and metabolic dysregulation. These authors stressed that, since the 1950s, pharmacotherapy for schizophrenia has involved the predominant administration of dopaminergic receptor antagonists with antipsychotic activity, including conventional antipsychotics, such as haloperidol and chlorpromazine [131]. However, during the last decade, atypical antipsychotics with unique pharmacological profiles involving modulation of several neurotransmitters, including serotonin, have become available [132]. With the significant and possibly broader spectrum of clinical efficacy observed with atypical antipsychotics, together with a lower risk of extrapyramidal symptoms (EPS), these agents have rapidly gained acceptance and have become the standard of care for patients with schizophrenia or schizoaffective disorder.

Simultaneously, increasing concern has been developed regarding the potential of antipsychotic drugs to produce a variety of neurologic adverse effects, ranging from acute dystonic reactions to akathisia, parkinsonism and tardive dyskinesia. While an acute response to appropriate dosages of FGAs may not differ much from SGAs, advantages of lower rates of extra-pyramidal side effects, tardive dyskinesia and, possibly, relapse may favour SGAs [125].

The more favoruable safety and tolerability profiles of SGAs seem also to reduce non-adherence, another relevant unmet need related to treatment and associated with several social negative consequences in patients with schizophrenia. However, SGAs may cause some adverse effects, including weight gain, metabolic disturbances, corrected QT interval prolongation and prolactin-related adverse effects: clozapine and olanzapine are most likely to induce weight gain and metabolic effects, whereas risperidone is more likely to induce EPS and prolactin elevations [125]. Therefore, it's important to note that SGAs treatment must be used in the context of appropriate periodical clinical assessments and medical monitoring.

Some issues remained still open. Particularly, whether specific pharmacological medications may be predominantly used in subgroups of patients showing a biological vulnerability to the early development of adverse effects or increased risk factors of poor prognosis is still a matter of debate. To improve treatment in schizophrenia, new research efforts are needed in order to discover biomarkers of the illness, predictors of treatment response as well as of the emergence of early adverse effects.

Taken together, these data show how relevant are currently considered the unmet needs in the treatment of schizophrenic patients. Psychopharmacological approach alone is only partially able to improve negative symptoms, cognitive dysfunctions, impaired social functioning in a complex and multifaceted disorder such as schizophrenia. Many patients continued to suffer of persistent symptoms and relapses, particularly if they do not adhere to prescribed medications.

These patients presumably require multimodal care including a combination of psychosocial treatments and antipsychotic medications. In synthesis, an integrated treatment approach in the management of schizophrenia is highly recommended; this approach needs to consider not only current symptoms, but also the presence of comorbid conditions, previous therapeutic response and adverse effects, as well as patient satisfaction and expectations. Overall, the possible benefits of combined pharmacological and non-pharmacological approaches need to be more closely investigated and novel treatment options need to be developed for those subjects who are currently considered as treatment resistant or showed poor adherence.

CONCLUSION

Schizophrenia is an invalidating mental disorder characterized by severe psychosocial impairment and functional disability and severely impacting the patients ability to engage in productive work and social relationships. It also determines tremendous societal effects, causing a strain on families, caregivers and mental healthcare systems. Although recent advances in identifying factors involved in the development of schizophrenia, the molecular mechanisms underlying its pathogenesis remain quite unclear. Neuroimaging studies in humans have documented, no doubt, the presence of several brain abnormalities resulted implicated in psychosis; however little is known about the biological meaning of these neuroanatomical alterations as well as about their potential to predict the course of the illness.

Many unmet needs regarding partial efficacy, treatment resistance, reduced safety and tolerability of modern antipsychotic drugs, reduced treatment adherence and stigmatizing attitudes may be still found among schizophrenic patients. Further longitudinal investigations including larger samples of patients are required in order to provide safer drugs in the treatment of schizophrenia in the present era as well as new treatment options to guarantee not only symptoms reduction but also relapse prevention, enhanced treatment adherence, increased efficacy for those who are non-responders.

REFERENCES

[1] J. Perälä, J. Suvisaari, S. I. Saarni, K. Kuoppasalmi, E. Isometsä, S. Pirkola, T. Partonen, A. Tuulio-Henriksson, J. Hintikka, T. Kieseppä, T. Härkänen, S. Koskinen and J. Lönnqvist, Lifetime prevalence of psychotic and bipolar I disorders in a general population, *Arch. Gen. Psychiatry* 64, 19–28 (2007).

[2] C. J. Murray and A. D. Lopez, *The Global Burden of Disease: A Comprehensive Assessment of Mortality and Disability from Diseases, Injuries and Risk Factors in 1990 and Projected to 2020*, Boston: Harvard School of Public Health (1996).

[3] J. L. Ayuso-Mateos, *Global Burden of Schizophrenia in the Year 2000* [Global Burden of Disease working paper], Geneva: WHO, 2006 at: http:// www.who.int/healthinfo /statistics/ bod_schizophrenia.pdf

[4] World Health Organization, *World Health Report 2001*, Mental Health: New Understanding, New Hope. Geneva: World Health Organization (2001).

[5] R. Freedman, Schizophrenia, *N. Engl. J. Med.* 349, 1738–1749 (2003).

[6] D. T. Balu and J. T. Coyle, Neuroplasticity signaling pathways linked to the pathophysiology of schizophrenia, *Neurosci. Biobehav. Rev.* 35, 848–870 (2011).

[7] N. S. Vyas, N. H. Patel and B. K. Puri, Neurobiology and phenotypic expression in early onset schizophrenia, *Early Interv. Psychiatry* 5, 3–14 (2011).

[8] R. E. Gur, Neuropsychiatric Aspects of Schizophrenia, *CNS Neurosci. Ther.* 17, 45–51 (2011).

[9] E. Kraepelin, *Dementia praecox and paraphrenia*. Edinburgh: E. & S. Livingston (1919).

[10] E. Bleuler, *Dementia praecox or the group of schizophrenias,* New York, NY: International Universities Press (1950).

[11] R. E. Gur, C. G. Kohler, J. D. Ragland, S. J. Siegel, K. Lesko, W. B. Bilker and R. C. Gur, Flat affect in schizophrenia: relation to emotion processing and neurocognitive measures, *Schizophr. Bull.* 32(2), 279–287 (2006).

[12] D. I. Leitman, J. Loughead, D. H. Wolf, K. Ruparel, C. G. Kohler, M. A. Elliott, W. B. Bilker, R. E. Gur and R. C. Gur, Abnormal superior temporal connectivity during fear perception in schizophrenia, *Schizophr. Bull.* 34(4), 673–678 (2008).

[13] P. F. Buckley, B. J. Miller, D. S. Lehrer and D. J. Castle, Psychiatric comorbidities and schizophrenia, *Schizophr. Bull.* 35(2), 383–402 (2009).

[14] P. F. Buckley, Prevalence and consequences of the dual diagnosis of substance abuse and severe mental illness, *J. Clin. Psychiatry* 67, 5–9 (2006).

[15] J. H. Boyd, Use of mental health services for the treatment of panic disorder, *Am. J. Psychiatry* 143, 1569–1574 (1986).

[16] V. Pokos and D. J. Castle, Prevalence of comorbid anxiety disorders in schizophrenia spectrum disorders: a literature review, *Curr. Psychiatry Rev.* 2, 285–307 (2006).

[17] A. Ciapparelli, R. Paggini, D. Marazziti, C. Carmassi, M. Bianchi, C. Taponecco, G. Consoli, V. Lombardi, G. Massimetti and L. Dell'osso Comorbidity with axis I anxiety disorders in remitted psychotic patients 1 year after hospitalization, *CNS Spectr.* 12, 913–919 (2007).

[18] M. Birchwood, R. Mason, F. MacMillan, J. Healy, Depression, demoralization and control over psychotic illness: a comparison of depressed and non-depressed patients with a chronic psychosis, *Psychol, Med,* 23, 387–395 (1993).

[19] J. van Os and S. Kapur, Schizophrenia, *Lancet* 374(9690), 635–645 (2009).

[20] B. A. Palmer, V. S. Pankratz and J. M. Bostwick, The lifetime risk of suicide in schizophrenia: a reexamination, *Arch. Gen. Psychiatry* 62(3), 247–253 (2005).

[21] M. Pompili, D. Lester, M. Innamorati, R. Tatarelli and P. Girardi, Assessment and treatment of suicide risk in schizophrenia, *Expert Rev. Neurother.* 8(1), 51–74 (2008).

[22] S. J. Borgwardt, A. Riecher-Rössler, P. Dazzan, C. Xavier, J. Aston, M. Drewe, U. Gschwandtner, S. Haller, M. Pflüger, E. Rechsteiner, M. D'Souza, R. D. Stieglitz, E. W. Radü and P. K. McGuire, Regional gray matter volume abnormalities in the at risk mental state, *Biol. Psychiatry* 61, 1148–1156 (2007).

[23] M. E. Shenton, C.C. Dickey, M. Frumin and R. W. McCarley, A review of MRI findings in schizophrenia, *Schizophr. Res.* 49, 1–52 (2001).

[24] I. C. Wright, S. Rabe-Hesketh, P.W. Woodruff, A. S. David, R. M. Murray and E. T. Bullmore, Meta-analysis of regional brain volumes in schizophrenia, *Am. J. Psychiatry* 157, 16–25 (2000).

[25] E. Bora, A. Fornito, J. Radua, M. Walterfang, M. Seal, S. J. Wood, M. Yücel, D. Velakoulis and C. Pantelis, Neuroanatomical abnormalities in schizophrenia: a multimodal voxelwise meta-analysis and meta-regression analysis, *Schizophr. Res.* 127(1-3), 46–57 (2011).

[26] T. D. Cannon, Clinical and genetic high-risk strategies in understanding vulnerability to psychosis, *Schizophr. Res.* 79, 35–44 (2005).

[27] T. H. McGlashan, Early detection and intervention in schizophrenia, *Schizophr. Bull.* 22, 327–345 (1996).

[28] A. R. Yung and P. D. McGorry, The prodromal phase of first episode psychosis: past and current conceptualizations, *Schizophr. Bull.* 22, 353–370 (1996).

[29] M. Keshavan, G. E. Berger, R. Zipursky, S. J. Wood and C. Pantelis, Neurobiology of early psychosis, *Br. J. Psychiatry* 187, 8–18 (2005).

[30] O. Mason, M. Startup, S. Halpin, U. Schall, A. Conrad and V. Carr, Risk factors for transition to first episode psychosis among individuals with 'at-risk mental states', *Schizophr. Res.* 71, 227–237 (2004).

[31] T. J. Miller, T. H. McGlashan, J. L. Rosen, K. Cadenhead, T. Cannon, J. Ventura, W. McFarlane, D. O. Perkins, G. D. Pearlson and S. W. Woods, Prodromal assessment with the structured interview for prodromal syndromes and the scale of prodromal symptoms: predictive validity, interrater reliability, and training to reliability, *Schizophr. Bull.* 29, 703–715 (2003).

[32] A. R. Yung, L. J. Phillips, H. P. Yuen, S. M. Francey, C. A. McFarlane, M. Hallgren and P. D. McGorry, Psychosis prediction: 12-month follow up of a high-risk ("prodromal") group, *Schizophr. Res.* 60, 21–32 (2003).

[33] S. Ruhrmann, F. Schultze-Lutter, R. K. Salokangas, M. Heinimaa, D. Linszen, P. Dingemans, M. Birchwood, P. Patterson, G. Juckel, A. Heinz, A. Morrison, S. Lewis, H. G. von Reventlow and J. Klosterkötter, Prediction of psychosis in adolescents and young adults at high risk: results from the prospective European prediction of psychosis study, *Arch. Gen. Psychiatry* 67(3), 241–251 (2010).

[34] G. Huber, The concept of substrate-close basic symptoms and its significance for the theory and therapy of schizophrenic diseases [in German], *Nervenarzt* 54(1), 23–32 (1983).

[35] F. Schultze-Lutter, Subjective symptoms of schizophrenia in research and the clinic: the basic symptom concept, *Schizophr. Bull.* 35(1), 5–8 (2009).

[36] J. Klosterkötter, F. Schultze-Lutter and S. Ruhrmann, Kraepelin and psychotic prodromal conditions, *Eur. Arch. Psychiatry Clin. Neurosci.* 258, Suppl 2, 74–84 (2008).

[37] J. Klosterkötter, M. Hellmich, E. M. Steinmeyer and F. Schultze-Lutter, Diagnosing schizophrenia in the initial prodromal phase, *Arch. Gen. Psychiatry* 58(2), 158–164 (2001).

[38] F. Schultze-Lutter, J. Klosterkötter, H. Picker, E. Steinmeyer and S. Ruhrmann, Predicting first-episode psychosis by basic symptom criteria, *Clin. Neuropsychiatry* 4(1), 11–22 (2007).

[39] P. D. McGorry, A. R. Yung, A. Bechdolf and P. Amminger, Back to the future: predicting and reshaping the course of psychotic disorder, *Arch. Gen. Psychiatry* 65(1), 25–27 (2008).

[40] A. R. Yung, L. J. Phillips, H. P. Yuen, P. D. McGorry, Risk factors for psychosis in an ultra high-risk group: psychopathology and clinical features, *Schizophr. Res.* 67, 131–142 (2004).

[41] A. Riecher-Rössler, U. Gschwandtner, S. Borgwardt, J. Aston, M. Pflüger and W. Rössler, Early detection and treatment of schizophrenia: how early? *Acta Psychiatr. Scand.* 429, 73–80 (2006).

[42] P. Fusar-Poli, J. M. Stone, M. R. Broome, I. Valli, A. Mechelli, M. A. McLean, D. J. Lythgoe, R. L. O'Gorman, G. J. Barker and P. K. McGuire, Thalamic Glutamate Levels as a Predictor of Cortical Response During Executive Functioning in Subjects at High Risk for Psychosis, *Arch. Gen. Psychiatry* in press (2011).

[43] P. Allen, C. A. Chaddock, O. D. Howes, A. Egerton, M. L. Seal, P. Fusar-Poli, I. Valli, F. Day and P. K. McGuire, Abnormal Relationship Between Medial Temporal Lobe and Subcortical Dopamine Function in People With an Ultra High Risk for Psychosis, *Schizophr. Bull.* in press (2011).

[44] N. Koutsouleris, K. Patschurek-Kliche, J. Scheuerecker, P. Decker, R. Bottlender, G. Schmitt, D. Rujesc, I. Giegling, C. Gaser, M. Reiser, H. J. Möller and E. M. Meisenzahl, Neuroanatomical correlates of executive dysfunction in the at-risk mental state for psychosis, *Schizophr. Res.* 123(2-3), 160-174 (2010).

[45] M. R. Broome, P. Matthiasson, P. Fusar-Poli, J. B. Woolley, L. C. Johns, P. Tabraham, E. Bramon, L. Valmaggia, S. C. Williams, M. J. Brammer, X. Chitnis and P. K. McGuire, Neural correlates of movement generation in the 'at-risk mental state, *Acta Psychiatr. Scand.* 122(4), 295-301 (2010).

[46] G. Modinos, A. Mechelli, J. Ormel, N. A. Groenewold, A. Aleman and P. K. McGuire, Schizotypy and brain structure: a voxel-based morphometry study, *Psychol. Med.* 40(9), 1423-1431 (2010).

[47] N. A. Crossley, A. Mechelli, P. Fusar-Poli, M. R. Broome, P. Matthiasson, L. C. Johns, E. Bramon, L. Valmaggia, S. C. Williams and P. K. McGuire, Superior temporal lobe dysfunction and frontotemporal dysconnectivity in subjects at risk of psychosis and in first-episode psychosis, *Hum. Brain. Mapp.* 30(12), 4129-4137 (2009).

[48] S. Benetti, A. Mechelli, M. Picchioni, M. Broome, S. Williams and P. McGuire, Functional integration between the posterior hippocampus and prefrontal cortex is impaired in both first episode schizophrenia and the at risk mental state, *Brain*, 132, 2426–2436 (2009).

[49] P. Fusar-Poli, J. Perez, M. Broome, S. Borgwardt, A. Placentino, E. Caverzasi, M. Cortesi, P. Veggiotti, P. Politi, F. Barale and P. McGuire, Neurofunctional correlates of vulnerability to psychosis: a systematic review and meta-analysis, *Neurosci. Biobehav. Rev.* 31(4), 465-484 (2007).

[50] L. J. Phillips, D. Velakoulis, C. Pantelis, S. Wood, H. P. Yuen, A. R. Yung, P. Desmond, W. Brewer and P. D. McGorry, Nonreduction in hippocampal volume is associated with higher risk of psychosis, *Schizophr. Res.* 58,145–158 (2002).

[51] C. Pantelis, D. Velakoulis, P. D. McGorry, S. J. Wood, J. Suckling, L. J. Phillips, A. R. Yung, E. T. Bullmore, W. Brewer, B. Soulsby, P. Desmond and P. K. McGuire, Neuroanatomical abnormalities before and after onset of psychosis: a cross-sectional and longitudinal MRI comparison, *Lancet* 361, 281–288 (2003).

[52] R. A. Morey, S. Inan, T. V. Mitchell, D. O. Perkins, J. A. Lieberman and A. Belger, Imaging frontostriatal function in ultra-high-risk, early, and chronic schizophrenia during executive processing. *Arch. Gen. Psychiatry* 62, 254–262 (2005).

[53] D. E. Job, H. C. Whalley, E. C. Johnstone and S. M. Lawrie, Gray matter changes over time in high risk subjects developing schizophrenia, *Neuroimage* 25,1023–1030 (2005).

[54] D. Velakoulis, S. J. Wood, M. T. Wong, P. D. McGorry, A. Yung, L. Phillips, D. Smith, W. Brewer, T. Proffitt, P. Desmond and C. Pantelis, Hippocampal and amygdala volumes according to psychosis stage and diagnosis: a magnetic resonance imaging study of chronic schizophrenia, first-episode psychosis, and ultra-high-risk individuals, *Arch. Gen. Psychiatry* 63,139 –149 (2006).

[55] J. Callicott, V. Mattay, B. Verchinski, S. Marenco, M. Egan and D. Weinberger, Complexity of prefrontal cortical dysfunction in schizophrenia: more than up or down, *Am. J. Psychiatry* 160, 2209–2215 (2003).

[56] W. M. Perlstein, C. S. Carte, D. C. Noll and J. D. Cohen, Relation of prefrontal cortex dysfunction to working memory and symptoms in schizophrenia. *Am. J. Psychiatry* 158, 1105–1113 (2001).

[57] D. C. Glahn, J Ragland, A. Abramoff, J. Barrett, A. Laird, C. Bearden, C. E. Bearden and D. I. Velligan, Beyond hypofrontality: a quantitative meta-analysis of functional neuroimaging studies of working memory in schizophrenia, *Hum. Brain. Mapp.* 25(1), 60-69 (2005).

[58] D. Manoach, Prefrontal cortex dysfunction during working memory performance in schizophrenia: reconciling discrepant findings, *Schizophr. Res.* 60, 285–298 (2003).

[59] A. Bertolino, G. Blasi, V. Latorre, V. Rubino, A. Rampino, L. Sinibaldi, G. Caforio, V. Petruzzella, A. Pizzuti, T. Scarabino, M. Nardini, D. R. Weinberger and B. Dallapiccola, Text Additive effects of genetic variation in dopamine regulating genes on working memory cortical activity in human brain, *J. Neurosci.* 26, 3918–22 (2006).

[60] V. A. Curtis, E. T. Bullmore, M. J. Brammer, I. C. Wright, S. C. Williams, R. G. Morris, T. S. Sharma, R. M. Murray and P. K. McGuire. Attenuated frontal activation during a verbal fluency task in patients with schizophrenia, *Am. J. Psychiatry* 155, 1056–1063 (1998).

[61] C. H. Fu, J. Suckling, S. C. Williams, C. M. Andrew, G. N. Vythelingum and P. K. McGuire, Effects of psychotic state and taskdemandon prefrontal function in schizophrenia: An fMRI study of overt verbal fluency, *Am. J. Psychiatry* 162, 485– 494 (2005).

[62] B. Garner, C. M. Pariante, S. J. Wood, D. Velakoulis, L. Phillips, B. Soulsby, W. J. Brewer , D. J. Smith, P. Dazzan, G. E. Berger, A. R. Yung, M. van den Buuse, R. Murray, P. D. McGorry and C. Pantelis, Pituitary volume predicts future transition to psychosis in individuals at ultra-high risk of developing psychosis, *Biol. Psychiatry* 58, 417–423 (2005).

[63] T. T. Kircher, M. J. Brammer, S. C. Williams and P. K. McGuire, Lexical retrieval during fluent speech production: an fMRI study, *Neuroreport* 11,4093–4096 (2000).

[64] B. McDonald, J. R. Highley, M. A. Walker, B. M. Herron, S. J. Cooper, M. M. Esiri and T. J. Crow, Anomalous asymmetry of fusiform and parahippocampal gyrus gray matter in schizophrenia: A postmortem study, *Am. J. Psychiatry* 157, 40–47 (2000).

[65] P. K. McGuire, D. A. Silbersweig, I. Wright, R. M. Murray, A. S. David, R. S. Frackowiak and C. D. Frith, Abnormal monitoring of inner speech: a physiological basis for auditory hallucinations, *Lancet* 346, 596–600 (1995).

[66] P. K. McGuire, D. J. Quested, S. A. Spence, R. M. Murray, C. D. Frith and P. F. Liddle, Pathophysiology of 'positive' thought disorder in schizophrenia, *Br. J. Psychiatry* 173, 231–235 (1998).

[67] L. J. Seidman, C. Pantelis, M. S. Keshavan, S. V. Faraone, J. M. Goldstein, N. J. Horton, N. Makris, P. Falkai, V. S. Caviness and M. T. Tsuang, A review and new report of medial temporal lobe dysfunction as a vulnerability indicator for schizophrenia: a magnetic resonance imaging morphometric family study of the parahippocampal gyrus, *Schizophr. Bull.* 29, 803–830 (2003).

[68] M. E. Shenton, R. Kikinis, F. A. Jolesz, S. D. Pollak, M. LeMay, C. G. Wible, H. Hokama, J. Martin, D. Metcalf, M. Coleman, et al, Abnormalities of the left temporal lobe and thought disorder in schizophrenia, A quantitative magnetic resonance imaging study, *N. Engl. J. Med.* 327,604–612 (1992).

[69] C. G. Wible, M. E. Shenton, H. Hokama, R. Kikinis, F. A. Jolesz, D. Metcalf and R. W. McCarley, Prefrontal cortex and schizophrenia. A quantitative magnetic resonance imaging study 2, *Arch. Gen. Psychiatry* 52,279 –288 (1995).

[70] I. C. Wright, P. K. McGuire, J. B. Poline, J. M. Travere, R. M. Murray, C. D. Frith, R. S. Frackowiak and K. J. Friston, A voxel-based method for the statistical analysis of gray and white matter density applied to schizophrenia, *Neuroimage* 2, 244–252 (1995).

[71] I. C. Wright, Z. R. Ellison, T. Sharma, K. J. Friston, R. M. Murray and P. K. McGuire, Mapping of gray matter changes in schizophrenia, *Schizophr. Res.* 35, 1–14 (1999).

[72] P. Falkai, B. Bogerts and M. Rozumek, Limbic pathology in schizophrenia: the entorhinal region–a morphometric study, *Biol. Psychiatry* 24(5), 515-521 (1988).

[73] L. E. DeLisi, M. Sakuma, W. Tew, M. Kushner, A. L. Hoff and R. Grimson, Schizophrenia as a chronic active brain process: A study of progressive brain structural change subsequent to the onset of schizophrenia, *Psychiatry Res.* 74,129–140 (1997).

[74] L. E. DeLisi, M. Sakuma, A. M. Maurizio, M. Relja and A. L. Hoff, Cerebral ventricular change over the first 10 years after the onset of schizophrenia, *Psychiatry Res.* 130,57–70 (2004).

[75] L. E. DeLisi and A. L. Hoff, Failure to find progressive temporal lobe volume decreases 10 years subsequent to a first episode of schizophrenia, *Psychiatry Res.* 138,265–268 (2005).

[76] Y. Hirayasu, M. E. Shenton, D. F. Salisbury, J. S. Kwon, C. G. Wible, I. A. Fischer, D. Yurgelun-Todd, C. Zarate, R. Kikinis, F. A. Jolesz and R. W. McCarley, Subgenual cingulate cortex volume in first-episode psychosis, *Am. J. Psychiatry* 156,1091–1093 (1999).

[77] T. G. van Erp, P. A. Saleh, M. Huttunen, J. Lonnqvist, J. Kaprio, O. Salonen, L. Valanne, V. P. Poutanen, C. G. Standertskjöld-Nordenstam and T. D. Cannon, Hippocampal volumes in schizophrenic twins, *Arch. Gen. Psychiatry* 61, 346–353 (2004).

[78] L. K. Jacobsen, J. N. Giedd, P. C. Berquin, A. L. Krain, S. D. Hamburger, S. Kumra and J. L. Rapoport, Quantitative morphology of the cerebellum and fourth ventricle in childhood-onset schizophrenia. *Am. J. Psychiatry* 154,1663–1669 (1997).

[79] J. J. Levitt, R. W. McCarley, P. G. Nestor, C. Petrescu, R. Donnino, Y. Hirayasu, R. Kikinis, F. A. Jolesz and M. E. Shenton, Quantitative volumetric MRI study of the cerebellum and vermis in schizophrenia: clinical an cognitive correlates, *Am. J. Psychiatry* 156,1105–1107 (1999).

[80] R. T. Loeber, C. M. Cintron and D. A. Yurgelun-Todd, Morphometry of individual cerebellar lobules in schizophrenia, *Am. J. Psychiatry* 158, 952–954 (2001).

[81] P. C. Nopoulos, J. W. Ceilley, E. A. Gailis and N.C. Andreasen, An MRI study of cerebellar vermis morphology in patients with schizophrenia: evidence in support of the cognitive dysmetria concept, *Biol. Psychiatry* 46, 703–711 (1999).

[82] S. M. Lawrie, H. Whalley, J. N. Kestelman, S. S. Abukmeil, M. Byrne, A. Hodges, J. E. Rimmington, J. J. Best, D. G. Owens and E. C. Johnstone, Magnetic resonance imaging of brain in people at high risk of developing schizophrenia, *Lancet* 353,30–33 (1999).

[83] T. D. Cannon, P.M. Thompson, T. G. van Erp, A. W. Toga, V. P. Poutanen, M. Huttunen, J. Lonnqvist, C. G. Standerskjold-Nordenstam, K. L. Narr, M. Khaledy, C. I. Zoumalan, R. Dail and J. Kaprio, Cortex mapping reveals regionally specific patterns of genetic and disease-specific gray-matter deficits in twins discordant for schizophrenia, *Proc. Natl. Acad. Sci. USA* 99, 3228–3233 (2002).

[84] H. E. Hulshoff Pol, R. G. Brans, N. E. van Haren, H. G. Schnack, M. Langen, W. F. Baaré, C. J. van Oel and R. S. Kahn, Gray and white matter volume abnormalities in monozygotic and same-gender dizygotic twins discordant for schizophrenia, *Biol. Psychiatry* 55,126–130 (2004).

[85] R. L. Suddath, G. W. Christison, E. F. Torrey, M. F. Casanova and D. R. Weinberger, Anatomical abnormalities in the brains of monozygotic twins discordant for schizophrenia. *N. Engl. J. Med.* 322,789 –794 (1990).

[86] C. C. Dickey, R. W. McCarley, M. M. Voglmaier, M. A. Niznikiewicz, L. J. Seidman, Y. Hirayasu, I. Fischer, E. K. Teh, R. Van Rhoads, M. Jakab, R. Kikinis, F. A. Jolesz and M. E. Shenton, Schizotypal personality disorder and MRI abnormalities of temporal lobe gray matter, *Biol. Psychiatry* 45(11), 1393–1402 (1999).

[87] Y. Kawasaki, M. Suzuki, S. Nohara, H. Hagino, T. Takahashi, M. Matsui, I. Yamashita, X. A. Chitnis, P. K. McGuire, H. Seto and M. Kurachi, Structural brain differences in patients with schizophrenia and schizotypal disorder demonstrated by voxel-based morphometry, *Eur. Arch. Psychiatry Clin. Neurosci.* 254, 406–414 (2004).

[88] D. R. Weinberger, Implications of normal brain development for the pathogenesis of schizophrenia, *Arch. Gen. Psychiatry* 44(7), 660–669 (1987).

[89] B. Bogerts, M. Ashtari, G. Degreef, J. Alvir, R. Bilder and Lieberman J. Reduced temporal limbic structure volumes on magnetic resonance images in first episode schizophrenia, *Psychiatry Res.* 35, 1–13 (1990).

[90] C. Carter, W. Perlstein, R. Ganguli, J. Brar, M. Mintun and J. Cohen, Functional hypofrontality and working memory dysfunction in schizophrenia, *Am. J. Psychiatry* 155, 1285–1287 (1998).

[91] S. Arnold and J. Trojanowski, Recent advances in defining the neuropathology of schizophrenia, *Acta Neuropathol.* 92, 217–231 (1996).

[92] P. Harrison and S. L. Eastwood, Neuropathological studies of synaptic connectivity in the hippocampal formation in schizophrenia, Hippocampus 11, 508–19 (2001).

[93] D. Weinberger, K. Berman, R. Suddath and E. Torrey, Evidence of dysfunction of prefrontal-limbic network in schizophrenia: a magnetic resonance imaging and regional cerebral blood flow study of discordant monozygotic twins, *Am. J. Psychiatry* 149, 890–897 (1992).

[94] A. Meyer-Lindenberg, R. Olsen, P. Kohn, T. Brown, M. Egan and D. Weinberger, Regionally specific disturbance of dorsolateral prefrontal-hippocampal functional connectivity in schizophrenia, *Arch. Gen. Psychiatry* 62(4), 379-86 (2005).

[95] Y. Zhou, N. Shu, Y. Liu, M. Song, Y. Hao, H. Liu, C. Yu, Z. Liu and T. Jiang, Altered resting-state functional connectivity and anatomical connectivity of hippocampus in schizophrenia, *Schizophr. Res.* 100, 120–132 (2008).

[96] P. Fletcher, The missing link: a failure of fronto-hippocampal integration in schizophrenia, *Nat. Neurosci.* 1, 266–267 (1998).

[97] L. D. Selemon and P. S. Goldman-Rakic, The reduced neuropil hypothesis: a circuit based model of schizophrenia, *Biol. Psychiatry* 45, 17–25 (1999).

[98] A. Bertolino, S. Nawroz, V. S. Mattay, A. S. Barnett, J. H. Duyn, C. T. Moonen, J. A. Frank, G. Tedeschi and D. R. Weinberger, Regionally specific pattern of neurochemical pathology in schizophrenia as assessed by multislice proton magnetic resonance spectroscopic imaging, *Am. J. Psychiatry* 153, 1554–1563 (1996).

[99] P. F. Buckley, C. Moore, H. Long, C. Larkin, P. Thompson, F. Mulvany, O. Redmond, J. P. Stack, J. T. Ennis and J. L. Waddington, 1H-magnetic resonance spectroscopy of the left temporal and frontal lobes in schizophrenia: clinical, neurodevelopmental, and cognitive correlates, *Biol. Psychiatry* 36, 792–800 (1994).

[100] J. A. Stanley, P. C. Williamson, D. J. Drost, T. J. Carr, R. J. Rylett, A. Malla and R. T. Thompson, An in vivo study of the prefrontal cortex of schizophrenic patients at different stages of illness via phosphorus magnetic resonance spectroscopy, *Arch. Gen. Psychiatry* 52, 399–406 (1995).

[101] L. J. Garey, W. Y. Ong, T. S. Patel, M. Kanani, A. Davis, A. M. Mortimer, T. R. Barnes and S.R. Hirsch, Reduced dendritic spine densityoncerebral cortical pyramidal neurons in schizophrenia, *J. Neurol. Neurosurg. Psychiatry* 65, 446–453 (1998).

[102] L. A. Glantz and D. A. Lewis, Decreased dendritic spine density on prefrontal cortical pyramidal neurons in schizophrenia, *Arch. Gen. Psychiatry* 57, 65–73 (2000).

[103] M. A. Niznikiewicz, M. Kubicki and M. E. Shenton, Recent structural and functional imaging findings in schizophrenia, *Curr. Opin. Psychiatry* 16, 123–147 (2003).

[104] S. G. Potkin, J. A. Turner, G. G. Brown, G. McCarthy, D. N. Greve, G. H. Glover, D. S. Manoach, A. Belger, M. Diaz, C. G. Wible, J. M. Ford, D. H. Mathalon, R. Gollub, J. Lauriello, D. O'Leary, T. G. van Erp, A. W. Toga, A. Preda and K. O. Lim, Working memory and DLPFC inefficiency in schizophrenia: the FBIRN study, *Schizophr. Bull.* 35, 19–31 (2009).

[105] M. Kyriakopoulos and S. Frangou, Recent diffusion tensor imaging findings in early stages of schizophrenia, *Curr. Opin. Psychiatry* 22, 168–176 (2009).

[106] F. J. Kallman and B. Roth, Genetic aspects of preadolescent schizophrenia. *Am. J. Psychiatry* 112, 599–606 (1956).

[107] B. Childs and C. R. Scriver, Age at onset and causes of disease, *Perspect. Biol. Med.* 29, 437–460 (1986).

[108] S. M. Purcell, N.R. Wray, J. L. Stone, P. M. Visscher, M. C. O'Donovan, P. F. Sullivan and P. Sklar, Common polygenic variation contributes to risk of schizophrenia and bipolar disorder. *Nature* 460, 748–752 (2009).

[109] C. A. Ross, R. L. Margolis, S. A. Reading, M. Pletnikov and J. T. Coyle, Neurobiology of schizophrenia, *Neuron* 52, 139–153 (2006).

[110] A. M. Addington, M. C. Gornick, A. L. Sporn, N. Gogtay, D. Greenstein, M. Lenane, P. Gochman, N. Baker, R. Balkissoon, R. K. Vakkalanka, D. R. Weinberger, R. E. Straub and J. L. Rapoport, Polymorphisms in the 13q33.2 gene G72/G30 are associated with childhood-onset schizophrenia and psychosis not otherwise specified, *Biol. Psychiatry* 55, 976–980 (2004).

[111] A. M. Addington, M. C. Gornick, P. Shaw, J. Seal, N. Gogtay, D. Greenstein, L. Clasen, M. Coffey, P. Gochman, R. Long and J. L. Rapoport, Neuregulin 1 (8p12) and childhood-onset schizophrenia: susceptibility haplotypes for diagnosis and brain developmental trajectories, *Mol. Psychiatry* 12, 195–205 (2007).

[112] M. C. Gornick, A. M. Addington, A. Sporn, N. Gogtay, D. Greenstein, M. Lenane, P. Gochman, A. Ordonez, R. Balkissoon, R. Vakkalanka, D. R. Weinberger, J. L. Rapoport and R. E. Straub, Dysbindin (DTNBP1, 6p22.3) is associated with childhood-onset psychosis and endophenotypes measured by the Premorbid Adjustment Scale (PAS), *J. Autism. Dev. Disord.* 35, 831–838 (2005).

[113] A. M. Addington, M. Gornick, J. Duckworth, A. Sporn, N. Gogtay, A. Bobb, D. Greenstein, M. Lenane, P. Gochman, N. Baker, R. Balkissoon, R. K. Vakkalanka, D. R. Weinberge, J. L. Rapoport and R. E. Straub, GAD1 (2q31.1), which encodes glutamic acid decarboxylase (GAD67), is associated with childhood-onset schizophrenia and cortical gray matter volume loss, *Mol. Psychiatry* 10, 581–588 (2005).

[114] A. E. Pulver, M. Karayiorgou, V. K. Lasseter, A. Sporn, N. Gogtay, A. Bobb, D. Greenstein, M. Lenane, P. Gochman, N. Baker, R. Balkissoon, R. K. Vakkalanka, D. R. Weinberger, J. L. Rapoport and R. E. Straub, Follow-up of a report of a potential linkage for schizophrenia on chromosome 22q12-q13.1: part 2, *Am. J. Med. Genet.* 54, 44–50 (1994b).

[115] A. E. Pulver, G. Nestadt, R. Goldberg, R. J. Shprintzen, M. Lamacz, P. S. Wolyniec, B. Morrow, M. Karayiorgou, S. E. Antonarakis, D. Housman, et al, Psychotic illness in patients diagnosed with velo-cardio-facial syndrome and their relatives, *J. Nerv. Ment. Dis.* 182, 476–478 (1994a).

[116] A. Sporn, A. Addington, A. L. Reiss, et al, 22q11 deletion syndrome in childhood onset schizophrenia: an update, *Mol. Psychiatry* 9, 225–226 (2004).

[117] O. Ousley, K. Rockers, M. L. Dell, K. Coleman and J. F. Cubells, A review of neurocognitive and behavioral profiles associated with 22q11 deletion syndrome: implications for clinical evaluation and treatment, *Curr. Psychiatry Rep.* 9, 148–158 (2007).

[118] C. E. Burgess, K. Lindblad, E. Sidransky, Q. P. Yuan, R. T. Long, T. Breschel, C. A. Ross, M. McInnis, P. Lee, E. I. Ginns, M. Lenane, S. Kumra, L. Jacobsen, J. L. Rapoport and M. Schalling, Large CAG/CTG repeats are associated with childhood onset schizophrenia, *Mol. Psychiatry* 3, 321–327 (1998).

[119] Canadian Psychiatric Association, Clinical practice guidelines. Treatment of schizophrenia, *Can. J. Psychiatry* 50, Suppl 1, 7–57 (2005).

[120] J. Geddes, N. Freemantle, P. Harrison and P. Bebbington, Atypical antipsychotics in the treatment of schizophrenia: systematic overview and meta-regression analysis, *B.M.J.* 321(7273), 1371–1376 (2000).

[121] R. Tandon and M. D. Jibson, Efficacy of newer generation antipsychotics in the treatment of schizophrenia, *Psychoneuroendocrinology* 28, Suppl. 1, 9–26 (2003).

[122] S. Leucht, T. R. Barnes, W. Kissling, R. R. Engel, C. Correll and J. M. Kane, Relapse prevention in schizophrenia with new-generation antipsychotics: a systematic review and exploratory meta-analysis of randomized, controlled trials, *Am. J. Psychiatry* 160(7), 1209–1222 (2003).

[123] C. U. Correll, S. Leucht and J. M. Kane, Lower risk for tardive dyskinesia associated with second-generation antipsychotics: a systematic review of 1-year studies, *Am. J. Psychiatry* 161(3), 414–425 (2004).

[124] J. M. Davis, N. Chen, I. D. Glick, A meta-analysis of the efficacy of second-generation antipsychotics, *Arch. Gen. Psychiatry* 60(6), 553–564 (2003).

[125] D. L. Kelly, R. R. Conley and W. T. Carpenter, First-episode schizophrenia: a focus on pharmacological treatment and safety considerations, *Drugs* 65(8), 1113–38 (2005).
[126] American Psychiatric Association, Practice Guideline for the Treatment of Patients With Schizophrenia, American Psychiatric Association, DC, USA (2004).
[127] M. F. Green, Stimulating the development of drug treatments to improve cognition in schizophrenia, *Annu. Rev. Clin. Psychol.* 3, 159–180 (2007).
[128] M. F. Green, What are the functional consequences of neurocognitive deficits in schizophrenia? *Am. J. Psychiatry* 153(3), 321–330 (1996).
[129] R. W. Heinrichs and K. K. Zakzanis, Neurocognitive deficit in schizophrenia: a quantitative review of the evidence, *Neuropsychology* 12(3), 426–445 (1998).
[130] H. A. Nasrallah and J. W. Newcomer, Atypical antipsychotics and metabolic dysregulation: evaluating the risk/benefit equation and improving the standard of care, *J. Clin. Psychopharmacol.* 24(5), Suppl. 1, S7–S14 (2004).
[131] H. T. Nagamoto, Antipsychotic medications. In: Psychiatric Secrets. J. L. Jacobson, A. M. Jacobson (Eds), Hanley and Belfus Inc, PA, USA, 253–259 (2001).
[132] J. M. Kane, Schizophrenia, *N. Engl. J. Med.* 334(1), 34–41 (1996).

In: Schizophrenia Research: Recent Advances
Editor: Tomiki Sumiyoshi
ISBN: 978-1-62808-703-1

Chapter 7

WHITE MATTER ABNORMALITIES IN SCHIZOPHRENIA PATIENTS AND GENETIC HIGH-RISK SUBJECTS

***Xiaobo Li*[1] *and Lynn E. Delisi*[2]**
[1]Gruss Magnetic Resonance Research Center
Department of Radiology,
Albert Einstein College of Medicine,
Yeshiva University, Bronx, NY, US
[2]VA Boston Healthcare System,
Harvard Medical School,
Brockton, MA, US

ABSTRACT

Schizophrenia is a brain disorder that is associated with disorganization in the fluency of language and thought. A significant genetic component is contributed to the etiology of the disorder. Thus the young family members with heightened genetic risk for developing the disorder have received increasing attention in clinical and neuroimaging studies aimed at determining the underlying genetic vulnerability that leads to schizophrenia.

The search for the presence of white matter (WM) abnormalities in patients with schizophrenia and the people at genetic high-risk has gained tremendous interest with recent advances in brain imaging techniques that allow the visualization of WM integrity. The significance of WM abnormalities is unknown. However, they could be associated with a developmental defect that weakens the neuronal connections necessary for cognitive processing, such as language processing. The early WM abnormalities in the young genetic high-risk people could play a role in the development of the disorder and the symptom of language dysfunction. In this study, we examined the voxel-based whole brain WM volume density and fiber track fractional anisotropy (FA) using the structural MRI and diffusion tensor imaging (DTI) data acquired from 19 patients with schizophrenia, 20 high-risk subjects, and 34 healthy controls. From the results of statistic analyses, schizophrenia patients showed significantly increased WM volume density in the right inferior longitudinal fasciculus (ILF) in the superior temporal lobe, compared with controls. The high-risk group showed significantly decreased WM density in right arcuate fasciculus (AF) close to the right supromarginal gyrus, compared with controls. Group comparisons of whole brain FA values showed that compared to controls, schizophrenia patients had significant FA reductions in a large number of regions from bilateral temporal and occipital lobe; and increased FA in bilateral frontal lobe. Genetic high-risk subjects showed significantly reduced FA in left superior temporal gyrus, right medial frontal gyrus, and right supramarginal gyrus, compared to controls. There was no significant group difference in WM density and FA between the schizophrenia patients and the high-risk people. The findings of this study suggested that structural brain abnormalities in the language-processing circuit exist before the onset of schizophrenia and may indicate the progressive pathology of the disorder.

INTRODUCTION

Schizophrenia is a brain disorder that is associated with disorganization in the fluency of language and thought, as well as misperceptions of internal and external experiences (i.e. hallucinations and delusions). It is heritable as a complex genetic disorder, with no specific biological marker that is known to be present in all affected individuals [1]. However, recent development of in vivo brain imaging techniques has made it possible to characterize the biological bases and brain mechanisms of the disorder.

Whole brain volumetric atrophy and regional gray matter reductions, especially in frontal and temporal lobe structures, have been consistently reported in brain imaging studies in patients with schizophrenia [2-6]. Examination of the white matter (WM) volume alone was not a focus of the early studies. The search for the presence of WM abnormalities in patients with schizophrenia has gained renewed interest with recent advances in diffusion tensor imaging (DTI) techniques that allow the visualization of the integrity of WM.

DTI is a magnetic resonance imaging (MRI) technique that measures the Brownian motion or free diffusion of water [7]. When applied to neural tissue, DTI assesses the degree to which water diffusion is constrained by barriers such as myelin sheaths, membranes or neuronal fiber tracts [8]. Diffusion in WM is anisotropic, i.e., in a given WM voxel, axial diffusion (parallel to the principal fiber direction) is much greater than radial diffusion (perpendicular to the principal fiber direction). The "diffusion tensor" of each WM voxel can be broken down into 3 component eigenvectors providing different anatomical information about the underlying diffusion of water along these separate axes. Diffusion anisotropy is expressed as fractional anisotropy (FA), a normalized measure derived from the 3 eigenvalues. White matter abnormalities with axonal disorganization might therefore be expected to decrease FA.

Some DTI studies have already been published in patients with schizophrenia. These studies tend to support that the structure of WM is abnormal in schizophrenia, although methods for MRI acquisition, image processing, overall analytic approach, and study sample sizes have varied considerably. Buchsbaum et al. [9] employed both DTI and PET in the same patients concluding that both methods supported diminished fronto-striatal connectivity in schizophrenia. Two studies demonstrated a loss of normal asymmetry in diffusion anisotropy in the uncinate fasciculus in male patients with schizophrenia [10; 11]. One recent study reported reduced FA values on the left superior longitudinal fasciculus (SLF) in recent-onset schizophrenia compared to controls, which implicated detectable WM changes in the early phases of the illness [12]. Another study by Seok et al. also reported significantly reduced FA in the left SLF, whereas increased WM density in the left inferior longitudinal fasciculus (ILF); and a significant positive correlation between the mean FA of the left frontal part of the SLF and the severity score of auditory hallucinations in the hallucinating patient group, suggesting that WM changes in the left fronto-temporal area may be an important step in the development of auditory hallucinations in schizophrenia [13]. Mori et al. confirmed the FA reduction in widespread WM structures, including uncinate fascicule and cingulum bundles, in patients with chronic schizophrenia compared to controls; and a significant negative correlation between FA and duration of illness in the patients, which suggested that decreased FA might be attributable, at least in part, to progressive changes after the onset of the illness [14].

Despite the existence of brain imaging studies examining the WM integrity in patients with schizophrenia, no study yet has examined the WM integrity in the young family members of the schizophrenia patients, who have heightened genetic high-risk for developing the disorder. In this study, we examined the voxel-based whole brain WM density and FA values in patients with chronic schizophrenia, subjects at genetic high-risk for developing schizophrenia, and healthy controls. We hypothesized that compared to healthy controls, the high-risk subjects and patients with schizophrenia would show abnormal WM densities and FA values in brain regions which associated with speech and language processing.

METHODS

Subjects

A total of 73 individuals (19 patients with schizophrenia, 20 subjects at genetic high-risk for developing schizophrenia, and 34 normal controls) were included in this study. Individuals in the normal control group did not have personal or family history of any psychotic disorder, psychiatric hospitalization, or suicide in any first and second-degree relatives and were not found to have any evidence of a psychotic illness (schizophrenia, bipolar disorder or psychosis not otherwise specified) upon evaluation. Subjects in the genetic high-risk group were within the peak age range of risk for developing schizophrenia [15; 16] , and originated from families in which at least one first-degree relative (parent or sibling) had a diagnosis of schizophrenia or schizoaffective disorder. Control subjects were solicited from the community by public advertisement. Patients with schizophrenia and subjects in the high-risk cohort were recruited by placing advertisements in newspapers and newsletters distributed by multiple chapters of the National Alliance on Mental Illness (NAMI) or from families who had previously participated in a genetic study of schizophrenia [1].

Every participant underwent an interview using the Diagnostic Interview for Genetic Studies (DIGS) [17], and was diagnosed by DSM-IV criteria. Evaluations were made based upon the interview, information collected from family members, and medical records. Anyone with an IQ less than 85 or higher than 145 was excluded from the study.

This study received Institutional Review Board Approval for human subjects' research at the Nathan S. Kline Institute for Psychiatric Research, a New York State Institution, and at

New York University School of Medicine, where this study was performed. Written informed consents were provided by all participants after being carefully explained the nature of the study and its procedures.

Imaging Acquisition Protocol

Magnetic resonance brain images were acquired on a 1.5T Siemens Vision scanner (Erlangen Germany). The high resolution 3D T1-weighted sequence was performed with the following parameters: TR = 11.6 s; TE = 4.9 ms; flip angle = 15°; FOV = 256 × 256 × 307 mm^3; voxel size = 1.0 × 1.2 × 1.2 mm^3. DTI sequence was performed with TR = 6 s, TE = 100 ms, b-value = 1000 s/mm^2, 8 non-collinear gradient orientations, 19 slices, 5 mm slice thickness, pixel size = 2.5 × 2.5 mm. We also acquired T2 weighted and field map data for possible spatial corrections.

Imaging Pre-Procession

All the image files were first converted from DICOM IMA format to NIfTI format. The tool to3d from AFNI (http://afni.nimh.nih.gov/afni) was used to assemble the data into AFNI-native format. Then the tool 3dAFNItoNIFTI was used to convert the data from AFNI to NIfTI format. FA map of each DTI data was computed using a software developed by Dr. Ardekani [18]. The latest version of the Statistical Parametric Mapping software package (SPM8), implemented in MATLAB 7.10.0 (R2010a) platform, was used to process the T1-weighted and DTI data.

Voxel-Based Whole Brain WM Density Analysis in Individuals

Voxel-based morphometry (VBM) was used to examine WM density differences between groups. For each subject, the T1-weighted image was normalized onto the MNI 152 (Montreal Neurological Institute) space. After spatial normalization, non-brain tissues in the T1-weighted images were removed. Relative differences in regional gray matter volume corrected for individual brain size were analyzed using the “modulated normalized-nonlinear only” option during the segmentation process into GM, WM, and cerebrospinal fluid (CSF) tissues. A bias corrected image volume and a partial volume effect (PVE) label image were used to remove noise. Covariance matrices were created to check the quality of the data procession before applying an 8mm FWHM Gaussian smoothing kernel to further eliminate spatial inhomogeneities in the data. Explicit masks for both the WM and the GM were created.

Voxel-Based Whole Brain FA Analysis in Individuals

The resulting transformation parameters of T1-weighted data normalization were applied to the b = 0 and FA images to ensure the accurate spatial normalization of the FA image. The white matter mask for FA analysis was created based on the average map computed from the normalized FA, which was then thresholded using a nonparametric histogram-based segmentation algorithm [19]. The FA value, instead of image intensity of each voxel, was used during the modulated normalization and comparison. Finally, 8mm FWHM Gaussian kernel was applied for spatial smoothing.

Group Statistical Analyses WM and FA Morphometry

One way ANOVA and post hoc *t* tests were performed to determine any demographic or clinical differences between groups.

ANCOVA was used to compare the voxel-based whole brain WM morphometry and FA values in the normal control, high-risk, and patient groups. Significance threshold was set up as $p < 0.05$ with cluster corrected clusters of 50 voxels or greater. Age, handedness, and gender impacts were corrected by add these measures as covariates. False discovery rate (FDR) was set at $p < 0.05$.

RESULTS

Table 1 showed the results of the group comparisons of the demographic and clinical characteristics, from which no group demographic differences were found, with the exception of age (There was no statistic age difference between the high-risk and control groups. But the patients were significantly older than the high-risk subjects and controls).

Table 1. Subject characteristics analyzed by one-way ANOVA

	Controls (n = 34)	High-risk (n = 20)	Schizophrenia (n = 19)	d.f.	*P*
Age	22.0 ± 5.1	21.1 ± 5.5	33.5 ± 8.3	2	0.000
(range)	(16-32)	(16-30)	(20-48)		
Male/Female (Chi-sq)	15/19	7/13	12/7	2	0.176
Left/Right Handed	2/32	2/18	2/17	–	–
Education(years)	14.8 ± 3.0	12.6 ± 2.75	14.5 ± 2.20	2	0.634
Mother's Education	13.8 ± 3.5	14.5 ± 2.5	12.5 ± 2.20	2	0.695
Father's Education	15.1 ± 2.05	15.0±2.225	14.5 ± 3.25	2	0.942
IQ	113.2 ± 17.4	108.07 ± 14.6	105.53 ± 14.3	2	0.88

The between-group comparisons of WM density showed that schizophrenia patients had one significantly increased cluster located in the right ILF in the superior temporal lobe with peak coordinates at [21 -9 -21], compared with controls. The high-risk group had one cluster with significantly decreased WM density in the right arcuate fasciculus (AF) with peak coordinates at [44 -31 25], close to the right supromarginal gyrus, compared with controls (Figure 1). There was no significant group difference of WM density between the schizophrenia patients and the high-risk people.

The between-group comparisons of FA morphometry showed that compared to controls, the schizophrenia patients had several clusters of significantly increased FA values located in the bilateral ILF (with local peaks of group differences at [-19 22 15], [24 34 3], and [23 24 20]), left middle frontal lobe [-44 49 20], and right caudate-frontal projection [19 11 11]. The schizophrenia patients also showed several clusters of significantly decreased FA values in left parietal-temporal-occipital association cortex [-23 -39 1], left limbic association cortex (beside Amygdala [-29 -2 -21] and Hippocampus [-24 -23 -25]), and right side visual cortex [19 -58 5], compared to controls.

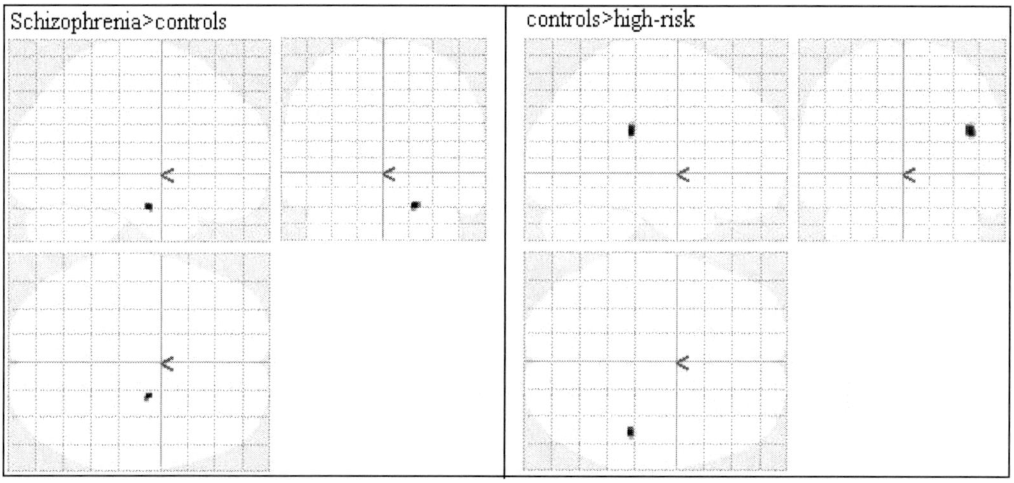

Figure 1. group comparisons of whole brain WM morphometry in the three groups.

FA comparisons between the high-risk and control groups showed that compared to controls, the high-risk subjects had significantly increased FA values in left fusiform gyrus with peak coordinates at [-24 -35 -15], left ILF close to angular gyrus [-28 -52 31], and significantly decreased FA values in left thalamus-temporal projection (-19, -22, 1), right side inferior frontal gyrus [43 28 21], and right side AF [43 -28 21].

Similar as the result of comparison of WM density between the patients and the high-risk cohort, there was no significant group difference of FA values between the schizophrenia patients and the high-risk people.

Conclusion

In the present study, we analyzed the voxel-based whole brain WM density and FA value in patients with chronic schizophrenia, subjects at genetic high-risk for developing schizophrenia, and healthy controls.

Group comparisons of the whole brain WM densities and FA values showed that compared to the normal controls, schizophrenia patients had one cluster of significantly increased WM density located in the ILF at superior temporal region, and had several clusters of significantly increased FA values located in the bilateral ILF, left middle frontal lobe, and right caudate-frontal projection. The schizophrenia patients also showed significantly decreased FA values in left parietal-temporal-occipital association cortex, left limbic association cortex, beside Amygdala and Hippocampus, and right side visual cortex, compared to controls.

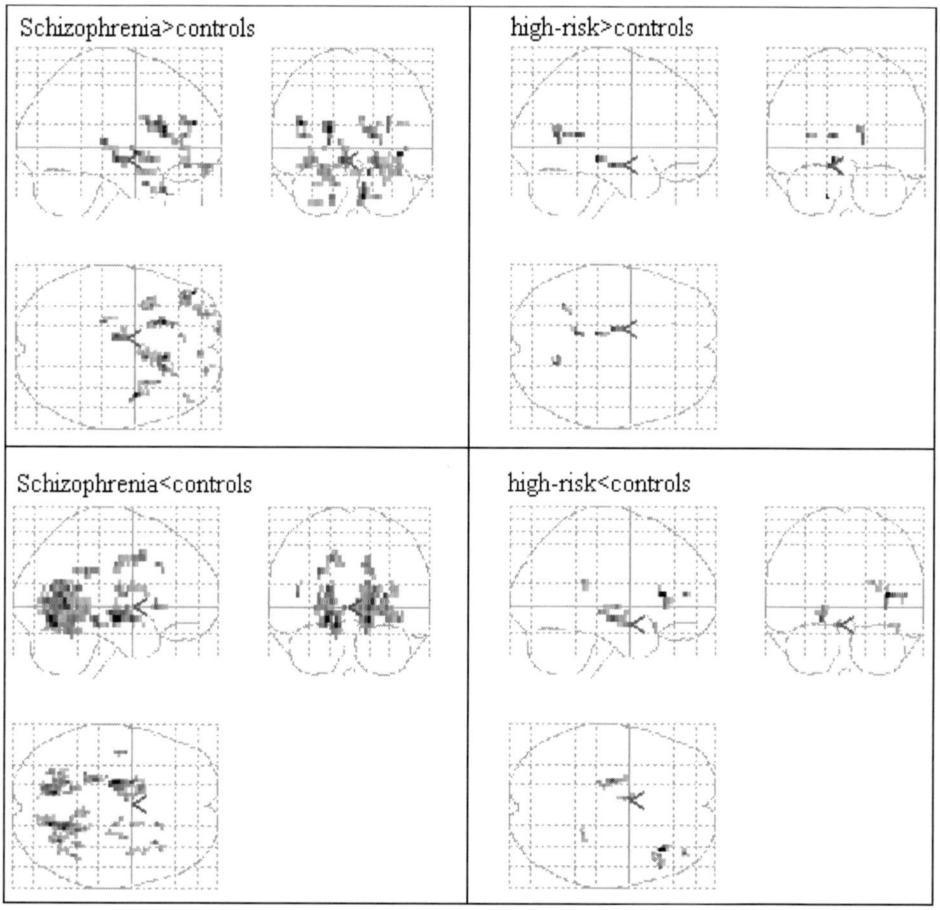

Figure 2. group comparisons of whole brain FA morphometry in the three groups.

Consistent with a lot of existing structural and functional neuroimaging studies [15; 20; 21], the finding of reduced FA in right side visual cortex reported in the present study suggests the impaired visual perception in patients with schizophrenia, which may be associated with the symptom of visual hallucination. Fibers in the ILF at the superior temporal area were suggested to contribute to visual perception and processing [22]. Thus, the increased WM density and FA in the ILF in patients with schizophrenia can be caused by neuronal compensation to the WM deficit in the right visual cortex.

The other regions of WM abnormalities, reported in the present study, include middle frontal area and parietal-temporal-occipital association cortex. These are important brain regions in the language processing pathways, referenced as Broca's and Vernicke's areas. The parietal-temporal-occipital association cortex is an important brain region in investigations of schizophrenia because of its association with auditory and language processing in its middle and more posterior regions, particularly the left posterior portion of Heschl's gyrus and the planum temporale. Several previous MRI studies suggest that reduced brain volume in this area is associated with the language disorder of schizophrenia [2] and also verbal memory deficits [23]. Converging evidence from behavioral and imaging studies suggests that anatomical abnormalities in these two areas could be the direct brain mechanism of the impaired language processing ability in schizophrenia [24-26]. In addition, the findings of abnormal FA values in the caudate-frontal projection and the limbic association cortex are consistent with existing findings from multiple studies [6; 27-29].

The results of this study also showed that compared to the normal controls, the genetic high-risk subjects had significantly decreased WM density in right AF close to the right supromarginal gyrus, significantly decreased FA in left thalamus-temporal projection, right side inferior frontal gyrus, and right side AF, and significantly increased FA in left fusiform gyrus, left ILF close to angular gyrus. Previous studies in the young high-risk subjects for developing schizophrenia reported gray matter abnormalities in the same brain regions, such as reversed hemispheric asymmetry in cingulate sulcal thickness [30]; increase of surface area in left parahippocampal gyri, and left middle temporal lobe [31]; and significantly increased right prefrontal cortical folding (associated with speech and thought) [32], compared with controls. These findings together suggest that the early abnormalities of the cortical neuron development in these cortical regions may contribute to the origins of the associated cognitive dysfunctions and psychotic symptoms, such as language impairment, thought and emotion.

Among the WM abnormalities in the patients with schizophrenia, the significantly increased FA in left ILF and significantly decreased FA in left superior temporal cortex are replicable in the subjects at high-risk for developing schizophrenia. This finding suggests that WM abnormalities in left ILF and superior temporal cortex may contribute to the early development of the disorder, and can be a valuable biomarker of the onset of schizophrenia.

There are some limitations to the present study. First, a few left-handed subjects were included in each group. However, this is unlikely to affect our results, as the majority of right-handed people have left brain language dominant, whereas left-handed people have 85% left hemispheric dominant, 15% bilaterally dominant, and rarely right side dominant [33]. In addition, the schizophrenia patients were significantly elder than the high-risk subjects and normal controls. WM density and integrity may change across the lifespan due to aging. As mentioned in (Cook et al., 2007), 60 is usually used as a cutoff age for aging. And in the same study they grouped the subjects in younger with 25.9 (SD 6.0) years and older with 68.3 (SD 4.9) years old. Similarly in (Sharp et al., 2006), they grouped the subjects in younger with 37-54 years and older with 60-83. In the current study, the patients were 33.5 (SD 8.3). The oldest patient was 51 and none of the subjects reached the cutoff age for aging. So we do not expect that the age differences would significantly affect the patterns of WM density and integrity among groups. Considering these concerns, we have also added age and handedness as the covariates to remove the effects of these factors in our analyses.

REFERENCES

[1] DeLisi LE, Shaw SH, Crow TJ, Shields G, Smith AB, Larach VW, Wellman N, Loftus J, Nanthakumar B, Razi K, Stewart J, Comazzi M, Vita A, Heffner T, Sherrington R: A genome-wide scan for linkage to chromosomal regions in 382 sibling pairs with schizophrenia or schizoaffective disorder. *Am.J.Psychiatry* 2002, **159:**803-812.

[2] Shenton ME, Kikinis R, Jolesz FA, Pollak SD, Lemay M, Wible CG, Hokama H, Martin J, Metcalf D, Coleman M: Abnormalities of the left temporal lobe and thought disorder in schizophrenia. A quantitative magnetic resonance imaging study. *N.Engl.J.Med.* 1992, **327:**604-612.

[3] DeLisi LE, Sakuma M, Tew W, Kushner M, Hoff AL, Grimson R: Schizophrenia as a chronic active brain process: a study of progressive brain structural change subsequent to the onset of schizophrenia. *Psychiatry Res.Neuroimaging* 1997, **74:**129-140.

[4] Gaser C, Volz HP, Kiebel S, Riehemann S, Sauer H: Detecting structural changes in whole brain based on nonlinear deformations-application to schizophrenia research. *Neuroimage.* 1999, 10:107-113.

[5] Jayakumar PN, Venkatasubramanian G, Gangadhar BN, Janakiramaiah N, Keshavan MS: Optimized voxel-based morphometry of gray matter volume in first-episode, antipsychotic-naive schizophrenia. *Prog.Neuropsychopharmacol.Biol.Psychiatry* 2005, 29:587-591.

[6] Shenton ME, Whitford TJ, Kubicki M: Structural neuroimaging in schizophrenia: from methods to insights to treatments. *Dialogues.Clin.Neurosci.* 2010, 12:317-332.

[7] Basser PJ, Mattiello J, LeBihan D: Estimation of the effective self-diffusion tensor from the NMR spin echo. *J Magn Reson.B* 1994, 103:247-254.

[8] Basser PJ, Mattiello J, LeBihan D: MR diffusion tensor spectroscopy and imaging. *Biophys.J* 1994, 66:259-267.

[9] Buchsbaum MS, Tang CY, Peled S, Gudbjartsson H, Lu D, Hazlett EA, Downhill J, Haznedar M, Fallon JH, Atlas SW: - MRI white matter diffusion anisotropy and PET metabolic rate in schizophrenia. *Neuroreport.1998 Feb 16;9(3):425 30.*

[10] Kubicki M, Westin CF, Maier SE, Frumin M, Nestor PG, Salisbury DF, Kikinis R, Jolesz FA, McCarley RW, Shenton ME: Uncinate fasciculus findings in schizophrenia: a magnetic resonance diffusion tensor imaging study. *Am.J.Psychiatry* 2002, 159:813-820.

[11] Burns J, Job D, Bastin ME, Whalley H, Macgillivray T, Johnstone EC, Lawrie SM: Structural disconnectivity in schizophrenia: a diffusion tensor magnetic resonance imaging study. *Br.J.Psychiatry* 2003, 182:439-443.

[12] Karlsgodt KH, van Erp TG, Poldrack RA, Bearden CE, Nuechterlein KH, Cannon TD: Diffusion tensor imaging of the superior longitudinal fasciculus and working memory in recent-onset schizophrenia. *Biol.Psychiatry* 2008, 63:512-518.

[13] Seok JH, Park HJ, Chun JW, Lee SK, Cho HS, Kwon JS, Kim JJ: White matter abnormalities associated with auditory hallucinations in schizophrenia: a combined study of voxel-based analyses of diffusion tensor imaging and structural magnetic resonance imaging. *Psychiatry Res.* 2007, 156:93-104.

[14] Mori T, Ohnishi T, Hashimoto R, Nemoto K, Moriguchi Y, Noguchi H, Nakabayashi T, Hori H, Harada S, Saitoh O, Matsuda H, Kunugi H: Progressive changes of white

matter integrity in schizophrenia revealed by diffusion tensor imaging. *Psychiatry Res.* 2007, 154:133-145.

[15] Li X, Branch CA, Ardekani BA, Bertisch H, Hicks C, DeLisi LE: fMRI study of language activation in schizophrenia, schizoaffective disorder and in individuals genetically at high risk. *Schizophr.Res.* 2007, 96:14-24.

[16] DeLisi LE: The significance of age of onset for schizophrenia. *Schizophr.Bull* 1992, 18:209-215.

[17] Nurnberger JI, Jr., Blehar MC, Kaufmann CA, York-Cooler C, Simpson SG, Harkavy-Friedman J, Severe JB, Malaspina D, Reich T: Diagnostic interview for genetic studies. Rationale, unique features, and training. NIMH Genetics Initiative. *Arch.Gen.Psychiatry* 1994, 51:849-59; discussion 863-4.

[18] Ardekani BA, Nierenberg J, Hoptman MJ, Javitt DC, Lim KO: MRI study of white matter diffusion anisotropy in schizophrenia. *NeuroReport* 2003, 14:2025-2029.

[19] Otsu N: A threshold selection method from gray-level histograms. *IEEE Trans Systems Man Cybernetics* 1979, 9:63-66.

[20] Li X, Branch CA, DeLisi LE: Language pathway abnormalities in schizophrenia: a review of fMRI and other imaging studies. *Curr.Opin.Psychiatry* 2009, 22:131-139.

[21] Wright IC, Rabe-Hesketh S, Woodruff PWR, David AS, Murray RM, Bullmore ET: Meta-analysis of regional brain volumes in schizophrenia. *Am.J.Psychiatry* 2000, 157:16-25.

[22] Geesaman BJ, Born RT, Andersen RA, Tootell RB: Maps of complex motion selectivity in the superior temporal cortex of the alert macaque monkey: a double-label 2-deoxyglucose study. *Cereb.Cortex* 1997, 7:749-757.

[23] Nestor PG, Shenton ME, McCarley RW, Haimson J, Smith RS, O'Donnell B, Kimble M, Kikinis R, Jolesz FA: Neuropsychological correlates of MRI temporal lobe abnormalities in schizophrenia. *Am.J.Psychiatry* 1993, 150:1849-1855.

[24] Watkins KE, Vargha-Khadem F, Ashburner J, Passingham RE, Connelly A, Friston KJ, Frackowiak RSJ, Mishkin M, Gadian DG: MRI analysis of an inherited speech and language disorder: structural brain abnormalities. *Brain* 2002, 125:465-478.

[25] Rajarethinam R, Sahni S, Rosenberg DR, Keshavan MS: Reduced superior temporal gyrus volume in young offspring of patients with schizophrenia. *Am.J.Psychiatry* 2004, 161:1121-1124.

[26] Jacobsen LK, Giedd JN, Tanrikut C, Brady DR, Donohue BC, Hamburger SD, Kumra S, Alaghband-Rad J, Rumsey JM, Rapoport JL: Three-dimensional cortical morphometry of the planum temporale in childhood-onset schizophrenia. *Am.J.Psychiatry* 1997, 154:685-687.

[27] Goldman AL, Pezawas L, Mattay VS, Fischl B, Verchinski BA, Chen Q, Weinberger DR, Meyer-Lindenberg A: Widespread reductions of cortical thickness in schizophrenia and spectrum disorders and evidence of heritability. *Arch.Gen.Psychiatry* 2009, 66:467-477.

[28] Welch KA, Stanfield AC, Moorhead TW, Haga K, Owens DC, Lawrie SM, Johnstone EC: Amygdala volume in a population with special educational needs at high risk of schizophrenia. *Psychol.Med.* 2010, 40:945-954.

[29] Witthaus H, Mendes U, Brune M, Ozgurdal S, Bohner G, Gudlowski Y, Kalus P, Andreasen N, Heinz A, Klingebiel R, Juckel G: Hippocampal subdivision and

amygdalar volumes in patients in an at-risk mental state for schizophrenia. *J.Psychiatry Neurosci.* 2010, 35:33-40.

[30] Goghari VM, Rehm K, Carter CS, MacDonald AW: Sulcal thickness as a vulnerability indicator for schizophrenia. *Br.J.Psychiatry* 2007, 191:229-233.

[31] Goghari VM, Rehm K, Carter CS, MacDonald AW, III: Regionally specific cortical thinning and gray matter abnormalities in the healthy relatives of schizophrenia patients. *Cereb.Cortex* 2007, 17:415-424.

[32] Stanfield AC, Moorhead TW, Harris JM, Owens DG, Lawrie SM, Johnstone EC: Increased right prefrontal cortical folding in adolescents at risk of schizophrenia for cognitive reasons. *Biol.Psychiatry* 2008, 63:80-85.

[33] Thilers PP, MacDonald SW, Herlitz A: Sex differences in cognition: the role of handedness. *Physiol Behav.* 2007, 92:105-109.

In: Schizophrenia Research: Recent Advances
Editor: Tomiki Sumiyoshi

ISBN: 978-1-62808-703-1

Chapter 8

DEPTH PERCEPTION DEFICITS IN SCHIZOPHRENIA

***Jamie K. Opper*[*], *Patrick Monnier*[†] *and Deana Davalos*[‡]**
Colorado State University, US

ABSTRACT

Previous research has established that patients with schizophrenia experience impairments in depth perception, distance perception, motion perception, and abnormal spatial frequency sensitivity, in addition to exhibiting reduced susceptibility to stereoptical illusions. These visual deficits affect a variety of processes that are needed to successfully navigate everyday life. One of the key questions regarding visual deficits in schizophrenia is whether there are shared neurophysiological and neurochemical substrates across all deficits or whether each type of deficit represents an etiologically unique and distinct type of visual deficit. Proposed accounts for these visual deficits range from attentional deficits in schizophrenia stemming from dysfunction of various neurochemicals and/or impaired connections between neural systems responsible for integrating top-down conceptual and bottom-up perceptual information to evidence implicating a specific neurotransmitter (e.g., endogenous cannabinoid/anandamide) system thought to affect multiple visual processes. One system that consistently appears dysfunctional in schizophrenia is the system responsible for depth perception, the ability to obtain and process 3D visual information about a scene based on monocular (information available to a single eye, such as the occlusion of one object by another) and binocular cues (information extracted by slightly disparate retinal images on both eyes). While a number of researchers have studied aspects of depth perception, there is little research integrating these findings to examine the neural underpinnings of depth perception deficits and the implications of such deficits on everyday living. In addition, there has been little research examining whether these deficits could be addressed via medication or therapy. To address these issues and the role that depth perception deficits play in overall visual processing in schizophrenia, we systematically review the literature and address possible explanations of these deficits and implications for possible interventions.

[*] E-mail address: Jamie.Opper@colostate.edu .
[†] E-mail address: Patrick.Monnier@colostate.edu.
[‡] E-mail address: Deana.Davalos@colostate.edu.

INTRODUCTION

Schizophrenia is arguably one of the most devastating mental illnesses, characterized by gross deficits across almost all domains: cognition, memory, volition, and motor abilities are all affected, and hallucinations and delusional beliefs are common [1]. While neuropsychological testing and brain imaging have done much to advance our understanding of the underlying causes of schizophrenia, there is still much to be learned, and in the meantime those who live with schizophrenia exist in a limbo where they must choose between living with the disabling symptoms of the illness or the unpleasant and occasionally equally disabling side effects of antipsychotic medications. A more thorough understanding of the neurological bases of schizophrenia would do much to help yield more effective medications with fewer detrimental side effects; however, the brain is a complex system, and it may be more efficient to study separate systems and/or structures of the brain independently to determine their contribution to the dysfunctions evident in schizophrenia.

One system that appears dysfunctional in schizophrenia is that responsible for depth perception, the ability to obtain and process visual information about a scene based on monocular (depth information available to a single eye, such as the occlusion of one object by another, perspective, texture gradient, etc.) and binocular cues (the extraction of depth by the processing of two slightly disparate retinal images). The human brain has neurons that are selective for retinal disparity; different binocular neurons are tuned to different levels of disparity. Since distance between the two eyes and an object determines the amount of retinal disparity, selectivity to such disparity can be used to estimate absolute distance (binocular disparity operates over a limited range of distances).

Both binocular and monocular vision appear to be disrupted in schizophrenia. In Freedman's [2] summary of autobiographical accounts of perceptual disturbance, many patients diagnosed with schizophrenia describe their experience of the world as "flat" or "unfocused" and report difficulty distinguishing background information from foreground information. Contrary to what one might expect, these disturbances seem to occur in the absence of visual hallucinations [2], indicating that the mechanism responsible for depth perception deficits in schizophrenia differs from that responsible for visual hallucinations.

There is a plethora of experimental evidence identifying deficits in processing both monocular and binocular information in schizophrenia, although overwhelmingly the focus is on stereopsis deficits (binocular vision), perhaps because stereopsisis easier to isolate and therefore to test experimentally—retinal disparity is the only way to achieve stereopsis, whereas individuals without binocular vision have many monocular cues upon which they can rely. In the next section, we review the relevant literature, as well as some of the techniques and instruments used to measure and estimate stereopsis acuity.

In the literature, the most widely used instrument to test stereopsis is the Howard-Dolman Depth Perception Apparatus. The instrument consists of a long box with a viewing aperture on one side [7]. Inside the box are two black rods suspended from parallel tracks which the subject can move back and forth along the tracks. During a typical session, one of the rods is set at a fixed distance from the subject, who is then required to move the other rod so that both rods appear aligned [7] (i.e., both rods appear to be the same distance away from the subject). As the box provides a scene devoid of any monocular depth cues, the subject can rely only on stereopsis to perform the task. The Howard-Dolman task is sometimes modified by changing the number of rods to be aligned [8]; attaching pictures of stimuli to rods [9], allowing for the inclusion of stimuli of varying affective value; or dividing the length of the box down the middle with an opaque partition so that the subject must use monocular, rather than binocular, cues [8, 9], thus testing depth perception that relies only on information from one eye instead of both. Regardless of the particular setup, the dependent variable is the error in the alignment of the rods. While there does not appear to be a universally established cutoff error that distinguishes "normal" from "deficient" subjects, Broota and Gupta [7] found that the mean error for subjects with schizophrenia is 10.73 cm, whereas that for control subjects is only 2.88 cm.

Another test of stereo vision is the Graded Circles Stereo Test, which uses polarized glasses and overlapping, disparate images (similar to the method used to achieve the illusion of depth in 3-D movies). The lenses of the glasses are polarized orthogonally so that each eye only perceives one of the images. Depth can only be perceived if the subject can process the disparate images. The amount of disparity between the images is varied systematically in different plates so as to measure stereoscopic acuity [10], depth perceived with smaller (larger) amounts of disparity indicating higher (lower) levels of stereoscopic acuity. The subject's task is to indicate which plate results in barely visible depth, and that amount of disparity is taken as a threshold [10].

An additional measure used to assess stereopsis, and one which has shown the most robust differences in depth perception between patients with schizophrenia and healthy controls, is known as the Binocular Depth Inversion Illusion (BDII). In the BDII, pictures of familiar objects are manipulated so that visual information usually presented to the right eye is presented to the left eye and vice versa [11-19]; in other words, images are presented with the depth information reversed. For subjects with normal stereo vision, objects that appear convex in the original photograph appear concave in the BDII, and vice versa. The BDII appears to be the most popular method of testing binocular disparity in schizophrenia patients, perhaps because it so clearly and reliably demonstrates differences in depth perception ability between subjects with schizophrenia and control subjects. It has therefore been used experimentally to compare stereopsis deficits among many clinical and non-clinical groups.

Experimental Evidence

Broota and Gupta found that subjects with schizophrenia were significantly less accurate than control subjects at matching the distance of the rods in a Howard-Dolman task, indicating that the subjects with schizophrenia had poorer depth perception [7]. In addition, subjects with schizophrenia exhibited much greater variability than did the control subjects, indicating that depth perception might be much more variable in people with schizophrenia than in the general population [7]. The authors do caution, however, that the higher variability seen among the subjects with schizophrenia may be due to their inability to tolerate concentrating on the task for long periods of time [7]. Similar studies have also shown that subjects with schizophrenia tend to perform more poorly than controls on Howard-Dolman tasks [20], including tasks involving such variations as replacing the stationary rod with a projected image and putting a divider between the two tracks to test monocular vision [8]. Similar studies have involved other manipulations, including enlarging the scale of the

Howard-Dolman Apparatus so that the experimenter physically carried a marker until informed by a subject that the moving marker appeared to be one yard away from a stationary marker [21], and attaching pictures of varying affective significance (a circle, a dog, a man, or a woman) to the rods of the Howard-Dolman Apparatus [9]. One study did not find significant differences between control subjects and subjects with schizophrenia, though it replicated Broota and Gupta's findings that variability was higher among subjects with schizophrenia [9]. The authors attribute the increased variability to a propensity for the subjects with schizophrenia to be more responsive to the affective properties of the stimuli, but this explanation does not seem to have clear support from the experimental evidence [9]. It is possible that the high variability in both cases was due to the inability on the part of the subjects with schizophrenia to maintain attention for long periods of time. This attentional instability may itself play a role in the poor depth perception of subjects with schizophrenia, as subjects may be unable to selectively attend to foreground stimuli and ignore cues from background stimuli.

Another study used the Graded Circles Stereo Test and a variety of optical illusions to determine the nature of depth perception deficits in schizophrenia and also found that subjects with schizophrenia exhibit reduced sensitivity to low spatial frequencies as well as reduced sensitivity to stereoptical illusions, such as those involved in the Graded Circles Stereo Test [10, 22]. In studies where there were no significant differences found in variability between subjects with schizophrenia and controls, the schizophrenia subjects consistently underestimated the distance of objects from them, performing worse than controls [8, 20, 21] with some evidence indicating that accuracy was even further impaired when the distance between subject and object increased [8, 21].

One study found that the depth perception of subjects with schizophrenia became less accurate as chronicity (i.e., the length of time elapsed since initial diagnosis) increased, but appeared to improve slightly for the most chronic groups (those for whom 20 or more years had elapsed since first diagnosis) [20]. The authors did not offer an explanation for this finding, although it is possible that it may be due to patients' adaptive development of compensatory strategies, such as learning to rely on monocular rather than binocular cues, or training themselves to better focus attention for sustained periods of time. The recovery of depth perception with increasing chronicity may also explain the nonsignificant findings for the study involving affective stimuli; however, this account is difficult to assess as the authors did not include chronicity data [9].

It is also possible that pharmaceutical interventions may play a role inpatients' depth perception, as levels of dopamine may influence ability to perceive object properties, such as fine detail or texture gradient [22]. One study tested the ability of patients with schizophrenia to perceive gratings of different spatial frequencies (vertical or horizontal bars of varying widths) before and after the injection of Stelazine, Modecate, or Haldol, drugs commonly used to treat schizophrenia as these drugs reduce dopamine levels in the brain [22]. Spatial frequency can provide cues to distance and hence depth perception: spatial frequency is determined by the size of an object and its distance from the viewer. The closer an object is to the viewer, the larger is its retinal image and small details are more visible (i.e., the lower its spatial frequency); likewise, the farther an object is from the viewer, the smaller is its retinal image and small details are less visible (i.e., the higher its spatial frequency). If patients with schizophrenia exhibit enhanced sensitivity to high spatial frequencies, then they will be better able than control subjects to discern objects' details regardless of an object's distance from them (i.e., object details will appear larger to them, and they may thus perceive objects as being closer than they really are). Impaired spatial frequency perception can thus affect depth perception. The authors [22] found that after administration of antipsychotic medication, when dopamine levels were lowest, subjects exhibited enhanced sensitivity to low spatial frequencies and reduced sensitivity to high spatial frequencies relative to their sensitivity prior to administration of antipsychotic medication, when dopamine levels were highest [22]. These results seem to suggest that when levels of dopamine are high, as in untreated schizophrenia, sensitivity to high spatial frequencies is enhanced relative to sensitivity to low spatial frequency, potentially leading to a tendency to underestimate the distance of objects from oneself. Further support for the role of dopamine in impaired depth perception in schizophrenia has been reported by Schneider and colleagues, who observed improved depth perception on a slightly different task following administration of antipsychotic medication. It may be that the higher variability found among subjects with schizophrenia noted in previous studies using the Howard-Dolman task may be determined by differences in dopamine levels.

A test of depth perception that has consistently found striking differences between subjects with schizophrenia and control subjects is the Binocular Disparity Inversion Index (BDII), wherein images are presented with the depth information reversed: for subjects with normal stereo vision, objects that appear concave in the original photograph appear convex in the BDII. Several studies [11-19] have established that, when tested with the BDII, control subjects are more likely to perceive the stimulus as convex, even though the presented depth information should be interpreted as concave. Not surprisingly, this effect is more pronounced for stimuli that are not encountered as concave in real life, such as human faces. Subjects with schizophrenia, however, are more likely to perceive the stimuli in accordance with the depth information presented to them by the inverted image, i.e., as concave, even for human faces. One study presented subjects with images of human faces with the depth information reversed (the images of the faces appear concave), and found that all subjects with schizophrenia reported seeing a human face stimulus as hollow, whereas none of the control subjects did [11]. In similar studies, when presented with stimuli depicting human faces with the depth information inverted, subjects with schizophrenia perceived a hollow face, as did healthy subjects who ingested delta-9-tetrahydrocannabinol (THC; the psychoactive compound in marijuana) before observing the stimuli [12, 18], and THC-intoxicated healthy controls performed similarly to patients in the prodromal phase of schizophrenia (i.e., patients who are still in the early stages of schizophrenia) on the BDII [13]. Subjects who had ingested nonpsychoactive cannabinoids (compounds chemically similar to THC) did not perceive hollow faces, but subjects who ingested psychoactive cannabinoids did [15]. The similarities in performance between subjects with schizophrenia and subjects intoxicated with psychoactive THC indicates that dysfunctional cannabinoid receptors in the brain may play a role in the depth perception abnormalities exhibited by subjects with schizophrenia.

DISCUSSION

The literature shows clear evidence of stereopsis deficits in schizophrenia; however, the cause of these deficits has yet to be definitively determined, although theories abound. Perhaps the simplest of these theories deal with the possibility of attentional dysfunction in schizophrenia. Broota and Gupta hypothesize that poor performance of subjects with schizophrenia might be due to their inability to selectively attend to foreground stimuli and ignore less relevant background stimuli [7]. This could explain the higher variability among subjects with schizophrenia, and may play a role in their poor performance on the Howard-Dolman task. While this account is reasonable, Broota and Gupta do not speculate about its cause. Emrich proposes a three-component model of psychosis to establish the relation between selective attention difficulties and depth perception dysfunction in schizophrenia [23]. Emrich proposes that there are three components to perception: the information actually being perceived by the sensory system, or the "sensualistic" component (also known as "bottom-up" processes); conceptual information based on prior experience in the world, or the "constructivistic" component (i.e.; "top-down" processes); and a "zensor" component, which is responsible for determining whether to use the "bottom-up" or "top-down" information [23]. The "zensor" component thus acts as a filter to determine which information the brain should give priority [23]. Emrich proposes that in psychosis (not limited to that found in schizophrenia), the equilibrium between the "top-down" processes and the "zensor" component is unbalanced, rendering patients with psychosis unable to use sensory information based in prior experience [23].

This theory is supported by the findings of the BDII experiments: control subjects are able to make use of "top-down" processes which inform them that in the world human faces do not occur as concave, whereas subjects with schizophrenia rely solely on the "bottom-up" information received by the visual system and thus are more likely to perceive human faces as hollow [11, 12, 15, 17-19]. Again, the cause of this dysfunctional informational filtering is unclear. There appear to be two main hypotheses as to its cause: neurotransmitter system dysfunction and impaired connections between neural systems (although these hypotheses are not mutually exclusive, as neurotransmitter system dysfunction may cause or be caused by impaired connections between neural systems, or both may exist concurrently).

Similarities in BDII performance between THC-intoxicated subjects and subjects with schizophrenia have been interpreted to indicate a role for the endogenous cannabinoid/anandamide system in schizophrenia [12, 13, 18]. Endogenous cannabinoids/anandamides are neurotransmitters that appear to have similar chemical composition to other cannabinoids, such as THC [12, 15, 18]. The discovery of the endogenous cannabinoid/anandamide system is relatively recent, so the function of endogenous cannabinoids in humans is still relatively poorly understood. Primary binding sites for cannabinoids appear to be in the dentate gyrus and other areas of the hippocampus, the cerebellum, the basal ganglia, the globus pallidus, and the substantia nigra [12, 18], areas that have historically been found to be dysfunctional in schizophrenia [1, 12]. The hippocampus in particular has been found to exhibit pronounced structural abnormalities in schizophrenia [1]. Gray and Rawlins (1986, as cited in [15]) suggest that the hippocampus may be the structure responsible for the "zensor" component, which is in keeping with Emrich's suggestion that the "zensor" component may be disturbed in schizophrenia [23].

Dima et al. provided some neurobiological evidence for the three-component model in neuroimaging studies involving controls and subjects with schizophrenia during a BDII task [11]. When shown inverted faces, fMRI scans of control subjects' brains showed an increased number of neural connections from the intraparietal sulcus (IPS, hypothesized to be responsible for the influence of "top-down" processes) to the lateral occipital cortex (LOC, implicated in visual processing), indicating the imposition of conceptual information onto sensory input [11]. In subjects with schizophrenia, however, increased activity was shown between V1 (the earliest stage of neural visual processing) and the LOC, indicating that, in schizophrenia, sensory information might take precedence over conceptual information [11]. This is in keeping with the relative insusceptibility of schizophrenia patients to the BDII.

Korn [3-6] puts forth a fascinating, but untested, theory regarding the inability of schizophrenia patients to filter background from foreground information. Korn distinguishes between two kinds of stereo vision: panoramic vision, which relies on depth information obtained from binocular disparity, and fixation vision, which relies on the convergence of the eyes upon a common fixation point, usually near the viewer [3]. Fixation vision, Korn suggests, allows one to determine the position of an object in the scene by comparing the distance from the fixation point to different horizontal points on the object; panoramic vision allows for a stereoscopic representation of the scene by integrating information from the disparate images projected to each eye [3]. Korn hypothesizes that dopamine is responsible for the switch from fixation (near) to panoramic (distance) vision, and the excess of dopamine that occurs in schizophrenia causes this switch to malfunction, thereby resulting in the simultaneous activation of fixation and panoramic vision and the inability to distinguish between background and foreground information. Korn further theorizes that this simultaneous activation causes hallucinations and delusions as the patient's brain attempts to makes sense of conflicting information [3].

Korn also suggests, based only on one case study, that foveal projections (i.e., the neural connections originating from the fovea, the area of the retina with highest acuity) are defective in schizophrenia [4]. In normal subjects, the optic nerve leaves the eye and goes to the optic chiasm, where the half of the optic nerve fibers closest to the bridge of the nose (i.e., the nasal half) cross to the other side of the body. Korn proposes that in schizophrenia, the temporal half, rather than the nasal half, of the optic nerve fibers cross in the optic chiasm (although this has not been supported by any postmortem research of which the authors are aware). This could account for the impaired performance of individuals with schizophrenia on the BDII [4]. Korn develops this hypothesis further, stating that vision-based proprioception (i.e., visual information about where one's body is in space based on movements of the eyeball) is ordinarily transmitted via the nasal half of the optic nerve fibers, which is to say that in normal controls, proprioception information would be projected to the side of the brain contralateral from the eye sending the information [5]. In schizophrenia, however, as the nasal fibers do not cross in the optic chiasm, proprioception information is received by the ipsilateral, rather than contralateral, side of the brain [5]. This, she explains, suggests that patients with schizophrenia receive proprioception information based on panoramic (i.e., distance) vision, rather than near visual field information, resulting in an inability to suppress attention to distance cues [5]. The inability to suppress distance information leads to a disconnect between spatial (panoramic) and object (fixation) vision, which in turn causes difficulty distinguishing between reality and illusion, as schizophrenia patients have difficulty integrating information regarding near and far objects [6]. Unfortunately, Korn's theory is based only on a single case study and has little anatomical, physiological, or empirical supporting evidence.

Another controversial theory regarding visual deficits in schizophrenia, but one better supported by empirical evidence (discussed below), is that the magnocellular pathway is dysfunctional in schizophrenia [10, 24]. The magnocellular pathway is the neural pathway responsible for rapidly transmitting low-resolution, low-spatial-frequency visual information (as distinguished from the parvocellular pathway, which transmits higher spatial frequency information more slowly) [24]. Magnocellular dysfunction in schizophrenia would explain the findings by Harris et al., Kantrowicz et al., and Schecter et al. that untreated schizophrenia patients have reduced sensitivity to low-spatial-frequency information [10, 22, 24]. Schecter et al. found that the average level of stereopsis achieved by subjects with schizophrenia was equivalent to that which is usually reached by age five in control subjects, suggesting a possible failure of neural development in schizophrenia [24].

The controversy regarding the selective impairment of the magnocellular system arises when Skottun and Skoyles point out that postmortem studies have found no abnormalities in the lateral geniculate nucleus (LGN; the brain structure containing both magno- and parvocellular neurons) in schizophrenia patients [25]. In addition, they argue that perception of both low- and high-frequency information is disrupted in schizophrenia patients [25]; indeed, Harris et al.'s findings seem to indicate that sensitivity to low-spatial-frequency information is reduced and sensitivity to high-spatial-frequency information is exaggerated in untreated schizophrenia [22]. Kantrowicz et al., however, found that subjects with schizophrenia did not differ significantly from control subjects on a task designed to selectively test the parvocellular system [10]. Skottun and Skoyles also explain that the magnocellular pathway does not convey stereopsis information; however, they do allow for the possibility that stereopsis could reflect indirect input from the magnocellular pathway to neurons selective to binocular disparity [25]. It is clear that more research is needed in this area, although Kantrowicz et al. caution that it is difficult to entirely separate out the effects of the magno- and parvocellular pathways, as there is some overlap in their function [10].

CONCLUSION

Schizophrenia is a devastating illness that can impact every facet of an individual's life. While great strides have been made toward determining neurological structures implicated in this disease, more research is needed, as the impact of schizophrenia on the brain is widespread and pervasive. Studying the various neural systems, such as the visual system, that seem to be affected can help add pieces to the puzzle, increasing the store of knowledge and leading us closer to the development of safer and more effective antipsychotic medications. Clearly more research is needed to determine precisely what the stereopsis deficits in schizophrenia might tell us about the disease, but every discovery narrows the gap between what we know and what remains to be found out.

Table 1. A Summary of Studies Investigating Depth Perception Deficits in Schizophrenia

Article	Schizophrenia Patients (SZ)	Other Subjects	Paradigm	Key Results
7	*N* = 25	Healthy controls (HC) = 25	Howard-Dolman Apparatus (HDA)	SZ less accurate at aligning rods; displayed more variability
8	*N* =50	HC = 50	HDA (monocular)	SZ underestimated distance of rod
9	*N* = 22	HC = 22	HAD (affective stimuli)	SZ placed stimuli w/ "higher" affective value further from them
10	*N* = 38	HC = 28	Graded Circles Stereo Test (GCST)	SZ have reduced sensitivity to optical low spatial frequencies illusions

Article	Schizophrenia Patients (SZ)	Other Subjects	Paradigm	Key Results
11	*N* = 13	HC = 16	Binocular Disparity Inversion Index (BDII)	SZ perceive faces as hollow and show bottom-up neural activity
12	*N* = 13	HC = 20; Cannabis-intoxicated (CI) = 7	BDII	SZ and CI were more likely to perceive objects' depth as inverted
13	*N* = 149	HC = 81; Prodromal psychosis (PP) = 22; Major depression (MD) = 35; Bipolar disorder = 20; Alzheimer's = 6	BDII	SZ and groups perceived depth information as inverted; other groups did not
14	*N* = 16	HC = 16; CI = 16; PP = 16	BDII	SZ, PP, and CI perceived depth information as inverted
17	*N* = 20	HC = 15; MD = 10	BDII	Antipsychotic treatment brought SZ performance on the BDII closer to that of HC and MD
18	*N* = 13	HC = 13; CI = 7	BDII	SZ and CI perceived depth information as inverted
19	*N* = 13	C = 51; Alcohol withdrawal (AW) = 10; Sleep deprived (SD) = 10	BDII	SZ, AW, and SD perceived depth information as inverted
20	*N* = 120	Non-psychiatric hospital patients (NHP) = 20	Variety of tasks including HDA	SZ performance on HDA task decreased as chronicity increased; rebounded for most chronic group
21	*N* = 20	Non-SZ psychiatric patients = 19	HDA (large scale)	SZ underestimated distance of marker from them
22	*N* = 8	None	Sinusoidal Gratings	SZ more sensitive to low frequency gratings after receiving neuroleptic
24	*N* =17	HC = 19	GCST	SZ stereopsis thresholds were below adult control norms

References

[1] Reichenberg and P. D. Harvey, *Psychol. Bull.* 133, 833 (2007).

[2] J. Freedman, *Arch. Gen. Psychiatry* 30, 333 (1974).

[3] H. Korn, *Med. Hypotheses* 52, 163 (1999).

[4] H. Korn, *Med. Hypotheses* 52, 539 (1999).

[5] H. Korn, *Med. Hypotheses* 55, 245 (2000).

[6] H. Korn, *Med. Hypotheses* 58, 305 (2002).

[7] A. Broota and G. C. Gupta, *J. Pers. Clin. Stud.* 1, 41 (1985).

[8] H. Kidd, *J. Abnorm.Psychol.* 68, 100 (1964).

[9] S. Nelson and W. E. Caldwell, *J. Gen. Psychol.* 67, 323 (1962).

[10] J. T. Kantrowicz, P. D. Butler, I. Schecter, G. Silipo, and D. C. Javitt, *Schizophrenia Bull.* 35, 1085 (2009).

[11] Dima, J. P. Rosier, D. E. Dietrich, C. Bonnemann, H. Lanfermann, H. M. Emrich, and W. Dillo, *NeuroImage* 46, 1180 (2009).

[12] H. M. Emrich, F. M. Leweke, and U. Schneider, *Pharmacol. Biochem. Behav.* 56, 803 (1997).

[13] Koethe, C. W. Gerth, M. A. Neatby, A. Haensel, M. Thies, U. Schneider, H. M. Emrich, J. Klosterkötter, F. Schultze-Lutter, and F. M. Leweke, *Schizophr. Res.* 88, 142 (2006).

[14] Koethe, L. Kranaster, C. Hoyer, S. Gross, M. A. Neatby, F. Schultze-Lutter, S. Ruhrmann, J. Klosterkötter, M. Hellmich, and F. M. Leweke, *Eur. Arch. Psychiatry Clin. Neurosci.* 259, 195 (2009).

[15] M. Leweke, U. Schneider, M. Radwan, E. Schmidt, and H. M. Emrich, *Pharmacol. Biochem. Behav.* 66, 175 (2000).

[16] T. Passie, M. Karst, M. Borsutzky, H. M. Emrich, and U. Schneider, *J. Psychopharmacol.* 17, 51 (2003).

[17] U. Schneider, M. Borsutzky, J. Seifert, F. M. Leweke, T. J. Huber, J. D. Rollnik, and H. M. Emrich, *Schizophr. Res.* 53, 101 (2002).

[18] U. Schneider, F. M. Leweke, K. R. Mueller-Vahl, and H. M. Emrich, *Pharmacopsychiatry* 31, 110 (1998).

[19] U. Schneider, F. M. Leweke, U. Sternemann, M. M. Weber, and H. M. Emrich, *Eur. Arch. Psychiatry Clin. Neurosci.* 246, 256 (1996).

[20] W. J. Johannsen, S. H. Friedman, and J. V. Liccione, *Br. J. Psychiatry* 467, 561 (1964).

[21] T. E. Weckowicz and R. Hall, *J. Clin. Psychol.* 16, 272 (1960).

[22] J. P. Harris, J. E. Calvert, J. A. Leendertz, and O. T. Phillipson, *Eye*4, 806 (1990).

[23] M. Emrich, *Br. J. Psychiatry* 155, 37 (1989).

[24] Schechter, P. D. Butler, M. Jalbrzikowski, R. Pasternak, A. M. Saperstein, and D. C. Javitt, *Biol. Psychiatry* 60, 1282 (2006).

[25] C. Skottun and J. R. Skoyles, *World J. Biol. Psychiatry* 10, 697 (2009).

In: Schizophrenia Research: Recent Advances
Editor: Tomiki Sumiyoshi
ISBN: 978-1-62808-703-1

Chapter 9

EMOTIONAL STARTLE MODULATION IN MALE PATIENTS WITH RECENT-ONSET SCHIZOPHRENIA

Roelie J. Hempel*[1,2]*, Hugo G. van Steenis*[1]*, Nico J. M. van Beveren*[1]*,
***Christian H. Röder*[1] *and Joke H. M. Tulen*[1]**
[1] Department of Psychiatry,
Erasmus MC, University Medical Center Rotterdam,
Rotterdam, The Netherlands
[2] Department of Psychology, University of Southampton,
Southampton, UK

ABSTRACT

Patients with schizophrenia suffer from both cognitive as well as emotional disturbances, leading to reduced social functioning and quality of life. This study investigated the ongoing emotional states of medicated and antipsychotic-free patients and healthy controls using an emotional startle paradigm. During positive, neutral and negative emotional pictures, aversive acoustic startle stimuli were presented at 4 different probe latencies (300, 800, 1300 and 3800 ms) from picture onset. In both patients and controls, positive pictures, and more specifically erotic pictures, elicited significantly smaller eye blinks compared with startle stimuli presented during neutral and negative pictures. With regard to the subjective ratings, medicated patients rated erotic pictures significantly less pleasant and the adventure, nature, and household pictures as significantly more arousing than healthy control subjects. The present results indicate the need to further investigate emotional responding to specific picture contents, with specific focus on the sexual needs and expectations of schizophrenic patients, so as to eventually improve the quality of life in these patients.

INTRODUCTION

Thus far, an extensive amount of research papers has been published on the impaired emotional functioning in patients with schizophrenia. Most of this research has focused on the impaired ability of these patients to recognize emotions from facial expressions [1], which is crucial for forming and maintaining interpersonal relationships [2, 3], and patients with schizophrenia are known to experience difficulties with social functioning [4-6].

Although patients with schizophrenia seem impaired in their ability to recognize and express emotional facial expressions, they do appear to experience emotions in a way similar to healthy controls. Several studies have found that patients and controls did not differ in their subjective ratings of valence when presented with emotion-eliciting pictures [7-13], although their experienced emotions have been found to differ from non-affected individuals. For example, schizophrenic patients reported that they experienced the same amount of pleasant emotions as healthy controls, but greater amounts of unpleasant emotions in response to emotion-eliciting stimuli [14, 15]. It has also been found that schizophrenic patients experience less positive emotions and more negative emotions in response to daily stressors [16] and emotion-eliciting pictures [17], compared with healthy control subjects. In their review, Kring and Moran [18] summarized that individuals with schizophrenia have a deficit in the expressive component but do not appear to be strongly deficient in the experiential and physiological components of emotion. Thus, previous studies indicate that individuals suffering from schizophrenia are able to correctly identify and classify stimuli, suggesting that previously reported emotional disturbances in patients with schizophrenia are limited to facial stimuli rather than more general emotion-eliciting stimuli.

It is important to accurately identify and interpret emotional meanings from situations in the environment. The idea that emotions serve as survival mechanisms is supported by the fact that emotions are accompanied by physiological reactions, such as changes in the somatic muscles and the viscera. These changes support the behavioral responses to the environmental stimuli [14, 19]. An experimental paradigm has been developed to investigate the ongoing positive and negative emotions of participants during the viewing of emotion-eliciting scenes: the emotional startle modulation paradigm [20, 21]. In this paradigm, different emotion-eliciting pictures are presented to participants on a screen, and occasionally loud startle noises are presented through headphones, to provoke a startle reflex in the participants. The startle reflex is measured by recording the electromyographic activity of the m. orbicularis oculi, the most reliable component of the whole body startle reflex [22].

The underlying theory of this paradigm defines emotions as action dispositions, which organize behavior along a valence dimension ranging from appetitive to aversive emotions [20]. The appetitive (positive) emotions can lead to approach and consummatory behavior, whereas the aversive (negative) emotions can lead to avoidance and defensive behavior. Behavior also includes several reflexes, which can be organized along the valence dimension, such as the salivary response and the startle reflex. If the emotional state and the reflex match in valence (i.e. both appetitive or both aversive), the reflex will be enhanced. Conversely, if there is a mismatch between the emotional state and the reflex, the reflex will be attenuated [20]. In the past two decades, this theory has received substantial support from numerous studies that investigated the effects of emotional picture viewing on the intensity of the startle eyeblink response: the startle reflex is reduced while viewing arousing pleasant slides, and enhanced while viewing arousing unpleasant slides [23]. Besides the valence dimension, the arousal dimension is also an important factor for emotional startle modulation to occur: startle potentiation occurs most reliably when unpleasant pictures are highly arousing [24, 25].

The magnitude of the startle response is modulated both by attention as well as emotion, depending on the duration between picture onset and startle onset. If the startle stimulus is presented early during the viewing of emotional pictures (300 to 500 ms; [21, 26], the startle response is influenced by attentional information processing: both pleasant and unpleasant pictures elicit smaller eyeblink responses compared with neutral pictures. This effect is explained by the attentional interpretation of prepulse inhibition: highly arousing pictures are more interesting and more complex than neutral pictures, resulting in longer periods of processing protection compared with less interesting pictures. Reflexes elicited around 800 ms were generally inhibited compared with neutral pictures, but they were sensitive to the affective contents of the pictures since differences in startle magnitude were found between pleasant and unpleasant pictures. At longer latency intervals (from 1300 ms till slide offset), the effects of stimulus content were more pronounced: negative pictures elicited larger eyeblink responses, and positive pictures elicited smaller responses compared with neutral pictures [26]. Bradley et al. [24] investigated whether specific picture contents elicited different startle response magnitudes. They found that negative pictures with animal threat, human threat, and contamination elicited the largest eyeblink responses. For the pleasant pictures, erotica (couples and opposite sex nudes) elicited the smallest blink reflexes. Finally, household objects were found to elicit neither inhibited nor potentiated startle, and thus can be considered most neutral. Thus, from a survival perspective, the two most relevant picture contents elicited the most pronounced responses: pictures signaling threat elicit the largest eyeblink responses, and pictures with erotic scenes elicit the smallest responses.

Five previous studies have been conducted thus far that have investigated the emotional startle responses in patients with schizophrenia. In the first study [8], the eyeblink responses of patients with schizophrenia to negative pictures were not potentiated, whereas healthy control subjects did show startle potentiation, and this difference was significant. Curtis et al. [17] did not find any differences between patients with schizophrenia, their first-degree relatives and healthy control subjects with regard to eyeblink responses during the viewing of emotion-eliciting pictures. Volz et al. [10] investigated the temporal course of emotional startle modulation in these patients. Following the study of Bradley et al. [26], startle stimuli were presented at varying intervals (150, 300, 800, 1300, and 3800 ms) during the viewing of emotion-eliciting pictures. Patients with schizophrenia and healthy controls did not differ in their startle responses when the startle stimulus was presented 3800 ms after picture onset. However, when the startle stimulus was presented earlier during picture viewing, patients did not show startle potentiation to unpleasant pictures, whereas the controls showed startle potentiation as early as 300 ms. For the pleasant and neutral pictures no differences between groups were found. The authors [10] concluded that patients with schizophrenia need more time than healthy control subjects to process the aversive information from unpleasant pictures, leading to a delay in the activation of the defense system. Yee et al. [13] did not find any differences in eyeblink responding to emotion-eliciting pictures between healthy controls and prodromal, first-episode, or chronic patients with schizophrenia. Finally, Kring et al. [12]found that patients with schizophrenia showed a similar startle pattern to emotion-eliciting stimuli as healthy control subjects during picture presentation. Controls also demonstrated this pattern shortly after pictures were removed from view, whereas patients did not. So, while the motivational system stayed engaged in the control group, possibly to help guide future behavioral responses, this was not the case in the patient group.

Summarizing, previous studies have demonstrated that individuals with schizophrenia report similar subjective responses and show similar eyeblink responses to emotion-eliciting pictures as healthy control subjects, indicating that their underlying motivational systems appear to be intact, at least when directly confronted with an emotional stimulus. However, except for Yee et al. [13], these studies only investigated the emotional responses of these patients to general picture types of positive, neutral, and negative pictures, whereas specific picture contents might be able to inform us about more specific underlying motivations to certain themes shown in these pictures. In addition, except for the study by Curtis et al. [17], none of these studies have compared the responses of patients with and without antipsychotic medication, while it has previously been shown that antipsychotics can modify physiological and subjective responding to emotion-eliciting stimuli in patients with schizophrenia [27].

The aim of the present study was to broaden our knowledge about the underlying motivations of patients with schizophrenia while viewing topic-specific emotion-eliciting pictures using startle eyeblink responses, whilst taking medication use into account. During the viewing of emotion-eliciting pictures, startle stimuli were presented at varying startle latencies from picture onset (300, 800, 1300 and 3800 ms) while eyeblink responses were measured, to allow us to investigate the temporal time course of emotional responding in this patient group. Based on previous research, we expected that individuals with schizophrenia and healthy control subjects would exhibit comparable reports of experienced subjective ratings and startle eyeblink responses when we would analyse the responses using general picture types, while the responses to topic-specific picture contents would be able to inform us more precisely about the underlying motivations of patients with schizophrenia. Because of the potential importance of antipsychotic medication use on psychophysiological responses, we analyzed our data separately for medicated and antipsychotic-free patients.

METHODS

Subjects

In this study, 33 male patients with schizophrenia (9 antipsychotic-free, 24 medicated) and 40 male control subjects participated. The patients were recruited from the early psychosis unit at the department of Psychiatry of Erasmus MC, University Medical Center Rotterdam. All patients were screened by a senior clinical psychiatrist using the Comprehensive Assessment of Symptoms and History (CASH) [28], and included in the study if they were diagnosed as suffering from schizophrenia according to the criteria of the DSM-IV [29]. All patients experienced a psychotic episode at the time of the study. All patients were inpatients and most of them were experiencing their first psychotic episode or were receiving treatment for the first time. In order to assess symptom severity, the Dutch translation of the Positive and Negative Syndrome Scale (PANSS) [30] was used. Antipsychotic treatment was administered according to the clinical treatment protocol of the Erasmus MC clinic for psychotic disorders, which is congruent with both the schizophrenia treatment guidelines of the Dutch Psychiatric Association and the American Psychiatric Association.

Controls were recruited by means of advertisements. All controls were healthy and drug-free at the time of testing as assessed by means of a short phone interview and a structured questionnaire. None of the controls or their first-degree relatives had experienced past or current psychiatric illnesses. Exclusion criteria for both patients and controls were respiratory and cardiovascular diseases, and we also excluded controls who indicated that they were using any type of medication that could influence the autonomic nervous system

After the subjects were given a complete description of the study, written informed consent was obtained. The study was approved by the Medical Ethics Committee of the Erasmus MC, University Medical Center Rotterdam, and was carried out in accordance with the Declaration of Helsinki.

Procedure

All experimental sessions took place between 09.00 and 11.00 hrs in the morning. The subject sat in a comfortable chair in a small, sound-attenuated dimly lit room. Both patients and controls were asked not to use any coffee or cigarettes before and during testing the day of the experimental session. Before the application of the electrodes participants were asked to complete a shortened version of the Dutch Profile of Mood States (POMS) [31]. Electrodes for the recordings of the startle eyeblink were applied according to standard laboratory procedures. After the application of the electrodes, the experimental session began with a rest period of five minutes in which subjects were asked to relax and not to speak. After this first rest period the headphones were put on, and the startle task was explained. The duration of the startle task was approximately 25 minutes. After completion of the task, all electrodes were removed from the subjects and they were asked to do the subjective rating task, which lasted approximately 15 minutes. All tasks were designed using E-prime (Psychology Software Tools, Inc., 2002).

Experimental tasks

Startle Task

Subjects were seated approximately 75 cm from the computer screen. All subjects were asked to relax, to breathe regularly and not to speak during the task. They were informed that they first would be hearing five loud noises through the headphones, but that they did not have to respond. These first five startle stimuli were presented to the subjects to allow them to get accustomed to these sounds and to decrease the impact of habituation effects during the experiment. The startle stimulus was a discrete white noise burst of 100 dB during 50 ms, with an instantaneous rise and fall time. The startle stimuli were presented binaurally through Sennheiser HD 265 linear headphones. The sound intensity of the startle stimulus was checked every week using a sound level meter to make sure that the startle stimulus was 100 dB for every participant.

After the first 5 startles, they were told that they were about to view a series of pictures, and that loud noises were occasionally presented through the headphones. They were asked to look at the pictures the entire time they were presented on the screen, but that they did not have to respond. Forty-eight pictures were selected from the IAPS [32]. The stimuli were chosen on the basis of their normative ratings provided with the IAPS, and could be divided into six different categories, based on their contents[1]. The positive pictures had erotic and adventure contents, the neutral pictures showed nature scenes and household objects, and the negative pictures contained pictures with mutilation and threat contents. The pictures were presented using a Dell Dimension M200a Personal Computer with a Pentium processor and a 17-inch Samsung SyncMaster monitor.

Each picture was presented for 6 seconds, with an inter-trial interval (ITI) ranging from 12-25 seconds. A total of 48 pictures were presented; during 12 of these pictures (4 positive, 4 neutral and 4 negative) no startle stimulus was presented. During the remaining 36 pictures, startle stimuli were presented either 300, 800, 1300 or 3800 ms after picture onset in such a way that each of these latency conditions occurred 3 times during the viewing of positive, neutral and negative pictures. In addition, 12 startle stimuli were randomly presented during the ITI's. Thus, a total of 48 pictures and 48 startle stimuli were presented. All pictures and startle stimuli were presented completely at random so that each subject was presented with a different order of stimuli.

Subjective Rating Task

The 48 pictures that were presented during the startle task were again presented in the subjective rating task, using a randomized order different from that of the startle task. The participants were asked to rate how they felt during the viewing of the pictures. They responded with their dominant hand using the numbers on the keyboard. A fixation cross was presented for 3 seconds on a 17-inch computer screen, followed by a 6-second presentation of a picture. After picture offset, the subjects were asked to rate each picture using the SAM (Self-Assessment Manikin; [33]. The SAM consisted of two subsequent screens, each containing five figures. On the first screen, the figures represented the degree of pleasantness of the pictures -ranging from very unpleasant to very pleasant- on a scale from 1 to 9. On the second screen, each figure represented the degree of arousal associated with each picture -ranging from very calm to very arousing- again on a scale from 1 to 9. After their response, the fixation cross appeared again for 3 seconds, followed by the next picture.

Psychophysiological Measurements

During the experiment, continuous measurements were made of electromyographic (EMG) activity. All data were sampled and stored on a flashcard by means of a portable digital recorder (Vitaport™ System; TEMEC Instruments B.V., Kerkrade, the Netherlands). Upon completion of the recording, all physiological data were imported and processed on a Personal Computer using a Vitascore™ software module (TEMEC Instruments BV, Kerkrade, the Netherlands).

---

[1] Positive IAPS pictures: 4220, 4290, 4608, 4660, 4670, 4680, 5260, 5470, 5621, 5910, 8030, 8170, 8490, 8501. Neutral IAPS pictures: 5120, 5260, 5510, 5530, 5535, 5711, 5731, 5740, 5900, 7000, 7002, 7004, 7006, 7009, 7010, 7020, 7025. Negative IAPS pictures: 3000, 3010, 3060, 3069, 3080, 3102, 3120, 3170, 6200, 6212, 6230, 6260, 6300, 6313, 6350, 6550.

Startle Eyeblink Responses

The EMG activity of the m. orbicularis oculi was measured using two Ag/AgCl cup electrodes filled with electrolyte paste (Spectra® 360; Parker Laboratories, Inc.). One electrode was placed in line with the pupil of the left eye over the skin above the m. orbicularis oculi when the subject was looking straight ahead, and the second electrode was placed 1 cm lateral to the first. A third electrode was attached to the forehead, serving as an isolated ground electrode.

The EMG data was sampled at 1024 Hz. First, a zero-phase bandpass finite impulse response (FIR-) filter with $\cos^2$-slopes was applied to the EMG-signal. The -6dB cutoff frequencies of the passband were defined at 28Hz and 500Hz [34], with a steepness at both slopes better than -20dB per octave. Subsequently, a Hilbert transform was applied to the signal, in order to calculate the envelope of the original signal. This signal conditioning technique does not require rectification of the signal and therefore does not affect the original values of the signal [35]. Finally, a lowpass filter of 40 Hz was applied.

The EMG-recording of each participant was examined visually for possible baseline contaminations (e.g., noise, movement artifacts) and spontaneous or voluntary blinks before the onset of the startle stimulus. In the case of artifacts, the blink response could not be accurately quantified for that particular trial, resulting in trial-rejection.

The baseline value of each individual eyeblink response was calculated as the mean voltage of the signal 50 ms before startle stimulus onset. Response onset was defined as the time point within 20-100 ms after startle onset at which the EMG signal exceeded two standard deviations above baseline value [22], searched from right to left in time, i.e. from peak back to startle onset, to avoid 'accidental/premature onsets'. Relative amplitude was computed as the difference between the peak and the baseline value of each response. If a peak did not exceed an amount of two standard deviations above baseline, the response was scored as zero. If the peak was detected outside the 20-150 ms scoring window, the response was scored as missing and excluded from further analyses. In case of multiple peaks within the 20-150 ms scoring window, the peak with the highest value was determined as response peak. Participants who did not show valid eyeblinks in more than 33% of the trials were excluded from further analysis [10, 36].

Statistical Analyses

All analyses were conducted using SPSS version 13.0 and MlWin 2.10 [37]. All alpha's were set at 0.05 unless otherwise specified.

Participant Demographics

We investigated whether the groups differed in age, smoking, symptom scores, and duration of illness by using Analyses of Variance (ANOVA), chi-square test, t-test, or non-parametric Mann-Whitney Test where appropriate. In case of unequal variances we used the corrected degrees of freedom to determine the level of significance.

Profile of Mood States (POMS)

To assess whether there were any differences in mood scores between the three groups (medicated, antipsychotic-free and controls), we used separate ANOVAs per subscale and for the total scale, which were followed up by Bonferroni-corrected post-hoc tests. The maximum scores for each of the scales were as follows: depression 32; fatigue 24; tension 24; anger 28; vigour 20. The total score was calculated by subtracting the vigour score from the sum of all the other scores (i.e. depression + fatigue + tension + anger – vigour = total), so that a higher score represented a more negative mood state.

Startle Eyeblink Responses

Because the Kolmogorov-Smirnov tests indicated that the data was not normally distributed, we normalized the EMG data using the natural logarithm. Two hierarchical linear models (HLM) were developed: one to examine the eyeblink responses to general picture types (Picture Type: positive, neutral, negative) and one to examine the eyeblink responses to specific picture contents (Picture Content: erotic, adventure, household, nature, mutilation, attack).

We entered Subject, Time, and Picture Type (for the 3 types) or Picture Content (for the 6 types) as repeated variables in the two HLM models. The following fixed variables were entered: Group (antipsychotic-free, medicated, and control), Time (300, 800, 1300 and 3800 msec) as a linear polynomial, Picture Type or Picture Content, Group x Time, Group x Picture Type/Content, Time x Picture Type/Content, and Group x Time x Picture Type/Content. The following covariates were entered: smoking (yes/no), age, illness duration (months), antipsychotic medication duration (weeks), and the total score on the Profile of Mood States (POMS; where a higher score indicates a more negative mood state). We started with a fully saturated model containing all factors and covariates, after which the best fit for the model was sought using the log likelihood method.

Subjective Ratings

Since the Kolmogorov-Smirnov tests indicated that the distributions of the SAM rating of pleasure and arousal were normally distributed within the groups (p-values ranged from 0.13 to 1.00), we performed two repeated measures ANOVA's with Pleasure or Arousal rating as the dependent variable, Group (medicated, antipsychotic-free and controls) as the between subjects factor, and Picture Type (for 3 types) or Picture Content (for 6 types) as the within subjects factor. In case of a significant interaction effect, we followed this up with separate ANOVAs.

RESULTS

Participant Demographics

Five patients and one control subject did not show eyeblinks in 33% of the trials, and data from these participants was excluded from further analyses. The five patients that were excluded did not differ in age, PANSS scores, POMS scores or medication use from the patients that were included in the present analysis. Table 1 presents the demographic data of the remaining 28 patients (8 antipsychotic-free, 20 medicated) and 39 control subjects while Table 2 presents the medication use of the remaining patients.

Table 1. Demographic characteristics of the patient and control groups

		Medicated patients (n=20)	*Antipsychotic-free patients (n=8)*	*Controls (n=39)*
Age (mean ± sd)		22 ± 7	21 ± 4	23 ± 4
Smokers (Yes/No)[a]		17/3	6/2	8/31
Duration of illness (months ± sd)		15 ± 19	3 ± 3	
Duration of current medication use (weeks ± sd)		4 ± 5		
PANSS[b] (mean ± sd)	Positive symptoms	17 ± 6	23 ± 7	
	Negative symptoms	15 ± 5	20 ± 5	
	General psychopathology	33 ± 9	44 ± 13	
	Total	64 ± 17	87 ± 15	

PANSS = Positive and Negative Syndrome Scale; sd = standard deviation

[a] There were significantly more smokers in both patient groups than in the control group ($\chi^2_{(2)} = 25.31$, $p < 0.001$)

[b] Antipsychotic-free patients had higher PANSS scores for all subscales than medicated patients (positive: $F[1,25] = 4.43$, $p < 0.05$; negative $F[1,25] = 6.35$, $p < 0.05$; general psychopathology $F[1,25] = 5.53$, $p < 0.05$; total score $F[1,25] = 10.35$, $p < 0.01$).

Table 2. Mean dosages and duration of current antipsychotic and benzodiazepine treatment

Antipsychotic	n	Mean dosage (mg) ± sd	Co-medication
No Antipsychotic	8		Lorazepam (n = 2)
Olanzapine	8	16.3 ± 6.9	Lorazepam (n = 2) Oxazepam (n = 1)
Risperidone	4	3.0 ± 0.7	Lorazepam (n = 1) Oxazepam (n = 1)
Haloperidol	4	2.8 ± 1.5	Lorazepam (n = 2)
Clozapine	3	300.0 ± 100.0	Lorazepam (n = 2)
Quetiapine	1	600.0	n/a

sd = standard deviation.

As can be seen in Table 1, there were significantly more smokers in both patient groups than in the control group ($\chi^2 = 29.71$, $p < 0.001$). With regard to symptom severity, antipsychotic-free patients had higher scores for all subscales and the total score of the PANSS than medicated patients (positive: $F[1,25] = 4.43$, $p < 0.05$; negative $F[1,25] = 6.35$, $p < 0.05$; general psychopathology $F[1,25] = 5.53$, $p < 0.05$; total score $F[1,25] = 10.35$, $p < 0.01$). The duration of illness seemed shorter in medicated versus antipsychotic-free patients, but due to the large standard deviations this was not a significant difference (Mann-Whitney $U = 47$, $p = 0.09$).

Profile of Mood States (POMS)

The POMS-scores of the three groups are reported in Table 3. The medicated and antipsychotic-free patients did not differ significantly in their mood scores for any of the subscales or the total score. However, the patients did significantly differ from the controls with regard to their mood scores (Depression F[2,64] = 12.51; Fatigue F[2,64] = 6.70; Tension F[2,64] = 13.85; Anger F[2,64] = 1.59; Vigor F[2,64] = 3.83; Total score F[2,64] = 14.63; all *p*s smaller than 0.05). Post-hoc tests indicated that the antipsychotic-free patients showed significantly decreased mood on all subscales and the total score, while the medicated patients had significantly decreased mood scores on all scales except the vigor subscale.

Table 3. Profile of Mood scores for medicated and antipsychotic-free patients and control subjects

		Medicated Patients (n=20)	Antipschotic-free Patients (n=8)	Controls (n=39)
POMS mean ± sd	Depression[a]	7.2 ± 7.4	7.6 ± 9.5	0.8 ± 1.6
	Fatigue[a]	6.3 ± 6.0	7.9 ± 5.5	2.9 ± 2.8
	Tension[a]	6.2 ± 4.7	5.8 ± 3.8	1.7 ± 2.2
	Anger[a]	4.5 ± 4.5	6.6 ± 5.6	1.3 ± 2.2
	Vigor[b]	10.6 ± 4.5	7.8 ± 4.9	11.8 ± 3.3
	Total[a]	11.7 ± 20.8	20.1 ± 23.0	-5.0 ± 7.2

sd = standard deviation;
[a] Significant difference between control subjects and both patient groups, $p < 0.05$
[b] Significant difference between control subjects and antipsychotic-free patients, $p < 0.05$.

General Picture Types

Eyeblink Responses

The following factors did not contribute significantly to the model and were therefore removed: the three-way interaction between Group x Time x Picture Type, the two-way interactions of Group x Picture Type, Group x Time, and Picture Type x Time, and the covariates Age, and Smoking.

As can be seen in Table 4 and Figures 1a-c, the main effect of Group (joint $\chi^2_{(1)} = 45.05$, $p < 0.001$) indicated that antipsychotic-free patients showed overall smaller eyeblink responses compared to medicated patients and healthy controls. The main effect for Time was also significant, indicating that eyeblink responses increased with increasing startle latency ($Z = 2.65$, $p < 0.01$). Finally, the main effect for Picture Type was also significant (joint $\chi^2_{(1)} = 7.61$, $p < 0.01$), indicating that the eyeblink responses to positive pictures were smaller than to neutral and negative pictures. With regard to the covariates, the significant effect for Duration of Medication use indicated that the longer a person received antipsychotic medication, the smaller their eyeblink responses, while the significant effect for Duration of Illness indicated that the longer a person was suffering from schizophrenia, the larger their startle eyeblink responses. Current mood also had a significant effect on eyeblink responses: higher POMS (i.e. more negative mood) scores were related to smaller eyeblinks.

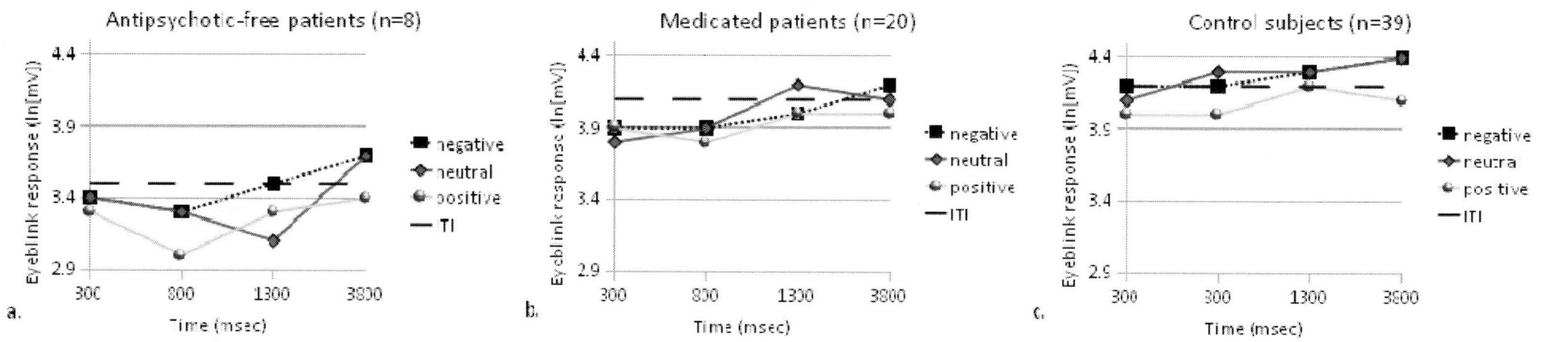

Figures 1 (a-c). Time series of the eyeblink responses to negative, neutral and positive picture stimuli in (a) antipychotic-free patients; (b) medicated patients; and (c) healthy control participants at 4 different startle latencies during picture presentation. Please note: ‘ITI’ refers to Inter-Trial Interval, i.e. the eyeblink responses to startle stimuli presented in between pictures.

Table 4. Beta coefficients of the HLM for eyeblink responses (ln[mV]) to positive, neutral, and negative pictures in antipsychotic-free patients, medicated patients, and healthy control subjects

Factor	Comparison	Beta coefficient	Standard error	**Z-score***
Constant		4.23	0.07	**65.12**
Group	AF vs C	-0.78	0.12	**-6.40**
	M vs C	-0.04	0.11	-0.36
	M vs AF	0.74	0.13	**5.76**
Picture Type	Neg vs Neu	0.01	0.08	0.16
	Pos vs Neu	-0.15	0.08	-1.81
	Pos vs Neg	-0.16	0.08	**-1.98**
Time[1]		0.18	0.07	**2.65**
Duration of illness (months)		0.01	0.004	**2.25**
Duration of medication use (weeks)		-0.06	0.02	**-4.00**
POMS total score		-0.004	0.002	**-2.00**

* Numbers expressed in bold indicate significant effects at the 0.05 level.
AF = Antipsychotic-free patients (n = 8); C = Control (n = 39); M = Medicated patients (n = 20).
Neg = negative pictures; Neu = neutral pictures; Pos = positive pictures.

Subjective Ratings

The mean SAM ratings for pleasure and arousal are presented in Figures 2a and b. For the pleasure ratings, we found a significant main effect for Picture Type ($F[1.7;111.0] = 32.85$, $p < 0.001$, partial $\eta^2 = 0.34$). Post-hoc comparisons showed that the positive pictures were rated as most pleasant, followed by the neutral pictures, while the negative pictures were rated as least pleasant (all ps < 0.001). No significant main or interaction effects for Group were found.

For the arousal ratings only the interaction effect between Picture Type and Group was significant ($F[1.6; 102.7] = 6.41$, $p < 0,01$, partial $\eta^2 = 0.09$). Follow-up ANOVAs showed that groups differed in their arousal ratings of neutral scenes ($F[2,64] = 6.25$, $p < 0.01$), and post-hoc comparisons showed that the medicated patients rated these scenes as more arousing than the control subjects.

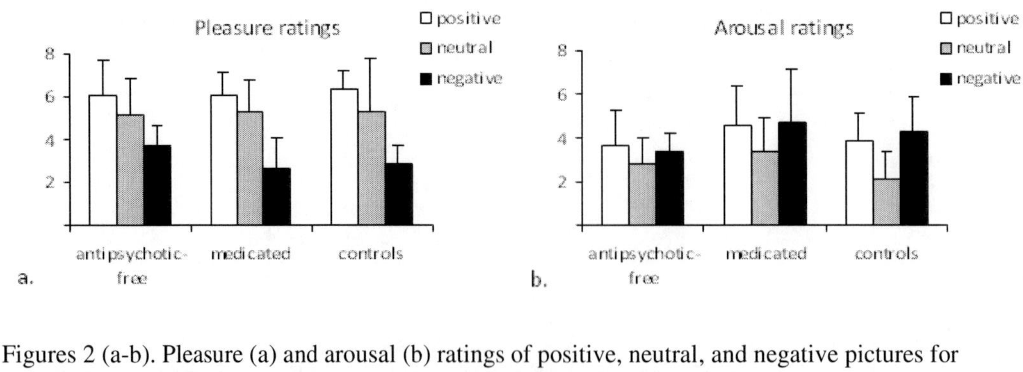

Figures 2 (a-b). Pleasure (a) and arousal (b) ratings of positive, neutral, and negative pictures for antipsychotic-free patients, medicated patients, and healthy control subjects.

Specific Picture types

Eyeblink Responses

The following factors did not contribute significantly to the model and were therefore removed: the three-way interaction between Group x Time x Picture Type, the two-way interactions of Group x Picture Type, Group x Time, and Picture Type x Time, and the covariate Age.

As can be seen in Table 5 and Figures 3a-f, the main effect of Group ($\chi^2_{(2)} = 54.35$, $p < 0.001$) indicated that antipsychotic-free patients showed overall smaller eyeblink responses compared to medicated patients and healthy controls. Similar to the previous analysis, the main effect for Time was significant, indicating that eyeblink responses increased with increasing startle latency ($Z = 3.15$, $p < 0.01$). There was also a main effect for Picture Type (($\chi^2_{(2)} = 19.41$, $p < 0.001$) indicating that the eyeblink responses to the erotic pictures were significantly smaller than to any of the other picture types.

With regard to the covariates, the significant effect for Smoking indicated that people who smoked had generally smaller eyeblink responses. The significant effect for Duration of Medication use indicated that the longer a person received antipsychotic medication, the smaller their eyeblink responses, while the significant effect for Duration of Illness indicated that the longer a person was suffering from schizophrenia, the larger their startle eyeblink responses. Current mood also had a significant effect on eyeblink responses: higher POMS (i.e. more negative mood) scores were related to smaller eyeblinks.

Subjective Ratings

The mean SAM ratings for pleasure and arousal are presented in Figures 4a and 4b. For the pleasure ratings, we found a significant main effect for Picture Content ($F[3.0;194.7] = 25.90$, $p < 0.001$, partial $\eta^2 = 0.29$). Post-hoc comparisons showed that all picture contents received different pleasure ratings, except for the erotic and nature pictures, which were not rated differently from each other. The interaction effect between Picture Content and Group was also significant ($F[3.0;194.7] = 3.75$, $p < 0.05$, partial $\eta^2 = 0.06$), indicating that the groups rated the pictures slightly different. Follow-up ANOVAs showed that the groups differed in their ratings of pictures displaying erotica ($F[2,64) = 5.51$, $p < 0.01$), attack ($F[2,64) = 3.70$, $p < 0.05$), and mutilation scenes ($F[2,64) = 3.19$, $p < 0.05$). Post-hoc comparisons further revealed that medicated patients rated erotic pictures as significantly less pleasant than the controls, while antipsychotic-free patients rated the mutilation pictures significantly less unpleasant than the controls. Finally, there was a trend for medicated patients to rate attack pictures as less pleasant compared to the controls and antipsychotic-free patients.

For the arousal ratings only the interaction effect between Picture Content and Group was significant ($F[2.8; 182.5] = 7.90$, $p < 0.001$, partial $\eta^2 = 0.11$). Follow-up ANOVAs showed that the groups differed in their ratings of pictures displaying adventure ($F[2,64) = 5.27$, $p < 0.01$), household ($F[2,64) = 6.83$, $p < 0.01$), and nature scenes ($F[2,64) = 5.37$, $p < 0.01$). Post-hoc comparisons indicated that the medicated patients rated these scenes significantly more arousing than control subjects.

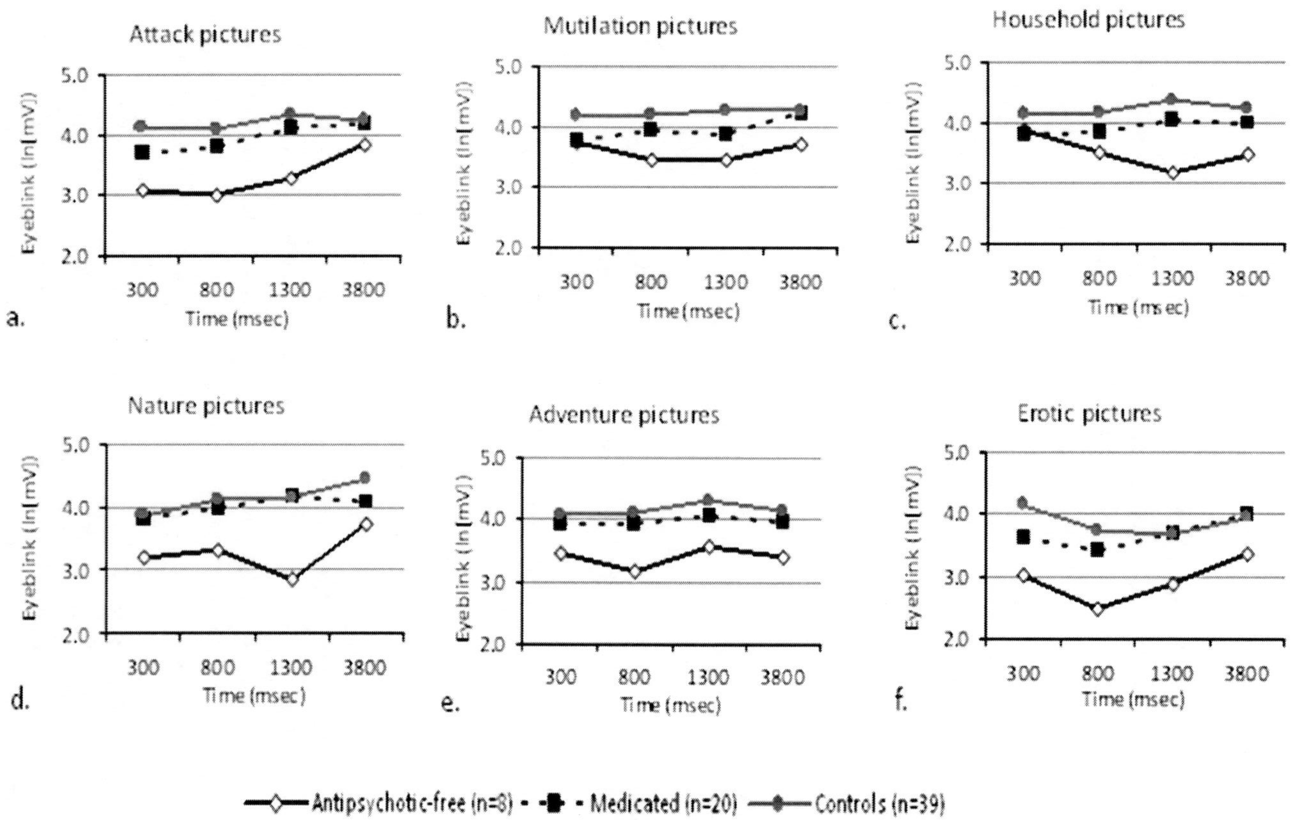

Figure 3 (a-f). Mean eyeblink responses of antipsychotic-free patients, medicated patients, healthy control participants at 4 different startle latencies (300, 800, 1300, and 3800 ms) during the presentation of (a) attack, (b), mutilation, (c) household, (d) nature, (e) adventure, and (f) erotic pictures.

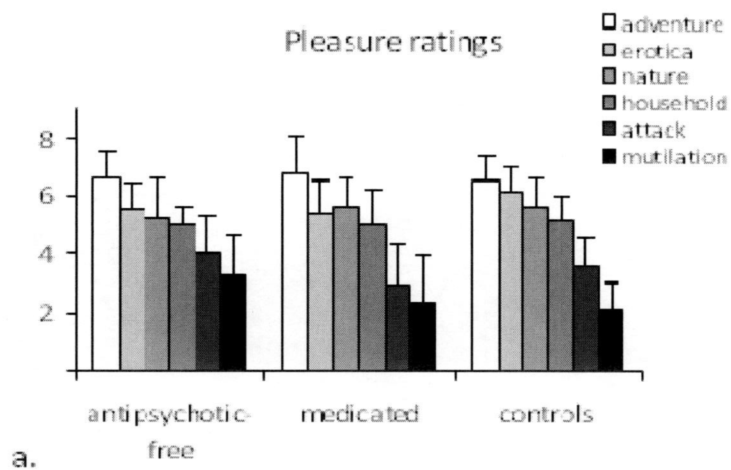

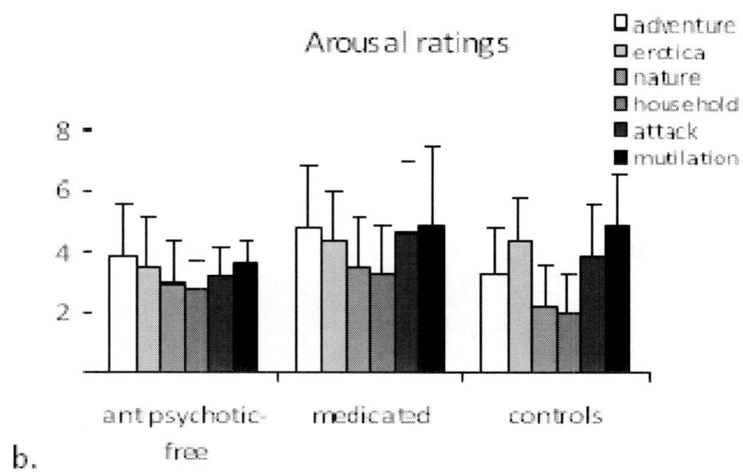

Figures 4 (a-b). Pleasure (a) and arousal (b) ratings of stimuli with specific picture contents for antipsychotic-free patients, medicated patients, and healthy control subjects.

Table 5. Beta coefficients of the HLM for eyeblink responses (ln[mV]) to emotion-eliciting pictures with specific contents in antipsychotic-free patients, medicated patients, and healthy control subjects

Factor	Comparison	Beta coefficient	Standard error	**Z-score***
Constant		4.19	0.07	**59.90**
Group	AF vs C	-0.63	0.10	**-6.08**
	M vs C	0.10	0.09	1.09
	M vs AF	0.73	0.10	**7.13**
Time[1]		0.17	0.05	**3.15**
Picture Type	Mutilation vs Attack	0.06	0.09	0.60
	Household vs Attack	0.03	0.09	0.32
	Nature vs Attack	0.01	0.09	0.08
	Adventure vs Attack	-0.01	0.09	-0.09
	Erotica vs Attack	-0.32	0.10	**-3.33**
	Household vs Mutilation	-0.03	0.09	-0.30
	Nature vs Mutilation	-0.05	0.09	-0.54
	Adventure vs Mutilation	-0.06	0.09	-0.69
	Erotica vs Mutilation	-0.38	0.10	**-3.91**
	Nature vs Household	-0.02	0.09	-0.24
	Adventure vs Household	-0.04	0.09	-0.40
	Erotica vs Household	-0.35	0.10	**-3.66**
	Adventure vs Nature	-0.01	0.09	-0.15
	Erotica vs Nature	-0.33	0.10	**-3.40**
	Erotica vs Adventure	-0.31	0.10	**-3.28**
Smoking		-0.20	0.07	**-2.88**
Duration of illness (months)		0.01	0.00	**3.67**
Duration of medication use (weeks)		-0.07	0.01	**-5.42**
POMS total score		-0.004	0.002	**-2.00**

* Numbers expressed in **bold** indicate significant effects at the 0.05 level.
AF = Antipsychotic-free patients (n = 8); C = Control (n = 39); M = Medicated patients (n = 20).

DISCUSSION

The aim of this study was to investigate whether male patients with schizophrenia differed from healthy control subjects in their startle eyeblink responses to emotion-eliciting pictures. A distinction was made between patients who were taking antipsychotic medication and patients who were not, because the demographic information indicated that these two groups differed significantly in terms of symptom severity and illness duration, and because antipsychotic medication is known for its ability to alter emotional responding [27].

We found that the antipsychotic-free patient group generally showed significantly smaller eyeblink responses than the control group. The overall decreased startle responses are most likely due to a generally decreased amount of attentional resources, in line with the existing literature on attentional deficits in these patients [38-40]. It should be noted, however, that there were no significant differences between patients with and without antipsychotic medication in terms of emotional startle modulation, a finding that is in line with Curtis et al. [17].

Across groups and analyses, we found that the eyeblink responses increased with increasing startle latency, in line with the attentional component of this paradigm [26]. We also found that the positive pictures, and more specifically the erotic pictures, elicited smaller eyeblink responses than neutral or negative pictures.

Eyeblink Responses

When the eyeblink responses to both the general and specific picture categories were analyzed, no differences between patients with schizophrenia, either on or off antipsychotic medication, and controls, were found. This finding is consistent with previous studies conducted in this field, which have generally shown comparable startle patterns in patients with schizophrenia compared with healthy control subjects [8, 10, 12, 13, 17]. Across all groups, positive pictures elicited smaller eyeblink responses than neutral and negative pictures. However, in contrast to previous studies, the negative pictures did not elicit startle potentiation, despite subjective ratings indicating that the negative pictures were experienced as unpleasant and more arousing than neutral pictures. Arousal has been found to be an important factor in the emotional modulation of eyeblink reflexes: Bradley et al. [24, 25] previously found that negative pictures rated low in arousal did not elicit startle potentiation reliably. The Self-Assessment Manikin [33] used in the present study had a rating scale ranging from 1 to 9, while the overall mean ratings from our subject samples did not exceed 5, which is considered 'moderately arousing'. Thus, it is possible that the pictures viewed passively in our experiment did not provoke the level of arousal necessary to modulate the startle response effectively. The arousal ratings found in our study were lower than what we would have expected based on the IAPS manual, from which the stimuli were selected. This finding is in line with a study by Libkuman et al. [41], who have also found lower arousal ratings to IAPS stimuli in their sample compared to the reported arousal ratings in the IAPS manual. One explanation they offer for this finding is that by now individuals have been exposed to this type of material in the media so frequently that people have habituated to shocking images of threat and mutilations. On the other hand, the positive pictures, and in particular the erotic stimuli, did elicit the expected startle inhibition despite the relatively low arousal scores. An alternative explanation may be that the subjects were already in a more negative state caused by the experimental procedures (i.e. loud noises and aversive pictures), and only the positive pictures were able to bring the subjects into a positive motivational state.

Subjective Ratings

With regard to the general picture types, there were no differences in valence ratings between the three groups, a finding that was consistent with previous studies [8, 10-13, 42, 43]. However, compared with healthy controls, the medicated patients rated the neutral pictures as more arousing. When we investigated valence ratings to the specific picture contents, we found that medicated patients rated the erotic pictures as significantly less pleasant than controls, while antipsychotic-free patients rated the mutilation pictures as significantly less unpleasant than controls. When analyzing the arousal ratings, we found that medicated patients rated nature, household, and adventure pictures more arousing than healthy control subjects. Previous studies investigating arousal ratings have found mixed results. While at least 3 previous studies [8, 10, 13] did not find any differences in arousal ratings, Kring et al. [12] found that patients with schizophrenia reported generally decreased arousal ratings, while Aminoff et al. [11] reported decreased arousal ratings in patients while viewing aversive pictures. However, none of these studies have focused on specific picture contents; a method that could be used to explore the nature of emotional responding in these patients in more depth. Below we offer some possible explanations about our findings.

Erotic Pictures

The present study found that medicated patients with schizophrenia rated erotic pictures as less pleasant than healthy control subjects. The patients in our study were all young male adults. We did not ask our patients about their sexual functioning or sexual needs, but previous studies have found that the social function needs of patients with schizophrenia are similar to those of healthy individuals, including social relationships, intimacy and sexual function [44-46]. Bengtsson-Tops and Hansson [44] found that, although having social relations is one of the five most important needs of schizophrenic patients, it is also one of the most often unmet needs, as was having intimate relationships. Thus, the decreased pleasure ratings in response to erotic pictures with may reflect a feeling of unmet sexual needs or expectations, eliciting a response suggestive of a more neutral or even negative feeling. Possibly, the erotic pictures did not only represent sexual behaviors, but also social and intimate relationships in a much broader sense. Having a serious mental illness can have severe consequences for the kind of lives the patients were used to before the onset of the illness. Indeed, several studies have found that persons with schizophrenia often experience feelings of hopelessness, and they may expect failure in the future and feel that they no longer can affect the course of their lives [47]. This explanation would also be in line with their reported deficit in 'anticipatory pleasure' [48, 49], i.e., the inability to anticipate that future events will be pleasurable as well as the ability to experience pleasure in anticipation of things to come.

An alternative and more straightforward explanation may be the loss of sexual interest due to the use of antipsychotic medication. Olfson et al. [50] found that 45.3% of the investigated 139 medicated male schizophrenic patients, receiving either haloperidol, olanzapine, risperidone or quetiapine, experienced sexual dysfunction. This group reported significantly lower ratings of quality of life and level of enjoyment of their life. However, the responses of the medicated patients did not differ significantly from those of the antipsychotic-free patients, suggesting that medication status alone does not explain the decreased pleasure ratings in response to erotic pictures. The quality of life of psychiatric patients is an important issue, and further research on the social and sexual needs and expectations of these patients may aid in the improvement of the quality of life of these patients.

Increased Arousal Ratings

Medicated patients rated adventure, nature, and household scenes as more arousing than healthy control subjects. This finding is in line with one of our previous studies, in which we found a trend for increased arousal ratings in response to neutral stimuli, which consisted of landscape pictures [43]. Other studies have not found increased arousal ratings [8, 10, 13], or have even found decreased arousal ratings [11, 12]. These other studies have mainly used a mixture of household objects and nature scenes as their neutral pictures. One possible explanation for increased arousal ratings may be that these pictures seemed slightly ambiguous to these patients. For example, a landscape can seem harmless, threatening, or lonely, and a single empty mug or a chair could represent loneliness too. Previous studies have shown that patients with schizophrenia respond differently to ambiguous stimuli compared with healthy control participants [51, 52], and Horan et al. [53] have shown that these patients have difficulty attributing the correct meaning to ambiguous stimuli in a social context. However, none of these studies directly explains our findings of increased arousal ratings to seemingly neutral stimuli. Future studies should aim to investigate the nature of emotional responses to specific stimuli in more detail, to inform us about the underlying motivations of patients with schizophrenia.

Limitations

With regard to our sample, there were several limitations. First, the sample size for the antipsychotic-free patients was very small, so any lack of a significant difference between antipsychotic-free patients and healthy control subjects could be due to a lack of statistical power. Second, we only included male participants in this study, which reduces the generalizability of our results. Third, due to the small sample sizes, we did not differentiate the patient group based on their symptom scores. This approach could have identified two sub-groups of patients, as in the study of Strauss en Herbener [54]. They found that 60% of their patient group reported subjective responses similar to healthy control subjects, while 40% rated negative stimuli as more unpleasant and more arousing than controls, and this same group rated a larger proportion of positive pictures as unpleasant. This 'atypical cluster' of patients displayed more severe symptoms on the PANSS Negative Symptom Scale and the Chapman Anhedonia Scale, as well as more functional impairment on the Heinrichs-Carpenter Quality of Life Scale than the patients in the normative group.

With regard to our findings, neither the patients nor the controls showed any significant startle potentiation during the viewing of negative slides compared with neutral slides, suggesting that our manipulation of bringing subjects into a negative emotional state may have failed. The subjective ratings did show the expected pattern for negative pictures, but it is possible that the negative pictures did not evoke a sufficient defensive emotional state in the subjects to elicit startle potentiation.

CONCLUSION

Generally, schizophrenic patients and healthy control subjects showed similar eyeblink response patterns during an emotional startle modulation paradigm. The eyeblink responses were smaller during the viewing of positive pictures compared with neutral and negative pictures. This finding suggests that emotion-eliciting pictures evoke similar motivational states in schizophrenic patients and controls. However, the decreased pleasure ratings of schizophrenic patients to erotic pictures and the increased arousal ratings to adventure, nature, and household pictures need further investigation.

Although the Self-Assessment Manikin is very useful for the rapid evaluation of pictures and increases the comparability of subjective ratings, more extensive subjective evaluations could provide further information about the experiences of these patients while viewing emotion-eliciting pictures. Finally, more research should focus on the sexual needs and expectations in general of these young male patients, since this is an important factor for the quality of life in this patient group.

REFERENCES

[1] Pinkham, A.E., R.E. Gur, and R.C. Gur, Affect recognition deficits in schizophrenia: neural substrates and psychopharmacological implications. Expert Rev Neurother, 2007. 7(7): p. 807-16.

[2] Davidson, R.J., et al., Neural Bases of Emotion Regulation in Nonhuman Primates and Humans, in Handbook of emotion regulation. 2007, Guilford Press: New York, NY US. p. 47-68.

[3] Beer, J.S., M.V. Lombardo, and J.J. Gross, Insights into Emotion Regulation from Neuropsychology, in Handbook of emotion regulation. 2007, Guilford Press: New York, NY US. p. 69-86.

[4] Hooker, C. and S. Park, Emotion processing and its relationship to social functioning in schizophrenia patients. Psychiatry Research, 2002. 112(1): p. 41-50.

[5] Mueser, K.T., et al., Emotion recognition and social competence in chronic schizophrenia. Journal of Abnormal Psychology, 1996. 105(2): p. 271-275.

[6] Meesters, P.D., et al., Social functioning among older community-dwelling patients with schizophrenia: a review. Am J Geriatr Psychiatry, 2010. 18(10): p. 862-78.

[7] Quirk, S.W. and M.E. Strauss, Visual exploration of emotion eliciting images by patients with schizophrenia. Journal of Nervous and Mental Disease, 2001. 189(11): p. 757-765.

[8] Schlenker, R., R. Cohen, and G. Hopmann, Affective modulation of the startle reflex in schizophrenic patients. European Archives of Psychiatry and Clinical Neuroscience, 1995. 245(6): p. 309-318.

[9] Takahashi, H., et al., An fMRI study of differential neural response to affective pictures in schizophrenia. NeuroImage, 2004. 22(3): p. 1247-1254.

[10] Volz, M., et al., Temporal course of emotional startle modulation in schizophrenia patients. International Journal of Psychophysiology, 2003. 49(2): p. 123-137.

[11] Aminoff, S.R., et al., Decreased self-reported arousal in schizophrenia during aversive picture viewing compared to bipolar disorder and healthy controls. Psychiatry Research, 2011. 185(3): p. 309-314.

[12] Kring, A.M., M. Germans Gard, and D.E. Gard, Emotion deficits in schizophrenia: Timing matters. Journal of Abnormal Psychology, 2011. 120(1): p. 79-87.

[13] Yee, C.M., et al., Integrity of Emotional and Motivational States During the Prodromal, First-Episode, and Chronic Phases of Schizophrenia. Journal of Abnormal Psychology, 2010. 119(1): p. 71-82.

[14] Kring, A.M., Emotion in schizophrenia: Old mystery, new understanding. Current Directions in Psychological Science, 1999. 8(5): p. 160-163.

[15] Kring, A.M. and J.M. Neale, Do schizophrenic patients show a disjunctive relationship among expressive, experiential, and psychophysiological components of emotion? Journal of Abnormal Psychology, 1996. 105(2): p. 249-257.

[16] Myin-Germeys, I., et al., Emotional reactivity to daily life stress in psychosis. Archives of General Psychiatry, 2001. 58(12): p. 1137-1144.

[17] Curtis, C.E., et al., Acoustic startle reflex in schizophrenia patients and their first-degree relatives: Evidence of normal emotional modulation. Psychophysiology, 1999. 36(4): p. 469-475.

[18] Kring, A.M. and E.K. Moran, Emotional response deficits in schizophrenia: Insights from affective science. Schizophrenia Bulletin, 2008. 34(5): p. 819-834.

[19] Bradley, M.M. and P.J. Lang, Measuring emotion: Behavior, feeling, and physiology, in Cognitive neuroscience of emotion., R.D. Lane and L. Nadel, Editors. 2000, Oxford University Press: New York, NY US. p. 242-276.

[20] Lang, P.J., M.M. Bradley, and B.N. Cuthbert, Emotion, attention, and the startle reflex. Psychological Review, 1990. 97(3): p. 377-395.

[21] Vrana, S.R., E.L. Spence, and P.J. Lang, The startle probe response: A new measure of emotion? Journal of Abnormal Psychology, 1988. 97(4): p. 487-491.

[22] Blumenthal, T.D., et al., Committee report: Guidelines for human startle eyeblink electromyographic studies. Psychophysiology, 2005. 42(1): p. 1-15.

[23] Grillon, C. and J. Baas, A review of the modulation of the startle reflex by affective states and its application in psychiatry. Clinical Neurophysiology, 2003. 114(9): p. 1557-1579.

[24] Bradley, M.M., et al., Emotion and motivation I: Defensive and appetitive reactions in picture processing. Emotion, 2001. 1(3): p. 276-298.

[25] Bradley, M.M., M. Codispoti, and P.J. Lang, A multi-process account of startle modulation during affective perception. Psychophysiology, 2006. 43(5): p. 486-497.

[26] Bradley, M.M., B.N. Cuthbert, and P.J. Lang, Pictures as prepulse: Attention and emotion in startle modification. Psychophysiology, 1993. 30(5): p. 541-545.

[27] Fakra, E., et al., Effect of risperidone versus haloperidol on emotional responding in schizophrenic patients. Psychopharmacology (Berl), 2008. 200(2): p. 261-72.

[28] Andreasen, N.C., M.C. Flaum, and S. Arndt, The Comprehensive Assessment of Symptoms and History (CASH): An instrument for assessing diagnosis and psychopathology. Archives of General Psychiatry, 1992. 49(8): p. 615-623.

[29] APA, Diagnostic and Statistical Manual of Mental Disorders. 4 ed. 1994, Washington DC: American Psychiatric Association.

[30] Kay, S.R., A. Fiszbein, and L.A. Opler, The positive and negative syndrome scale (PANSS) for schizophrenia. Schizophr Bull, 1987. 13(2): p. 261-76.
[31] Wald, F.D.M. and G.J. Mellenbergh, De verkorte versie van de Nederlandse vertaling van de Profile of Mood States (POMS). Nederlands Tijdschrift voor Psychologie, 1990. 45: p. 86-90.
[32] Center for the Study of Emotion and Attention, C.S.E.A.N.I.M.H., The international affective picture system (IAPS): digitized photographs. 1999.
[33] Bradley, M.M. and P.J. Lang, Measuring emotion: The Self-Assessment Manikin and the semantic differential. Journal of Behavior Therapy and Experimental Psychiatry, 1994. 25(1): p. 49-59.
[34] van Boxtel, A., A.J.W. Boelhouwer, and A.R. Bos, Optimal EMG signal bandwidth and interelectrode distance for the recording of acoustic, electrocutaneous and photic blink reflexes. Psychophysiology, 1998. 35(6): p. 690-697.
[35] Gabor, D., Theory of communication. IEE Proceedings, 1946. 93(3): p. 429-457.
[36] Graham, F.K. and G.M. Murray, Discordant effects of weak prestimulation on magnitude and latency of the reflex blink. Physiological Psychology, 1977. 5(1): p. 108-114.
[37] Rasbash, J., et al., MLwiN. February 2009, Centre for Multilevel Modelling, University of Bristol: Bristol.
[38] Braff, D.L., Information Processing and Attention Dysfunctions in Schizophrenia. Schizophrenia Bulletin, 1993. 19(2): p. 233-259.
[39] Nuechterlein, K.H., et al., Identification of separable cognitive factors in schizophrenia. Schizophrenia Research, 2004. 72(1): p. 29-39.
[40] Nuechterlein, K.H. and M.E. Dawson, Information processing and attentional functioning in the developmental course of schizophrenic disorders. Schizophr Bull, 1984. 10(2): p. 160-203.
[41] Libkuman, T.M., et al., Multidimensional normative ratings for the International Affective Picture System. Behavior Research Methods, 2007. 39(2): p. 326-334.
[42] Hempel, R.J., et al., Subjective and physiological responses to emotion-eliciting pictures in male schizophrenic patients. International Journal of Psychophysiology, 2007. 64(2): p. 174-183.
[43] Hempel, R.J., et al., Physiological responsivity to emotional pictures in schizophrenia. Journal of Psychiatric Research, 2005. 39(5): p. 509-518.
[44] Bengtsson-Tops, A. and L. Hansson, Clinical and social needs of schizophrenic outpatients living in the community: The relationship between needs and subjective quality of life. Social Psychiatry and Psychiatric Epidemiology, 1999. 34(10): p. 513-518.
[45] Hansson, L., et al., The relationship of needs and quality of life in persons with schizophrenia living in the community. A Nordic multi-center study. Nordic Journal of Psychiatry, 2003. 57(1): p. 5-11.
[46] McDonald, J. and T.A. Badger, Social function of persons with schizophrenia. J Psychosoc Nurs Ment Health Serv, 2002. 40(6): p. 42-50.
[47] Lysaker, P.H., L.W. Davis, and N.L. Hunter, Neurocognitive, social and clinical correlates of two domains of hopelessness in schizophrenia. Schizophrenia Research, 2004. 70(2-3): p. 277-285.

[48] Gard, D.E., et al., Anhedonia in schizophrenia: Distinctions between anticipatory and consummatory pleasure. Schizophrenia Research, 2007. 93(1-3): p. 253-260.

[49] Chan, R.C.K., et al., Anticipatory and consummatory components of the experience of pleasure in schizophrenia: Cross-cultural validation and extension. Psychiatry Research, 2010. 175(1-2): p. 181-183.

[50] Olfson, M., et al., Male Sexual Dysfunction and Quality of Life in Schizophrenia. Journal of Clinical Psychiatry, 2005. 66(3): p. 331-338.

[51] Constant, E.L., et al., Deficit in negative emotional information processing in schizophrenia: Does it occur in all patients? Psychiatry Research, 2010. 185(3): p. 315-320.

[52] Trémeau, F., et al., In support of Bleuler: Objective evidence for increased affective ambivalence in schizophrenia based upon evocative testing. Schizophrenia Research, 2009. 107(2-3): p. 223-231.

[53] Horan, W.P., et al., Disturbances in the spontaneous attribution of social meaning in schizophrenia. Psychol Med, 2009. 39(4): p. 635-43.

[54] Strauss, G.P. and E.S. Herbener, Patterns of emotional experience in schizophrenia: Differences in emotional response to visual stimuli are associated with clinical presentation and functional outcome. Schizophrenia Research, 2011. 128(1-3): p. 117-123.

In: Schizophrenia Research: Recent Advances
Editor: Tomiki Sumiyoshi
ISBN: 978-1-62808-703-1

Chapter 10

THE PROSPECTIVE EPIGENETIC KEYS FOR THE INFLAMMATORY PUZZLE OF SCHIZOPHRENIA

A. Khoyetsyan* and A. Boyajyan
Institute of Molecular Biology
Armenian National Academy of Sciences
Yerevan, Republic of Armenia

Abstract

The present chapter addresses the gene-environment epigenetic interplay of inflammatory mediators and its potential involvement in pathogenesis of schizophrenia. Epigenetics is the study of heritable changes in gene expression that do not involve changes in DNA sequence. The epigenetic code, the sum and interaction of epigenetic regulations, is dynamic and modified by environmental factors. There is increasing evidence that epigenetic changes play a critical role in the development of many human diseases, such as neurodevelopmental and neurodegenerative disorders, cardio- and cerebrovascular diseases, type-2 diabetes mellitus, obesity and infertility. The importance of epigenetic regulatory mechanisms in generation and development of the immune response, including both chronic and acute inflammation, is emerging. On the other hand, a chronic inflammation has been implicated in the pathogenesis of schizophrenia. There is abundant evidence (including our own) suggesting that immune-mediated inflammatory mechanisms at systemic level as well as within the central nervous system contribute to immunological impairments in schizophrenia. In addition, both inherited risk factors, including different variants of genes encoding the inflammatory mediators as well as epigenetic regulators of gene expression, such as DNA methylation state, have been implicated in the pathophysiology of schizophrenia. Probably, the epigenetic code in schizophrenia can bring together environmental and genetic factors in a way that can explain the psychoneuroimmunological impairments observed in this pathology.

* E-mail address: a.g.khoyets@gmail.com.

INTRODUCTION

Affecting 24 million people worldwide, schizophrenia is a heterogeneous illness with a range of clinical expression (chronic psychosis, social, occupational, behavioral and cognitive impairments). The molecular pathomechanisms responsible for the generation and development of schizophrenia remains unclear. However, several lines evidence including genetic, epidemiological, neuropathological and neurochemical suggest that immune-based neurodevelopmetal abnormalities play the importment role in the etiopathogenesis of schizophrenia. This pathology affects the *neuro-immune-endocrine axis* of the organism (Figure 1) [1-16].

There is considerable evidence, including results of our own studies, to suggest a key role for upregulated immune response in the pathogenesis of schizophrenia, since alterations in both the innate and adaptive immunity were described in this pathology [1-3, 9, 16-19]. The important role of these interrelated and interdependent mechanisms in generation and development of schizophrenia has been increasingly considered. In this term, the Th1/Th2 polarization and a chronic neuroinflammation have been implicated in the pathogenesis of this disorder [9].

On the other hand, the importance of epigenetic regulatory mechanisms in generation and development of the immune response, both chronic and acute inflammation, is emerging. There is increasing evidence that epigenetic changes play a critical role in the development of many human diseases, such as neurodevelopmental and neurodegenerative disorders, cardio- and cerebrovascular diseases, type-2 diabetes mellitus, obesity and infertility [20-23].

In this commentary review we aim to present brief road map for the epigenetic mechanisms of the gene expression, in general, next take a focus on epigenetic code of inflammation and, from this prism, try to highlight the possible mechanisms responsible for the implication of the inflammatory component in schizophrenia

Epigenetics

Epigenetics is the study of heritable changes in gene expression that does not involve changes in DNA sequence. In a broad sense, epigenetics is a bridge between genotype and phenotype. These heritable differences in the programs of gene expression that result in the development of the different cells as well as tissues and organs do not involve changes in DNA sequence. The epigenetic code, the sum and interaction of epigenetic regulations, is dynamic and can be modified by environmental factors [20, 24-26]. There are three epigenetic mechanisms of the gene expression regulation: (1) DNA methylation, (2) chromatin variation, and (3) non coding RNA mechanism which are known to collaborate together. Figure 2 represents a brief road map for the three main mechanisms of epigenetic modifications highlighting molecular levels and targets of these dynamic regulations.

DNA Methylation

DNA Methylation is perhaps the best characterized chemical modification of chromatin, which inhibits gene transcription mainly depending on the position of the methylation change relative to the position of the transcription start site (promoter region). DNA methylation plays a critical role in gene regulation and chromatin organization during embryogenesis and gametogenesis. Methylated cytosine residius are mainly located on so-called CpG islands throughout the human genome that are 200bp region of DNA and with more than 60 % of GC content. Non-CpG sequences may also exhibit methylation, but generally at a much lower frequency.

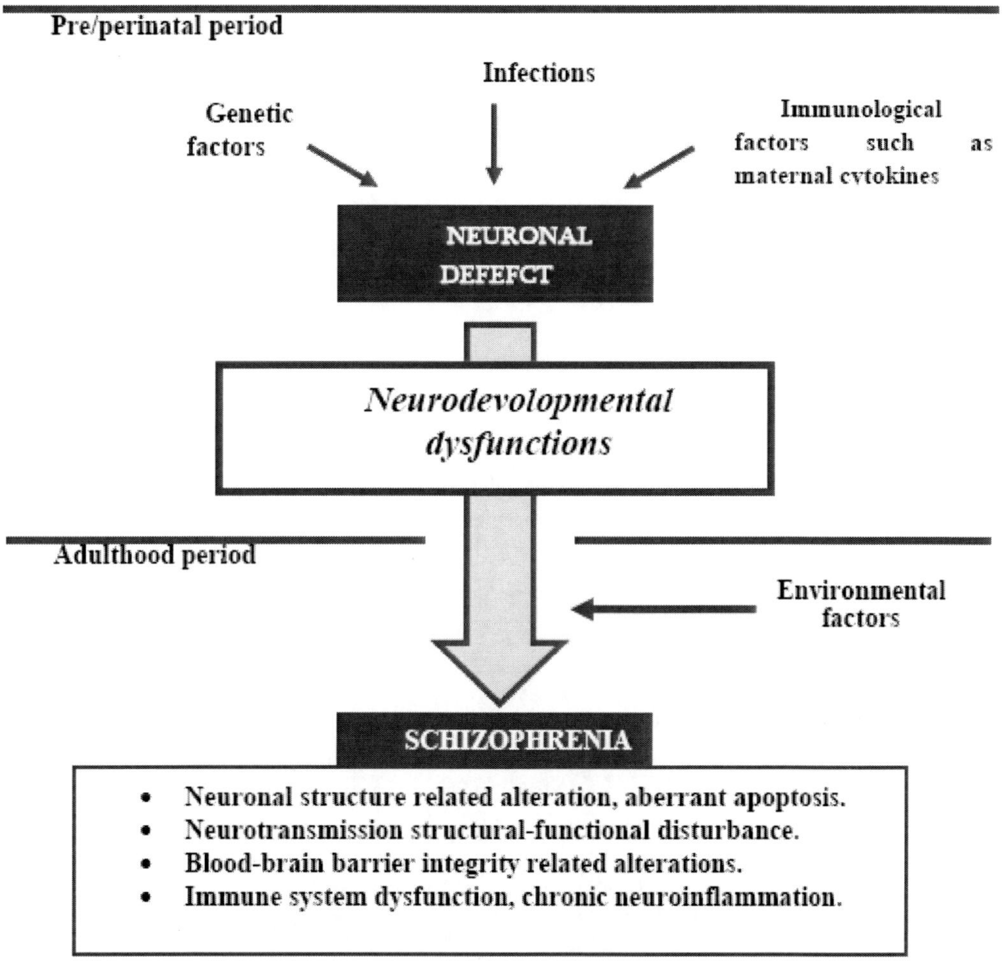

Figure 1. The brief scheme for the mechanisms of the generation and development of schizophrenia.

These reactions are catalysed by DNA methyl transferases (DNMTs) methylated cytosine at five carbon positions by transfering methyl group from the S-adenosyl-methionie. Four DNA methyltransferases named DNMT1, DNMT2, DNMT3A and DNMT3B have been identified. There are two essential cofactors, folate and vitamin B12, for this methylation cycle. Methylated cytosine residues are recognized by methyl DNA binding complexes consisting of methyl CpG binding protein 1 and 2 (MeCP1, MeCP2). DNA methylation provides a stable, heritable, long-term,and critical component of epigenetic regulation [27-31].

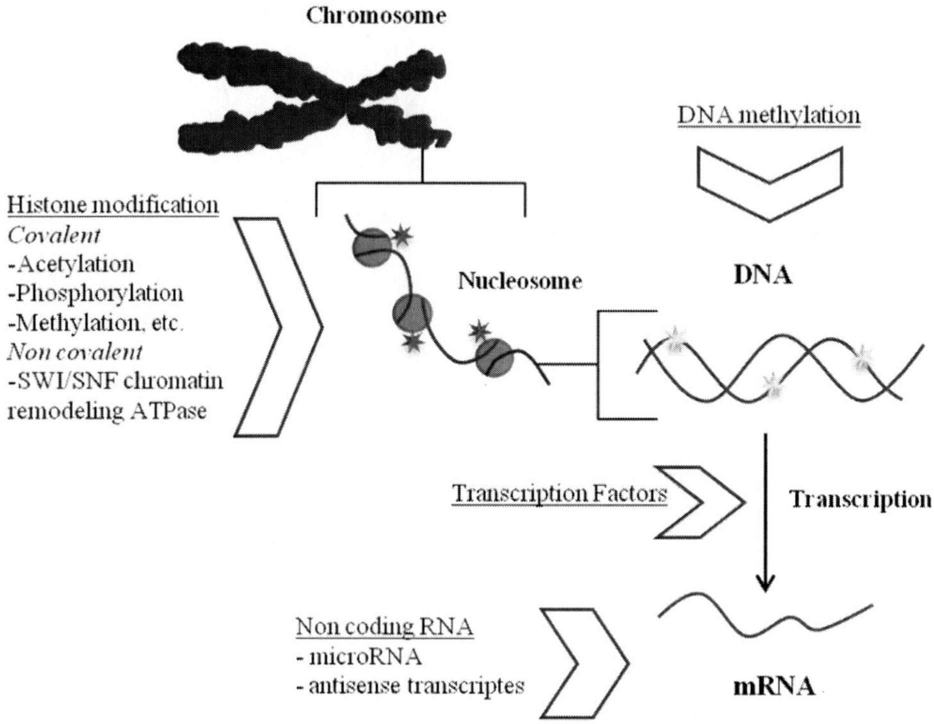

Figure 2. The road map of the main three epigenetic modification mechanisms.

Chromatin Variation

There are two mechanisms for chromatin variation: covalent and non covalent. *Covalent variation* of chromatin is a chemical modificiation of histones, which includes acethylation, phosporylation, methylation, ubiquination, ADP-ribosilation, carbonylation, SUMOylation, glycosylation and biotinylation [20, 25, 32-34]. In contrast to DNA methylation, the chemical modification of N-terminal tail of histone molecules is complexity regulatory process and confers short-term, therefore, flexible epigenetic regulation. The list of covalent modifications of histone proteins continues to grow. For example, there have been discovered over 150 different combinations for H3 [35] and more than 60 different modifiactaion on histone positions [36].

In general, the both acetylation and phosphorylation modification mechanisms regulate the gene expression by adding a single negative charge to the histone, increasing histone-DNA interaction repulsive force and decreasing histones affinity for DNA. As a result, the modified chromatin relaxes and is maked more accessible to transcription machinary binding and functioning [20]. The 18 different groups of enzymes for histone acetylation modification have been characherized, which are organized in 4 main classes: class I (HDAC1, 2, 3 and 8), class II (HDAC4, 5, 6,7, 9 and 10), class III sirtuins (SIRT1, 2, 3, 4, 5, 6 and 7) and class IV (HDAC11) [32].

There is a direct link between the histone phosphorylation code of the gene expression regulation and a key enzymes (protein kinases, protein phosphatases) of cellular signaling.

Contrary to acetylation and phosphorylation modification mechanisms, histone methylation has been linked to both activation and repression of gene expression. The targets are lysine and occasionally serine residues, which can be methylated (mono-, di-, or trimethylation) by histone methylases and demethylases. The epigenetic mechanisms of histone modifications are detailed described in a number of reviews [20, 21, 26, 32-34].

There is a cross regulation between all these three epigenetic mechanisms. Particularly, in case of DNA methylation and histone acetylation cross regulation is achieved through the interaction between methylated CpG islands and co-regulating complexes of histone modifying enzymes such as HDACs [37-39].

The *noncovalent mechanisms* such as covalent modifications of histone N-tail are additional tools for introducing variation into the chromatin template. Nucleosome remodeling is achieved by ATP-dependent processes, which result in repositioning of nucleosomes by altering DNA-histone interactions. Here the SWI/SNF (switching-defective-sucrose non fermenting; also known as BAF) chromatin remodeling ATPase has been considered as the central unit of noncovalent mechanism of the chromatin variation [40, 41].

Non-coding RNA

Third level of epigenetic regulation of the gene exspression is transcript modification mechanism. The key players of this modification are non-coding RNAs, particularly, microRNAs, siRNA, antisense transcript, etc. All these RNA-associated modification mechanisms can also induce transcriptional silencing of genes by facilitating histone modification and DNA methylation. MicroRNAs are single-stranded non-coding RNAs with approximately 19-25 nucleotides in length. The biogenesis of miRNAs is a complex, multistep process, which includes several enzyme clusters and molecular interactions [42-44]. There has been discovered that human miRNAs have a very high copy numbers per cell (from 100 copies to 10000 copies in some cases). Each miRNA can regulate about hundreds of mRNA targets [45, 46]. Another example of the cross regulatory epigenetic mechanism is the transcript modification by antisence oligonucleotids that are complementary to mRNA of human DNMT1 [47, 48].

It is important that among the epigenetic mechanisms heritable and more stable modifications are mainly considered. The stability, heritability and long-term modification decrease as well as flexibility, irreversibility increase in this direction: DNA methylation > Histone modification > non coding RNA > transcription factors.

Schizophrenia and the Epigenetic Code of Inflammation

In this section we briefly highlighted the main alterations of immune system associated with schizophrenia, mostly focusing on epigenetic regulation level both the innate and adaptive mechanisms of chronic inflammation in schizophrenia.

Based upon the existing knowledge related to etiology and pathology of schizophrenia, three major milestones for the immune system alterations in schizophrenia have been considered [1, 7] (see Figure 1):

(a) *neurodevelopmnetal stage,*
(b) *first clinical manifestation or symptomatic stage,*

(c) *chronic, degenerative stage.*

It is important to consider these three stage-associated immune system alterations in the context of long- and short term epigenetic modifications. For example, DNA methylation as a long-term and heritable modification has an essential role in embriogensis and gametogenesis [24]. And, a from view point of the immune-mediated neurodevelopmental theory of schizophrenia the maternal infections as well as elevated cytokines levels considered as an etiological factors [1, 8-11].

Here two major questions may arise: *whether immune system alterations result from aberrant neurodevelopment are (a) primary etiological or (b) secondary pathological mechanisms of schizophrenia?*

There is abundant evidence, results of our own studies that immune-mediated inflammatory mechanisms at a systemic level as well as within the central nervous system contribute to immunological impairments in schizophrenia [1-3, 9, 16-19]. The Th1/Th2 imbalance as well as polarized cytokine signature has been implicated in the pathogenesis of schizophrenia [9].

Inflammation is a multicomponent response to tissue stress, injury and infection, with complicated cluster of genes of the several types of mediators such as cytokines, prostaglandins, reactive oxygen radicals, etc. This recovery response depends upon (a) the origin of pathological factors, (b) localization of injury and (c) intensity of damage. The response may be either acute or chronic, each implicating different initiation and progression mechanisms [49]. The acute inflammatory response leads to the rapid elimination of pathogen followed by tissue recovery. Continious exposure to pathogens, (auto)antigens, or cytotoxic factors, leads to long-term (chronic) inflammation. However, both the innate and adaptive components of immune response are in a close relationships assisting each other during recognition, initiation, adaptation and resolution stages of inflammation. In contrast to the acute inflammatory response, in case of chronic inflammation there is no apparent switch to an adaptive phase and resolution is uncommon.

The peripheral immune access to the CNS is limitied and strongly controlled by the blood-brain barrier, the CNS has the local innate immune defense mechanisms which are capable to initiate and develop dynamic immune and inflammatory responses to variety of insults (such as infections, trauma, stroke, toxins and other stimuli). *Microglial cells* are the main innate immune cells within the brain complex cellular structure. These cells are present throughout the CNS (about 10% of CNS glia); some regions are more heavily populated than others. Microglial cells express Toll-like receptors (TLRs), produce complement system proteins and pro-inflammatory mediators. Normally microglial cells are down-regulated, but can be activated in different pathological conditions, quickly responding to several pathogens and injury [50-54]. It is clear that microglia is a key cellular mediator of neuroinflammatory process. The acute neuroinflammatory response, an immediate and short term activation of the brain local innate immune mechanisms, includes activation of the microglia resulting in a phagocytic phenotype as well as the release of inflammatory mediators such as cytokines, chemokines. On the other hand, the continuous release of inflammatory mediators leads to chronic neuroinflammation, a long-term, often self-perpetuating inflammatory process. [51-55].

Two different microglia cell activation models, liner and plasticity models are proposed for neurodegenerative diseases (Alzheimer, Prion, etc.). Interestingly, that microglia cells can be activating without morphology changing [55]. Juckel and colleages [56] in their pilot study, have shown that maternal infection during embryogenesis contributes to microglial activation in the offspring, which therefore represent a contributing factor to the pathogenesis of schizophrenia. However, this field is still in its infancy.

The NF-κB family of transcription factors is defined as a family of latent cytoplasmic factors, which in inactive form reside in the cytoplasm, but, when activated, are translocated into the nucleus. The NF-κB family of transcription factors has a key role in regulation of the cluster of inflammatory genes as well as in activation of monocytes, macrophages and microglia. Since quite a number of genes contain NF-κB responsible elements in their regulatory regions, their expression regulation can significantly vary. There is considerable evidence suggesting that NF-κB signaling, regulating the appropriate gene expression and transcriptional activity, depends on epigenetic modifications [reviewed in 57]. For example, it was demonstrated that, upon triggering cells by the inflammatory stimuli, different target genes can recruit NF-κB with different rates (fast, slow), depending on constitutive or inducible H4 acetylation modifications in their chromatin structure [58].

Rajendrasozhan and colleagues have considered NF-κB-dependent gene regulation in term of chromatin covalent modification mechanisms, particularly accounting for the changes in deacetylases, such as HDACs and sirtuins [59]. From this view point, it is interesting that recently published suggest that schizophrenic patients showed activation of cytokine system, which correlated with NF-κB activation [60].

Lipopolysacharide (LPS) modulating model of macrophage and microglia cell activation is well investigated and presented in [61]. LPS triggers microglia activation by TLR4 through NF-κB transcriptional factor pathway. Three classes of transcriptional factors, as well as various transcriptional co-regulators and chromatin modification are considered as inflammatory response regulators in this model. Thus, it is proposed that the H3S10 (histone 3 at serine 10) phosphorylation might have a gene specific role in NF-κB pathway activation or repression [62]. Chromatin remodeling can also regulate the generation and development of the inflammatory response; the main requirements for chromatin remodeling differ between LPS-inducible primary and secondary response genes [63].

The chromatin covalent and non-covalent variations in term of rapid activation or repression of NF-κB transcriptional factor signaling pathway also well reviewed by McCall and colleagues [64]. In case of the acute inflammatory response supression (initiation stage) and anti-inflammatory activation (adaptation) are described in term of chromatin variations. Mainly NAD^+-dependent deacetylase, Sirtuin 1 and NF-κB dependent transcription regulators are involved in this regulation. However, in case of chronic inflammation only recognition and initation stages and adaptation stage dysfunction may be considered. Thus, lack of adaptation stage response may associate with the long-term silencing of this stage responsible inflammatory mediators gene cluster, which is induced during the first stage of schizophrenia generation, particularly due to the influence of maternal factors such as IL-8, infections, etc.

In addition, several recent findings have discovered pathogen-mediated chromatin remodeling mechanisms. For instance, inhibition of TNFα (but not IL-10) production by *Toxoplasma gondii* infection is associated with decreased H3 acetylation and H3S10 phosphorylation, and decreased recruitment of p56 to the *Tnf* promoter [65]. In addition, several other pathogens also downregulate H3S10 phosphorylation [66]. In this context, the recent finding on the association of *Toxoplasma gondii* infection with etiopathology of schizophrenia is of great importance [67].

Next target point for innate mechanism of inflammation is TLRs family, including key mediators involved in inflammation and acting on the interface of the adaptive and innate immunity. The activation of TLRs leads to the expression of co-stimulating factors on the phagocytes followed by the change in the latests phenotype from phagocyte to antigen-presenting cell and the activation of T cell response [49]. Moreover, TLRs are important in recognition of the inflammatory stimuli and have to be considered in the recognition stage of the inflammation as well as in the initation stage. However, up to now mainly LPS-TRL4 modulation pathway is well investigated [61, 63].

The epigenetic code of chronic inflammation is well reviewed and discussed by Backdahl et al [21]. In the regulation of the chronic inflammation the adaptive immune response is among the most important mechanisms. CD4+ T helper cells (Th1, Th2, Th17, Treg) have a crucial role in the regulation of the inflammatory response. On the other hand, epigenetic modifications as well as transcriptional factors initate and regulate differnataion and maturation of these T-cell subpopulations. For example, Th1/Th2 differentiation process depends on chromatin modifications, such as histone methylation, histone acetylation and DNA methylation. Th2 lineage differentiation is regulated by epigenetic silencing of the Th1 cytokine locus (INF-γ), and differentiation of Th2 cytokine locus (IL4/IL13/Rad50/IL5) [68, 69]. Hence, activation of the Th2 locus is associated with silencing of Th1 locus and *vise versa* in order to generate Th1 and Th2 differentiated T helper cells [70, 71]. There are many conflicting data concerning the Th1/Th2 paradigm in chronic inflammation. In term of new T helper cell lineage, Th17 cells, this paradigm needs updating. For example, TGFβ suppresses Th1 and Th2 differentation and, interestingly, avctivates Treg cell lineage [72]. FOXP3 is important in activation of Treg and Th17, which regulate Th1 and Th2 cell lineage development. It is interesting, that miR-155 activates Th1 response, and suppresses Th2. In this review are presented and discussed considerable evidence, which suggest NF-κB, IL-12, FOXP3, RORγt, miR-146 and miR-155 to be key regulators in immune cell differentiation during chronic inflammation [21]. Epigenetic control of FOXP3 was reviewed by Huehn and colleages [73]. This review is focused on the conversion of Treg cells to Th17 cells, which can be induced by dendritic cell- derived Il-6, which downregulates the expression of FOXP3 in a STAT3-dependent manner. In addition, the mechanisms of the epigenetic modifications (DNA methylation and histone acetylation) of FOXP3 are also considered.

There are some published data, which indicate that chromatin remodeling of the IL-4 locus is accompanied by CpG demethylation during Th2 differentation, whereas these changes do not occur during Th1 differentation [74]. In addition, the differentiation of naïve CD4+ T cells to the Th2 phenotype is characterized by rapid acquisition of H3 acetylation at the IL-4/IL-13 gene cluster [75].

There are recently published review on DNA methylation epigenetic modification mechanism for implication of the immune system dysfunction in schizophrenia [76]. Interestingly, the relationship between high levels of homocysteine (participate in methyl donation metabolic pathway) and activation of the immune response (production of various cytokines, etc).

Finally, there is emerging evidence for the non-coding RNA mechanisms by which miRNAs regulate gene expression, particularly related to the development of immune cells and in modulating innate and adaptive immune responses (detail review is presented in [77]). There have been also found that miRNAs both the host (miR -155,-150, -181a, -146) and viral

(SV40, miR-LAT) have an important role in the development and functioning of the immune cells and/or in host–pathogen interactions.

CONCLUSION

In this chapter we tried to introduce the major epigenetic modification mechanisms in term of target molecules and action duration as well as heritable aspects. There are not data for epigenetic code of inflammation in schizophrenia. We have summarized and presented the mostly well studied points of epigenetic regulation of inflammation mechanisms through NF-κB and FOXP3 signaling, Treg cell differentiation, and some other, highlighting key regulatory mechanisms of schizophrenia-associated chronic inflammation. Here, for the first time, the epigenetic regulatory dysfunction was considered as a key mechanism of regulation of the chronic inflammation in schizophrenia on different stages of the disease progression.

REFERENCES

[1] G. Stöber, et al., *The World Journal of Biological Psychiatry,* 10 (2), 127-155 (2009).

[2] M. Herberth, E. Schwartz, S. Bahn, *Biomarkers Med.,* 2 (4) (2008).

[3] D. R. Hanson, I. I. Gottesman, *BMC Medical Genetics*. 6(7), 1-17 (2005).

[4] P. J. Harrison, *Psychiatry*. 4(10), 18-21 (2005).

[5] P. J. Harrison, D. R. Weinberger, *Mol. Psychiatry* 10, 40-68 (2005).

[6] K. Ishizuka, M. Paek, A. Kamiya, A. Sawa, *Biol. Psychiatry* 59, 1189-1191 (2006).

[7] Y. K. Kim, L. Kim, M. S. Lee, *Schizophr Res*. 44, 165-75 (2000).

[8] A. Khoyetsyan, A. Boyajyan, *Journal of Neurology and Psychiatry S.S. Korsakova* 2 (110), 97-101 (2010).

[9] N. Müller, M. J. Schwarz, *Neurotoxicity Research.* 10 (2), 131-148 (2010).

[10] S. E. Arnold, K. Talbot, C. G. Hahn, *Prog. Brain Res*. 147, 319-345 (2005).

[11] S. C. Bakker, M. C. Hoogendoom, R. J. Sinke, K. F. Verzibergen, K. A. Kusters, H. G. Otten, P. L. Pearson, R. S. Kahn, *Association study of the neuregulin, dysbindin and G72 genes in a large sample of Dutch schizophrenic patients.* In: N. Barden, M. Cote, L. DeLisi, M. Gill, J. Kelsoe, M. Schalling (Eds.), XIth World Congress of Psychiatric Genetics, Quebec, 2003; 19.

[12] D. H. Blackwood, A. Fordyce, M. T. Walker, D. M. St. Clair, D. J. Porteous, W. J. Muir, *Am. J. Hum.Genet.* 69, 428-433 (2001).

[13] A. S. Brown, C. A. Schaefer, R. J. Wyatt, et al., *Schizophr Bull*. 26, 287-95 (2000).

[14] J. T. Coyle, *Biochemical Pharmacology*. 68, 1507-1514 (2004).

[15] M. Di Forti, J. M. Lappin, R. M. Murray, *European Neuropsychopharmacology*. 17, S101-S107 (2007).

[16] L. Drzyzga, E. Obuchowicz, A. Marcinowska, Z. S. Herman, *Brain, Behavior, and Immunity*. 20, 532–545 (2006).

[17] R. D. Strous, Y. Shoenfeld, Schizophrenia, autoimmunity and immune system dysregulation: A comprehensive model updated and revisited, *J. Autoimmun*. 27, 71-80 (2006).

[18] A. Boyajyan, A. Khoyetsyan, G. Tsakanova, R. B. Sim, *Clinical Biochemistry*, 41(6), 355-360 (2008).

[19] Boyajyan, A. Khoyetsyan, A. Chavushyan. *Neurochemical Research* (2010) DOI 10.1007/s11064-010-0126-2

[20] P. Narayan and M. Dragunow, *British Journal of Pharmacology*, 159, 285-303 (2010).

[21] L. Backdahl, A. Bushell, S. Beck, *The International Journal of Biochemistry and Cell Biology*, 41, 176-184 (2009).

[22] A. G. Wilson, *J. Periodontal,* 79 (S8), 1514-1519 (2008).

[23] M. Trenkmann, M. Brock, C. Ospelt, S. Gay, *Clinic. Rev. Allerg. Immonol.* 39, 10-19 (2010).

[24] W. Reik, *Nature* 447, 425-432 (2007).

[25] A. D. Goldberg, C.D. Allis, E. Bernstein, *Cell* 128, 635-638.

[26] J. Peedicayil, *Indian J. Med. Res.* 123, 17-24 (2006).

[27] S. Saxonov, P. Berg, D. L. Brutlag, *Proc Natl Acad Sci USA* 103, 1412-1417.

[28] P. A. Jones, D. Tankai, *Science*, 293, 1068-1070 (2001).

[29] J. F.Costelo, C. Plass, *J. Med. Genet.* 38, 285-303 (2001).

[30] J. A. McKay, E. A. Williams, J. C. Mathers, *Biochem. Soc. Trans.* 32, 1006-1007 (2004).

[31] E. Reynolds. *Lancet. Neurol.* 5, 949-960 (2006).

[32] A. Mai, *Expert. Opin. Ther. Targets* 11, 835-851 (2007).

[33] B. R. Kepler, T.K. Archer, *Expert. Opin. Ther. Targets* 12, 1301-1312 (2008a).

[34] B. R. Kepler, T.K. Archer, *Expert. Opin. Ther. Targets* 12, 1457-1467 (2008b).

[35] B. A. Garcia, J. J. Pesavento, C. A. Mizzen, N. L. Kelleher, *Nat. Methods* 4, 487-489 (2007).

[36] T. Kouzardies, *Cell* 128, 693-705 (2007).

[37] F. Fuks, W. A. Burgers, A. Brehm, L. Hughes-Davis, T. Kouzarides, *Nat. Genet.* 24, 88-91 (2000).

[38] M. R. Rountree, K. E. Bachman, S. B. Baylin, *Nat. Genet.* 25, 269-277.

[39] W. A. Burgers, F. Fuks, T. Kouzarides, *Trends. Genet.* 18, 275-277 (2002).

[40] C. L. Smith and C. L. Peterson, *Curr. Top. Dev. Biol.* 65, 115-148 (2005).

[41] C.S. Known and D. Wagner, *Trends. Genet.* 23(8), 403-412 (2007).

[42] G. Egger, G. Liang, A. Aparicio, P. A. Jones, *Nature* 429, 457-463 (2004).

[43] D. P. Bartel, *Cell* 116, 281-297 (2004).

[44] B. R. Cullen, *Mol Cell* 16, 861-865 (2004).

[45] H. Z. Sheng, P. X. Lin, P. G. Nelson, *Anal. Biochem.* 222, 123-130 (1994).

[46] M. G. Carter, A.A. Sharov, V. VanBuren, et. al., *Genome. Biol.* 6, R61 (2005).

[47] L. Yan, S. J. Nass, D. Smith, W. G. Nelson, J. G. Herman, N. E. Davidson, *Cancer. Biol. Ther.* 2, 552-556 (2003).

[48] A. J. Davis, K. A. Gelmon, L. L. Siu, M. J. Moore, et al., *Invest. New Drugs* 21, 85-87 (2003).

[49] I. Royt, J. Brostoff, D. Male, D. Rath, Immunology, 7th edition, Elsevier Ltd., England, 2006.

[50] M. L. Block, J. S. Hong. *Prog. Neurobiol.* 76(2), 77-98 (2005).

[51] W. J. Streit, R. E. Mrak, W. S. Griffin, *J. Neuroinflammation.* 1(1), 14. (2004).

[52] T. C. Frank-Cannon, L. T. Alto, F. E. McAlpine, M. G. Tansey, *Mol. Neurodegener.* 16(4), 47 (2009).

[53] B. A. Barres. *Neuron.* 6(3), 430-40 (2008).
[54] M. A. Yenari, T. M. Kauppinen, R. A. Swanson, *Neurotherapeutics.* 7(4), 378-91 (2010).
[55] V. H. Perry, C. Cunningham, C. Holmes, *Nat. Rev. Immunol.* 7(2), 161-7 (2007).
[56] G. Juckel et al., *Schizophrenia Research*, 2011 doi:10.1016/j.schres.2011.06.018
[57] W. Vanden Berghe, M. N. Ndlovu, R. Hoya-Arias, N. Dijsselbloem, S. Gerlo, G. Haegeman, *Biochemical Pharmacology* 72, 1114-1131 (2006).
[58] S. Saccani, S. Pantano, G. Natoli, *J. Exp. Med.* 193(12), 1351-1359 (2001).
[59] S. Rajendrasozhan, S.-R. Yang, I. Edrisinghe, H. Yao, D. Adenuga, I. Rahman, *Antioxid. Redox. Signal.* 10(4), 799-811 (2008).
[60] X.-Q. Song, L.-X. Lv, W.-Q. Li, Y.-H. Hao, J.-P. Zhao, *Biol. Psychiatry* 65, 481-488 (2009).
[61] R. Medzhitov, T. Horng, *Nature Reviews/Immunology* 9, 692-703.
[62] S. Saccani, S. Pantano, G. Natoli, *Nature Immunology* 3, 69-75 (2002).
[63] V. R. Ramirez-Carrozi, et al., *Genes. Dev.* 20, 282-296 (2006).
[64] E. McCall, M. El Gazzar, T. Liu, V. Vachharajani, B. Yoza, *Journal of Leukocyte Biology* 90, 1-8 (2011).
[65] J. Leng, B. A. Butcher, C. E. Ergan, D. S. Abdallah, E. Y. Denkers, *J. Immunol.* 182, 489-497 (2009).
[66] M. A. Hamon, et al., *Proc. Natl. Acad. Sci. USA* 104, 13467-13472 (2007).
[67] R. Schwarcz, C. A. Hunter, *Schizophrenia Bulletin,* doi:10.1093/schbul/sbm030 (2007).
[68] A. S. Hutchins, D. Artis, B. D. Hendrich, A. P. Bird, P. Scott, S. L. Reiner, *J. Immunol.* 175(9), 5606-5610 (2005).
[69] G. R. Lee, S. T. Kim, C. G. Spilianakis, P. E. Fields, R. A. Flavell, *Immunity* 24(4), 369-379 (2006).
[70] K. M. Ansel, I. Djuretic, B. Tanasa, A. Rao, *Annu. Rev. Immunol.* 24, 607-656 (2006).
[71] I. M. Djuretic, D. Levanon, V. Negreanu, Y. Groner, A. Rao, K. M. Ansel, *Nat. Immunol.* 8(2), 145-153 (2007).
[72] M. Veldhoen, R. J. Hocking, C. J. Atkins, R. M. Locksley, B. Stockinger, *Immunity* 24(2), 179-89 (2006).
[73] J. Huehn, J. Polansky, A. Hamann, *Nature Reviews. Imuunology*, 9, 83-89 (2009).
[74] S. Agarwal, A. Rao, *Immunity* 9(6), 765-75 (1998).
[75] A. Baguet, M. Bix, *Proc. Natl. Acad. Sci. USA* 101, 11410-11415 (2004).
[76] M. Khojasteh-Fard, M. Tabrizi, M. M. Amoli, *Medical Hypotheses* doi:10.1016/j.mehy.2011.06.034 (2011).
[77] H. F. Lodish, B. Zhou, G. Liu, C.-Z. Chen, *Nature Reviews/Immunology* 8, 120-130 (2008).

In: Schizophrenia Research: Recent Advances
Editor: Tomiki Sumiyoshi
ISBN: 978-1-62808-703-1

Chapter 11

MOLECULAR AND GENETIC INDICATORS OF ABERRANT IMMUNITY AND APOPTOSIS IN SCHIZOPHRENIA

Anna Boyajyan**, *Roksana Zakharyan and Aren Khoyetsyan
Institute of Molecular Biology,
National Academy of Sciences of the Republic of Armenia

ABSTRACT

Schizophrenia is a multifactorial and polygenic chronic disease affecting around 24 million people worldwide. Current progress in schizophrenia research has created a strong background for understanding the molecular etiopathomechanisms and identification of vital biomarkers of schizophrenia and may contribute to improved diagnosis and treatment. The present chapter provides overview of our recent studies on the involvement of immune system abnormalities in schizophrenia pathogenesis. The investigations include human studies focused on a major mediators of the immune response, the complement cascade, immune complexes, cytokine network, C-reactive protein (CRP), brain-derived neurotrophic factor (BDNF), and neuroprotein netrin G1 (NTNG1) in a large cohort of paranoid schizophrenia patients (ICD-10 code: F20.0; DSM-IV-TR code: 295.30) and controls. Methodological design is mainly based on enzyme-linked immunosorbent assays, hemolytic assays, immunochemical procedures, protein chemistry methods, different electrophoretic and immunoblotting procedures, flow-cytometry, and polymerase chain reaction. Detailed evaluation of the complement functional activity in schizophrenia-affected subjects on the level of total activities of its classical and alternative pathways, activities and levels of its individual components (C1Q, C2, C3, C4, and factor B) was performed. Also, formation of the complement activation end product, membrane attack complex (MAC), levels of complement regulatory protein factor H, and expression of complement receptor 1 (CR1) on erythrocytes and leukocytes was studied. In addition, association of the functional single nucleotide polymorphisms of the C1Q complement component and CR1 genes with susceptibility to schizophrenia was investigated. Furthermore, the levels and

* E-mail addresses: aboyajyan@sci.am, r_zakharyan@mb.sci.am, akhoyetsyan@mb.sci.am.

immunochemical composition of different populations of immune complexes circulating in the blood of schizophrenia-affected subjects were assessed. The main attention was focused on pathogenic small-sized immune complexes, cryoglobulins, and immune complexes containing natural ligands of CR1, C1Q, and opsonic fragments of C3, originating during complement activation. Evaluating the state of cytokine network in schizophrenia, protein levels and genetic polymorphisms for a number of proinflammatory and immunoregulatory cytokines, including monocyte chemotactic protein-1, tumor necrosis factor-a, interleukin-6, interleukin-8, and macrophage migration inhibitory factor were assessed. For acute phase protein CRP, BDNF, an important modulator of immune-cell produced immunity, and NTNG1, a regulator of immunological synapse, protein level estimations and genotyping were performed. Our data clearly demonstrate the involvement of inflammatory and autoimmune processes and aberrant apoptosis in schizophrenia pathomechanisms and provide detailed information on the consequence of molecular and genetic alterations contributing to development of these alterations. Contributions of other research groups provided. The results obtained are discussed in the context of prominent existing theories of schizophrenia.

INTRODUCTION

Schizophrenia (SCH) is a multifactorial and polygenic chronic psychiatric disorder affecting around 24 million people worldwide [1, 2]. Current progress in SCH research has created a strong background for understanding the molecular etiopathomechanisms and identification of vital biomarkers of schizophrenia and may contribute to the development of improved diagnosis and treatment of this complex disorder. Evidence from epidemiological and genetic studies suggest a high degree of heritability of SCH and point to a number of potential candidate genes that may be perturbed early in development leading ultimately to the development of psychotic symptoms [1, 2].

A number of studies suggest the involvement of alterations in the immune response, including autoimmune and inflammatory mechanisms, in etiopathogenesis of SCH [3-10]. Also, both structural and functional brain imaging experiments and postmortem histopathological and molecular-level studies that have examined markers of apoptosis and levels of apoptotic regulatory proteins in postmortem SCH brain tissue suggest that apoptotic vulnerability in SCH patients (SP) is increased and that non-lethal localized apoptosis may contribute to the pathophysiology of this disorder [11-17]. Promising studies indicate that both neuronal and glial as well as peripheral apoptotic markers are altered in SCH [11-17]. According to the neurodevelopmental theory, these changes may result from pathological processes in the brain induced by environmental factors during the early stage of brain formation [18-20], and both neuroinflammation and autoimmune sensitization could be accounted for an increased rate of apoptosis recently demonstrated in SCH-related studies [11-17]. These processes result in genetic abnormalities leading to dysfunction of specific neural network, which might contribute to the premorbid signs for the later developed SCH [18-20].

The present chapter provides overview of our recent studies on the involvement of immune system abnormalities and aberrant apoptosis in the pathogenesis of SCH. The investigations include human studies in a large cohort of patients with paranoid form of SCH (ICD-10 code: F20.0; DSM-IV-TR code: 295.30) [21, 22] and age-, sex-matched healthy subjects (controls), in total 400 subjects in each group. Contributions of other research groups to this field are also indicated.

1. Alterations in the Complement Cascade in SCH

1.1. General Presentation of the Complement System

The complement system is an important effector on the innate and adaptive immunity, mediator of a variety of cellular and humoral interactions in the immune response. Complement has an important role in the immune recognition, host defense against invading pathogens (bacteria, viruses, fungi) and defective host cells (transformed or damaged), in maintaining immunologic memory, as well as in cell proliferation and differentiation, tissue regeneration, aging, and growth [23-27].

The complement system is a network of 35-40 soluble and membrane-bound proteins (enzymes, receptors, regulators, etc). Mostly all tissues and organs, including brain, are able to produce complement proteins, but liver is their main source. Many of complement soluble proteins (mostly serum glycoproteins) are proenzymes (serine proteases), producing and circulating in inactive forms (zymogens), but activating when cleaved into two peptides. One peptide binds to immune complexes (IC), pathogen, altered host cell or to complement receptors (CR) CR1, CR2, CR3, CR4, C1QR, C5aR, and C3aR expressed by various cells and acts as opsonin, inflammatory mediator, chemotaxin, or anaphylatoxin. The other peptide continues to act in cascade as protease, activating the next component directly or after assembling with proteolytic cleavage product of another complement protein (formation of convertases). Some molecules of this peptide may also act as opsonins or inflammatory mediators (directly or after further cleavage). Thus, activation of the complement leads to a sequential cascade of proteolytic and complex formation reactions resulting in generation of fragments of the complement C2, C3, and C4 proteins (C2a, C2b, C3a, C3b, C4a, C4b) and their further degradation products (iC3b, C3c, C3dg, C3d, C3g, C4c, C4d), which are inflammatory mediators, opsonins, chemotaxins, and anaphylatoxins [23-27].

Complement activation is known to occur through three pathways, classical, alternative, and lectin, differed in components and initiation mechanisms. Complement proteins mostly exist as inactive zymogens that are then sequentially cleaved and activated (Fig.1). All pathways converge at C3 complement protein. Final sequence of reactions in the complement cascade, the terminal pathway, is identical for all 3 pathways and results in the assembly of membrane attack complex (MAC), a terminal end product of the complement activation. MAC is a powerful cytolytic agent, which puts pores in membranes of host cells to which antibodies are bound, outer and inner membranes of Gram-negative bacteria, and damages envelope of virus resulting in their lysis [23-27].

The complement system is tightly controlled through several regulatory mechanisms. Many regulatory proteins block activity through binding to target. Decay accelerating factor for complement (CD55), complement membrane cofactor protein (CD46), and membrane inhibitor of reactive lysis (CD59; complement regulatory protein; protectin) represent membrane-bound regulatory proteins of the complement system. Among soluble proteins are both positive regulators (properdin, mannan-binding lectin (MBL) associated protein of 19 kDa (MAp19)) and negative regulators (CI-inhibitor, C4b-binding protein, factor H, factor I, carboxypeptidase, S-protein, clusterin, MBL-associated serine peptidase 3 (MASP-3), MBL-associated protein of 44 kDa (MAp44)) [23-27].

Inappropriate complement activation, complement upregulation as well as complement deficiencies and downregulation are the underlying causes of the pathophysiology of many diseases [23, 27-29].

Promising findings, implicating complement in neurogenesis, synapse remodeling and pruning during brain development [30-32], suggest a potential role of complement in neurodevelopmental processes contributing to SCH susceptibility [18, 33-35]. A number of studies, including also our own research presented below suggest that alterations in the complement cascade are involved in pathogenesis of SCH.

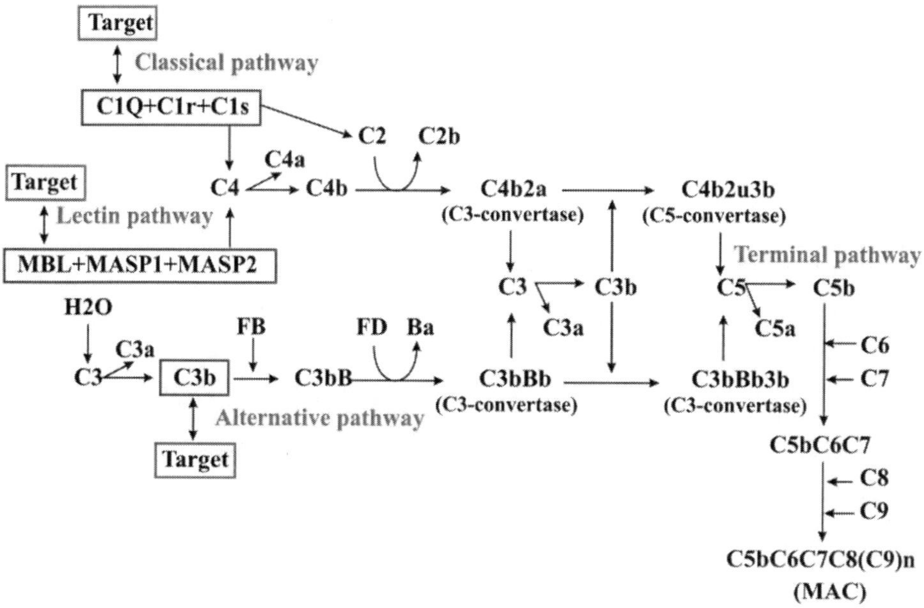

MBL - mannan-binding lectin, MASP1 - MBL-associated serine peptidase 1, MASP2 - MBL-associated serine peptidase 2, FD - factor D, FB - factor B.1.2. Classical complement pathway in SCH.

Figure 1. Complement activation pathways.

The classical pathway of the complement cascade (Fig.1) is initiated when IC are formed after immunoglobulin (Ig) G or IgM binds to pathogens or to other foreign and non-self antigens or autoantigens. The C1 multimeric complex consists of three serine proteases, namely C1Q, C1r, and C1s. The binding of C1Q to crystallizable fragment (Fc) of IC leads to auto-activation of C1r, which activates C1s. C1s cleaves C4 and C2 to form the classical pathway C3 convertase, C4bC2a, that cleaves C3, leading to activation of C3-C9 components and formation of MAC. Pentraxins including the long pentraxin 3 (PTX3), C-reactive protein (CRP), and serum amyloid P (SAP) can substitute IgG and IgM in the IC, bind C1Q and activate the classical pathway. In addition, MBL-SAP complexes, myocardial damage products, membranes of apoptotic cells, C4 nephritic factor, myelin, phosphatidylcholine, bacterial polysacharides, capsular polysacharides of Gram-positive bacteria, lipid A (component of cell wall lipopolysacharides of Gram-negative bacteria), DNA, RNA, chromatin, polyanions, polycations, Rodent leukemia virus, and HIV may also activate the classical complement pathway through direct interaction with C1Q [23-29, 36].

Several studies have focused on the total activity of the complement classical pathway in SCH. Spivak et al. [37] reported a decrease in total hemolytic activity of the complement classical pathway (CH50) in the blood of SP versus controls, while more recent studies, including our own, suggest a modest insignificant increase in the blood CH50 levels when comparing SP with controls [38-42]. Measurements were performed according to earlier described hemolytic assay utilizing sheep erythrocytes sensitized with rabbit anti-sheep antibodies as target cells [43]. Also, in one report significantly raised CH50 blood levels in SP versus controls were observed [44]. It is conceivable that differences in the disease stage and course as well as disease duration may influence complement total hemolytic activity.

1.2. C1 Complement Protein in SCH

As it was already mentioned, C1 is the initial component of the complement classical pathway. We determined hemolytic activity of C1 protein in the blood serum samples of SCH-affected subjects and controls [41, 42]. Measurements were performed according to earlier described hemolytic assay utilizing sheep erythrocytes sensitized with rabbit anti-sheep antibodies as target cells and C1 depleted serum [43, 45]. According to the results obtained, the mean value of the serum C1 hemolytic activity in SP was 1.7 times higher than in controls ($p<0.002$), and no significant difference was found between males and females in each group. Also, there was no significant difference between the mean value of the C1 hemolytic activity when comparing neuroleptic-treated and neuroleptic-free SP. Our data related to the increased hemolytic activity of the C1 component of complement in the serum of SP is in agreement with previous data reported by Shcherbakova et al [39, 40]. Currently no data on C1 blood levels in SCH are reported.

Increased hemolytic activity of the complement C1 protein in SP is of special interest accounting for a positive linkage of SCH with chromosome 1p36 loci located nearby the C1Q encoding *C1QA* and *C1QB* genes (1p36.12) [46, 47]. No data regarding association of the mentioned genes polymorphisms with SCH have been published yet. To explore whether the alterations in C1Q activity in SCH are genetically determined or not, we evaluated the possible association of complement C1Q component gene variants with susceptibility to SCH in Armenian population, focusing on *C1QA* and *C1QB* four intronic single nucleotide polymorphisms (SNPs) [48].

Two tagged SNPs were selected by Martens et al. using HapMap project [49], and other two we chose according to their frequent appearance in European Caucasoid population with minor allele frequency >10% and also their potential functional effect (gain/loss of binding site for transcription factors) [50-53]. All DNA samples were genotyped for four SNPs, namely *C1QA:* rs292001, *C1QB:* rs913243, rs291982 and rs631090 by polymerase chain reaction with sequence-specific primers (PCR-SSP) and quantitative real-time (qRT) PCR. The genotype distributions of studied SNPs in *both SP and controls complied with Hardy-Weinberg (H-W) equilibrium ($p>0.05$).* Statistical power of the study, indicating the difference in the carriage of the *C1QB* rs291982*G allele between the SP and controls for the odds ratio (OR) 2.5, reached 98.4% while for OR=1.2 was 38%.

The frequencies of all studied genetic variants in the groups of SP and control subjects are shown in Table 1. *C1QA* rs292001 and *C1QB* rs913243 polymorphisms were almost equally represented in both groups (p>0.05). By contrast, significant differences in the *C1QB* rs631090*C (22% versus 17%, OR=1.4, 95%CI: 1.01-1.95, $p_{nominal}$=0.044) and rs291982*G (58% vs 46%, OR=1.64, 95%CI: 1.26-2.13, $p_{nominal}$=0.0002) minor allele between SP and controls were found. After Bonferroni correction for the number of tested loci (n=4) *C1QB* rs291982*G minor allele remained more frequent at significant level in schizophrenics compared to controls ($p_{corrected}$=0.0008). The overall distribution of *C1QB* rs291982 genotypes differed between the patients and controls ($p_{corrected}$=0.0004, 2 degrees of freedom, d.f.) due to the overrepresentation of rs291982 GG homozygotes among schizophrenics (36% vs 19%, $p_{nominal}$=2.4E-5, $p_{corrected}$=9.6E-5, 1 d.f., OR=2.5, 95%Cl: 1.62-3.85). Further, the rs291982 GG genotype was associated with increased risk for schizophrenia when compared to both TG ($p_{corrected}$=0.0004) and TT ($p_{corrected}$=0.0016) genotypes. In contrast, the susceptibility to schizophrenia was almost equal in rs291982 TG and TT genotypes ($p_{nominal}$=0.82). These results suggest that the *C1QB* rs291982*G minor allele might be considered as a risk factor for schizophrenia at least in Armenian population

Table 1. Distribution of *C1QA / C1QB* genotypes and carriage of minor alleles in SP and controls. The data are presented as absolute numbers with proportions (%) in parentheses

SNP ID	Genotype 1	Genotype 2	Genotype 3	Allele 1	Allele 2	Carriage
rs292001	GG	GA	AA	G	A	A
SP	76 (0.34)	112 (0.50)	37 (0.16)	264 (0.59)	186 (0.41)	149 (0.66)
Controls	59 (0.26)	119 (0.53)	47 (0.21)	237 (0.53)	213 (0.47)	166 (0.74)
p					0.070[a]	0.080[b]
rs913243	GG	GT	TT	G	T	T
SP	68 (0.30)	123 (0.55)	34 (0.15)	259 (0.58)	191 (0.42)	157 (0.70)
Controls	64 (0.28)	124 (0.56)	37 (0.16)	254 (0.56)	196 (0.44)	161 (0.72)
p					0.638[a]	0.679[b]
rs291982	TT	TG	GG	T	G	G
SP	46 (0.20)	97 (0.44)	82 (0.36)	189 (0.42)	261 (0.58)	179 (0.80)
Controls	61 (0.27)	122 (0.54)	42 (0.19)	244 (0.54)	206 (0.46)	164 (0.73)
p					0.0002[a]	0.003[b]
rs631090	TT	TC	CC	T	C	C
SP	135 (0.60)	79 (0.35)	11 (0.05)	349 (0.78)	101 (0.22)	90 (0.40)
Controls	153 (0.68)	67 (0.30)	5 (0.02)	373 (0.83)	77 (0.17)	72 (0.32)
p					0.044[a]	0.077[b]

[a] *p*-values for comparison of Allele 2 proportion between SP and controls;
[b] *p*-values for comparison of Allele 2 carriage between SP and controls.

Haplotype analysis was performed to confirm the observed association and to estimate the maximum-likehood *C1QA*/*C1QB* (rs292001/rs913243/rs291982/rs631090) haplotype frequencies. In total, 16 haplotypes in each group of study subjects were estimated. Interestingly, haplotype comparison between SP and controls revealed four haplotypes with nominally significant differences groups, namely, A-T-T-T (haplotype frequencies in SP versus controls: 13% versus 19%, OR=0.57, 95%CI: 0.40-0.81, $p_{nominal}$=0.02, $p_{corrected}$=0.32),

A-G-T-T (4% versus 11%, OR=0.41, 95%CI: 0.23-0.74, $p_{nominal}$=0.002, $p_{corrected}$=0.03), A-G-G-T (8% versus 4%, OR=2.02, 95%CI: 1.13-3.63, $p_{nominal}$=0.015, $p_{corrected}$=0.24), G-G-G-C (8% versus 2%, OR=1.99, 95%CI: 1.03-3.84, $p_{nominal}$=0.049, $p_{corrected}$=0.78) and A-T-G-C (1% versus 0.6%, OR=4.43, 95%CI: 1.25-15.66, $p_{nominal}$=0.009, $p_{corrected}$=0.14), only one of which (A-G-T-T) remained significant after the correction for the number of haplotypes.

The difference in A-G-T-T haplotype between SP and controls suggested that the *C1QB* rs291982*G minor allele is more frequent in SP than in controls. Importantly, this data are in complete concordance with minor allele frequencies in both groups. The haplotype analysis, therefore, confirmed detected association of the *C1QB* rs291982 variant with SCH.

In both patients and controls pair-wise linkage disequilibrium (LD) between the investigated *C1QB* rs913243, rs291982 and rs631090 SNPs was determined. LD blocks of *C1QB* gene SNPs and values of absolute D′ (r^2) for both groups are presented in Fig. 2.

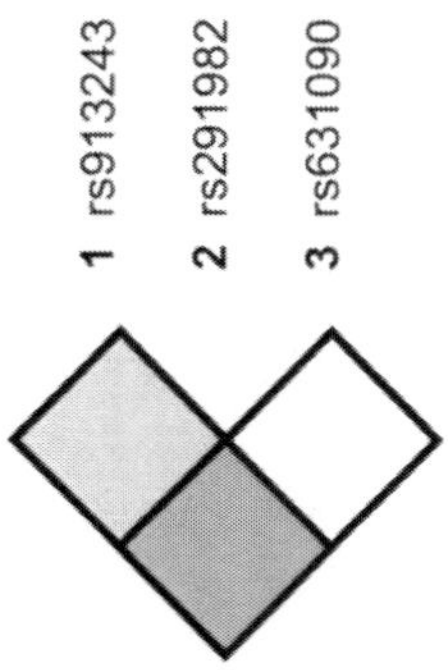

SP

|D'| (r^2)	marker		
marker	rs913243	rs291982	rs631090
rs913243		0.22 (0.03)	0.41 (0.04)
rs291982	0.22 (0.03)		0.11(0.005)
rs631090	0.41 (0.04)	0.11(0.005)	

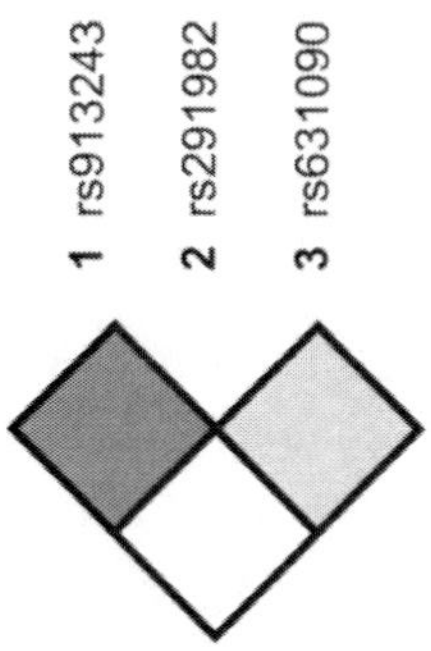

Controls

|D'| (r^2)	marker		
marker	rs913243	rs291982	rs631090
rs913243		0.49 (0.15)	0.23 (0.01)
rs291982	0.49 (0.15)		0.33 (0.02)
rs631090	0.23 (0.01)	0.33 (0.02)	

Figure 2. LD blocks of *C1QB* gene rs913243 / rs291982 / rs631090 SNPs and values of absolute D′ (r^2) for SP and controls.

Thus, we observed no association of *C1QA* rs292001, *C1QB* rs913243 and rs631090 variants with SCH, whereas positive association of *C1QB* rs291982*G variant, namely its GG genotype with SCH was found. The results suggest that the *C1QB* rs291982*G minor allele might be a risk factor for SCH at least in Armenian population. Therefore, *C1QB* gene may be considered as a relevant candidate gene for susceptibility to SCH. To our knowledge, this is the first study investigating association of the *C1QA* and *C1QB* genetic variants with SCH. This study might contribute to understanding the molecular pathomechanisms responsible for generation and development of SCH.

Whereas the functionality of *C1QA* rs292001 and *C1QB* rs631090 has been previously shown in lupus erythematosus [49], our study revealed no association of these two functional variants with SCH. At present, there are no published data on functionality of the *C1QB* rs291982 and rs913243 polymorphisms. In order to explore possible functional role of these genetic variants, we use the web server ALGGEN, a convenient tool for identification of the functional effects of SNPs [54]. Analysis showed that both *C1QB* rs291982 and rs913243 SNPs were found to be intronic enhancers. Thus, the *C1QB* rs291982 minor G allele contains binding sites for transcription factors forkhead box P3 (FOXP3, also known as hepocyte nuclear factor 3 (HNF3) forkhead homologue 2 or HFH-2), progesterone receptor isoform A (PRA) and B (PRB), absent in the T major allele. Further, the rs913243 G/T polymorphism of the *C1QB* gene leads to loss of binding sites of glucocorticoid receptor-alpha (GR-alpha) and retinoid X receptor-alpha (RXR-alpha) transcription factors. Whereas these types of functional effects have low phenotypic risk [55], the results of our analysis might indicate the functionality of the *C1QB* rs291982 and rs913243 SNPs as enhancers, transcription-stimulating DNA regulatory elements [56]. Importantly, these transcription factors might have an indirect impact on immune system [50-53], therefore, might contribute to the immune system alterations in SCH.

The association between the *C1QB* gene rs291982*G genetic variant with SCH obtained in our study may suggest the etiological significance of *C1QB* gene in SCH in Armenian population. Furthermore, this finding may reflect implication of neurodegenerative component in SCH [20]. Thus, Grewal et al demonstrated overexpression of *C1QB* in the areas undergoing neurodegeneration [57]. In addition, recent study showing alterations in expression of *C1QB* gene in hippocampus and cerebral cortex in the animal models of Alzheimer's disease [58], having some clinical features shared with SCH, such as neuron loss and cognitive impairment [21].

There may be another possible explanation of the association observed in our study in the light of the vascular-inflammatory theory of SCH [8]. This theory is based on observations that inflammatory vascular disease of the brain leads to psychosis and exhibits a fluctuating course as seen in SCH, and that disturbances of central nervous system blood flow have repeatedly been observed in people with SCH [8]. Interestingly, it has been demonstrated that the human cerebrovascular smooth muscle cells (HCSMC) isolated from cortical vessels derived from postmortem brains can express mRNAs for complement *C1QB* gene. As HCSMC are closely associated with amyloid beta deposits in vessels in the brain, their production of complement proteins could amplify the proinflammatory effects of amyloid in the perivascular environment, further compromising brain vascular integrity [59].

Also, the observed differences in the *C1QB* gene LD blocks between SP and controls may suggest that *C1QB* rs291982*G allele is a marker of a haplotype carrying "causative" variant located nearby on the first chromosome. In this context it is quite important to note that chromosomal region 1p36 carrying *C1QB* gene has already been associated with SCH in two genome-wide linkage scans [46, 47].

1.3. C2 complement Protein in SCH

The C2 component participates in both classical and lectin pathways of the complement activation (Fig. 1). Both partial and acquired C2 complement component deficiency has been known to associate with a number of autoimmune disorders and an increased risk of autoimmune disease [60].

According to our data, SCH is characterize by decreased C2 hemolytic activity, since the mean value of the blood serum C2 hemolytic activity in SP was 1.94 times lower than in controls ($p<0.001$); and no significant difference was found between males and females in each group. Also, there was no significant difference between the mean value of the C2 hemolytic activity when comparing neuroleptic-treated and neuroleptic-free SP or males and females in each study group [41, 42]. Measurements were performed according to earlier described hemolytic assay utilizing sheep erythrocytes sensitized with rabbit anti-sheep antibodies as target cells and C2 depleted serum [43, 44].

The observed decreased activity of C2 in SCH might be one of the possible reasons for why in SCH the classical pathway activity of the complement remains practically unchanged, whereas the activity of its C1 component increases [38, 43, 45]. However, it has to be mentioned that Scherbakova et al detected significant 1.3 times increase in serum C2 hemolytic activity in SP, while reporting insignificant changes in CH50 and significant increase in hemolytic activities of C1 protein [39, 40]. Therefore, the influence of population-specific genetic or environmental factors on C2 serum levels in SP also cannot be excluded. The C2 protein belongs to those components of the complement, whose genes are located at the HLA class III region of the human genome. Wang et al investigated the C2 allotypes of HLA class III in SP, but found no significant difference in C2 allotypes between the patients and controls [61]. However, only population-associated studies with the involvement of different ethnic groups will help to reveal if there are any SCH-associated population specific functional variants of the C2 gene polymorphisms.

1.4. C3 Complement Protein in SCH

C3 is a central protein of the complement system. This protein is the initial component of the complement alternative pathway, and the converge point of all three complement activation pathways, i.e. starting point of the complement terminal pathway (Fig.1). It is also involved in the complement classical and lectin pathways. Of the 35-40 distinct complement proteins recognized to date, C3 is probably the most versatile and multifunctional molecule known, interacting with at least 20 different proteins. C3 is also involved in the control of the intracellular processing of the antigen, plays a central role in complement activation and participates in phagocytic and multiple immunoregulatory processes. Fragments of C3 interact with various proteins and fulfill diverse functions, i.e. complement activation, participation in phagocytosis and enhancement of antigen processing. C3 fragments increase cell to cell interactions, induce intracellular signaling after binding to their receptors and increases intracellular processing of antigens [23-27, 62, 63].

The C3 allotypes (F and S) appear to have the same hemolytic activity and blood levels of the component, but have been reported to have different capacity to bind to C3 receptors, e.g. the F type has higher affinity to the receptors compared to the S allotype [64-66]. Data related to difference in C3 phenotype and allotype frequencies [67-69] as well as in the C3 protein blood levels [37, 70] between SP are controversial.

We focused our attention on the activity of C3 in SCH. According to our data [41, 42], the mean value of the serum C3 hemolytic activity in SP was 2 times higher than in controls ($p<0.004$). Measurements were performed according to earlier described hemolytic assay utilizing sheep erythrocytes sensitized with rabbit anti-sheep antibodies as target cells and C3 depleted serum [43, 45].

The results obtained are consistent with those previously reported by Shcherbakova et al [39, 40]. No difference in the mean value of the C3 hemolytic activity was observed when comparing males and females in each study group. However, we found that the mean value of the hemolytic activity of C3 was 2.17 times higher in neuroleptic-treated SP than in neuroleptic-free SP ($p<0.001$).

1.5. C4 Complement Protein in SCH

The complement protein C4 is a non-enzymatic component of the complement system. C4 is activated proteolytically when complement is activated via the classical or lectin activation pathways. The product of activation, C4b, is itself an opsonin, and binds covalently to the complement activating target. It also serves as a subunit of the C3 and C5 convertases of these pathways. C4 is a major factor in the complement cascade, and, therefore, in the innate immune system [71]. C4 deficiency may lead to defective processing of immune complexes, and impairment of B-cell memory, and, in turn, to persistence of bacterial and viral infections [72-74]. On the other hand, an excess activity/production of C4 may cause overactivation of the complement pathways and exacerbate the inflammatory response [75].

Our study indicated that the mean value of the blood serum C4 hemolytic activity in SP is 1.38 times significantly higher than in controls ($p<0.001$) [41, 42]. Measurements were performed according to earlier described hemolytic assay utilizing sheep erythrocytes sensitized with rabbit anti-sheep antibodies as target cells and C4 depleted serum [43, 45]. The results obtained are consistent with the previously reported data [39, 40].

There was no significant difference between the mean value of the C4 hemolytic activity when comparing neuroleptic-treated and neuroleptic-free SP. Also, no significant difference was found between males and females in each group [41, 42].

C4 has two C4A and C4B isotypes, which have diversified thereby probably improving (i) the opsonization/immune clearance function and (ii) the function of inhibiting infection by microbial lysis and neutralization. Many infectious and autoimmune diseases are associated with complete or partial deficiency of C4A and/or C4B [76, 77]. Some association between mental diseases and decreased C4B protein levels in serum has been reported. Thus, decreased C4B was observed in children with attention-deficit hyperactivity disorder, and it was also shown that low concentration of C4B was plausibly associated with autism [78-80].

The genes encoding C4A and C4B proteins are located at the HLA class III region of the human genome and are highly polymorphic with variation at many residues, but the difference in activity between the two proteins correlates with differences in only four amino acids [81, 82]. Significantly higher frequency of the C4A*4 allele in SP compared with controls was found; the relative risk of this allotype to SCH was 4.18 and the etiologic fraction was 0.042 [61]. According to the C4 protein isotyping data of Rudduck et al. [83], the significant increase in the frequency of C4B (Q0Q0) homozygous deficiency was found among Swedish SP compared with controls ($p<0.0005$). However, the C4 genotyping data obtained from a German population [84] contradict this as they report C4B (Q0Q0) homozygote deficiency at similar frequency among patients and controls.

The data concerning the levels of C4 in the blood of SP, accounting for total protein concentration (C4A+C4B) or C4A and C4B concentrations separately have been inconsistent [37, 83-87]. To clear this question and to test whether there is an association of homozygous C4B deficiency with SCH in Armenian population, we investigated the C4B phenotypes by sodium dodecylsulphate polyacrylamide gel electrophoresis [88] and concentration by sandwich enzyme-linked immunosorbent assay (ELISA) [89] in the blood serum of SP and controls [90-93].

Our data on serum C4B protein concentrations in SP and controls are shown in Table 2. A significant difference was seen in this respect between SP and controls. The patients had decreased C4B concentration in serum in comparison with controls ($p<0.01$, 95% CI: (-61.5)-(-7.11)). In subjects with 4BB the mean level of the protein was 2 times higher than in C4BQO haploinsufficient individuals ($p<0.00001$, Fig.3). The last observation is in accordance with literature data [94]. No association between C4B serum level and age, gender, age at first onset and duration of SCH was found. No difference in the mean values of the C4B level between neuroleptic-free and neuroleptic-treated SP as well as females and males in each studied group was detected [90-93].

Our data do not confirm a positive association between a homozygous deficiency in complement factor C4B and SCH previously reported by Rudduck et al [83]. Also, we do not observe the significant increase in homozygous C4B (Q0Q0) phenotype in SCH as Schroers et al [84]. Only one patient had complete deficiency of this protein. However, we did find decreased serum C4B protein concentrations in SP versus controls. On average, C4B protein was 22.5% lower in serum of SP than in controls [90-92].

Table 2. Concentration of C4B in the blood serum of SP and controls

Group	Mean±SD	p	95% CI of mean	Median [IQR]	p	95% ICR of median
SP	141±53.0	<0.01	125.2-157.0	159,1[62.9]	<0.01	142.5-175.7
Controls	182±81.7		159,2-205.1	180.0[102]		148.0-196.0

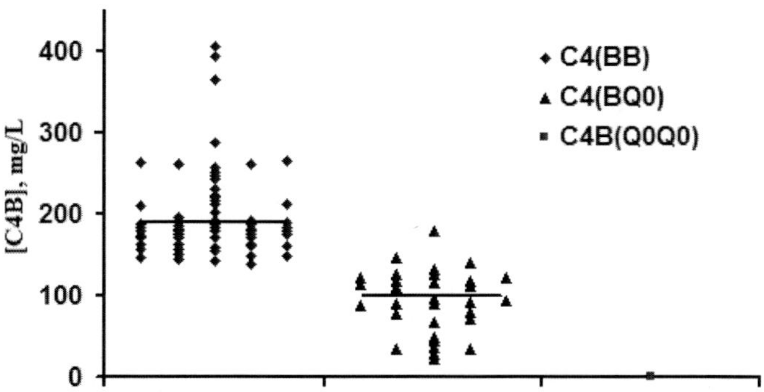

Figure 3. Concentration of the C4B protein in the serum of individuals with one (C4BQO) or both (C4BB) alleles, as well as in an individual with complete C4B deficiency.

Our data clearly demonstrate a decrease in complement C4B protein level in the blood of SP and indicate that the increased hemolytic activity of the C4 protein in SCH may result from the increased level of its C4A isotype.

1.6. CR1 and Its Ligands in SCH

CR1 (CD35, C3b/C4b receptor) is a multifunctional receptor, which is expressed in the majority of peripheral blood cells [95-98], with high affinity to complement components C1Q, C3, C4 [99-102], and MBL [103]. Binding of CR1 to opsonic fragments of the complement C3 and C4 components (C3b, C4b, iC3b, and C3dg) and to the complement component C1Q attached to IC, foreign or altered host cells serves to mediate clearance of IC (on erythrocytes) [98, 104] and phagocytosis of complement-coated particles (on leukocytes) [95, 105, 106]. In addition, interaction of CR1 with its ligands plays further roles in regulation of leukocytes activity by promoting secretion of interleukin (IL)-1α, IL-1β, and prostaglandins [107]. Furthermore, CR1 plays a role in antigen presentation to B cells [106]. In addition to membrane-bound CR1, leukocytes also release soluble form of CR1, which is a potent inhibitor of both classical and alternative pathways of complement activation by exhibiting decay-accelerating activity for both C3 and C5 convertases, as well as cofactor activity for factor I (FI)-mediated cleavage of C3b and C4b [104, 107, 108].

CR1 represents a special interest, accounting for a positive genome-wide linkage of SCH with the *CR1* gene encoding locus (1q32) [109]. A common *CR1* C5507G SNP in exon 33 has been shown to be associated with some diseases characterized by altered inflammatory response [110, 111], and changes in CR1 expression have been shown in patients with a variety of inflammatory and autoimmune diseases [112-114].

We investigated the expression of CR1 on erythrocytes and leukocytes in SP and controls and evaluated the possible association of the *CR1* C5507G functional polymorphism with this disorder. In addition, in the blood of SP the levels of IC containing natural ligands of CR1, C1Q, and fragments of C3 (C1Q-IC and C3d-IC, respectively), were also determined [115, 116].

The expression of CR1 on blood cells was quantified by flow cytometry. The results obtained are shown in Table 3. According to the data obtained, the CR1 expression levels for erythrocytes were significantly higher in SP compared to controls and were positively correlated with the duration of SCH (rho=0.637, p<0.004). The same applies to the percentage of CR1-positive erythrocytes (SP: 83.84 [2.66] % versus controls: 75.94 [6.74] %, p<7.48E-07). Interestingly, the CR1 expression on subpopulation of leukocytes (lymphocytes, monocytes, and neutrophils) in patients was significantly higher than in controls, whereas the percentage of CR1 positive lymphocytes (SP: 11.69 [4.03] % versus controls: 17.26 [6.60] %, p<4.02E-05) and monocytes (SP: 1.49 [0.91] % versus controls: 5.19 [1.83] %, p<1.42E-10) was significantly lower. No significant difference was observed in the number of positive neutrophils among studied groups (SP: 64.18 [12.15] % versus controls: 59.93 [9.60] %, p>0.52).

Table 3. CR1 expression on blood cells in SP and controls

Type of blood cells	CR1 expression, relative fluorescence intensity, median [interquartile range]		
	SP	Controls	p
Erythrocytes	6.85 [0.89]	6.21 [0.67]	<0.001
Lymphocytes	22.35 [8.35]	19.30 [7.90]	<0.011
Monocytes	85.55 [46.35]	47.30 [10.00]	<1.20E-08
Neutrophils	185.5 [80.00]	140.00 [44.5]	<0.003

Distribution of genotypes for *CR1* C5507G SNP corresponded to the H-W equilibrium. We found no significant differences in distribution of genotypes, allele and carriage frequencies between the groups of SP and controls (p>0.05, Table 4). The intergroup comparisons showed that in the CC genotype the levels of CR1 expression on erythrocytes, monocytes, and neutrophils were higher in patients than in controls (p<0.006), whereas in lymphocytes practically equal levels of CR1 expression in both groups were detected (p>0.05). Further, we compared the levels of CR1 expression on the blood cells of normal allele homozygotes and minor allele carriers (CG+GG) in SP and controls. Both groups showed increased CR1 expression on erythrocytes in CC homozygous subjects compared to minor allele carriers (Fig. 4), whereas the levels of CR1 expression on lymphocytes, monocytes, and neutrophils did not differ between these genotypes (p>0.05, Table 5). No correlation between the *CR1* 5507G carriers and clinical characteristics of SP has been observed. In SP, the fractions of CR1 positive lymphocytes (CC: 10.45 [5.41] %, CG+GG: 13.51 [4.90] %, p=0.047) and neutrophils (CC: 62.95 [10.90] %, CG+GG: 70.75 [14.98] %, p=0.026) were higher in minor allele carriers, whereas in controls the number of CR1 positive erythrocytes were significantly higher in CC homozygotes (CC: 80.10 [4.54] %, CG+GG: 75.09 [6.48] %, p=0.023).

The median level of C1Q-IC in the blood serum was significantly higher in SP compared to controls (SP 27.25 [4.17] ug/mL versus controls: 24.23 [3.88] ug/mL, p=0.017), whereas the levels of C3d-IC were practically the same in both groups (SP: 14.20 [2.68] ug/mL versus controls14.09 [3.77] ug/mL, p=0.66). No difference in C3d-IC and C1Q-IC levels was observed between *CR1* 5507 CC homozygotes and minor allele carriers in SP (p>0.05). In contrast, the G allele carriers in controls had significantly elevated C1Q-IC levels (CG+GG: 25.18 [3.16] ug/mL versus CC: 22.27 [3.73] ug/mL, p=0.015).

Correlation analysis showed that CR1 expression levels on blood cells in controls positively correlated with C3d-IC levels (rho=0.44, p=0.049) and negatively correlated with C1Q-IC levels (rho=-0.42, p=0.058). No significant correlation between these parameters was observed in SP.

Table 4. Distribution of the *CR1* C5507G genotypes and carriage rates for minor alleles in SP and controls. The data are presented as absolute numbers with proportions in parenthesis

		SP	Controls	OR, 95%CI, p
		Frequency, absolute (relative)		
Genotype	CC	75 (0.64)	84(0.59)	p>0.05
	CG	38 (0.32)	55 (0.39)	
	GG	4 (0.03)	3 (0.02)	
Allele	C	188 (0.80)	223 (0.79)	OR: 1.15, 95CI%: 0.85-1.36, p>0.05
	G	46 (0.20)	61 (0.21)	
Carriage	C	113 (0.98)	139 (0.97)	OR: 0.78, 95%CI: 0.66-1.16, p>0.05
	G	42 (0.41)	58 (0.36)	

Our study has extended the current knowledge on the state of the complement system in SCH by studying CR1 expression on blood cells, the levels of IC bound to CR1 ligands, the products of the complement activation, and the *CR1* C5507G functional polymorphism in SP and controls.

The results obtained for the first time demonstrated an increased expression of CR1 on erythrocytes and subpopulations of leukocytes (lymphocytes, monocytes, and neutrophils), accompanied by the elevated number of CR1 positive erythrocytes and reduced number of CR1 positive lymphocytes and monocytes in SP as compared to controls. Regarding IC bound to complement-derived CR1 ligands, the increased levels of C1Q-IC in SP compared to controls were detected, whereas no significant difference in the levels of C3d-IC between SP and controls was observed.

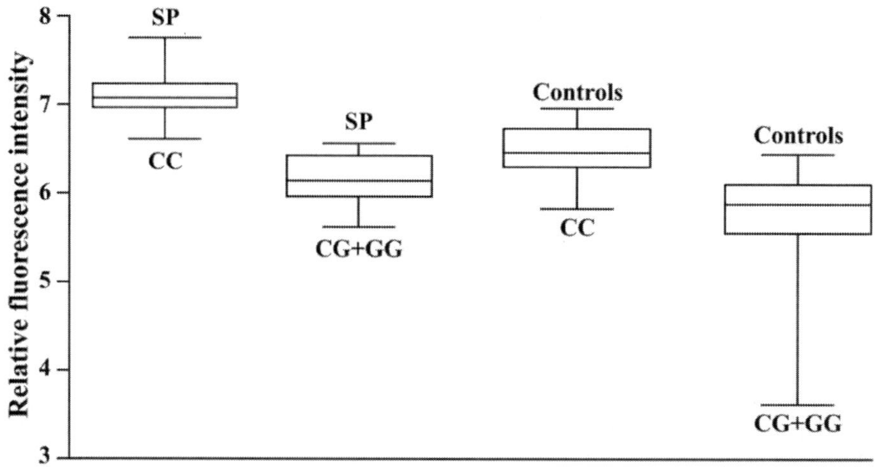

Figure 4. The intragroup comparison of CR1 surface expression with regard to the *CR1* 5507 major allele homozygotes (CC) versus G minor allele carriers (CG+GG). Surface expression is given in relative fluorescence intensity units (excitation 488 nm, emission max 518 nm) as median [interquartile range]. The data are expressed as whisker box plots; the box represents the 25-75th percentiles, the median is indicated by a horizontal bar across the box, the whiskers on each box represent the minimum and maximum level. P<0.0003 when comparing levels between SP and controls.

Table 5. Comparison of CR1 expression (median [interquartile range]) on blood cells (erythrocytes (E), lymphocytes (L), monocytes (M), and neutrophils (N)) of SP and controls depending on the *CR1* C5507G genotypes

Type of cell	CR1 expression in SP			CR1 expression in controls		
	CC	CG+GG	p	CC	CG+GG	p
E	7.07 [0.31]	6.15 [0.52]	6.57E-08	6.46 [0.46]	5.87 [0.52]	<6.88E-06
L	21.70 [8.48]	24.15 [9.33]	>0.05	19.5 [8.25]	18.5 [8.5]	>0.05
M	80.8 [49.35]	89.6 [45.88]	>0.05	48.86 [9.00]	45.45 [16.75]	>0.05
N	190 [91.30]	174.5 [65.00]	>0.05	128 [42.50]	149.5 [97]	>0.05

Changes in CR1 expression on blood cells have been implicated in a variety of diseases (systemic lupus erythematosus, acute immunodeficiency syndrome, rheumatoid arthritis, malarial anaemia, insulin-dependent diabetes, myocardial infarction, etc) associated with the immune system dysfunction, development of inflammatory and autoimmune reactions [113, 114, 117-121]. Depending on diseased condition, these changes may be determined by either genetic or environmental factors. For instance, increase of CR1 expression on leukocytes can be induced by tumor necrosis factor-α (TNF-α) and IL-1 [122, 123], which are elevated in the blood of SP [124].

We also observed an enhanced number of CR1 positive erythrocytes in SP, while fractions of CR1 positive lymphocytes and monocytes were significantly decreased in SP compared to controls. Increased number of CR1 positive erythrocytes in circulation might be related to the enhanced hematopoiesis in response to cytokines and other inflammatory agents [125], while reduced number of CR1 positive leukocyte subpopulations might be explained by increased rate of apoptosis induced by antipsychotic treatment [126-128].

In summary, on the basis of our results we suggested that SCH is associated with the increased expression of CR1 on erythrocytes, lymphocytes, monocytes, and neutrophils accompanied by the elevated number of CR1 positive erythrocytes, reduced number of CR1 positive lymphocytes and monocytes, and increased level of C1Q-IC. The levels of CR1 expression on erythrocytes were higher in *CR1* 5507 CC homozygotes when compared to those in G allele carriers both among SP and controls.

1.7. Alternative Complement Pathway in SCH

The alternative pathway is initiating upon binding of C3b to foreign or non-self and non-normal or altered-self surfaces. C3 is constantly hydrolyzed at a low level ("tick over") to form C3b. C3b binds to charged parts of cell surface, carbohydrates, lipids, and proteins. FB is then recruited to the bound C3b followed by FD that cleaves FB to form the C3 convertase C3bBb (Fig.1), which is stabilized by the presence of plasma properdin. Properdin is a protein released by activated neutrophils (properdin is also found in macrophages and T cells) and which stabilizes the convertase by binding to C3b and preventing its cleavage by the alternative pathway inhibitors, factor H (FH) and FI [23-27]. Recent studies suggest that properdin can directly bind to apoptotic and necrotic cells and initiate complement activation [129]. The alternative pathway is triggered by pure carbohydrates (agarose, inuline), membranes of apoptotic cells, necrotic cells, endotoxins (lipopolysacharides, lipooligosacharides) from the outer membrane of Gram-negative bacteria, some viruses, and virally infected cells (measles, influenza, Epstein-Barr), some tumor cells (Human Burkitt's lymphoma, Raji tumor cell line), IgA-containing IC, Ig light chains, Ig aggregates, C3 nephritic factor, Cobra venom factor, Heterologous erythrocytes, anionic polymers (dextran sulfate), fungi: *Cryptococcus, Saccharomyces, Candida, Histoplasm) (*through cell wall zymosan), β-D-glucans, parasites: protozoa (trypanosomes) and helminthes, many strains of Gram-positive bacteria (staphylococcus, streptococcus) through cell wall peptidoglicans and teichoic acids, many strains of Gram-negative bacteria (*Escherichia coli* K12, bacterioids) through cell wall lipopolysacharides [23-27, 129].

We evaluated the alternative pathway complement activity in SCH by measuring the alternative pathway hemolytic activity (AH50) in the blood serum samples of SP and controls [130-133] using rabbit erythrocytes as target cells [43]. That is the only data on the total activity of the complement alternative pathway in SCH reported to date. In addition, correlation analysis between AH50 and hemolytic activity of the C3 protein (C3H50) was also performed [130-133] as described in 2.5. According to the results obtained, the mean values of the serum AH50 in both neuroleptic-treated and neuroleptic-free SP were significantly higher than in controls (2.4 ($p<0.001$) and 1.7 times ($p<0.001$), respectively). In addition, in neuroleptic-treated SP AH50 was 1.4 times significantly higher than in neuroleptic-free ($p<0.001$). The results with serum C3H50 levels were similar to those we reported earlier for another cohort of SP [41, 42] described in 2.5. Thus, the mean value of C3H50 in both neuroleptic-treated and neuroleptic-free SP groups were significantly higher than in controls group (2.96 ($p<0.001$) and 1.4 times ($p<0.002$), respectively); the mean value of C3H50 in neuroleptic-treated SP was 2.1 times higher than in neuroleptic-free SP ($p<0.001$). Notably, there was a positive correlation between the increased hemolytic activities of the alternative complement pathway and the C3 complement component in both neuroleptic-free ($r = 0.68$, $p<0.014$) and neuroleptic-treated SP ($r=0.81$, $p<0.001$). The results are summarized in Table 6.

Table 6. Levels of AH50 and CH50 (units*/mL) in the blood serum of SP and controls

Study group	AH50 (mean±SE)	C3H50 (mean±SE)
Neuroleptic-treated SP	228.3±28.1	294.1±23.0
Neuroleptic-free SP	155.6±13.0	138.5±17.1
Controls	93.7±1.7	99.5±4.1

* - an AH50 unit is defined as the amount of serum that causes a 50% hemolysis of rabbit erythrocytes in the reaction mixture. A C3H50 unit is defined as the amount of serum that causes a 50% hemolysis of antibody-sensitized sheep erythrocytes in the reaction mixture. The hemolytic titer is the number of CH50/AH50 units per ml of serum, and is calculated as the reciprocal of the serum dilution which gives 50% cell lysis.

No significant difference was found while comparing patients with family history of SCH and those with a sporadic form of the disease within both neuroleptic-free and neuroleptic-treated groups of SP. In addition, no significant correlation was observed between serum AH50 or C3H50 levels of SP and such variables as age, age at onset and duration of SCH as well as between serum AH50 or C3H50 levels and age in the controls group. Also, no significant difference in the mean values of serum AH50 or C3H50 was found between males and females in each of the examined groups.

The results of our study clearly demonstrate upregulation of the alternative complement cascade in SCH, confirmed our previous data with C3 [41, 42] and, in addition, reveal the existence of a strong correlation between the increased serum levels of C3H50 and AH50 in SP. Therefore, it becomes clear that the elevated hemolytic activity of C3 in SP [39-42] reflects upregulation of the alternative complement cascade.

Since apoptotic cells are known as potent activators of the complement cascade, particularly its alternative pathway, and, on the other hand, C3 is one of the complement proteins, which is directly responsible for opsonization of the apoptotic cells [25, 134-136], we propose that hyperactivation of the alternative complement pathway in SCH is stimulated by apoptotic cells.

The deposition of activated C3 on apoptotic cells is shown to increase the efficiency of their uptake by phagocytic cells [134] by helping phagocytes to dispose of the corpses of the cells. The C3 activation product C3b binds covalently to the activator particle, and acts as an opsonin. Further cleavage of C3b occurs to form a more effective opsonin named iC3b.

Fragments of C3 deposited on the apoptotic cells will bind the phagocyte-expressed complement receptors to further aid recognition and clearance [25, 134-136]. In this context we proposed that elevated levels of C3 activity in SCH [39-42] may result from hyperactivation of the alternative complement pathway by apoptotic cells, which may activate the alternative pathway directly through the complement protein C3 [11, 25, 135, 136].

In addition, the detected difference in both AH50 and C3H50 serum levels between neuroleptic-free and neuroleptic-treated SP suggest an activating effect of neuroleptics on complement alternative pathway. This finding is also consistent with the data obtained in our previous study, where we found the same effect at the level of the C3 complement protein [41, 42]. Furthermore, this finding provides additional support to our hypothesis on the stimulatory effect of apoptotic cells on the alternative complement cascade in SCH, as neuroleptics have been shown to be potent inducers of apoptosis [137-140].

1.8. FB Complement Protein in SCH

Complement FB provides the catalytic subunit of the C3/C5 convertases of the alternative complement pathway. Assembly of the C3 convertase (C3bBb) requires binding of complement FB to C3b, originating during spontaneous hydrolysis of C3, and factor D-mediated cleavage of bound FB resulting in the release of Ba. The C3 convertase is stabilized by the binding of properdin. This provides a positive amplification loop for the classical and alternative complement pathways. Bb is the serine protease element of C3 convertase, which cleaves C3. After cleavage of C3, the C5 convertase C3bBb3b is formed (Fig. 5) [23-27].

According to data reported by Yang et al [141], FB precursor showed significant overexpression in SP as compared to controls ($p<0.022$). The genes encoding FB protein, consisting from one polypeptide chain, are located at the HLA class III region of the human genome. Currently recognized major allotypes of factor B are F, S non-classified, and hypomorphic [142]. Singer et al. [143] found a significant increase in frequency of the FB*F allele of factor B among paranoid SP (54% vs. 33% of controls). Wang et al reported significantly higher frequencies of FB*F and BF*SO7 variants of F and S allotypes, respectively, in SP as compared to controls; the relative risk of these allotypes to SCH was estimated as 1.81, 7.79, and the etiologic fraction were 0.086, 0.060, respectively [61]. However, Rudduck et at found a significant decrease of the S type of FB in patients with a family history of SCH, and no significant difference in this allotype between patients without a family history of SCH and controls [144]. Probably the observed inconsistency of data related to FB allotypes in SCH reflects the population differences of study subjects. Thus, low prevalence of FS in SCH was detected in Spanish population [68], whereas in British population a significantly raised frequency of the FB*S07 in SP was detected [69].

No data regarding FB activity in SP have been published yet.

In our study we performed a comparative determination of the levels of FB in SP using sandwich ELISA utilizing monoclonal antibodies specific to FB and and its Bb fragment, but not to Ba [unpublished data]. This is the only study were the levels of FB in SP were estimated. According to the results obtained, presented on Fig. 5, in SP a significant 1.3 times decrease in the blood serum levels of FB is detected as compared to controls (mean±SD, ug/mL: 220.0±61.04 vs 276.8±65.46, $p<0.01$). We detected no significant difference in the mean value of FB between neuroleptic-free and neuroleptic treated SP. Also, no significant difference was found while comparing patients with family history of SCH and those with a sporadic form of the disease as well as between serum FH levels and such variables as age, age at onset and duration of SCH. The mean value of serum FB levels was not differed between males and females in each of the examined groups.

The observed decline of FB level in SCH may reflect the increased activity of the alternative pathway [130-133] and, consequently, the enhanced degradation of FB.

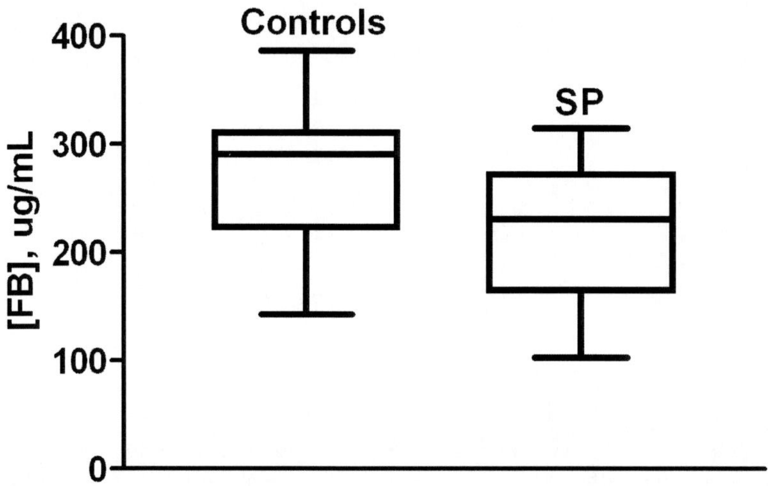

Figure 5. The levels of FB in SP and controls. The data are expressed as whisker box plots; the box represents the 25-75th percentiles, the median is indicated by a horizontal bar across the box, the whiskers on each box represent the minimum and maximum levels (10th and 90th percentiles, respectively). P<0.01 when comparing SP and controls.

1.9. Complement Regulatory Protein FH in SCH

FH is a plasma glycoprotein that plays a key role in controlling complement activation, providing critical negative regulation to the alternative pathway of the complement cascade. It is secreted by Kupffer cells, hepatocytes, vascular endothelial cells, and platelets, and circulates in the blood at high concentration. It prevents local complement activation by sequestering complement component C3b, accelerating the decay of C3 and C5 convertases, competes with factor B for binding to C3b, and functions as a cofactor for the C3b inactivator, FI in the degradation of newly formed C3b molecules to form iC3b (Fig.1) [23-27].

FH interacts with cell surface polyanions including heparin and sialoglycoproteins, and immobilized FH supports the CD11b/CD18 integrin-dependent adhesion of neutrophils. Within the FH molecule there are binding sites for heparin and C3b, as well as for the peptide hormone adrenomedullin [145-147].

A *common* T>C single nucleotide *polymorphism* in exon 9 of the *FH* gene (rs1061170) resulting in *Tyr(Y)* to *His (H)* substitution at position 402 (Y402H) of the FH polypeptide chain, has been shown to associate with some diseased conditions characterised by altered inflammatory response, including atypical hemolytic uremic syndrome, age-related macular degeneration, and coronary heart disease [148-151]. Our recent data also indicated the implication of FH through its 402H variant in the development of systemic inflammatory response developed after ischemic stroke onset [152, 153]. The Y402H polymorphism occurs in the SCR7 region of the gene which has the overlapping binding sites for FH ligands indicated above [145-147].

FH represents a subject of particular interest in SCH research in the light of the observed alterations in the alternative complement pathway in SP [130-133] as stated in 1.8. However, no data relevant to FH in SCH have been published yet.

We performed comparative determination of the blood levels of total FH and its 402H and 402Y variants in SP and controls and assessed genotype frequency of *FH* Y402H polymorphism among both study groups [unpublished data]. Concentrations of total FH and *FH* 402H variant in the serum of study subjects were measured by in-house ELISA as described earlier [155]. Concentration of FH 402Y variant was calculated by subtraction of FH 402H variant level from total FH concentration and expressed in milligrams per 1 liter of blood serum (mg/L).

According to the results obtained, no significant difference was detected in the total FH serum levels between SP and controls (mean±SD: 241.9±52.1 vs 265.6±28.4, p=0.07). Also, there was no difference in total FH serum levels between 402H minor variant carriers (YH+HH) and major variant (YY) homozygotes both in SP (247.4±56.1 vs 235.9±49.2, p>0.05) and controls (259.8±35.6 vs 270.9±44.2, p>0.05). Further, we performed intragroup analysis of the 402H and 402Y levels. Among the controls, the mean level of 402H variant tended to be lower in 402H minor variant carriers (YH+HH) than in YY homozygotes (254.2±24.4 vs 272.4±27.3, p=0.05). In SP the levels of 402Y variant were lower in YH+HH minor variant carriers than in YY homozygotes (71.92±57.9 vs 216.2±79.9, p<0.0003). The levels of 402H in SP were marginally lower compared to 402Y levels (89.6±30.1 vs 144.1±100.5, p=0.06), whereas in controls a significantly increased 402H levels in comparison to 402Y levels were observed (263.3±25.9 vs 79.6±71.9, p<0.0001). The results obtained are presented on Fig. 6, 7.

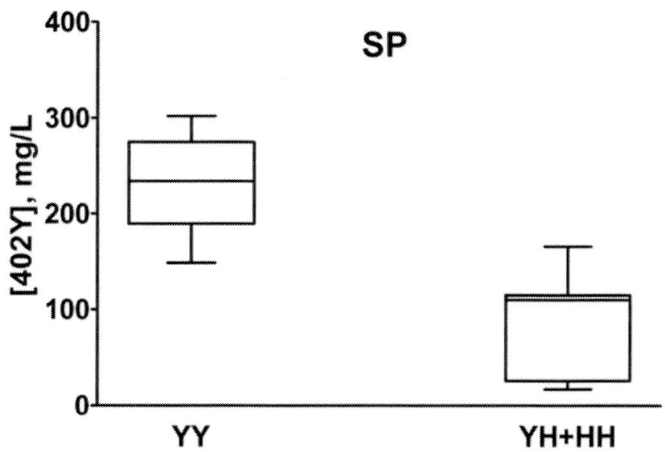

Figure 6. The levels of FH 402Y in the blood serum of YH+HH and YY SP. The data are expressed as whisker box plots; the box represents the 25-75th percentiles, the median is indicated by a horizontal bar across the box, the whiskers on each box represent the minimum and maximum levels (10th and 90th percentiles, respectively). P<0.0001 when comparing 402Y levels between YH+HH versus YY.

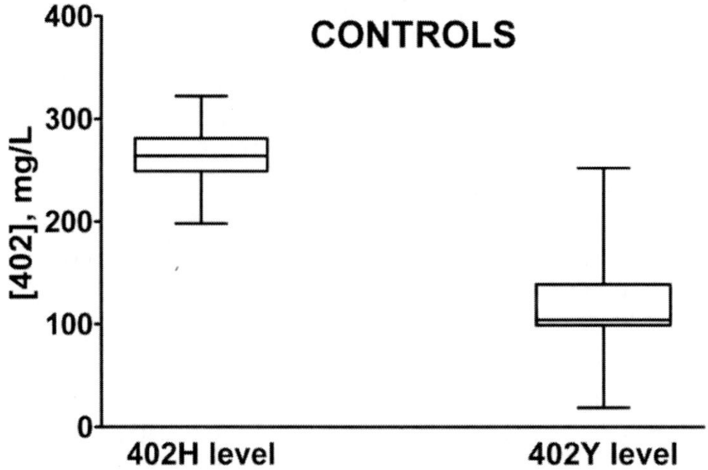

Figure 7. The levels of FH 402H and 402Y variants in the blood serum of controls. The data are expressed as whisker box plots; the box represents the 25-75th percentiles, the median is indicated by a horizontal bar across the box, the whiskers on each box represent the minimum and maximum levels (10th and 90th percentiles, respectively). P<0.0001 when comparing 402H and 402Y in controls.

1.10. Terminal Complement Pathway and MAC in SCH

As it was already stated in 1.1, all 3 complement activation pathways converge at C3 level, leading to activation of terminal pathway and MAC formation (Fig. 1). The assembly of MAC includes the following steps: C5 convertase, generated by any of the pathways described above cleaves C5 into C5a and C5b; C5b instantaneously binds C6 and subsequently C7 to yield a hydrophobic C5b67 complex, which attaches quickly to the plasma membrane. C5b binds C6 while still bound to C5convertase; on binding C7; 3-molecular C5b67 is released and inserts into membrane; C8 then inserts, traversing the membrane; C9 binds initially in its folded state, and then unfolds and polymerizes to form MAC pore. If complement is activated on an antigen without a lipid membrane to which the C567 can attach, the C567 complex may bind to nearby cells and initiate bystander lysis. C9 is the key protein in MAC, an amphipathic molecule that inserts through cell membrane and then polimerizes and forms a pore (100 Å) thus lysing the cell. There may be 16-18 C9 molecules per 1 MAC [23-29, 155, 156].

The soluble regulatory protein S (vitronectin) prevents insertion of C5b67 MAC component into the membrane. Homologous restriction factor (HRF) or membrane inhibitor of reactive lysis (CD59; glycosyl-phosphatidyl inositol-anchored protein) bind C5b678, preventing assembly of poly-C9 and blocking formation of MAC (Fig.8) [23-29, 155, 156].

MAC has a variety of other non-lytic effects that differ according to the nature of the target cell and the system interrogated. On phagocytes, which are intrinsically resistant to complement-mediated lysis, MAC induces profound activation, with the production and release of infammatory mediators - prostaglandins, thromboxanes, leukotrienes, and reactive oxygen species. MAC can also act as apoptotic trigger, initiate production of inflammatory mediators, reactive oxygen species, and expression of adhesion molecules. Effect depends on cell type and other environmental factors (Fig.8) [23-29, 155, 156].

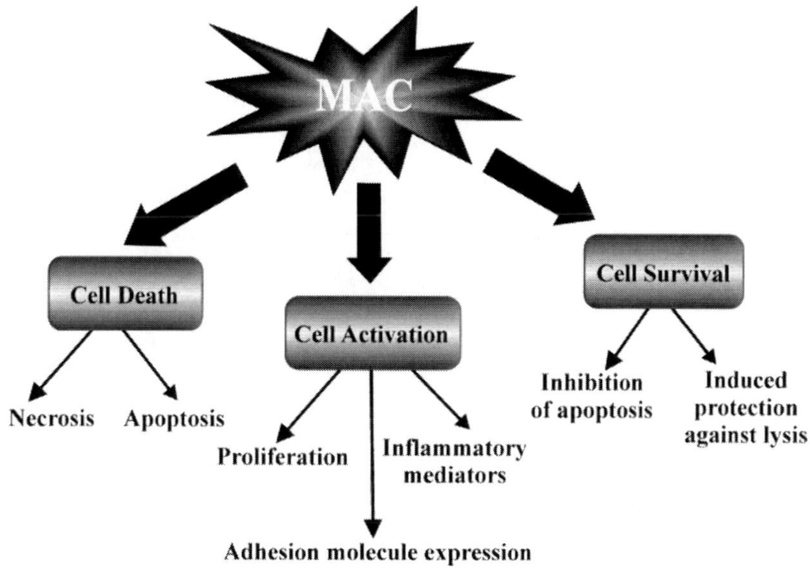

Figure 8. Range of cellular effects of MAC.

Alterations in the components, activity, or regulation of terminal complement pathway as well as MAC formation are detected under various pathologic conditions, including the central nervous system disorders, and, depending on diseased condition, may have etiological, pathogenic, or protective role [157-163].

Practically no data on the state of TCC, MAC or its regulatory proteins in SCH are available. Two studies have been addressing association of functional polymorphisms of C6 component of the terminal pathway/MAC with SCH. So far, no associations has been reported and no significant differences in C6 gene or phenotype frequencies between SP and controls have been found [67, 68]

Our own data, yet unpublished, revealed significantly increased levels of soluble MAC in the blood serum of SCH as compared to controls (mean±SD, mg/mL: 7.66±2.13 versus 5.35±1.82, $p<0.001$). The methodological design includes in-house ELISA developed by Morgan et al. [164]. Further we plan more detailed evaluation of the terminal complement pathway and MAC to assess the molecular mechanisms leading to its rise in SCH.

2. IC and Their Atypical Populations in SCH

2.1. IC at a Glance

Formation of IC is a normal physiological reaction of the organism to foreign or autoantigens. IC may interact with both humoral and cellular components of the immune recognition system, activate the complement cascade, and thus affect the immune response on multiple levels [165, 166]. In healthy conditions IC are easily eliminating from circulation through complement deposition, followed by their opsonization, ***phagocytosis***, and further processing by proteases [95, 105, 106, 165, 166]. Phagocytosis of IC might occur directly in the blood or in the over tissues, mostly in liver and spleen (Fig.9, see also 1.7) [95, 105, 106, 165, 166].

In pathologic conditions inappropriate clearance or deposition of IC might occur concentration of the IC in circulation increase and the efficiency of their elimination decrease. IC may deposit in endothelial or vascular structures provoking prolonged inflammatory response through permanent activation of the complement cascade [165]. Accumulating in the blood and other tissues, IC may induce a number of destructive processes resulting in generation of cytotoxic agents and tissue injury [167-170]. IC deposition is a prominent feature of several autoimmune, infectious, and autoinflammatory diseases [171-176], as well as in diseased conditions characterized by neuroinflammation and low-grade systemic inflammation, such as diabetes mellitus [177, 178], ischemic and hemorrhagic stroke [179-181], and posttraumatic stress disorder [182, 183]. The most aggressive and hardly eliminated populations of IC represent so called small-sized or pathogenic IC [184-186] and cryoglobulins [185, 187-192]. Both have atypical physico-chemical properties. Pathogenic IC generate in excess of antibodies or antigens, are smaller in size than classic or so called large-sized IC, therefore are poorly recognized by the immunocompetent cells [184-186]. Cryoglobulins are abnormal IC, where both antigen and antibody are presented by Ig, and which reversibly precipitate at temperature below 37^0C [187-192].

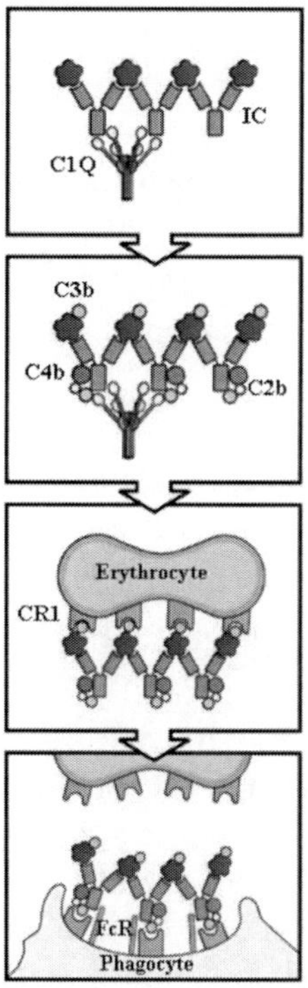

Figure 9. Clearance of IC.

Cryoglobulins can deposit in blood vessels, stimulating infiltration of endothelial cells by neutrophils and monocytes [193, 193], bind complement [181], C-reactive protein [195], and stimulate production of TNFα [196]. The presence of small-sized IC and cryoglobulins in circulation has been associated with a number of diseased conditions and considered as a nonspecific marker of upregulated immune response, inflammation, and autoimmune sensitization [184-192, 197]. Investigations of the IC in SCH, identification and study of their atypical populations in SP, described in details below (2.3; 2.4), provided strong evidence on the important role of inflammatory and autoimmune components in disease-associated disordered immunity.

2.2. Large and Small-Sized IC in SCH

Several studies have demonstrated the increased total IC blood levels in SP compared to controls [197-201], and only one report was inconsistent with those studies indicating no changes in IC levels when comparing SP to controls [202]. However, no data regarding different IC populations in SCH were provided. In our studies [203-205] we determined the levels of large- and small-sized IC circulated in the blood of SP and controls by spectrophotometric assay [206, 207]. Firstly, we separated these populations of IC from each by differential precipitation with 3.5 and 7.0% polyethylene glycol (6kDa) followed by affinity chromatography on protein-G sepharose. According to the results obtained, the levels of large-sized IC in the blood serum of SP were similar to those of controls, whereas a significant 2 times increase in the levels of small-sized IC in SP as compared to controls ($p<4E-8$) was detected [203-205]. The results obtained are presented on Fig.10.

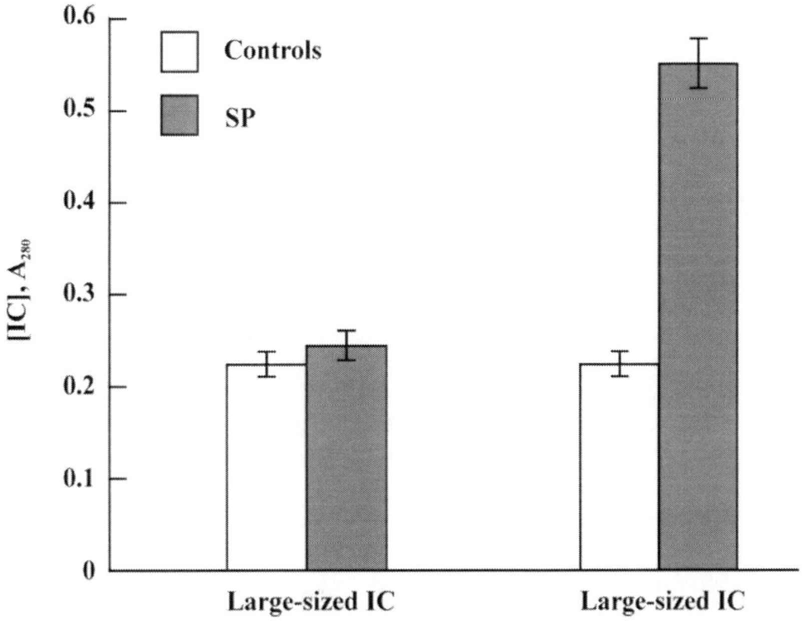

Figure 10. Mean value (±SD) of large- and small-sized IC in the blood serum of SP and controls.

The data obtained may explain the earlier observation of Vetlugina et al, which detected (*in vitro*) that leukocytes of SP are considerably less active against IC than those of controls [208] that was probably related to increased levels of small-sized IC in the total IC fraction.

We detected no difference in both large- and small-sized IC blood levels between neuroleptic-treated and neuroleptic-free patients [203-205]. However, Koliaskina et al reported decreased total IC blood levels in neuroleptic-treated SP as compared to controls [201, 202]. This inconsistency may result from the type of neuroleptics used: in our studies mostly patients treated with typical neuroleptics were included [203-205], whereas in the above mentioned investigations SP treated with atypical neuroleptics were recruited [200, 201].

Notably, we found that concentrations of both large and small-sized IC in the blood of SCH-affected female patients were significantly higher than in SCH-affected male patients, 1.28 ($p<0.035$) and 1.23 times ($p<0.04$), respectively [203-205]. This observation is consistent with the earlier reported by Vertlugina et al [208]. In this regard, it is interesting to note that there are certain clinical and epidemiologic observations of male and female differences in the expression of SCH. For instance, in case of paranoid type of SCH onset of illness is delayed in women by a mean of 4 to 6 years [cited in 209], also residual and catatonic types of SCH in men are detected more often than in woman [210]. There is also evidence that the effect of gender on age at onset may vary as a function of clinical subtypes of SCH. In several early studies [cited in 211] the early onset in males was particularly evident in paranoid SCH. Beratis et al [212] found a significantly earlier onset in males than in females among the paranoid SP and an earlier onset in females among patients with the disorganized subtype. In the same vein, the severity of illness expression in women is less debilitating than in men during the first decade following onset [cited in 211]. Other reported SCH differences in men and women include differences in extrapyramidal effects and tardive dyskinesia, different symptoms, brain abnormalities, premorbid competencies, etc [cited in 211]. It is proposed that these differences may reflect the difference in sex hormones (gonadal steroids) having different effects on structures and functionality of the brain [213-217]. The same may applies to the differences in the IC levels, as it is known that sex hormones are modulators of the immune system activity participate in formation of the immune response and development of autoimmunity reactions [218-221]. On the other hand, the detected differences in IC levels between SCH-affected males and females may also reflect sex chromosome aberrations detected in SCH. While there is no linkage between SCH and X or Y chromosome, there are data suggesting that aneuploidy of the X chromosome is observed in many SP representing a risk factor for this disorder. It is proposed that aneuploidia-associated disbalance in the expression products of genes localized on X chromosome is responsible for susceptibility to SCH, since the excess of these products induces pathological processes in the brain upon neuronal development [222- 224].

2.3. Cryoglobulins in SCH

Our studies, for the first time, revealed the presence of cryoglobulins in the blood of SP [225-227]. We determined blood levels of cryoglobulins in SCH, isolated this abnormal population of IC from the blood of SP using earlier developed approaches and recommendations [187, 228, 229] and investigated their immunochemical composition using different electrophoretic and immunoblotting systems [225-227].

According to the data obtained (Fig.11), significantly increased levels of cryoglobulins were detected in the blood serum of all SP (2.1 times in average; $p<0.00001$), as compared to controls. Here, similarly to our previous findings with large- and small-sized IC (see 2.1), serum levels of cryoglobulins in female patients were higher (1.3 times in average, $p<0.04$)

than in male [225-227]. As it was discussed in 2.1, our observation probably reflects gender-dependent different manifestation of the disease [210, 212] and/or sex chromosome abnormalities (excess of sex chromosome aneuploidies - XXY, XXX, and possibly XYY) [222-224] detected in SCH. This phenomenon may be also caused by different influences of sexual hormones on the neurodevelopmental processes and the main brain functions [213] as well as on the basic immune responses [230-232]. We detected no gender differences in controls. No significant difference in the mean values of serum cryoglobulins was found between neuroleptic-treated and neuroleptic-free SP, patient with family history of SCH and those with sporadic form of the disease [225-227]. In addition, no significant correlation was observed between serum levels of cryoglobulins and such variables as age, age at onset, and duration of SCH [225-227].

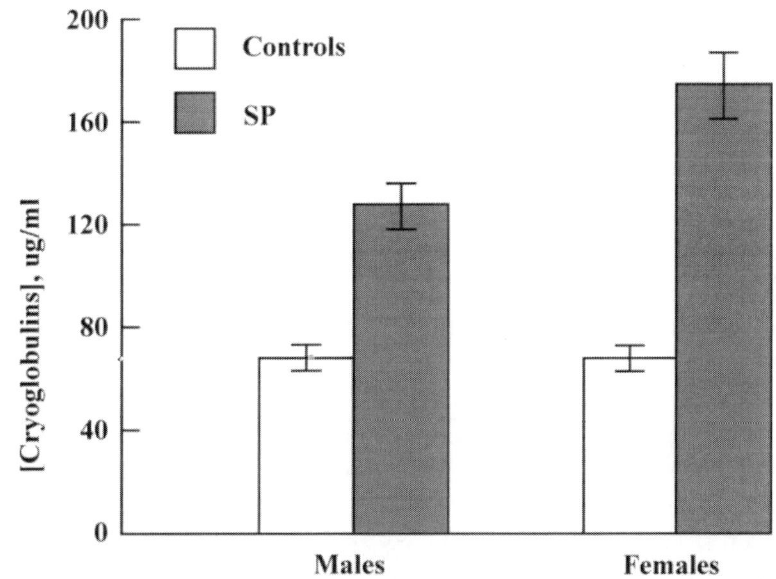

Figure 11. Mean values (mean±SD) of cryoglobulins in the blood serum of SP and controls.

Our data obtained upon investigating the composition of cryoglobulins isolated from the blood of SP are briefly summarized in Table 7. For comparison, data related to controls are also presented. As it was revealed by immunoblotting, cryoglobulins isolated from the serum of all SP contained a mixture of polyclonal IgG, IgM, and IgA. Semi-quantitative analysis showed that IgG was the most abundant among others, with the mean level being 5 times higher than that of IgM and 2 times higher than that of IgA. On the basis of their Ig composition and concentration in the blood cryoglobulins can be classified into three types, according to Brouet et al [233]. Type I (>5 mg/mL) consists of a monoclonal component alone and is usually found in multiple myeloma, Waldenström's macroglobulinemia, and lymphoma; type II (>1 mg/mL), which is common in hepatitis C and Sjögren's syndrome, is a mixture of monoclonal and polyclonal Igs, and type III (<1 mg/mL) consists of a mixture of polyclonal Igs with other serum proteins and is detected in the connective tissue diseases, chronic infections and ischemic stroke [181, 187-192, 233]. Our data (Table 7) indicated the presence of type III cryoglobulins in the blood of SP.

Table 7. Immunochemical composition of cryoglobulins isolated from the blood of SP and controls

Study group	[Cryoglobulins], ug/mL serum	Immunochemical composition of cryoglobulins	
		Igs	C1Q and C3
SP	149	Polyclonal IgG+IgA+ IgM (100%)	C1QA, C1QB, C1QC, C3-β, C3bi, C3c
Controls	71	Polyclonal: IgG (12.5%), IgG + IgA (17.5%), IgG+IgA+IgM (30%), IgG + IgM (40%)	N/A

In cryoglobulins isolated from the serum of controls only polyclonal Igs were found as well. However, in this case the picture was very variable among individuals. Thus, 12.5% of controls contain IgG, 17.5% - a mixture of IgG and IgA, 30% - a mixture of IgG, IgM, and IgA, and 40% - a mixture of IgG and IgM. The presence of trace amounts of cryoglobulins in the blood of controls detected in this study is consistent with the earlier reported observations [234, 235]. Our data have shown that cryoglobulins isolated from the blood of controls are different from those of SP. Here, together with individual variations in Igs composition, the absence of complement proteins was detected. Probably, in controls cryoglobulins simply represent cryo-aggregates of serum Igs. With regard to the presence of the complement proteins, both C1Q and C3 proteins (C1QA, C1QB, C1QC, and C3-β subunits) and their activated split products (C3bi, C3c) were found in all cryoglobulins isolated from the serum of SP, whereas in case of cryoglobulins isolated from the serum of controls nothing was detected. Typical patterns of Western blot analysis of C1Q and C3 in cryoglobulins isolated from the serum of SP and controls are shown in Fig.12. Here, our data demonstrating the presence of the complement proteins C1Q and C3, and their activated split products in cryoglobulins of SP indicate that cryoglobulins are involved in SCH-associated upregulated immune response by binding the complement proteins and activating the complement cascade.

Also, finding of the activated split products of C3 complement protein, iC3b and C3c, in cryoglobulins of SP together with our recent observation on increased blood activity of C3 in SCH [41, 133] provide additional evidence to the involvement of aberrant apoptosis in pathomechanisms of this disease. The data obtained also provide an additional evidence to the involvement of aberrant apoptosis in pathomechanisms of SCH. Complement influences apoptosis at two distinct levels: first, in deciding the fate of the cell, and secondly, in helping phagocytes to dispose of the corpses of apoptosed cells. Apoptotic cells may affect the complement directly through the complement protein C3. The C3 split product, C3b, binds covalently to the apoptotic cell and acts as an opsonin activating leukocytes bearing complement receptors. Cleavage of C3b occurs to form a more effective opsonin named iC3b, which further cleaved to C3c and C3d. Fragments of C3 deposited on the apoptotic cells bind the phagocyte-expressed complement receptors CR1, CR3, and CR4 to further aid recognition and clearance [25, 136].

Involvement of the autoimmune processes in the etiopathogenesis of SCH has been reported for many years. While the question about autoimmune origin of SCH is still open, numerous studies have indicated that at least secondary autoimmune reactions are associated with this disease. Thus, the increased blood and CSF levels of autoantibodies to neurospecific protein, neuroreceptors, neuromediators, DNA, histones, cardiolipin, etc. as well as elevated levels of IL-6 together with B lymphocytes activity have been detected in SP [3, 236-239]. In this context the increased levels of type III cryoglobulins may be considered as another independent evidence of SCH-associated autoimmunity.

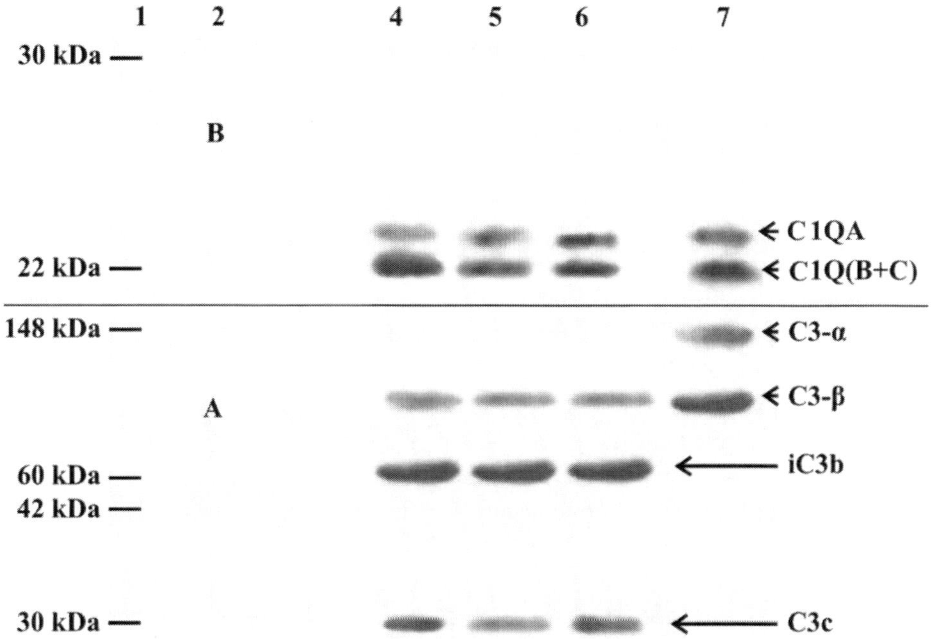

Figure 12. Typical Western-blot patterns of C1Q (A) and C3 (B) detection in cryoglobulins isolated from the blood of SP and controls.
1 - marker proteins, 2, 3 - cryoglobulins isolated from the blood of controls, 4-6 - cryoglobulins isolated from the blood of SP, 7 - C1Q and C3 subinuts (standards): C1QA -24 kDa; C1Q(B+C) - 22 kDa; C3-α -120 kDa; C3-β - 75 kDa. iC3b (68 and 43 kDa) and C3c (25 kDa) - C3 activation split products.

On the other hand, according to genetic-inflammatory-vascular theory of SCH, which integrates all existing theories of SCH including autoimmune, neurodevelopmental, neurodegenerative, and viral, SCH in the result of damage to the micro-vascular system in the brain initiated by genetically influenced abnormal inflammatory processes acting in response to ubiquitous environmental factors (infection, trauma, or apoxia) that trigger inflammatory responses [8]. From this viewpoint, the ability of cryoglobulins to induce immune complex vasculitis, to deposit in vessels and induce inflammatory response through subsequent infiltration of neutrophils and mononuclear cells, to bind complement components, activate the complement system, and TNF-α production [193, 194, 196] suggests that these abnormal immune complexes are implicated in pathomechanisms of SCH at multiple levels. Another argument for this suggestion is that cryoglobulinemia is often detected in several infection diseases [148], and in case of SCH the infection may have an etiological significance [7, 8, 238].

3. Cytokines in SCH

3.1. Brief Presentation of Cytokines

Cytokine is a generic name for a diverse group of small proteins that act in nano-picomolar concentrations as humoral regulators and modulate the functional activities of individual cells and tissues. Cytokines, expressed in response to stimulation by mostly all cells in the body, regulate many essential functions including cell proliferation and differentiation, hematopoiesis, tissue repair, immunity, and inflammation. Cytokines upregulate expression of adhesion molecules on endothelial cells, leukocytes, and platelets, mediating interaction between endothelial cells and leukocytes leading to infiltration of leukocytes into tissues and may cause both local and acute phase immune responses [239].

Some cytokines are produced by a rather limited number of different cell types while others are produced by almost the entire spectrum of known cell types. Cytokines also mediate interactions between cells and regulate processes taking place in the extracellular environment. Many cytokines act as cellular survival factors by preventing programmed cell death. Cytokines represent the major factors involved in the communication between T cells, macrophages, and other immune cells in the course of an immune response to antigens and infectious agents. Resembling hormones in their biological activity and systemic level cytokines act on a wider spectrum of target cells than hormones. The major feature distinguishing cytokines from hormones is the fact that cytokines do not produced by specialized cells organized in specialized glands. Cytokines are secreted proteins, i.e. their expression sites do not predict where they exert their biological function. Many cytokines are secreted by cells using secretory pathways [239].

Most genes encoding cytokines give rise to variety of cytokines by means of alternative splicing, yielding molecules with slightly different but biologically significant bioactivities. The switching between soluble and membrane forms of cytokines is an important regulatory event. Cytokines expression is regulated tightly at the transcription level, translation level, and protein synthesis. The production and secretion of cytokines is context dependent, i.e. their expression is influenced by individual signals received but also by the balance of signals received through one or more receptors (which themselves may be subject to inducible/repressible expression). The expression of cytokines also seems to be regulated differentially, depending on cell type and developmental age. Secretion or release from the producer cells is also a regulated process. Once released, their behavior in the circulation may be regulated by soluble receptors and specific or unspecific binding proteins. Regulation also is at work at the receptor level on target cells and at the level of signaling pathways governing alterations in the behavior of responder cells [239].

Numerous cytokines are pleiotropic effectors showing multiple biological activities. Currently about 100 cytokines have been described, and they can have synergistic or antagonistic activities. Multiple cytokines have overlapping activities therefore a single cell frequently interacts with multiple cytokines with identical responses. A possible consequence of this functional overlap is the observation that one factor may frequently functionally replace another factor completely or at least partially compensates the lack of another factor. Since most cytokines have ubiquitous biological activities, their physiologic significance as normal regulators of physiology is often difficult to assess. Cytokine biological activity is mediated by specific membrane receptors, which are expressed on all cell types known. The expression of receptors is usually regulated, although some receptors are expressed constitutively [239].

Cytokines act in cascades, influence a large number of signal transduction mechanisms, affect the expression of various inflammatory and apoptotic genes. Cytokines and their receptors are highly regulated by a net of endogen mediators at translational, transcriptional, and posttranscriptional levels [239]. When the balance is broken the massive self-destroying reactions are produced, which are implicated as either etiological or pathogenic factors in many diseased conditions including neuroinflammatory and neurodegenerative diseases, stress and depression. Many neurological and psychiatric diseases are characterized by altered cytokine network. Changes regarding the cytokine system have been shown to be involved in the development of multiple sclerosis, Parkinson's and Alzheimer's disease, depression, narcolepsy, or stroke. Imbalances in the regulation of pro-inflammatory cytokines have been increasingly correlated with a number of severe and prevalent neurodevelopmental disorders, including autism spectrum disorder, Down syndrome, and SCH. Although several studies have shown that cytokines have potent effects on neural function, their role in neural development is still poorly understood [239-246].

Several studies indicated the involvement of cytokines in SCH-associated immune system abnormalities, demonstrating elevated levels of pro-inflammatory and immunoregulatory cytokines in this pathology and leading to a hypothesis that SCH is associated with an imbalance in inflammatory cytokines, leading to a decrease in Th1 and an increase in Th2 cytokine secretion [247-256].

Cytokines demonstrate diverse actions in the brain and modulate systemic and CNS responses to injury, infection, and inflammation. Prenatal exposure to infection appears to increase the risk of SCH and other neurodevelopmental disorders. Proinflammatory cytokines are critical in brain development, and are believed to play an important role in neurodevelopmental disorders associated with prenatal exposure to infection. Cytokines, generated in response to maternal infection, play a key mechanistic role in this association, and cytokine-mediated neuronal injury during development may contribute to SCH pathophysiology, causing subtle alterations in neuronal number and density. Promising data suggest a role for cytokines in the modulation of neuronal survival during neurodevelopment, a finding potentially relevant to SCH pathophysiology [257, 258].

Our particular attention has been focused on the role of IL-6 and TNF-α interleukines, IL-8, and MCP-1 chemokines, and macrophage migration inhibitory factor (MIF) in SCH. These cytokines play a central role in mediating cellular and physiological responses [239]. The results obtained together with the data reported by other researchers related to these cytokines are presented below.

3.2. IL-6 in SCH

IL-6 (interferon-2beta; B cell stimulatory factor-2) belongs to the IL-6 family of cytokines, signaling through the common receptor subunit (glycoprotein), subsequently activates signal transducers and activators of transcription (STAT3), mitogen-activated proteinkinase, and phosphatidylinositol 3-kinase. IL-6 is a multifunctional pleiotropic cytokine with a variety of biological functions such as regulation of immune system and generation of acute phase reactions. This cytokine functions in inflammation and the maturation of B cells. IL-6 is primarily produced at sites of acute and chronic inflammation, where it is secreted into the serum and induces a transcriptional inflammatory response through membrane bound receptor and soluble receptor (IL-6R and sIL-6R, respectively), and IL-6 specific binding molecule [259, 260]. The functioning of this cytokine is implicated in a wide variety of inflammation- and autoimmunity-associated disease states. IL-6 is also involved in hematopoiesis, bone metabolism, and cancer progression and is implicated in age-related and psychiatric disorders [246, 247, 261].

A number of studies have demonstrated increased IL-6 blood levels in SP as compared to controls [262-284], and recent report also shown the increased levels of IL-6 mRNA in SCH [285]. However, there are also controversial data indicating unchanged [286-289] or decreased blood IL-6 levels in SP in comparison to controls [290-292]. In addition, Ganguli et al and Akiyama showed positive correlation between the increased IL-6 blood levels and duration of SCH [263, 270], whereas Pae et al observed no such correlation [277]. Very inconsistent are data related to the influence of neuroleptics on IL-6 blood levels in SP. Thus, no effect [263, 265, 267, 270, 272, 274, 279, 282, 293], diminished/normalizing effect [264, 277, 283, 286] as well as rising effect [268, 269, 291, 292] on IL-6 blood levels in SP treated with both typical and atypical neuroleptics has been shown.

Regarding IL-6 receptors, Maes et al found medication-independent decreased blood levels of this receptor in SCH [264], but later reported increased sIL-6R blood levels in neuroleptic-free SP [265], while Lin et al indicated no changes in sIL-6R blood levels in SCH [269].

Few reports addressed possible changes in *IL-6* and *IL-6R* genes in SCH [283, 294, 295]. Sun et al demonstrated association between *sIL-6R* polymorphism and SCH in Chinese population [294]. Liu et al [295] studies association of genetic variants of *IL-6* and *IL-6R* with SCH in Taiwan through genotyping of three SNPs for each *IL-6* (*IL-6-1*, *IL-6-2*, and *IL-6-3*) and *IL-6R* (*IL-6R1*: rs4845617, *IL-6R2*: rs4553185, and *IL-6R3*, rs4379670) gene. All six SNPs and their haplotypes failed to show a significant association with SCH. However, the *IL-6-2* SNP showed a nominally significant association with the positive symptoms of SCH (p=0.0472) [295]. Sasayama et al [284], investigated association of plasma IL-6 and soluble IL-6R levels with the Asp358Ala polymorphism of the *IL-6R* gene in SP, suggested that SCH is associated with elevated IL-6 levels, whereas sIL-6R levels are mainly predetermined by the Asp358Ala genotype and are not associated with the disease status. They proposed that the increased IL-6 levels without alterations in sIL-6R levels may result in excessive IL-6 signaling in SCH.

Recently Paul-Samojedny et al. [296] studying *IL-6* promoter -174G/C (rs 1800795) polymorphism in SP and controls, using PCR-restriction fragment length polymorphism method, found that the existence of genotype GC at position -174 of *IL*-6 promoter sequence correlates with increasing risk of paranoid SCH in the Polish population [296]. SNP in the promoter region of the *IL-6* gene at position -174 is known to affect IL-6 release, suggesting about functional role of mentioned polymorphism [297, 298].

We explored the possible association of the *IL-6* -174(G/C) polymorphism with SCH in the Armenian population using PCR-SSP [299]. Distributions of the *IL-6* -174 alleles and genotypes in the groups of SP and controls were in compliance with H-W equilibrium. Statistical power of our study, the difference in the carriage of the *IL-6* -174*C allele between

SP and controls, for OR=2.0 reached 94.6%. The allele and phenotype frequencies of the studied genetic variant in SP and controls are shown in the Table 8.

We observed that the *IL-6* -174G allele was less frequent in SP than in controls (38% vs 24%, p=0.002, OR=1.95, 95% CI: 1.18-2.14). Accordingly, the carriers of the -174*C allele were overrepresented in the group SP compared to controls (62% vs 42%, p=0.003, OR=2.28, 95% CI: 1.13-1.94).

Table 8. Distribution of the *IL-6* -174G/C SNP genotypes and carriage of minor allele in SP and controls. The data are presented as absolute numbers with proportions (%) in parentheses

IL-6 -174G/C rs1800795		Controls	SP	*P*
	GG	61 (0.58)	39 (0.38)	
Genotypes	GC	38 (0.36)	50 (0.49)	
	CC	6 (0.06)	14 (0.14)	
Alleles	G	160 (0.76)	128 (0.62)	
	C	50 (0.24)	78 (0.38)	0.002[a]
Carriers	C	44 (0.42)	64 (0.62)	0.003[b]

[a] p-values for comparison of C allele proportion (allele frequency) between SP and controls;
[b] p-values for comparison of C allele carriage (phenotype frequency) between SP and controls.

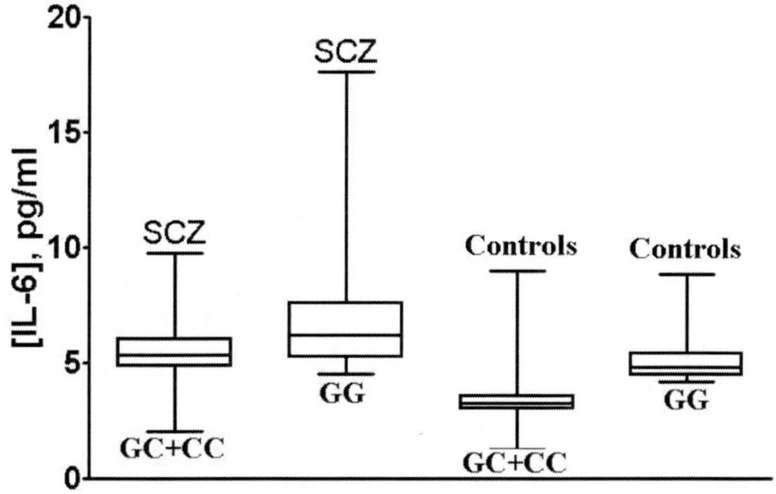

Figure 13. IL-6 levels (median [interquartile range]) in the plasma of SP and control regarding the *IL-6* -174G/C genotypes. The data are expressed as whisker box plots; the box represents the 25-75th percentiles, the median is indicated by a horizontal bar across the box, the whiskers on each box represent the minimum and maximum level. P<0.0001 when comparing IL-6 levels between SP and controls.

Therefore, we found a positive association of the *IL-6* -174*C genetic variant with SCH in Armenian population. This study demonstrated that the -174*C variant of the *IL*-6 gene is associated with increasing risk to SCH in Armenian population, which is in accordance with the previous finding in the Polish population [294], and suggest that *IL-6* gene localized on chromosome 7 (7p21) may be considered as a relevant candidate gene for SCH.

Further, we performed a comparative determination of the IL-6 plasma levels in neuroleptic-treated, neuroleptic-free SP, and controls using sandwich ELISA. Group statistics was presented as mean±SD in pg/ml. According to the data obtained, in neuroleptic-treated SP the mean value of the IL-6 plasma level was 1.54 times higher than in controls (6.41±2.47 vs 4.15±1.42, $p<0.0001$). Importantly, the mean value of IL-6 level in our small sample size of the neuroleptic-free SP was significantly higher compared to controls (SP vs controls: 7.32±2.72 vs 4.15±1.42, $p<0.0001$). Also, we found no significant difference in the mean values of IL-6 plasma level between neuroleptic-free and neuroleptic-treated SP (7.32±2.72 vs 6.41±2.47, $p=0.27$). Correlation analysis between the IL-6 plasma levels and its -174G/C genotypes revealed higher IL-6 plasma level in -174GG homozygotes than in -174*C minor allele carriers (GC+CC) both in SP and controls (GG vs GC+CC, SP: 7.02±2.8 vs 5.39±1.2, $p=0.0006$; controls: 5.21±1.17 vs 3.38±1.03, $p=1.6E-15$, Fig.13).

3.3. TNF-α in SCH

TNF-α (cachectin; tumor necrosis factor ligand superfamily member 2) is the prototypic ligand of the TNF superfamily, a proinflammatory cytokine that is mainly produced by activated monocytes and macrophages. TNF-α production has also been reported for a wide variety of immune and non-immune cells, including T cells, NK cells, neutrophils, and astrocytes [239]. TNF-α was first isolated by Carswell et al. in 1975 [300] in an attempt to identify tumor necrosis factors responsible for necrosis of the sarcoma Meth A. TNF-α has a broad spectrum of biological activities. In addition to its central role in inflammation, TNF-α is noted for its cytotoxic and tumoricidal abilities either by necrosis or apoptosis induction. It is a pleiotropic molecule that plays a central role in inflammation, apoptosis, and immune system development. Its functions also include growth modulation and induction of cellular differentiation. Depending on its concentration, TNF-α can exert neurotrophic and neurotoxic effects and also influence neural cell growth and proliferation. TNF-α regulates lymphoid tissue development through control of apoptosis. It also promotes inflammatory responses by inducing the activation of vascular endothelial cells and macrophages. Human TNF-α consists of a 35 amino acid (aa) cytoplasmic domain, a 21 aa transmembrane segment, and a 177 aa extracellular domain (ECD). Within the ECD, human TNF-α shares 97% aa sequence identity with rhesus and 71% - 92% with bovine, canine, cotton rat, equine, feline, mouse, porcine, and rat TNF-α. The 26 kDa type 2 transmembrane protein is assembled intracellularly to form a noncovalently linked homotrimer. Ligation of this complex induces reverse signaling that promotes lymphocyte costimulation but diminishes monocyte responsiveness. Cleavage of membrane bound TNF-α by TACE/ADAM17 releases a 55 kDa soluble trimeric form of TNF-α. TNF-α trimers bind the ubiquitous TNF-α receptor-1 and the hematopoietic cell-restricted TNF-α receptor-2, both of which are also expressed as homotrimers [239].

Despite its various beneficial actions, TNF-α also plays a detrimental role in several diseased conditions, including neurological and psychiatric disorders. Changes regarding the immune system and specifically the cytokine system, of which TNF- α is a part, have been shown to be involved in the development of neurological and psychiatric disorders such as stroke, multiple sclerosis, Parkinson's and Alzheimer's diseases, depression, narcolepsy, and

SCH [244-247, 301]. It is proposed that TNF-α might contribute to the pathogenesis of these diseases by an activation of the hypothalamo-pituitary-adrenocortical axis, an activation of neuronal serotonin transporters, the stimulation of the indoleamine 2,3-dioxygenase, which leads to tryptophan depletion, by immunologically mediated destruction of neurons, or neurotoxic release of glutamate [301].

The increased TNF-α blood levels [126, 267, 287, 283, 302-305], elevated levels of TNF-α mRNA in the blood [303] and prefrontal cortex of SP [306], as well as increased blood levels of TNF-α soluble receptors [304, 307, 308] in SCH have been demonstrated in several studies. However, there are also controversial data indicating unchanged blood levels of TNF-α [273, 282, 289, 290, 309, 310], TNF-α soluble receptors [305], or decreased expression of TNF-α mRNA [311] in SP as compared to controls.

Psychotropic drugs influence the TNF-α system too, increasing its levels in SP [291, 301, 304]. It is proposed that during psychopharmacological treatment of SCH, some antipsychotics might act on neurotransmitter metabolism via inducing the proinflammatory cytokine system. This hypothesis may lead to new therapeutical strategies for psychiatric patients [301]. However, some studies demonstrated that usage of atypical neuroleptics results in suppression of blood levels of TNF-α or its receptors in SP [267, 302, 312, 313]. Furthermore, Kowalski et al. [314] demonstrated that the monocytes of SP stimulated by lipopolisaccharide *in vitro* released significantly higher amounts of TNF-α than those of controls. Further, treatment with the typical neuroleptics haloperidol and perazine decreased the release of TNF-α to the control levels [314]. In addition, there are reports indicating no influence of typical or atypical neuroleptic treatment on these parameters [278, 126, 307].

Interestingly, Liu et al. [313] revealed that TNF-α is overexpressed in the peripheral blood mononuclear cells of SP and their siblings as compared to controls, indicating the influence of hereditary factors on SCH-associated increased TNF-α levels.

In our recent study (unpublished data) comparative determination of TNF-α plasma levels in neuroleptic-treated and neuroleptic-free SP, and controls has been performed using sandwich ELISA. Group statistics was presented as mean±SD in pg/ml. We found 1.16 times higher TNF-α levels in neuroleptic-treated SP compared to controls (62.17±10.61 vs 53.55±17.54, $p<0.0001$). Further, TNF-α levels were 1.22 times higher in neuroleptic-free SP when compared to controls (65.6±10.76 vs 53.55±17.54, $p=0.025$). However, no significant difference in TNF-α levels between neuroleptic-treated and neuroleptic-free subjects was found (62.17±10.61 vs 63.00±22.65, $p=0.38$).

Several research groups have examined whether the observed alterations in TNF-α expression in SCH are genetically determined. This question is of particular interest, since TNF-α gene is located on the small arm of chromosome 6 (6p21.1-21.3), a locus associated with genetic susceptibility to SCH [315, 316]. The majority of the research was concentrated on the -308G/A biallelic base exchange polymorphism of the *TNF-α* gene promoter region, which directly affects TNF-α blood levels and associates with the increased production of this cytokine. Other polymorphisms of this region were also assessed. Nevertheless, the data presented till now are very discrepant, probably, reflecting variability in *TNF-α* gene depending on ethnicity [317-337]. Interestingly, Zhang et al. found association of the -1031T/C polymorphism of *TNF-α* gene with age of onset of SCH [338].

3.4. IL-8 and MCP-1 Chemokines in SCH

Chemokines constitute a complex superfamily of mostly small chemoattractant cytokines (8-12 kDa) that function in leukocyte trafficking, recruiting, and recirculation. They can be released by many different types of tissue cells and in some cases platelets. Chemokines selectively recruite monocytes, neutrophils, lymphocytes and induce chemotaxis through the activation of G-protein-coupled receptors. More than 30 chemokines have been discovered, and are at least seventeen known chemokine receptors, and many of these receptors exhibit promiscuous binding properties whereby several different chemokines can signal through the same receptor. Chemokines are divided into subfamilies based on conserved aa sequence motifs. Most family members have at least four conserved cysteine residues that form two intramolecular disulfide bonds. The subfamilies are defined by the position of the first two cysteine residues. There are four subfamilies of the chemokines, the CXC, the CC, the CX_3C, and the C. The CXC subfamily has an aa separating the two cysteines. The CC subfamily has adjacent cysteines. The CX_3C has three aa separating the cysteines and the C subfamily has only one cystiene in its N terminus. The CXC chemokines are found on chromosome 4 and the CC chemokines are found on chromosome 17. All chemokine receptors have two conserved cysteines that are assumed to form a disulfide bond critical for the conformation of the ligand-binding pocket [339, 340].

In addition to central role in autoimmune and inflammatory conditions, the chemokine system plays a critical role in many pathophysiological processes such as allergic responses, infectious, and autoimmune diseases, angiogenesis, inflammation, tumor growth, and hematopoietic development [341-343].

While interleukins and their genetic variants have been intensively studied in schizophrenia [249-252, 254], little attention has been focused on chemokines to date. However, recent promising findings suggest dysregulation of chemokine network in SCH [344].

3.4.1. IL-8

IL-8 (CXCL8), the best known and the most potent member of the CXC chemokines, is one of the major mediators of the inflammatory response [339, 340]. This chemokine is secreted by several cell types. It functions as a chemoattractant, and is also a potent angiogenic factor. It is believed to play a role in the pathogenesis of diseased conditions accompanied with the development of inflammatory, autoinflammatory and autoimmune processes including bronchiolitis, pulmonary diseases, cardiovascular diseases, Crohn's and Graves diseases, inflammatory bowel disease, systemic lupus erythematosus, and_psoriasis [341-343]. Alterations in IL-8 expression levels have been also reported for a number of psychiatric disorders including autism spectrum disorders [345, 346], major depressive disorder [347, 348], posttraumatic stress disorder [246], and non-traumatic stress [349].

A limited number of reports exploring a possible implication of IL-8 in pathomechanisms of SCH have underlined its involvement in disease-associated immune abnormalities. The important finding here, reported by several research groups, is demonstration that *in utero* exposure to elevations in IL-8 may partially account for brain disturbances commonly found in SP [350-353]. These findings have provided further support for the hypothesis that prenatal exposure to infection contributes to the etiology of SCH [250, 257, 258]. In addition, Reale et al. demonstrated that peripheral blood mononuclear cells of SP released significantly higher levels of constitutively and LPS-induced IL-8 as compared with controls [344]. Also, the increased levels of IL-8 in the blood of SP as compared to controls were reported [274, 275, 354, 355], whereas Erbağci et al. [290] observed no changes in IL-8 levels between SP and controls. It was reported that neither typical nor atypical neuroleptics showed significant influence on the higher blood IL-8 concentration in SCH [275].

The *IL-8* gene is localized on the chromosome 4 of the human genome (4q12-q21). We studied functional polymorphism +293 (G/T) SNP in intron 1 of the *IL-8* gene in SP and controls using PCR-SSP genotyping (unpublished data). Lower *IL-8* +293*T allele frequency was found in SP when compared to controls (0.22 vs 0.32, p=0.0007). Accordingly, the carriers of the *IL-8* +293*T minor allele were less frequent in SP than in controls (0.37 vs 0.52, p=0.001). Based upon these results we concluded that the *IL-8* +293*T minor allele might be nominated as a risk factor for SCH at least in the Armenian population.

3.4.2. MCP-1

MCP-1(CCL2) is one of the best characterized members of the chemokine CC family involved in the inflammatory processes. MCP-1 is considered to be a potent mediator for attraction of monocytes and macrophages to the sites of inflammation [356, 357]. MCP-1 regulates migration of monocytes from the blood stream across the vascular endothelium required for routine immunological surveillance of tissues, as well as in response to inflammation [356, 357]. Both MCP-1 and its receptor CCR2 have been demonstrated to be induced and involved in various diseases, particularly those accompanied by neuroinflammation including multiple sclerosis [358], ischemic stroke [245, 359, 360], myocardial infarction [360], and HIV-1 encephalitis [361]. High levels of MCP-1 in circulation have been found in patients with the above mentioned disorders [245, 358-361].

Very *few studies* have *addressed* the possible role of MCP-1 in SCH. Here the association of A/G biallelic polymorphism at the position -2518 (rs1024611) of the *MCP–1* gene promoter with clinical heterogeneity of SCH [362] as well as with resistance to antipsychotic treatment [363] was shown. Also, higher levels of non-stimulated and lipopolysaccharide-stimulated peripheral blood mononuclear cells of SP as compared with controls were found [344].

To reveal possible contribution of MCP-1 to SCH, we evaluated the 2518A/G genetic polymorphism and blood levels of MCP-1 in SP and controls through PCR-SSP genotyping and sandwich ELISA, respectively [364, 365]. According to the results obtained, the distribution of genotypes for the *MCP-1* -2518A/G SNP in *both SP and controls complied with H-W equilibrium (p>0.05).* Statistical power of the present study, indicating the difference in the carriage of the *MCP-1* -2518*G allele between the SP and controls for the OR=2.0 reached 94.9%. The allele and phenotype frequencies of the studied genetic variant in the groups of SP and controls are shown in Table 9. According to the data obtained, the *MCP-1* -2518*G minor allele was significantly more frequent in SP than in controls (35% vs 23%, p=0.009, OR=1.77, 95%CI: 1.1-2.04). Also, the carriers of the *MCP-1* -2518*G allele were overrepresented in SP compared to controls (60% vs 40%, p=0.003, OR=2.27, 95% CI: 1.13-2.01). Comparative determination of the MCP-1 plasma levels in SP and controls (presented as mean ±SD, pg/mL) indicated that in neuroleptic-treated SP the mean value of the MCP-1 plasma level was 1.6 times higher than in controls (455.7±187.7 vs 282.7±144.1, p=0.0003) (Fig. 14). Also, we found no significant difference in the mean value of MCP-1 plasma levels between neuroleptic-free and neuroleptic-treated patients (404.2±75.6 vs

455.7±187.7, p=0.23). Notably, the mean value of MCP-1 level in neuroleptic-free SP was significantly higher compared to controls (404.2±75.6 vs 282.7±144.1, p=0.001). Further, we assessed whether there is a difference between the mean value of the MCP-1 plasma levels in SP and controls depending on their -2518 genotype. The SP with the GG genotype had the highest MCP-1 mean level (711.4±211.4), followed by those with the AG genotype (472.1±135.8) and AA (372.4±180.2) homozygotes.

Table 9. Distribution of *MCP–1* –2518A/G SNP genotypes and carriage of minor allele in SP and controls. The data are presented as absolute numbers with proportions (%) in parentheses

MCP-1 -2518A/G		SP	Controls	P
	AA	41 (0.40)	63 (0.60)	
Genotypes	AG	52 (0.50)	35 (0.33)	
	GG	10 (0.10)	7 (0.07)	
Alleles	A	134 (0.65)	161 (0.77)	
	G	72 (0.35)[a]	49 (0.23)	0.009
Carriers	G	62 (0.60)[b]	42 (0.40)	0.003

[a] *p*-values for comparison of G allele proportion (allele frequency) between SP and controls;
[b] *p*-values for comparison of G allele carriage (phenotype frequency) between SP and controls.

The detected differences were statistically significant (GG vs AG: p=2.0E-4; GG vs AA: p=3.0E-6; AG vs AA: p=0.048). The same relationship was detected in controls; MCP-1 level in the GG, AG and AA genotypes were 566±52.5, 409.8±47.8, and 181±67.4, respectively (GG vs AG: p=6.0E-4; GG vs AA: p=4.0E-5; AG vs AA: p=1.0E-4). The data given above also indicate that for all three genotypes separately the mean value of MCP-1 plasma levels in SP were higher than in controls (p<0.001).

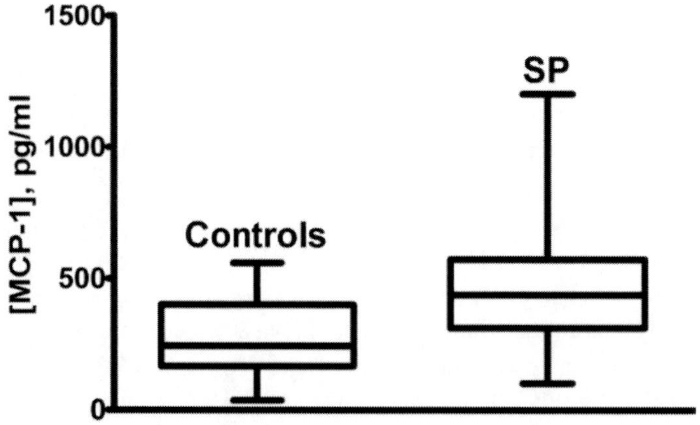

Figure 14. MCP-1 levels (pg/ml) in plasma of SP and controls. The data are expressed as whisker box plots; the box represents the 25–75th percentiles, the median is indicated by a bar across the box, the whiskers on each box represent the minimum and maximum level. P=0.0003 when comparing levels between SP and controls.

We found that the *MCP-1* -2518*G minor allele was more frequent in SP than in control subjects. Also, the *MCP-1* -2518*G carriers were overrepresented in SP compared to controls. Our results did not confirm the previous data suggesting no significant association between the *MCP-1* -2518A/G polymorphism and susceptibility to SCH [250, 256]. However, the *MCP-1* -2518A/G polymorphism was found be associated with clinical heterogeneity of SCH [256] as well as with resistance to neuroleptic treatment in SP [250].

Concerning the levels of MCP-1 protein, our findings showed higher MCP-1 plasma levels in both neuroleptic-treated and neuroleptic-free SP compared to controls. Our data are in concordance with those reported previously by Drexhage et al. [366]. By contrast, Teixeira et al. [367] found no significant difference in serum levels of MCP-1 between healthy subjects and SP treated with neuroleptics [367]. This mismatch may reflect population/ethnic differences between subjects enrolled in our study and those examined in previous investigations. In addition, our data revealed a difference between the MCP-1 protein blood levels in individuals depending on the -2518A/G genotype; subjects carrying the AG or GG genotype had significant higher MCP-1 levels than those with the AA genotype.

3.5. MIF in SCH

MIF is an important mediator of the innate immune system involved in chronic inflammation, a pleiotropic protein, participating in inflammatory and immune responses. MIF was originally discovered as a lymphokine involved in delayed hypersensitivity and various macrophage functions, including phagocytosis, spreading, and tumoricidal activity. MIF was reevaluated as a proinflammatory cytokine and pituitary-derived hormone potentiating endotoxemia. The evolutionary conserved MIF exhibits prominent proinflammatory and proatherogenic functions. The latest findings on its chemotactic and chemokine-like properties nonecanonic chemokines and imply MIF as a crucial drug target for the treatment of inflammatory diseases and further as none-canonic chemokine. This protein is ubiquitously expressed in various organs, such as the brain and kidney. Among cytokines, MIF is unique in terms of its abundant expression and storage within the cytoplasm and, further, for its counteraction against glucocorticoids [368, 369]. De la Fontaine et al. [370] performed comparative investigation of -173G/C (rs755622) SNP and the tetranucleotide repeat CATT (5-8) at position -794 of the *MIF* gene in SP and controls. They found that *MIF* genotypes were equally distributed in both groups [370].

We explore whether the functional single nucleotide polymorphism rs1007888 A/G in the 3′-flanking region of the *MIF* gene (22q11.23) is associated with susceptibility to schizophrenia. A total of 208 Armenians (103 patients with paranoid form of schizophrenia and 105 healthy subjects) were genotyped using polymerase chain reaction with sequence-specific primers (PCR-SSP). The distribution of *MIF* rs1007888 genotypes complied with the H-W equilibrium in both groups. No significant difference was found in frequency of the *MIF* rs1007888*G allele between the patients and healthy subjects (0.49 vs 0.45 p=0.44). The rs1007888*G carriers were slightly overrepresented among the SP compared to controls, but the difference was not statistically significant (0.78 vs 0.70, p=0.18, OR=1.52, 95%CI: 0.95-1.31). To summarize, our results suggest that the *MIF* gene rs1007888A/G variant does not contribute to the susceptibility to SCH in the Armenian population.

4. CRP IN SCH

CRP, an acute and chronic phase inflammation marker, produced by liver and plays an important role in the immune response [371, 372]. There is plausible evidence on the implication of CRP in the pathogenesis of schizophrenia, particularly in disease-associated immune system abnormalities [39, 40, 373-383]. Increased CRP or high sensitivity C-reactive protein (hsCRP) serum levels in SP and related psychiatric disorders were observed in different populations [39, 40, 373-377]. Also, serum CRP levels were associated with the severity of cognitive impairment [378] and more severe psychopathology in SCH [377, 379]. C-reactive protein has also emerged as a target for cardiovascular (CV) risk outcomes in SP [380] and found to correlate with the type of neuroleptics used for SP treatment [381, 382]. However, there are also studies on association between the CRP levels and SCH with conflicting results [383, 384].

Concerning the gene coding CRP protein, it is located on the first chromosome 1q loci positively linked to schizophrenia [385]. Recent genetic analysis revealed a positive association between Center for Epidemiological Studies-Depression (CESD) scores and CRP levels among individuals with the *CRP* A-G-T [rs1417938 (A/T), rs1800947 (C/G), rs1205 (C/T)] haplotype [386]. Also, it has been shown that *CRP* gene polymorphisms are independently associated with increased (rs1205) and decreased (rs1800947) CRP level and that *CRP* genotypes/haplotypes interact with obesity to set CRP level [387]. In our studies, we evaluated the possible association of *CRP* rs1417938, rs1800947, and rs1205 genetic variants with susceptibility to SCH. No significant differences in allele frequencies and carriers between SP and controls were observed. Nevertheless, the rs1417938 AA homozygotes and rs1205*T carriers tended to be overrepresented in SP when compared to controls (p=0.1 in both cases). Thus, despite *CRP* gene might be considered as relevant candidate gene for susceptibility to SCH or as a gene modifier of this disease symptomatology, we observed no association of investigated genetic variants within *CRP* gene and the SCH in Armenians that might reflect some ethnic differences as well as absence of acute inflammation signs in SP.

5. BRAIN-DERIVED NEUROTROPHIC FACTOR AND NEUROPROTEIN NETRIN G1 IN SCH

Proteins with neuroimmunomodulatory properties represent a special interest in SCH research, and the genes encoding these proteins are considered as important candidate susceptibility genes for SCH [388, 389].

Brain-derived neurotrophic factor (BDNF) promotes several functions of neurons, modulates neurotransmission, contributes to neuronal growth, survival, differentiation, and regulates synaptic transmission and cognitive processes [390]. Also, BDNF produced by several immune-cell subtypes is an important modulator of immunity, therefore, considered as neurotrophin with neuroimmunomodulatory properties [391].

The *BDNF* gene (locus 11p13) maps to human chromosomes linked to SCH [392, 393]. The functional missense polymorphism of the *BDNF* gene (Val66Met, rs6265) affects activity-dependent secretion of BDNF, memory, and hippocampal functions [394], which may have significant consequences in SCH. Interestingly, the rs6265 polymorphism alters the intracellular trafficking and packaging of proBDNF, important in the context of synaptic plasticity [395]. Moreover, the association of the rs6265 with human cortical morphology and bilateral reductions of hippocampal gray matter volumes in Met carriers compared with Val/Val subjects was indicated [396]. Gallinat et al. [397] found that Val66Met genotype appears to predict the BDNF blood level in controls that linked the Met allele to higher concentrations of BDNF in the blood.

A number of studies indicated reduced BDNF levels in SP compared to controls [398-402], and an association of BDNF blood level with some clinical and demographic characteristics of SCH-affected subjects was observed [401, 402].

A crucial role of *BDNF* rs6265 polymorphism in neuroplasticity related to SCH was demonstrated [403], and a relationship of *BDNF* rs6265 genotypes with age of onset and the psychotic symptoms of SCH was observed [404]. Furthermore, *BDNF* 66Met allele was shown to associate with increased aggressive behavior in SP [405]. However, the results from the meta-analyses concerning association of the *BDNF* rs6265 polymorphism with SCH are controversial, which may reflect the ethnic differences between studied groups [406, 407].

In our studies we evaluated the association of the *BDNF* rs6265 polymorphism with susceptibility to SCH and its manifestation in an Armenian population [408, 409]. In order to reveal if there is any association between selected genes and SCH, SP and controls were genotyped for BDNF rs6265 functional polymorphism by PCR-SSP. The genotypes of the studied polymorphism in *both groups complied with H-W equilibrium* ($p>0.05$). The genotype and allele distributions obtained for target SNP are similar to those reported for European population in public genetic databases (http://www.ncbi.nlm.nih.gov/SNP). Statistical power of this study, indicating the difference in the carriage of the *BDNF* 66Met allele between the patients and controls at level for the OR=2.0, reached 93.9%.

The distribution of the *BDNF* rs6265 gene variant in both groups is shown in Table 10. The *BDNF* 66Met minor allele frequency was higher in SP than in controls (31% versus 19%, p=0.004, OR=1.93, 95%CI: 1.12-1.65). Accordingly, the *BDNF* 66Met carriers were overrepresented in SP compared to controls (55% versus 35%, p=0.003, OR=2.28, 95%CI: 1.14-1.98) [408, 409].

Table 10. The frequencies of *BDNF* genotypes, alleles, and carriage of minor alleles in SP and controls. The data are given as absolute numbers with proportions in parentheses

BDNF rs6265		SP	Controls	*P*
	GG	46 (0.45)	68 (0.65)	
Genotypes	GA	51 (0.50)	35 (0.33)	
	AA	6 (0.06)	2 (0.02)	
Alleles	G	143 (0.69)	171 (0.81)	
	A	63 (0.31)	39 (0.19)	0.004[a]
Carriage	A	57 (0.55)	37 (0.35)	0.003[b]

[a] p-values for comparison of Allele 2 proportion (allele frequency) between SP and controls;
[b] p-values for comparison of Allele 2 carriage (phenotype frequency) between SP and controls.

Categorical survival analysis was performed to evaluate the potential correlation between *BDNF* genotype and particular clinical and demographic characteristics of SP. No significant correlation between the *BDNF* rs6265 genotypes and the age at SCH onset, gender, and family history of SCH was observed. By contrast, the rs6265 genotypes correlated with the age at disease onset in affected subjects. Survival analysis revealed dependence between the mean age at SCH onset and the *BDNF* rs6265 genotypes (Val/Val: 30.3±2.1 years; Val/Met: 25.1±1.4 years; Met/Met: 18.0±1.5 years). Accordingly, patients with the *BDNF* Met/Met genotype had lower age at onset compared to those with Val/Val+Val/Met genotypes ($p<0.024$) [408, 409]. Our results demonstrated a relationship between the *BDNF* rs6265 genotype and age at SCH onset, indicating that the Met/Met genotype may confer earlier onset at the disease, and are in concordance with the data obtained for other ethnic groups (Spaniards, African-Americans and Japanese) [404, 406, 412]. Notably, Malla et al. found that age at the onset itself has an impact on SCH severity [411]. Further, Douaud et al. indicated larger anatomically related grey and white matter abnormalities in adolescent SP compared to adult patients and suggested etiological mechanisms for adolescent- and adult-onset SP with an altered neurodevelopmental time course in patients [412].

Further, we measured BDNF in the blood plasma of SP and controls using sandwich ELISA and assess possible association between the *BDNF* Val66Met genetic variant and BDNF plasma levels [unpublished data]. The results obtained demonstrated that in SP the mean value of the BDNF plasma levels was 1.67 times significantly lower than in controls (p<0.0001) and are in agreement with the data presented by other research groups [397-402]. Notably, in both groups the mean value of BDNF levels in females was significantly lower compared to males (SP: p<0.0001; controls: p<0.019). This tendency was in concordance with recently reported data indicating a trend for a great reduction of BDNF level in SCH-affected females [402].We observed no significant difference between the mean value of BDNF level in neuroleptic-free and neuroleptic-treated SP, confirming data reported by Rizos et al. [400].

Regarding the association between the *BDNF* Val66Met genetic variant and BDNF plasma levels, our results showed that in SP as well as in controls the Met allele carriers had significantly higher BDNF plasma levels when compared to subjects with Val/Val genotype (p<0.0001). While no association between the family history of SCH and Val66Met genotypes as well as BDNF plasma levels was observed, lower BDNF levels were found in SP with long duration of SCH (p<0.004) [unpublished data]. Our findings on the association of BDNF levels with SCH duration, gender, and Val66Met genotypes are in concordance with the data from other populations [397, 401, 402].

Thus, our study indicates that the *BDNF* 66Met allele was positively associated with susceptibility to SCH and earlier onset at the disease. Based upon the detected overrepresentation of the *BDNF* Met allele carriers in SP, and positive association between this allele and high BDNF blood levels, we nominate *BDNF* 66Met minor allele and high BDNF levels as risk factors for SCH.

Neuroprotein netrin G1 (NTNG1), a vertebrate-specific axon guidance molecule, promotes neurite outgrowth and regulates formation and function of synapse [413], particularly, an immunological synapse formed by interaction of T cells with antigen-presenting cells, and as a guidance cues might be involved immune cell interactions and trafficking [414, 415].

The *NTNG1* gene (locus 1p13.3), like the *BDNF* gene, map to human chromosome 1 linked to schizophrenia [5, 6]. There are few data elevating NTNG1 in SCH. Fukasawa et al. found association of SCH with the *NTNG1* IVS8-1467C>T polymorphism and related haplotype block in a Japanese population [416]. Another study indicated association of SCH with specific haplotypes encompassing alternatively spliced exons of *NTNG1* [417]. In particular, an SNP, namely rs628117, located within the intron 9 of the *NTNG1* gene and leading to an A to G substitution was recently found to be associated with SCH in a Japanese population [417]. However, our own study, based on the same methodological design as presented above for BDNF, found no association of the *NTNG1* rs628117 polymorphism with susceptibility to SCH and its manifestation in an Armenian population [408, 409]. Thus, the *NTNG1* rs628117 genotype and allele frequencies were equally distributed among SP and controls. Also, no significant correlation between the *NTNG1* rs628117 genotypes and the age at SCH onset, gender, and family history of SCH was observed [408, 409]. The data obtained do not confirm the previous data indicating important role of *NTNG1* rs628117 variant in SCH reported in a Japanese family-based study [417] that might reflect the ethnic differences between Japanese and Armenians. Nevertheless, our finding does not exclude the association of other polymorphisms covering the *NTNG1* gene with SCH in Armenian as well as in other populations.

CONCLUSION

1. Pathogenesis of SCH is characterized by alterations in the functional activity of the complement system, including:
    - increased activities of the complement alternative and terminal pathway, and the individual activities of the complement C1, C3, and C4 proteins and decreased activity of the complement C2 protein;
    - decreased levels of the complement protein FB and the C4B isotype of the C4 complement protein;
    - increased level of MAC, the terminal end product of the complement cascade;
    - increased expression of CR1 on erythrocytes, lymphocytes, monocytes, and neutrophils, accompanied by the elevated number of CR1 positive erythrocytes and reduced number of CR1 positive lymphocytes and monocytes.
2. Pathogenesis of SCH is characterized by the increased levels of complement derived triggers of inflammation and apoptosis.
3. Pathogenesis of SCH is characterized by the increased levels of atypical populations of IC in circulation including small-sized IC and type 3 cryoglobulins as well as of C1Q-CIC.
4. Pathogenesis of SCH is characterized by the increased levels of IL-6, TNF-α, and MCP-1 cytokines.
5. Pathogenesis of SCH is characterized by the increased level of neuroimmunomodulatory protein BDNF.
6. Immune dysregulation in SCH has a genetic component. Among the candidate genes are the *C1QB* gene, the *IL-6* gene, the *IL-8,* the *MCP-1* gene, and the *BDNF* gene, as follows:

- the rs291982*G minor allele of the *C1QB* gene might represent a risk factor for SCH;
- the -174*C variant of the *IL*-6 gene is associated with increasing risk to SCH;
- the *IL-8* +293*T minor allele might be nominated as a risk factor for SCH;
- the *MCP-1* -2518*G minor allele was more frequent in SP than in control subjects, and the *MCP-1* -2518*G carriers were overrepresented in SP compared to controls;
- the *BDNF* gene 66Met minor allele positively associates with susceptibility to SCH and earlier onset of the disease.

REFERENCES

[1] M. Baron M, *Am. J. Hum. Genet.* 68, 299 (2001).

[2] P. A. Holmans, B. Riley, A. E. Pulver, M. J. Owen, D. B. Wildenauer, P. V. Gejman, B. J. Mowry, C. Laurent, K. S. Kendler, G. Nestadt, N. M. Williams, S. G. Schwab, A. R. Sanders, D. Nertney, J. Mallet, B. Wormley, V. K. Lasseter, M. C. O'Donovan, J. Duan, M. Albus, M. Alexander, S. Godard, R. Ribble, K. Y. Liang, N. Norton, W. Maier, G. Papadimitriou, D. Walsh, M. Jay, A. O'Neill, F. B. Lerer, D. Dikeos, R. R. Crowe, J. M. Silverman and D. F. Levinson, *Mol. Psychiatry* 14, 786 (2009).

[3] M. Rothermundt, V. Arolt and T. A. Bayer, *Brain Behav. Immun.* 15, 319 (2001).

[4] F. Gaughran, *Int. Rev. Neurobiol.* 52, 275 (2002).

[5] D. Hinze-Selch D, *Bipolar Disord.* 4, 81 (2002).

[6] N. Müller, *Eur. Arch. Psychiatry Clin. Neurosci.* 254, 1 (2004).

[7] A. L. Jones, B. J. Mowry, M. P. Pender and J. M. Greer, *Immunol. Cell. Biol.* 83, 9 (2005).

[8] D. R. Hanson and I. I. Gottesman, *BMC Med. Genet.* 6, 7 (2005).

[9] A. Monji, T. Kato and S. Kanba, *Psychiatry Clin. Neurosci.* 63, 257 (2009).

[10] S. Y. Yum, S. K. Yum, T. Kim and M. Y. Hwang, *Psychiatr. Clin. North Am.* 32, 795 (2009).

[11] L. F. Jarskog, L. A. Glantz, J. H. Gilmore and J. A. Lieberman, *Prog. Neuropsychopharmacol. Biol. Psychiatry*, 29, 846 (2005).

[12] L. F. Jarskog, E. S. Selinger, J. A. Lieberman and J. H. Gilmore, *Am. J. Psychiatry*, 161, 109 (2004).

[13] G. E. Berger, S. Wood and P. D. McGorry, *Psychopharmacol. Bull.* 37, 79 (2003).

[14] N. Kozlovsky, R. H. Belmaker and G. Agam, *Eur. Neuropsychopharmacol.* 12, 13 (2002).

[15] V. S. Catts and S. V. Catts, *Schizophr. Res.* 41, 405 (2000).

[16] D. A. Lewis and J. A. Lieberman, *Neuron*, 28, 325 (2000).

[17] R. L. Margolis, D. M. Chuang and R. M. Post, *Biol. Psychiatry*, 35, 946 (1994).

[18] D. A. Lewis and P. Levitt, *Annu. Rev. Neurosci.* 25, 409 (2002).

[19] J. L. Rapoport, A. M. Addington, S. Frangou and M. R. Psych, *Mol. Psychiatry*, 10, 434 (2005).

[20] S. H. Fatemi and T. D. Folsom, *Schizophr. Bull.* 35, 528 (2009).

[21] World Health Organization, *The international statistical classification of diseases and related health problems.* ed. 10, Geneva (1992).
[22] American Psychiatric Association, *Diagnostic and statistical manual of mental disorders, ed. 4, text revised* (*DSM-IV-TR*), American Psychiatric Pub, Washington, DC (2000).
[23] M. Sakamoto, Y. Fujisawa and K. Nishioka, *Nutrition*, 14, 391 (1998).
[24] R. B. Sim and A. Laich, *Biochem. Soc. Trans.* 28, 545 (2000).
[25] D. S. Cole and B. P. Morgan, *Clin. Sci.* 104, 455 (2003).
[26] A. J. Nauta, A. Roos and M. R. Daha, *Int. Arch. Allergy Immunol.* 134, 310 (2004).
[27] J. V. Sarma and P. A. Ward, *Cell Tissue Res.* 343, 227 (2011).
[28] J. E. Volankis and M. Frank, *The human complement system in health and disease.* Marcel Dekker, New York (1998)
[29] M. V. Carroll and R. B. Sim, *Adv. Drug Deliv. Rev.* 63, 965 (2011).
[30] Y. Rahpeymai, M. A. Hietala, U. Wilhelmsson, A. Fotheringham, I. Davies, A. K. Nilsson, J. Zwirner, R. A. Wetsel, C. Gerard, M. Pekny and M. Pekna, *EMBO J.* 25, 1364.
[31] L. Fourgeaud amd L. M. Boulanger, *Cell*, 131, 1034 (2007).
[32] B. Stevens, N. J. Allen, L. E. Vazquez, G. R. Howell, K. S. Christopherson, N. Nouri, K. D. Micheva, A. K. Mehalow, A. D. Huberman, B. Stafford, A. Sher, A. M. Litke, J. D. Lambris, S. J. Smith, S. W. John and B. A. Barres, *Cell*, 131, 1164.
[33] B. T. Woods, *Am. J. Psychiatry*, 155, 1661 (1998).
[34] P. C. Ashe, M. D. Berry and A. A. Boulton, *Prog. Neuropsychopharmacol. Biol. Psychiatry*, 25, 691 (2001).
[35] H. Jaaro-Peled, A. Hayashi-Takagi, S. Seshadri, A. Kamiya, N. J. Brandon and A. Sawa, *Trends Neurosci.* 32, 485 (2009).
[36] E. Gout, C. Moriscot, A. Doni, C. Dumestre-Pérard, M. Lacroix, J. Pérard, G. Schoehn, A. Mantovani, G. J. Arlaud and N. M. Thielens, *J. Immunol.* 186, 5815 (2011).
[37] B. Spivak, M. Radwan, J. Brandon, Y. Baruch, M. Stawski, S. Tyano and A. Weizman, *Psychol. Med.* 23, 315 (1993).
[38] T. Sasaki, S. Nanko, R. Fukuda, T. Kawate, H. Kunugi and H. Kazamatsuri, *Biol. Psychiatry*, 35, 173 (1994).
[39] A. V. Shcherbakova, E. A. Neshkova, V. L. Dotsenko, L. V. Kozlov, A. A. Mishin, T. P. Platonova, E. G. Shcherbakova and G. A. Iarovaia, *Zh. Nevrol. Psikhiatr. Im. S. S. Korsakova*, 98, 38 (1998).
[40] Shcherbakova, E. Neshkova, V. Dotsenko, T. Platonova, E. Shcherbakova and G. Yarovaya, *Immunopharmacology*, 43, 273 (1999).
[41] S. Hakobyan, A. Boyajyan and R. B. Sim, *Neurosci. Lett.* 374, 35 (2005).
[42] A. Boyajyan, S. Hakobyan and R. B. Sim, *World J. Biol. Psychiatry,* 6 (Suppl.1), 244 (2005).
[43] K. Whaley and J. North, *Haemolytic assays for whole complement activity and individual components. Complement. A practical approach.* Oxford University press, Oxford (1997).
[44] K. R. Mayilyan, J. N. Arnold, J. S. Presanis, A. F. Soghoyan and R. B. Sim, *Neurosci. Lett.* 404, 336 (2006).

[45] B. P. Morgan, *Measurement of complement hemolytic activity, generation of complement-depleted sera, and production of hemolytic intermediates.* In *B. P. Morgan, ed. Complement methods and protocols),* Human Press, Totowa, New Jersey (2000).
[46] B. Xu, A. Woodroffe, L. Rodriguez-Murillo, J. L. Roos, E. J. van Rensburg, G. R. Abecasis, J. A. Gogos and M. Karayiorgou, *Proc. Natl. Acad. Sci. USA*, 106, 16746 (2009).
[47] K. S. Hong, H. H. Won, E. Y. Cho, H. O. Jeun, S. S. Cho, Y. S. Lee, D. Y. Park, Y. L. Jang, K. S. Choi, D. Lee, M. J. Kim, S. Kim, W. S. Han and J. W. Kim, *Am. J. Med. Genet. B Neuropsychiatr. Genet.* 150B, 647 (2009).
[48] R. Zakharyan, A. Khoyetsyan, A. Arakelyan, A. Boyajyan, A. Gevorgyan, A. Stahelova, F. Mrazek, and M. Petrek. *BMC Med. Genet.*_12, 126 (2011).
[49] H. A. Martens, M. W. Zuurman, A. H. de Lange, I. M. Nolte, G. van der Steege, G. J. Navis, C. G. Kallenberg, M. A. Seelen and M. Bijl M, *Ann. Rheum. Dis.* 68, 715 (2009).
[50] D. J. Campbell and M. A. Koch, *Nat. Rev. Immunol.* 11, 119 (2011).
[51] S. Muñoz-Cruz, C. Togno-Pierce and J. Morales-Montor, *Curr. Top. Med. Chem.* 11, 1714 (2011).
[52] E. Freier, C. S. Weber, U. Nowottne, C. Horn, K. Bartels, S. Meyer, Y. Hildebrandt, T. Luetkens, Y. Cao, C. Pabst, J. Muzzulini, B. Schnee, M. C. Brunner-Weinzierl, M. Marangolo, C. Bokemeyer, H. C. Deter and D. Atanackovic, *Psychoneuroendocrinology*, 35, 663 (2010).
[53] V. Núñez, D. Alameda, D. Rico, R. Mota, P. Gonzalo, M. Cedenilla, T. Fischer, L. Boscá, C. K. Glass, A. G. Arroyo and M. Ricote, *Proc. Natl. Acad. Sci. USA* 107, 10626 (2010).
[54] D. Farré, R. Roset, M. Huerta, J. E. Adsuara, L. Roselló, M. M. Albà and X. Messeguer, *Nucleic Acids Res.* 31, 3651 (2003).
[55] H. K. Tabor, N. J. Risch and R. M. Myers, *Nat. Rev. Genet.* 3, 391 (2002).
[56] D. N. Arnosti and M. M. Kulkarni, *J. Cell. Biochem.* 94, 890 (2005).
[57] R. P. Grewal, T. E. Morgan and C. E. Finch, *Neurosci. Lett.* 271, 65 (1999).
[58] Y. Zheng, X. R. Cheng, W. X. Zhou and Y. X. Zhang, *Neurosci. Lett.* 439, 119 (2008).
[59] D. G. Walker, J. E. Dalsing-Hernandez and L. F. Lue, *Microvasc. Res.* 75, 411 (2008).
[60] K. E. Sullivan, *Curr. Opin. Pediatr.* 10, 600 (1998).
[61] C. Wang, B. X. Jian, X. D. Jiang and X. Z. Zhao, *Chin. Med. J.* 105, 316 (1992).
[62] J. D. Lambris, I. Zarkadis, L. Tort and O. J. Sunyer, Phylogeny and diversity of the third complement component C3, *Dev. Comp. Immunol.* 21, 143 (1997).
[63] C. L. Villiers, M. B. Villiers and P. N. Marche, *Ann. Biol. Clin.* 57, 127 (1999).
[64] H. R. Colten and C. A. Alper, *J. Immunol.* 108, 1184 (1972).
[65] D. P. Agarwal, H. G. Benkmann and H. W. Goedde, *Hum. Hered.* 22, 356 (1972).
[66] H. Arvilommi, *Nature*, 251, 740 (1974).
[67] C. Rudduck, L. Beckman, G. Franzén and L. Lindström, *Hum. Hered.* 35, 255 (1985).
[68] L. Fañanás, P. Moral, M. A. Panadero and J. Bertranpetit, *Hum. Hered.* 42, 162 (1992).
[69] D. H. Blackwood, W. J. Muir, A. Stephenson, J. Wentzel, A. Ad'hiah, M. J. Walker, S. S. Papiha, D. M. St Clair and D. F. Roberts, *Psychiatr. Genet.* 6, 51 (1996).
[70] C. T. Wong, W. F. Tsoi and N. Saha, *Schizophr. Res.* 22, 165 (1996).
[71] S. A. Johnson, G. M. Pasinetti and C. E. Finch, *Brain Res. Dev. Brain Res.* 80, 163 (1994).

[72] H. R. Colten and F. S. Rosen, *Annu. Rev. Immunol.* 10, 809 (1992).
[73] M. C. Carroll, *Annu. Rev. Immunol.* 16, 545 (1998).
[74] G. Hauptmann, G. Tappeiner and J. A. Schifferli, *Immunodefic. Rev.* 1, 3 (1988).
[75] C. A. Blanchong, E. K. Chung, K. L. Rupert, Y. Yang, Z. Yang, B. Zhou, J. M. Moulds and C. Y. Yu, *Int. Immunopharmacol.* 1, 365 (2001).
[76] T. Höhler, B. Stradmann-Bellinghausen, R. Starke, R. Sänger, A. Victor, C. Rittner and P. M. Schneider, *J. Hepatol.* 37, 387 (2002).
[77] C. Y. Yu, E. K. Chung, Y. Yang, C. A. Blanchong, N. Jacobsen, K. Saxena, Z. Yang, W. Miller, L. Varga and G. Fust, *Prog Nucleic Acid Res Mol Biol.* 75, 217 (2003).
[78] R. P. Warren, R. A. Burger, D. Odell, A. R. Torres and W. L. Warren, *Arch. Pediatr. Adolesc. Med.* 148, 180 (1994).
[79] R. P. Warren, J. D. Odell, W. L. Warren, R. A. Burger, A. Maciulis and A. R. Torres, *J. Am. Acad. Child Adolesc. Psychiatry* 34, 1009 (1995a).
[80] R. P. Warren, J. Yonk, R. W. Burger, D. Odell and W. L. Warren, *Neuropsychobiology*, 31, 53 (1995b).
[81] D. E. Isenman and J. R. Young, *J. Immunol.* 132, 3019 (1984).
[82] S. K. Law, A. W. Dodds and R. R. Porter, *EMBO J.* 3, 1819 (1984).
[83] C. Rudduck, L. Beckman, G. Franzén, L. Jacobsson and L. Lindström, *Hum. Hered.* 35, 223 (1985).
[84] R. Schroers, M. M. Nöthen, M. Rietschel, M. Albus, W. Maier, S. Schwab, D. Wildenauer, R. Fimmers, P. Propping and G. Dewald, *Hum. Hered.* 47, 279 (1997).
[85] B. Spivak, M. Radwan, D. Elimelech, Y. Baruch, G. Avidan and S. Tyano, *Biol. Psychiatry* 26, 640 (1989).
[86] M. Maes, J. Delange, R. Ranjan, H. Y. Meltzer, R. Desnyder, W. Cooremans and S. Scharpé, *Psychiatry Res.* 66, 1 (1997).
[87] C. L. Cazzullo, M. Saresella, K. Roda, M. G. Calvo, P. Bertrando, S. Doria, M. Clerici, A. Salvaggio and P. Ferrante, *Schizophr. Res.* 31, 49 (1998).
[88] M. H. Roos, E. Mollenhauer, P. Démant and C. Rittner, *Nature*, 298, 854 (1982).
[89] J. Chrispeels, S. Bank, C. Rittner and D. Bitter-Suermann, *J. Immunol. Methods* 125, 5 (1989).
[90] K. Mayilyan, P. Schneider, A. Dodds, D. Rujescu, B. Stradmann-Bellinghausen, A. Harmann, A. Soghoyan, A. Boyajyan and R. Sim, *Immunology*, 113, 125 (2004).
[91] K. R. Mayilyan, A. W. Dodds, A. S. Boyajyan, J. S. Presanis, J. N. Arnold, A. S. Soghoyan and R. B. Sim, *World J. Biol. Psychiatry*, 5, 143 (2004).
[92] K. R. Mayilyan, R. B. Sim, A. S. Boyajyan, J. S. Presanis, A. S. Soghoyan and A. W. Dodds, *Mol. Immunology*, 41, 274 (2004).
[93] K. R. Mayilyan, A. W. Dodds, A. S. Boyajyan, A. S. Soghoyan and R. B. Sim, *World J. Biol. Psychiatry*, 9, 225 (2008).
[94] C. A. Blanchong, B. Zhou, K. L. Rupert, E. K. Chung, K. N. Jones, J. F. Sotos, W. B. Zipf, R. M. Rennebohm and C. Yung Yu, *J. Exp. Med.* 191, 2183 (2000).
[95] D. T. Fearon, *J. Exp. Med.* 152, 20 (1980).
[96] D. Liu and Z. X. Niu, *Immunopharmacol. Immunotoxicol.* 31, 524 (2009).
[97] J. A. Schifferli, Y. C. Ng and D. K. Peters, *N. Engl. J. Med.* 315, 488 (1986).
[98] C. Hess and J. A. Schifferli, *News Physiol. Sci.* 18, 104 (2003).
[99] L. B. Klickstein, S. F. Barbashov, T. Liu, R. M. Jack and A. Nicholson-Weller, *Immunity*, 7, 345 (1997).

[100] P. Eggleton, A. J. Tenner and K. B. Reid, *Clin. Exp. Immunol.* 120, 406 (2000).
[101] E. McGreal and P. Gasque, *Biochem. Soc. Trans.* 30, 1010 (2002).
[102] Ghiran, S. R. Tyagi, L. B. Klickstein and A. Nicholson-Weller, *Immunobiology*, 205, 407 (2002).
[103] Ghiran, S. F. Barbashov, L. B. Klickstein, S. W. Tas, J. C Jensenius and A. Nicholson-Weller, *J. Exp. Med.* 192, 1797 (2000).
[104] M. Krych-Goldberg and J. P. Atkinson, *Immunol. Rev.* 180, 112 (2001).
[105] L. A. Hebert, *Am. J. Kidney Dis.* 17, 352 (1991).
[106] B. P. Thornton, V. Větvicka and G. D. Ross, *J. Immunol.* 152, 1727 (1994).
[107] F. Bacle, N. Haeffner-Cavaillon, M. Laude, C. Couturier and M. D. Kazatchkine, *J. Immunol.* 144, 147 (1990).
[108] A. Rochowiak Z. I. Niemir, *Pol. Merkur. Lekarski* 28, 84 (2010).
[109] S. Mah, M. R. Nelson, L. E. Delisi, R. H. Reneland, N. Markward, M. R. James, D. R. Nyholt, N. Hayward, H. Handoko, B. Mowry, S. Kammerer and A. Braun, *Mol. Psychiatry* 11, 471 (2006).
[110] M. Zorzetto, I. Ferrarotti, R. Trisolini, L. Lazzari Agli, R. Scabini, M. Novo, A. De Silvestri, M. Patelli, M. Martinetti, M. Cuccia, V. Poletti, E. Pozzi and M. Luisetti, *Am. J. Respir. Crit. Care Med.* 168, 330 (2003).
[111] M. Katyal, S. C. Tiwari, A. Kumar, A. K. Dinda, V. Arora, R. Kumar and N. Das, *Mol. Immunol.* 40, 1325 (2004).
[112] A. L. Hepburn, J. C. Mason and K. A. Davies, *Rheumatology* 43, 547 (2004).
[113] A. Erdei, A. Isaák, K. Török, N. Sándor, M. Kremlitzka, J. Prechl and Z. Bajtay, *Mol. Immunol.* 46, 2767 (2009).
[114] R. Khera and N. Das, *Mol. Immunol.* 46, 761 (2009).
[115] A. Arakelyan, R. Zakharyan, A. Khoyetsyan, D. Poghosyan, R. Aroutiounian, F. Mrazek, M. Petrek and A. Boyajyan. *BMC Clin. Pathol.* 11, 10 (2011).
[116] A. Khoyetsyan and A. Boyajyan, "Implication of abnormal immune complexes in term of schizophrenia-associated immune system alterations", FEBS advanced lecture course "Trends in genetics: genomic instability and pathways of response", 20-26, Feb. 2011 (Yerevan, Armenia) pp53.
[117] M. D. Kazatchkine, M. H. Jouvin, J. G. Wilson, E. Fischer and A. Fischer, *Immunol. Lett.* 14, 191 (1987).
[118] P. E. Ruuska, I. Ikäheimo, S. Silvennoinen-Kassinen, M. L. Käär and A. Tiilikainen, *Clin. Exp. Immunol.* 89, 18 (1992).
[119] N. Waitumbi, M. O. Opollo, R. O. Muga, A. O. Misore and J. A. Stoute, *Blood*, 95, 1481 (2000).
[120] V. L. Serebruany, D. Atar, S. R. Murugesan, S. Jerome, H. Semaan and P. A. Gurbel, *J. Thromb. Thrombolysis* 10, 197 (2000).
[121] D. McCarthy, M. J. Taylor, J. Bernhagen, J. D. Perry and A. S. Hamblin, *Ann. Rheum. Dis.* 51, 307 (1992).
[122] M. Berger, E. M. Wetzler and R. S. Wallis, *Blood*, 71, 151 (1988).
[123] D. Ogle, J. G. Noel, R. M. Sramkoski, C. K. Ogle and J. W. Alexander, *Cytokine*, 2, 447 (1990).
[124] S. Theodoropoulou, G. Spanakos, C. N. Baxevanis, M. Economou, A. D. Gritzapis, M. P. Papamichail and C. N. Stefanis, *Schizophr. Res.* 47, 13 (2001).

[125] T. Mardi, S. Toker, S. Melamed, A. Shirom, D. Zeltser, I. Shapira, S. Berliner and O. Rogowski, *Diabetes Res. Clin. Pract.* 69, 249 (2005).
[126] A. Pillai, K. M. Dhandapani, B. A. Pillai, A. V. Terry Jr and S. P. Mahadik, *Neuropsychopharmacology*, 33, 1942 (2008).
[127] N. R. Kim, S. W. Park, J. G. Lee and Y. H. Kim, *Prog. Neuropsychopharmacol. Biol. Psychiatry* 32, 633 (2008).
[128] D. P. Williams, M. Pirmohamed, D. J. Naisbitt, J. P. Uetrecht and B. K. Park, *Mol. Pharmacol.* 58, 207 (2000).
[129] C. Kemper, J. P. Atkinson and D. E. Hourcade, *Annu. Rev. Immunol.* 28, 131 (2010).
[130] A. G. Khoyetsyan, S. S. Hakobyan, G. V. Tsakanova and A. S. Boyajyan, *Blood (Yerevan)*, 1, 60 (2007).
[131] A. S. Boyajyan, A. G. Khoyetsyan, S. S. Hakobyan, G. V. Tsakanova and V. A. Ayvazyan, *Dokl. Biochem. Biophys.* 419, 56 (2008).
[132] A. Khoyetsyan, S. Hakobyan and A. Boyajyan, Alternative complement pathway in schizophrenia. *Int. J. Neuropsychopharmacol.* 11, 144 (2008).
[133] S. Boyajyan, A. G. Khoyetsyan and A. S. Chavushyan, *Neurochem. Res.* 35, 894 (2010).
[134] S. Tsuji, K. Kaji and S. Nagasawa, *J. Biochem.* 116, 794 (1994).
[135] F. Takizawa, S. Tsuji and S. Nagasawa, *FEBS Lett.* 397, 269 (1996).
[136] Verbovetski, H. Bychkov, U. Trahtemberg, I. Shapira, M. Hareuveni, O. Ben-Tal, I. Kutikov, O. Gill and D. Mevorach, *J. Exp. Med.* 196, 1553 (2002).
[137] R. Galili, Mosberg, I. Gil-Ad, A. Weizman, E. Melamed and D. Offen, *J. Neural Transm.* 107, 479 (2000).
[138] Sachdev P.S. The current status of tardive dyskinesia, Aust. N. Z. J. Psychiatry 34 (3) (2000) 355-369.
[139] Gil-ad, B. Shtaif, R. Shiloh and A. Weizman, *Cell. Mol. Neurobiol.* 21, 705 (2001).
[140] S. N. Marandi, N. Trimble and S. Lee, *Biopharm. J.* 8, 4 (2004).
[141] Y. Yang, C. Wan, H. Li, H. Zhu, Y. La, Z. Xi, Y. Chen, L. Jiang, G. Feng and L. He, *Anal. Chem.* 78, 3571 (2006).
[142] WHO-IUIS Nomenclature Sub-Committee, *Nomenclature for human complement factor B**, WHO Bulletin OMS. Vol 70, 1992, 541-546.
[143] Singer, S. Mayer, M. M. Tongio, M. Roos, J. M. Danion, H. Bernard, P. Leclercq, G. Hauptmann, M. T. Kapfer, J. Bindler and P. Mandel, *Encephale*, 8, 9 (1982).
[144] Rudduck, G. Franzén, A. Hansson and B. Rorsman, *Hum. Hered.* 34, 331 (1984).
[145] E. Giannakis, T. S. Jokiranta, D. A. Male, S. Ranganathan, R. J. Ormsby, V. A. Fischetti, C. Mold and D. L. Gordon, *Eur. J. Immunol.* 33, 962 (2003).
[146] E. Giannakis, D. A. Male, R. J. Ormsby, C. Mold, T. S. Jokiranta, S. Ranganathan and D. L. Gordon, *Int. Immunopharmacol.* 1, 433 (2001).
[147] H. Jarva, T. S. Jokiranta, J. Hellwage, P. F. Zipfel and S. Meri, *J. Immunol.* 163, 3957 (1999).
[148] S. Zareparsi, K. E. Branham, M. Li, S. Shah, R. J. Klein, J. Ott, J. Hoh, G. R. Abecasis and A. Swaroop, *Am. J. Hum. Genet.* 77, 149 (2005).
[149] S. P. Mooijaart, K. M. Koeijvoets, E. J. Sijbrands, M. R. Daha and R. G. Westendorp, *Exp. Gerontol.* 42, 1116 (2007).
[150] K. Pai, J. E. Manson, K. M. Rexrode, C. M. Albert, D. J. Hunter and E. B. Rimm, *Eur. Heart J.* 28, 1297 (2007).

[151] K. Kim, F. Ji, M. A. Morrison, S. Adams, Q. Zhang, A. M. Lane, A. Capone, T. P. Dryja, J. Ott, J. W. Miller and M. M. DeAngelis, *Mol. Vis.* 14, 1487 (2008).
[152] G. Tsakanova, E. Arakelova, T. Hovsepyan, L. Zhamgaryan, M. Hambardzumyan, G. Avetisyan, V. Ayvazyan, A. Arakelyan and A. Boyajyan, *Blood (Yerevan)*, 1, 21 (2010).
[153] A. Arakelyan, S. Hakobyan, L. Zhamgaryan, M. Hambardzumyan, E. Arakelova, T. Hovsepyan, G. Grigoryan, P. B. Morgan amd A. Boyajyan, *Biolog Journal of Armenia,* 62, 34 (2010).
[154] S. Hakobyan, C. L. Harris, A. Tortajada, E. Goicochea de Jorge, A. García-Layana, P. Fernández-Robredo, S. Rodríguez de Córdoba and B. P. Morgan, *Invest. Ophthalmol. Vis. Sci.* 49, 1983 (2008).
[155] Klaska and J. Z. Nowak, *Postepy Hig. Med. Dosw (Online)*, 61, 167 (2007).
[156] S. C. Kondos, T. Hatfaludi, I. Voskoboinik, J. A. Trapani, R. H. Law, J. C. Whisstock and M. A. Dunstone, *Tissue Antigens*, 76, 341 (2010).
[157] H. Rus, C. Cudrici, S. David and F. Niculescu, *Autoimmunity*, 39, 395 (2006).
[158] F. Qiao, C. Atkinson, M. S. Kindy, A. Shunmugavel, B. P. Morgan, H. Song and S. Tomlinson, *Am. J. Pathol.* 177, 3061 (2010).
[159] R. D. Lewis, C. L. Jackson, B. P. Morgan and T. R. Hughes, *Mol. Immunol.* 47, 1098 (2010).
[160] Bjerre, C. Kistorp, T. K. Hansen, J. Faber, G. Y. Lip, P. Hildebrandt and A. Flyvbjerg, *Scand. Cardiovasc. J.* 44, 260 (2010).
[161] E. A. Arakelova, A. A. Arakelyan, A. S. Boyajyan, G. V. Tsakanova, S. S. Hakopyan, B. P. Morgan and G. S. Grigoryan, *Immunology (Moscow)*, 31, 316 (2010).
[162] V. Yanamadala and R. M. Friedlander, *Trends Mol. Med.* 16, 69 (2010).
[163] J. Carter, *Neurochem. Int.* 58, 301 (2011).
[164] P. Morgan, R. H. Daniels and B. D. Williams, *Clin. Exp. Immunol.* 73, 473 (1988).
[165] M. Moulds, *Transfus. Apher. Sci.* 40, 185 (2009).
[166] H. W. Schroeder Jr and L. Cavacini, *J. Allergy Clin. Immunol.* 125, S41 (2010).
[167] Konstantinova N.A. Immune complexes and tissue injury. Moscow: Medicine, 1996, 1-256.
[168] F. Pratesi, S. Moscato, D. Chimenti, A. Sabbatini, M. P. Dolcher, B. Marchini and P. Migliorini, *J. Chemother.* 10, 167 (1998).
[169] V. Shmagel and V. A. Chereshnev, *Biochemistry (Mosc)*, 74, 469 (2009).
[170] F. Burut, Y. Karim and G. A. Ferns, *Angiology*, 61, 679 (2010).
[171] A. N. Theofilopoulos and F. J. Dixon, *Am. J. Pathol.* 100, 529 (1980).
[172] N. Theofilopoulos, *Prog. Clin. Immunol.* 4, 63 (1980).
[173] S. McDougal and F. C. McDuffie, *Adv. Clin. Chem.* 24, 1 (1985).
[174] R. A. Mageed, J. R. Kirwan, P. W. Thompson, D. A. McCarthy and E. J. Holborow, *Ann. Rheum. Dis.* 50, 231 (1991).
[175] G. M. Mkrtchyan, A. S. Boyajyan, K. G. Karageuzyan, A. A. Aivazyan, S. A. Pashinyan and E. E. Nazaretyan, *Dokl. Biol. Sci.* 385, 329 (2002).
[176] S. G. Childs, *Orthop. Nurs.* 25, 140 (2006).
[177] Hovsepyan, A. Boyajyan, V. Aivazyan, K. Mayilyan, A. Guevorkyan and A. Mamikonyan, *Diabetes Mellitus (Moscow)*, 17, 44 (2002).

[178] R. Ovsepyan, A. S. Boyadjyan, A. A. Mamikonyan and A. A. Gevorkyan, Circulating immune complexes at the late stages of diabetes mellitus. *Immunology (Moscow)*, 25, 375 (2004).
[179] A. Arakelian, A. Boiadzhian, A. Pogosian, G. Bakunts, G. Sil'vanian and L. Egiian, *Zh. Nevrol. Psikhiatr. Im. S. S. Korsakova,* Suppl. 8, 44 (2003).
[180] S. Boiadzhian, E. A. Arakelova, A. A. Arakelian, G. V. Avetisian, V. A. Aivazian, G. G. Manucharian, G. M. Mkrtchian, R. B. Sim and A. K. Willis, *Zh. Nevrol. Psikhiatr. Im. S. S. Korsakova,* Suppl. 21, 43 (2007).
[181] Manukyan, A. Boyajyan, A. Arakelyan, V. Ayvazyan, E. Arakelova, R. Sim and G. Grigoryan, *J. Clin. Immunol.* 29, 274 (2009).
[182] Hovhannisyan, G. Mkrtchyan, A. Boyajyan, S. Sukiasian and A. Kalashyan, *Scand. J. Immunol.* 68, 204 (2008).
[183] P. Hovhannisyan, G. M. Mkrtchyan, A. S. Boyajyan and S. H. Sukiasian, Immune complexes and complement classical cascade in posttraumatic stress disorder. *Immunology (Moscow, www.medline.ru)*, 9, 269 (2008).
[184] P. V. Struchkov, N. A. Konstantinova, V. V. Lavrent'ev and A. G. Chuchalin, *Lab. Delo* 7, 410 (1985).
[185] C. Edwards and G. Cambridge, *Br. J. Rheumatol.* 37, 126 (1998).
[186] Hilhorst, P. van Paassen, P. van Breda Vriesman P and J. W. Cohen Tervaert, *Nephrol. Dial. Transplant* 2011, doi: 10.1093/ndt/gfr149.
[187] U. Kallemuchikkal and P. D. Gorevic, *Arch. Pathol. Lab. Med.* 123, 119 (1999).
[188] A. Dispenzieri, *Curr. Treat. Options Oncol.* 1, 105 (2000).
[189] C. Ferri, A. L. Zignego and S. A. Pileri, *J. Clin. Pathol.* 55, 4 (2002).
[190] Mohammed and H. U. Rehman, *Acta Med. Austriaca*. 30, 65 (2003).
[191] P. Hilgard, U. Treichel, V. Dries, H. P. Dienes and G. Gerken, *Hepatogastroenterology*, 52, 1534 (2005).
[192] A. Tedeschi, C. Baratè, E. Minola and E. Morra, *Blood Rev*. 21, 183 (2007).
[193] B. Hellmich, P. Lamprecht, P. M. Aries and W. L. Gross, *Z. Rheumatol.* 64, 538 (2005).
[194] C. Ferri and M. T. Mascia, *Curr. Opin. Rheumatol.* 18, 54 (2006).
[195] S. M. Weiner, V. Prasauskas, D. Lebrecht, S. Weber, H. H. Peter and P. Vaith, *Clin. Exp. Immunol.* 125, 316 (2001).
[196] Mathsson, A. Tejde, K. Carlson, M. Höglund, B. Nilsson, K. Nilsson-Ekdahl and J. Rönnelid, *Br. J. Haematol.* 129, 830 (2005).
[197] G. A. Vilkov, Ola Siletskiĭ, L. I. Mezhova and L. S. Volcho, *Zh. Nevropatol. Psikhiatr. Im. S. S. Korsakova*, 79, 581 (1979).
[198] T. P. Vetlugina, G. V. Logvinovich, S. N. Maslennikova and O. A. Vasileva, *Zh. Nevropatol. Psikhiatr. Im. S. S. Korsakova* 84, 422 (1984).
[199] G. I. Kolyaskina, O. A. Burbaeva and Ya. M. Tsutsulkovskaya, *Schizophr. Res.* 36, 106 (1999).
[200] G. I. Koliaskina, T. P. Sekirina, L. V. Androsova, S. G. Kushner, E. F. Vasileva, O. A. Burbaeva and M. A. Morozova, *Zh. Nevrol. Psikhiatr. Im. S. S. Korsakova*, 104, 39 (2004).
[201] G. I. Koliaskina, T. P. Sekirina, L. V. Androsova, S. G. Kushner, E. F. Vasileva, O. A. Burbaeva and M. A. Morozova, *Vestn. Ross. Akad. Med. Nauk.* 3, 14 (2007).
[202] A. Fontana, U. Storck, J. Angst, R. Dubs, A. Abegg and P. J. Grob, *Neuropsychobiology,* 6, 284 (1980).

[203] S. S. Hakobyan and A. S. Boyajyan, *Psychopharmacol. Biol. Narcol.* 4, 687 (2004).
[204] R. Mailian, A. S. Boiadzhian, A. F. Sogoian, R. B. Sim and L. A. Manukian, *Zh. Nevrol. Psikhiatr. Im. S. S. Korsakova*, 105, 55 (2005).
[205] S. Hakobyan, G. Avetisyan, A. Boyajyan, S. Torosyan, G. Khachatryan and S. Tatevosyan, *Dokl. Biochem. Biophys.* 380, 343 (2001).
[206] Digeon, M. Laver, J. Riza and J. F. Bach, *J. Immunol. Methods,* 16, 165 (1977).
[207] Tarnacka, G. Gromadzka and A. Czlonkowska, *Stroke*, 33, 936 (2002).
[208] T. P. Vetlugina, S. A. Ivanova, G. V. Logvinovich and O. A. Vasileva, *Zh. Nevrol. Psikhiatr. Im. S. S. Korsakova,* 89, 102 (1989).
[209] V. Seeman, *J. Psychiatry Neurosci.* 21, 123 (1996).
[210] S. Beratis, J. Gabriel and S. Hoidas, *Schizophr. Res.* 28, 239 (1997).
[211] H. Y. Meltzer, J. Rabinowitz, M. A. Lee, P. A. Cola, R. Ranjan, R. L. Findling and P. A. Thompson, *Am. J. Psychiatry*, 154, 475 (1997).
[212] S. Beratis, J. Gabriel and S. Hoidas, *Schizophr. Bull.* 20, 287 (1994).
[213] V. Seeman and M. Lang, *Schizophr. Bull.* 16, 185 (1990).
[214] M. Goldstein and M. T. Tsuang, *Schizophr. Bull.* 16, 179 (1990).
[215] R. Scholten, A. Aleman, B. Montagne and R. S. Kahn, *Schizophr. Res.*78, 61 (2005).
[216] F. Kritzer and L. M. Creutz, *J. Neurosci.* 28, 9525 (2008).
[217] R. Weinberger and P. Harrison, *Schizophrenia*, 3rd ed., John Wiley and Sons, USA (2011).
[218] Verthelyi, *Int. Immunopharmacol.* 1, 983 (2001).
[219] Cutolo, A. Sulli, S. Capellino, B. Villaggio, P. Montagna, B. Seriolo and R. H. Straub, *Lupus*, 13, 635 (2004).
[220] A. Bouman, M. J. Heineman and M. M. Faas, *Hum. Reprod. Update*, 11, 411 (2005).
[221] S. Ackerman, *Arch. Dermatol.* 142, 371 (2006).
[222] E. DeLisi, U. Friedrich, J. Wahlstrom, A. Boccio-Smith, A. Forsman, K. Eklund and T. J. Crow, *Schizophr. Bull.* 20, 495 (1994).
[223] S. Kumra, E. Wiggs, D. Krasnewich, J. Meck, A. C. Smith, J. Bedwell, T. Fernandez, L. K. Jacobsen, M. Lenane and J. L. Rapoport, *J. Am. Acad. Child Adolescent Psychiatry*, 37, 292 (1998).
[224] A. S. Bassett, E. W. Chow and R. Weksberg, *Am. J. Med. Genet.* 97, 45 (2000).
[225] Khoyetsyan, A. Boyajyan and M. Melkumova, "Level and chemical composition of cryoglobulins in schizophrenia", In: Brilliant Light in Life and Material Sciences (Editors: Tsakanov V., Wiedemann H.), NATO Security through Science Series B: Physics and Biophysics, Springer, Netherlands, 2007, 295-298.
[226] Boyajyan, A. Khoyetsyan, G. Tsakanova and R. B. Sim, *Clin. Biochem.* 41, 355 (2008).
[227] Khoyetsyan, A. Boyajyan, G. Tsakanova and R. B. Sim, *Neurochem. J.* 2, 329 (2008).
[228] Musset, M. C. Diemert, F. Taibi, L. Thi Huong Du, P. Cacoub, J. M. Leger, G. Boissy, O. Gaillard, J. Galli, *Clin. Chem.* 38, 798 (1992).
[229] J. A. Hardin, *Proc. Natl. Acad. Sci. USA*, 78, 4562 (1981).
[230] T. Giglio, M. A Imro, G. Filaci, M. Scudeletti, F. Puppo, L. De Cecco, F. Indiveri and S. Costantini, *Life Sci.* 54, 1305 (1994).
[231] Arniaud, J. P. Mattei, J. Boyer and H. Roux, *Rev. Rhum. Engl. Ed.* 65, 21 (1998).
[232] A. J. Silman and J. E. Pearson, *Arthritis Res.* 4, S265 (2002).
[233] J. C. Brouet, J. P. Clauvel, F. Danon, M. Klein and M. Seligmann, *Am. J. Med.* 57, 775 (1974).

[234] A. Maire, M. Mittey and P. H. Lambert, *Autoimmunity*, 2, 155 (1989).
[235] Oliver, T. Coton, C. Ragot, D. Chianéa, J. L. Moalic and J. M. Debonne, *Ann. Biol. Clin. (Paris)* 63, 59 (2005).
[236] Müller, M. Riedel, M. Ackenheil and M. J. Schwarz, *World J. Biol. Psychiatry*, 1, 173 (2000).
[237] R. D. Strous and Y. Shoenfeld, *Isr. Med. Assoc. J.* 7, 43 (2005).
[238] R. D. Strous and Y. Shoenfeld, *J. Autoimmun.* 27, 71 (2006).
[239] A. W. Thomson and M. T. Lotze, *The Cytokine Handbook*, 4th ed., *Academic Press*, USA (2003).
[240] R. Dantzer, E. E. Wollman and R. Yirmiya, *Cytokines, stress, and depression (series Advances in Experimental Medicine and Biology),* Springer (1999).
[241] R. E. Mrak and W. S. Griffin, *Neurobiol. Aging*, 26, 349 (2005).
[242] A. P. Kallaur, D. R. Kaimen-Maciel, H. K. Morimoto, M. A. Ehara Watanabe, S. M. Georgeto and E. M. Reiche, *Int. J. Mol. Med.* 28, 467 (2011).
[243] M. B. Trotta, J. B. Serro Azul, M. Wajngarten, S. G. Fonseca, A. C. Goldberg and J. E. Kalil, *Immun. Ageing*, 8, 4 (2011).
[244] M. Di Napoli, A. Arakelyan, A. Boyajyan, A. Godoy and F. Papa, Chapter III*: The acute phase inflammatory response in stroke: systemic inflammation and neuroinflammation. In: Progress in Inflammation Research (Editor: J. A. Pitzer),* Nova Science Publishers Inc., USA (2006).
[245] A. S. Boyajyan, E. A. Arakelova, V. A. Ayvazyan and L. A. Manukyan, *Cytokines and inflammation*, 7, 41 (2008).
[246] A. Hoge, K. Brandstetter, S. Moshier, M. H. Pollack, K. K. Wong amd N. M. Simon, *Depress. Anxiety*, 26, 447 (2009).
[247] Müller, *Nervenarzt.* 68, 11 (1997).
[248] Belardelli, *APMIS* 103, 161 (1995).
[249] Y. K. Kim, A. M. Myint, B. H. Lee, C. S. Han, H. J. Lee, D. J. Kim and B. E. Leonard, *Prog. Neuropsychopharmacol. Biol. Psychiatry*, 28, 1129 (2004).
[250] A. Schuld, D. Hinse-Selch and T. Pollmacher, *Nervenarzt.* 75, 215 (2004).
[251] R. C. Drexhage, E. M. Knijff, R. C. Padmos, L. Heul-Nieuwenhuijzen, W. Beumer, M. A. Versnel and H. A. Drexhage, *Expert. Rev. Neurother.* 10, 59 (2010).
[252] S. Potvin, E. Stip, A. A. Sepehry, A. Gendron, R. Bah and E. Kouassi, *Biol. Psychiatry*, 63, 801 (2008).
[253] S. Hope, I. Melle, P. Aukrust, N. E. Steen, A. B. Birkenaes, S. Lorentzen, I. Agartz, T. Ueland and O. A. Andreassen, *Bipolar Disord.* 11, 726 (2009).
[254] Y. Watanabe, T. Someya and H. Nawa, *Psychiatry Clin. Neurosci.* 64, 217 (2010).
[255] P. Karanikas, *Psychiatrike*, 22, 43 (2011).
[256] R. H. Lee, E. A. Mills, N. Schwartz, M. R. Bell, K. E. Deeg, E. S. Ruthazer, N. Marsh-Armstrong and C. D. Aizenman, *Neural. Dev.* 5, 2 (2010).
[257] E. Marx, L. F. Jarskog, J. M. Lauder, J. A. Lieberman and H. H. Gilmore, *Biol. Psychiatry*, 50, 743 (2001).
[258] A. Urakubo, L. F. Jarskog, J. A. Lieberman and H. H. Gilmore, *Schizophr. Res.* 47, 27(2001).
[259] T. Kishimoto, *Blood*, 74, 1 (1989).
[260] S. A. Jones, S. Horiuchi, N. Topley, N. Yamamoto and G. M. Fuller, *FASEB*, 15, 43 (2001).

[261] S. Omoigui, *Immun. Ageing*, 4, 1 (2007).
[262] Shintani, S. Kanba, N. Maruo, T. Nakaki, M. Nibuya, E. Suzuki, Y. Kinoshita and G. Yagi, *Life Sci.* 49, 661 (1991).
[263] R. Ganguli, Z. Yang, G. Shurin, K. N. Chengappa, J. S. Brar, A. V. Gubbi and B. S. Rabin, *Psychiatry Res.* 51, 1 (1994).
[264] M. Maes, H. Y. Meltzer and E. Bosmans, *Acta Psychiatr. Scand.* 89, 346 (1994).
[265] M. Maes, E. Bosmans, J. Calabrese, R. Smith and H. Y. Meltzer, *J. Psychiatr. Res.* 29, 141 (1995).
[266] J. Naudin, J. L. Mège, J. M. Azorin and D. Dassa, *Schizophr. Res.* 20, 269 (1996).
[267] Monteleone, M. Fabrazzo, A. Tortorella amd M. Maj, *Psychiatry Res.* 71, 11 (1997).
[268] M. Maes, E. Bosmans, G. Kenis, R. De Jong, R. S. Smith and H. Y. Meltzer, *Schizophr. Res.* 26, 221 (1997).
[269] A. Lin, G. Kenis, S. Bignotti, G. J. Tura, R. De Jong, E. Bosmans, R. Pioli, C. Altamura, S. Scharpé and M. Maes, *Schizophr. Res.* 32, 9 (1998).
[270] K. Akiyama, *Schizophr. Res.* 37, 97 (1999).
[271] P. van Kammen, C. G. McAllister-Sistilli, M. E. Kelley, J. A. Gurklis and J. K. Yao, *Psychiatry Res.* 87, 129 (1999).
[272] M. Maes, L. Bocchio Chiavetto, S. Bignotti, G. Battisa Tura, R. Pioli, F. Boin, G. Kenis, E. Bosmans, R. de Jongh, A. Lin, G. Racagni and C. A. Altamura, *Eur. Neuropsychopharmacol.* 10, 119 (2000).
[273] T. Kamińska, A. Wysocka, H. Marmurowska-Michalowska, H. Dubas-Slemp and M. Kandefer-Szerszeń, *Arch. Immunol. Ther. Exp. (Warsz)* 49, 439 (2001).
[274] X. Y. Zhang, D. F. Zhou, P. Y. Zhang, G. Y. Wu, L. Y. Cao and Y. C. Shen, *Schizophr. Res.* 57, 247 (2002).
[275] X. Y. Zhang, D. F. Zhou, L. Y. Cao, P. Y. Zhang, G. Y. Wu and Y. C. Shen, *J. Clin. Psychiatry*, 65, 940 (2004).
[276] X. Y. Zhang, D. F. Zhou, L. Y. Cao, G. Y. Wu and Y. C. Shen, *Neuropsychopharmacology*, 30, 1532 (2005).
[277] U. Pae, C. H. Yoon, T. S. Kim, J. J Kim, S. H. Park, C. U. Lee, S. J. Lee, C. Lee and I. H. Paik, *Int. Immunopharmacol.* 6, 666 (2006).
[278] Hori, R. Yoshimura, Y. Yamada, A. Ikenouchi, M. Mitoma, Y. Ida and J. Nakamura, *Int. Clin. Psychopharmacol.* 22, 21 (2007).
[279] X. Y. Zhang, D. F. Zhou, L. Y. Qi, S. Chen, L. Y. Cao, C. Chen da, M. H. Xiu, F. Wang, G. Y. Wu, L. Lu, T. A. Kosten and T. P. Kosten, *Psychopharmacology (Berl)*, 204, 177 (2009).
[280] Y. K. Kim, A. M. Myint, R. Verkerk, S. Scharpe, H. Steinbusch and B. Leonard, *Neuropsychobiology*, 59, 123 (2009).
[281] García-Miss Mdel, J. Pérez-Mutul, B. López-Canul, F. Solís-Rodríguez, L. Puga-Machado, A. Oxté-Cabrera, J. Gurubel-Maldonado and J. Arankowsky-Sandoval, *J. Psychiatr. Res.* 44, 441 (2010).
[282] M. Kunz, K. M. Ceresér, P. D. Goi, G. R. Fries, A. L. Teixeira, B. S. Fernandes, P. S. Belmonte-de-Abreu, M. Kauer-Sant'anna, F. Kapczinski and C. S. Gama, *Rev. Bras. Psiquiatr.* 33, 268 (2011).
[283] J. Miller, P. Buckley, W. Seabolt, A. Mellor and B. Kirkpatrick, *Biol. Psychiatry* 70, 663 (2011).

[284] Sasayama, C. Wakabayashi, H. Hori, T. Teraishi, K. Hattori, M. Ota, M. Ishikawa, K. Arima, T. Higuchi, N. Amano and H. Kunugi, *J. Psychiatr. Res.* 45, 1439 (2011).
[285] H. Chang, S. Y. Chiang, C. C. Chiu, C. C. Tsai, H. H. Tsai, C. Y. Huang, T. C. Hsu and B. S. Tzang, *Psychiatry Res.* 187, 341 (2011).
[286] M. M. Behrens and T. J. Sejnowski, *Neuropharmacology*, 57, 193 (2009).
[287] Naudin, C. Capo, B. Giusano, J. L. Mège and J. M. Azorin, *Schizophr. Res.* 26, 227 (1997).
[288] Baker, J. Masserano and R. J. Wyatt, *Schizophr. Res.* 20, 199 (1996).
[289] V. Barak, Y. Barak, J. Levine, B. Nisman and I. Roisman, *J. Basic Clin. Physiol. Pharmacol.* 6, 61 (1995).
[290] A. B. Erbağci, H. Herken, O. Köylüoglu, N. Yilmaz and M. Tarakçioglu, *Mediators Inflamm.* 10, 109 (2001).
[291] M. Haack, D. Hinze-Selch, T. Fenzel, T. Kraus, M. Kühn, A. Schuld and T. J. Pollmächer, *J. Psychiatr. Res.* 33, 407 (1999).
[292] Pollmächer, D. Hinze-Selch amd J. Mullington, *J. Clin. Psychopharmacol.* 16, 403 (1996).
[293] J. Kim, W. Kim, S. J. Yoon, H. J. Go, B. M. Choi, T. Y. Jun and Y. K. Kim, *Int. J. Neurosci.* 111, 11 (2001).
[294] Sun, F. Wang, J. Wei, L. Y. Cao, L. Y. Qi, M. H. Xiu, S. Chen, X. H. Li, T. A. Kosten, T. R. Kosten amd X. Y. Zhang, *Schizophr. Res.* 102, 346 (2008).
[295] Y. L. Liu, C. M. Liu, C. S. Fann, W. C. Yang, Y. H. Chen, L. J. Tseng, S. K. Liu, M. H. Hsieh, T. J. Hwang, H. Y. Chan, J. J. Chen, W. J. Chen and H. G. Hwu, *Neurosci. Lett.* 468, 330 (2010).
[296] M. Paul-Samojedny, M. Kowalczyk, R. Suchanek, A. Owczarek, A. Fila-Danilow, A. Szczygiel and J. Kowalski. *J. Mol. Neurosci.* 42, 112 (2010).
[297] J. Brull, H. E. Montgomery, J. Sanders, S. Dhamrait, L. Luong, A. Rumley, G. D. Lowe and S. E. Humphries, *Arterioscler. Thromb. Vasc. Biol.* 21, 1458 (2001).
[298] Wypasek, A. Undas, M. Sniezek-Maciejewska, B. Kapelak, D. Plicner, E. Stepien and J. Sadowski, *Ann. Clin. Biochem.* 47, 343 (2010).
[299] R. Zakharyan, *Biolog Journal of Armenia*, 62, 130 (2010).
[300] A. Carswell, L. J. Old, R. L. Kassel, S. Green, N. Fiore and B. Williamson, *Proc. Natl. Acad. Sci. U S A*, 72, 3666 (1975).
[301] Himmerich, M. Berthold-Losleben and T. Pollmächer, *Fortschr. Neurol. Psychiatr.* 77, 334 (2009).
[302] P. Francesconi, K. M. Ceresér, R. Mascarenhas, L. Stertz, C. S. Gama and P. Belmonte-de-Abreu, *Neurosci. Lett.* 502, 143 (2011).
[303] X. Q. Song, L. X. Lv, W. Q. Li, Y. H. Hao and J. P. Zhao, *Biol. Psychiatry*, 65, 481 (2009).
[304] Kluge, A. Schuld, A. Schacht, H. Himmerich, M. A. Dalal, P. M. Wehmeier, D. Hinze-Selch, T. Kraus, R. W. Dittmann and T. Pollmächer, *Psychoneuroendocrinology*, 34, 118 (2009).
[305] S. M. O'Brien, P. Scully and T. G. Dinan, *Psychiatry Res.* 160, 256 (2008).
[306] J. Paterson, Y. Ohashi, G. P. Reynolds, J. A. Pratt and B. J. Morris, *J. Psychopharmacol.* 20, 636 (2006).
[307] Pollmächer, D. Hinze-Selch, T. Fenzel, T. Kraus, A. Schuld and J. Mullington, *Am. J. Psychiatry*, 154, 1763 (1997).

[308] M. Coelho, H. J. Reis, R. Nicolato, M. A. Romano-Silva, M. M. Teixeira, M. E. Bauer and A. L. Teixeira, *Neuroimmunomodulation,* 15, 140 (2008).
[309] A. Schmitt, T. Bertsch, H. Tost, A. Bergmann, U. Henning, A. Klimke and P. Falkai, *Neuropsychiatr. Dis. Treat.* 1, 171 (2005).
[310] A. Schattner, Y. Cori, T. Hahn and P. Sirota, *J. Autoimmun.* 9, 661 (1996).
[311] O. Freudenreich, M. A. Brockman, D. C. Henderson, A. E. Evins, X. Fan, J. P. Walsh and D. C. Goff, *Psychiatry Res.* 176, 99 (2010).
[312] Sugino H, Futamura T, Mitsumoto Y, Maeda K, Marunaka Y. *Prog. Neuropsychopharmacol. Biol. Psychiatry*, 33, 303 (2009).
[313] L. Liu, F. Jia, G. Yuan, Z. Chen, J. Yao, H. Li and C. Fang, *Psychiatry Res.* 176, 1 (2010).
[314] J. Kowalski, P. Blada, K. Kucia, A. Madej and Z. S. Herman, *Schizophr. Res.* 50, 169 (2001).
[315] W. Maier, S. Schwab and M. Rietschel, *Curr. Opin. Psychiatry*, 13, 3 (2000).
[316] L. Peltonen, *Nature*, 378, 665 (1995).
[317] F. Boin, R. Zanardini, R. Pioli, C. A. Altamura, M. Maes and M. Gennarelli, *Mol. Psychiatry*, 6, 79 (2001).
[318] M. Riedel, H. Krönig, M. J. Schwarz, R. R. Engel, K. U. Kühn, C. Sikorski, S. Sokullu, M. Ackenheil, H. J. Möller and N. Müller, *Eur. Arch. Psychiatry Clin. Neurosci.* 252, 232 (2002).
[319] T. Y. Jun, C. U. Pae, J. H. Chae, W. M. Bahk, K. S. Kim, H. Han and A. Serretti, *Schizophr. Res.* 61, 39 (2003).
[320] H. Y. Handoko, D. J. Nancarrow, N. K. Hayward, J. U. Ohaeri, H. Aghanwa, J. J. McGrath, D. F. Levinson, C. Johns, M. K. Walters, D. A. Nertney, T. N. Srinivasan, R. Thara and B. J. Mowry, *Am. J. Med. Genet. B Neuropsychiatr. Genet.* 121B, 1 (2003).
[321] R. Zanardini, L. Bocchio-Chiavetto, C. Scassellati, C. Bonvicini, G. B. Tura, G. Rossi, J. Perez and M. Gennarelli, *J. Psychiatr. Res.* 37, 457 (2003).
[322] I. V. Meira-Lima, A. C. Pereira, G. F. Mota, M. Floriano, F. Araújo, A. J. Mansur, J. E. Krieger and H. Vallada, *Mol. Psychiatry*, 8, 718 (2003).
[323] S. G. Schwab, S. Mondabon, M. Knapp, M. Albus, J. Hallmayer, M. Borrmann-Hassenbach, M. Trixler, M. Gross, T. G. Schulze, M. Rietschel, B. Lerer, W. Maier and D. B. Wildenauer, *Schizophr. Res.* 65, 19 (2003).
[324] C. U. Pae, J. H. Chae, W. M. Bahk, H. Han, T. Y. Jun, K. S. Kim, Y. S. Kwon and A. Serretti, *Psychiatry Clin. Neurosci.* 57, 399 (2003).
[325] E. C. Tan, S. A. Chong, C. H. Tan, Y. Y. Teo, K. Peng and R. Mahendran, *Biol. Psychiatry*, 54, 1205 (2003).
[326] S. J. Tsai, C. J. Hong, Y. W. Yu, C. H. Lin and L. L. Liu, *Schizophr. Res.* 65, 27 (2003).
[327] R. Hashimoto, M. Yoshida, N. Ozaki, Y. Yamanouchi, N. Iwata, T. Suzuki, T. Kitajima, M. Tatsumi, K. Kamijima and H. Kunugi, *J. Neural Transm.* 111, 217 (2004).
[328] S. Duan, Y. Xu, W. Chen, Z. Liu, T. Guo, J. Gao, L. Bian, Y. Zhen, X. Li, Y. Zhang, Y. Pan, N. Gu, G. Feng and L. He, *Neurosci. Lett.* 366, 139 (2004).
[329] O. Kampman, S. Anttila, A. Illi, K. M. Mattila, R. Rontu, E. Leinonen and T. Lehtimäki, *Eur. Arch. Psychiatry Clin. Neurosci.* 255, 279 (2005).
[330] K. Hänninen, H. Katila, R. Rontu, K. M. Mattila, M. Hurme and T. Lehtimäki, *Neurosci. Lett.* 385, 76 (2005).

[331] C. U. Pae, A. Serretti, P. Artioli, T. S. Kim, J. J. Kim, C. U. Lee, S. J. Lee, I. H. Paik and C. Lee, *J. Neural. Transm.* 113, 887 (2006).
[332] B. H. Shirts, M. Bamne, J. J. Kim, M. Talkowski, J. Wood, R. Yolken and V. L. Nimgaonkar, *Schizophr. Res.* 83, 7 (2006).
[333] G. Zai, D. J. Müller, J. Volavka, P. Czobor, J. A. Lieberman, H. Y. Meltzer and J. L. Kennedy, *Psychopharmacology (Berl)*, 188, 171 (2006).
[334] B. Morar, S. G. Schwab, M. Albus, W. Maier, B. Lerer and D. B. Wildenauer, *Am. J. Med. Genet. B Neuropsychiatr. Genet.* 144B, 318 (2007).
[335] Y. Watanabe, T. Muratake, N. Kaneko, N. Fukui, Y. Nara and T. Someya, *Psychiatry Res.* 153, 1 (2007).
[336] P. M. Czerski, F. Rybakowski, P. Kapelski, J. K. Rybakowski, M. Dmitrzak-Weglarz, A. Leszczyńska-Rodziewicz, A. Słopień, M. Skibińska, M. Kaczmarkiewicz-Fass and J. Hauser, *Neuropsychobiology*, 57, 88 (2008).
[337] M. Naz, M. Riaz and M. Saleem, *Mol. Biol. Rep.* 38, 4709 (2010).
[338] X. Y. Zhang, C. N. Haile, Y. L. Tan, L. J. Zuo, B. Z. Yang, L. Y. Cao and D. F. Zhou, *Mol. Psychiatry*, 10, 897 (2005)
[339] D. Rossi and A. Zlotnik, *Annu. Rev. Immunology*, 18, 217 (2000).
[340] E. J. Fernandez and E. Lolis, *Annu. Rev. Pharmacol. Toxicol*, 42, 469 (2002).
[341] A. Garin and A. E. Proudfoot, *Exp. Cell Res.* 317, 602 (2011).
[342] C. L. Speyer and P. A. Ward, *J. Invest. Surg.* 24, 18 (2011).
[343] D. Raman, T. Sobolik-Delmaire and A. Richmond, *Exp. Cell Res.* 317, 575 (2011).
[344] M. Reale, A. Patruno, M. A. De Lutiis, M. Pesce, M. Felaco, M. Di Giannantonio, M. Di Nicola and A. Grilli, *BMC Neurosci.* 12, 13 (2011).
[345] P. Ashwood, P. Krakowiak, I. Hertz-Picciotto, R. Hansen, I. Pessah and J. Van de Water, *Brain Behav. Immun.* 25, 40 (2011).
[346] K. Suzuki, H. Matsuzaki, K. Iwata, Y. Kameno, C. Shimmura, S. Kawai, Y. Yoshihara, T. Wakuda, K. Takebayashi, S. Takagai, K. Matsumoto, K. J. Tsuchiya, Y. Iwata, K. Nakamura, M. Tsujii, T. Sugiyama and N. Mori, *PLoS One*, 6, e20470 (2011).
[347] L. Hallberg, S. Janelidze, G. Engstrom, A. G. Wisén, A. Westrin and L. Brundin, *J. Affect. Disord.* 126, 262 (2010).
[348] S. M. Lehto, L. Niskanen, K. H. Herzig, T. Tolmunen, A. Huotari, H. Viinamäki, H. Koivumaa-Honkanen, K. Honkalampi, H. Ruotsalainen and J. Hintikka, *Psychoneuroendocrinology*, 35, 226 (2010).
[349] Y. Song, D. Zhou, Z. Guan and X. Wang, *Neuroimmunomodulation*, 14, 248 (2007).
[350] S. L. Buka, M. T. Tsuang, E. F. Torrey, M. A. Klebanoff, R. L. Wagner and R. H. Yolken, *Brain Behav. Immun.* 15, 411 (2001).
[351] A. S. Brown, J. Hooton, C. A. Schaefer, H. Zhang, E. Petkova, V. Babulas, M. Perrin, J. M. Gorman and E. S. Susser, *Am. J. Psychiatry*, 161, 889 (161).
[352] A. S. Brown, *Schizophr. Bull.* 32, 200 (2006).
[353] U. Meyer, I. Weiner, G. M. McAlonan and J. Feldon, *Expert Rev. Neurother.* 11, 29 (2011).
[354] M. Maes, L. Bocchio Chiavetto, S. Bignotti, G. J. Battisa Tura, R. Pioli, F. Boin, G. Kenis, E. Bosmans, R. de Jongh and C. A. Altamura, *Schizophr. Res.* 54, 281 (2002).
[355] T. P. Klushnik, T. M. Syriachenko, O. S. Brusov, Z. V. Sarmanova, I. N. Otman, A. M. Dupin and R. E. Sokolov, *Zh. Nevrol. Psikhiatr. Im. S. S. Korsakova*, 108, 31 (2008).
[356] L. Gu, S. C. Tseng and B. J. Rollins, *Chem. Immunol.* 72, 7 (1999).

[357] S. L. Deshmane, S. Kremlev, S. Amini and B. E. Sawaya, *J. Interferon Cytokine Res.* 29, 313 (2009).
[358] J. Losy, G. Michałowska-Wender, A. Kurdyńska and M. Wender, *Folia Neuropathol.* 43, 153 (2005).
[359] J. Losy and J. Zaremba, *Stroke*, 32, 2695 (2001).
[360] A. Arakelyan, J. Petrkova, Z. Hermanova, A. Boyajyan, J. Lukl and M. Petrek. *Mediators Inflamm.* 2005, 175 (2005).
[361] P. Cinque, L. Vago, M. Mengozzi, V. Torri, D. Ceresa, E. Vicenzi, P. Transidico, A. Vagani, S. Sozzani, A. Mantovani, A. Lazzarin and G. Poli, *AIDS*, 12, 1327 (1998).
[362] C. U. Pae, K. I. Chung, J. J. Kim, H. S. Yu, C. U. Lee, S. J. Lee, C. Lee, T. Y. Jun, A. Serretti and I. H. Paik, *Psychiatr. Genet.* 14, 65 (2004).
[363] E. Mundo, A. C. Altamura, S. Vismara, R. Zanardini, S. Bignotti, R. Randazzo, C. Montresor and M. Gennarelli, *Am. J. Med. Genet. B Neuropsychiatr. Genet.* 132B, 1 (2005).
[364] R. Zakharyan, A. Khoyetsyan, A. Chavushyan, Z. Navratilova, A. Arakelyan, A. Boyajyan, F. Mrazek and M. Petrek, *Tissue Antigens*, 75, 628 (2010).
[365] R. Zakharyan, A. Boyajyan, A. Arakelyan, M. Melkumova, F. Mrazek and M. Petrek, *Cytokine*, 2011 [*submitted to publication*].
[366] R C. Drexhage, R. C. Padmos, H. de Wit, M. A. Versnel, H. Hooijkaas, A. J. van der Lely, N. van Beveren, R. H. deRijk and D. Cohen, *Schizophr. Res.* 102, 352 (2008).
[367] A. L. Teixeira, H. J. Reis, R. Nicolato, G. Brito-Melo, H. Correa, M. M. Teixeira and M. A. Romano-Silva, *Prog. Neuropsychopharmacol. Biol. Psychiatry*, 32, 710 (2008).
[368] J. Nishihira, *J. Interferon Cytokine Res.* 20, 751 (2000).
[369] H. Noels, J. Bernhagen and C. Weber, *Trends Cardiovasc. Med.* 19, 76 (2009).
[370] L. de la Fontaine, M. J. Schwarz, M. Riedel, S. Dehning, A. Douhet, I. Spellmann, N. Kleindienst, P. Zill, H. Plischke, R. Gruber and N. Müller, *Psychiatry Res.* 144, 39 (2006).
[371] E. B. Windgassen, L. Funtowicz, T. N. Lunsford, L. A. Harris and S. L. Mulvagh, *Postgrad. Med.* 123, 114 (2011).
[372] J. P. Casas, T. Shah, A. D. Hingorani, J. Danesh and M. B. Pepys, *J. Intern. Med.* 264, 295 (2008).
[373] I. V. Shcherbakova, G. V. Kozlovskaia, M. A. Kalinina and T. P. Kliushnik, *Zh. Nevrol. Psikhiatr. Im. S. S. Korsakova*, 105, 45 (2005).
[374] V. Mazzarello, A. Cecchini, G. Fenu, M. Rassu, L. A. Dessy, L. Lorettu and A. Montella, *Ital. J. Anat. Embryol.* 109, 177 (2004).
[375] A. O. Akanji, J. U. Ohaeri, S. Al-Shammri and H. R. Fatania, Association of blood levels of C-reactive protein with clinical phenotypes in Arab schizophrenic patients. *Psychiatry Res.* 169, 56 (2009).
[376] T. P. Kliushnik, T. M. Sirachenko, Z. V. Sarmanova, I. N. Otman and A. M. Dupin, *Zh. Nevrol. Psikhiatr. Im. S. S. Korsakova*, 109, 55 (2009).
[377] M. H. Fawzi, M. M. Fawzi, M. M. Fawzi and N. S. Said, *Psychiatry Res.* 2011 [*in press*].
[378] F. Dickerson, C. Stallings, A. Origoni, J. Boronow and R. Yolken, *Schizophr. Res.* 93, 261 (2009).
[379] X. Fan, C. Pristach, E. Y. Liu, O. Freudenreich, D. C. Henderson and D. C. Goff, *Psychiatry Res.* 149, 267 (2007).

[380] J. M. Meyer, J. P. McEvoy, V. G. Davis, D. C. Goff, H. A. Nasrallah, S. M. Davis, J. K. Hsiao, M. S. Swartz, T. S. Stroup and J. A. Lieberman, *Biol. Psychiatry*, 66, 1013 (2009).

[381] T. Baptista, A. Dávila, Y. El Fakih, E. Uzcátegui, N. N. Rangel, Y. Olivares, T. Galeazzi, D. Vargas, R. Peña, D. Marquina, V. Villarroel, L. Teneud and S. Beaulieu, *Int. Clin. Psychopharmacol.* 22, 205 (2007).

[382] E. Carrizo, V. Fernández, J. Quintero, L. Connell, Z. Rodríguez, M. Mosquera, A. Acosta and T. Baptista, *Schizophr. Res.* 103, 83 (2008).

[383] T. P. Klushnik, T. M. Syriachenko, O. S. Brusov, Z. V. Sarmanova, I. N. Otman, A. M. Dupin and R. E. Sokolov, *Zh. Nevrol. Psikhiatr. Im. S. S. Korsakova*, 108, 31 (2008).

[384] E. Fernandez-Egea, M. Bernardo, T. Donner, I. Conget, E. Parellada, A. Justicia, E. Esmatjes, C. Garcia-Rizo and B. Kirkpatrick, *Br. J. Psychiatry*, 194, 434 (2009).

[385] W. Hennah, P. Thomson, L. Peltonen and D. Porteous, *Schizophr. Bull.* 32, 409 (2006).

[386] I. Halder, A. L. Marsland, J. Cheong, M. F. Muldoon, R. E. Ferrell and S. B. Manuck, *Brain Behav. Immunity*, 24, 160 (2010).

[387] M. S. Teng, L. A. Hsu, S. Wu, H. H. Chang, H. H. Chou and Y. L. Ko, *Atherosclerosis*, 204, e64 (2009).

[388] Y. Le Strat, N. Ramoz and P. Gorwood, *Curr. Mol. Med.* 9, 506 (2009).

[389] H. Stefansson, R. A. Ophoff and S. Steinberg, *Nature,* 460, 744 (2009).

[390] C. Cunha, R. Brambilla and K. L. Thomas, *Front. Mol. Neurosci.* 3, 1 (2010).

[391] A. M. Stanisz and J.A. Stanisz, *Ann. N. Y. Acad. Sci.* 917, 268 (2000).

[392] T. Arinami, T. Ohtsuki, H. Ishiguro, H. Ujike, Y. Tanaka, Y. Morita, M. Mineta, M. Takeichi, S. Yamada, A. Imamura, K. Ohara, H. Shibuya, K. Ohara, Y. Suzuki, T. Muratake, N. Kaneko, T. Someya, T. Inada, T. Yoshikawa, T. Toyota, K. Yamada, T. Kojima, S. Takahashi, O. Osamu, T. Shinkai, M. Nakamura, H. Fukuzako, T. Hashiguchi, S. I. Niwa, T. Ueno, H. Tachikawa, T. Hori, T. Asada, S. Nanko, H. Kunugi, R. Hashimoto, N. Ozaki, N. Iwata, M. Harano, H. Arai, T. Ohnuma, I. Kusumi, T. Koyama, H. Yoneda, Y. Fukumaki, H. Shibata, S. Kaneko, H. Higuchi, N. Yasui-Furukori, Y. Numachi, M. Itokawa and Y. Okazaki, *Am. J. Hum. Genet.* 77, 937 (2005).

[393] B. K. Scguarez, J. Duan, A. R. Sanders, A. L. Hinrichs, C. H. Jin, C. Hou, N. G. Buccola, N. Hale, A. N. Weilbaecher, D. A. Nertney, A. Olincy, S. Green, A. W. Schaffer, C. J. Smith, D. E. Hannah, J. P. Rice, N. J. Cox, M. Martinez, B. J. Mowry, F. Amin, J. M. Silverman, D. W. Black, W. F. Byerley, R. R. Crowe, R. Freedman, C. R. Cloninger, D. F. Levinson and P. V. Gejman, *Am. J. Hum. Genet.* 78, 315 (2006).

[394] M. F. Egan, M. Kojima, J. H. Callicott, T. E. Goldberg, B. S. Kolachana and A. Bertolino, *Cell*, 112, 257 (2003).

[395] A. Cattaneo, L. Bocchio-Chiavetto, R. Zanardini, E. Marchina, D. Bellotti, E. Milanesi, S. Moraschi, F. Calabrese, S. Barlati, M. A. Riva and M. Gennarelli, *BMC Neurosci.* 11, 16 (2010).

[396] L. Pezawas, B. A. Verchinski, V. S. Mattay, J. H. Callicott, B. S. Kolachana, R. E. Straub, M. F. Egan, A. Meyer-Lindenberg and D. R. Weinberger, *J. Neurosci.* 24, 10099 (2004).

[397] J. Gallinat, F. Schubert, R. Brühl, R. Hellweg, A. A. Klär, C. Kehrer, C. Wirth, T. Sander and U. E. Lang, *Neuroimage*, 49, 767 (2010).

[398] P. Mackin, P. Gallagher, S. Watson, A. H. Young and I. N. Ferrier, *Aust. N. Z. J. Psychiatry,* 41, 321 (2007).

[399] Y. Ikeda, N. Yahata, I. Ito, M. Nagano, T. Toyota, T. Yoshikawa, Y. Okubo and H. Suzuki, *Schizophr. Res.* 101, 58 (2008).
[400] E. N. Rizos, A. Papadopoulou, E. Laskos, P. G. Michalopoulou, A. Kastania, D. Vasilopoulos, K. Katsafouros and L. Lykouras, *World J. Biol. Psychiatry*, 11, 251 (2010).
[401] E. N. Rizos, P. G. Michalopoulou, N. Siafakas, N. Stefanis, A. Douzenis, I. Rontos, E. Laskos, A. Kastania, V. Zoumpourlis and L. Lykouras, *Neuropsychobiology*, 62, 87 (2010).
[402] R. D. Jindal, A. K. Pillai, S. P. Mahadik, K. Eklund, D. M. Montrose and M. S. Keshavan, *Schizophr. Res.* 119, 47 (2010).
[403] P. F. Buckley, A. Pillai and K. R. Howell, *Curr. Opin. Psychiatry*, 24, 122 (2011).
[404] S. Numata, S. Ueno, J. Iga, K. Yamauchi, S. Hongwei, K. Ohta, S. Kinouchi, S. Shibuya-Tayoshi, S. Tayoshi, M. Aono, N. Kameoka, S. Sumitani, M. Tomotake, Y. Kaneda, T. Taniguchi, Y. Ishimoto and T. Ohmori, *Neurosci. Lett.* 401, 1 (2006).
[405] G. Spalletta, D. W. Morris, F. Angelucci, I. A. Rubino, I. Spoletini, P. Bria, G. Martinotti, A. Siracusano, G. Bonaviri, S. Bernardini, C. Caltagirone, P. Bossu, G. Donohoe, M. Gill and A. P. Corvin, *Eur. Psychiatry*, 25, 311 (2010).
[406] M. Gratacos, J. R. Gonzalez, J. M. Mercader, R. de Cid, M. Urretavizcaya and X. Estivill, *Biol. Psychiatry*, 61, 911 (2007).
[407] T. Kanazawa, S. J. Glatt, B. Kia-Keating, H. Yoneda and M. T. Tsuang, *Psychiatr.* Genet. 17, 165 (2007).
[408] R. Zakharyan, A. Boyajyan, A. Arakelyan, F. Mrazek and M. Petrek, *Tissue Antigens*, 77, 493 (2011).
[409] R. Zakharyan, A. Boyajyan, A. Arakelyan, A. Gevorgyan, F. Mrazek and M. Petrek, *Hum. Immunol.* 72, 746 (2011).
[410] H. M. Chao, H. T. Kao and B. Porton, *Am. J. Med. Genet. B. Neuropsychiatr. Genet.* 147B, 505 (2008).
[411] A. K. Malla, R. M. Norman, R. Manchanda, M. R. Ahmed, D. Scholten, R. Harricharan, L. Cortese and J. Takhar, *Schizophr Res.* 54, 231 (2002).
[412] G. Douaud, C. Mackay, J. Andersson, S. James, D. Quested, M. K. Ray, J. Connell, N. Roberts, T. J. Crow, P. M. Matthews, S. Smith and A. James, *Brain*, 132, 2437 (2009).
[413] S. W. Moore, M. Tessier-Lavigne and T. E. Kennedy, *Adv. Exp. Med. Biol.* 621, 17 (2007).
[414] K. Padhan and R. Varma, *Immunology*, 129, 322 (2010).
[415] H. Takamatsu, T. Okuno and A. Kumanogoh, *Cell. Mol. Immunol.* 7, 83 (2010).
[416] M. Fukasawa, M. Aoki, K. Yamada, Y. Iwayama-Shigeno, H. Takao, J. Meerabux, T. Toyota, T. Nishikawa and T. Yoshikawa, *J. Med. Dent. Sci.* 51, 121 (2004).
[417] T. Ohtsuki, Y. Horiuchi, M. Koga, H. Ishiguro, T. Inada, N. Iwata, N. Ozaki, H. Ujike, Y. Watanabe, T. Someya and T. Arinami, *Neurosci. Lett.* 435, 194 (2008).

SECTION III

STRATEGIES FOR NOVEL THERAPEUTICS

In: Schizophrenia Research: Recent Advances
Editor: Tomiki Sumiyoshi
ISBN: 978-1-62808-703-1

Chapter 12

ANTIPSYCHOTICS, SOCIAL COGNITION AND OUTCOME

*Alessandro De Risio**
NHS, Health Trust "Veneto Orientale"
Unit of Psychiatry of Portogruaro,
Venezia, Italia

ABSTRACT

Introduction: Although use of antipsychotics is widespread in treating severe mental disorders, their relations with social cognition, the ability to perceive the intentions and dispositions of others, is controversial. A host of studies evidenced few or little improvements in social cognition domains, such as emotion perception or reasoning biases in schizophrenic persons treated with antipsychotics. Atypicals were no better than first-generation antipsychotics in improving social cognition, at least in short time.

An interesting domain of social cognition is Theory of Mind, ToM, the ability to understand and represent one's own and other people's beliefs, intentions and desires. An impaired ToM is associated to the negative symptoms and poor empathy in predicting poor functional outcome of schizophrenic persons. Although antipsychotic treatment showed so far no correlations with ToM abilities in people with schizophrenia, single antipsychotic drugs have displayed different actions in modifying or improving ToM capacities.

Our study investigated to what extent antipsychotics and impaired social cognition were related in predicting social behaviour, considering that intelligence and duration of illness are confounders.

Methods. We examined 21 persons with schizophrenia by testing them for intelligence, executive functioning, psychopathology, social cognition (ToM, emotion recognition, problem-solving, empathy) and social functioning. The participants, who were all taking antipsychotics, were compared to an equal number of healthy controls, matched for age and sex.

Results. Poor emotion recognition and negative symptoms correlated with impaired ToM abilities. Unexpectedly, the interaction of ToM with medication explained more

* E-mail address: alessandroemilio.derisio@tin.it.

than 40% of the social functioning variance. In contrast with previous research, antipsychotic treatment added to social cognition measures to predict functional outcome in people with schizophrenia. The modulating effect of serotonin system on dopamine transmission might represent the biological basis of antipsychotics "ToM-repairing" activity.

Conclusion. Our data might confirm the unstructured observation of outcome improvement in long-term schizophrenic persons administered with a combination of atypicals. Our results should be replicated in wider samples to validate the effectiveness of antipsychotics on social cognition and functional outcome.

INTRODUCTION

Since the second half of twentieth century, the introduction of antipsychotic drugs represented a milestone in the treatment of severe mental disorders, for its contribution in reducing admission to psychiatric hospitals and in formulating innovative pathways of care. The most disabling mental disorder, schizophrenia, is the first target of antipsychotic treatment. First Generation Antipsychotics, FGAs, that were marketed from 1950s-1960s onwards, block the dopamine D_2 receptor, effectively reducing positive symptoms of schizophrenia, i.e. delusions and persecutory beliefs, while Second Generation Antipsychotics, SGAs, that appeared in the 1990s with a combined serotonin-dopamine antagonism, are mainly focused on contrasting the negative symptoms, such as anhedonia, emotional blunting and social withdrawal.

A third, functional dimension, targeted by SGAs, is represented by cognitive dysfunctions, a host of impairments concerning all aspects of understanding and knowing the world around oneself, preventing severely affected psychotic patients from reaching social adaptation. Cognitive deficits affect short-term or working memory, long-term or "semantic" memory, attention and executive functions, i.e. the ability to solve problems, use abstract concepts and successful skills and adaptive strategies [1].

With the expression "social cognition" cognitive psychologists refer to the way in which information is processed in social contexts, that is how persons think about themselves and the others in social interactions [2-3]. In severe psychotic illnesses, such as schizophrenia, relevant dysfunctions of social cognition are reported [4]. Social cognition shares with cognitive dysfunctions the disruption of relevant neural mechanisms governing social functioning and differentiates from them for a stronger relation to social adaptation [5-8]. The necessity to treat or overcome social cognition impairment adds to the need to provide persons with severe mental disorders with adequate pharmacological treatment in order to reach a good adaptation to the environment, that is better defined with the expressions of "functional outcome" [9-10].

Anyway, there are few contributions exploring how non-pharmacological social cognitive interventions and the use of antipsychotics might combine in rehabilitating treatment of the severe mental disorders, with research actively sustaining that the two conditions are mutually exclusive [11-12]. The aim of this chapter is to provide evidence in support of the possible synergistic action of the pharmacological treatment and of social-cognitive interventions in improving the functional outcome of people affected by schizophrenia.

Antipsychotics and the Boundaries of Social Cognition

It is acknowledged that FGAs in 1950s proved a determinant factor in the development of deinstitutionalization process, with a reduction of two thirds in the population of psychiatric hospitals at least fifteen years after their introduction [1]. Even the radical anti-istitutional psychiatry in the 1960s recognized the importance of FGAs in facilitating the enactment of no-restraint procedures and social milieu therapies in the care of schizophrenic persons [13]. The use of FGAs determines a better lifetime outcome due to symptoms reduction, the decrease of violent behaviours and the improvement in caregivers' quality of life [14]. What is more, research conducted in the 1990s outlined how the newly developed SGAs, with their serotonin-dopamine antagonizing action were effective in improving a host of cognitive dysfunctions ranging from better verbal fluency or verbal memory to enhanced executive functions in people with schizophrenia [15-17]. From this evidence, it would have been expected that SGAs acted as a "magic bullet" to improve the poor outcome typically seen in schizophrenia, with a powerful action in contrasting the cognitive decline [1]. Ten years after, such a condition was only partially reached, with SGAs proving to be at least as effective as FGAs in improving quality of life and outcome in schizophrenic persons, despite their high increase in consume and their relevant cost [18]. To explain why SGAs were partially ineffective in the cognitive remediation and outcome of schizophrenia there are several reasons. First of all, it may be interesting to describe the boundaries of social cognition, for the importance gained by this construct in defining the goals and the objective of integrated rehabilitative treatment of schizophrenia.

The wide reviews of Green [9], Green et al. [10] and Couture et al. [19] outlined how neurocognitive deficits as a whole were only able to explain from 20% to 60% of the variance of "functional outcome", that is a broad definition including self- or interpersonal behaviours of people with schizophrenia, their behavior in community settings, their skill in independent living, such as self-care or financial skills, together with abilities in laboratory settings, such as role-playing or problem-solving abilities. On the other hand, this host of research emphasized social cognition, for the importance of processing social stimuli, as an essential issue in reaching autonomy. As neurocognition and social cognition, although related, are different constructs [6], it is necessary to provide an exhaustive definition of the latter, to understand how it can impact with antipsychotic treatment of schizophrenic persons in reaching functional outcome. Along with Green et al.'s [20] position, social cognition encompasses the following constructs, (i) Emotion Perception, EP, the capacity of understand other people's feelings observing a combination of facial expressions and vocal inflexions; (ii) Social Peception, SP, the ability to understand social hints from the social context; (iii) Theory of Mind, ToM, the ability to infer the state of the world and other people's intentions, beliefs and desires; (iv) Attributional Style, AS, the capacity to ascribe the cause of life events, with people affected by persecutory delusions attributing the negative outcomes of a situation to others for a "personalizing bias" [21].

Research also outlined how social cognition might represent a mediator between the "classical" neurocognitive indices, such as executive functioning, and functional outcome [22]. The mediating relationship between neurocognitive indices and social cognition would be stronger than the one between neurocognition and negative symptoms of schizophrenia [23]. From these considerations, it would have been expected to evidence at least a similar pattern for antipsychotic treatment and social cognition. Antipsychotics have gained a remarkable impact on the persons affected by severe mental disorders. Firstly, use of antipsychotics in schizophrenic subjects is widespread. From 1994 onwards, the pharmaceutical expenditure for antipsychotics in USA increased from 1.4 billion dollars to the current 10 billion [18]. Moreover, the existence of cognitive remediating properties of SGAs has been postulated since the early studies [24]. If neurocognition, although a discrete construct, is in some ways related to social cognition, social cognition itself has a relation to functional outcome and functional outcome is improved by antipsychotics, for strict logical reasons it would have been possible to establish a similar connection between antipsychotic treatment and social cognition. Anyway, none of this sort happened, and even though antipsychotic drugs, as a class, proved effective in treating positive and negative symptoms of schizophrenia [25], and in improving functional outcome of schizophrenic persons [26-27] no studies have so far exhibited a straightforward relation between antipsychotic treatment and social cognition in the definition of outcome improvement [12]. The reasons explaining this condition will be discussed further on in the chapter.

The Controversial Relation between Antipsychotics and Social Cognition

The first reason to explain the difficulties in combining antipsychotic treatment and social cognition measures to improve the outcome of people with schizophrenia is that the improvement in psychosocial functioning provided by the drugs over time is only modest. This position is supported by the results of the CATIE study conducted by the National Institute of Mental Health, NIMH [26], [28]. The Authors evidenced how all antipsychotics, FGAs and SGAs induced a small change in the scores at Quality of Life Scale, QLS [29] especially between baseline and 6 months, that tended to stabilize after 12 months. The best gains in psychosocial functioning induced by antipsychotics was reported in QLS subscale investigating engagement in vocational, recreational or task-related activities. Other significant improvements were observed in QLS subscales evaluating purposes, motivation and curiosity. The lower gains were noticed for the QLS subscale measuring occupational and educational functioning. After analyzing by multiple regression other significant predictors of outcome, NIMH researchers evidenced how the female sex, the non urban residence and a higher neurocognitive baseline functioning were good predictors, while the concomitant substance abuse and the presence of extrapiramidal side effects were poor predictors of outcome.

Another relevant research, the CUtLASS study [30] has also outlined how no single class of antipsychotic drugs was superior to another one in increasing psychosocial functioning.

In any case, these data have explored a global dimension, the Quality of Life, that is a general, multifaceted construct encompassing several dimensions, with a highly subjective characterization. Jones et al.'s study [30] also pointed out how quality of life in schizophrenia is difficult to ascertain and this raises the question on which measure can best describe the relation between antipsychotic treatment and outcome.

A second aspect is that the impact of antipsychotic treatment on neurocognition had not proved totally effective. Although the clinical studies [15-17] and meta-analyses conducted in the 1990s [24], [31], together with at least three meta-analyses realized in the following years independently from the pharmaceutical companies [32-34] had outlined an established neurocognitive advance of SGAs compared to FGAs, the results of the CATIE study [35] displayed how a FGA, perphenazine, had induced slightly better neurocognitive improvement than all the other SGAs. The CATIE results also evidenced how improvement on neurocognition was small for all antipsychotic drugs, typicals and atypicals, and that some apparently favourable properties of perphenazine might have been induced by a metabolite, N-dealkylperphenazine, whose relatively elevated affinity for serotonin 5-HT-$_{2A}$ receptors had been previously documented [36]. The fact that the CATIE was an open study, with at least 60% of participants already taking SGAs before inclusion, has raised the possibility that some favourable effects of SGAs on neurocognition might have been masked. Moreover, the CATIE study evidenced how the relation between neurocognitive improvement and treatment compliance was also weak, indicating either that cognitive improvement was increased by adherence to treatment or compliance supported an ameliorated cognition. Finally, the small size of cognitive improvement cannot exclude the likelihood of practice effect, that is impossible to distinguish from treatment effects in most studied on medication in mental disorders. In any case, these results have evidenced how the alleged superiority of SGAs on neurocognition was questionable and have fostered the need for a better comprehension of the whole topic [27], [203].

A third reason explaining the difficulties in associating antipsychotic treatment and social cognition is that studies conducted on the subdomains of social cognition have provided contrasting findings. The most consistent results have been reported for Social Perception, SP, a subdomain of social cognition that has been found to be somewhat linked to pharmacological treatement. The studies of Kee et al. [37] and Littrell et al. [38] have evidenced how risperidone and, respectively, olanzapine were associated to amelioration of social perception with respect to typical antipsychotic drugs. Both studies had limited sample sizes and the latter was uncontrolled. Contrariwise, another small study conducted by Herbener et al. [11] found no evidence for the association of emotion perception with antipsychotic treatment. Research performed on a higher number of participants also have evidenced the lack of association between social perception and antipsychotics, as in the study of Harvey et al. [39], in which neither risperidone nor quetiapine improved social perception on 289 persons affected by schizophrenia. Sergi et al.'s [221] comparative study, conducted on 100 persons with schizophrenia or schizoaffective disorder being treated with two atypicals, risperidone and olanzapine and a typical comparator, haloperidol, also evidenced how neither the two atypicals, nor the typical antipsychotic managed in improving Social Perception.

The results of the CATIE study on Social Perception [40], that involved 1460 persons affected by schizophrenia randomly adminidstered with olanzapine, risperidone, quetiapine, ziprasidone and haloperidol, have evidenced how the participants showed small non-significant improvements in Social Perception from baseline to two months. The outcome measure employed in the study was the Face Emotion Discrimination Test, FEDT, composed of 30 pairs of faces presented concurrently without limitation of time and requiring the respondent to identify if in each presented pair of faces the emotion was the same or different [222]. An improvement in Social Perception had a significant association to lower baseline emotion perception and better neurocognition.

Studies on Social Perception are important for the relation of this social cognitive subdomain with working capacity and independent living skills [19], [20], but even the other subdomains of this construct may attain a close relation to outcome and deserve to be explored in their association with psychopharmacological treatment. Other than Social

Perception, SP, the other two social cognition subdomains that have conquered the attention of research are Attributional Style, AS and Theory of Mind, ToM: the first one refers to the tendency, expressed by persons with paranoid or persecutory delusions to blame the others for the negative events, while the second concerns the capacity to represent human conditions and to make inferences about others' intentions. Attributional Style is associated to other social cognition dysfunctions, such as the tendency to "jump to conclusions" and to display a "confirmation bias", that is the research of a confirmatory, rather than disconfirmatory evidence for a belief [3], [41]. As deficits in ToM and in personalizing bias are associated [42-43] and ToM impairments have proved to be a trait deficit, having been found in first-degree relatives of schizophrenic persons [44-46], this array of impairments might represent a core dysfunction in schizophrenic processes. Their association with negative symptoms and a poor social outcome has already been outlined [47-50]. Still has to be demonstrated, however, the association between ToM impairments, AS deficits and the action of antipsychotic drugs. In this sight, the review of So et al. [51] has evidenced how antipsychotic treatment might determine the amelioration of belief flexibility and Theory of Mind, while the "jumping to conclusion" distortions, as a trait feature, were unlikely to improve under the action of antipsychotics. Although well conducted, this review outlined how the available data belonged to studies conducted unsystematically on small samples. In any case, the evidence for a link between ToM impairments and the negative symptoms underscores how it's likely that drug treatment might have a weak, but definite connection with the domains of social cognition. Further data sustaining this position might come from biological and basic cognition evidence. Even in this case, research evidence is contrasting and will be discussed further on in the chapter.

The Biological Determinants of the Relation between Antipsychotics and Social Cognition

A further issue that could explain why the association between antipsychotics and social cognition was difficult to recognize in the literature is represented by the biological determinants of the different actions conducted by typical and atypical antipsychotics. As neurocognition and social cognition have been regarded as independent constructs from the symptoms dimensions [1], it should have been expected that different biological mechanisms determined their malfunctioning, with separated neural and biochemical pathways. For this reason, antipsychotics and interventions on social cognition dysfunctions would act on different and separated biological targets from those remediating for the "classical" neurocognitive dysfunctions. The same consideration may be stated for the mechanisms underlying the activity of typical and atypical antipsychotic drugs in the neural pathways related to neurocognitive and social cognition dysfunctions. The literature investigating the relation of antipsychotics with neural dysfunctions in schizophrenia is widespread and an analysis of the evidence goes far beyond the aims of this chapter. A careful overview of studies investigating neural mechanisms closely related to activity of antipsychotics, social cognition and functional outcome is instead necessary. An interesting measure of cognitive performance is Procedural Learning, PL. Procedural Learning acquires a relevant clinical importance in determining functional outcome in schizophrenic persons for its connection to everyday skills and activities. In fact, PL pertains to cognitive and motor learning processes, such as learning by doing, whose associated executive functioning strategies cannot be explicitly displayed, but are learned through a trial-and-error process [52]. Procedural Learning is essential in engaging finalized behaviours. The capacity to perform goal-directed activities adds to the ability to understand others' intentions and beliefs in the set of domains pertaining to functional outcome in schizophrenia persons.

Early studies on PL provided contrasting results after the administration of antipsychotics. In fact, increase in execution of PL tasks in healthy volunteers is facilitated by dopamine activity and inhibited by non-selective D_2 receptor antagonists, such as haloperidol [53]. Functional magnetic resonance imaging performed during administration of a PL task in healthy subjects and schizophrenic persons on typical antipsychotics showed significant PL gains in healthy controls, but not in the schizophrenics. PL was associated with increased activation in the striatum, thalamus, cerebellum, precuneus, medial frontal lobe, and cingulate gyrus. Only the anterior inferior gyrus was significantly activated in patients [54]. Administration with risperidone or haloperidol led to no difference in execution of activities of daily living sustained by PL in persons affected by schizophrenia, whose working memory and executive functions improved after antipsychotic treatment. Improvements in activities of daily living were attributed to reinforcerment and behavioral training, independently from the drug action [55].

Further studies tried to evidence a differential activity between FGAs and SGAs on procedural learning by proposing a direct effect of the antipsychotics, apparently through a D_2 dopamine blockade in the striatum. In the study of Purdon et al. [56], schizophrenia patients, divided into three groups according to their pharmacological treatment with haloperidol, olanzapine and risperidone were compared to normal controls on a PL task: the problem solving learning task of the Tower of Toronto. PL abilities were preserved in patients administered with olanzapine, while haloperidol and risperidone were associated with the decline of PL after 6 months.

These results may be explained by the differential effects of drugs on the striatal dopamine receptors, despite their classification as conventional or atypical neuroleptics and the specific process implicated in each of these PL tasks. In fact, tracer studies with radioactive benzamides specific to striatal D receptors outlined a relationship between striatal D_2 receptor occupancy and PL performance. Using this method, studies on schizophrenia patients treated with olanzapine and haloperidol have shown that the coefficient of determination in a visuomotor PL task was inversely associated with D_2 receptor saturation [52]. Earlier research had already evidenced how D_4 receptor-blocking atypical drugs, such as clozapine, would also facilitate PL tasks, presumably by a selective action [57].

Studies on PL abilities have proven the effect of impaired cognitive functions on schizophrenia patients' outcome. Cognitive deficits found in schizophrenia affect planning, together with the capacity to begin and control a goal-directed behavior. The association between damaged executive functions and impairments in planning daily activities has been investigated in persons with schizophrenia, who gained scores significantly lower than controls, with high perseveration, in tasks concerning daily living activities such as going for shopping or the ability to cook a meal [52], [58-62].

An interesting issue should be represented by the finding of a link between the activity of antipsychotic drugs and the impact on procedural learning and problem-solving abilities on people affected by schizophrenia. This connection might be found by examining which cognitive processes are critical determinants of social competence. The relation between performance in social cognition and the capacity to solve concrete interpersonal problems had already been established [8], [63]. Most PL, and hence problem-solving tasks rely on Theory of Mind, the subdomain of social cognition involved in metarepresentation, that is the awareness of one's own and others' intentions, goals and beliefs. In this view, impairments in PL and problem-solving may be induced by patients' difficulties in inferring other people's state of mind and translating their own intentions into adaptive social acts [64]. In this context, Theory of Mind must be regarded as a complex social cognition subdomain as compared with more elementary ones, such as action-monitoring, the processing of social cues and Emotion Perception [8]. For this reason, an overview of how the activity of antipsychotic drugs might impact on Theory of Mind might help in combining the biochemical action of these drugs with social cognitive outcomes.

ANTIPSYCHOTICS AND THEORY OF MIND

At the beginning of the 1990s Christopher Frith [65] proposed that some symptoms of schizophrenia could be explained by a Theory of Mind deficit, giving birth to a wide array of studies that became the leading theme of research in severe mental disorders in the following years. The expression "Theory of Mind", however, was first used by primatologists [66], who investigated whether great apes had the capacity to represent one own' s and other's mental states. Such a capacity, in humans, would have allowed the adaptation to the environment, according to the social brain hypothesis [67]. The persons with good mind-reading properties would be more able to deceive, manipulate and take advantage over others, thus acquiring high social advantage in controlling food sources and sexual partners [68]. Individuals with psychotic illnesses, on the other hand, would be less able to understand the state of the world and the beliefs of the others, with significant impairments in social adaptation [49], [69-70]. Frith's model of Theory of Mind [65] established a direct connection between the nuclear symptoms of schizophrenia and ToM, with a selective model hierarchically linking the negative and disorganised symptoms with disorders of willed actions, the paranoid symptoms with defective monitoring of other people's intentions or defective mentalising and the passivity symptoms with impaired self-monitoring. Qualitative evidence displayed how ToM deficits in schizophrenia are specific of the disease, being not induced by general cognitive impairment [49], [71], while meta-analytic research evidenced a strong effect size from studies on ToM, with Theory of Mind performance of individuals with schizophrenia being at least one standard deviation below healthy controls [72]. ToM deficits have been evidenced during remission from schizophrenia [73] and have been found in persons with subclinical schizotypal traits [44], [74-77] and, most of all, in first-degree relatives of schizophrenic persons [46], [78]. For these reasons, impairment in mentalizing is nowadays considered a trait-dependent marker of vulnerability of schizophrenia, a real "cognitive endophenotype" of this condition [46]. The specificity of mentalizing deficits [47], [79], that represents a core part of the social cognition concept [6] raises the question of how impairments of mental states might be reduced or at least modified by the activity of antipsychotic treatment. In fact, ToM deficits represent a strong predictor of the chances of being a schizophrenic person [50] and, mostly, of the poor social competence in schizophrenics [12]. By demonstrating that antipsychotics might help in recovering from social cognitive deficits, it would be easier to utilize pharmacological treatment in addition to non-pharmacological rehabilitative interventions for schizophrenia persons. An overview of the biological structures and the neurochemical pathways most involved in the formation of mental state attribution impairments might help in understanding to what extent a pharmacological treatment of ToM deficit would be effective.

Neurotransmitters and Theory of Mind Dysfunctions

The introduction of the SGAs coincided with a modification of the "classical" theory of hyperactivity of dopaminergic system, according to which an excess of dopamine transmission in the forebrain would be responsible for the onset of psychotic symptoms [80], with the "evidence" of the clinical effectiveness of FGAs, for their activity in blocking postsynaptic dopamine receptors [81-82]. The newly "atypical" antipsychotics, in fact, had two main activities that distinguished their action from the former "typical" drugs: (i) a lower degree of occupancy of striatal D_2 dopamine receptors, from 30% to 60%, compared to 70-80% of the traditional drugs [83]; (ii) a differentiated multisite activity, mainly on dopamine and serotonin receptors and transmission systems, but also on adrenergic and histaminergic receptors. An hyperactivity in the mesolimbic system, i.e. the dopaminergic neurons projecting from midbrain A10 Ventro-Tegmental Area, VTA to the Nucleus accumbens, and an hypoactivity of the mesocortical system, i.e. the dopaminergic neurons projecting from the VTA to the Prefrontal cortex, has been documented in persons with schizophrenia. Excess in dopamine mesolimbic activity would be caused by a dysfunctional feedback inhibitory loop of the cortical over subcortical areas [84]. This dysregulation in dopamine transmission would produce a hypodopaminergic state in the prefrontal cortex of schizophrenic patients, with the decreased mesocortical dopaminergic activity inducing the negative symptoms and poor performance in frontally-mediated cognitive tasks. Moreover, in the prefrontal cortex, where levels of dopamine are reduced, SGAs, with their low affinity for D_2 receptors, may realize the occupation of a significantly higher proportion of these receptors compared to the striatum. On the other hand, FGAs evidence a high affinity for D_2 receptor, with high D_2 receptor occupancy both in the striatum and in the cortex [83].

Probably all the serotonin receptors are also involved in cognitive functions like executive functioning and memory. Serotonin modulates dopaminergic transmission, with blockade of 5-HT_2 receptors inducing an increase of extracellular dopamine levels [85]. As early studies on SGAs, with dual dopamine-serotonin activity, evidenced better cognitive outcomes compared to FGAs, blocking dopamine receptors only, it was proposed that the dopaminergic-serotoninergic system, DS, was the neurochemical basis of the ability to mentalize [86].

Over the years, such a view has been partially modified by evidence from neurobiological and functional neuroimaging research. First of all, it has been acknowledged that mental state attribution abilities originate from the integrated activity of several functionally interconnected brain regions. According to Abu-Akel's [87] theories, self and other's mental states are detected in two posterior brain regions, the Inferior Parietal Lobe, IPL, and the Superior Temporal Sulcus, STS. Information from these posterior regions is then fed forward to the limbic-paralimbic structures, including the Amygdala, the Orbitofrontal Cortex, OFC, the Ventral Medial Prefrontal Cortex, VMPFC, in which the integration of the detected mental states with emotions and motivationally salient instance take place. Finally, information about mental states is relayed to the Prefrontal Cortex, PFC where mental state attribution is processed for application and action. In the prefrontal cortex, two areas had acquired the most relevant importance in the execution of Theory of Mind performance: the Dorsal and Lateral Prefrontal Cortex, DLPFC and the Inferolateral Frontal Cortex, ILFC.

The positron emission tomography, PET study of Spence et al. [88] evidenced how in normal subjects there is a replicable cerebral pattern of activation when performing voluntary motor acts, while persons with schizophrenia experiencing passivity phenomena show abnormal IPL hyperactivation in executing the same acts.

From a methodological point of view, functional Magnetic Resonance Imaging, fMRI of the frontal lobe while performing an experimentally controlled task is the only measurement clearly distinguishing between persons with schizophrenia and healthy controls, with schizophrenia patients failing to activate their frontal cortex when required [52]. Two seminal fMRI neuroimaging studies have shown that at least two areas of PFC are necessary for the representation of mental states.

Fletcher et al.'s [89] fMRI study evidenced that there is increased cortical activity in left dorsal MPFC (Brodmann's areas 8 and 9) in healthy adults presented with a narrative containing a ToM task as compared to a narrative without such a task. Russell et al.'s fMRI study [90] on schizophrenics has evidenced how, during the execution of a ToM task, the patients, compared to normal controls, had significantly less activation of the ILFC. The last study becomes even more relevant when considering that ILFC contains a group of cells, the Mirror Neurons, MNs, that are believed to be implicated in mental attribution processes. The MNs were first detected in monkeys in the ventral premotor area F5 [91] and are probably also localized in Broca's area of the frontal operculum in humans. Broca's area is part of ILFC and controls the oro-laryngeal, oro-facial and brachio-manual movements that are acted in speech production. The properties of MNs are unique, for they discharge congruent firing patterns both when the subject executes specific goal-directed motor activities with their face, arms and hands and when the subject is passively witnessing the same goal-directed actions performed by another [87], [92-93]. The ILFC is probably the PFC area most involved in mental state attribution [87].

Secondly, the dopaminergic pathways and transmission acquired further importance in determining how emotional, social cognitive and mental state attribution functions are influenced by the neurochemical status in persons with schizophrenia [8]. Most of the research conducted on dopamine function in paralimbic and limbic structures evidenced how this neurotransmitter mediates adaptive and goal-directed behaviours [94]. Dysregulation of VMPFC dopamine function may contribute to maladaptive states, where behaviour dissociates from its consequences. VMPFC is, in fact, necessary for the generation of autonomic responses guiding effective decision making [95]. The different subtypes of dopamine receptors showed different properties in these patterns of functional connectivity. Dopamine levels increase after completing Working Memory tasks in PFC (VLFC, Left Inferior Frontal Gyrus) and in Left Inferior Frontal Cortex, probably due to a specific effect on D_1 receptors [96]. D_1 receptors, that are more highly expressed in the cortex than in the striatum, were believed to be a sensible target of novel antipsychotics, for their greater impact on cognitive and negative symptoms [83]. D_1 and D_2 receptors have different properties, with the first facilitating conditioned-unconditioned associations, while the others favouring adaptive responses to cope with aversive environmental stimuli [97]. The blocking of another subtype of dopamine receptors, D_4, within the medial PFC prevents the acquisition of fear-related behaviours and emotional associative learning [94]. In clozapine-administered schizophrenics, dopamine D_4 receptors had a somewhat facilitating effect on Procedural Learning, the construct that is the cognitive base of problem-solving and social adaptation, that are in turn related to Theory of Mind [57], [63-64]. The crucial role of dopamine D_4 receptors in modulating the encoding of emotional memory in schizophrenia and other psychotic illnesses has been extensively evidenced [98]. As nearly all dopamine receptors are localized in high concentrations in limbic-paralimbic areas, basal ganglia and the frontal cortex, dopamine activity and transmission acquires a highly relevant function in modulating motivationally-salient stimuli [94]. Dopamine transmission fluctuates, however, in persons with schizophrenia, with high increases in psychotic states [8], [99]. It has been proposed that dopamine cognitive action in the production of psychotic symptoms takes place by interfering with the ability to attribute the right "salience to external objects and internal representation" [100]. According to another theory dopamine would stabilize the neural representations by modifying the signal-to-noise ratio in the cortical microcircuits [101]. Other studies [102-103] focused on the balance between D_1 and D_2 receptors, that would modify or stabilize stored representations in the prefrontal cortical maps, with short-term D_1 receptors stimulation reversing cognitive impairment induced by chronic FGA stimulation. The evidence of a higher proportion of dopamine afferences on the Anterior Cingulate Cortex, Acc, postulated another research hypothesis, according to that dopamine transmission might normalize the updating of the short-term contextual representations to match the input of externally or internally generated information, with different levels of this neurotransmitter being associated to abnormal social cognition patterns [8], [104]. To support this, administration of dopamine receptor agonists displayed that D_2 and D_4 receptors quenches amygdalar-induced inhibition, while D_1 receptors attenuate amygdalar-elicited firing of mPFC neurons. This combined action modifies the balance of excitatory and inhibitory transmission in this pathway, producing a net increase in the excitatory influence exerted by the amygdala over populations of mPFC neurons [105]. Genetic findings have, however, associated the increase in dopamine transmission with Catechol-O-methyl transferase (COMT) Val(158/108)Met lower activity allele in caucasian schizophrenic adults with 22q11 deletion syndrome (22q11DS), a highly prevalent syndrome in schizophrenia [106], suggesting a possible explanation for the origin of the imbalances in dopamine transmission.

Thirdly, results from new evidence postulate that impairments in social cognition might be a consequence of the dysregulation in the activity of other several functionally interconnected neurotransmitters.

The nonapeptide hormone oxytocin, well-known for its pro-lactation and uterine-contracting properties, in the last decade has also been associated to social cognition. Although primarily synthesized in magnocellular neurons of Paraventricular, PVN and Supraoptic, SON nuclei of hypothalamus, in humans oxytocin is as well generated in small amounts in lateral amygdala and it is widely distributed in many brain areas [107]. An already well-documented cognitive activity of oxytocin is reinstatement of Pre-Pulse Inhibition, PPI that is disrupted by dizocilpine, a non-competitive NMDA antagonist and amphetamine, that is an indirect dopamine agonist [107-108]. Prepulse inhibition, PPI of the startle reflex is a variety of sensorimotor gating presented by different species in which the reflexive reaction to a abrupt, powerful sensory stimulus is reduced by another, weaker sensory stimulus that precedes the first one. This gating process is an attentional mechanism aimed at filtering potentially distracting stimuli, in order to concentrate attention on relevant information [107]. Deficits in sensorimotor gating are a key feature of schizophrenia and have been considered an endophenotype of this disease [109-110]. Abnormal filtering of sensory inputs and information from multiple sources might contribute to obstacle everyday life functioning in persons with schizophrenia. Some SGAs, like clozapine, a dopamine and partial serotonin agonist, significantly increase oxytocin plasma levels, that are reported low in persons with schizophrenia indicating that this substance may act as a natural antipsychotic [107], [111]. In fact, higher oxytocin levels were correlated with improved pro-social behaviours, while oxytocin hematic levels were inversely related to symptom severity in women with schizophrenia [112], [113]. In humans, oxytocin has reduced the activation of amygdala in a fMRI face recognition task [114-115] and, more generally, facilitates the recognition of happy or angry faces [116]. More specifically, intranasal oxytocin boosts the gazing at the eye region of human faces [117] as well as the chance of evoking a happy face [118]. Most interestingly, intranasal oxytocin, had enhanced the capacity to infer the mental state of others from social cues in the eye region [119]. It has been proposed that oxytocin might amplify sensations of trust and empathy by increasing eye gaze and the subsequent comprehension of social hints, thus supporting the detection and the understanding of others' feelings, in other words the feelings of empathy toward others [107]. Theory of Mind has been related to empathy, that has been viewed as the capacity to understand and experience others' feelings in relation to oneself [120-121], with psychotic subjects showing a dissociation between "hot", affective ToM abilities, closely related to empathic abilities and "cold", cognitive ToM capacities, more associated to false belief understanding [122].

In any case, if ToM and empathy have close similarities, oxytocin might affect this construct. In this view, plasma levels of oxytocin in schizophrenic persons have been recognized as predictors of the capacity to recognize facial emotions, further associating this hormone to the social aspects of schizophrenia [111]. The functional properties of oxytocin involve an increase in the activity of dopamine release in the Ventro-Tegmental Area, VTA, that in turn would abnormally modulate the mesocorticolimbic dopaminergic transmission, with impaired emotional salience processing inducing the deficit in social cognition [123-124].

The other nonapaptide arginine vasopressin, AVP synthesized in the suprachiasmatic nuclei and then transported in the hypothalamus, has also been involved in social cognition mechanisms. Although vasopressin receptors, V_1 and V_2 are mainly distributed in the kidney (V_1), the vascular tree, the adrenal glands, the uterus and other tissues (V_2), AVP releasing neurons of the hypothalamus also project in central nervous system, with effects on memory and aggression. In monogamous rodents, AVP has exerted effects on affiliation, with the creation of stronger, enduring selective preference for their mate, while the same does not happen for polygamous rodents, with V1a receptor antagonists not suppressing mating and affiliative behaviour suggesting that there are different neurochemical pathways for AVP activity in different species. In pair-bonding rodents, in fact, AVP neurons are located in ventral pallidum, most involved with reward, while in non pair-bonding species those neurons are highly represented in lateral septum and amygdala. Some evidences have related pair-bonding maintenance to dopamine D_1 receptors [125]. However, as there is little information about V_1 receptor expression in humans and non-human primates, interactions between AVP and dopamine are yet to be demonstrated [126].

If striatal dopamine transmission may be influenced by the two small nonapeptides, further evidence highlight the function of serotonin in regulating dopamine transmission in the cortex. Dopaminergic-serotoninergic interactions at cortical level acquired a critical importance in originating the main mentalizing abilities [86]. In this context, the analysis of a specific effect of a functional polymorphism of the serotonin 1A receptor, $5\text{-}HT_{1A}$-R, regulating both serotonin and dopamine transmission in stabilized persons with schizophrenia performing neuropsychological and, most importantly, ToM tasks, has evidenced a significant $5\text{-}HT_{1A}$-R genotype effect on ToM performances, with the CC genotype achieving significantly better results [127]. This evidence highlights the consequence of $5\text{-}HT_{1A}$-R polymorphism on ToM functioning in persons with schizophrenia. It is most likely that the interactions between dopaminergic and serotoninergic systems in Theory of Mind are multifaceted and more intricate that how it was believed. The reported evidence on neurobiological determinants of the social cognitive abilities allow to propose a model in which the capacity to attribute mental states might stem from a complex effect of mesolimbic dopamine transmission on the frontal cortex. To account for the dysregulation of the dopaminergic transmission not only there would be a failure in the modulatory, inhibiting control of serotonin system [86], but also a deeper striatal activity of other "atypical" neurotransmitters, such as oxytocin and AVP. The result would be an aberrant modulation of the different levels of dopamine responsible for the impairments in the social domain in at least three regions of the brain, the amygdala, the inferior parietal lobule and the medial prefrontal cortex [8], [87]. Interestingly, violent schizophrenic persons imprisoned on account of severe offences perform better at Theory of Mind tasks, but worse on an empathic inferencing tasks than non violent psychotic patients, suggesting that empathy might inhibit violence and aggression [128]. As levels of oxytocin in schizophrenic patients are reported low [111] and AVP V_1 receptor are overexpressed in the prefrontal cortex of male marmosets when they become fathers – a pro-social behaviour - [126], it is possible to speculate that the dysregulation of other neurotransmitters than dopamine would impair as well the expression of some social cognitive abilities and, in turn, enhance the manifestation of others. To sustain this, it is of note that the different subtypes of dopamine receptors have different, but related functions. The activity of D_1 and D_2 receptors in the amygdala has a role in the modulation of fear and anxiety, while the dopamine D_4 towards D_1 transmission from the basolateral amygdala, BLA to the medial prefrontal cortex, mPFC modulates within the mPFC the processing of emotional learning and memory, two constructs related to social cognition [97], [129]. The model describing the striato-cortical interactions of neurotransmitters accounting for the maintenance and the disruption of the mental state attribution abilities is showed in figure 1.

From this data, there is at least some possibility that antipsychotic drugs might influence complex social cognition domains, as Theory of Mind is. A revision of the evidence will provide further highlights on this relation.

The Pros and Cons of the Activity of Antipsychotics on Theory of Mind

A striking feature of Theory of Mind is that, although there has been a definite demonstration that subjects with schizophrenia have a poorer performance on ToM tasks with respect to healthy individuals, the measurement of this social cognitive domain is difficult to perform, for the divergent psychometric properties of the rating instruments.

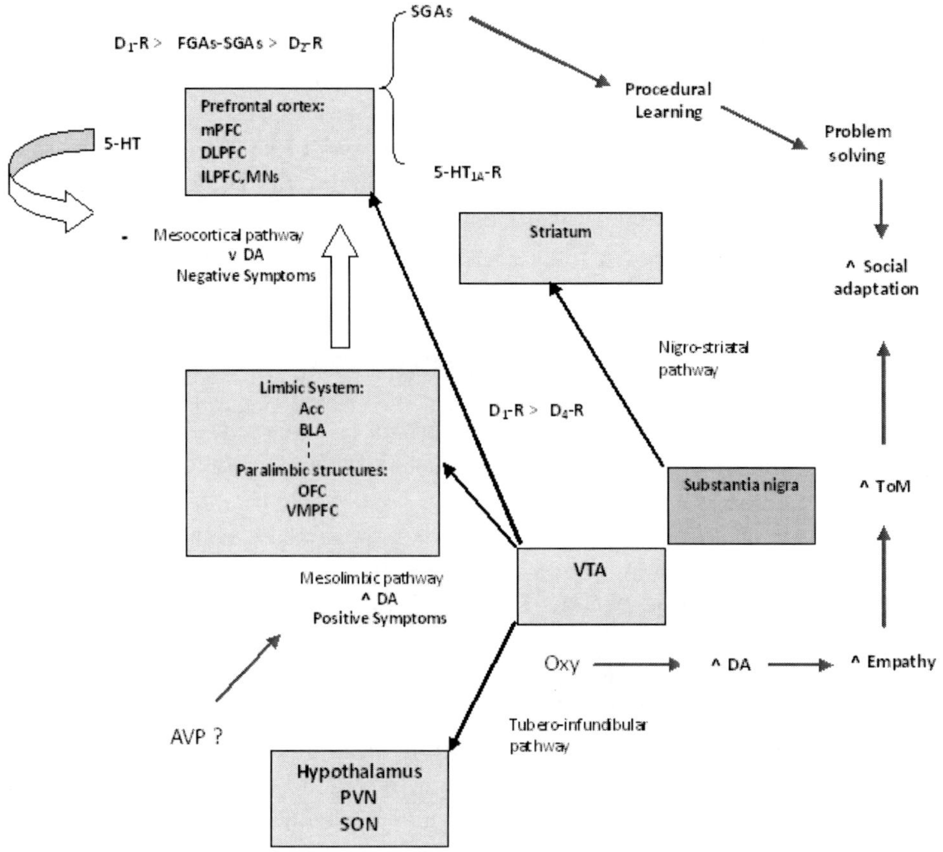

Figure 1. The combined putative effect of serotonin-dopamine transmission and APs on the neural pathways subserving Theory of Mind.
The impairment of social cognition subdomains, especially of Theory of Mind may originate from an imbalance of serotonin-dopamine system [8], [86], [100]. At cortical level, a failure in the modulatory, inhibiting control of serotonin system on dopamine transmission would induce the negative symptoms [86], while at striatal level, the excess of dopamine would be responsible for the onset of positive symptoms. An imbalance in the activity of the nonapeptides oxytocin and probably Arginin Vasopressine, AVP would play a part in the aberrant modulation of the levels of dopamine, responsible for the impairments in the social domain, in the amygdala, the inferior parietal lobule and the medial prefrontal cortex [8], [87], [100], [107-108]. According to their degree of receptorial occupancy [52], FGAs and, more appropriately, SGAs would contribute to revert the dopamine disequilibrium by enhancing Procedural Learning pro-social activities in the cortex through the stabilization of the transmission between D_2 and D_1 receptors and a direct activity on D_4 receptors [57], [83], [98]. By acting on D_2 and D_4 receptors in the striatum, APs would enhance amygdalar inhibiting firing, thus modulating the excitatory influence induced by the amygdala on mPFC neurons [105].
Abbreviations: Acc: Anterior cingulated cortex; APs: antipsychotic drugs; AVP: Arginin Vasopressine; BLA: Basolateral Amygdala; DLPFC: Dorso-Lateral Prefrontal Cortex; FGAs: First Generation Antipsychotics; ILPFC: Infero-Lateral Prefrontal Cortex; MNs: Mirror Neurons; mPFC: medial Prefrontal Cortex; OFC: Orbitofrontal Cortex; Oxy: Oxytocin; PVN: Paraventricular Nucleus; SGAs: Second Generation Antipsychotics; SON: Supraopticus Nucleus; VMPFC: Ventral Medial Prefrontal Cortex; VTA: Vental Tegmental Area.

Table 1. The Different Theory of Mind Tasks

Type of task	Characteristics of the tasks	Psychological features	Relation to psychopathology	Relation to outcome
False belief or deception	✓ First order false belief: assesses the ability to understand that someone believes something different from the real state of the world; ✓ Second order false belief: participants have to infer the false belief of a character about the beliefs of a second character	Involves linguistic aspects and knowledge of context, hints and conversational rules for proper understanding, Mazza et al., 2001[47]	Impaired first order and second order false belief in schizophrenic persons with positive symptoms, Frith and Corcoran, 1996[133]; Drury et al., 1998[134]; Doody et al., 1998[135]; impaired first and second order false belief in schizophrenics with negative symptoms, Mazza et al., 2001[47]; Corcoran and Frith, 1996[136]; Mazza et al., 2007[137]; first order false belief impaired in schizophrenics with disorganized symptoms, Zalla et al., 2006[138]	Second order false belief tasks predict social functioning, Roncone et al., 2002[48]; First and second order false belief tasks predict social behaviour, Brüne, 2005b[50]; Brüne et al., 2007[12]
Machiavellian Intelligence	✓ Assesses the ability to deceive and manipulate others and the degree of accordance with statements depicting a "cynical" lifestyle	Assesses awareness and social functioning in a social context characterized by "interpersonal deception", Mazza et al., 2003a[70]	Subjects with negative schizophrenic symptoms are more prone to disagree with sentences expressing the need for deception and manipulation in the Mach IV Scale; the reverse is true for persons with positive symptoms, Mazza et al., 2003a[70]	No associations with other social cognitive measures, Mazza et al., 2007[137]
Intention-inferencing	✓ Evaluates the ability to infer a character's intention from information included in a short story	Requires the interpretation of social inferences behind indirect speech (eg.: a child says to his mother: "please, close the window", meaning "I feel cold", Mazza et al., 2001[47])	Intention-inferencing tasks are impaired in negative schizophrenics, Langdon et al., 1997 [139] and in disorganized schizophrenics, Sarfati and Hardy-Baylè, 1999[140]; Sarfati et al., 2000[141];	Predicts social behavior (pooled with false belief tasks, Brüne, 2005b[50]; Brüne et al., 2007[12]
Understanding of indirect speech	✓ Measures the ability to understand indirect speech from irony, banter, hints and metaphors§	Another person's mental states understanding is required for the comprehension of indirect speech; comprehension of irony is not related to the understanding of metaphors, Sprong et al., 2007[72]	Indirect speech tasks are impaired in negative schizophrenics or in subjects with passivity phenomena, Corcoran et al., 1995 [142]	No relation with outcome measures

Table 1. (Continued)

Type of task	Characteristics of the tasks	Psychological features	Relation to psychopathology	Relation to outcome
Geometrical shapes	✓ Assesses the attribution of mental states to animated geometrical shapes interacting in a "socially complex way"	Requires a high level of abstraction, Sprong et al., 2007[72]	Related to positive symptoms of schizophrenia, Blakemore et al., 2003 [143]; Russel et al., 2006[144]	No relation with outcome measures
"Eyes" task	✓ Mental states are detected by looking at pictures of eyes	More related to emotion recognition and empathy, Sprong et al., 2007[72]	Related to the negative symptoms of schizophrenia, Kelemen et al., 2005[145]; Bora et al., 2006[146]	Predictor of social functioning, Bora et al., 2006[146]
Faux pas	✓ Ascertains a mental representation that the persons saying something were unaware of they should not say it, and another that the person hearing would feel insulted or hurt	Bridges the gap between the cognitive and the "affective" parts of Theory of Mind, Decety and Jackson, 2004[121]	Related to positive paranoid symptoms of schizophrenia, Abu-Akel and Abushua'leh, 2004[128]	Adequate empathic capacities, with a good understanding of faux pas predict a reduction in hostility and violence in positive schizophrenics, Abu-Akel and Abushua'leh, 2004[128]

§ an understanding of other's mental states is required for the comprehension of indirect speech, Sprong et al., 2007[72].

Table 2. The Current Studies on Theory of Mind and Antipsychotics

Studies	Psychopathological features of participants	No. of participants	Type(s) of antipsychotics/medication utilized	ToM Task utilized	Main results on ToM and/or outcome
Sarfati et al., 1999[140]	Persons with Schizophrenia and Major Depression	26 participants with Schizophrenia; 13 with Major Depression; 13 normal controls	Antipsychotic medication	Intention-inferencing tasks	No effects of antipsychotics on mental state attribution tasks
Mazza et al., 2005[147]	Persons with Schizophrenia	14 participants	Risperidone (8 subjects); risperidone + donepezil (7 subjects)	First- and Second Order False Belief tasks	Improvements in attention, executive functions and in First Order False Belief Task understanding in the group treated with Risperidone + donepezil
Savina and Beninger, 2007[148]	Persons with Schizophrenia and Schizoaffective Disorder	84 participants; 24 healthy controls	SGAs: - clozapine (18 subjects); - olanzapine (20 subjects); - risperidone (23 subjects);	First- and Second Order False Belief tasks; faux pas test	Olanzapine group scoring best in first and second order false belief tasks and faux pas; risperidone had a performance between FGAs and

			FGAs:		olanzapine in first order tasks;
Studies	**Psychopathological features of participants**	**No. of participants**	**Type(s) of antipsychotics/medication utilized**	**ToM Task utilized**	**Main results on ToM and/or outcome**
			- perphenazine (2 subjects); - fluphenazine (8 subjects); - flupenthixol (6 subjects); - zuclopenthixol (4 subjects); - stelazine (1 subject); - haloperidol (2 subjects) Concomitant use of mood stabilizers; no use of anticholinergics		FGAs had the worst performance on both tasks; risperidone had the worst score on faux pas task
Shamay-Tsoory et al., 2007[122]	Persons with Schizophrenia	22 participants; 55 healthy controls	SGAs: - olanzapine (8 subjects); - clozapine (5 subjects); - risperidone (3 subjects); - quetiapine (1 subject); FGAs: - fluphenazine (2 subjects); - zuclopenthixol (1 subject); - perphenazine (1 subject); - penfluridolum (1 subject)	Computerized task with combined verbal and "eye task" elements assessing "cognitive", "affective" and "physical" ToM conditions	Schizophrenia patients more impaired in "affective" ToM than controls; participants on SGAs perform better in "affective" ToM tasks
Mizrahi et al., 2007[149]	Persons with Schizophrenia, Schizoaffective Disorder and Schizophreniform Disorder	71 participants (cross-sectional component); 17 drug-free participants (due to receive APs for at least 6 weeks in the longitudinal component of the study)	SGAs (risperidone, olanzapine, clozapine, 88.6%); FGAs (loxapine, 11.4%)	Hinting task	Improvement of ToM performance during the 6 weeks of the longitudinal component, particularly in the first 2 weeks
Brüne et al., 2007[12]	Persons with Schizophrenia	38 participants	SGAs (risperidone, quetiapine, amisulpride, aripiprazole, clozapine)	Computerized task pooling false belief, intention-inferencing and picture-sequencing tasks	No interference between medication and performance on ToM tasks
Corcoran et al., 2008[150]	Persons with Schizophrenia, Schizoaffective Disorder and Major Depression	68 participants with Schizophrenia; 27 with Major Depression; 33 healthy controls	FGAs and SGAs	False belief ToM stories and false belief ToM picture-sequencing tasks	No interference between medication and performance on ToM tasks
Mazza et al., 2008[46]	Persons with Schizophrenia	38 participants with Schizophrenia, 34 First-Degree relatives; 44 healthy controls	Antipsychotic medication	False belief ToM stories and pragmatic conversation tasks	No interference between medication and performance on ToM and pragmatic conversation tasks

This has raised the question as to whether ToM is a unitary concept or not [72]. In fact, attempts to standardize social cognition measures in the wide cognitive test set realized in the MATRICS Consensus Cognitive Battery, MCCB [130], although promising, have proved only partially effective, due to the fact that the Mayer-Salovey-Caruso Emotionally Intelligence Test, MSCEIT [223], included in the MCCB, only addresses emotion perception without considering social cognition constructs related to mentalizing abilities, such as social judgment [131-132]. To effectively rate mental state attribution abilities there are at least seven different kinds of measuring tasks, each of them with unique properties [72], [128]. The different Theory of Mind tasks are shown in Table 1.

Interestingly, the tasks that are more prone to assess the capacity to perceive, understand and represent the emotional features of other people's mental states are the ones that best predict social functioning and an appropriate behaviour in schizophrenic persons. If the false belief tasks, directly related to linguistic abilities, have been related to everyday life functioning and social behaviour capacities since the first investigation on social cognition and outcome [48], the "eyes" tasks of Theory of Mind have been added to the predictors of an overall good functioning in more recent times [146]. Clinical evidence on the faux pas task outlined a dissociation between social cognition abilities allowing to deceive, manipulate or hurt the others and the capacities that are necessary for the comprehension of the other people's feelings, being therefore not associated to improper, unethical or violent conduct [128]. Such evidence raises the question as to whether the impact of antipsychotic drug on mentalizing abilities may have remediating properties or only a "moderating" function, along with So et al.'s [51] position about the action of drug treatment on the reasoning biases. Reasoning biases may be conceptualized as subdomains of Attributional Style, AS, a construct that, in turn, pertains to the boundaries of social cognition [3]. Considering the evidence supporting reasoning biases as a trait marker of psychosis, just as Theory of Mind is now considered [3], [21], [46], [51], [72], it is conceivable that APs might influence ToM function, just as it happens with reasoning biases. To explore this, an overview of the studies describing the activity of antipsychotics on ToM will be helpful. The studies in which an association between antipsychotic treatment and Theory of Mind indices are reported in Table 2.

Four of the eight studies with data on mentalizing abilities and antipsychotic drugs [12], [46], [140], [150] reported no association between Theory of Mind and the effect of pharmacological treatment. To sustain this evidence, one of the best conducted study on the issue [12] proposed that dysfunctional emotionally-based social cognition abilities are impervious to medical treatments, or that at least only simple metacognitive functions would benefit from APs. The other four studies, on the other hand, evidenced a differentiated pattern of activity of antipsychotic treatment on mental state attribution abilities. In the study of Mazza et al. [147], the association between risperidone and donepezil, an anticholinergic drug, improved the understanding of a first order false belief task. The following study of Savina and Beninger [148] displayed a multifaceted pattern of activity of antipsychotics on ToM, in which a SGA, olanzapine, determined good performances on first and second order false belief tasks and, interestingly, in the empathically-oriented faux pas task, while subject treated with FGAs gained the worst performance on the whole ToM and faux pas tasks. Another SGA, risperidone, obtained, however, an intermediate score on first order false belief tasks, but a poor performance on faux pas. In the interesting study of Shamay-Tsoory et al. [122], outlining for the first time a dissociation between "cognitive" and "affective" Theory of Mind, SGAs appeared more related to a better performance in the "affective" ToM tasks. Finally, in the methodologically well-conducted Mizrahi et al.'s study [149], Theory of Mind performance quickly improved on drug-naïve subjects, at least for the first order false belief tasks, during the first two weeks of administration of antipsychotic treatment, and then become stabilized over a definite amount of time, six weeks. The fact that the overall majority of Mizrahi et al.'s [149] participants were on SGAs may underlie how the new antipsychotics might act on Theory of Mind impairment better than the older FGAs. However, both typical and atypical antipsychotics have few or none effect on behavioural changes in the long term [12], [140]. After the results of the landmark studies of Geddes et al. [25] and Lieberman et al. [26] displaying how atypicals were no better than typicals in clinical and neuropsychological activity, one might wonder whether it is possible to figure out a differentiated activity on Theory of Mind for FGAs and SGAs. To do so, a short revision of the evidence linking FGAs and SGAs on social cognition and ToM is needed.

FGAs, SGAs, Social Cognition and Theory of Mind: Are There Class-Related Differences?

Only a few studies so far have specifically addressed the question on how typical or atypical antipsychotics might assume a different function on social cognitive measures. Most of the research focused on different constructs from Theory of Mind, such as Emotion Perception, EP. The studies of Kee et al. [37] and Williams et al. [151] evidenced the superiority of SGAs in remediating EP dysfunctions. Another seminal study [11] displayed that, although the negative symptoms, closely related to EP impairment, responded well to SGAs, a similar, direct response on EP disruption did not occur. A peculiar result was evidenced in the study of Mo et al. [152], in which a partial correlation between scores at second order false belief tasks and the understanding of metaphors was evidenced in negative and disorganized schizophrenics after controlling for years of education, IQ and, most of all, medication daily dosage. Unfortunately, it was not reported in this study whether the participants were on typical or atypical antipsychotics. As already described, antipsychotics displayed differentiated effects on Procedural Learning tasks, closely related to Theory of Mind, with olanzapine and risperidone achieving better results than haloperidol, probably due to the different degree of occupancy of dopamine D_2 receptors irrespective of the classification in typicals and atypicals. It is therefore conceivable that the capacity of performing a PL task varied inversely with D_2 receptor saturation [52]. Considering the reduced pattern of D_2 receptor occupancy that SGAs display in comparison to the higher affinity FGAs [83], this could represent an explanation of the alleged superiority of SGAs compared to FGAs in the remediation of social cognitive dysfunctions [51], [148].

Antipsychotic Drugs, Theory of Mind and Empathy

To better understand why it is important to associate APs to social cognition, we have to remind that, in clinical terms, the pharmacological treatment is a landmark feature of rehabilitation of persons with schizophrenia, while adjunctive psychosocial treatment may help in maintaining the motivation to stay on medication [153]. The discovery of a relation between mental state attribution abilities, helping in maintaining the relation with others, and APs, effective in reducing the symptom of the disease, would effectively facilitate users of psychiatric services in reaching an acceptable level of social adaptation and of quality of life. In the following paragraphs, some experimental evidence relating APs, ToM and outcome will be presented to show how pharmacological treatment may have a role in the definition of functional outcome of persons with schizophrenia

Background: The Evolutionary and Clinical Features of Theory of Mind

From an evolutionary perspective, Theory of Mind represents an interesting subdomain of social cognition for its adaptive characteristics and properties. In fact, the capacity to deceive and manipulate other people allows to increase the amount of food sources and the number of sexual partners [68]; in persons with schizophrenia such adaptive capacity is lacking, as well as ToM abilities [69-70].

Other studies have related ToM to empathy, that is the capacity to understand and experience others' feelings in relation to oneself [120-121]. In this context, the faux pas situation, in which a person must recognize s/he has said or done something embarrassing someone else [128], provide a specific link between ToM and the capacity to empathize about other people's feelings. In addition, psychotic subjects evidenced a dissociation between "affective" ToM abilities, closely related to empathic abilities and "cognitive" ToM capacities, more associated to false belief understanding [122]. In any case, integration between emotional features and mentalizing capacities in schizophrenia is impaired [154].

From a clinical point of view, poor ToM abilities improve in rehabilitation programs involving cognitive remediation and problem-solving approaches [155-158]. Problem-solving is a self-directed cognitive process aimed at identifying and performing effective solutions to everyday problems [159] and has been considered as a social cognition mediator, i.e. a mediating construct between basic cognition and social functioning [22-23], [160]. As impairments in problem-solving abilities may be viewed as a consequence of the disruption of mental state attribution processes [64], the actions aimed at remediating ToM dysfunctions involve the execution of problem-solving related tasks, that are in turn based on Procedural Learning, PL [52]. The remediation of problem-solving deficits involves patients' perception of their needs and of the help received by mental health services and institutions [157], [161].

In the previous paragraphs it was extensively reviewed how it is difficult to find out an association between ToM and antipsychotic treatment. A striking feature in the studies on the issue is that antipsychotics might improve – at least in short time – some basics aspects of ToM, such as first order false belief tasks [149], but in no way they can predict social adaptation [12].

Furthermore, although impaired emotion recognition is quite common in schizophrenic persons [162], its association with a weakened ToM has been questioned, and the two domains are considered independent of each other [50]. As emotion recognition and perception are a landmark feature of social adaptation [3], it should be relevant to weight the impact of this construct in the building of a model aimed at predicting which pro-social behaviours are useful for persons with schizophrenia.

For this reason, this chapter's research sought to determine to what extent the association of ToM impairments to antipsychotic medication, intelligence level, empathy, problem-solving skills, emotion recognition and other executive functions is effective in predicting the impairment of social behaviour and functional outcome in schizophrenic persons.

The first working hypothesis was that impairment of mental state attribution had enough strength to predict the disruption of social capacities in schizophrenic patients, regardless of the effects of medication and the confounding action of intelligence level and duration of illness [48-50]. It is of note that the effects of antipsychotic treatment were considered a confounder at this stage, for the scarcity of evidence related to a definite activity on mental state attribution abilities.

A further hypothesis was that poor mental state attribution could undermine problem solving attitudes, hampering patients' social skills. This assumption was supported for the alleged similarities between problem solving and Procedural Learning tasks [52]. It was also hypothesized, along with Brüne's position [50] that mental state attribution impairment and dysfunctional emotion perception were unrelated, due to the existence of dissimilar neural pathways differently impaired that underlies the dysfunction in the two constructs. Finally, it was tested how an impaired ToM might reduce patients' perception of their needs and of help received from formal or informal networks of care.

Methods

Participants

Twenty-one persons (14 males, 7 females) with a diagnosis of schizophrenia, according to DSM-IV-TR [163], who were receiving day-treatment at the local Community Mental Health Centre, were included in the study. All the participants furnished written informed consent, according to the latest version of the Declaration of Helsinki and to the local ethical committee guidelines. Nineteen participants were treated with second-generation antipsychotics (quetiapine, aripiprazole, risperidone and olanzapine) and two persons with first-generation antipsychotics (perphenazine and haloperidol).

Mean chlorpromazine, CPZ equivalents were 457.14±373.86 mg per day, calculated according to American Psychiatric Association guidelines [164] and to the rules provided by Woods [165]. Patients with a history of alcohol and substance abuse, mental retardation, head trauma and other neurological illnesses were excluded from the study.

Participants mean age at onset was 23.52 years (range 11-38 years, sd ± 5.58) and mean duration of the illness was 16.29 years (range 1-29, sd ± 9.01). The mean age at the time of the assessment was 39.81 (range 25-59, sd ± 8.43).

The participants have been confronted to an equal number of healthy controls with no history of psychiatric illness and no first-degree relatives with schizophrenia (9 males; 12 females, mean age 36.71 years; range 20-60, sd ±10.85), who were mainly students of psychology, their relatives and hospital staff. No difference between participants and controls were observed between age ($t=-1.033$; $p= 0.308$), and sex ($\chi^2=1.538$; $p=0.215$).

Socio-demographic and psychopathological characteristics of the sample, including scores at the outcome measures, are better described in Table 3.

Neurocognitive Tasks

To assess mean intelligence level, IQ we used a combination of Wilson's [166] Rapid Approximate Intelligence Test, consisting in a multiplication task, and Kent's Intelligence Test [167], involving higher verbal and thought problem-solving capacities. Scoring rules are those reported by Othmer and Othmer [168]. Executive functioning were assessed by Wisconsin Card Sorting Test, WCST [169], administered with standard instructions as described by Spreen and Strauss [170], whereas scoring followed Heaton's rules [171], while planning skills were assessed with Tower of London test [172]. Scoring and administration of Tower of London were those described by Krikorian et al. [173]. Verbal memory estimation took place with the Verbal Memory test [174].

Table 3. Demographic characteristics for participants to the study and healthy controls, including comparison of intelligence and education level (IQ>95 in *italics*)

	Participants	Controls	*P*
n.	21 *(11)*	21	
Sex ratio (M:F)	14:7 *(9:2)*	9:12	
Years of education	10.67±3.02 *(10.45±3.05)*	13.14±3.53	0.019 *(0.040)*
IQ (Kent + Wilson score)	94.57±19.34 *(110±11.62)*	122.14±2.54	<0.0001 *(<0.0001)*
GAF score	49.00±16.86 *(57.55±13.03)*		*(0.575, n.s.)*
BPRS total score	44.48±11.51 *(42.55±18.08)*		*(0.142, n.s.)*
BPRS Disorganization score	5.90±2.41 *(5.18±1.17)*		*(0.020)*
BPRS Elevated Affect score	5.10±1.26 *(5.55±1.44)*		*(0.045)*
BPRS Negative Affect score	13.38±4.58 *(12.09±3.51)*		*(0.302, n.s.)*
BPRS Negative Symptoms score	6.43±3.96 *(5.64±3.04)*		*(0.960, n.s.)*
BPRS Positive Symptoms score	10.29±5.51 *(10.09±4.70)*		*(0.345, n.s.)*
HoNOS Roma, total score	18.48±9.26 *(17.36±8.18)*		*(0.291, n.s.)*
Camberwell 1, unmet needs score	9.33±5.30 *(7.82±3.66)*		*(0.255, n.s.)*
Camberwell 2, informal help score	6.81±3.84 *(5.18±3.71)*		*(0.042)*
Camberwell 3, institutional help score	10.86±6.57 *(6.00±3.49)*		*(0.002)*

Mental State Attribution and Social Cognition Tasks

Mental state attribution was estimated with a combination of four verbal ToM stories and a picture sequencing task. The ToM stories task examined the ability to understand first- and second-order false belief. First-order ToM stories, requiring a subject to make an inference about the state of the world, were the Sally-Anna story [175] and the Cigarettes story [176].

Second-order ToM stories, testing the ability to understand a false belief about a belief of another character, were the Ice-Cream Van story [177] and the Burglar story [178]. The stories were read to the subjects who were shown a series of cartoon drawings presenting the action sequences of the stories. Scoring was performed according to Mazza et al.'s [47] rules, involving a first, ToM question, concerning the false belief of a character, and a second, control question, reflecting the subject's comprehension of the stories. A correct answer to both ToM and control question was rated 1, while a wrong or incomplete answer was rated 0.

The picture sequencing task was inspired by Brüne's [12], [50] picture stories, and consisted of four cartoon-picture stories depicting, in the paper and pencil fashion, (i) one scenario describing a state of the world; (ii) one scenario showing cooperation of two characters; (iii) one scenario illustrating deliberate deception of one character by another, and (iv) one scenario showing two characters cooperating at the cost of a third one. Similarly to Brüne's [50] rules, each picture story consisted of four cards, presented in a jumbled order, and the participants were asked to order the cards in a logical sequence of events. Rating included two points given for the first and the last correctly sequenced card, and one point each for correct sequencing of the two middle cards (6 points maximum per picture story, with maximum sum 24 pts). Differently from Brüne's [50] rules, mental state questions about the picture sequencing task were not provided, and the sequencing was simply rated as accomplished by participants by summing the score to the points obtained by answering to verbal ToM stories. A total score of maximum 28 pts was therefore obtained, for first-, second-order ToM stories and picture sequencing task.

Empathy and emotion recognition were then assessed to measure broader social-cognitive capacities of participants. The Faux Pas, FP test measures the ability to empathize. In the FP task, the participants were read a story to ascertain a mental representation that the persons saying something were unaware of they should not say it, and another that the person hearing would feel insulted or hurt, and then heard a series of six questions, the first three used to determine the ability to recognize a Faux Pas, the latter three to examine individual cognitive and empathic components of the task. The first three questions were rates as the ToM stories. FP questions 4 and 5, testing the mental understanding of the listener and the speaker, were rated 0 if both failed, 1 if one question was correctly answered, and 2 if they both were correct. For question 6, specifically testing the ability to empathize, the participants received a score of 0, fail, and 1, pass [128].

Emotion recognition was assessed through a face recognition test developed and rearranged from a similar child psychology task studying affect recognition in autistic children [179], involving recognition of the face emotions in four different groups of figures representing the emotions of happiness, fear, anger and sadness with increasing levels of complexity: (1) four schematic faces through right or curved lines corresponding to the essential traits of a face; (2) four hand-made pictures, "emoticons" representing non-schematic faces; (3) five pictures representing a cartoon character; (4) seven human faces, taken from Ekman and Friesen's [180] Pictures of Facial Affect. For each series of faces, an answer sheet with all the possible choices was continuously presented, to make the participants' choice unambiguous. Scoring was obtained by rating 1 for each face correctly recognised and 0 for wrong or ambiguous recognition, with a maximum of 20 pts.

Psychopathological, Behavioural and Functional Outcome Measures

Psychopathology was assessed by Brief Psychiatric Rating Scale, BPRS version 4.0 [181-182] translated into Italian by Morosini and Casacchia [183]. To ascertain the relation of symptom cluster with ToM performance in schizophrenia, BPRS scores were grouped in the five-factor model of Roncone et al. [184]: Disorganised, Negative Affect, Positive Symptoms, Elevated Affect, and Negative Symptoms.

The participants' attitude to Problem-solving skills was assessed with the Problem Solving Inventory, PSI [185]. This is a 35-item instrument measuring how individuals react to personal problems of their daily lives, consisting of three sub-scales: PSI A, *"Confidence in Problem-Solving"*, PSI B, *"Approach-Avoidance Style related to Problem-Solving Activities"*, and PSI C, *"Degree of Personal Control of Emotions and Behaviours while engaging in Problem-Solving Activities"*. Low scores indicate a positive view of problem-solving skills.

Participants' perception of the needs of care was assessed with Camberwell Assessment of Needs, CAN [186-187], obtaining three different sub-scores for (1) the total number of unmet needs of the participants; (2) the informal help received by significant others; (3) the institutional help of the mental health services and the other health care providers.

A revision of participants' status was attained by Health of the Nation Outcome Scale, HoNOS [188], in its Italian version, HoNOS Roma [189], a functional outcome measure also taking into account caregiver distress.

The evaluation of global functioning was achieved by Global Assessment of Functioning scale, GAF, corresponding to DSM-IV-TR, axis V [163].

All social cognition, psychopathology and behavioural measures were rated blind to the participants' performance on neuropsychological and mental state attribution tasks. Statistical analyses were performed with SPSS 13.0 for Windows.

Results

Between-Group Differences

Student *t* test was used to calculate group differences for all the normally distributed variables, while Mann-Whitney-*U* non-parametric test was used for determining between-group differences for variables with large differences in between-group variance. In spite of the relatively normal IQ level of the participants, significant IQ differences were observed between participants and controls (t=6.478; p<0.0001). Participants also significantly differed from controls for years of education (t=2.444; p=0.019). As expected, there were significant difference between groups in executive functioning, problem solving attitudes, mental state attribution tasks, emotion recognition and empathic competences (Table 4). Persons with schizophrenia were also significantly more impaired in action planning, as measured using the Tower of London test (t=7.228; p<0.0001). A subgroup (n=11) of persons with schizophrenia with an IQ above or equal to 95 pts (mean=110; sd ± 11.62) – still with a lower IQ (t=4.647; p<0.0001) and fewer years of education than controls (t=2.141; p=0.040), but showing no significant age differences between schizophrenia patients (mean age 41.36 yrs.; sd ± 9.72) and controls (mean age 36.71; sd ± 10.85; t=-1-192; p=0.243) – even made poorer performance in PSI A, *"Confidence in Problem-Solving"*, PSI B, *"Approach Avoidant style related to Problem-Solving activities"*, mental state attribution, empathy, emotion recognition and perseverative errors at WCST. The group differences disappeared, however, with respect to PSI C, *"Degree of Personal Control of Emotions and Behaviours while engaging in Problem-Solving activities"*, and statistical significance was only marginally reached for the number of total errors at WCST. Significant differences between the low and the high IQ group emerged between BPRS Disorganisation (t=1.487; p=0.020), and Elevated Affect symptoms cluster (t=-1.811; p=0.045), and were also observed in CAN 2, informal help (t=1.367; p=0.042) and CAN 3, help from institutions scores (t=3.808; p=0.002). No differences emerged for the other BPRS or behavioural measures. Means and p-values for the high IQ subgroup are shown in italics in round brackets in Tables 3 and 4.

Table 4. Non-parametric Mann-Whitney between-group comparison outlining the performance of participants and controls in problem-solving, executive functioning and mental state attribution task (IQ≥95 in *italics*)

Item	Mean rank		Mann-Whitney-U	P
	Participants	Healthy Controls		
PSI A	13.33 *(10.97)*	29.07 *(26.40)*	61.500 *(33.500)*	<0.0001 *(<0.0001)*
PSI B	14.24 *(11.50)*	28.76 *(25.98)*	68.000 *(42.500)*	<0.0001 *(<0.0001)*
PSI C	16.60 *(16.48)*	26.40 *(23.24)*	117.500 *(115.000)*	0.009 *(0.064)*
Verbal memory	12.62 *(10.91)*	30.38 *(26.45)*	34.000 *(32.500)*	<0.0001 *(<0.0001)*
ToM 1st Order	17.52 *(15.47)*	25.48 *(22.76)*	137.000 *(110.000)*	0.013 *(0.045)*
ToM 2nd Order	14.53 *(12.97)*	28.07 *(24.79)*	82.500 *(67.500)*	<0.0001 *(<0.0001)*
ToM Stories total score	14.90 *(12.76)*	28.10 *(24.55)*	82.000 *(64.000)*	<0.0001 *(<0.0001)*
ToM Sequence	12.14 *(20.35)*	30.86 *(26.90)*	24.000 *(23.000)*	<0.0001 *(<0.0001)*
WCST general errors	25.45 *(22.76)*	17.55 *(16.86)*	137.500 *(123.000)*	0.036 *(0.107, n.s.)*
WCST perseverative errors	2.68 *(2.55)*	1.61 *(1.46)*	108.500 *(76.500)*	0.003 *(0.002)*
Empathy (Faux Pas)	13.07 *(11.44)*	31.83 *(26.02)*	43.500 *(41.500)*	<0.0001 *(<0.0001)*
Emotion Recognition total score	11.17 *(9.21)*	31.83 *(27.83)*	3.500 *(3.000)*	<0.0001 *(<0.0001)*
Mental states total score	11.76 *(9.91)*	31.24 *(27.76)*	16.000 *(15.500)*	<0.0001 *(<0.0001)*

PSI A=Problem Solving Inventory, Factor A, "*Confidence in Problem-Solving*" score; PSI B=Problem Solving Inventory, Factor B, "*Approach Avoidant style to Problem-Solving Activities*" score; PSI C=Problem Solving Inventory, Factor C, "*Degree of Personal Control of Behaviour and Emotions while engaging in Problem-Solving Activities*" score; Mental states total score=total score of ToM stories (1st + 2nd Order) and ToM Sequencing, max 28 pts; Emotion Recognition total score=total score of schematic faces, emoticons, cartoons and human faces recognition, max 20 pts.

Correlations within the Participants Group

Pearson's correlation coefficients were calculated, since skewness and kurtosis of the variables were within an adequate range. IQ was positively correlated with mental states and Tower of London, while mental states total score had a relevant, positive correlation with GAF, that was not statistically significant in the high IQ group. For this group, it is worth mentioning the very strong positive correlation of IQ with mean drug dosage and PSI A, *"Confidence in Problem-Solving"*. Due to the participants' relevant length of illness, partial correlations were calculated. After partialling out duration of illness, the correlation between IQ and drug dosage remained strong (r=0.774; p=0.009), while after ruling out intelligence, partial correlation between medication and length of illness lost its significance (r=0.103, p=0.665, n.s.).

The association between mental states total score and GAF lost significance after partialling out the duration of illness (r=0.500; p=0.141, n.s.), but still was statistically significant when intelligence was ruled out (r=0.460; p=0.034), evidencing the length of illness as a confounder. No statistically significant correlations were observed between IQ, WCST total and perseverative errors and Faux Pas scores.

Other, very strong positive correlations were observed between mental states total score and Tower of London, with variance increasing when IQ was above 95. Mental states had strong, positive correlation with Emotion recognition with increasing variance in the high IQ group, while correlation of mental state attribution with HoNOS Roma outcome scores was inverse and only significant in the high IQ group. All these correlations remained strong and stable in high IQ group after ruling out the duration of illness: mental states total score vs. Tower of London: r=0.682; p=0.030; mental states total score vs. Emotion recognition total score: r=0.606; p=0.031; mental states total score vs. HoNOS Roma total score: r=-0.539; p=0.035. On the other hand, when IQ was partialled out, the relationship between mental states and Tower of London remained significant (r=0.505; p=0.023), and the same was for the correlation between mental states and Emotion recognition (r=0.390, p=0.045), while the association between mental states and HoNOS Roma lost significance (r=-0.312, p=0.180, n.s.).

Faux Pas was inversely correlated with HoNOS Roma outcome score; WCST total errors had a strong, positive correlation with Tower of London; the variance increased in the high IQ group, and after partialling out the length of illness (r=0.691; p=0.027). GAF score was positively correlated with Emotion recognition, with statistical significance disappearing in the high IQ group, and was negatively correlated with HoNOS Roma score. In the latter correlation, variance increased when IQ was above 95, and remained stable after ruling out the duration of illness (r=-0.794; p=0.006). Verbal memory had only a significant direct correlation with Emotion recognition, with a loss of significance in the high IQ group. All these correlations support the relationship between disruption of social cognition capacities and poor functional outcome.

For psychopathology measures, although BPRS sub-scores showed multiple correlations with GAF and the other functional outcome measures, no statistically significant correlations were observed between BPRS Disorganisation, mentalising abilities and executive functions. BPRS Negative Affect had inverse correlations with PSI A, *"Confidence in Problem-Solving"*. On the other hand, in the high IQ group, a very strong, positive correlation was noticed between BPRS Positive Symptoms and PSI C, *"Degree of Personal Control of Emotions and Behaviours while engaging in Problem-Solving Activities"*.

BPRS Negative Symptoms had inverse correlations with mental states total score, WCST total score, Emotion recognition total score, GAF score, and a positive correlation with HoNOS Roma total score, whose variance increased in the high IQ group. Correlation between BPRS Negative Symptoms and Tower of London was inverse and statistically significant for high IQ group. After ruling out years of illness, partial correlations between BPRS Negative Symptoms and mental states total score became positive, (r=0.790; p=0.007), while the association between BPRS Negative Symptoms and HoNOS Roma total score (r=0.710; p=0.021) remained significant. Poor mentalising capacities are associated to psychopathology, as well as functional outcome is. No statistically significant correlations have been observed between mental states attribution and CAN sub-scores, with no evidence of association between mentalising capacities and participants' perception of their needs.

More details for correlations within participants are observed in Table 5.

Regression Analyses

In the light of the multiple correlations with GAF, we sought to evidence which of the variables would best predict functional outcome of the participants. For this reason, we performed a stepwise linear regression analysis with GAF score as the dependent variable and total score of mental states, emotion recognition, mean daily drug dosage, scores at Faux Pas test, verbal memory and HoNOS Roma and IQ level as independent variables. Mental state attribution entered the equation first, with an R^2 value of 0.334 (adjusted R^2 as a more careful estimate was 0.249), showing that, conservatively estimated, at least a quarter of the variance of the GAF score could be accounted for by mentalising abilities alone (F(1,19)=8.670; p=0.002). Unexpectedly, the mean daily drug dosage was included, adding a further 15.9% of the variance to the model. Emotion recognition and faux pas score were excluded in the first step (Emotion recognition: Beta in: 0.228; t=-1.079; p=0.299; faux pas: Beta in: 0.266, t=1.368; p=0.188), intelligence level in the second (Beta in: 0.182; t=0.933; p=0.365). More surprisingly, after regressing the same set of variables to the duration of the illness, scores at Faux Pas test remained the only significant predictor, explaining near 50% of the variance (R^2 =0.486; adjusted R^2 =0.429; F(1,9)=8.515; p=0.017), with the exclusion of mental states (Beta in: 0.153; t=0.515; p=0.620) and mean daily drug dosage (Beta in: -0.299; t=-1-185; p=0.270).

The regression model is shown in Figure 2.

Antipsychotics Effectively Predict the Functional Outcome of Persons with Schizophrenia

The most relevant finding presented in this chapter is that, in addition to mental state attribution impairments, the mean daily drug dosage contributes to predict the global functional outcome of the participants, with both variables explaining more than 40% of the overall variance. This result was unexpected and in contrast with the studies of Sarfati et al. [140], Herbener et al. [11], and, most of all, Brüne et al. [12], that found no evidence of relationship between antipsychotics as a class and impairment in social cognition. It is also noteworthy that Sergi et al. [23] did not find an association of single antipsychotics to broad social cognitive indices. Considering, on the other hand, the studies that have found an association between single APs and social cognition measures, Mazza et al. [147] first discovered that risperidone improved attention, memory and ToM capacity, Mizrahi et al. [149] demonstrated that ToM performance improved after 6 weeks of therapy with SGAs, especially after the first two weeks, and Savina and Beninger [148] found that patients on olanzapine and clozapine had a performance similar to controls on ToM tasks, while the scores of participants on typical and risperidone were poorer.

In the first study, the adjunct of donepezil, an acetylcholinesterase inhibitor directly acting on neuropsychological functions, might have contributed to ToM improvement, in the second research the improvement was noticed in "physically-based" first order ToM tasks, while in the third study the overall performance of the patients was poorer than controls in all the ToM tasks and there was no confrontation with other social cognitive or neuropsychological variables. In any case, the results of the present research may add to Mazza et al.'s [147], Mizrahi et al.'s [149] and Savina and Beninger's [148] to demonstrate that, not only ToM improves with antipsychotic treatment, but it may also influence the functional outcome of schizophrenic people. Besides, a further issue of interest is the comparison with Shamay-Tsoory et al.'s study [122], in which participants on SGAs achieved a better performance on the "affective" component of ToM, that is related to empathic capacities.

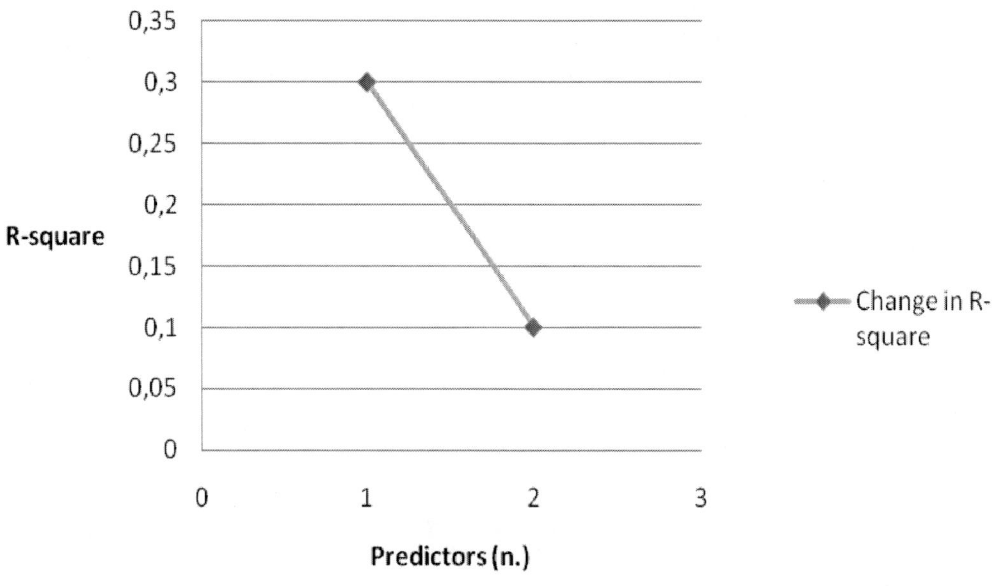

Figure 2. The regression model exploring predictors of functional outcome and duration of the illness of the participants to the study.
Linear regression on GAF score indicating modification in variance amount operated by each single predictor entering the model Predictors of GAF score: 1. Mental state attribution: Adj-R^2=0.249; p=0.002; 2. mean daily drug dosage: Adj-R^2=0.159; p=0.029.
Predictors of years of illness: 1. Faux pas test scores: Adj-R^2=0.486; p=0.017; Excluded variables: mean daily drug dosage: βIn: -0.299; t=-1.185; p=0.270, n.s.; Mental state attribution: βIn:0.153; t=0.515; p=0.620, n.s.

Table 5. Correlations of participants' psychopathological and behavioural measures with problem-solving, executive functioning, social perception, and social cognition indices (IQ≥95 group in *italics*)

(A)

	BPRS Tot	BPRS Diso	BPRS Ea	BPRS Na	BPRS Ns	BPRS Ps	CAN 1	CAN 2	CAN 3	mgEq CLZ/day
BPRS Tot		0.741** *(0.359)*	0.157 *(0.385)*	0.868** *(0.754**)*	0.357 *(0.225)*	0.746** *(0.652*)*	**0.561*** *(-0.071)*	0.095 *(-0.124)*	**0.558**** *(-0.245)*	0.227 *(-0.246)*
BPRS Diso			0.020 *(-0.303)*	0.671** *(0.069)*	0.367 *(0.330)*	0.349 *(0.051)*	0.355 *(-0.202)*	-0.062 *(-0.355)*	**0.477**** *(-0.417)*	0.255 *(0.451)*
BPRS Ea				0.080 *(0.227)*	-0.269 *(-0.270)*	0.253 *(0.450)*	-0.274 *(-0.321)*	-0.404 *(-0.357)*	-0.310 *(-0.338)*	-0.417 *(-0.357)*
BPRS Na					0.148 *(-0.006)*	0.614** *(0.424)*	**0.586**** *(0.431)*	0.193 *(0.391)*	**0.528**** *(0.106)*	0.092 *(-0.457)*
BPRS Ns						-0.130 *(-0.473)*	0.081 *(-0.456)*	0.116 *(-0.047)*	0.167 *(-0.489)*	0.170 *(-0.301)*
BPRS Ps							**0.643**** *(0.170)*	0.200 *(-0.116)*	**0.560**** *(0.250)*	0.418 *(0.091)*
CAN 1								0.678** *(0.666*)*	0.805** *(0.736**)*	**0.578**** *(-0.031)*
CAN 2									0.470* *(0.756**)*	0.396 *(-0.212)*
CAN 3										**0.530*** *(0.077)*
mgEq CLZ/day										
PSI A										
PSI B										
PSI C										
Men tot										
Empathy (Faux pas)										
WCST Tot										
WCST Pers										

Table 5A (Continued)

	BPRS Tot	BPRS Diso	BPRS Ea	BPRS Na	BPRS Ns	BPRS Ps	CAN 1	CAN 2	CAN 3	mgEq CLZ/day
GAF										
Verbal Memory										
ToL										
Ertot										
KW										
HoNOS Roma tot										

* Correlation is significant at the 0.05 level (two-tailed)

** Correlation is significant at the 0.01 level (two-tailed)

BPRS Tot = BPRS, Total score; **BPRS Diso** = BPRS Disorganization cluster; **BPRS Ea** = BPRS Elevated Affect cluster; **BPRS Na** = BPRS Negative Affect cluster; **BPRS Ns** = BPRS Negative Symptoms cluster; **BPRS Ps** = BPRS Positive Symptoms cluster (Roncone et al., 1999, 2002); **CAN 1** = Camberwell Assessment of Needs, Total Needs score; **CAN 2** = Camberwell Assessment of Needs, Informal Help score; **CAN 3** = Camberwell Assessment of Needs, Help from Institutions score (Phelan et al., 1995; Ruggeri et al., 1999).

(B)

	PSI A	PSI B	PSI C	Men tot	Empathy (Faux pas)	WCST tot	WCST pers	GAF	Verbal memory	ToL	Er tot	KW	HoNOS Roma tot
BPRS Tot	-0.329 *(-0.062)*	-0.069 *(-0.227)*	0.207 *(0.252)*	-0.082 *(-0.102)*	**-0.446**** *(-0.070)*	-0.024 *(-0.522)*	-0.465 *(-0.306)*	**-0.581**** *(-0.264)*	-0.029 *(0.031)*	0.159 *(-0.322)*	-0.214 *(-0.149)*	-0.145 *(-0.218)*	**0.522*** *(0.319)*
BPRS Diso	0.019 ***(0.624*)***	0.171 ***(0.632*)***	0.242 *(-0.253)*	-0.361 *(-0.507)*	-0.369 *(0.083)*	0.136 *(-0.128)*	-0.200 *(0.099)*	**-0.653**** *(-0.500)*	-0.378 *(-0.179)*	0.072 *(-0.366)*	-0.171 *(-0.149)*	-0.232 *(0.258)*	0.393 *(0.181)*
BPRS Ea	0.118 *(-0.317)*	-0.425 *(-0.596)*	0.137 *(0.457)*	0.234 *(0.395)*	-0.148 *(-0.243)*	0.001 *(-0.197)*	-0.200 *(-0.027)*	0.303 *(0.356)*	0.128 *(-0.102)*	0.360 *(0.356)*	0.416 *(-0.469)*	0.317 *(-0.120)*	-0.158 *(-0.180)*
BPRS Na	**-0.441*** *(-0.366)*	-0.103 *(-0.103)*	0.111 *(-0.042)*	-0.040 *(-0.015)*	-0.294 *(0.085)*	0.196 *(-0.231)*	-0.393 *(-0.283)*	-0.393 *(0.227)*	-0.179 *(-0.108)*	0.151 *(-0.215)*	-0.073 *(-0.244)*	-0.345 *(-0.442)*	0.432 *(0.044)*
BPRS Ns	-0.130 *(-0.149)*	-0.218 *(0.288)*	0.096 *(-0.527)*	**-0.528*** ***(-0.809**)***	-0.337 *(-0.134)*	**-0.567**** *(-0.521)*	-0.305 *(-0.188)*	**-0.622**** ***(-0.608*)***	-0.418 *(0.047)*	-0.293 ***(-0.834*)***	**-0.635**** ***(-0.657**)***	-0.267 *(-0.481)*	**0.518*** ***(0.709*)***
BPRS Ps	-0.331 *(0.196)*	-0.336 *(-0.519)*	0.198 ***(0.825**)***	0.323 *(0.590)*	-0.184 *(0.018)*	0.126 *(-0.173)*	-0.282 *(-0.198)*	0.231 *(0.024)*	-0.051 *(0.157)*	0.427 *(0.296)*	0.071 *(0.395)*	0.164 *(0.330)*	0.129 *(-0.209)*

	PSI A	PSI B	PSI C	Men tot	Empathy (Faux pas)	WCST tot	WCST pers	GAF	Verbal memory	ToL	Er tot	KW	HoNOS Roma tot
CAN 1	**-0.559**** *(-0.223)*	-0.096 *(-0.051)*	0.088 *(0.059)*	0.004 *(0.360)*	-0.090 *(0.422)*	0.185 *(0.466)*	-0.259 *(-0.169)*	-0.257 *(0.448)*	-0.280 *(0.273)*	0.068 *(0.158)*	-0.166 *(0.029)*	-0.130 *(-0.022)*	0.210 *(-0.429)*
CAN 2	**-0.596**** *(-0.386)*	-0.221 *(0.045)*	-0.097 *(-0.211)*	-0.014 *(0.166)*	0.142 *(0.122)*	-0.258 *(-0.040)*	-0.032 *(-0.303)*	0.106 *(0.513)*	-0.387 *(-0.130)*	-0.182 *(-0.156)*	-0.090 *(-0.446)*	-0.220 *(-0.336)*	0.119 *(-0.355)*
CAN 3	-0.402 *(-0.063)*	0.004 *(-0.182)*	0.317 *(0.337)*	-0.248 *(0.554)*	-0.293 *(0.082)*	-0.137 *(0.164)*	-0.217 *(-0.105)*	**-0.529*** *(0.431)*	**-0.464*** *(0.064)*	0.018 *(0.252)*	-0.364 *(0.063)*	**-0.471*** *(0.111)*	0.131 *(-0.529)*
mgEq CLZ/day	-0.056 ***(0.855**)***	0.235 *(0.311)*	0.230 *(0.067)*	0.007 *(0.207)*	-0.018 *(0.442)*	0.023 *(0.466)*	-0.236 *(-0.169)*	-0.395 *(0.448)*	-0.361 *(0.273)*	0.130 *(0.158)*	-0.290 *(-0.014)*	0.071 ***(0.777**)***	0.138 *(-0.360)*
PSI A		0.421 *(0.413)*	0.238 *(0.136)*	0.003 *(-0.066)*	0.101 *(0.181)*	-0.009 *(-0.057)*	0.334 *(0.298)*	0.057 *(-0.407)*	0.082 *(-0.179)*	-0.059 *(-0.033)*	0.050 *(-0.061)*	0.281 ***(0.620*)***	-0.322 *(-0.108)*
PSI B			-0.121 *(-0.703*)*	-0.352 ***(-0.642*)***	-0.252 *(-0.027)*	0.111 *(0.158)*	0.103 *(0.442)*	-0.240 *(-0.175)*	-0.268 *(-0.491)*	-0.217 *(-0.253)*	**-0.522*** *(-0.591)*	-0.004 *(0.091)*	-0.078 *(-0.087)*
PSI C				-0.183 ***(0.708*)***	-0.366 *(-0.137)*	-0.030 *(-0.079)*	-0.107 *(-0.033)*	**-0.439*** *(0.032)*	-0.128 *(0.303)*	0.061 *(0.458)*	0.032 *(0.647*)*	-0.275 *(0.367)*	0.119 *(-0.276)*
Mental States					0.333 *(0.170)*	0.245 *(0.303)*	-0.145 *(-0.290)*	**0.578**** *(0.572)*	0.389 *(0.214)*	**0.620*** ***(0.788*)***	**0.471*** ***(0.611*)***	**0.503*** *(0.472)*	-0.339 ***(-0.668*)***
Empathy (Faux pas)						0.115 *(0.340)*	0.033 *(-0.481)*	0.428 *(-0.005)*	0.345 *(0.542)*	-0.082 *(-0.162)*	0.218 *(-0.043)*	0.149 *(0.246)*	**-0.453*** *(-0.133)*
WCST Tot							0.001 *(0.140)*	0.034 *(0.280)*	0.406 *(0.311)*	**0.492*** ***(0.642*)***	0.389 *(0.473)*	0.076 *(0.493)*	-0.110 *(-0.257)*
WCST Pers								0.345 *(-0.015)*	-0.079 *(-0.489)*	-0.095 *(0.221)*	0.391 *(0.161)*	0.026 *(-0.016)*	-0.262 *(-0.041)*
GAF									0.255 *(-0.349)*	0.159 (0.518)	**0.450*** *(0.103)*	0.399 *(-0.106)*	**-0.558**** ***(-0.806*)***
Verbal memory										0.057 *(-0.041)*	**0.515*** *(0.385)*	0.342 *(0.177)*	0.027 *(0.274)*
ToL											0.373 ***(0.767**)***	**0.462*** *(0.569)*	-0.190 *(-0.506)*
ER tot												0.300 *(0.404)*	-0.001 *(-0.087)*
KW													-0.143 *(-0.274)*
HoNOS Roma tot													

PSI A = Problem Solving Inventory, Factor A, "*Confidence in Problem-Solving*"; **PSI B** = Problem Solving Inventory, Factor B, "*Approach Avoidant Style to Problem-Solving Activities*"; **PSI C** = Problem Solving Inventory, Factor C, "*Degree of Personal Control of Behaviour and Emotions while engaging in Problem-Solving Activities*" (Heppner, 1988); **Men tot** = Mental states, total score; **WCST Tot** = WCST Total score; **WCST pers** = WCST perseverative errors score; **ToL** = Tower of London planning time (s); **Er tot** = Emotion recognition total score; **HoNOS Roma tot** = HoNOS Roma total score (Morosini et al., 2003); **KW**= IQ as measured with Kent's Intelligence Test (Kent, 1946) + Rapid Approximate Intelligence Test (Wilson, 1967).

Although this chapter's results provided no differentiation of SGAs and FGAs activity on ToM, they also showed another relevant finding: poor empathy can predict the duration of illness in the participants. In this context, two functional brain imaging studies using ToM tasks [190-191] established a relation between reduced activation of insula, medial prefrontal cortex, or temporal gyrus and poor performance at ToM and empathy tasks in schizophrenic persons. In the first study, [190] the authors propose how underactivation of insular region might reflect a lack of empathic involvement, that would in turn explain the difficulties of schizophrenic patients in judging a scenario fair or unfair. In the latter [191], a reduced activation in an empathy tasks was noticed in right posterior and superior temporal gyrus, whose grey matter volume was lower than controls and inversely correlated with the duration of the illness. Taken together, these findings would propose a physiological explanation of empathy's predictive role of the course of the disease in our participants and of how antipsychotic treatment might in some way influence or remediate the poor empathic capacities of schizophrenic persons.

A possible explanation of the results evidenced in this chapter might rely on the research hypotheses proposing that dopaminergic transmission - crucial in signalling predictions about consequences of future events and regulating the update of short-term contextual representations in response to externally or internally generated information - might have represented a natural evolutionary mechanism of ToM abilities [8], [86-87]. Increased levels of dopamine facilitate the origin of psychotic symptoms by interfering with the capacity to attribute an adequate relevance to external entities and internal symbols. The modulating effect of serotonin system on the dopamine transmission may adequately represent the biological substrate of mental state attribution [87], [127]. For this reason, atypical antipsychotics, assumed by the majority of our participants, with their dual activity on dopamine and serotonin receptors, other than improving cognitive functions, may restore the 'lost' ToM abilities [86]. As antipsychotics improve Procedural Learning tasks according to their degree of striatal D_2-receptor occupancy [52], the dopamine system might modulate both the related constructs of problem-solving and ToM. After considering the putative activity of the newly social cognition-related neurotransmitters, such as oxytocin and arginine vasopressin, AVP [107-108], [125], it is conceivable that they both could affect dopamine mesocorticolimbic transmission, contributing to its dysregulation and to the induction of abnormally modulated emotionally-salient representations. To sustain the better results of SGAs with respect to FGAs on ToM remediation, it is also possible to speculate that at least some of them might influence the D_1 versus D_2 dopamine receptor activity and, most of all, the dopamine D_4 towards D_1 transmission, especially modulating emotional learning and memory [83], [97].

Apart from drug-related results, the evidence in this chapter confirm previous findings outlining mental state attribution impairment as a strong predictor of poor social functioning in persons with schizophrenia [12], [48]. This chapter's data also outline the "selectivity" of ToM deficits, that is they are independent from intelligence level. To explain this, it must be made a reference to a core, central problem in neural sciences, the concept of domain specificity in mental and ontogenetic processes [192]. If ToM construct is considered as an innate, domain specific cognitive module, with a distinct neuroanatomical location, according to Fodor's [193] concept, in severe mental diseases mental state attribution performances should remain intact or become impaired regardless of severe intellectual damage [194]. The disruption of mental state attribution competence in schizophrenic persons should be therefore attributable to the impairment of a selected neural network [47]. To confirm these results, in the correlation analysis, the loss of significance between mental states and GAF score after controlling for the years elapsed from disease onset indicates how the relevant duration of the illness in the participants might have hampered their overall performance more than IQ, thus emerging as the only confound [48].

The strong association between ToM and Emotion recognition is a finding in contrast with previous studies that postulated their mutual independence [50]. The more skilled are our participants in ToM abilities, the more they are able to recognize other people's emotions. An evolutionary perspective might help in interpreting these results. In ontogenesis, the origin of ToM abilities involves that simple, non-verbal inputs, such as facial mimics, posture, gesture, and tune of voice were progressively decoded and transformed into more complex stimuli aimed at recognizing emotions and understanding complex social interactions [181], [195]. The behavioural deficits of schizophrenic persons might have developed in a hierarchically stepwise fashion that, in agreement with the Edelman model [196-197], hinders the integrity of the final output by interrupting the sequence of reasoning, actions and events needed to plan and accomplish tasks. In the negative symptom schizophrenia, that appeared early in the phylogenesis, the behavioural deficits might correspond to a premature damage of the modular neural networks, preventing persons from using fundamental functions like emotion recognition. In the positive symptoms psychoses, that developed later in evolutionary terms, the behavioural deficit would be located further down the neural network, precluding patients from performing more complex forms of reasoning, such as understanding other peoples' intentions and beliefs [70], [198]. The absence of correlations between faux pas and ToM scores might, on the other hand, support the different anatomical localization of "hot" empathic and "cold" cognitive ToM [122]. Such a functional model would account for the impairment in the integration of emotions with mental state attributions observed in schizophrenia [154].

The impairment in social cognition did not appear correlated to patients' perception of their needs. Although participants with higher IQ seemed more aware of the need for help from informal or institutional networks, neither there was found any correlation between ToM or social cognition impairment with participants' perception of their needs or of the necessity of institutional help, nor CAN subscores entered the regression model. To explain this, some studies highlighted how the unmet needs of schizophrenic persons are more associated to practical factors outside the individual control, such as financial means, personal resources or psychiatric services availability, than to the impaired ability of mentalising [19], [199].

From a clinical perspective, this chapter's data emphasize how the combination of antipsychotics, psychopathology and social cognition may induce an adaptation of our participants to environmental stimuli and requests. Although there were not found statistically significant correlations between ToM and problem solving indices, the participants' attitude to problem solving skills was associated to positive symptoms and negative affectivity. These results are very similar to studies evidencing a relationship between positive and negative BPRS items and problem-solving skills, explained by the mean drug dosage [64]. The strong association between intelligence and medication dosage in the participants should confirm this hypothesis. As problem solving tasks rely on ToM [200], this chapter's findings support the relationship between ToM and antipsychotics and indicate how medication can help our participants in finding the right way to solve problems and consequently adapt to the environment.

Further support for the activity of APs in sustaining the functional outcome of schizophrenic persons is provided by unstructured observations linking the action of a combination of SGAs to improved social competence in a group of persons affected by psychotic symptoms for a long term.

ANTIPSYCHOTIC DRUGS, THEORY OF MIND AND OUTCOME

In the light of the current debate on which kind of antipsychotics – typicals vs. atypicals – best provide advances for treatment, the current indications outlined how the overall effect size of this class of drugs on neurocognition is scarce [33], [35]. Furthermore, social cognition measures still remain a weak predictor of outcome with a great amount of the variance left unexplained, compared to the long-term memory, working capacity, female sex and to living in a nonurban environment [22], [28]. The discovery of a small, but definite relation between antipsychotic treatment, social cognition indices and functional outcome in schizophrenic persons is therefore a remarkable issue, for the opportunity to utilize non-pharmacological psychosocial treatments involving social cognition, such as Cognitive Behavioural Therapy, Family Intervention Therapies, Cognitive Remediation Therapy, or Social Skills Training in support of drug therapy in treatment-resistant individuals [153]. In this view, evidence linking antipsychotic treatment to improvements in functional outcome of people affected with schizophrenia will be reviewed, to provide a comprehensive synopsis of data in support of the remediating action of this class of drugs.

Combination of Antipsychotics May Enhance Psychosocial Outcomes in Schizophrenia

All in all, the results of the two main studies on the clinical effectiveness of antipsychotics, the CATIE [26], [28], [40] and the CUtLASS trials [30] have evidenced that social cognitive indices, although weak, are a definite predictor of social functioning in persons affected with schizophrenia or other similar severe mental disorders. This chapter's results, although conducted on a small sample, are in line with the evidence of the abovementioned larger studies, because of the attribution of a limited, but significant proportion of the outcome variance to a combined index of mental state attribution capacity in the regression analysis. The superiority of antipsychotic treatment in reducing hospital stay of schizophrenic persons compared to psychotherapy alone, placebo or electroconvulsive therapy has been documented since the second half of the Twentieth Century [201], while the clinical effectiveness of APs in preventing relapses and in restoring social functioning has been ascertained as well, with a greater efficacy of some SGAs compared to FGAs [27], [202]. Antipsychotic drugs, in particular SGAs, are not, however an homogeneous class, and this implicates the need of an individualized treatment plan for the patients [203]. Other critical issues in the cognitive remediating activity of antipsychotics are the unexpected finding of improvements in cognition induced by a FGA, perphenazine in the CATIE study [26], and the results of another large study, the European First Episode Schizophrenia Trial, EUFEST [204], in which no differential cognitive advantages of SGAs with respect to FGAs

[154]. The statistically significant correlations between daily drug dosage, problem solving indices and a Theory of Mind measure supports, in this chapter, the possibility that antipsychotics, as a class, may become a mediator between basic neurobiological dysfunctions and social adaptation, as well as it has been proposed for the entire domain of social cognition [22-23], [160]. Interestingly, a mediating role on the severity of symptoms has been outlined for another subdomain of social cognition, the Reasoning Biases, because of the fact that reasoning processes ameliorate in response to the antipsychotic treatment [51]. If there is the possibility that antipsychotics may improve symptoms by modifying the processes of reasoning, pharmacological treatment might as well ameliorate social adaptation through the restoration of the "lost" Theory of Mind abilities [51], [86].

With respect to other social cognitive domains, an intact Theory of Mind may induce a more thorough adaptation to the social context because of the fact that the metacognitive abilities need a valid attitude to interpret other people's thoughts to deceive and manipulate them [7], [12], [68-70]. From these assumptions, it appears that Theory of Mind is a useful construct allowing to sustain the complex social interactions that are needed for the everyday life. If dopamine system activity is able to modulate Theory of Mind and Emotion Perception dysfunctions by acting on fronto-cortical dopaminergic pathways, it would be possible to assume that the drugs producing an effect on the dopamine receptors might influence the behavioural outcome [8], [86], [100], [122].

The results in this chapter, in this view, are similar to Bae et al.'s study [218] that, after using a complex data mining decision tree statistical algorithm, evidenced how social functioning of persons with schizophrenia might be influenced by social cognitive Theory of Mind abilities, the recognition of disgust - a negative emotion, the clinical symptoms, the capacity of insight and the kind of pharmacological treatment. Such a result would confirm that the pharmacological treatment may predict behavioural outcomes as well as clinical and social cognition indices. It is of note that the participants in this chapter, although with a higher duration of the illness, had a mean daily drug dose comparable to Bae et al.'s (457.14±373.86 mg equivalents of chlorpromazine per day vs. 457.76±256.37 mg equivalents per day). The relatively low dose of antipsychotics further supports the hypothesis attributing to the different degree of D_2 receptor occupancy the modulation of dopaminergic pathways involved in problem solving-related social cognition tasks [52], [64]. The theory of a differential modulation of serotonin on dopamine receptors function operated by the single antipsychotics to induce the enactment of social cognition activities [86], [127] would also be explained by the fact that, in this chapter, the participants were taking a combination of typical and atypical antipsychotics, while in Bae et al.'s study [218] all the enrolled subjects were administered only with atypicals. Interestingly, one of the participants in this chapter was on perphenazine, a typical AP whose neurocognitive remediating properties are slightly better than the majority of the older drugs [35-36].

Although conducted on a number (n=67) of participants allowing to achieve valid statistically significant results, Bae et al.'s study [218], however, was based on an uncommon statistical procedure relatively different from traditional methods emphasizing inference and estimation. It is therefore necessary to design studies on the functions of antipsychotics on the social competence of persons with schizophrenia that utilize statistical procedures allowing to obtain a proper estimate of the results and the identification of clinically effective predictors of outcome.

Future Research Should Consider Aps as a Mediator between Social Cognition Impairment and Functional Outcome

The evidence from this research was obtained by means of a correlation analysis on a small sample of participants. Such an approach is obviously limited and needs further confirmation of the presented results, for the implications on the enactment of pharmacological and adjunctive psychosocial treatments for the affected patients [48], [153]. To actively sustain that antipsychotic drugs may be a mediator between basic cognitive dysfunctions and social adaptation, there will be the necessity to plan *ad hoc* studies allowing to discover whether social dysfunctions normalize in response to drug treatment or not. A condition that hinders the opportunities to perform similar studies is that large trials have exhibited only a weak relation between neurocognition, social cognition and antipsychotics [30], [35], [40], [204]. Some methodological consideration on these trial's design may help, however, in the definition of the methods and the statistical procedures to be utilized for a larger study on the impact of antipsychotics on social cognition. Both CATIE [35] and CUtLASS [30] studies have utilized classical inferential procedures such as the analysis of covariance, ANCOVA or the χ^2 test, that are best suited for multiple treatment group comparison trials. In any case, the methodological analysis by Leucht et al. [27], [203] showed that the CATIE study was flawed by a remarkable number of drop-outs and in the CUtLASS study the choice between FGAs and SGAs was not randomized, with the impossibility to conclude which individual drug had the better clinical effectiveness. Furthermore, in many large trials the participants were maintained in the initial randomization group even after the switch to a different AP from the drug prescribed at the beginning of the assessment. The conclusion of the Authors are the following: (i) the design of CATIE and CUtLASS, although sometimes useful, might induce distortions in drug efficacy and side effects; (ii) evidence from other meta-analyses sustaining limited, but clinically effective remediating properties of some SGAs on the overall cognitive dysfunctions are confirmed [33]; (iii) a few studies have evidenced how only three SGAs, clozapine, amisulpride and sertindole are really effective on a outcome measure, the quality of life. From these data, it is possible to state how the larger trials were unable to evidence the real effect of antipsycotics on the social outcome of schizophrenic patients and further studies are needed to explore this condition.

A further methodological question arise from studies that have explored the possibility that social cognition may be a mediating construct between basic neurocognitive dysfunctions and social outcome. Sergi et al.'s studies [22-23] have defined that a variable acquires the function of a "mediator" when (i) this variable is significantly correlated with the predictor variable; (ii) the mediating variable is also significantly correlated with the outcome variable; (iii) the association between the predictor variable and the outcome variable achieves the statistical significance before the introduction of the potential mediator but becomes not significant when the potential mediator is introduced.

A particular statistical procedure, Structural Equation Modeling, SEM, allows to perform a statistical test of mediation that may confirm the reaching of the condition of mediator. In any case, in the first study of Sergi et al. using SEM [22] only a small portion of the outcome variance (18%) was explained by a mediation model, while in the second [23] it was evidenced how social cognition and neurocognition were separate constructs and, when the negative symptoms were introduced in the model, the association between negative symptoms and social cognition was weaker than the one between social cognition and neurocognition. From these considerations, it appears that SEM studies are a confirmation of data already investigated in the studies of the 1990s [1], [9-10], [160] outlining the association between negative symptoms, cognitive dysfunctions and functional outcome indices. When conducted on the antipsychotic treatment, these studies have evidenced how the single APs can induce an amelioration of selected cognitive dysfunction measures [15-17].

The search for a mediation between social outcome and cognitive impairment acquires, however, a relevant importance in the planning of the intensity of service activities and facilities, and most of all, of vocational rehabilitation outcomes for the schizophrenic patients [219-220]. To effectively state that antipsychotic treatment may obtain such a mediating function, along with So et al.'s [51] position, two distinct pathways might be useful in the planning of a future study: (i) a longitudinal observation design in which the impact of the outcome measures is influenced by the antipsychotic treatment, that is changes in the outcome are measured before and after the onset of antipsychotic treatment; (ii) a less-powerful cross-sectional design, in which the association between the modification of the outcome and the activity of the drug treatment is investigated in a group of patients with different cognitive dysfunctions intensity and severity. The first opportunity is challenging, because it implies the necessity of investigating a group of drug-free patients, that in general are difficult to find, unless the experimenters make the choice of studying a sample of persons with psychosis at onset.

In this context, it is of note that the EUFEST trial, conducted on first episode schizophrenia patients [204] displayed a statistically significant improvement in cognitive dysfunctions after six months from the introduction of antipsychotics, with no difference between FGAs and SGAs. Moreover, the Mizrahi et al.'s [149] study, in the first, longitudinal part conducted on drug-free patients, displayed that mental state attribution improved with APs, but there was no relation between changes in ToM and symptoms modification. It is therefore necessary to overcome such difficulties by realizing a longitudinal study on the impact of the antipsychotic treatment on Theory of Mind and social outcomes that would include a sufficient number of participants and explore the outcomes with an adequate array of measures.

The second possibility is relatively simpler to enact, and it was, actually, the method followed by most of the studies on social cognition and antipsychotics [12], [122], [147-150] and by this chapter's research. The contrasting results evidenced in the correlation analysis utilized in the majority of these papers raises the question of how to identify a statistically significant relation between social cognitive dysfunctions, antipsychotics and behavioural outcome of schizophrenia patients.

The evidence reported by Bae et al. [218] show, at least that, by using an unconventional statistical procedure, the antipsychotic drugs display a predictive role for the social outcomes of the participants to that study. These results are in line with those displayed in this chapter, that were obtained, instead, from a relatively simpler correlational approach. The utilization of more complex statistical models on a cross-sectional study conducted on a relatively higher sample of participants than those reported in most studies [48], [122], [147] would probably allow a better definition of the activity of antipsychotic treatment on the variables defining social adaptation of the persons with schizophrenia.

Conclusion

The relation between antipsychotic treatment, social cognition and psychosocial functioning of schizophrenic persons is complex and needs to be further explored in order to define how the drug treatment might influence their behavioural outcomes. In this context, it is important to point out that two psychosocial factors, the service intensity [219] and the social discomfort for the job [220], have exhibited a mediating function between social cognition impairments and functional change in the rehabilitation of patients with schizophrenia. As antipsychotic treatment, by reducing the intensity and the severity of the symptoms, provides a sensible help in the recovery of the affected persons, it would be a remarkable step forward to evidence a relation, albeit indirect, between APs and social behavioural measures involved in rehabilitation. This chapter's results have evidenced the existence of a relationship, although weak, between these constructs, whose strength and impact on the patients in terms of quality of life, subjective satisfaction for their health and social skills capacities still need to be addressed. This chapter's results have found, however, that antipsychotic treatment was not associated with patient's awareness of their personal necessities. A similar result was evidenced for what concerns patient's expectations to receive help from the treating institutions and the informal networks of care. Future studies should also address this issue, to explore whether APs are effective in favouring the improvement of the subjective dimensions of patient's well-being, or they just perform a supportive function of their routine activities. This issue is justified by APs high costs, especially of SGAs [18], that implicate an evaluation of the appropriateness of the prescriptions, an assessment of the clinical effectiveness of these drugs and the consequences of their perceived benefits. These dimensions have acquired a relevant impact in the realization of service models aimed at promoting the recovery of schizophrenia patients [199]. In this context, a modulation of social cognition functions may acquire a fundamental importance. The results from a retrospective case series study on a combination of two SGAs, clozapine and aripiprazole [217] have shown, in fact, that the atypicals may enhance two specific aspects of functional outcome, autonomy in everyday life and the capacity to collaborate with rehabilitation goals. It should be necessary, therefore, to design studies aimed at the investigation of the capacity of APs to enhance social cognition performances in the light of reporting their efficacy in producing changes in psychosocial competences.

References

[1] P. Harvey, and T. Sharma. *Understanding and Treating Cognition in Schizophrenia: A Clinician's Handbook*. Martin Dunitz, London (2002)

[2] R. Adolphs, *Curr. Opin. Neurobiol.* 11, 231 (2001)

[3] D.L. Penn, L.J. Sanna and D.L. Roberts, *Schizophr. Bull.* 34, 3 (2008)

[4] D.L. Penn, D.L. Roberts, D. Combs and A. Sterne, *Psychiatry. Serv.* 58, 4 (2007)

[5] T.M. Ostrom, *The sovereignity of social cognition.* In: R.S. Wyer and T.K. Srull (eds.) Handbook of social cognition (Vol 1, pp1-37) Erlbaum, Hillsdale, NJ. (1984)

[6] D.L. Penn, P.W. Corrigan, R.P. Bentall, J.M. Racenstein and L. Newman, *Psychol. Bull.* 121, 114 (1997)

[7] M. Casacchia, M. Mazza and R. Roncone, *Curr Psychiatry Rep.* 6, 3 (2004)
[8] E. Brunet-Gouet and J. Decety, *Psychiatr. Res. Neuroimaging* 148, 75 (2006)
[9] M.F. Green, *Am. J. Psychiatry* 153, 321 (1996)
[10] M.F. Green, R.S. Kern, D.L. Braff and J. Mintz, *Schizophr. Bull.* 26, 1 (2000)
[11] E.S. Herbener, S.K. Hill, R.W. Marvin and J.A. Sweeney, *Am. J. Psychiatry* 162, 1746 (2005)
[12] M. Brüne, M. Abdel-Hamid, C. Lehmkämper and C. Sonntag, *Schizophr. Res.* 92, 151 (2007)
[13] F. Basaglia "La distruzione dell'ospedale psichiatrico come luogo di istituzionalizzazione. Mortificazione e libertà dello «spazio chiuso». Considerazioni sul sistema «open door» (Itl.)" 1st International Congress on Social Psychiatry, London, 1964, *Ann. Neurol. Psichiatry*, LIX, 1 (1965)
[14] R.J. Wyatt, *Schizophr. Bull.* 17, 325 (1991)
[15] R.W. Buchanan, C. Holstein and A. Breier, Biol. Psychiatry 36, 717 (1994)
[16] E. Stip and I. Lussier, *Can. J. Psychiatry* 41, 2 (1996)
[17] A. Rossi, F. Mancini, P. Stratta et al. *Acta Psychiatr. Scand.* 95, 40 (1997)
[18] J.K. Patel, D.A. Pinals and A. Breier, *Schizophrenia and other Psychotic Disorders*. In A. Tasman, J. Kay, J.A. Lieberman, M.B. First and M. Maj (Eds) Psychiatry, Third Edition Wiley-Blackwell, England (2009)
[19] S.M. Couture, D.L. Penn and D.L. Roberts, *Schizophr. Bull.* 32, S1 (2006)
[20] M.F. Green, B. Olivier, J.N. Crrawley, D.L. Penn and S. Silverstein, *Schizophr. Bull.* 31, 882 (2005)
[21] P.A. Garety, P. Bebbington, D. Fowler, D. Freeman and E. Kuipers, *Psychol. Med.* 37, 1377 (2007)
[22] M. Sergi, Y. Rassovsky, K.H. Nuechterlein and M.F. Green, *Am. J. Psychiatry* 163, 3 (2006)
[23] M. Sergi, Y. Rassovsky, C. Widmark, C. et al., *Schizophr. Res.* 90, 316 (2007)
[24] R.S.E. Keefe, S. Perkins, S.M. Silva and J.A. Lieberman, *Schizophr. Bull.* 25, 201 (1999)
[25] J. Geddes, N. Freemantle, P. Harrison and P. Bebbington, *BMJ* 321, 1371 (2000)
[26] J.A. Lieberman, T.S. Stroup, J.P. Mac Evoy et al. *N. Engl. J. Med.* 353, 1209 (2005)
[27] S. Leucht, C. Corves, D. Arbter, R.R. Engel, C. Li and J.M. Davis, *Lancet*, 373, 3 (2009)
[28] M.S. Swartz, D.O. Perkins, T. Scott-Stroup et al. *Am. J. Psychiatry* 164, 428 (2007)
[29] D.W. Heinrichs, T.E. Hanlon, W.T. Carpenter, *Schizophr. Bull.* 10, 388 (1984)
[30] P.B. Jones, T.R.E. Barnes, L. Davies et al. *Arch. Gen. Psychiatry* 63, 1079 (2006)
[31] P.D. Harvey and R.S.E. Keefe, *Am. J. Psychiatry* 158, 176 (2001)
[32] R.S.E. Keefe, L.J. Seidman, B.K. Christiensen et al. *Am. J. Psychiatry* 161, 985 (2004)
[33] N.D. Woodward, S.E. Purdon, H.Y. Meltzer and D.H. Zald, Int. J. Neuropsychopharmacol. 6, 457 (2005)
[34] R.S.E. Keefe, L.J. Seidman, B.K. Christiensen et al. *Biol. Psychiatry* 59, 97 (2006)
[35] R.S.E. Keefe, R.M. Bilder, S.M. Davis et al. *Arch. Gen. Psychiatry* 64, 633 (2007)
[36] R.A. Sweet, B.G. Pollock, B.H. Mulsant et al. J. Clin Psychopharmacol. 20, 181 (2000)
[37] K.S. Kee, R.S. Kern, B.D. Marshall, Jr. and M.F. Green, *Schizophr. Res.* 31, 159 (1998)
[38] K.H. Littrell, R.G. Petty, N.M. Hilligoss, C.D. Kirshner and C.G. Johnson, *Schizophr. Res.* 66, 2 (2004)

[39] P.D. Harvey, T.L. Patterson, L.S. Potter, K. Zhong and M. Brecher, *Am. J. Psychiatry* 163, 11 (2006)
[40] D.L. Penn, R.S.E. Keefe, S.M. Davis et al. *Schizophr. Res.* 115, 1 (2009)
[41] D. Freeman, *Clin. Psychol. Rev.* 27, 425 (2007)
[42] J.L. Taylor and P. Kinderman, *Br. J. Psychiatry* 93, 137 (2002)
[43] F. Randall, R. Corcoran, J.C. Day and R.P. Bentall, *Cognit. Neuropsychiatry* 8, 287 (2003)
[44] F. Irani, S.M. Platek, I.S. Panyavin et al. *Schizophr. Res.* 88, 151 (2006)
[45] O. Kelemen, S. Keri, A. Must, G. Benedek and Z. Janka, *Acta Psychiatr. Scand.* 110, 146 (2004)
[46] M. Mazza, V. Di Michele, R. Pollice, R. Roncone and M. Casacchia, *Psychopathology*, 708 (2008)
[47] M. Mazza, A. De Risio, L. Surian, R. Roncone and M. Casacchia, *Schizophr. Res.* 47, 299 (2001)
[48] R. Roncone, I.R.H. Falloon, M. Mazza et al. *Psychopathology* 35, 280 (2002)
[49] M. Brüne, *Schizophr. Bull.* 31, 1 (2005)
[50] M. Brüne, *Psychiatry Res.* 133, 135 (2005)
[51] S.H. So, P.A. Garety, E.R. Peters and S. Kapur, *Psychosom. Med.* 72, 7 (2010)
[52] E. Stip, *Encephale* 32, 341 (2006)
[53] V. Kumari, P.J. Corr, O.F. Mulligan, P.A. Cotter, S.A. Checkley and J.A. Grant, *Psychopharmacology*, 129, 3 (1997)
[54] V. Kumari, J.A. Gray, G.D. Honey et al., *Schizophr. Res.* 57, 1 (2002)
[55] R.P. Liberman, D. Gutkind, J. Mintz, M. Green, B.D. Marshall, Jr., M.J. Robertson and J. Hayden, *Compr. Psychiatry* 43, 6 (2002)
[56] S.E. Purdon, N. Woodward, S.R. Lindborg and E. Stip, *Psychopharmacology*, 169, 3-4 (2003)
[57] M.A. Bédard, H. Scherer, J. Delorimier, E. Stip and P. Lalonde, *Can. J. Psychiatry*, 41 (7 Suppl 1) (1996)
[58] M. Knight, *Cognitive function and food preparation ability in schizophrenia.* Doctoral dissertation, University of Rhode Island, Department of Nursing (2000)
[59] M. Semkovska, E. Stip, L. Godbout et al., *Schizophr. Res.* 69, 289 (2004)
[60] D. Velligan, P. Diamond, D. Glahn et al., *Psychiatry Res.* 151, 55 (2007)
[61] L. Godbout, F. Limoges, I. Allard et al., *Compr. Psychiatry* 48, 293 (2007)
[62] G. Aubin, E. Stip, I. Gélinas, C. Rainville and C. Chapparo, *Psychiatr. Serv.* 60, 6 (2009)
[63] P.W. Corrigan and R. Toomey, *Schizophr. Bull.* 21, 395 (1995)
[64] A. Zanello, L. Perrig and P. Huguelet, *Psychiatry Res.* 142, 67 (2006)
[65] C. Frith, *The Cognitive Neuropsychology of Schizophrenia.* Lawrence Erlbaum Associates: Hove, U.K. (1992)
[66] D. Premack and G. Woodruff, *Behav. Brain Sci.* 4, 515 (1978)
[67] L. Brothers, *Concepts Neurosci.* 1, 27 (1990)
[68] R.W. Bryne and A. Whiten (eds.) *Machiavellian intelligence: Social expertise and the evolution of intellect in monkeys, apes, and humans.* Oxford University Press, Oxford (1988)
[69] R.J. Sullivan and J.S. Allen, *Acta Psychiatr. Scand.* 99, 148 (1999)

[70] M. Mazza, A. De Risio, C. Tozzini, R. Roncone, M. Casacchia, *Brain Cogn.* 51, 262 (2003)
[71] L. Harrington, R.G. Siegert and J. McClure, *Cognit. Neuropsychiatry* 10, 249 (2005)
[72] M. Sprong, P. Schothorst, E. Vos, J. Hox and H. Van Engeland, *Br. J. Psychiatry* 191, 5 (2007)
[73] R. Herold, T. Tenyi, K. Lenard et al., *Psychol. Med.* 32, 1125 (2002)
[74] R. Langdon and M. Coltehart, *Cognition* 71, 43 (1999)
[75] R. Langdon and M. Coltehart, *Psychiatry Res.* 125, 9 (2004)
[76] G.J. Pickup, *Cognit. Neuropsychiatry* 11, 177 (2006)
[77] C.S. Jahshan and M.J. Sergi, *Schizophr. Res.* 88, 151 (2007)
[78] I. Janssen, L. Krabbendam, J. Jolles et al., *Acta Psychiatr. Scand.* 110, 146 (2003)
[79] M. Abdel-Hamid, C. Lehmkämper, C. Sonntag, G. Juckel, I. Daum and M. Brüne, *Psychiatry Res.* 165, 19 (2009)
[80] A. Carlsson, *Neuropsychopharmacology* 1, 179 (1988)
[81] P. Seeman, T. Lee, M. Chau-Wong et al. *Nature* 261, 717 (1976)
[82] S.H. Snyder, *Am J Psychiatry* 133, 197 (1976)
[83] P.F. Spano, M. Ballmaier and E. Sacchetti. *D_1 and D_2 receptors in schizophrenia: retrospective and prospective views.* In: E. Sacchetti and P.F. Spano (eds.): Novel Antipsychotics: Facts and Promises at the Turn of the Millennium (pp. 37-46) Excerpta Medica, Reed Elsevier Group, Milano, Italia (2000)
[84] B.K. Lipska and D.R. Weinberger. *Cortical regulation of the mesolimbic dopamine system: implications for schizophrenia.* In: P. W. Kalivas, C. D. Barnes (eds). Limbic Motor Circuits and Neuropsychiatry. CRC Press, London (pp. 329–349) (1993)
[85] L.L. Devaud, E.B. Hollingsworth and B.R. Cooper, *J. Neurochem* 59, 1459 (1992)
[86] A. Abu-Akel, *Med Hypotheses* 60, 3 (2003)
[87] A. Abu-Akel, *Brain Res. Rev.* 43, 29 (2003)
[88] S.A. Spence, D.J. Brooks, S.R. Hirsch, P.F. Liddle, J. Meehan and P.M. Grasby, *Brain*, 120 (Pt11) (1997)
[89] P.C. Fletcher, F. Happé, U. Frith, S.C. Baker and S.J. Frackoviak, *Cognition* 57, 109 (1995)
[90] T.A. Russell, K. Rubia, E.T. Bullmore et al., *Am. J. Psychiatry* 157, 2040 (2000)
[91] V. Gallese and A. Goldman, *Trends Cogn. Sci.* 2, 493 (1998)
[92] G. Rizzolatti and M.A. Arbib, *Trends Neurosci.* 15, 188 (1998)
[93] G. Rizzolatti and C. Sinigaglia. *So quel che fai. Il cervello che agisce e i neuroni specchio* (Itl.) Raffaello Cortina Editore, Milano (2000)
[94] S.R. Laviolette, *Schizophr. Bull.* 33, 4 (2007)
[95] P.K. Hitchcott, J.J. Quinn and J.R. Taylor, *Cereb. Cortex* 17, 2820 (2007)
[96] S. Aalto, A. Brück, M. Laine, K. Någren and J.O. Rinne, *J. Neurosci.* 25, 10 (2005)
[97] M.P. de la Mora, A. Gallegos-Cari, Y. Arizmendi-Garcìa, D. Marcellino and K. Fuxe, *Prog. Neurobiol.* 90, 2 (2010)
[98] N.M. Lauzon and S.R. Laviolette, *Behav. Brain Res.* 17, 208 (2010)
[99] A. Abi-Dargham, R. Gil, J. Krystal et al., *Am. J. Psychiatry* 155, 761 (1998)
[100] S. Kapur, *Am. J. Psychiatry* 160, 13 (2003)
[101] G. Winterer and D.R. Weinberger, *Trends Neurosci.* 27, 683 (2004)
[102] S.A. Castner, *Science* 287, 2020 (2000)
[103] J.K. Seamans, C.R. Yang, *Progr. Neurobiol.* 74, 1 (2004)

[104] J.M. Allman, A. Hakeeem, J.M. Erwin, E. Nimchimsky and P. Hof, *Ann NY Acad Sci* 935, 107 (2001)
[105] S.B. Floresco and M.T. Tse, *J. Neurosci.* 27, 8 (2007)
[106] A.S. Bassett, O. Caluseriu, R. Weksberg, D.A. Young and E.W. Chow, *Biol. Psychiatry* 61, 10 (2007)
[107] H.J. Lee, A.H. Machbeth, J. Pagani and W.S. Young 3rd, *Prog. Neurobiol.* 88, 2 (2009)
[108] D. Feifel and T. Reza, *Psychopharmacology (Berl)* 141, 93 (1999)
[109] D.L. Braff and R. Freedman. *Endophenotypes in studies of the genetics of schizophrenia, in Neuropsychopharmacology: The Fifth Generation of Progress.* In: K.L. Davis, D.S. Charney, J.T. Coyle and C. Nemeroff (eds.) Neuropsychopharmacology: The Fifth Generation of Progress. (pp. 703-716). Lippincott Williams & Wilkins, Philadelphia (2002)
[110] I.I. Gottesman, T.D. Gould, *Am. J. Psychiatry* 160, 636 (2003)
[111] M. Goldman, M. Marlow-O'Connor, I. Torres and C.S. Carter, *Schizophr. Res.* 98, 247 (2008)
[112] D. Feifel, K. Macdonald, A. Nguyen et al., *Biol. Psychiatry* 68,7 (2010)
[113] D. Feifel, *Expert. Rev. Neurother.* 11, 2 (2011)
[114] P. Kirsch, C. Esslinger, Q. Chen, et al., *J. Neurosci.* 25, 11489 (2005)
[115] G. Domes, M. Heinrichs, A. Michel, C. Berger and S.C. Herpertz, *Biol. Psychiatry* 61, 731 (2007)
[116] E. Savaskan, R. Erhardt, A. Shultz, M. Walter and H. Schachninger, *Psychoneuroendocrinology* 33, 368 (2008)
[117] A.J. Guastella, P.B. Mitchell and M.R. Dadds, *Biol. Psychiatry* 63, 3 (2008)
[118] A.J. Guastella, P.B. Mitchell and F. Mathews, *Biol. Psychiatry* 64, 256 (2008)
[119] G. Domes, M. Heinrichs, J. Glascher, C. Buchel, D.F. Braus and S.C. Herpertz, *Biol. Psychiatry* 62, 1187 (2007)
[120] E.J. Lawrence, P. Shaw, D. Baker, S. Baron-Cohen and A.S. David, *Psychol. Med.* 34, 911 (2004)
[121] J. Decety and P.L. Jackson, *Behav. Cognit. Neurosci. Rev.* 3, 71 (2004)
[122] S. Shamay-Tsoory, S. Shur, L. Barcai-Goodman, S. Medlovich, H. Harari and Y. Levkovitz, *Psychiatr. Res* 149, 11 (2007)
[123] M.R. Melis, S. Succu, C. Cocco et al., *Neuropsychopharmacology* 58, 7 (2010)
[124] A.J. Rosenfeld, J.A. Lieberman and L.F. Jarskog, *Schizophr. Bull.* 22 (2010)
[125] B.J. Aragona and Z. Wang, *Front. Behav. Neurosci.* 3, 15 (2009)
[126] T.R. Insel, *Neuron.* 65, 6 (2010)
[127] M. Bosia, S. Anselmetti, M. Bechi et al., *Psychiatry Res.* 29 (2010)
[128] A. Abu-Akel and K. Abushua'leh, *Schizophr. Res* 69, 45 (2004)
[129] N.M. Lauzon, S.F. Bishop and S.R. Laviolette, *J. Neurosci.* 29, 15 (2009)
[130] M.F. Green, K.H. Nuechterlein, J. Gold et al., *Biol. Psychiatry* 56, 5 (2004)
[131] S.M. Eack, M.F. Pogue-Geile, C.G. Greeno and M.S. Keshavan, *Schizophr. Res.* 114, 1-3 (2009)
[132] S. Shamsi, A. Lau, T. Lencz et al., *Schizophr. Res.* 126, 1-3 (2011)
[133] C.D. Frith and R. Corcoran, *Psychol. Med.* 26, 521 (1996)
[134] V.M. Drury, E.J. Robinson and M. Birchwood, *Psychol. Med.* 28, 1101(1998)
[135] G.A. Doody, M. Gotz, E.C. Johnstone, C.D. Frith and D.G. Cunningham Owens, *Psychol. Med.* 28, 397 (1998)

[136] R. Corcoran and C.D. Frith, *Cognit. Neuropsychiatry* 1, 305 (1996)
[137] M. Mazza, C. Costagliola, V. Di Michele et al., *Eur. Arch. Psychiatry Clin. Neurosci.* 257, 12 (2007)
[138] T. Zalla, N. Bouchilloux, N. Labruyere et al., *Brain Res. Bull.* 68, 195 (2006)
[139] R. Langdon, P.T. Michie, P.B. Ward et al., *Cognit. Neuropsychiatry* 2, 167 (1997)
[140] Y. Sarfati, M.C. Hardy-Baylé, J. Nadel et al., *Schizophr. Res.* 37, 183 (1999)
[141] Y. Sarfati, C. Passarieux and M.C. Hardy-Baylé, *Psychopathology* 33, 246 (2000)
[142] R. Corcoran, G. Mercer and C.D. Frith, *Schizophr. Res.* 17, 5 (1995)
[143] S.J. Blakemore, Y. Sarfati, N. Bazin et al., *Psychol. Med.* 33, 1433 (2003)
[144] T.A. Russell, E. Reynaud, C. Herba et al., *Schizophr. Res.* 81, 101
[145] O. Kelemen, R. Erdelyi, I Pataki et al., *Neuropsychology* 19, 494 (2005)
[146] E. Bora, A. Eryavuz, B. Kayahan, G. Sungu and B. Veznedaroglu, *Psychiatry Res.* 145, 2-3 (2006)
[147] M. Mazza, R. Pollice, V. Gaspari et al., *Clin. Ter.* 156, 5 (2005)
[148] I. Savina and R.J. Beninger, Schizophr. Res. 94, 128 (2007)
[149] R. Mizrahi, M. Korostil, S.E. Starkstein, R.B. Zipursky and S. Kapur, *Psychol. Med.* 37, 4 (2007)
[150] R. Corcoran, G. Rowse, R. Moore et al., *Psychol. Med.* 38, 1577 (2008)
[151] L.M. Williams, C.M. Loughland, M.J. Green, A.W. Harris and E. Gordon, *Psychiatry Res.* 120, 13 (2003)
[152] S. Mo, Y. Su, R.C.K. Chan and J. Liu, Psychiatry Res 157, 21 (2008)
[153] T.L. Patterson and O.R. Leeuwenkamp, *Schizophr. Res.* 100, 108 (2008)
[154] S. Shur, S.G. Shamay-Tsoory and Y. Levkovitz, *Cognit. Neuropsychiatry* 13, 472 (2008)
[155] R. Roncone, M. Mazza, I. Frangou et al., *Neuropsychol. Rehab.* 14, 421 (2004)
[156] I.R.H. Falloon, L. Barbieri, I. Boggian and D. Lamonaca, *J. Men. Health* 16, 553 (2006)
[157] L. Barbieri, I. Boggian and D. Lamonaca. *Problem solving nella riabilitazione psichiatrica. Guida pratica.* (Itl) Erickson, Gardolo, TN (2008)
[158] A. Mastroeni, C. Bellotti, E. Pellegrini, F. Galletti, E. Lai and I.R.H. Falloon, *Clin. Practice & Epidemiol. Mental Health*, 23, (2005)
[159] T.J. D'Zurilla and M.R. Goldfried, *J. Abnormal Psychology* 78, 107 (1971)
[160] T. Sharma and P. Harvey. *Cognition in schizophrenia. Impairments, importance and treatment strategies.* Oxford University Publishing, Oxford, UK (2002)
[161] M. Ruggeri and A. Dall'Agnola. *Come valutare l'esito nei dipartimenti di salute mentale.* (Itl) Il Pensiero Scientifico Editore, Roma (2000)
[162] K.T. Mueser, R. Doonan, D.L. Penn et al., *J. Abnormal Psychology* 105, 271 (1996)
[163] American Psychiatric Association. *Diagnostic and Statistical Manual of Mental Disorders, 4th edn., Text Revision.* American Psychiatric Association, Washington, DC (2000)
[164] American Psychiatric Association, *Am. J. Psychiatry* 154 (Suppl.), 1-63 (1997)
[165] S.W. Woods, *J. Clin. Psychiatry* 64, 663 (2003)
[166] I.C. Wilson, *Am. J. Psychiatry* 123, 1289 (1967)
[167] G.H. Kent. *E-G-Y scales. The Psychological Corporation.* Williams & Wilkins, New York (1967)

[168] E. Othmer and S.C. Othmer. *The Clinical Interview Using DSM-IV. Volume 1: Fundamentals.* American Psychiatric Press, Inc., Washington, DC (1994)
[169] D.A. Grant and E.A. Berg, *J. Experiment. Psychology* 38, 404 (1948)
[170] O. Spreen and E. Strauss. *A compendium of neuropsychological tests: administration, norms, and commentary, 2nd edn.* Oxford University Press, London (1988)
[171] R.K. Heaton. *A Manual For The Wisconsin Card Sorting Test.* Psychological Assessment Resources, Odessa, FL (1981)
[172] T. Shallice, *Philos. Trans. R. Soc. Lond. B. Biol. Sci.* 25, 298 (1982)
[173] R. Krikorian, J. Bartok and N. Gay, J. Clin. Experiment. Neuropsychology 16, 840 (1994)
[174] G. Novelli, C. Papagno, E. Capitani, M. Laiacona, G. Vallar and F.S. Cappa, *Arch. Psicol. Neurol. Psichiatr.* 47, 477 (1986)
[175] S. Baron-Cohen, A. Leslie and U. Frith, *Cognition* 21, 37 (1985)
[176] F. Happé, *J. Autism Dev. Disorders* 24, 129 (1994)
[177] S. Baron-Cohen, *J. Child Psychol. Psychiatry* 30, 285 (1989)
[178] F. Happé and U. Frith. *Theory of mind in autism.* In: E. Schopler, G. Mesibov (eds) Learning and cognition in autism. Plenum Press, New York (1994)
[179] S. Baron-Cohen. *Mindblindness. An essay on autism and theory of mind.* MIT Press, Cambridge, Mass. (1995)
[180] P. Ekman and V.W. Friesen, *Pictures of Facial Affect.* Consulting Psychologists Press, Palo Alto, CA (1976)
[181] J. Ventura, M.F. Green, A. Shaner and R.P. Liberman, *Int. J. Methods Psychiatr. Res.* 3, 221 (1993)
[182] J. Ventura, D. Lukoff, K.H. Nuechterlein, R.P., M.F. Green and A. Shaner, *Int. J. Methods Psychiatr. Res.* 3, 227 (1993)
[183] P.L. Morosini and M. Casacchia, *Riv. Riab. Psichiatr. Psicosociale* 3, 199 (1995)
[184] R. Roncone, J. Ventura, M. Impallomeni et al., *Acta Psychiatr. Scand.* 100, 3 (1999)
[185] P.P. Heppner, *The Problem Solving Inventory: Manual.* Consulting Psychologists Press, Palo Alto, CA (1988)
[186] M. Phelan, M. Slade, G. Thornicroft et al., *Br. J. Psychiatry* 167, 589 (1995)
[187] M. Ruggeri, A. Lasalvia, S. Nicolau and M. Tansella, *Epidemiol. Psichiatr. Soc.* 8, 135 (1999)
[188] J.K. Wing, A.S. Beevor, R.H. Curtis, S.B. Park, S. Hadden and A. Burns, *Br. J. Psychiatry* 172, 11 (1998)
[189] P. Morosini, A. Gigantesco, A. Mazzarda and L. Gibaldi, *Epidemiol. Psichiatr. Soc.* 12, 53 (2003)
[190] M. Brüne, S. Lissek, N. Fuchs et al., *Neuropsychologia* 46, 1992 (2008)
[191] F. Benedetti, A. Bernasconi, M. Bosia et al., *Schizophr. Res.* 114, 154 (2009)
[192] L. Surian. *Autismo. Indagini sullo sviluppo mentale.* (Itl) Gius. Laterza & Figli Spa, Bari (2002)
[193] J.A. Fodor. *The modularity of mind (USA ed.).* MIT Press, Cambridge, MA (1983)
[194] M. Moscovitch and C.A. Umiltà. *Conscious and nonconscious aspects of memory: a neuropsychological framework of modules and central systems.* In: R.G. Lister and H.J. Weingartner (eds.), Perspectives on cognitive neuroscience. (pp. 229-266).Oxford University Press, Oxford UK (1991)
[195] A.M. Leslie, *Psychol. Rev.* 94, 412 (1987)

[196] G.M. Edelman, *The remembered present. A biological theory of consciousness.* Basic Books, New York (1989)
[197] G.M. Edelman and G. Tononi. *A universe of consciousness. How matter becomes imagination* (itl.: Un universo di coscienza. Come la materia diventa immaginazione. Einaudi, Torino) (2000)
[198] L. Cosmides and J. Tooby. (1992). *Cognitive adaptations for social exchange.* In J. H. Barkow, L. Cosmides, & J. Tooby (Eds.), The adapted mind. Evolutionary psychology and the generation of culture. Oxford University Press, New York (1992)
[199] V. Kovess-Masféty, D. Wiersma, M. Xavier et al., *Clin. Practice & Epidemiol. Mental Health* 2, 22 (2006)
[200] A. Carcione and M. Falcone. *Il concetto di metacognizione come costrutto clinico fondamentale per la psicoterapia.* In: A. Semerari (ed.), Psicoterapia Cognitiva del Paziente Grave. (pp. 9– 42) (Itl) Raffaello Cortina Editore, Milano (1999)
[201] P.R. May, A.H. Tuma, C. Yale, P. Potepan and W.J. Dixon, *Arch. Gen. Psychiatry* 33, 481 (1976)
[202] J.M. Davis and N. Chen, *Eur. Psychiatry* 20, 7 (2005)
[203] S. Leucht, W. Kissling and J.M. Davis, *Psychol. Med.* doi:10.1017/S003329 1709005455 (2009)
[204] M. Davidson, S. Galderisi, M. Weiser et al., *Am. J. Psychiatry* 166, 6 (2009)
[205] B.W. Palmer, S.E. Dawes and R.K. Heaton, *Neuropsychol. Rev.* 19, 365 (2009)
[206] M. De Hert, V. Schreurs, D. Vancampfort and R. Van Vinkel, World Psychiatry 8, 15 (2009)
[207] M. Zink, S. Englisch and A. Meyer-Lindenberg, *Curr. Opin. Psychiatry* 23, 2 (2010)
[208] S. Englisch and M. Zink, *Progr. Neuro-Psychopharmacol. Biol. Psychiatry* 32, 1386 (2008)
[209] E. Stip and V. Tourjman, *Clin Ther.* 32, Suppl 1:S3-20 (2010)
[210] D.C. Henderson, L. Kunkel, D.D. Nguyen et al., *Acta Psychiatr. Scand.* 113, 142 (2006)
[211] M.R.A. Muscatello, A. Bruno, G. Pandolfo et al., *Schizophr. Res.* 127, 1-3 (2011)
[212] A. Benedetti, A. Di Paolo, M. Lastella et al., *Clin. Practice & Epidemiol. Mental Health* 6, 30 (2010)
[213] J.S. Chang, Y.M. Ahn, H.J. Park et al., *J. Clin. Psychiatry* 69,720 (2008)
[214] M. Nosé, S. Accordini, P. Artioli et al., *Trials* 10, 31 (2009)
[215] W.W. Fleischhacker, M.E. Heikkinen, J.P. Olia et al., *Int. J. Neuropsychopharmacol.* 12, 1 (2010)
[216] C. Mitsonis, N.P. Dimopoulos, P.A. Mitropoulos et al., *Progr. Neuro-Psychopharmacol. Biol. Psychiatry* 31, 373 (2007)
[217] A. De Risio, A. Pancheri, G. Simonetti, D. Giannarelli and B. Gentile, *Progr. Neuro-Psychopharmacol. Biol. Psychiatry* 35, 1112 (2011)
[218] S.M. Bae, S.H. Lee, Y.M. Park, M.H. Hyun and H. Yoon, *Psychiatry Investig.* 7, 93 (2010)
[219] J.S. Brekke, M. Hoe, J. Long and M.F. Green, *Schizophr. Bull.* 33, 5 (2007)
[220] M. Bell, H.W.H. Tsang, T.C. Greig and G.J. Bryson, *Schizophr. Bull.* 35, 4 (2009)
[221] M.J. Sergi, M.F. Green, C. Widmark et al., *Am J. Psychiatry* 164, 1585 (2007)
[222] S.L. Kerr and J.M. Neale, *J. Abnorm. Psychol. 102*, 2 (1993)
[223] J.D. Mayer, P. Salovey, D.R. Caruso and G. Sitarenios, *Emotion* 3, 1 (2003)

[224] R.L. Borison, A. Pathiranja, S. Haverstock, S. Gowda and B.I. Diamond. *Classical and New Antipsychotic Drugs in the Treatment of Schizophrenia.* In: C.L. Shriqui and H.A. Nasrallah (eds.). Contemporary Issues in the Treatment of Schizophrenia. American Psychiatric Press, Inc., Washington, D.C. and London, England (1996)
[225] J.L.F. Casey, L.E. Hollister, C.J. Klett et al., *Am. J. Psychiatry* 17, 997 (1961)
[226] M.S. Terrel, *Dis. Nerv. Syst.* 23, 41 (1962)
[227] D.W. Swanson, J.A. Smith and H. Perez, *Dis. Nerv. Syst.* 28, 756 (1967)
[228] B. Jones, H.E. Lehmann, B.M. Saxena et al., *Curr. Ther. Res.* 10, 276 (1968)
[229] C. Sheppard, V. Beyel, J. Fracchia et al., *Dis. Nerv. Syst.* 35, 83 (1974)
[230] L.S. Godleski, R. Kerler, J.W. Barber et al., *J. Nerv. Ment. Dis.* 177, 686 (1989)
[231] S.D. Soni, G. Sampath, A. Shah et al., *Acta Psychiatr. Scand.* 85, 354 (1992)

In: Schizophrenia Research: Recent Advances
Editor: Tomiki Sumiyoshi
ISBN: 978-1-62808-703-1

Chapter 13

COGNITIVE DEFICITS IN PHARMACOLOGICAL RODENT MODELS OF SCHIZOPHRENIA: EVALUATION OF SPATIAL COGNITION

Tereza Nekovarova[1,2], Ales Stuchlik[1], Karel Vales[1], Lukas Rambousek[1,3] and Tomiki Sumiyoshi[4]

[1] Institute of Physiology, Academy of Sciences of the Czech Republic, Prague, Czech Republic

[2] Third Faculty of Medicine, Charles University, Prague. Czech Republic

[3] Department of Organic Technology, Institute of Chemical Technology, Prague, Czech Republic

[4] Department of Neuropsychiatry, University of Toyama Graduate School of Medicine and Pharmaceutical Sciences, Toyama, Japan

ABSTRACT

Disturbances of various domains of cognition, e.g. several types of memory, attention, and executive functions, are considered to provide a major determinant of outcome in patients with schizophrenia. Nevertheless, these symptoms continue to represent one of the least surmountable “unmet needs” in the development of the therapeutics for the illness. Cognitive deficits have also attracted considerable attention from the viewpoint of biomarkers of animal models of schizophrenia. Neurodevelopmental, genetic and pharmacological manipulations have been found to simulate behavioral abnormalities reminiscent of the disease in experimental animals. Although the etiology and pathophysiology of schizophrenia is not fully understood, these animal models have been used in the search for novel antipsychotic drugs.

A role for the glutamatergic neurotransmitter system in the etiopathogenesis of schizophrenia has been supported by various levels from molecular interactions, as well as observations on the structural layout of neuronal networks in the human brain. Non-competitive antagonists at N-methyl-D-aspartate (NMDA) receptors produce hallucinations, cognitive disorganization, and other schizophrenia-like symptoms in healthy human subjects. Accordingly, various cognitive deficits, e.g.

impaired coordination, working memory, attention, latent learning, reversal learning, and attentional set-shifting, are observed in animals administered NMDA blockers. The dopaminergic and serotonergic systems have also been a focus of extensive research from the perspective of the neural circuits involved in the development of schizophrenia. For example, a number of existing antipsychotic drugs modulate serotonin receptors, which is thought to be related to the ability of these compounds to improve negative symptoms and cognitive deficits.

Pharmacologically induced cognitive deficits can be quantified by behavioral methods, e.g. Morris water maze and radial maze. In particular, the active allothetic place avoidance task, or Carousel maze, provides a strategy to evaluate spatial learning and memory. We have developed a novel operant task in which rats observe distant objects on the computer screen, and discriminate their positions. These tests of spatial cognition provide efficient tools not only for studying spatial perception itself, but also for evaluating impairments of memory, learning, and attention both in human subjects and model animals.

In this chapter, we will provide a review of the major pharmacological rodent models of schizophrenia and their performance on cognitive tasks, with particular emphasis on spatial cognition. The use of effective behavioral tasks of spatial perception facilitates evaluation of novel antipsychotic drugs and obtaining further insights into the pathophysiology of schizophrenia. Despite some difficulties in modeling specific symptoms, e.g. hallucinations, cognitive impairments in rodents are thought to effectively mimic the counterparts in clinical subjects.

1. Introduction

Schizophrenia is a complex neurodevelopmental psychiatric disorder induced by interaction between predisposing genes and environmental factors. The symptomatology of schizophrenia is manifold and the symptoms could be divided into negative symptoms, positive symptoms and cognitive deficits. Positive symptoms include conceptual disorganization, thought disorders, hallucinations and abnormal though contents, while negative symptoms are characterized by a decrease in normal functioning, flattened emotions, alogia, anhedonia and diminished motivation for social behavior. Recently, cognitive deficits are considered by some authors to be the most important feature of schizophrenia, particularly from the perspective of long-term outcome. Several domains of cognition are affected, e.g. aggravated attention and information processing, decreased flexibility, impaired verbal learning, working memory and executive functions. These disturbances of the illness may be related with deficits in social behavior. [1]

As research into cognitive aspects of the illness may be of value, as it may represent a complex neurodevelopment derangement accompanied with typical clinical manifestations, e.g. psychotic symptoms. This concept has to be taken into consideration when designing animal models of schizophrenia.

Abnormalities have been reported in all major neurotransmitter systems. Also, structural changes in the brains of patients with schizophrenia may be diverse. For example, ventricular enlargement and reduction in the volume of the cerebral cortex, thalamus, basal ganglia, hippocampus and amygdala have been reported compared to controls [2,3,4,5]. Among them, findings with the prefrontal cortex are consistent, including reduced volume of gray and white matters, decrease in total number of dendrites and axons, and decrease in the size of cortical pyramidal neurons [6].

These aberrations are thought to be inherited, but may be covered early in life. They become clinically overt in early adulthood, due, possibly, to the timing of maturation and axonal pruning in particular brain areas [7]. Thus, the first manifestations of psychotic symptoms commonly take place in late adolescence or early adulthood. This phase of schizophrenia is usually characterized by positive symptoms. On the other hand the prodromal phase preceding the active phase is often accompanied by nonspecific behavioral changes [8]. Thus, the crucial properties of schizophrenia include the latency between early neurodevelopment aberrations and clinically detectable manifestations. This "time gap" is expected to promote the study of early interventions during prodromal stage, and even the investigations of the fundamental pathophysiology or etiology of the disease. Here, genetic and/or neurodevelopment animal models offer valuable tools for studying the link between genetic backgrounds and environmental factors, and for the development of pharmacological strategies to prevent the manifestation of psychosis in high-risk individuals. Various neurodevelopmental and genetics animal models have been reviewed (for example in [9,10,11]) .

Interactions between environmental factors and genetic backgrounds in vulnerable subjects play a major role in the initiation of neurodevelopmental and pathophysiologic processes of the disorder. Environmental risk factors (from prenatal infections to trauma) could affect gene expression by epigenetic mechanisms. However, the direction of the genetic research is not well established; most of the candidate genes pose only small impact, and are not specific to schizophrenia.

1.1. Cognitive Deficits as Markers of Schizophrenia

One of the main problems in developing animal models of psychiatric disorder is to define specific markers. So far, no precise etiopathogenic mechanisms or biomarkers have been identified for schizophrenia. This is why many studies focus on behavioral variables that are related with neurobiological mechanisms underlying the illness.

Cognitive deficits belong to the most prominent symptoms in patients with schizophrenia. It is possible to mimic these deficits in animal models to some extent, as one of the markers of schizophrenia. Therefore, an increasing number of researchers have paid attention to developing behavioral tasks relevant to both humans and animals for the study of cognitive impairments, including sensory gating, attention, working memory, abstraction and social cognition.

In the following sections, we will summarize the current picture of cognitive tests used for rodents, with emphasis on the assessment of spatial cognition.

1.2. Animal Models and Their Validity

Research into the neurobiology of schizophrenia and development of novel pharmacotherapy is benefitted by implementation of appropriate animal models. Although controversy exists, such approach is widely used in various species, e.g. non-human primates and rodents. This allows more precise approach towards elucidating the connection among the neurophysiology, neurochemistry, and behavior. Although it is not possible to mimic the entire symptomatic spectrum of psychiatric illnesses in humans, data from animal studies are required for a compound to be tested clinically for therapeutic potentials.

To be considered an appropriate animal model of mental disorders, the relevance to the etiology, treatment, and underlying neurophysiological processes [13] must be fulfilled. In other words, face validity, predictive validity, and construct validity [14] are required.

The "resemblance" between behavioral abnormalities of animal models and pathological phenotypes in humans is usually termed as "face validity". This relates to similar pathophysiology and strong phenomenological similarities between behaviors exhibited by animals and specific symptoms of diseases. Nevertheless, one should be cautious about if a particular condition would manifest itself identically in different species [15]. For example, there are only a few behavior patterns shared by rodents and humans (e.g. prepulse inhibition).

In general, the construct validity refers to correlation between the theorized outcome of measuring and measuring itself. In the case of animal model, it concerns whether similar processes underlying the relevant behaviors exist across species, e.g. human and experimental animals. The concept of construct validity is closely related to the etiological validity [16]. However, it is difficult to assess etiological validity for complex human diseases, such as psychiatric disorders. For this purpose, the core biological processes shared by a particular disorder and manipulated animals should be clearly defined [13].

Predictive validity generally means the extent to which outcome of one measurement predicts that of another measurement or some other criteria. The predictive validity in psychopharmacology primarily concerns the ability of model animals to identify drugs with potentially therapeutic values for human [17]. Reliability applies to the accuracy with which the observations, both clinical and experimental, are made.

Rang [18] defined three types of animal models: homologous, isomorphic and predictive models. An animal model is regarded as homologous if the symptoms and the course of the disease are well represented by the model. There are only a few models that fulfill these conditions (for example well-defined lesion syndromes), while others are considered as "only partial". Isomorphic models have symptoms similar to those in humans, but their causes are different. Isomorphic, homologous, and predictive models are considered to show face, construct, and predictive validity, respectively, although this typology may have exceptions [19].

Schizophrenia is heterogeneous in terms of both the clinical course and symptoms. Besides psychosis and cognitive deficits, some patients experience catatonic phenomena, such as catalepsy, stereotypies, and unusual posturing and mannerisms [20].

In order to get better insight into the complexity of schizophrenia, model animals play an essential part in, for example, the development of novel antipsychotic drugs. Neurodevelopmental animal models mimic the anomaly of brain structures and functions as a result of environmental risk factors, such as viral infection, malnutrition, stress, trauma etc. in most cases, genetic models carry mutation or manipulation of genes involved in brain development, which affects behavior and cognition. These models usually have higher constructive validity. On the other hand, pharmacological models demonstrate high predictive validity. Here, psychotomimetic drugs have been used to test the dopaminergic, serotonergic or glutamatergic theory of schizophrenia. Many of these pharmacological models can be created also in human subjects. In this chapter, we will discuss some of the major pharmacological rodent models of schizophrenia and their performance on cognitive tasks, using the spatial cognition.

2. Pharmacological Animal Models of Schizophrenia

2.1. Dopaminergic Models

Dopamine (DA) is one of the major monoamine neurotransmitters in the brain. The dopamine hypothesis has dominated the study of the pathophysiology of schizophrenia for the past several decades. In particular, hyperactivity of dopaminergic pathways in mesolimbic areas underlies positive symptoms, while hypo-activity in frontocortical areas underlies negative and cognitive symptoms of the disease. The hypothesis has been based on the fact that application of dopamine agonists (cocaine, amphetamine, and apomorphine) exacerbates psychotic symptoms [21], and that conventional, or "typical" antipsychotic drugs, such as haloperidol and chlorpromazine, treat these symptoms by selective inhibition of DA-D_2 dopamine receptors.

The correlation between clinical efficacy of typical antipsychotics and their potency to antagonize D_2 receptors is robust. In addition, overstimulation of dopaminergic receptors by psychotomimetic drugs induces positive symptoms of schizophrenia in healthy subjects and causes their exacerbation in schizophrenia patients. Neuroimaging studies show increased dopamine transmission in the brains of subjects with schizophrenia, and enhanced release of dopamine after amphetamine administration [22,23]. Lower concentrations of homovanillic acid, a major metabolite of dopamine, have been found in the frontal cortex of subjects with schizophrenia [24]. A recent large-scale study of psycho-stimulant-induced psychosis showed that these patients display both positive and negative symptoms [25].

Acute or repeated administration of dopamine agonists, such as methamphetamine, has been produces schizophrenia-like symptomatology in animals. These drugs facilitate dopamine release, inhibit its re-uptake by blockade of dopamine transporters, and inhibit degradation of dopamine metabolites through actions on monoamine oxidase (MAO), all of which lead to an increase in extracellular concentrations of dopamine. In animals, application of psycho-stimulants induces stereotypic behaviors, and hyperlocomotion, and impairs performance on cognitive tests, such as prepulse inhibition (PPI) and latent inhibition. These behavioral alterations are ameliorated by administration of typical or atypical antipsychotics, supporting the predictive validity of these pharmacological models. [26,27]

Repeated applications of psycho-stimulants, such as amphetamine in escalating dosage regimen, produce sensitization, and augmented neurochemical and behavioral responses to the drugs. Behavioral sensitization to amphetamine in rats requires stimulation of dopaminergic neurons, and is blocked by D_1 or D_2-receptor selective antagonists [28, 29]. Current evidence supports the use of amphetamine sensitization as a model of the positive symptoms of schizophrenia. Additionally, there is increasing evidence for long-lasting cognitive deficits in sensitized animals, especially in the area of attention and cognitive flexibility. Rodent studies report impaired sustained attention, executive function and attentional set-shifting. In some studies, this model failed to produce deficits in working memory and hippocampus-dependent long-term memory in rodents [30, 31, 32, 33]. A recent study report a relationship between deficits in working memory and hyper-phosphorylation of extracellular signal-regulated kinase 1/2 in hippocampus after repeated treatment with methamphetamine in rats. This impairment was reversed by clozapine but not haloperidol, suggesting the involvement of neurotransmitter receptors other than dopamine receptors [34]. Schizophrenia-like behaviors have been observed in non-primate species after repeated treatment with amphetamine [35,36,37]. Another study reports impairments in working memory in association with reduced dopamine turnover in prefrontal cortex and striatum following amphetamine-induced sensitization [38]. On the other hand, a failure of amphetamine to produce working memory impairment has also been noticed [39].

Although nearly all antipsychotic drugs have certain affinity for D_2 receptors, they are not capable of satisfactorily ameliorating cognitive disturbances and negative symptoms of schizophrenia. Furthermore, there is a delay in the onset of action of antipsychotics, suggesting a role for other neurotransmitter systems in the efficacy of these compounds [40].

2.2. Serotonergic Models

The involvement of serotonin (5-hydorxytryptamin, 5-HT) in the pathophysiology of schizophrenia has been elucidated by experiments with hallucinogens. Based on their chemical structures, they are divided into indolamines (e.g. psilocybin, N,N-dimethyl tryptamine; DMT), ergolines (e.g., lysergic acid diethylamide; LSD), and fenylethylamines (e.g., mescaline, 4-methyl-2.5-dimetoxyamfetamine; DOM). Administration of LSD produces symptoms similar to early stage of schizophrenia in psychiatric healthy humans [41]. These symptoms have been classified by Hollister into three categories: somatic, perceptual and psychic [42]. Based on experiments with 5-HT_{2A} receptor antagonists, the behavioral and subjective effects of hallucinogens have been thought to be mediated mainly by activation of these receptors [43,44,45].

5-HT_{2A} receptors are expressed on dopaminergic, GABAergic, glutamatergic and cholinergic neurons in prefrontal cortex, basal ganglia and limbic structures, such as nucleus accumbens and hippocampus. They are involved in regulation of attention, working memory, and are considered to play important role in development of prefrontal cognitive dysfunctions in schizophrenia [46]. Later experiments elucidated the role of 5-HT_{2A}, 5-HT_{2C} and 5-HT_{1A} receptors in the action of hallucinogens. Modulation of 5-HT_{1A} receptors in the prefrontal cortex, which interact with N-methyl-D-aspartic (NMDA) receptors, plays an important role in learning and memory. Specifically, 5-HT_{1A} partial agonists have been reported to be effective in the treatment of psychotic symptoms and cognitive deficits of schizophrenia [47,48,49,50]. Moreover, 5HT_{1A} receptors are thought to mediate attentional deficits induced by hallucinogens [51]. LSD interacts also with 5-HT_5, 5HT_6, 5HT_7, α-adrenergic, and dopaminergic receptors. The pharmacological profiles of hallucinogens have been reviewed in great detail elsewhere [43].

In rodent studies, acute administration of hallucinogens affects sensorimotor gating, exploratory activity, locomotion, and social behavior, and stereotypy, as well as flat body posture and head twitches [43, 52]. LSD is known for its ability to produce a biphasic behavioral pattern [53]; an initial phase characterized by anxiety and a decrease in locomotor activity is followed by a phase of hyperlocomotion [52,54]. Chronic administration of LSD causes a persistent neuro-adaptive state that functionally resembles the acute effect of NMDA antagonists. Hypolocomotion persists for 3 months after cessation of chronic treatment, and is reversed by antipsychotic treatment, suggesting another animal model of schizophrenia [55].

Animal models with LSD have been associated with behavioral tolerance which develops after repeated administration of the agent, unlike the situation for schizophrenia. Reduced 5-HT_{2A} receptors density has been found after chronic administration of LSD, DOM and DOI in cortical areas of rats [56,57,58]. However, a recent study revealed that tolerance may not occur after administration of DMT [59]. Furthermore, these hallucinogens induce predominantly visual, rather than auditory hallucinations, with the latter more typical in schizophrenia. Taken together, serotonergic animal models provide face and predictive validities for positive symptoms of schizophrenia, but their construct validity remains to be established.

2.3. Glutamatergic Models

Glutamate is major excitatory neurotransmitters in mammalian species. Glutamatergic neurotransmission is executed via two families of receptors: inotropic (NMDA, AMPA and kainite) and metabotropic receptors. Non-competitive blockade of NMDA receptors by ketamine, phencyclidine (PCP), or dizocilpine (MK-801) induces positive, negative and cognitive symptoms of schizophrenia in both recreational users and healthy volunteers. The glutamatergic hypothesis of schizophrenia presumes hypofunction of NMDA receptors, resulting in an increase in cortical glutamate release and secondary activation of the mesolimbic dopamine circuits, thus inducing psychosis. Acute or repeated exposure to NMDA blockers has been established as a pharmacological tool to produce schizophrenia symptomatology in rodents. Their administrations induce motor dysfunction, hyperlocomotion, stereotypic behaviors, PPI and LI deficits, complex impairments in cognitive functions and social interactions, which are reversed by antipsychotics. PPI deficits by non-competitive NMDA antagonists have been described in rats, mice, primates and humans, providing a tool for testing atypical antipsychotics and candidate compounds [60].

Effects of non-competitive NMDA antagonists on biochemical and behavioral abnormalities in animal models and their relevance to schizophrenia have been reviewed (e.g., [61]). On the neurochemical level, acute administration causes increased levels of glutamate in prefrontal cortex (PFC), increased levels of dopamine in PFC and nucleus accumbens. Contrary to acute administration, repeated administration decreases glutamate and dopamine turnover in PFC. Glutamatergic models have been viewed to reconcile the dopaminergic and serotonergic hypotheses, and these three neurotransmitter systems are regarded to be interdependent. MK-801 is a selective NMDA antagonist [62], while PCP interacts also with dopamine transporters, D2 receptors, and sigma receptors [63,64]. Single administration of these agents to rodents produces behavioral abnormalities reminiscent of acute form of schizophrenia.

Systemic treatment with MK-801 results in hippocampal plasticity impairment and parallel deficits in memory and spatial learning in rodents [65,66,67]. It is known that MK-801 impairs hippocampal-dependent behavior, blocks long-term potentiation *in vitro* [68], and alters expression levels of NMDA and dopamine receptors [69,70]

The ability of NMDA blockers to impair cognitive performance depends on dose and type of task. In acute experiments, MK-801 given at 0.1 or 0.2 mg/kg disturbed reference memory, as measured by Morris Water Maze task (MWM), whereas only the higher dose impaired learning memory in the Active Allothetic Place Avoidance (AAPA) task [71]. In another study, MK-801, at 0.2 mg/kg, was found to disrupt the reinforced retention of the AAPA. Re-acquisition of AAPA in the novel environment was impaired by both doses of MK-801 [72]. In accordance with our results, another study also reports impaired working memory at a dose equal or higher than 0.2 mg/kg in reinforced alternation task and radial arm maze [73]. Although MWM is more sensitive to MK-801-induced behavioral deficits than the AAPA, we found working memory impairment, measured by AAPA in Wistar rats treated with 0.1 mg/kg MK-801 but not in Long-Evans rats [74]. The observed effect of strain on performance on visual orientation tests may be related to the visual system deficits associated with albinism [75]. Although higher doses of MK-801 produce cognitive deficits more reliably, they also disturbed motor functions that affect performance on some of the tasks. Thus, appropriate dosage regimen should be considered depending on cognitive tasks used. Impaired working memory, evaluated by the delayed alteration task has been reported [76]. Comparison of the effects of ketamine, PCP, MK-801 with other NMDA antagonists on attention and working memory has been made [77].

Rats treated sub-chronically with low-dose MK-801 showed deficits in the working memory task from MWM and the object-in-context recognition task, but not in the object recognition task [78]. Affected protein translation, synapse formation, hippocampus-dependent learning and neuronal development have been found by postnatal administration of 0.1mg/kg MK-801 for 15 days [79]. Furthermore, alterations in NMDA receptor subunits composition in the hippocampus, similar to the pattern of patients with schizophrenia, have been observed [80].

Increased expression of the NR2B and NR1 subunits in the hippocampus after chronic treatment with MK-801 have been described [81]. Both acute and chronic treatment with PCP induces behavioral and cognitive changes similar to those with MK-801 (reviewed in [82]). Withdrawal from repeated PCP administration has been suggested as another glutamatergic model of schizophrenia. Seiller and Giuffrida [83] reported impairments in working memory after withdrawal from PCP (10 mg/kg, 1 × 14 days), whereas other authors found no such deficit under different dosage regimen (5 mg/kg, 2 × 5 days) [84].

Manipulation with metabotropic glutamate (mGlu) receptors may provide a strategy to treat aberrant behaviors related with schizophrenia, especially cognitive symptoms. Thus, two subtypes of mGlu receptors, i.e. mGlu2/3 and mGlu5 receptors,have been shown to ameliorate deficits in schizophrenia. Data from our laboratory have shown a difference in effect of the activation of mGlu5 and mGlu2/3 receptors on MK-801-induced cognitive deficits. While activation of mGlu5 receptor leads to an improvement of cognitive parameters without affecting locomotion, activation of mGlu2/3 receptor does not [85,86]. However, other investigators observed pro-cognitive effects of mGlu2/3 agonists in PCP-induced animal models [87,88]. LY2140023, an mGlu2/3 receptor agonist, has been demonstrated to be effective for treating positive and negative symptoms of schizophrenia in a phase II study [86] .

Taken together, current data indicate that mGlu5 receptor agonists are effective in the treatment of cognitive deficits, while positive symptoms can be treated by mGlu2/3 receptor agonists, supporting predictive validity for the glutamatergic model of schizophrenia.

Some of the key features of dopaminergic, serotonergic, and glutamatergic models are presented in Table 1.

Table 1. Characteristics of pharmacological animal models of schizophrenia-like behaviors

Clinical symptoms and relevant behavioral measures	Positive symptoms	Negative symptoms	Cognitive deficits	Validity	Limitations
	Hyper-locomotion, stereotypic behavior	Social withdrawal	Prepulse inhibition, Morris water maze, Carousal maze, and etc.		
Dopaminergic model	+	-	+	P	Negative symptoms, not represented
Serotonergic model	+	+	+	F, P	Drug tolerance, present
Glutamatergic model	+	+	+	F, P	Construct validity, to be tested

+, represented; -, not represented; F, face validity; P, predictive validity.

3. Spatial Cognition in Model Animals and Cognitive Abnormalities in Schizophrenia

The search for appropriate biomarkers of psychiatric diseases is crucial for developing suitable animal models. This may be especially difficult for schizophrenia, because of the complexity of its etiology, symptoms and clinical courses. Furthermore, many of typical symptoms cannot be mimicked in rodent models. Therefore, cognitive functions, such as spatial memory, are useful, because the mechanisms underlying their deficits can be shared by humans and animals.

Some studies have shown that patients suffering from schizophrenia performed worse on spatial working memory tasks [89,90]. Spatial memory is easily measured in animal models using spatial tasks, as described in this section.

3.1. Spatial Cognition

Spatial cognition is a widely used model to study cognitive processes both in animals and humans. In a broad sense, we can define spatial cognition as an ability to deal effectively with spatial relations and geometric properties of objects in space. One aspect of this domain of cognition is the capability to orient oneself in a given environment relative to other objects and the knowledge of self-location [91]. This is a key ability for every organism [92], and allows us to design experimental tasks that are natural for animals even in an artificial laboratory environment.

We can distinguish two mechanisms that take part in a goal-directed navigation: idiothetic and allothetic processes [93]. Idiothesis is based on self-motion information produced by active or passive movement of animals [94]. It integrates information from the vestibular system measuring inertial forces originated from acceleration and signals from proprioceptors sensing the subject's locomotion with respect to a substrate [95]. Idiothetic cues are permanently changing – they are generated by self-movement and efferent copies of motion commands [96].

By contrast, allothesis is based on external and more stable information; it represents perception of spatial relationships between remote and visual landmarks vs. the subject [92].

When encoding the same position, the allothetic and idiothetic modes are mutually independent. When one of these processes is removed, it could be compensated by the other, and their contribution rates differ according to the environment in which the subject is located. In darkness, the influence of path integration usually increases [97], but if not updated with external cues, estimation errors in task performance are rapidly increased. The influence of allothesis is enhanced when a subject is navigating on an unstable substrate (water or moving arena) with available distal cues surrounding it [98]. Many lesion studies demonstrated that allothesis is dependent on hippocampus [99,100,101]. There is evidence for the role of hippocampus also in idiothesis, but neuronal substrates for idiothesis are not fully identified [96,102,103].

Therefore, it is advantageous to develop behavioral tests to measure a specific navigational strategy that is not affected by the other. Such tests enable us to learn particular brain areas and mechanisms underlying these strategies separately.

3.2. Morris Water Maze (Fig. 1)

The Morris water maze (MWM) is a classical and perhaps the most abundantly used test of spatial learning and memory. MWM was designed by Richard G.M. Morris in 1981 [104, 105]. The maze is represents by a circular pool, filled with opaque water, in which a rodent (typically a rat) released from various place at the pool periphery searches for an escape platform hidden under the water surface. The trial usually stops either when a rat found the platform, or after a defined maximum duration is completed (e.g., 60 s), after which the animal is gently guided to the goal. In any case, the animal is allowed to stay on the platform for a fixed period of time (e.g., 15 s). This test is unique because virtually all proximal (olfactory etc.) cues are abolished (an animal swims in the water), and only distal landmarks outside a pool can be used to localize the platform in a "cognitive map-like" fashion (in the classical version of the task). Moreover, the test exploits the natural ability of rats to swim while not causing a major distress to the animals despite significant stress response induced by the task [106,107]. Another advantage of the MWM is its simplicity, which has contributed significantly to its success and massive use. Indeed, the hardware part of the apparatus can be constructed at minimum costs and many commercial software solutions are available on the market to operate the maze, ranging from simple and cheap software to large and powerful packages.

Performance of rats on the MWM is evaluated by a number of criteria. Beside mere *escape latency,* i.e., the time needed to find the platform, swim speed and path length should be simultaneously analyzed because they may also provide an indication of sensorimotor disturbance. In many cases, the total path to the platform measured at a given sampling frequency provides better solution than escape frequency. It is preferred to use also a measure of *thigmotaxis,* such as time at the wall. There are a number of other measures, including *direction angle, Whishaw error* and etc., which are reviewed elsewhere [107,108].

Type of the Morris Water Maze Tasks

The MWM is typically used in two basic experimental configurations. The reference (or long-term) memory version (also incremental version or place version; [108]) involves training of rats released from the periphery of the pool to find a hidden platform, the position of which is stable across daily sessions. There are usually more swims (trials) in every daily session, e.g., 8, 10 or 12. The learning of this task is incremental, and for example, healthy animals of the Long-Evans strain from the breeding colony of the Institute of Physiology usually reach the asymptote escape latency by the fourth daily session (with 8 swims; [71,74,109). An early study by Morris showed that place navigation in this version is impaired by hippocampal lesions. However, this version can also be made hippocampus-independent as well as resistant to several pharmacological manipulations after extensive pre-training or specific training protocols. An interesting procedure is so-called non-spatial pre-training (NSP; [110,111]) in which animals are first made familiar with all procedural aspects of the task (´rules´), e.g., there is a platform in the maze, no way how to get on the wall, and etc. The pre-training is usually pursued by closing a dark curtain (without any cues) around the pool and putting submerged platform in random places in the pool. Animals thus get fully acquainted with searching for the platform, but do not know where to search it. Such pre-training was found to eliminate a number of deficits, such as those by NMDA receptor or cholinergic blockade [110,112], diazepam treatment [111], and 5-HT depletion [113] .

Another variant of the MWM task is a *delayed-matching-to place* version (DMP; [114,115]), in which animals are released in four trials a day and the platform position is changed between days (but always stays the same within four trials in a particular day). Therefore, rats cannot locate the platform correctly or find it just by chance in the first swim of a day. However, the second swim already contains a memory trace from the first one, and typically, this swim is evaluated. Moreover, multiple inter-trial intervals (ITIs) between the first and second swims can be used (e.g., 15s; 20min and 90 min). There should be no interference between positions in particular days, i.e. each position should be used only once; in this sense, the task represents a paradigm for assessment of one-trial spatial learning. With short delays (e.g., 15s), this modification is essentially a test of working memory [114] and longer delays are aimed at evaluating persistence of the memory trace [115]. The DMP version of the MWM is strictly hippocampus-dependent, in that animals with hippocampal lesions were not capable of performing better on the second swim than on the first one [114].

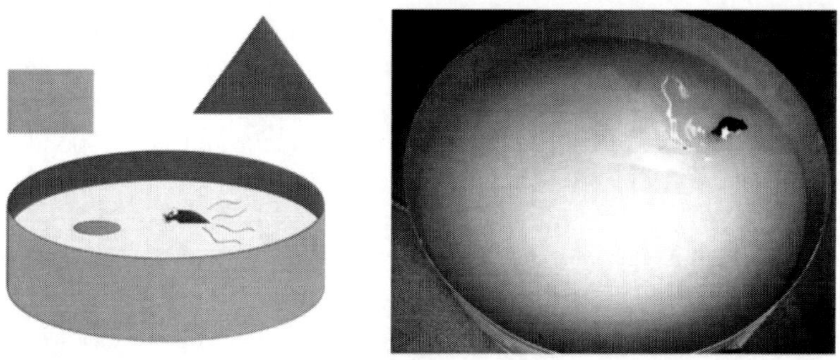

Figure 1. Morris water maze. A) Scheme of the apparatus: A rat is swimming towards a hidden platform according to external visual cues; B) Photograph of a rat on a hidden platform (photos by Jan Svoboda).

As in other tasks, it is important to control for confounding factors from a more general impairment, such as in perceptual, motivational, and procedural dysfunctions. This can be tested by a control test, e.g. *visible platform test*, in which the platform is raised above the water and animals are allowed to swim directly to it. Moreover, performance on the spatial versions should be carefully analyzed in order to rule out a "non-cognitive impairment". After completion of the whole training or each daily session [116], a *'probe trial'* may be conducted, during which a rat is allowed to swim freely in the pool showing a potential preference for a given zone, e.g. time in particular quadrants of the maze or number of crossings through the previous platform-location. Researchers sometimes use a variety of more sophisticated designs of the basic MWM configurations, often together with analysis of behavioral strategies (e.g., [117]). There are also other modifications and protocols, including 'working memory version' (e.g., eight swims daily with the target position changed between days - however, this might be confounded by long-term memory). Other versions use insets (annular water maze), an on-demand or Atlantis platform [118,119]. Some studies sought to assess "self-motion", "idiothetic" navigation [97,120], or path integration [121] in this task.

MWM Performance in Animal Models of Schizophrenia

As a classical and sensitive test of spatial learning and memory, MWM has attracted much attention from scientists interested in cognitive symptoms in animal models of schizophrenia and other diseases. Such studies focus on cognitive deficits in both acute and chronic models of this disorder.

The MWM also has been regarded as a benchmark behavioral test of prediction of antipsychotic-like activity (e.g., [122,123]). For example, behavioral abnormalities following acute application of PCP [124] or MK-801 [125] have been examined as hypoglutamatergic models. These changes are reversed by sertindole, risperidone, and the alpha-7 nicotine receptor agonist SSR180711, but not haloperidol [124, 125] (reviewed in [123]). These results suggest that the MWM can be used to test predictive validity of cognitive disturbances in animal models of schizophrenia. Another recent study has shown that risperidone, at 0.125 mg/kg, significantly shortened MK-801-induced elongation of the distance to platform in the MWM [126].

The MWM can also be used to evaluate behavioral changes caused by chronic exposure to NMDA antagonists (e.g., PCP, MK-801). Such procedure was represented, for example, by 2-week administration of 0.2 mg/kg MK-801, followed by testing in the water maze [127], or shorter administration of a higher dose (0.5 mg/kg; [128]). Repeated PCP administration was also found to elicit deficits in the MWM with a modified design for mice. These animals were administered subcutaneously with PCP (0.25-4.0 mg/kg) for 12 days, and the MWM test was conducted. Deficits in two-trial daily sessions were found to respond to the atypical antipsychotic drug clozapine but not haloperidol (typical antipsychotic drug) [129]. Data from this study suggest that, by carefully titrating dose, it is possible to induce cognitive deficits both in acute and chronic paradigms, which is independent of locomotor activity (e.g., hyperlocomotion) and other functions, such as dis-coordination.

Interestingly, antipsychotics per se were found to impair the Morris water maze performance [130]. Rats were trained in a reference memory version involving four daily sessions, each consisting of three swims. Atypical antipsychotic compounds, sertindole and quetiapine, did not yield any effect on spatial performance, while clozapine disrupted learning on the first two daily sessions but had no effect on the final two daily sessions. Ziprasidone and olanzapine profoundly disrupted spatial memory without effect on swimming speed. Risperidone and haloperidol deteriorated memory, and additionally, decreased swimming speed [130]. This shows that the MWM is a suitable test not only for psychosis-related deficits, but also for the assessment of side-effects of putatively "pro-cognitive" antipsychotic drugs.

Results from our laboratory indicate that performance on the reference memory version of MWM is affected by dopamine D_1 or D_2 receptor blockade [109]. It was also disrupted after acute systemic treatment with NMDA antagonists, such as MK-801 [71]. The latter study showed that the cognitive deficit induced by MK-801 was evident at lower doses than those used in the Carousel maze in Long-Evans rats, which is supported by others [131]. Performance on the ′working memory′ version of the MWM (8 swims a day, platform position changed daily) was found not to be affected by 0.1mg/kg of MK-801 both in Long-Evans and Wistar rats [74]. These results are in agreement with the view that the NMDA receptor may not contribute much to some forms of visuospatial working memory [114].

Controversy exists as to learning impairments, measured by water maze, in animal models of schizophrenia based on the NMDA receptor hypothesis. As noted above [110], the procedure of non-spatial pre-training eliminated the NMDA blocker-induced deficits in performance on the long-term memory version of the MWM. Moreover, systemic or intra-hippocampal treatment with competitive or non-competitive antagonists at NMDA receptors failed to affect working memory [74,114,132], whose deficit is considered a core feature of schizophrenia [133]. These results suggest that physiological inactivation of NMDA receptors (via local application of some antagonists) may elicit behavioral effects that are different from those by systemic administration. This may be due to secondary functional changes in the brain following acute application of non-competitive NMDA receptor antagonists [134,135]. Indeed, systemic administration of MK-801 was found to impair working memory in some studies using the MWM [136,137] and radial-arm maze [138]. Working memory is impaired both in humans and animals after acute administration of sub-anesthetic doses of ketamine (reviewed in [139]).

3.3. Carousel Maze (Fig. 2)

The Carousel maze (also referred to as active allothetic place avoidance) task [71,74,140,141,142,] is a variant of the place avoidance task [143,144,145,146,147,148,149]. In this task, a rat is placed on a dry circular arena, and is required to avoid a directly imperceptible to-be-avoided sector. Rats are typically used, but the maze can be adapted to mice as well. The experimental arena continuously rotates with a fixed speed (1 rpm) in the enlightened room. The to-be-avoided sector (60 degree) in the arena is defined in the stable position in the coordinate frame of the room. Each animal must therefore recognize the distal visual cues in the room, and navigate according to them. He has to ignore self-generated arena-based cues (urine, droppings, scent marks) which are dissociated from the to-be-avoided sector position by arena rotation. Animals also perceive arena rotation (which facilitates learning; [150]), and have to find an appropriate active strategy to move to the safe part of surface constantly or in interrupted runs (hence, active place avoidance).

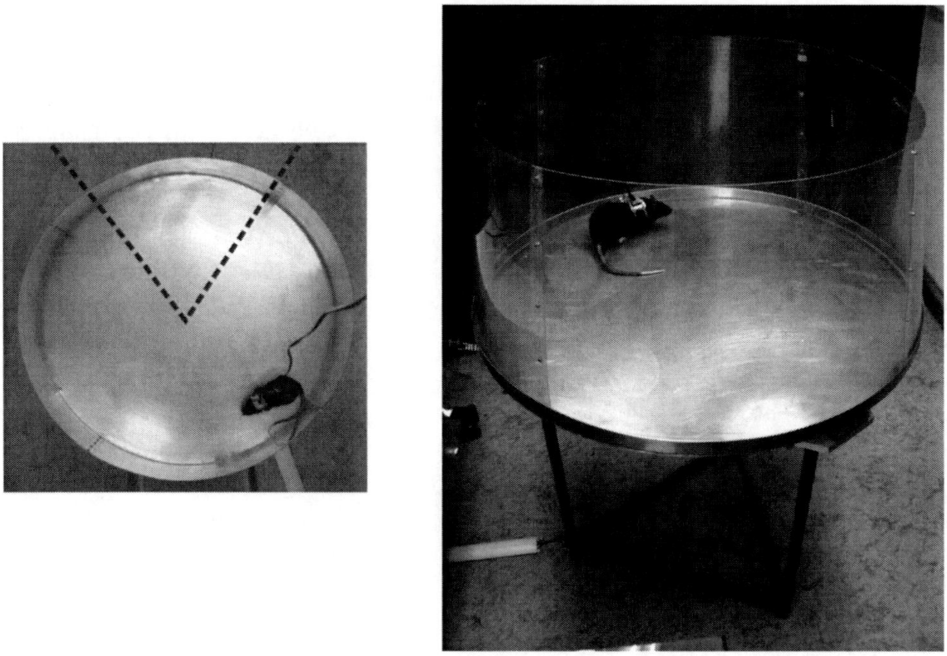

Figure 2. *Carousel maze*. A) View from above. An aversive sector is marked by dashed line; B) A side view.

Performance on the Carousel maze is evaluated with many parameters. Most frequently used measures include total distance traversed per session (as a measure of locomotion) and the number of entrances into the to-be-avoided sector (i.e. errors). The maximum time between two errors (maximum time avoided) is regarded as cumulative performance within a session. The latency from the start of a session to the first error (latency to first error) shows the memory trace established on the previous day, and serves as a measure of retrieval of avoidance, representing "memory retrieval" [151]. There are additional parameters featuring the track by a tested rat in a quantitative way, i.e., linearity of the trajectory, dwell-time in particular radial and annular zones, and total number of shocks. Many of such measures are provided by a commercial solution for the place avoidance arena (Tracker, TrakAnalysis, Biosignal Group, USA).

Place Avoidance and Carousel Maze Tasks

The original "place avoidance" tasks were developed in late nineties [143]. The group initially elaborating place avoidance tasks included M. Wesierska, José M. Cimadevilla, Boldizsár Czéh and others. Scientific leadership was provided by André A. Fenton and Jan Bures.

Designing such ´dry-land´ spatial maze tasks has produced several advantages:

1) These tasks facilitated place-cell recordings; an important paper on place-cells´ attitudes during performance on the two-frame place avoidance task was first published in 2010 [152].

2) They evaluate spatial learning and memory in a more natural environment than other similar tasks, e.g. MWM, and have been considered convenient for the assessment of animal

models of schizophrenia [71,72,74,142,153]. These tasks, together with the selective use of a constantly rotating arena under light/dark conditions, allow identification of a to-be-avoided sector in the coordinate frames of the room and arena; these two are dissociated by slow arena rotation. This has facilitated insights into organization of information by means of reference frames [145,149], and, ultimately, the discovery of ´cognitive coordination´ function of the hippocampus [154], whose ´frame-segregation´ function is dissociable from navigational function [155]). Moreover, the above-mentioned electrophysiological paper [152] has provided evidence that representations of the arena and room frames alternate in the hippocampus during solution of the two-frame place avoidance task. It is noteworthy that the Carousel maze led to the finding that blockade of maintenance phase of long-term potentiation (LTP) erases a previously established memory trace [151].

3) Especially, the Carousel maze has been recommended for the study of behavioral abnormalities in animal models of schizophrenia [71,72,74,142,153].

Features of the Carousel Maze Tasks

Performance on the place avoidance tasks generally requires simultaneous and independent knowledge for arena- and room-frame memories (or representations) [145]. Variants of these tasks include those with no conflict of the two frames (e.g., both frames are made stable, and etc., [154]).

Passive versions of the task, where animals do not have to actively move in order to solve it, are usually used together with ´pellet-retrieval´ or ´pellet-chasing´ manipulation [156]. In these versions, food-deprived rats are trained to collect small food pellets periodically dispersed onto random places of the arena floor from an overhead feeder. Contrary to passive versions, the Carousel maze (active place avoidance), with or without shallow water suppressing the disturbing intra-maze cues (conflict between frames minimized), it is not necessary to motivate the animals to collect food. However, our experience suggests that random collecting of scattered food during performance yields less variability of data, and provides a more sensitive measure of drug effects [157]. It should be noted that mice should be tested on the arena covered with a grid, unlike the case with rats.

Performance on the Carousel maze requires spatial learning. The sector is defined with respect to distal room cues, so the animals are required to use a purely allothetic [158] strategy to determine its position. The allothetic mode of information consists of distal orienting, mainly visual cues. It was demonstrated that rats cannot acquire this task in darkness [159]. The idiothetic mode of navigation (e.g., collection and integration of self-motion signals, [158,160] and substratal exteroceptive cues, such as scent marks) is irrelevant and animals need to ignore them. Another feature of the task is that it requires an active approach for successful avoidance behavior. Passive approach, such as freezing or simple escape upon shock exposure, represents an inefficient strategy, since arena rotation repeatedly transports the rat into the shock sector if the animal does not actively avoid it. The typical strategy to avoid punishment is to recognize the position of the shock sector and stay away from it by walking in a direction opposite to arena rotation. Effective performance on the task is acquired very rapidly. In the case for some variant methods, the acquisition is even faster than in the MWM or radial maze. It is therefore possible to assess short-term changes in performance of animals, e.g. during the estrous cycle [146]. Since the Carousel maze uses a dry-arena, it does not require swimming, and thus can be applied to young or even weaning rats [148].

Carousel Maze in the Study of Animal Models of Schizophrenia

A modern theory about the pathogenesis of schizophrenia concerns neurodevelopmental anomalies coupled with disruption of the glutamatergic neurotransmitter system. This concept is based on the findings that systemic administration of non-competitive antagonists of the N-methyl D-aspartate (NMDA) subtype of glutamate receptors (e.g., ketamine, PCP) cause schizophrenia-like symptoms in healthy humans, and exacerbate psychotic symptoms in schizophrenic patients [161]. These effects might be mediated by greater sensitivity of inhibitory interneurons to the action of NMDA receptor antagonists (e.g., [162]). This results in an increase in excitation of pyramidal neurons in the cortex (e.g., [163]). Genetically-engineered mice with ablated NMDA receptor function in cortical and hippocampal GABAergic interneurons during postnatal ontogenesis elicit schizophrenia-like phenotypes emerging in the post-adolescent period [164].

Systemic administration of MK-801, which causes a cognitive deficit at lower doses and hyperlocomotion at higher doses can be used as a model with predictive validity (e.g., [142,165].

The first study on NMDA receptor blockade compared the effects of MK-801 (0.1 and 0.2 mg/kg) on performance of rats on the Carousel maze and MWM, measures of reference memory [71]. In the MWM, even the lower dose MK-801 significantly increased the latency to find the hidden platform, and retarded the learning. The higher dose caused a severe procedural deficit, so that animals were unable to climb upon the platform. On the other hand, data from the Carousel maze showed the lower dose did not alter either the total path or the total number of errors, whereas the higher dose induced pronounced hyperactivity and prevented effective avoidance [71].

The effect of pre-training on the ability of MK-801 to disrupt behaviors was examined in a follow-up study [72]. Rats were trained in the Carousel maze for 4 daily sessions, and then received systemic MK-801 administration (0.15 or 0.2mg/kg), followed by a reinforced memory retention test with the same position of the to-be-avoided sector on the 5th day. Next week, MK-801-treated rats were trained on a different arena located in a different room for task re-acquisition. The results showed that only the higher dose impaired retention, while both doses disrupted re-acquisition. The higher dose (0.2 mg/kg) also caused hyperactivity, in accordance with previous studies [71, 165]. MK-801 (0.15 mg/kg) was demonstrated to impair spatial avoidance (re-acquisition) despite pre-training, which was accompanied by increased locomotion.

Some strain-related differences were found in performance on the Carousel maze in this animal model of schizophrenia between Long-Evans and Wistar rats. An inter-strain study [74] compared performance of these rat strains (both from breeding colony of the Institute of Physiology ASCR, Prague, Czech Republic) on working memory version of the MWM and the Carousel maze 30 min after systemic administration of MK-801 (0, 0.1, 0.2 and 0.3 mg/kg). The lowest dose did not affect performance on working memory by means of the MWM. The other doses induced motor impairment, and affected the ability of rats to find the platform. Wistar rats administered with 0.1 mg/kg MK-801 performed significantly worse than did Long-Evans rats. The performance was slightly impaired in saline-treated Wistar animals compared to Long-Evans counterparts.

In the Carousel maze, only the Wistar strain displayed an increased number of errors and reduced duration of the maximum time avoided, following treatment with MK-801 (0.1 mg/kg). Locomotor activity in the Carousel maze was not significantly increased by this dose.

Both strains performed significantly worse regarding these cognitive parameters with MK-801, at 0.2 and 0.3 mg/kg, which was accompanied with increased locomotion. These results suggested that Wistar rats are more sensitive to NMDA receptor antagonists than Long-Evans rats in the Carousel maze tasks.

MK-801 at lower doses impaired long-term memory rather than short-term memory. The relative sparing of short-term memory is not similar to findings from humans; schizophrenia patients typically exhibit working memory deficits [133]. This discrepancy may be explained by a minor involvement of the NMDA receptor system at least in the hippocampus, as suggested by neurochemical studies (e.g., [114]).

The predictive validity of this animal model of schizophrenia was tested by administering DA and/or 5-HT related compounds, including typical and atypical antipsychotic drugs (ritanserin, risperidone, haloperidol) [142]. This study investigated the effects of these compounds on schizophrenia-like behaviors induced by MK-801. Male adult albinotic Wistar rats were injected with 0.1 mg/kg MK-801, which impaired avoidance without altering locomotion. Additionally, animals received ritanserin (5-$HT_{2A/2C}$ antagonist; 2.5 and 5mg/kg), the atypical antipsychotic risperidone (D_2/5-$HT_{2A/2C}$ antagonists; 0.1 and 1 mg/kg), or typical antipsychotic haloperidol (D_1/D_2 antagonist; 0.1 and 1 mg/kg). Haloperidol markedly decreased locomotion but did not alleviate cognitive deficits induced by low dose (0.1 mg/kg) MK-801. By contrast, risperidone and ritanserin significantly ameliorated MK-801-induced cognitive deficits. These results suggest that 5$HT_{2A/2C}$ receptor antagonism may be a crucial factor in treating cognitive deficits in MK-801-induced animal models of psychosis.

Research to date suggests that MK-801 may interact *in vivo* with other neurotransmitter systems, including the noradrenergic system. This may be related to the alpha-adrenergic antagonist property of many atypical antipsychotic drugs. There is evidence that both locomotor stimulation and deficits in avoidance behavior in the Carousel maze induced by MK-801 is reversed by systemic application of the alpha1-adrenergic antagonist prazosin, at 1 and 2 mg/kg [140]. This study showed that both doses of prazosin partly alleviated hyperlocomotion induced by MK-801, as well as avoidance-behavior deficits, as measured by the number of entrances into the shock sector. Importantly, MK-801-induced decrease in maximum time between two entrances, another index of cognitive function, was not affected by prazosin. On the other hand, MK-801-induced hyperlocomotion by prazosin was inhibited under the ′forced-locomotion′ condition in the Carousel maze. Results of this experiment also showed variable degrees of the link between spatial cognition parameters and locomotion in MK-801 treated animals [140].

Disturbances of glutamatergic transmissions may represent a potential target for pharmacotherapy of schizophrenia. This is based on the idea that enhancement of glutamatergic transmission via. metabotropic glutamate (mGlu) receptor subtypes, mGlu2/3 and mGlu5, would ameliorate cognitive performance. We recently evaluated cognitive deficits induced by 0.1 mg/kg MK-801 in Long-Evans rats and the effects of non-specific mGlu receptor agonists using Carousel maze (with 4 daily acquisition sessions) [153]. The test drugs were: (1S,3R)-1-aminocyclopentane-1,3-dicarboxylic acid (1S,3R-ACPD), as an mGlu5 receptor agonist; (RS)-2-Chloro-5-hydroxyphenylglycine (CHPG), (3-Fluoro-phenyl)methylene]hydrazone-3-fluorobenzaldehyde (DFB), and 3-Cyano-N-(1,3-diphenyl-1H-pyrazol-5-yl)benzamide (CDPPB) as positive modulators; and (2,2,2-Trifluoro-N-[4-(2-methoxyphenoxy)phenyl]-N-(3-pyrdinylmethyl) ethanesulfonamide hydrochloride (LY-487379) as an mGlu2/3 receptor agonists.

1S,3R-ACPD, but not LY-487379 ameliorated cognitive performance without affecting locomotion [153]. These results support the concept that mGlu5 receptor agonism may provide a novel strategy for the treatment of cognitive deficits in patients with schizophrenia. Above all, our study suggests the usefulness of the Carousel maze in the search of new drugs to treat cognitive disturbances of the illness.

3.4. Radial Maze (Fig. 3)

The radial maze is one of the most frequently used standard measures of spatial cognition and learning memory. It was invented by Olton and Samuelson in 1976 [166], and rapidly became popular in neurobiological research. In the original version, the maze has a central octogonal platform and eight arms with the same length. The "standard version" of the maze consists of platform and eight identical arms radiating from it, like a spoke on a wheel. The number of arms can vary from four (known as a "plus maze" [167]) to 12 [168] in rats, and can be 17 or even 24 in mice [169,170,171].

The apparatus is commonly elevated about the floor, and placed in a room with many salient visual cues that can be used for allothetic orientation. In the standard version, the maze is fully baited, which means a food reward placed at the end of each arm. Animals are provided with only limited time to choose arms; in this situation the optimal strategy is to visit every arm only once.

There are modifications of the radial maze, e.g. the aquatic version using aversive stimuli rather than apetitive stimuli [172], or a version combined with both "win-shift" and "win-stay" strategies [173].

The *number of errors* is the parameter most often used in the radial maze. We define an error as a return of a rat to the previously visited arm. Another parameter is the *rank of the first error,* i.e., the number of consecutive correct responses before an error occurred. These two parameters evaluate the efficiency of performance on the test. After training, the number of errors decreases and the rank of the first error increases. Quantification of the *angles between two successfully visited arms* represents strategic aspects, in addition to efficacy [174]. Another parameter is the *degree of divergence* [175]. This parameter is counted only for successful trials without errors, and reflects the number of arms between two subsequent correct choices plus one. The number could by averaged for trials during the whole daily session. Degree of divergence equals 7 in case rats use a clockwise strategy, representing visits to all 8 arms [170].

The *sequential position of error* is another parameter that determines relative probability of repetition of a choice [166]. On each day of testing, the first seven choices were ordered, and the observed relative probability of repeating the correct choice is calculated. Scores range from 0 to 100 percent. One hundred percent indicates all errors were made by repeating a particular arm, while 0 percent suggests that this choice was not repeated. This provides information on whether animals tend to enter the arm they have already chosen at the beginning of the session.

In the original Olton's version, all arms were initially open and rats could freely explore all of them without any restrictions. However, Olton and his colleagues later introduced a new version of the task with the inter-choices time intervals, i.e. the period during which access to the arms is prevented ("confinement intervals") [170,176,177]. They implemented this step to prevent rats from stereotypic behavior he observed.

Dubreuil and her colleagues systematically tested the performance of rats on the maze with or without confinement of different durations [174]. They found that both versions – with or without confinement of 10 sec produced similar efficiency after 12 days of training, although the confined rats made more errors during the training. However, some differences were noted in behavioral strategies for solving the task between the two conditions. Rats from *no* confinement condition used a clockwise strategy, so that they visited all arms; confinement probably prevents the development of this strategy. Furthermore, confined rats did not show any preference for a particular angle. The authors argued the clockwise strategy is based on locomotor activity, and that implementation of a few second delay is necessary to remove this motor-based strategy and allow animals to develop spatial representation of environment. Confinement intervals vary depending on versions of radial mazes, ranging from seconds to tens of minutes (e.g., [174,178]).

The original version of radial maze, which was fully baited, was designed to assess "working memory" of animals, as defined by Olton and his colleagues. It should be emphasized that this term is slightly different from the definition by Miller al. [179] for humans. Working memory in human studies originated from the unitary model of Atkinson and Shiffrin [180], who proposed that this cognitive ability represents a system controlling the flow of information into and out of long-term memory [181]. Presently, the multiple-system model proposed by Baddeley and Hitch [182] predominates. According to it, working memory is a system providing temporary storage and manipulation of information, which underlies complex cognitive tasks, such as language comprehension, learning, and reasoning. It can be divided into some components; 1) the central executive system, which is assumed to control attention, 2) the visuospatial sketch pad manipulating visual images, and (3) the phonological loop, which stores and rehearses speech-based information [183,184]. Recently, another subsystem, i.e. the episodic buffer that holds multidimensional episodes combining different modalities, has been proposed [181]. However, the animal model of working memory overlaps with these human models in some respects [185].

In a broader, sense working memory in animals is defined as a representation of object, stimulus or spatial location, which is used to guide behaviors within a testing session [186]. Sometimes, it may be problematic to distinguish working memory from other subtypes of short-term memory.

To measure reference memory and working memory at the same time, a modified version of radial maze was developed [177]. It consists of two sets of arms, one baited and the other not. Food is placed on the same arms every day during the training. An animal is considered to perform optimally if entering each of the baited arms only once, avoiding the unbaited arms. The entry to a never-baited arm is regarded as an error linked to reference memory. On the other hand, repeated entry to one of the baited arms within one session is considered an error related to working memory (Fig. 3).

Several lines of evidence suggest both working memory and long-term memory are disrupted in schizophrenia, although controversy exists as to whether neurocognition is generally or domain-dependently impaired (for review see [133,187,188]). Performance on the radial maze is disrupted in some pharmacological animal models of schizophrenia. In line with the glutamatergic hypothesis, many studies demonstrate systemic administration of

NMDA antagonists impairs cognition, depending on their type (competitive or non-competitive antagonists) and actions on other receptors [190,191].

A meta-analysis revealed that DA exerts less influence on performance on radial maze than on MWM, due to the difference in motivational procedure [201]; performance on radial maze is affected by DA levels in the nucleus accumbens after food deprivation [192].

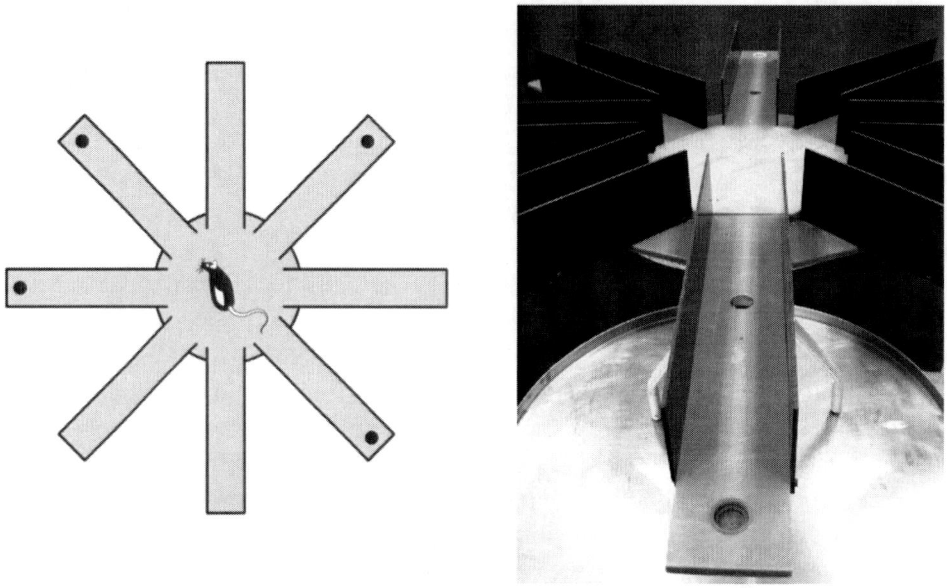

Figure 3. Radial maze. A) Scheme of an experiment measuring working and reference memory. Half of the arms are baited. B) Photograph of the apparatus.

Kay and colleagues [193] compared the effects of MDMA and scopolamine on performance on working memory and reference memory in an eight-arm radial maze task. They demonstrated that scopolamine produced a greater impairment with respect to the working memory component of the task, whereas acute exposure to 3,4-methylenedioxymethaphemtamine (MDMA, a DA/5-HT releaser) produced a greater impairment in reference memory. These authors postulated that the 5-HT agonist properties of MDMA provide a neurochemical mechanism underlying the specific influence on reference memory.

Buhot et al. [194] studied the effect of 5-HT on spatial memory performance in the rat by using both working and reference memory versions of the radial maze. Animals received intra-hippocampal micro-injections of 8-hydroxy-2-(di-n-propylamino)tetralin (8-OH-DPAT, a 5-HT_{1A} agonist, 3-(1,2,5,6-tetrahydropyrid-4-yl)pyrrolo[3,2-b]pyrid-5-one (CP-93,129, a 5-HT $_{1B}$ agonist), or scopolamine. Whereas 8-OH-DPAT increased running speed, with no effect on spatial memory, both CP-93,129 and scopolamine disrupted spatial memory performance. CP-93,129 showed a greater effect on reference memory in a dose-dependent manner, whereas scopolamine affected working and reference memory to a similar extent.

Confounding factors of the radial maze include the use olfactory cues that could provide animals with information on which arms have already been visited. Various methods to prevent olfactory cues are; to allow animals freely explore the maze before the test, to clean the arms between the tests, to rotate them around the platform while the positions of the food remain the same [195], and so on.

As mention before, spatial cognition is intrinsic to rodents' behaviors, and radial maze, especially the standard version, is appetitive and causes only little stress to animals. The ability of radial maze to separate and quantify the deficit of working and reference memory performances makes the task a powerful tool to study psychiatric diseases, including schizophrenia, and develop their therapeutics.

3.5. Operant Tasks Using a Computer Screen (Fig. 4)

Spatial cognition of rodents has been studied mainly by tasks in which animals are actively moving throughout a space (e.g., [104,166,196]). Impaired performance could therefore be caused by deficits in recognizing subject's own position and/or planning and executing goal-directed movements. Only a few attempts have been made to minimize the influence of locomotor components, while extracting recognition components of animals' behavior. In experiments by Klement and Bures [197], rats were passively transported onto a rotating arena through an environment. They were trained to recognize a specific position by reinforcing lever presses in that location. Pašťálková and colleagues [198] studied rats watching a rotating scene. These animals were trained to respond when the scene was within a particular sector by reinforcing lever presses while the object was there.

We have developed a novel behavioral test in which rats observe distant objects on the computer screen, and discriminate their positions [199,200,201]. Food-deprived rats were placed in a modified Skinner box with an open front wall allowing them watching the screen. The operant chamber was placed in front of a computer screen where the visual stimuli were presented. The rats were trained to press a lever according to these stimuli. The operant responses were rewarded when a particular stimulus or configuration was displayed. We used this experimental apparatus for tasks measuring various types of cognition, i.e., brightness discrimination, object discrimination, and position-discrimination. In the position-discrimination task, rats are trained to press a lever when a stationary object was displayed in a particular position, or when a moving object was passing through a particular region.

We demonstrated rats elicit an increased number of responses before the object entered the rewarded area. This suggests these animals recognized the position of the virtual object moving on the computer screen by estimating distance between the object and the rewarded position [199,201].

To test the suitability of this method for pharmacological research, Levcik and colleagues examined the effect of systemic injection of MK-801, (RS)-2-chloro-5- hydroxy-phenylglycine (CHPG, a mGluR5-agonist), and their co-administration on cognitive performance of rats in the novel spatial task [202]. Food deprived rats were trained to press a lever when an object (white rectangle) moving from one side of the screen to the other was in the particular "rewarded area". After the rats had reached the point of asymptotic performance, the effect of MK-801 and CHPG on spatial cognition was tested.

Whereas intact rats showed increased frequency before the object entered into the rewarded area, MK-801 (0.1 mg/kg, i.p.) impaired the ability of animals to recognize the position of the distant objects on the screen, without affecting motor activity. Administration of CHPG (0.1 mg/kg, i.p.) did not elicit effect on either the cognitive or motor component of the performance. Treatment with CHPG reduced MK-801-induced impairment of performance on the task, consistent with findings in other laboratories. These observations suggest that the test we are proposing [202] provides a novel tool suitable for evaluating disturbances of spatial cognition in animal models of schizophrenia.

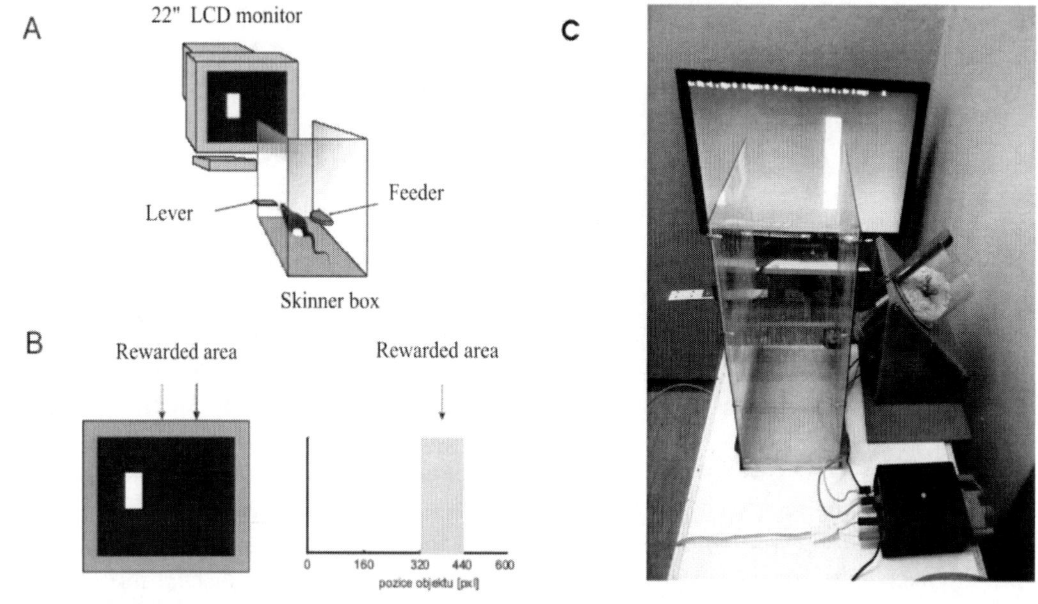

Figuew 4. Operant tasks using a computer screen A) Scheme of the apparatus: B) Visual stimulus shown on the screen (experiment with a moving object); C) Photograph of the apparatus (scheme adapted from [202] with permission of authors).

One of the benefits of this novel task, in comparison with MWM and radial maze, is the ability to distinguish between cognitive and motoric components of animals' behavior. This is advantageous particularly in pharmacological research, because some (antipsychotic) drugs also affect the former component interacting with the latter.

A shortcoming of this method is a relatively lengthy training time compared with other spatial tasks. Another concerns the mixture of spatial and temporal strategies; rats may use both temporal and spatial cues to solve this version of operant tasks. Therefore, it is important to design these tasks in the way that allows distinction between these strategies.

A computer monitor for presenting stimuli has been used in other experiments with rodents (e.g., [203,204,205,206,207,208]). This method provides a better control of the shape of objects, their positions, velocity, and trajectories, as well as the precise timing of experiments. These manipulations are difficult with physical objects. Moreover, these "virtual reality" tasks are applicable also to primates and humans. This allows better understanding of the difference in neuronal mechanisms and functions across species, and, thus, better prediction of the ability of novel drugs to ameliorate cognitive impairments in clinical subjects.

Conclusion

Association and linkage studies in humans have so far produced inconsistent results, and have provided only limited information as to the relations between risk factors and the development of schizophrenia. On the other hand, experimental models have provided more consistent evidence. Specifically, experimental paradigms with animals allow us to test causalities and mechanistic hypotheses in the ways that are not feasible in patients. Therefore, the role for the animal models will remain essential for the study of the pathophysiology of schizophrenia and the development of novel therapeutics.

A crucial issue in designing these animal models is that some of the most prominent symptoms (e.g., hallucinations, abstract thinking, language, complex social cognition etc.) cannot be fully replicated. On the other hand, a number of biological markers (e.g., cognitive deficits) relevant to schizophrenia are likely to be reproduced.

Cognitive deficits are one of the biomarkers bridging the psychology in humans and experimental approaches. For this reason, it is important to develop cognitive evaluation sensitive enough to detect specific features of schizophrenia. Tests of spatial cognition provide a promising candidate for this purpose. They are used to measure not only spatial cognition itself, but also impairments of other key cognitive domains, such as learning memory and attention [89,90,209,210].

Acknowledgments

The authors declare no conflict of interest for this chapter. This work was supported by research goal MSM 0021620816, grants GACR P309/10/J032 and 309/09/0286, MSMTCR (1M0517 and LC554), the research project AVOZ 50110509, the bilateral project of Academy of Sciences of the Czech Republic, Health and Welfare Ministry of Japan, Takeda Science Foundation, and Japan Society for the Promotion of Science.

References

[1] N. L. Lazar, R. W. J. Neufeld, D. P. Cain, *J Psychiatry Neurosci*, 36(4), 1-25, (2011)
[2] N. C. Andreasen, J. C. Ehrhardt, V. E. Swayze et al., *Arch Gen Psychiatry*, 47, 35-44, (1990)
[3] J.R. Kelsoe Jr, J. L. Cadet, D. Pickar, et al., *Arch Gen Psychiatry*, 45, 533-41, (1988)
[4] R. Rajarethinam, J. R. DeQuardo, J. Miedler, et al., *Psychiatry Res*, 108, 79-87, (2001)
[5] S. Heckers, C. Konradi, *J Neural Transm,* 109, 891-905, (2002)
[6] R. W. Buchanan, K. Vladar, P. E. Barta, et al., *Am J Psychiatry*, 155, 1049-55, (1998)
[7] S. Marenco, D. R. Weinberger, *Dev Psychopathol,* 12, 501-27, (2000)
[8] J. A. Lieberman, D. Perkins, A. Belger, M. Chakos, F. Jarskog, J. Gilmore, *Biol Psychiatry*, 50(11), 884-897, (2001)
[9] B. K. Lipska, D. R. Weinberger, *Neuropsychopharmacology*, 23(3), 223-39, (2000)
[10] B. K. Lipska, D. R. Weinberger, *Neurotox Res*, 4(5-6), 469-475, (2002)
[11] A. S. Brown, E. J. Derkits, *Am J Psychiatry*, 167(3), 61-80, (2001)
[12] J. E. Schijndel, G. J. Martens, *Curr Neuropharmacol*, 8(4), 382-93, (2010)

[13] R. E. Lubow, Schizophr Bull, 31(1), 139-153 (2005)
[14] P. Willner, *Prog Neuropsychopharmacol Biol Psychiatry*, 10(6), 677-90, (1986)
[15] C. Maximino, T. M. de Brito, A. Gouveia Jr., *Psychology & Neuroscience, 3(1), 117 – 123 (2010)*
[16] S. Tordjman, D. Drapier, O. Bonnot, R. Graignic, S. Fortes, D. Cohen, B. Millet, C. Laurent, Behav Genet, 37, 61–78, (2007)
[17] P. Willner. Behavioural models in psychopharmacology. In P. Willner (Ed.), *Behavioural models in psychopharmacology: Theoretical, industrial and clinical perspectives* (pp. 3-18). Cambridge: Cambridge University Press. (1991)
[18] M. S. Rand, Selection of animal models. Research animal methods. University of Arizona, Tucson, (2004)
[19] S. Tordjman, Behav Genet, 37, 61–78, (2007)
[20] E. R. Marcotte, D. M. Pearson, L. K. Srivastava, *J Psychiatry Neurosci,* 26(5), 395-410, (2001)
[21] A. Carlsson, *Neuropsychopharmacology*, 1(3), 179-86. (1988)
[22] M. Laruelle, A. Abi-Dargham. *J Psychopharmacol*. 13(4), 358-71, (1999)
[23] A. Abi-Dargham, *Int J Neuropsychopharmacol,* 7(1), 1-5, (2004)
[24] D. R. Weinberger, K. F. Berman, B. P. Illowsky, *Arch Gen Psychiatry*, 45(7), 609-15, (1988)
[25] M. Srisurapanont, R. Ali, J. Marsden, A. Sunga, K. Wada, M. Monteiro, Int J Neuropsychopharmacol, 6(4), 347-52, (2003)
[26] Y. Goto, A. A. Grace, *Int Rev of Neurobiol*, 78, (2007)
[27] O. Guillin, A. Abi-Dargham, M. Laruelle, *Int Rev of Neurobiol*, 78, (2007)
[28] H. Ujike, T. Onoue, K. Akiyama, T. Hamamura, S. Otsuki, *U Psychopharmacology* (Berl), 98(1), 89-92, (1989)
[29] T. Hamamura, K. Akiyama, K. Akimoto, K. Kashihara, K. Okumura K, H., S. Otsuki. *Brain Res*. 546(1), 40-6, (1991)
[30] J. R. Shoblock, I. M. Maisonneuve, S. D. Glick, *Psychopharmacology (Berl)*, 170(2), 150-6, (2003)
[31] M. R. Stefani, B. Moghaddam, *Behav Brain Res,* 134(1-2), 267-74, (2002)
[32] H. Russig, A. Durrer, B. K. Yee, C. A. Murphy, J. Feldon. *Neuroscience*. 119(1), 167-79, (2003)
[33] T. Shuto, A. Nishi, *CNS Neurosci Ther*. 17(2), 133-9, (2011)
[34] T. Nagai, K. Takuma, M. Dohniwa, D. Ibi, H. Mizoguchi, H. Kamei, T. Nabeshima, K. Yamada, *Psychopharmacology (Berl),* 194(1), 21-32. (2007)
[35] S. A. Castner, P. S. Goldman-Rakic, *Biol Psychiatry*, 54(2), 105-10, (2003)
[36] S. A. Castner, P. S. Goldman-Rakic, *Neuropsychopharmacology*. 20(1), 10-28, (1999)
[37] F. Sams-Dodd, J. D. Newman, *Pharmacol Biochem Behav*. 56(3), 471-80, (1997)
[38] S. A. Castner, P. S. Goldman-Rakic, *J Neurosci*, 24(6), 1446-50, (2004)
[39] T. L. Sills, A. O. Onalaja, J. N. Crawley. *Eur J Neurosci.* 10(5), 895-902, (1998)
[40] M. J. Marino, L. J. Knutsen, M. Williams, *J Med Chem*, 51(5), 1077-107, (2008)
[41] M. B. Bowers Jr, D. X. Freedman, Arch Gen Psychiatry, 15(3), 240-8, (1966)
[42] L. E. Hollister, *Psychiatr Clin North Am*, 7(3), 435-52, (1984)
[43] D. E. Nichols, *Pharmacol Ther*. 101(2), 131-81, (2004)
[44] F. X. Vollenweider, K. L. Leenders, C. Scharfetter, P. Maguire, O. Stadelmann, J. Angst, *Neuropsychopharmacology*, 16(5), 357-72, (1997)
[45] F. X. Vollenweider, *Pharmacopsychiatry*, 31(2), 92-103, (1998)
[46] G. V. Williams, S. G. Rao, P. S. Goldman-Rakic. *J Neurosci*, 22(7), 2843-54, (2002)
[47] T. Sumiyoshi, V. Bubenikova-Valesova, J. Horacek, B. Bert, *Adv Ther*, 25(10), 1037-56. (2008)

[48] Y. Higuchi, T. Sumiyoshi, Y. Kawasaki, T. Ito, T. Seo, M. Suzuki, *J Clin Psychopharmacol.* 30(6), 732-4, (2010)
[49] V. Bubenikova-Valesova, J. Svoboda, J. Horacek, T. Sumiyoshi, *Psychopharmacology (Berl)*, 212(2), 267-76, (2010)
[50] T. Sumiyoshi, M. Tsunoda, Y. Higuchi, T. Itoh, T. Seo T, H. Itoh, M. Suzuki, M. Kurachi, Adv Ther, 27(5), 307-13, (2010)
[51] O. L. Carter, D. C. Burr, J. D. Pettigrew, G. M. Wallis, F. Hasler, F. X. Vollenweider, *J Cogn Neurosci*, 17(10), 1497-508, (2005)
[52] L. Grossman, E. Utterback, A. Stewart, S. Gaikwad, K. M. Chung, C. Suciu, K. Wong, M. Elegante, S. Elkhayat, J. Tan, T. Gilder, N. Wu, J. Dileo, J. Cachat, A. V. Kalueff, *Behav Brain Res*, 214(2), 277-84, (2010)
[53] D. X. Freedman, Pharmacol Biochem Behav, 24(2), 407-15, (1986)
[54] T. Pálenícek, M. Balíková, V. Bubeníková-Valesová, J. Horácek, *Psychopharmacology (Berl)*, 196(1), 51-62, (2008)
[55] D. Marona-Lewicka, C. D. Nichols, D. E. Nichols, *Neuropharmacology*, 61(3), 503-12, (2011)
[56] P. J. Gresch, R. L. Smith, R. J. Barrett, E. Sanders-Bush, *Neuropsychopharmacology*, 30(9), 1693-702, (2005)
[57] J. E. Leysen, P. F. Janssen, C. J. Niemegeers, *Eur J Pharmacol*, 163(1), 145-9, (1989)
[58] R. L. Smith, R. J. Barrett, E. Sanders-Bush, *Psychopharmacology (Berl),* 144(3), 248-54, (1999)
[59] R. J. Strassman, C. R. Qualls, L. M. Berg, *Biol Psychiatry*, 39(9), 784-95, (1996)
[60] M. Geyer, B. Ellenbroek, *Prog Neuropsychopharmacol Biol Psychiatry*, 27(7), 1071-1079, (2003)
[61] V. Bubeníková-Valesová, J. Horácek, M. Vrajová, C. Höschl, *Neurosci Biobehav Rev*, 32(5), 1014-23, (2008)
[62] E. H. Wong, J. A. Kemp, T. Priestley, A. R. Knight, G. N. Woodruff, L. L. Iversen, *Proc Natl Acad Sci U S A*, 83(18), 7104-8. (1986)
[63] M. J. Crosby, J. E. Hanson, A. E. Fleckenstein, G. R. Hanson, *Eur J Pharmacol*, 438(1-2), 75-8, (2002)
[64] J. W. Sharp, *Brain Res*, 758(1-2), 51-8, (1997)
[65] M. Ahlander, I. Misane I, P. A. Schött, S. O. Ogren, *Neuropsychopharmacology*, 21(3), 414-26, (1999)
[66] I. Q. Whishaw, R. N. Auer, *Psychopharmacology (Berl)*, 98(4), 500-7, (1989)
[67] D. Manahan-Vaughan, D. von Haebler, C. Winter, G. Juckel, U. Heinemann, *Hippocampus*, 18(2), 125-34, (2008)
[68] A. S. Fix, J. F. Ross, S. R. Stitzel, R. C. Switzer, *Toxicol Pathol*, 24, 291–304, (1996)
[69] G. Duncan, S. Miyamoto, H. Gu, J. Lieberman, B. Koller, J. Snouwaert, *Brain Res*, 951, 166–176, (1996)
[70] D. J. Healy, J. H. Meador-Woodruff, *Eur J Pharmacol*, 306, 257–264, (1996)
[71] A. Stuchlik, L. Rezacova, K. Vales, V. Bubenikova, S. Kubik, *Neurosci Lett*, 12, 366(2), 162-6, (2004)
[72] A. Stuchlík, K. Vales, *Behav Brain Res*, 159(1), 163-71, (2005)
[73] D. F. Wozniak, J. W. Olney, L. Kettinger, M. Price, J. P. Miller, *Psychopharmacology (Berl)*, 101(1), 47-56, (1990)
[74] K. Vales, V. Bubenikova-Valesova, D. Klement, A. Stuchlik, *Neurosci Res*, 55(4), 383-8, (2006)
[75] D. J. Creel, R. E. Dustman, E. C. Beck, *J Comp Physiol Psychol*, 73(3), 490-3, (1970)
[76] W. Zajaczkowski, A. Czyrak, K. Wedzony, *Pol J Pharmacol*, 55(5), 703-11 (2003)

[77] J. W. Smith, F. Gastambide, G. Gilmour, S. Dix S, J. FossJ, K. Lloyd, N. Malik, M. A. Tricklebank, *Psychopharmacology (Berl)*, [Epub ahead of print] Apr 12. (2011)
[78] J. T. Li, Y. A. Su, C. M. Guo, Y. Feng, Y. Yang, R. H. Huang, T. M. Si.. Eur J *Pharmacol.,* 652(1-3), 65-72, (2010)
[79] M. Elhardt, L. Martinez, M. V. Tejada-Simon, *Neurosci Lett*, 468(2), 166-71, (2010)
[80] X. M. Gao, K. Sakai, R. C. Roberts, R. R. Conley, B. Dean, C. A. Tamminga, Am J *Psychiatry*, 157(7), 1141-9. (2000)
[81] D. Rujescu, A. Bender, M. Keck, A. M. Hartmann, F. Ohl, H. Raeder, I. Giegling, J. Genius J, R. W. McCarley, H. J. Möller, H. A. Grunze, *Biol Psychiatry*, 59(8), 721-9, (2006)
[82] J. D. Jentsch, R. H. Roth, *Neuropsychopharmacology*, 20(3), 201-25 (1999)
[83] A. Seillier, A. Giuffrida, *Behav Brain Res*, 204(2), 410-5, (2009)
[84] M. R. Stefani, B. Moghaddam B, *Behav Brain Res*, 134(1-2), 267-74, (2002)
[85] K. Vales, J. Svoboda, K. Benkovicova, V. Bubenikova-Valesova, A. Stuchlik. Eur J *Pharmacol*, 639(1-3), 91-8, (2010)
[86] S. Chaki, H. Hikichi, *Curr Pharm*, 17(2), 94-102, (2011)
[87] J. Cartmell, J. A. Monn, D. D. Schoepp, *J Pharmacol Exp Ther*, 291(1), 161-70, (1999)
[88] B. Moghaddam, B. W. Adams, *Science*, 281(5381), 1349-52, (1998)
[89] G. Weniger, E. Irle, *Schizophr. Res*, 101, 201-209, (2008).
[90] S. Landgraf, M. O. Krebs, J. P. Olie, G. Committeri, A. Berthoz, I. Amado, *Neuropsychologia*, 48, 2922-2930, (2010)
[91] A. S. Reber, *The Penguin Dictionary of Psychology*. England, Clays Ltd., (1985)
[92] J. O'Keefe, L. Nadel, *The hippocampus as a cognitive map*. Clarendon Press, Oxford. (1978)
[93] B. Czeh, A. Stuchlik, M. Wesierska, J. M. Cimadevilla, J. Pokorny, L. Seress, J. Bures, *Neurobiology of Learning and Memory*, 75, 190–213, (2001)
[94] M. Mittelstaedt, H. Mittelstaedt, *Naturwissenschaften*, 68, 566. (1980)
[95] A. Stuchlik, A. A. Fenton, and J. Bures, PNAS 98(6), 3537–3542, (2001)
[96] I. Q. Whishaw, B. Gorny B, J Neurosci, 19(11), 4662-73, (1999)
[97] Moghaddam, J. Bures, Behav Brain Res., 78(2), 121-9, (1996)
[98] A. Stuchlik, J. Bures, Behav Brain Res, 128(2), 179-88, (2002)
[99] R. G. M. Morris, P. Garrud, J. Rawlings, J. O'Keefe, *Nature (London),* 297, 681–683, (1982)
[100] J. P. Bouffard, L. E. Jarrard, *Behav Neurosci*, 102(6), 828-34, (1988)
[101] L. E. Jarrard, *Behav Brain Res*, 71(1-2), 1-10, (1995)
[102] I. Q. Whishaw, D. J. Hines, D. G. Wallace DG, *Behav Brain Res*, 127(1-2), 49-69, (2001)
[103] D. G. Wallace, D.J. Hines, J. H. Gorny, I. Q. Wishaw, A role for the hippocampus in dead reckoning: an ethological analysis using natural exploratory and food-carrying tasks. In K. J. Jeffery (Ed) The Neurobiology of Spatial Behavior, Oxford University Press, 316 pages. (2003)
[104] R. G. Morris, *Learning and Motivation*, 12, 239-260, (1981)
[105] R. G. Morris, *J. Neurosci.* Methods, 11, 47-60, (1984)
[106] C. Hölscher, *Behav Brain Res*, 100(1-2), 225-35, (1999)
[107] R. D'Hooge, P. P. De Deyn, *Brain Res Brain Res Rev*, 36(1), 60-90, (2001)
[108] R. E. Clark, S. J. Martin, *Curr Opin Neurobiol*, 15(5), 593-8, (2005)
[109] A. Stuchlik, L. Rehakova, P. Telensky, K. Vales, *Neurosci Lett*, 422(3), 169-74, (2007)
[110] D. Saucier, E. L. Hargreaves, F. Boon, C. H. Vanderwolf, D. P. Cain, *Behav Neurosci*, 110(1), 103-16, (1996)
[111] D. P. Cain, *Psychopharmacology (Berl),* 130(4), 313-9, (1997)

[112] D. P. Cain, D. Saucier, F. Boon, *Behav Brain Res*, 84(1-2), 179-93, (1997)
[113] J. Beiko, L. Candusso, D. P. Cain, *Behav Brain Res*, 88(2), 201-11, (1997)
[114] R. J. Steele, R. G. Morris, *Hippocampus*, 9(2), 118-36, (1999)
[115] C. M. O'Carroll, S. J. Martin, J. Sandin, B. Frenguelli, R. G. Morris, *Learn Mem*, 13(6), 760-9, (2006)
[116] A. L. Markowska, J. M. Long, C. T. Johnson, D. S. Olton, *Behav Neurosci*, 107(4), 627-32, (1993)
[117] A. Garthe, J. Behr, G. Kempermann, *PLoS One*, 4(5), e5464, (2009)
[118] O. Buresová, I. Krekule, A. Zahálka, J. Bures, *J Neurosci Methods*, 15(1), 63-72, (1985)
[119] R. I. Spooner, A. Thomson, J. Hall, R. G. Morris, S. H. Salter, Learn Mem, 1(3), 203-11, (1994)
[120] M. Moghaddam, J. Bures, *Neurobiol Learn Mem*, 68(3), 239-51, (1997)
[121] S Benhamou, *Anim Behav*, 54(2), 321-7, (1997)
[122] J. Arnt, T. Skarsfeldt, J. Hyttel, *Int Clin Psychopharmacol*, 12(1), 9-17, (1997)
[123] V. Castagné, P. C. Moser, R. D. Porsolt, *Adv Pharmacol*, 57, 381-418, (2009)
[124] M. Didriksen, T. Skarsfeldt, J. Arnt, *Psychopharmacology (Berlin)*, 193, 225–233, (2007)
[125] P. Pichat, O. E. Bergis, J. P. Terranova, A. Urani, C. Duarte, V. Santucci, et al., *Neuropsychopharmacology*, 32, 17–34, (2007)
[126] I. K. Celikyurt, F. Y. Akar, G. Ulak, O. Mutlu, F. Erden, *Pharmacology*, 87(3-4), 187-94, (2011)
[127] J. T. Li, Y. A. Su, C. M. Guo, Y. Feng, Y. Yang, R. H. Huang, T. M. Si, *Eur J Pharmacol*, 52(1-3), 65-72, (2011)
[128] R. J. Beninger, J. K. Forsyth, M. Van Adel, J. N. Reynolds, R. J. Boegman, K. Jhamandas, *Pharmacol Biochem Behav*, 91(4), 495-502, (2009)
[129] S. Beraki, A. Kuzmin, F. Tai, s. O. Ogren, *Eur Neuropsychopharmacol*, 18(7), 486-97, (2008)
[130] T. Skarsfeldt, *Psychopharmacology (Berl)*, 124(1-2), 126-33, (1996)
[131] F. J. van der Staay, K. Rutten, C. Erb, A. Blokland, *Behav Brain Res*, 220(1), 215-29, (2011)
[132] R. P. Kesner, M. Dakis, *Psychopharmacology (Berl)*, 120(2), 203-8, (1995)
[133] J. X. Van Snellenberg, *Psychiatry Res*, 174(2), 89-96, (2009)
[134] E. D. French, A. Mura, T. Wang, *Synapse*, 13(2), 108-16, (1993)
[135] L. Lecourtier, H. Homayoun, G. Tamagnan, B. Moghaddam, *Biol Psychiatry*, 62(7), 739-46, (2007)
[136] A. Boultadakis, N. Pitsikas, *Neuropsychopharmacology*, 35(12), 2357-66, (2010)
[137] Enomoto T, Ishibashi T, Tokuda K, Ishiyama T, Toma S, A. Ito, *Behav Brain Res*. 186(2), 197-207, (2008)
[138] M. Pitkänen, J. Sirviö, E. MacDonald, S. Niemi, T. Ekonsalo, P. Riekkinen Sr., Eur *Neuropsychopharmacol*, 5(4), 457-63, (1995)
[139] J. J. Chrobak, J. R. Hinman, H. R. Sabolek, *J Neurosci*, 28(17), 4512-20, (2008)
[140] A. Stuchlík, T. Petrásek T, K. Vales, *Physiol Res*, 58(5), 733-40, (2009)
[141] A. Stuchlík, K. Vales, *Behav Brain Res*, 159(1), 163-71, (2005)
[142] V. Bubenikova-Valesova, A. Stuchlik, J. Svoboda, J. Bures, K. Vales, *Proc Natl Acad Sci U S A*, 105(3), 1061-6, (2008)
[143] J. Bures, A. A. Fenton, Y. Kaminsky, L. Zinyuk, *Proc Natl Acad Sci U S A*, 94(1), 343-50, (1997)
[144] J. Bures, A. A. Fenton, Y. Kaminsky, M. Wesierska, A. Zahalka, *Neuropharmacology*, 37(4-5), 689-99, (1998)

[145] A. A. Fenton, M. Wesierska, Y. Kaminsky, J. Bures, *Proc Natl Acad Sci U S A*, 95(19), 11493-8, (1998)
[146] J. M. Cimadevilla, A. A. Fenton, J. Bures, *Behav Brain Res*, 107(1-2), 161-9, (2000)
[147] J. M. Cimadevilla, Y. Kaminsky, A. Fenton, J. Bures, *J Neurosci Methods*, 102(2), 155-64, (2000)
[148] J. M. Cimadevilla, A. A. Fenton, J. Bures, *Behav Neurosci*, 115(3), 695-703, (2001)
[149] J. M. Cimadevilla, M. Wesierska, A. A. Fenton, J. Bures, *Proc Natl Acad Sci U S A*, 98(6), 3531-6, (2001)
[150] K. Blahna, J. Svoboda, P. Telensky, D. Klement, *Behav Brain Res*, 216(1), 207-13, (2011)
[151] E. Pastalkova, P. Serrano, D. Pinkhasova, E. Wallace, A. A. Fenton, T. C. Sacktor, *Science*, 313(5790), 1141-4, (2006)
[152] E. Kelemen, A. A. Fenton, *PLoS Biol*, 8(6), e1000403, (2010)
[153] K. Vales, J. Svoboda, K. Benkovicova, V. Bubenikova-Valesova, A. Stuchlik, Eur J *Pharmacol*, 639(1-3), 91-8, (2010)
[154] M. Wesierska, C. Dockery, A. A. Fenton, *J Neurosci*, 25(9), 2413, (2005)
[155] S. Kubík, A. A. Fenton, *J Neurosci*, 25(40), 9205-12, (2005)
[156] R. A. Muller, *Neuron*, 17(5), 813-22, (1996)
[157] *Kubik* et al., *in preparation*
[158] M. L. Mittelstaedt, H. Mittelstaedt, *Naturwissenschaften*, 67, 566-567, (1980)
[159] *Kenney* et al., *in preparation*
[160] M. L. Mittelstaedt, S. Glasauer, *Zool. Jb. Physiol*, 95, 427-435 (1991)
[161] J. W. Newcomer, J. H. Krystal, *Hippocampus*, 11, 529–542, (2001)
[162] Q. Li, S. Clark, D. V. Lewis, W. A. Wilson, *J Neurosci*, 22, 3070–3080, (2002)
[163] M. E. Jackson, H. Homayoun, B. Moghaddam, *Proc Natl Acad Sci USA*, 101, 8467–8472, (2004)
[164] J. E. Belforte, V. Zsiros, E. R. Sklar, Z. Jiang, G. Yu, Y. Li, E. M. Quinlan, K. Nakazawa, *Nat Neurosci*, 13(1), 76-83, (2010)
[165] M. Nilsson, S. Waters, N. Waters, A. Carlsson, M. L. Carlsson, *J Neural Transm*, 108(10), 1181-96, (2001)
[166] D. S. Olton, R. J. Samuelson, *J Exp Psychology: Animal Behavior Processes*, 2(2), 97-116, (1976)
[167] R. K. Zeldin, D. S. Olton DS, *J Exp Psychol Anim Behav Process*, 12(4), 412-9, (1986)
[168] R. G. Cook, M. F. Brown, D. A. Riley, *J Exp Psychol Anim Behav Process*, 11(3), 453-69, (1985)
[169] G. E. Demas, R. J. Nelson, B. K. Krueger, P. J. Yarowsky PJ, Behav Brain Res, 90(2), 199-201, (1998)
[170] D. S. Olton, C. Collison, M. A. Werz, *Learning and Motivation*, 8(3), 289-314, (1977)
[171] O. Buresova, J. Bures, *Psychopharmacology (Berl)*, 77(3), 268-71, (1982)
[172] O. Buresova, J. Bures, M. S. Oitzl, A. Zahálka, *Physiol Behav*, 34(6), 1003-5, (1985)
[173] M. G. Packard, R. Hirsh, N. M. White, *The Journal of Neuroscience*, g(5): 1465-1472, (1969)
[174] D. Dubreuil, C. Tixier, G. Dutrieux, J. M. Edeline, *Neurobiol Learn Mem*, 79(1), 109-17, (2003)
[175] M. Ammassari-Teule, A. Caprioli, *Behav Brain Res*, 17(1), 9-16, (1985)
[176] D. S. Olton, J. T. Becker, G. E. Handelmann, *Behav Brain Sci*, 2, 313–65, (1979)
[177] D. S. Olton, B. C. Paras, *Neuropsychologia*, 17(6), 669-682, (1979)
[178] J. J. Bolhuis, S. Biljlsma, P. Ansmink, *Behav Neural Biol*, 46, 115–22, (1986)
[179] G. A. Miller, E. Galanter, K. H. Pribram, *Plans and the Structure of Behavior*, Holt, Rinehart & Winston, New York, (1960)

[180] R.C. Atkinson, R.M. Shiffrin, *Human memory: A proposed system and its control processes.* In K. W. Spence and J. T. Spence (Eds.), The Psychology of Learning and Motivation: Advances in Research and Theory. (Vol. 2, pp. 89–195). New York: Academic Press, (1968)
[181] A. Baddeley, *Curr Biol*, 20(4), 136-40, (2010)
[182] A. D. Baddeley, G. J. Hitch, In G. A. Bower (Ed.) *Recent Advances in Learning and Motivation,* 47–89, Academic, New York, (1974)
[183] A. D. Baddeley, *Science*, 255(5044), 556-559, (1992)
[184] A. D. Baddeley, *Nature Review Neuroscience*, 4, 829-839, (2003)
[185] J. F. Keeler, T. W. Robbins, *Biochem Pharmacol*, 81(12), 1356-66, (2011)
[186] P. A. Dudchenko, *Neurosci Biobehav Rev*, 28(7), 699-709, (2004)
[187] N. F. Forbes, L. A. Carrick, A. M. McIntosh, S. M. Lawrie, *Psychol Med*, 39(6), 889-905. (2009)
[188] M. Conklin, C. E. Curtis, M. E. Calkins, W. G. Iacono, *Neuropsychologia*, 43, 930–942, (2005)
[189] C. Bischoff, P. I. Tiedtke, Eur. J. Pharmacol. Res., 129, 211–216. (2002)
[190] H. B. Li, K. Matsumoto, M. Yamamoto, H. Watanabe, *Pharmacol. Biochem. Behav.*, 58, 249–253, (1997)
[191] H. B. Li, K. Matsumoto, M. Tohda, M. Yamamoto, H. Watanabe H., Brain Res., 725(2), 268-71, (1996)
[192] T. Myhrer. *Brain Research Reviews*, 41, 268–287, (2003)
[193] C. Kay, D.N. Harper, M. Hunt, *Neurobiology of Learning and Memory*, 93(2), 151-156, (2010)
[194] M. Buhot, S. K. Patra, S. Naili, *European Journal of Pharmacology*, 285, 221–228, (1995)
[195] S. Sharma, S. Rakoczy, H. Brown-Borg, *Life Sciences*, 87, 521–536, (2010)
[196] C. A. Barnes, *J Comp Physiol Psychol,* 93, 74-104, (1979)
[197] D. Klement, J. Bures, *Proc Natl Acad Sci U S A*. 97(6), 2946-51, (2000)
[198] E. Pastalkova, E. Kelemen, J. Bures, *Proc Natl Acad Sci U S A*, 100(4), 2094-9, (2003)
[199] T. Nekovarova, D. Klement. *Physiol Res*, 55, 105-113, (2006)
[200] D. Klement, K. Blahna, T. Nekovarova, *Physiol Res*, 57(3), 161-5, (2008)
[201] D. Klement, D. Levcik, D. Duskova L, Nekovarova T, *Behav Brain Res*., 207(2), 480-9, (2010).
[202] D. Levcik D, D. Klement, K. Vales, T. Nekovarova, A. Stuchlik, *Psychiatrie*, 14(2), 15-18, (2010)
[203] A. Sahgal, T. Steckler, *J Neurosci Methods*, 55(1), 59-64, (1994)
[204] Steckler T, Sahgal A, *Psychopharmacology (Berl)*, 118(2), 226-9, (1995)
[205] J. Keller, H. Strasburger, D. T. Cerutti, S. A. Sabel, *J Neurosci Methods,* 97, 103-10, (2000).
[206] G. T. Prusky, R. M. Douglas, L. Nelson, A. Shabanpoor, R. J. Sutherland, *Proc Natl Acad Sci USA,* 101, 5064-5068, (2004)
[207] E. A. Gaffan, M. J. Eacott, *J Neurosci Methods,* 60, 23-37, (1995)
[208] T. J. Bussey, L. M. Saksida, L. A. Rothblat,*Behav Neurosci,* 115, 957-960, (2001)
[209] D. Piskulic, J. S. Olver, T. R. Norman, P. Maruff, *Psychiatry Research*, 150, 111–121, (2007)
[210] F. M. Hanlon, M. P. Weisend, D. A. Hamilton, A. P. Jones, R. J. Thoma, M. Huang, K. Martin, R. A. Yeo, G. A. Miller, J. M. Cañive, *Schizophrenia Research*, 87, 67–80, (2006)

Reviewed by Masayoshi Kurachi.

In: Schizophrenia Research: Recent Advances
Editor: Tomiki Sumiyoshi
ISBN: 978-1-62808-703-1

Chapter 14

MANAGEMENT OF COGNITIVE IMPAIRMENTS IN SCHIZOPHRENIA: THE THERAPEUTIC ROLE OF 5-HT RECEPTORS

Yukihiro Ohno[1*], Ayaka Tatara[1], Saki Shimizu[1] and Masashi Sasa[2]
[1] Laboratory of Pharmacology,
Osaka University of Pharmaceutical Sciences, Japan
[2] Nagisa Clinic, Japan

Abstract

Patients with schizophrenia exhibit diverse psychotic symptoms including positive symptoms (e.g., hallucinations and delusions), negative symptoms (e.g., apathy and emotional withdrawal) and cognitive impairments (e.g., inattention, deficits in social recognition, learning and memory). Although newly-developed atypical antipsychotic drugs (e.g., risperidone, olanzapine, quetiapine, perospirone and aripiprazole) provide benefits in the treatment of schizophrenia, clinical reports do not show significant advantages of the above 2nd generation antipsychotics beyond typical (classical) ones (e.g., haloperidol), especially in their efficacy against neurocognitive impairments. Recently, several lines of studies revealed the therapeutic role of 5-HT receptors in treating cognitive impairments in schizophrenia and other disorders (e.g., Alzheimer's disease). Specifically, 5-HT_{1A}, 5-HT_3, 5-HT_4 and 5-HT_6 receptors seem to be promising targets for alleviating cognitive impairments. In this chapter, the therapeutic role and functional mechanisms of 5-HT receptors in modulating cognitive deficits in schizophrenia are reviewed.

INTRODUCTION

Schizophrenia is a heterogenous disease with diverse psychotic symptoms including positive symptoms (e.g., hallucinations, delusions and excitation), negative symptoms (e.g.,

* E-mail address: yohno@gly.oups.ac.jp.

apathy, flattened affect, social and emotional withdrawal), and cognitive impairments (inattention, deficits in social recognition, learning and memory) [1-4]. Although the precise mechanisms for the etiology of schizophrenia are still uncertain, the "Dopamine hypothesis" that hyperactivity of the meso-limbic and meso-cortical dopaminergic systems is responsible for the development of schizophrenia is now widely accepted as a causative mechanism [5, 6]. Based on the "Dopamine hypothesis", a variety of dopamine antagonists which commonly possess dopamine D_2 blocking action have been developed as antipsychotic drugs (Fig. 1). These include phenothiazine- (e.g., chlorpromazine and perphenazine), butyrophenone- (e.g., haloperidol and spiroperidol) and benzamide- (e.g., sulpiride and raclopride) derivatives. These agents have been widely used since the 1950's and contributed to controlling schizophrenia symptoms, especially the positive symptoms. However, these classical antipsychotics frequently induce severe extrapyramidal side effects (e.g., akathisia, bradykinesia, akineisa, tremors, muscle rigidity, dystonia and dyskinesia) and increase the plasma prolactin level (i.e., hyperprolactinemia). In addition, they are not so effective for the negative and other symptoms (e.g., cognitive impairments and affective symptoms) [1, 3, 7, 8].

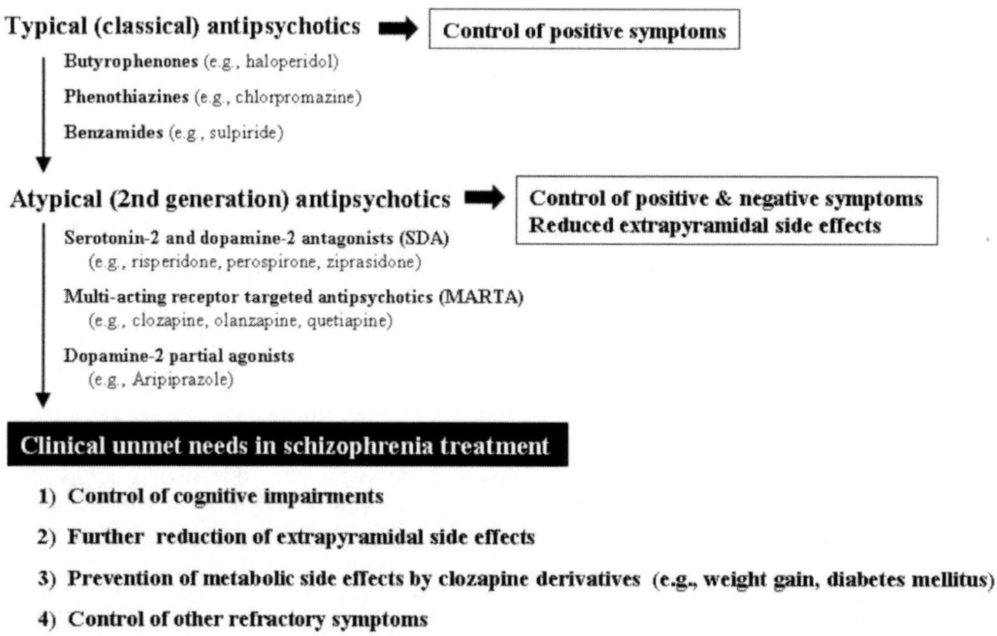

Figure 1. Development of antipsychotic drugs and clinical unmet needs in schizophrenia treatment.

Since the 1980's, numerous studies have shown the therapeutic role of $5\text{-}HT_{2A}$ receptors in schizophrenia in that the blockade of $5\text{-}HT_{2A}$ receptors can ameliorate the negative symptoms and attenuate the antipsychotic-induced extrapyramidal side effects [1, 2, 7-10]. Based on this “serotonin hypothesis in schizophrenia", a line of 2nd generation antipsychotic drugs (e.g., risperidone, olanzapine, quetiapine, perospirone and ziprasidone) have been developed in the past two decades (Fig. 1). These agents commonly show a higher affinity to $5\text{-}HT_{2A}$ receptors than to D_2 receptors and inhibit $5\text{-}HT_{2A}$ receptor-mediated abnormal behaviors. They are now called “atypical” antipsychotics and are differentiated from "typical (classical)" drugs based on their pharmacological features, a superior efficacy for the negative symptoms and a reduced liability to induce extrapyramidal side effects [1, 2, 7]. In addition, the dopamine D_2 partial agonist aripiprazole has also been developed as an atypical antipsychotic [11].

The 2nd generation antipsychotics are now used as first line drugs in the treatment of schizophrenia. With the development of these new antipsychotics, pharmacotherapy for schizophrenia has progressed and the quality of life of the patients with schizophrenia has significantly improved. Nonetheless, there remain several clinical unmet needs to be resolved in the treatment of schizophrenia (Fig. 1) [3, 4]. Among them, controlling cognitive impairments (e.g., inattention, deficits in social recognition, learning and memory) in schizophrenia is the primary concern and a major hurdle to overcome. Indeed, recent comprehensive clinical reports, the Clinical Antipsychotic Trials of Intervention Effectiveness (CATIE) and European First-Episode Schizophrenia Trial (EUFEST), did not show significant advantages of 2nd generation antipsychotics (e.g. risperidone, olanzapine and quetiapine) over typical ones (e.g., haloperidol), especially in their efficacy against neurocognitive impairments [12-14]. On the other hand, several lines of recent studies revealed the therapeutic role of the serotonergic nervous system in treating cognitive impairments in schizophrenia and other disorders (e.g., Alzheimer's disease) [4, 15, 16]. In this chapter, the therapeutic role and functional mechanisms of 5-HT receptors in modulating cognitive deficits in schizophrenia are reviewed.

SEROTONERGIC NERVOUS SYSTEM

The serotonergic system plays an important role in regulating various physiological functions, including psychoemotional, cognitive, sensory-motor, and autonomic functions [17, 18]. Serotonin neurons are located in the raphe nuclei, which are located in the lower brain stem (pons and medulla oblongata), and send axons to various brain regions including the cerebral cortex, limbic regions, basal ganglia, diencephalon and the spinal cord (Fig. 2). The serotonergic neurotransmissions are mediated by various 5-HT receptor subtypes, which consist of 7 families (5-HT_1 to 5-HT_7) and 14 subtypes (5-HT_{1A}, $_{1B}$, $_{1D}$, $_{1E}$, $_{1F}$, 5-HT_{2A}, $_{2B}$, $_{2C}$, 5-HT_3, 5-HT_4, 5-HT_{5A}, $_{5B}$, 5-HT_6 and 5-HT_7) according to their signal transduction pathways [18]. Thus, 5-HT_1 receptors (i.e., 5-HT_{1A}, $_{1B}$, $_{1D}$, $_{1E}$, $_{1F}$) are coupled to $G_{i/o}$ protein and inhibit the adenylate cyclase and protein kinase A (PK-A) cascade. 5-HT_2 receptors (i.e., 5-HT_{2A}, $_{2B}$, $_{2C}$) are G_q-coupled receptors, enhance the phosphatidilinositol (PI) turnover and activate the protein kinase C (PK-C)- and/or Ca^{2+}/calmodulin-cascades. 5-HT_3 receptors are ion channel-type receptors and 5-HT_4 to 5-HT_7 receptors are G_s-coupled receptors which activate the adenylate cyclase and PK-A cascades. All these 5-HT receptors act as postsynaptic receptors and regulate activity of the target neurons to which 5-HT neurons are innervated (Fig. 2). In addition, 5-HT_{1A}, 5-HT_{1B} and 5-HT_{1D} receptors also act as presynaptic 5-HT autoreceptors and negatively regulate the activity of 5-HT neurons by themselves. Specifically, 5-HT_{1A} receptors are located on the cell bodies and dendrites of 5-HT neurons in the raphe nuclei and inhibit the firing of 5-HT neurons. On the other hand, 5-HT_{1B} and 5-HT_{1D} receptors are located on membranes of nerve terminals of 5-HT neurons, where stimulation of 5-$HT_{1B/1D}$ receptors inhibits the synaptic synthesis and release of 5-HT. Through these mechanisms, 5-

HT_{1A} and 5-$HT_{1B/1D}$ receptors control the overall tone of the serotonergic nervous system (Fig. 2).

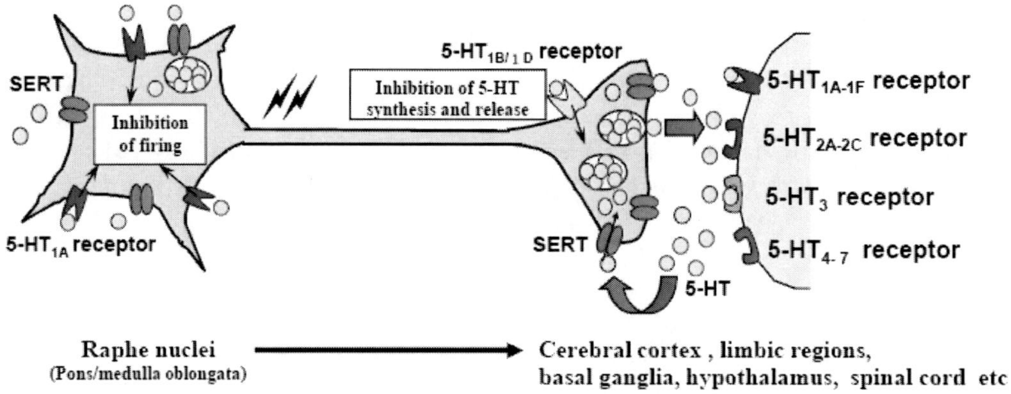

Figure 2. Schematic illustration of the serotonin neuron and 5-HT receptors. SERT: Serotonin transporter.

5-HT receptors are implicated in the pathogenesis and treatment of various central nervous system diseases such as anxiety (e.g., 5-HT_{1A}, 5-HT_{2A}, 5-HT_{2C}, 5-HT_3 receptors), depression (e.g., 5-HT_{1A}, 5-HT_{2A}, 5-HT_{2C}, 5-HT_6, 5-HT_7, receptors), schizophrenia (e.g., 5-HT_{1A}, 5-$HT_{2A,\ 2C}$, 5-HT_6 receptors), and migraine (5-HT_3 receptors) [17, 18]. Besides the above diseases, there is accumulating evidence that 5-HT receptors play an important role in regulating cognitive functions (e.g., learning and memory). Especially, 5-HT_{1A}, 5-HT_3, 5-HT_4, and 5-HT_6 receptors are expected to be promising targets for alleviating cognitive impairments in central nervous system diseases.

5-HT Receptors and Cognitive Functions

5-HT_{1A} Receptors

5-HT_{1A} receptors are $G_{i/o}$ protein-coupled receptors with a 7-transmembrane-spanning structure and are predominantly expressed in the limbic areas (e.g., hippocampus, amygdala and lateral septum) and the raphe nuclei (e.g., raphe nuclei) (Fig. 3) [4, 18, 19]. Moderate to low levels of 5-HT_{1A} receptors are also expressed in the cerebral cortex, basal ganglia (e.g., striatum) and diencephalon (e.g., thalamus and hypothalamus). 5-HT_{1A} receptors function both as presynaptic autoreceptors and postsynaptic receptors, as described previously. Stimulation of 5-HT_{1A} receptors inhibits adenylate cyclase, cAMP formation and PK-A activity. In addition, 5-HT_{1A} receptors also activate G-protein-gated inwardly rectifying potassium (GIRK) channels and hyperpolarize (inhibit) target neurons (Fig. 3) [20-25]. Numerous 5-HT_{1A} agonists with different intrinsic activities (e.g., full agonists: 8-OH-DPAT, flesinoxan and F-11440, partial agonists: buspirone, tandospirone ipsapirone and gepirone) and 5-HT_{1A} antagonists (e.g., WAY-100135, WAY-100635 NAD-299 and Lecozotan) have been synthesized, but so far only buspirone and tandospirone are clinically available (Fig. 3).

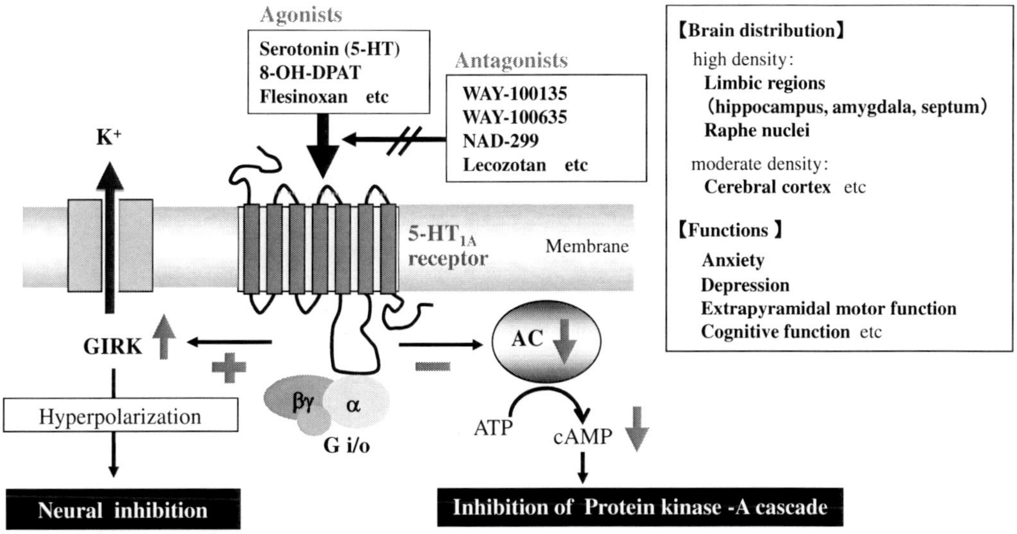

Figure 3. Structure and functions of 5-HT1A receptors. AC: Adenylate cyclase, GIRK: G protein-coupled inwardly rectifying K+ channel .

5-HT_{1A} receptors have long been implicated in the pathogenesis and treatment of anxiety and depressive disorders [26-30]. It is now documented that activation of 5-HT_{1A} receptors alleviates anxiety and psychosomatic disorders by inhibiting neuronal activities in the limbic areas (e.g., hippocampus, amygdale and lateral septum). In addition, it is also known that the density of 5-HT_{1A} receptors is elevated in the brains of patients with chronic schizophrenia [31, 32], implying a close relationship between 5-HT_{1A} receptors and the pathogenesis of schizophrenia. Specifically, recent clinical studies have shown that a partial 5-HT_{1A} agonist, tandospirone, significantly improved the cognitive deficits (assessed by Wisconsin Card Sort test or California verbal learning test) in patients with schizophrenia [33, 34]. Since cognitive deficits are a core symptom of schizophrenia for which the currently available antipsychotics are not very effective, 5-HT_{1A} receptors have received attention as a promising therapeutic target for schizophrenia [4, 35, 36]. Besides these functions, 5-HT_{1A} receptors are also expected to provide benefits in the treatment of schizophrenia such that activation of 5-HT_{1A} receptors reduces antipsychotic-induced extrapyramidal side effects [4, 37, 38-44] and ameliorates affective disorders (e.g., anxiety and depression) [3, 4, 28, 45].

Animal studies revealed that 5-HT_{1A} antagonists (e.g., WAY-100635, WAY-101405, NAD-299 and Lecozotan) reversed the cognitive impairment induced by mACh receptor antagonists (e.g., scopolamine) or N-methyl-D-aspartate (NMDA) receptor antagonists (e.g., MK-801) [15, 46-49]. On the other hand, full 5-HT_{1A} agonists (e.g., 8-OH-DPAT) reportedly exhibit biphasic effects on cognitive functions, showing facilitation at low doses and inhibition at high doses [15, 48]. These facilitatory and inhibitory effects of 5-HT_{1A} agonists are thought to be mediated by stimulation of presynaptic and postsynaptic 5-HT_{1A} receptors, respectively (Fig. 4). Stimulation of postsynaptic 5-HT_{1A} receptors inhibits cognitive functions probably through 1) reducing the activity of cholinergic or glutamatergic neurons in the basal forebrain regions (e.g., diagonal band of Broca and medial septum) projecting to the cerebral cortex or the hippocampus, 2) reducing the activity of the hippocampal and cortical neurons receiving the above cholinergic or glutamatergic inputs, and 3) reducing ACh release in the hippocampus (Fig. 4). Although further validations are required, the above findings indicate that antagonism/partial agonism of 5-HT_{1A} receptors provides benefits in treating cognitive impairment in schizophrenia. In this regard, novel 5-HT_{1A} antagonists or antipsychotic drugs which interact with 5-HT_{1A} receptors are now being developed (Table 1). For example, the new antipsychotic candidate lurasidone, with a 5-HT_{1A} antagonistic (weak partial agonistic) action [50], has been shown to improve the learning and memory impairment induced by MK-801 [51] and to ameliorate the cognitive impairment in schizophrenia patients [52].

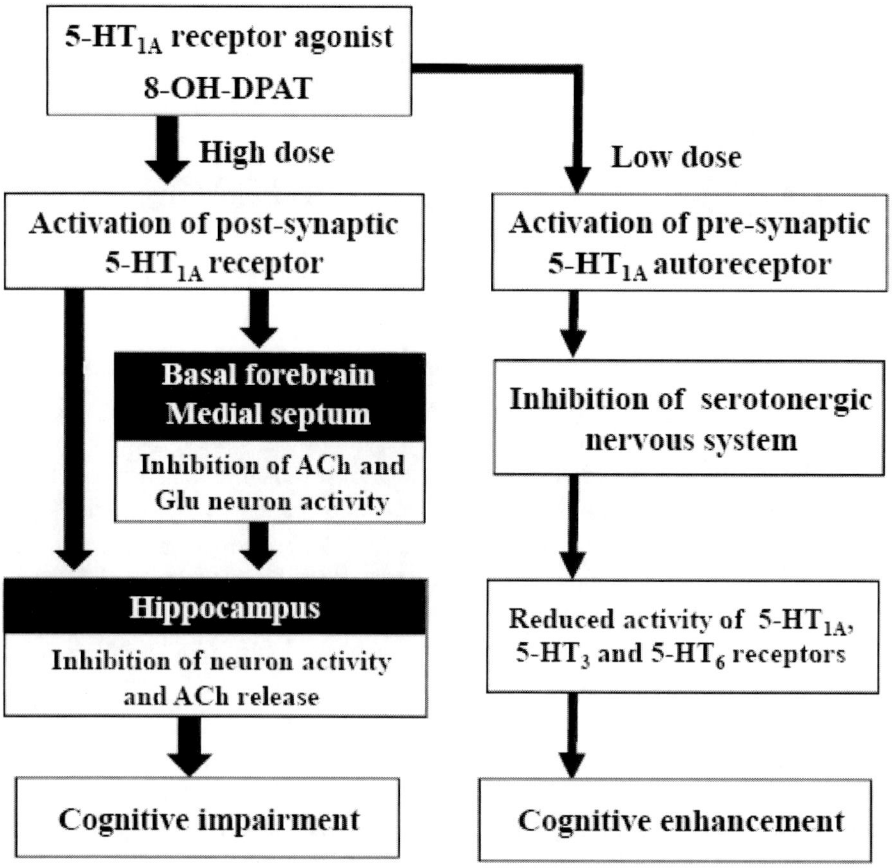

Figure 4. Action mechanisms of 5-HT_{1A} agonists in regulating cognitive function.

5-HT_3 Receptors

5-HT_3 receptors are the only ion channel-type receptor among the 5-HT receptors. 5-HT_3 receptors are composed of a heteropentamer consisting of 5-HT_{3A} to 5-HT_{3E} subunits and act as a cation channel permeable for Na^+ and Ca^{2+} (Fig. 5) [17, 18, 53]. Thus, the activation of 5-HT_3 receptors depolarizes postsynaptic membranes and excites the target neurons. 5-HT_3 receptors are also located on nerve terminals of acetylcholinergic and glutamatergic neurons and regulate neurotransmitter release. It is well known that 5-HT_3 receptors play a role in regulating emetic responses and 5-HT_3 antagonists effectively inhibit nausea and vomiting, especially elicited by antitumor agents (e.g., cisplatin) (Fig. 5). In the central nervous system, 5-HT_3 receptors are implicated in the pathogenesis of anxiety and cognitive disorders. 2-Methyl-5-HT and chlorophenylbiguanide are known as 5-HT_3 agonists and many 5-HT_3 antagonists (e.g., ondansetron, granisetron, azasetron and tropisetron) are clinically available as antiemetic drugs [17, 18].

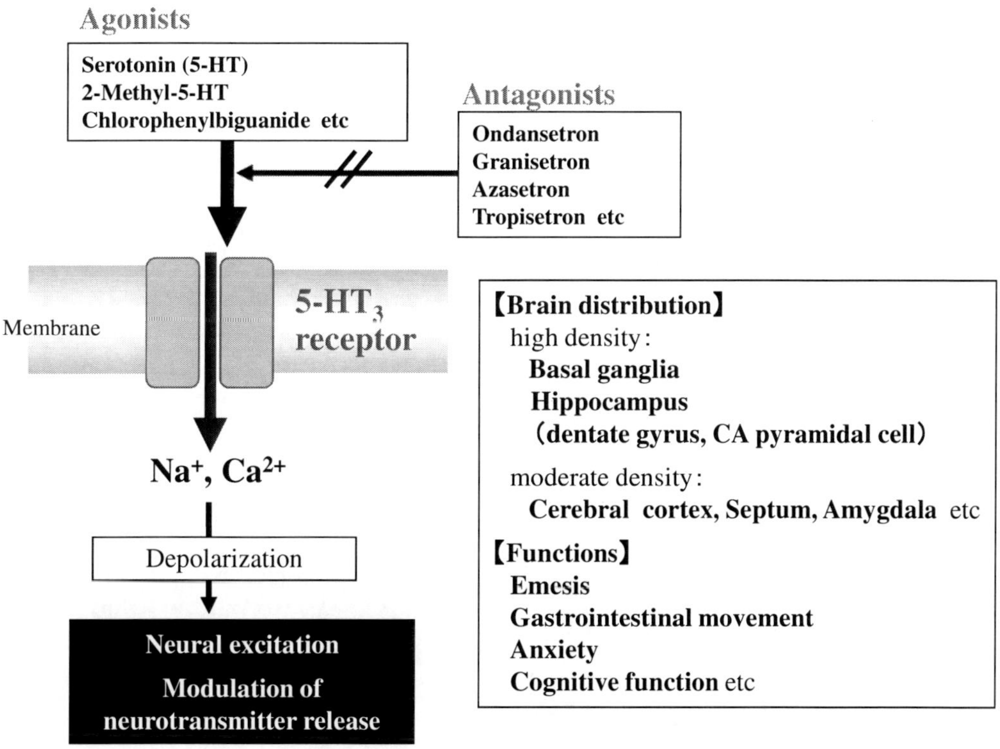

Figure 5. Structure and functions of 5-HT_3 receptors.

Previous studies showed that 5-HT_3 antagonists enhance cognitive functions and alleviate cognitive deficits associated with aging or drug treatment in various animal models (e.g., Morris water maze test and novel object recognition test) [54-57]. These actions of 5-HT_3 antagonists are thought to be mediated by enhanced release of acetylcholine in the cerebral cortex (Table 1) [55, 57, 58]. Interestingly, recent clinical studies have shown that the 5-HT_3 antagonist ondansetron significantly improved cognitive impairments in schizophrenia [59, 60]. These were double-blind, randomized, placebo-controlled studies using chronic schizophrenia patients and ondansetron was added to the treatment with haloperidol [59] or risperidone [60]. The add-on therapy of ondansetron for 8-12 weeks significantly improved the overall scale of the Positive and Negative Syndrome Scale (PANSS) and the subscale for cognition, negative symptoms and general psychopathology. Furthermore, consistent with a recent study [61], combination of ondansetron with antipsychotic drugs (even with atypical risperidone) significantly reduced the incidence and severity of antipsychotic-induced extrapyramidal side effects (e.g., akathisia and parkinsonism) [59, 60]. It is therefore likely that antagonism of 5-HT_3 receptors is useful as an adjunctive therapy for chronic schizophrenia, especially for improving the cognitive impairments, negative symptoms and also reducing adverse reactions associated with antipsychotic treatments.

5-HT$_4$ Receptors

5-HT$_4$ receptors are G$_s$ protein-coupled receptor and activate adenylate cyclase, cAMP formation and PK-A cascade (Fig. 6) [17, 18]. 5-HT$_4$ receptors are expressed at high density in the hippocampus and basal ganglia (e.g., striatum). Moderate levels of 5-HT$_4$ receptors are also expressed in the cerebral cortex, medial septum and amygdala [15, 17, 18]. Interestingly, the density of 5-HT$_4$ receptors has been shown to be reduced in the cerebral cortex and hippocampus in patients with Alzheimer's disease [62], suggesting the potential role of 5-HT$_4$ receptors in cognitive functions.

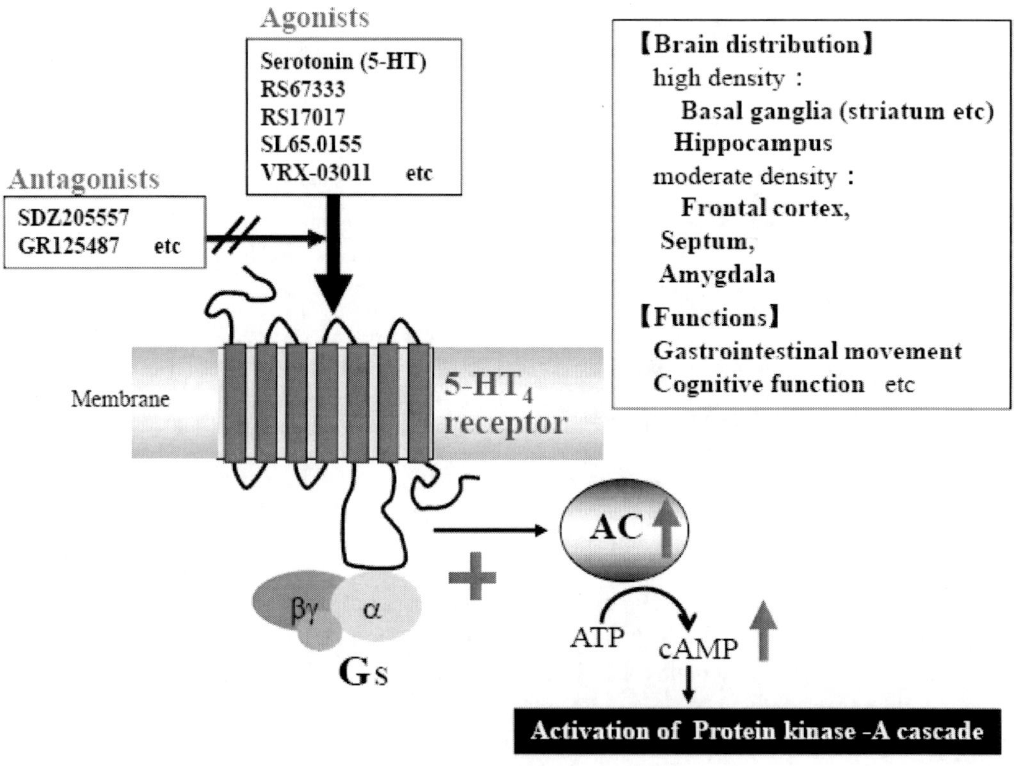

Figure 6. Structure and functions of 5-HT4 receptors. AC: Adenylate cyclase .

Previous studies have shown that 5-HT$_4$ agonists (e.g., RS67333 and RS17017) enhance cognitive functions and, conversely, 5-HT$_4$ antagonists (e.g., SDZ20557 and GR125487) cause impairments in learning and memory formation [63-66]. Especially, 5-HT$_4$ receptors are thought to play an important role in the acquisition and consolidation of memory [15, 65]. Although the mechanisms for the procognitive action of 5-HT$_4$ agonists are still uncertain, stimulation of 5-HT$_4$ receptors is known to enhance acetylcholine release in the cerebral cortex and hippocampus (Table 1) [15, 67, 68]. Besides these actions, 5-HT$_4$ receptors block

Ca^{2+}-dependent K^+ currents via activating PK-A cascade and inhibit afterhyperpolarization of the action potentials [69], which leads to neural excitation in the cerebral cortex and hippocampus. Several new 5-HT_4 agonists or partial agonists are now being developed (Table 1).

5-HT_6 Receptors

5-HT_6 receptors are coupled to Gs protein and their stimulation activates the adenylate cyclase-cAMP-PK-A cascade (Fig. 7) [15, 17, 18]. 5-HT_6 receptors are predominantly expressed in the brain, specifically in the basal ganglia (e.g., striatum and nucleus accumbens), limbic regions (e.g., olfactory tubercles and hippocampus) and cerebral cortex at high density. In addition, immunohistochemical studies revealed that 5-HT_6 receptors are mainly located in GABAergic neurons [70-72]. 5-HT_6 receptors are implicated in psychoemotional disorders (e.g., schizophrenia and depression), eating disorders, cognitive deficits in schizophrenia and Alzheimer's disease. Indeed, polymorphism of the gene HTR6 encoding human 5-HT_6 receptors shows a significant association to Alzheimer's disease and the patients with Alzheimer's disease have a reduced number of 5-HT_6 receptors in the cerebral cortex [15], suggesting a close relationship between 5-HT_6 receptor functions and cognition.

Studies using transgenic animals overexpressing 5-HT_6 receptors show deficits of learning behaviors, which could be reversed by a 5-HT_6 antagonist [73]. Conversely, treatment of animals with antisense of 5-HT_6 receptor mRNA improves the performance in the Morris water maze test [74]. Many other studies have shown that 5-HT_6 antagonists enhance cognitive functions or reverse amnesia induced by ACh antagonists [75-78]. These procognitive actions of 5-HT_6 antagonists are brought about by relieving the GABAergic neural inhibition in the cerebral cortex and/or limbic structures (Table 1) since 5-HT_6 receptors are mainly located on GABAergic neurons [70, 71, 72] and since stimulation of 5-HT_6 receptors increased GABA release [79]. In addition, 5-HT_6 antagonists are also known to enhance ACh release in the above structures [72, 80].

Another important fact is that 5-HT_6 receptors are the potential target for clozapine, to which clozapine binds with high affinity [81]. In addition, a genetic association is found between HTR6 (C267T) polymorphism and clinical responses to clozapine of patients with treatment-resistant schizophrenia [82]. Thus, it is possible that blockade of 5-HT_6 receptors improves the treatment-resistant symptoms of schizophrenia, including cognitive impairments.

Furthermore, antagonism of 5-HT_6 receptors improves antipsychotics-induced extrapyramidal side effects [61]. Thus, many new 5-HT_6 antagonists (e.g., BGC20-761, LY-483518, Ro 4368554, PRX-07034, SB-742457) are now being developed (Table 1).

Other 5-HT Receptors

Other 5-HT receptors, which are suggested to have a role in regulating cognitive functions include 5-$HT_{2A/2C}$, 5-HT_7 and 5-$HT_{1B/1D}$ receptors. 5-HT_{2A} receptors are G_q-coupled and, upon stimulation, activate PI turnover and the subsequent PK-C-signaling cascade [17,

18]. It is generally known that 5-HT_{2A} receptors counteract NMDA receptor-mediated glutamatergic transmission in the cerebral cortex and striatum, and thereby 5-HT_{2A} antagonists can reverse the learning deficits induced by NMDA antagonists (e.g., MK-801 and phencyclidine) [83, 84]. However, a recent study suggests that 5-HT_{2A} antagonism does not improve, but rather worsens, cognitive functions [85]. Thus, the role of 5-HT_{2A} receptors in regulating cognitive functions is still elusive and remains to be clarified. Furthermore, several studies suggest that 5-HT_7 and 5-$HT_{1B/1D}$ receptors are also involved in cognitive functions, but further evidences are required.

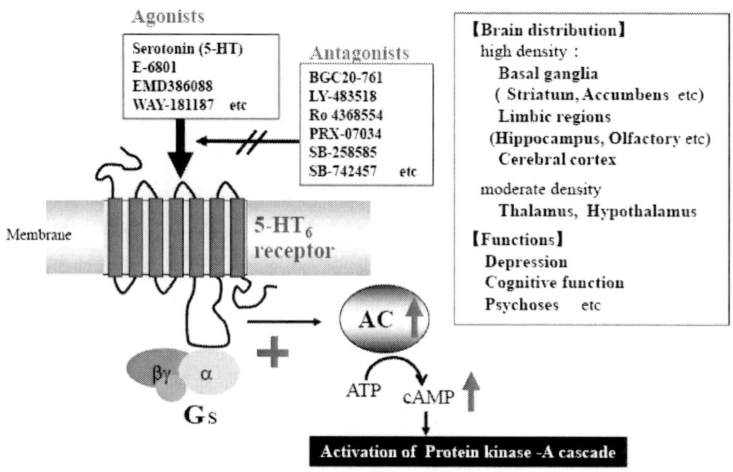

Figure 7. Structure and functions of 5-HT6 receptors. AC: Adenylate cyclase .

Table 1. Serotonergic strategies for the treatment of cognitive impairment

5-HT receptor	Treatment strategy	Action mechanisms	Related compounds
5-HT_{1A} receptor	Antagonist Partial agonist	Enhancement of neuron activities and ACh release in the hippocampus Enhancement of activities of ACh and Glu neurons in the basal forebrain and medial septum	Lurasidone PF-217830 Lacozotan Xaliproden WAY-211612 PRX-00023
5-HT_3 receptor	Antagonist Partial agonist	Enhancement of ACh and Glu release in the cerebral cortex	Ondansetron Granisetron Azasetron Tropisetron
5-HT_4 receptor	Agonist Partial agonist	Enhancement of neuron activities and ACh release in the cerebral cortex and hippocampus	SL65.0155 PRX-03140
5-HT_6 receptor	Antagonist Partial agonist	Enhancement of neuron activities and ACh release in the cerebral cortex and hippocampus by inhibiting GABA neurons	SB-742457 SAM-531 SGS-518 LY-483518 PRX-07034 SUVN-502

SEROTONERGIC MODULATION OF COGNITIVE IMPAIRMENTS IN SCHIZOPHRENIA

As described previously, the serotonergic nervous system plays an important role in regulation of cognitive functions and it may be a novel therapeutic target for the management of cognitive impairments in schizophrenia. The 5-HT receptor subtypes which have therapeutic potential include 5-HT_{1A}, 5-HT_3, 5-HT_4 and 5-HT_6 receptors. Table 1 summarizes their functional mechanisms underlying the modulation of cognitive functions and therapeutic applications. Indeed, many new compounds are now being developed as drug candidates. The therapeutic strategy for the treatment of schizophrenia with the serotonergic system is shown in Fig. 8. 5-HT_{1A}, 5-HT_3, and 5-HT_6 receptors serve as a promising target for the management of cognitive impairments in schizophrenia. In addition, stimulation (agonist or partial agonist) of 5-HT_4 receptors also seems to be effective (Fig. 8). Furthermore, it is noteworthy that blockade of 5-HT_3 and 5-HT_6 receptors or stimulation of 5-HT_{1A} receptors also reduces the incidence of extrapyramidal motor disorders associated with the D_2 receptor blockade [3, 61]. Therefore, an antagonist or partial agonist for 5-HT_{1A}, 5-HT_3 and 5-HT_6 receptors is expected to improve both cognitive impairments and antipsychotics-induced extrapyramidal side effects in schizophrenia treatment (Fig. 8) as in the case of the ondansetron add-on therapy [59, 60].

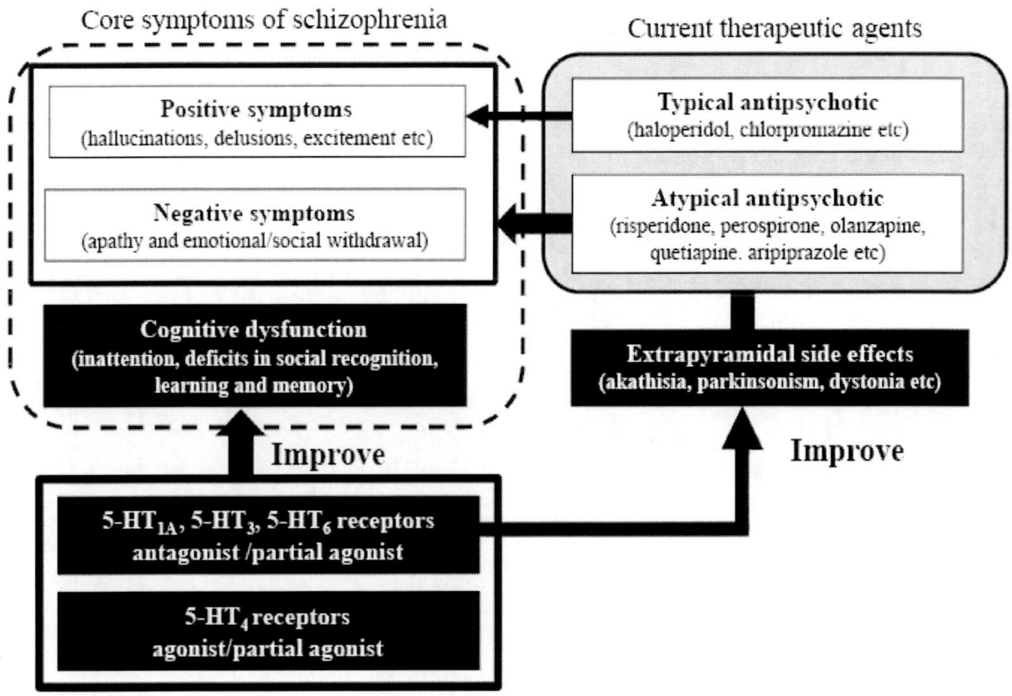

Figure 8. Therapeutic role of 5-HT_{1A}, 5-HT_3, 5-HT_4 and 5-HT_6 receptors in the treatment of schizophrenia.

CONCLUSION

Cognitive deficits are the core symptom of schizophrenia which is relatively resistant against current drug therapy even with 2nd generation antipsychotics (e.g., 5-HT_2 and D_2 antagonists). This chapter reviewed the role and functional mechanisms of the serotonergic system in regulating cognitive functions and introduced potential strategy for the treatment of cognitive impairments in schizophrenia. Specifically, 5-HT_{1A}, 5-HT_3, 5-HT_4 and 5-HT_6 receptors serve as a promising target to alleviate cognitive deficits. These serotonergic strategies, especially add-on therapy with serotonergic agents, may provide benefits in clinical treatment of schizophrenia and facilitate further clinical investigations. Furthermore, drug discovery research designing new 5-HT receptor ligands, which possess combine affinities to the current therapeutic sites (e.g., D_2 and 5-HT_{2A} receptors) and the pro-cognitive sites (e.g., 5-HT_{1A}, 5-HT_3, 5-HT_4 and 5-HT_6 receptors), will contribute to future schizophrenia therapy.

REFERENCES

[1] H. Y. Meltzer, *Schizophrenia Bull.* 17, 263 (1991).
[2] S. Kapur and G. Remington, *Ann. Rev. Med.* 52, 503 (2001).
[3] Y. Ohno, *Cent. Nerv. Syst. Agents Med. Chem.* 10, 148 (2010).
[4] Y. Ohno, *CNS Neurosci. Ther.* 17, 58 (2011).
[5] H. Y. Meltzer and S. M. Stahl, *Schizophr Bull.* 2, 19 (1976).
[6] P. Seeman, Synapse. 1, 133 (1987).
[7] Y. Ohno, K. Ishida-Tokuda, T. Ishibashi, H. Sakamoto, R. Tagashira, T. Horisawa, et al. *Pol. J. Pharmacol.* 49, 213 (1997).
[8] H. Y. Meltzer, Z. Li, Y. Kaneda and J. Ichikawa, *Prog. Neuro-Psychopharmacol Biol. Psychiat.* 27, 1159 (2003).
[9] A. Bleich, S. L. Brown, R. Kahn and H. M. van Praag, *Schizophr Bull.* 14, 297 (1988).
[10] A. Breier, Schizophr Res. 14, 187 (1995).
[11] M. Wood and C. Reavill, *Expert. Opin. Investig. Drugs.* 16, 771 (2007).
[12] J. A. Lieberman, T. S. Stroup, J. P. McEvoy, M. S. Swartz, R. A. Rosenheck, D. O. Perkins, et al. *N. Engl. J. Med.* 353, 1209 (2005).
[13] R. S. Keefe, R. M. Bilder, S. M. Davis, P. D. Harvey, B. W. Palmer, J. M. Gold, et al. *Arch. Gen. Psychiatry.* 64, 633 (2007).
[14] M. Davidson, S. Galderisi, M. Weiser, N. Werbeloff, W. W. Fleischhacker, R. S. Keefe, et al. *Am. J. Psychiatry.* 166, 675 (2009).
[15] M. V. King, C. A. Marsden and K. C. Fone, *Trends Pharmacol. Sci.* 29, 482 (2008).
[16] J. Walstab, G. Rappold and B. Niesler, *Pharmacol. Ther.* 128, 146 (2010).
[17] B. L. Roth, *Ann. Clin. Psychiatry.* 6, 67 (1994).
[18] N. M. Barnes and T. Sharp, *Neuropharmacology.* 38, 1083 (1999).
[19] T. J. Pucadyil, S. Kalipatnapu and A. Chattopadhyay, *Cell. Mol. Neurobiol.* 25, 553 (2005).
[20] A. Hirose, M. Sasa, A. Akaike and S. Takaori, *Neuropharmacology.* 29, 93 (1990).
[21] P. Van den Hooff and M. Galvan, *Br. J. Pharmacol.* 106, 893 (1992).

[22] V. Hadrava, P. Blier, T. Dennis, C. Ortemann and de Montigny C. *Neuropharmacology.* 34, 1311 (1995).

[23] Y. Ohno, K. Ishida, T. Ishibashi, H. Tanaka, H. Shimizu and M. Nakamura, Effects of tandospirone, a selective 5-HT_{1A} agonist, on activities of the lateral septal nucleus neurons in cats., In "*Serotonin in the Central Nervous System and Periphery*." edited by Y. Takada and G, Curzon, pp. 159, Elsevier Science BV, Amsterdam (1995).

[24] J. R. Raymond, Y. V. Muklin, T. W. Gettys, and M. N. Garnovskaya, *Brit. J. Pharmacol.* 127, 1751 (1999).

[25] K. Tada, K. Kasamo, N. Ueda, T. Suzuki, T. Kojima, and K. Ishikawa, *J. Pharmacol. Exp. Ther.* 288, 843 (1999).

[26] J. P. Feighner, and W. F. Boyer, *Psychopathology.* 22, 21 (1989).

[27] R. W. Fuller, *J. Clin. Psychiatry.* 52, 52 (1991).

[28] Y. Ohno, Tandospirone citrate, a new serotonergic anxiolytic agent: A potential use in Parkinson's disease. In "*Mapping the Progress of Alzheimer's and Parkinson's Disease.*" edited by Y. Mizuno, A. Fisher and I. Hanin, pp. 423, Kluwer Academic/Plenum, New York (2002).

[29] H. Kusserow, B. Davies, H. Hörtnagl, I. Voigt, T. Stroh, B. Bert, et al. *Brain. Res. Mol Brain Res.* 129, 104 (2004).

[30] E. Akimova, R. Lanzenberger and S. Kasper, *Biol. Psychiatry.* 66, 627 (2009).

[31] T. Hashimoto, N. Nishino, H. Nakai and C. Tanaka, *Life Sci.* 48, 355 (1991).

[32] E. V. Gurevich and J. N. Joyce, *Biol. Psychiatry.* 42, 529 (1997).

[33] T. Sumiyoshi, M. Matsui, S. Nohara, I. Yamashita, M. Kurachi, C. Sumiyoshi, et al. *Am. J. Psychiatry.* 158, 1722 (2001).

[34] T. Sumiyoshi, S. Park, K. Jayathilake, A. Roy, A. Ertugrul and H. Y. Meltzer, *Schizophrenia Res.* 95, 158 (2007).

[35] H. Y. Meltzer and T. Sumiyoshi, *Behav. Brain Res.* 195, 98 (2008).

[36] T. Sumiyoshi, V. Bubenikova-Valesova, J. Horacek and B. Bert, *Adv. Ther.* 25, 1037 (2008).

[37] M. J. Millan, *J. Pharmacol. Exp. Ther.* 295, 853 (2000).

[38] M. L. Wadenberg, K. A. Young, J. T. Richter and P. B. Hicks, *Neuropharmacology.* 38, 151 (1999).

[39] E. P. Prinssen, F. C. Colpaert and W. Koek, *Eur. J. Pharmacol.* 453, 217 (2002).

[40] T. Ishibashi and Y. Ohno, *Biog. Amines* 8, 329 (2004).

[41] Y. Ohno, S. Shimizu, J. Imaki, S. Ishihara, N. Sofue, M. Sasa, et al. *Neuropharmacology* 55, 717 (2008).

[42] Y. Ohno, S. Shimizu, J. Imaki, S. Ishihara, N. Sofue, M. Sasa, et al. *Prog. Neuro-Psychopharmacol Biol. Psychiat.* 32, 1302 (2008).

[43] Y. Ohno, S. Shimizu and J. Imaki, *J. Pharmacol. Sci.* 109, 593 (2009).

[44] S. Shimizu, A. Tatara, J. Imaki and Y. Ohno, *Prog. Neuro-Psychopharmacol Biol. Psychiat.* 34, 877 (2010).

[45] P. Blier and N. M. Ward, *Biol. Psychiatry.* 53,193 (2003).

[46] I. Misane and S. O. Ögren, *Brit. J. Pharmacol.* 28, 253 (2003).

[47] M. Lüttgen, E. Elvander, N. Madjid and S. O. Ögren, *Neuropharmacology.* 48, 830 (2005).

[48] N. Madjid, E. E. Tottie, M. Lüttgen, B. Meister, J. Sandin, A. Kuzmin, et al. *J. Pharmacol. Exp. Ther.* 316, 581 (2006).

[49] S. O. Ögren, T. M. Eriksson, E. Elvander-Tottie, C. D'Addario, J. C. Ekström, P. Svenningsson, et al. *Behav. Brain Res.* 195, 54 (2008).
[50] T. Ishibashi, T. Horisawa, K. Tokuda, T. Ishiyama, M. Ogasa, R. Tagashira, et al. *J. Pharmacol. Exp. Ther.* 334, 171 (2010).
[51] T. Ishiyama, K. Tokuda, T. Ishibashi, A. Ito, S. Toma and Y. Ohno, *Eur. J. Pharmacol.* 572, 160 (2007).
[52] M. Nakamura, M. Ogasa, J. Guarino, D. Phillips, J. Severs, J. Cucchiaro, et al. *J. Clin. Psychiatry.* 70, 829 (2009).
[53] M. R. Livesey, M. A. Cooper, T. Z. Deeb, J.E. Carland, J. Kozuska, T.G. Hales, et al. J. Biol. Chem. 283, 19301 (2008).
[54] J. M. Barnes, B. Costall, J. Coughlan, A. M. Domeney, P.A. Gerrard, M.E. Kelly, et al. *Pharmacol. Biochem. Behav.* 35, 955 (1990).
[55] H. Hodges, P. Sowinski, J. J. Turner and A. Fletcher, *Psychopharmacology* (Berl). 125, 146 (1996).
[56] A. F. Arnsten, C. H. Lin, C. H. Van Dyck, and K.J. Stanhope, Neurobiol. Aging. 18, 21 (1997).
[57] F. J. Gil-Bea, J. Domínguez, M. García-Alloza, B. Marcos, B. Lasheras and M.J. Ramirez, *Neuropharmacology. 47*, 225 (2004).
[58] M. G. Giovannini, I. Ceccarelli, B. Molinari, M. Cecchi, J. Goldfarb and P. Blandina, *J. Pharmacol. Exp. Ther.* 285, 1219 (1998).
[59] Z. J. Zhang, W. H. Kang, Q. Li, X. Y. Wang, S. M. Yao and A.Q. Ma, *Schizophr. Res.* 88, 102 (2006).
[60] S. Akhondzadeh, N. Mohammadi, M. Noroozian, N. Karamghadiri, A. Ghoreishi, A.H. Jamshidi, et al. *Schizophr. Res.* 107, 206 (2009).
[61] Y. Ohno, J. Imaki, Y. Mae, T. Takahashi and A. Tatara, *Neuropharmacology.* 60, 201 (2011).
[62] G. P. Reynolds, S. L. Mason, A. Meldrum, S. De Keczer, H. Parnes, R. M. Eglen, et al. *Br. J. Pharmacol.* 114, 993 (1995).
[63] D. J. Fontana, S. E. Daniels, E. H. Wong, R. D. Clark and R. M. Eglen, *Neuropharmacology.* 36, 689 (1997).
[64] N. Galeotti, C. Ghelardini and A. Bartolini, *J. Pharmacol. Exp. Ther.* 286, 1115 (1998).
[65] L. Lamirault and H. Simon, *Neuropharmacology.* 41, 844 (2001).
[66] E. G. Mohler, S. Shacham and S. Noiman, *Neuropharmacology.* 53, 563 (2007).
[67] S. Consolo, S. Arnaboldi, S. Giorgi, G. Russi and H. Ladinsky, *Neuroreport.* 5, 1230 (1994).
[68] A. Siniscalchi, I. Badini, L. Beani and C. Bianchi, *Neuroreport.* 10, 547 (1999).
[69] U. Bickmeyer, M. Heine, T. Manzke and D. W. Richter, *Eur. J. Neurosci.* 16, 209 (2002).
[70] R. P. Ward and D. M. Dorsa, *J. Comp. Neurol.* 370, 405 (1996).
[71] M. L. Woolley, C. A. Marsden and K. C. Fone, Curr. Drug Targets CNS Neurol. Disord. 3, 59 (2004).
[72] B. Marcos, F. J. Gil-Bea, W. D. Hirst, M. García-Alloza and M. J. Ramirez, *Eur. J. Neurosci.* 24, 1299 (2006).
[73] E. S. Mitchell, T. Sexton and J. F. Neumaier, *Neuropsychopharmacology.* 32, 1520 (2007).

[74] M. L. Woolley, J. C. Bentley, A. J. Sleight, C. A. Marsden and K. C. Fone, *Neuropharmacology.* 41, 210 (2001).

[75] M. L. Woolley, C. A. Marsden, A. J. Sleight, C. A. Marsden and K. C. Fone, *Psychopharmacology (Berl).* 170, 358 (2003).

[76] M. V. King, A. J. Sleight, M. L. Woolley, I. A. Topham, C. A. Marsden and K. C. Fone, *Neuropharmacology.* 47, 195 (2004).

[77] C. K. Lieben, A. Blokland, A. Sik, E. Sung, P. van Nieuwenhuizen and R. Schreiber, *Neuropsychopharmacology.* 30, 2169 (2005).

[78] W. D. Hirst, T. O. Stean, D. C. Rogers, D. Sunter, P. Pugh, S.F. Moss, et al. *Eur. J. Pharmacol.* 553, 109 (2006).

[79] L. E. Schechter, Q. Lin, D. L. Smith, G. Zhang, Q. Shan, B. Platt, et al. *Neuropsychopharmacology.* 33, 1323 (2008).

[80] C. Riemer, E. Borroni, B. Levet-Trafit, J. R. Martin, S. Poli, R. H. Porter, et al. *J. Med. Chem.* 46, 1273 (2003).

[81] R. Kohen, M. A. Metcalf, N. Khan, T. Druck, K. Huebner, J. E. Lachowicz, et al. *J. Neurochem.* 66, 47 (1996).

[82] Y. W. Yu, S. J. Tsai, C. H. Lin, C. P. Hsu, K. H. Yang and C. J. Hong, Neuroreport. 10, 1231 (1999).

[83] G. A. Higgins, M. Enderlin, M. Haman and P.J. Fletcher, *Psychopharmacology* (Berl). 170, 309 (2003).

[84] C. Mirjana, M. Baviera, R. W. Invernizzi and C. Balducci, *Neuropsychopharmacology.* 29, 1637 (2004).

[85] V. Boulougouris and T. W. Robbins, *J. Neurosci.* 30, 930 (2010).

In: Schizophrenia Research: Recent Advances
Editor: Tomiki Sumiyoshi
ISBN: 978-1-62808-703-1

Chapter 15

GENE POLYMORPHISM AT SEROTONIN 5-HT_{1A} RECEPTORS: MOVING TOWARD PERSONALIZED MEDICINE FOR PSYCHOSIS AND MOOD DEFICITS?

Adrian Newman-Tancredi[1] and Paul R. Albert[2]
[1] NeuroAct Communication, Castres, France
[2] University of Ottawa, Ottawa, Canada

ABSTRACT

Compelling evidence indicates that serotonin 5-HT_{1A} receptors play an important role in the pathophysiology of schizophrenia and in the therapeutic profiles of antipsychotics. Indeed, recent antipsychotics, such as aripiprazole and lurasidone, have increasingly been selected on the basis of their capacity to act as agonists at 5-HT_{1A} receptors. However, new evidence indicates that a common 5-HT_{1A} gene (HTR1A) promoter polymorphism (rs6295, C-1019G), which occurs in about 20-40% of the population, leads to changes in 5-HT_{1A} receptor function that markedly affect vulnerability to psychiatric disorders. Thus, rs6295 is associated with mood deficits, cognitive dysfunction and suicidality, as well as treatment resistance to antipsychotics and antidepressants. At a molecular level, rs6295 dis-inhibits 5-HT_{1A} autoreceptor expression and impairs cortical (post-synaptic) 5-HT_{1A} receptor expression, thus causing a dual imbalance in serotonergic neurotransmission. Patients expressing rs6295 polymorphism may preferentially benefit from pharmacotherapy aiming to re-establish normal 5-HT_{1A} function by treatment with antipsychotics possessing 5-HT_{1A} agonist properties, such as aripiprazole, or by treatment with 5-HT_{1A} agonists as adjunct to other antipsychotics. Such a therapeutic strategy would constitute a step towards gene profile-based personalized medicine, but several issues require further clarification. For example, not all studies have reported an association of rs6295 with psychosis, and the relevance of rs6295 to patients may vary in different ethnic backgrounds depending on genotype frequency. In addition, current 5-HT_{1A} agonists activate 5-HT_{1A} autoreceptors as well as post-synaptic 5-HT_{1A} receptors: it would be desirable to develop drugs that exhibit "biased agonism" at cortical 5-HT_{1A} receptors, such as the prototypical compound, F15599. Indeed, agonists that stimulate cortical 5-HT_{1A} receptor neurotransmission without suppressing serotonergic neuron activity may constitute promising personalized pharmacotherapies for patients with rs6295-elicited psychiatric disorders.

INTRODUCTION

Serotonergic systems are of fundamental importance to the pathophysiology of schizophrenia and to the mechanism of action of antipsychotics. Thus although currently-available antipsychotics act as D_2 receptor antagonists (or weak partial agonists), most atypical antipsychotics also exhibit potent antagonist properties at serotonin 5-HT_{2A} receptors [1-3]. The combination of these two properties improves management of negative symptoms and cognitive deficits which are insufficiently controlled by D_2 receptor blockade alone [2,4,5]. However, accumulated evidence has indicated that the 5-HT_{1A} receptor subtype also plays a major role in the control of non-psychotic symptoms in schizophrenia and in the reduction of neuroleptic-elicited extrapyramidal symptoms (EPS) [1,6]. Indeed, activation of 5-HT_{1A} receptors with selective agonists opposes catalepsy in rodents, dystonia in primates and EPS in human [7-10]. Further, co-treatment with 5-HT_{1A} partial agonists does not compromise the capacity of D2 antagonists, such as haloperidol, to achieve antipsychotic clinical efficacy against positive symptoms [11,12]. Thus, associating 5-HT_{1A} agonism with D_2 receptor antagonism in a single molecule is an attractive strategy to widen the "therapeutic window" between antipsychotic actions and EPS induction [13,14]. However, the benefits of 5-HT_{1A} agonism in the pharmacotherapy of schizophrenia extend beyond EPS suppression. Indeed, 5-HT_{1A} receptors are highly expressed in the prefrontal cortex (PFC), a region that is profoundly involved in the control of cognition and mood [5,15,16]. Thus, atypical antipsychotics such as risperidone and olanzapine increase dopamine levels in PFC, partly via indirect 5-HT_{1A} receptor activation [17,18], a property that likely underlies their superior capacity to improve negative symptoms and cognitive deficits in schizophrenia. 5-HT_{1A} agonists stimulate PFC dopamine release in rodent microdialysis studies [18-20], and improve cognitive performance in schizophrenia patients when administered as adjunct to neuroleptic treatment [12,21-23]. Such observations have attracted attention to antipsychotics that exhibit dual D_2 antagonist / 5-HT_{1A} agonist properties, as is the case for some established antipsychotics and several exploratory novel drugs [24]. Thus, clozapine acts as a weak partial agonist at 5-HT_{1A} receptors [25], as well as potently blocking 5-HT_{2A} receptors and modestly antagonizing D_2 receptors [1]. The 5-HT_{1A} agonist properties of clozapine are sufficient to be expressed in animal models of anxiety (ultrasonic vocalization test, [26]), neurotransmitter release (microdialysis measures of dopamine and serotonin levels [27,28]) and EPS (attenuation of haloperidol-induced catalepsy [29]), as demonstrated by blockade with selective 5-HT_{1A} receptor antagonists and suggesting that even modest 5-HT_{1A} activation may be therapeutically relevant. Another established antipsychotic with dual D_2/5-HT_{1A} properties is aripiprazole, which exhibits partial agonism at both receptors, and several other compounds, including lurasidone and cariprazine, have been reported and are undergoing various stages of investigation (see [24] for review). However, increasing data indicates that substantial diversity exists between these drugs depending on their respective balance of affinity and agonist / antagonist properties at D_2 and 5-HT_{1A} receptors [1,6]. Thus low affinity or antagonism at 5-HT_{1A} receptors may fail to provide protection against EPS or desired benefits on negative symptoms and cognitive function. Conversely, excessively potent and efficacious 5-HT_{1A} agonism provides antidepressant-like properties but may compromise satisfactory antipsychotic actions [6]. Hence it may be surmised that a "one size fits all" approach to novel D_2/5-HT_{1A} antipsychotics may be inappropriate: some of these drugs may be better suited to patients with predominantly psychotic symptoms whereas others may be more suitable for those patients that display persistent cognitive deficits, negative symptoms or co-morbid mood disorders. The relevance of such a "personalized medicine" approach in the use of antipsychotics has become even more pertinent in view of recent studies showing that 5-HT$_{1A}$ receptor function can be substantially influenced by genetic factors [30,31]. Indeed, a gene promoter variant (rs6295 HTR1A polymorphism) of the 5-HT$_{1A}$ receptor affects its expression in a brain region-dependent manner. Subjects carrying this gene variant exhibit exacerbated vulnerability to psychiatric disorders and impaired therapeutic response to antipsychotics and other psychotropic agents [32]. Here, we review the molecular mechanisms underlying the rs6295 polymorphism and how they influence clinical outcomes. The implications for the pharmacotherapy of schizophrenia are discussed, and the desirability of preferentially targeting 5-HT$_{1A}$ receptor subpopulations is considered in the light of the recent discovery of "biased agonists" at this site.

5-HT$_{1A}$ Receptor Polymorphism: Molecular Mechanisms

The rs6295 polymorphism was initially reported in 1999 [33] as a common polymorphism C(-1018)G in the promoter region of the human HTR1A gene. With the consensus HTR1A sequence (Genbank) it is currently denoted as C(-1019)G. It was subsequently found that this polymorphism is located in a palindrome sequence and that the G-allele reduces the binding of nuclear proteins to this sequence [34]. Two transcription factors were identified that are affected by the G-allele, NUDR/Deaf-1 and Hes5. Transcriptional reporter studies revealed that in 5-HT$_{1A}$-expressing serotonergic raphe cells as a model of 5-HT$_{1A}$ autoreceptors and in cells that lack the receptor, both factors repress the expression of the 5-HT$_{1A}$ receptor gene, however Deaf-1 displays enhancer activity in several 5-HT$_{1A}$-expressing neuronal cell lines that do not express serotonergic markers, and constitute models of post-synaptic neuronal 5-HT$_{1A}$ heteroreceptors [35,36]. Importantly, these actions were blocked by the G-allele, which also modified basal receptor expression, leading to de-repression in raphe cells but reduced activity in non-serotonergic 5-HT$_{1A}$-positive cells. When co-expressed, Deaf-1 had the dominant effect compared to Hes5 [36,37]. This suggests that the major factor regulating HTR1A expression in these cells is Deaf-1, which displays enhancer activity in the post-synaptic cells. Consistent with this, in post-mortem tissue from female depressed subjects, decreases in both Deaf-1 and 5-HT$_{1A}$ receptor levels were observed suggesting coupling between the two [38]. Conversely, in PET imaging studies, the G-allele was associated with increased 5-HT$_{1A}$ autoreceptor expression in depression and bipolar depression [39-41], although not in normal subjects [42], suggesting that normal subjects may be able to compensate for the genetic dys-regulation imparted by the 5-HT$_{1A}$ receptor G-allele. It should be noted that there are multiple regulators that act at other sites of the HTR1A promoter [31]. For example, stress-induced down-regulation of 5-HT$_{1A}$ receptors in the prefrontal cortex does not involve changes in Deaf-1 protein levels [43,44], and could instead be mediated by glucocorticoid-induced repression of 5-HT$_{1A}$ receptor transcription [45,46]. However, Deaf-1 appears to be particularly important for dys-regulation of HTR1A expression by the rs6295 polymorphism.

Since the initial studies, the role of additional transcription factors to regulate the 5-HT_{1A} receptor at the rs6295-containing palindrome site has been addressed. In addition to Hes5, Hes1 was identified as a key regulator at the polymorphism that induced even stronger repression than Hes5 [37]. Hes6, a negative regulator of Hes1 and Hes5, antagonized their activity. The Hes proteins are expressed in the brain primarily in neural progenitors, where they repress the expression of neuronal genes to maintain pluripotency and prevent neuronal differentiation. Upon signaling to induce neuronal differentiation in embryogenesis, Hes proteins are down-regulated [47]. Hence the effect of a lack of Hes1 on the developmental expression of 5-HT_{1A} receptor RNA was addressed in vivo using Hes1 -/- mice. This mutation is embryonically lethal due to premature neuronal differentiation, and in midbrain sections of Hes1 -/- tissue the expression of 5-HT_{1A} receptors were prematurely induced and displayed an expanded expression [37]. These results indicate that Hes1 represses 5-HT_{1A} autoreceptor expression in development, and suggest that the G-allele may lead to premature expression of 5-HT_{1A} autoreceptors. Transgenic over-expression of 5-HT_{1A} receptors has been shown to inhibit serotonergic projections [48], and reduce differentiation of 5-HT neurons [49], and may do so by 5-HT_{1A} autoreceptor coupling to inhibition of ERK1/2 activation [50].

In contrast to Hes proteins, Deaf-1 is expressed in the brain throughout development and adulthood and is likely to mediate altered regulation HTR1A expression by the G-allele in the adult [34]. Deaf-1 is widely expressed throughout the brain and is colocalized with 5-HT_{1A} autoreceptors in raphe neurons, and with 5-HT_{1A} heteroreceptors in cortical neurons in human tissue [34,38,51]. It remains unclear how Deaf-1 activity as a repressor or enhancer is regulated. Recent evidence indicates that Deaf-1 may be a direct target for the action of mood stabilizers such as lithium, via GSK3β-induced phosphorylation of Deaf-1 [52]. Inhibitors of GSK3β such as lithium, increased Deaf-1 enhancer activity, suggesting that mood stabilizers may act in part by activating Deaf-1 leading to increased 5-HT_{1A} heteroreceptor expression. Consistent with this, a preliminary PET imaging study of bipolar depression patients found that chronic treatment with mood stabilizers increases 5-HT_{1A} receptor levels in specific cortical sub-regions [53].

Interestingly, preliminary data suggest that in mice lacking Deaf-1, a 50% induction of 5-HT_{1A} autoreceptor expression is observed, while in the cortex there is a reduction in 5-HT_{1A} heteroreceptor expression [54]. The opposite regulation of pre- and post-synaptic 5-HT_{1A} receptor expression by Deaf-1 is expected to have a synergistic effect on serotonergic neurotransmission. Transgenic mice engineered with a 30% decrease in 5-HT_{1A} autoreceptors have augmented 5-HT neurotransmission, leading to increased 5-HT release, and increased resistance to behavioral despair in animal models [55]. Most strikingly, they respond to SSRI treatment within days, whereas the wild-type littermates failed to respond. On the other hand, selective reduction of 5-HT_{1A} heteroreceptors leads to an anxiety phenotype [56]. Based on these mouse models, the loss of Deaf-1 regulation at the G-allele would be expected to confer risk to both depression (via up-regulation of 5-HT_{1A} autoreceptors) and anxiety (via reduction in post-synaptic 5-HT_{1A} heteroreceptors), and is expected to produce resistance to chronic SSRI treatment [57]. As described above, the most prominent effect of the G/G genotype in human depression and bipolar depression appears to be upregulation of 5-HT_{1A} autoreceptors as detected by PET imaging techniques [39-41]. However, there are several reports of global reductions in 5-HT_{1A} receptors in depression and anxiety disorders [58], and it remains unclear which effect is more important in these different diseases. It is likely that brain region-specific alterations in 5-HT$_{1A}$ receptor expression, which are not readily detected by PET imaging but can be observed in post-mortem studies [58], will dictate susceptibility to various mental illnesses.

A key question is whether the heterozygous genotype (CG) behaves more like the CC (wild-type) or the (GG) genotype. In theory, the heterozygous genotype would exert 50% of the effect of the GG genotype, which could lead to a partial dys-regulation of 5-HT$_{1A}$ receptor expression. For example, instead of a 50% increase in 5-HT$_{1A}$ autoreceptors, a less dramatic 25% increase might be observed. Depending on the sensitivity of the phenotype to 5-HT$_{1A}$ receptor expression this could be sufficient to mimic the GG genotype. Thus, a 30% relative increase in 5-HT$_{1A}$ autoreceptors was sufficient to abrogate SSRI activity [55], and thus the CG genotype could be considered similar to the GG genotype for this outcome [57]. On the other hand, a complete suppression of 5-HT$_{1A}$ autoreceptors produced a more robust depression phenotype, and hence for depression association the CG could be considered like CC. Thus improved animal models may be very instructive to guide genetic association studies and their analysis.

5-HT$_{1A}$ Receptor Polymorphism: Influence on Neuropsychiatric Disorders

Although some literature reviews are available regarding the influence of the rs6295 polymorphism in diverse psychiatric disorders, [31,32,59], the rapidity with which the field has advanced renders necessary an up-to-date summary of the numerous studies that have been reported over recent years. As indicated in Tables 1-3, these range from small studies with a few dozen patients to others with several hundred patients. Studies have been carried out in nearly twenty different countries covering numerous ethnic groups, ranging from French-Canadian to Spanish, Taiwanese, Italian, Finnish and South Korean. The pathologies examined include major (unipolar) depression (MD), bipolar depression, psychosis / schizophrenia and panic disorders. Despite a wide variety of clinical study designs, it is striking that a majority of the studies report convergent data, with rs6295 carriers showing greater vulnerability to mood deficits and impaired response to drug treatments (Tables 1-3). However, beyond this broad generalization, several issues remain to be clarified.

Firstly, although most studies of the rs6295 polymorphism in patients suffering from MD have reported an association, several studies have reported diverging conclusions, raising the possibility that methodological and/or other factors may mask underlying genetic vulnerability. In particular, ethnic groups and gender may influence clinical outcomes. For example, although a Japanese study failed to find an association of rs6295 with MD, it did report an association with MD in Asian patients when a meta-analysis was conducted [60]. Conversely, the studies that have failed to observe an association with MD were mainly carried out in Caucasians [61-63]. These observations therefore raise the possibility that patients from different ethnic backgrounds may be differentially affected by changes in 5-HT$_{1A}$ receptor function elicited by the rs6295 polymorphism. Indeed, a study comparing Korean and Caucasian volunteers concluded that the rs6295 polymorphism could result in divergent psychological outcomes, depending on an individual's cultural context [64]. In addition, the frequency of the "risk allele" in the population can vary with ethnicity. For example, the G-allele is present in 5-10% of Oriental populations but 40% in Caucasian population [32]; hence a 10% increase in allele frequency may be statistically significant in the former but not the latter population.

In addition to ethnic differences, a gender influence may also be present. Thus, a Chinese study reported that the rs6295 polymorphism is likely to be the susceptible gene locus for female late-onset MD, a conclusion consistent with an American study which found that female geriatric patients expressing the G allele of rs6295 exhibited higher rates of Geriatric Depression Scale scores following hip fracture [65]. Finally, in a Canadian study, female GC genotype MD patients responded less well to antidepressant treatment than males [66] although the sample size was too small to draw firm conclusions. Nevertheless, there was a statistically significant difference in response between patients carrying the CC genotype and those with the CG or GG genotypes, suggesting that the heterozygous genotype elicits resistance to antidepressant treatment, and that the G-allele appears to be dominant for this phenotype (cf. comments above on molecular mechanisms).

Secondly, rs6295 appears to differentially affect various mood disorders. For example, rs6295 may, in some cases, predispose patients to exhibit co-morbid mood deficit symptoms. Thus, an Anglo-Spanish study reported that no association was detected between the G allele and MD or General Anxiety Disorder (GAD) but that a significant association was observed in patients suffering from co-morbid MD and GAD [67]. A German study reported that rs6295 was associated with Panic Disorder in those patients that exhibited concurrent agoraphobia [68]; by contrast, a Korean study found an association of rs6295 with panic disorder in patients without agoraphobia [69]. More recently, a Brazilian study associated an HTR1A haplotype including the G-allele of rs6295 with panic disorder, suggesting that additional polymorphisms in linkage disequilibrium with rs6295 may contribute to HTR1A dys-regulation. Conversely, the presence of the G allele may actually decrease risk of certain disorders, as reported for premenstrual dysphoric disorder [70] or attention deficit and hyperactivity disorder (ADHD) [71]. Thus, it seems clear that rs6295 does not equally predispose to all mood deficits although measurable modifications in brain region volume may be observed even in cases where clinical symptoms may not be systematically detected. Thus, significant decreases in amygdala volumes were reported in borderline personality disorder (BPD) patients [72] although expression of the G allele was not found to be associated with BPD [73].

Thirdly, the influence of rs6295 on psychiatric pathologies may be accentuated in the presence of additional genetically-determined characteristics. In particular, the short variant of the 5-HT transporter-linked polymorphic region (5-HTTLPR) is associated with increased incidence of depression [74,75], cognitive deficits [76] and suicide risk [77], possibly by influencing 5-HT_{1A} receptor expression levels [78]. Importantly, the short-variant 5-HTTLPR "risk gene" is independent of the rs6295 5-HT_{1A} receptor polymorphism. Indeed, rs6295 increased the incidence and severity of interferon-induced depression independently of 5-HTTLPR genotype [79]. Further, antidepressant response to fluvoxamine was significantly less in G allele MD patients, independently of their 5-HTTLPR genotype [80]. It may therefore be hypothesized that if both the 5-HTTLPR and 5-HT_{1A} "risk genes" are dys-regulated due to functional polymorphisms, patients may be synergistically vulnerable to psychiatric disorders. This hypothesis is supported by a Chinese study that reported a combined effect for 5-HTTLPR and 5-HT_{1A} rs6295 polymorphisms on modifying the response to negative life events conferring susceptibility to MD [81]. In addition, MD patients expressing both the 5-HTTLPR and 5-HT$_{1A}$ "risk alleles" responded poorly to the selective serotonin reuptake inhibitor, citalopram, whereas normal response was observed in patients that only expressed the rs6295 polymorphism [82]. Finally, a study of response to emotional stimuli showed significantly increased bilateral amygdala activation in panic disorder patients with either the rs6295 G allele or the 5-HTTLPR polymorphism [83], consistent with an additive effect of the genotypes [84]. Similarly an association of MD with risk alleles of both HTR1A and BDNF genes was reported, although neither allele was individually associated with MD [85].

Fourthly, the relative contribution of the heterozygous rs6295 CG genotype to psychiatric disorders requires clarification. Indeed, different studies have adopted inconsistent methodologies for statistical purposes. In some cases, patients expressing the CG genotype were pooled with those expressing the CC genotype and compared with those expressing the GG genotype [86,87]. In other cases, patients expressing the CG and GG genotypes were pooled and compared to patients expressing the CC genotype [88-90]. Such disparate approaches to data analysis may underlie some divergent results and, potentially, obscure differences between subjects. Ideally each of these subgroups of subjects would be characterized separately, as has been reported in some cases [64,69,91]. For example, one study [92] reported that attentional processing was aggravated in patients with the GG genotype relative to those with the CG genotype, which, in turn, was worse than that in patients with the CC genotype, implying that increasing numbers of -1019G alleles lead to a reduction of attentional processes.

Taken together, the above considerations indicate that additional research is necessary to fully elucidate the influence of rs6295 in mood / psychiatric disorders. Nevertheless, available information supports the concept that rs6295 represents a genetic risk factor for vulnerability to mood and cognition-related deficits.

5-HT$_{1A}$ Receptor Polymorphism: Influence in Schizophrenia

As concerns studies in schizophrenia or psychotic patients (Table 2), the existence of a genetic association with rs6295 is currently under debate. Indeed, association was reported by one group [93] but not by another [94], and a third group reported a haplotype association of rs6295 with a tagging polymorphism of the 5-HT$_{1A}$ receptor (rs878567). In contrast, other studies have consistently indicated that schizophrenia patients expressing rs6295 show impaired therapeutic response to antipsychotic treatment, particularly atypical antipsychotics which have a serotonergic component of their pharmacology. The studies supporting this conclusion are summarized below.

Firstly, a Spanish study pooled 63 Spanish Caucasian patients receiving a variety of different antipsychotics, including risperidone (N=19 patients), olanzapine (N=18), quetiapine (N=10), other antipsychotics (N=11) or even no antipsychotic at all (N=5). Those patients expressing GG or CG genotypes showed less improvement in negative symptom scores (using the Positive and Negative Syndrome Scale, PANSS) and depressive symptoms (Calgary Depression Scale) than those expressing CC genotype [95]. No genotype-related differences were observed on positive symptom scores.

Secondly, a larger study of Chinese subjects examined response to an 8-week treatment with risperidone (dose range 2-6 mg) and controlled for blood plasma levels of risperidone, 9-OH-risperidone and prolactin [96]. 70 subjects had the CC genotype, 44 were heterozygous (CG genotype) and 11 had the GG genotype. The latter displayed significantly less improvement in negative symptoms (32% reduction in negative PANSS scores) that those with the CC genotype (48% reduction). Once again, no significant difference was observed on positive symptom scores.

Thirdly, a German study examined two cohorts of Caucasian schizophrenia patients. The first cohort (68 patients) was treated with either risperidone or haloperidol (dose range 2-8 mg) for 4 weeks. GG genotype patients treated with risperidone responded poorly on negative symptoms (scores decreased by only 1.22 points) whereas those with CC or CG genotypes responded better (negative symptom scores decreased by 4.38 points). Curiously, patients treated with haloperidol did not show a significant difference in response between genotypes, the reason for this being unclear. A second cohort (130 patients) was also examined. These patients were treated for 4 weeks with a variety of antipsychotics including olanzapine (N=59), amisulpride (N=47), clozapine (N=16), quetiapine (N=15), risperidone (N=13) and other antipsychotics. Patients with the GG genotype showed a mean improvement of 2.81 points in negative symptoms scores, whereas patients with at least one C allele improved by 4.99 points. Thus the second cohort of patients confirmed and extended the findings of the risperidone-treated patients in the first cohort.

Fourthly, a Japanese study investigated 30 patients treated for 3 months with either lurasidone or olanzapine [97]. All genotype groups (CC or CG+GG) showed improvement in scores of positive symptoms (Scale for Assessment of Positive Symptoms, SAPS) and negative symptom (Scale for Assessment of Negative Symptoms, SANS). However, subjects with the CC genotype showed improved attention scores on the SANS-Attention subscale, whereas the subjects with the CG or GG genotypes did not.

Fifthly, an Italian study investigated the performance of 118 clinically stabilized schizophrenia patients on verbal memory, executive function, attention and a Theory-of-Mind (ToM) test. In the latter, subjects with the CC genotype performed significantly better than subjects with CG or GG genotypes, supporting the importance of 5-HT$_{1A}$ receptors in cognitive function in schizophrenia.

5-HT$_{1A}$ Receptor Polymorphism: Implications for Pharmacotherapy of Schizophrenia

The clinical studies described above indicating an rs6295-associated treatment resistance to antipsychotics raise important questions concerning pharmacotherapy in schizophrenia. Indeed, negative symptoms and cognitive deficits underlie poor social function and contribute to healthcare and economic costs of schizophrenia [98,99]. Thus, it seems warranted to identify "personalized medicine" strategies for patients expressing rs6295 who respond poorly to some current antipsychotic drugs. In fact, the imbalance in 5-HT$_{1A}$ receptor function elicited by rs6295 may require pharmacological intervention with drugs specifically targeting this receptor subtype in order to re-establish appropriate serotonergic neurotransmission. Thus, it would be interesting to determine whether patients expressing rs6295 respond better (for negative and cognitive symptoms) to antipsychotics that possess some level of 5-HT$_{1A}$ receptor agonist activity. As mentioned above, aripiprazole is a partial agonist at 5-HT$_{1A}$ receptors, as are clozapine, ziprasidone and lurasidone. It may be hypothesized that these antipsychotics would favor normalization of deficient post-synaptic 5-HT$_{1A}$ receptor function and thus improve mood and cognition better than antipsychotics that lack 5-HT$_{1A}$ agonist properties, such as risperidone or olanzapine. However, two elements should be emphasized.

Firstly, all atypical antipsychotics act at a panoply of receptor subtypes, including dopamine D_2, D_3 and D_4 receptors, where they exhibit various activities (either partial agonism, as in the case of aripiprazole, or antagonism, as in the case of ziprasidone and lurasidone), noradrenergic alpha1 and alpha2 receptors, and various other serotonin receptors, including 5-HT$_{2A}$ and 5-HT$_{2C}$. Atypical antipsychotics such as clozapine and olanzapine also potently interact with various sites that may mediate side-effects, including muscarinic and histaminergic receptors. Thus, these drugs exhibit complex or "rich" pharmacological profiles in which their 5-HT$_{1A}$ properties may not be optimally expressed. For example, aripiprazole exhibits 5-HT$_{1A}$ receptor agonism in some animal models [100,101], but not others [18], possibly due to obscuring effects of its other pharmacological properties.

Secondly, it may be undesirable to activate all the 5-HT$_{1A}$ receptor subpopulations located in different brain regions. Indeed, 5-HT$_{1A}$ autoreceptors are likely to be hyper-active in patients expressing rs6295 so it would seem unwise to administer exogenous 5-HT$_{1A}$ agonists which would further inhibit serotonergic neurotransmission. Conversely, cortical 5-HT$_{1A}$ receptors may be hypo-functional in patients expressing rs6295, so it would be desirable to preferentially activate 5-HT$_{1A}$ receptors in this brain region which is pivotal to control of mood and cognition. It is interesting that a microdialysis study in mice suggested that aripiprazole preferentially activates postsynaptic cortical 5-HT$_{1A}$ receptors controlling dopamine release, and more weakly activates 5-HT$_{1A}$ autoreceptors controlling 5-HT release [102]. Such an activity may compensate for deficient cortical 5-HT$_{1A}$ receptor function whilst not exacerbating hyperactivity of 5-HT$_{1A}$ autoreceptors. Flibanserin is another compound that exhibits 5-HT$_{1A}$ agonism, as well as 5-HT$_{2A}$ antagonism and dopamine D_4 receptor partial agonism [103,104]. In a clinical trial, depressed patients expressing the GG or CG genotypes responded less well to flibanserin than patients expressing the CC genotype [57]. This indicates that flibanserin's combination of pharmacological properties did not compensate for underlying genetic vulnerability. Flibanserin has been proposed to exhibit preferential cortical activity but the precise pharmacological basis for this activity (5-HT$_{1A}$/5-HT$_{2A}$/D_4) remains to be clarified. Indeed, exploration of preferential post-synaptic 5-HT$_{1A}$ agonism would require selective 5-HT$_{1A}$ "biased agonists" capable of targeting cortical sites without additional interactions with other receptor subtypes or with 5-HT$_{1A}$ receptor subpopulations. Although commercialized therapeutic agents of this kind are unavailable at present, a recent selective 5-HT$_{1A}$ receptor "biased agonist", F15599, exhibits preferential activation of cortical 5-HT$_{1A}$ receptors in a panoply of pharmacology tests [105]. Thus, F15599 activates cortical pyramidal cell electrical activity at doses that do not inhibit raphe cell firing and stimulates cortical dopamine release, via activation of post-synaptic 5-HT$_{1A}$ receptors, at doses that do not inhibit serotonin release via activation of 5-HT$_{1A}$ autoreceptors [106]. In measures of mood and cognition, F15599 shows potent antidepressant-like activity [107] and reverses working and reference memory deficits elicited by the non-competitive NMDA receptor antagonist, phencyclidine [108]. Thus the profile of action of F15599 appears promising to treat negative symptoms and cognitive deficits such as those observed in schizophrenia patients. The favorable brain region-selective profile of F15599 appears to be based on its distinctive "signaling fingerprint", whereby it preferentially activates Gαi versus Gαo G-proteins and potently activates Extracellular Regulated Kinase (ERK1/2) phosphorylation *in vitro* and *ex vivo*, with weaker potency for other signaling responses [109]. Overall, it may be surmised that pharmacotherapy of schizophrenia patients with the G allele of the rs6295 polymorphism would be improved by the use of antipsychotics that preferentially activate post-synaptic 5-HT_{1A} receptors in cortical areas, or possibly by co-administration of a biased agonist acting at these sites.

Table 1. Studies of 5-HT_{1A} promoter polymorphism in patients with major depression

Effect?	Influence of rs6295	No. of patients, country	Ref.
Yes	Higher baseline symptoms, lower response rate	153 MD patients; USA	[111]
Yes	No overall association, but meta-analysis indicates association with MD in Asian patients.	331 MD patients, 804 controls; Japan	[60]
Yes	Increased incidence of co-morbid MD-GAD	1059 MD patients; Spain & UK	[67]
Yes	Association with MD in patients with 5-HTTLPR polymorphism and stressful life events	401 MD patients, 391 controls; China	[81]
Yes	Association with MD in female and late-onset subjects.	400 MD patients, 400 controls; China	[112]
Effect?	**Influence of rs6295**	**No. of patients, country**	**Ref.**
Yes	Higher geriatric depression scores, poorer functional recovery	145 elderly females with hip fractures; USA	[65]
Yes	Decreased response to transcranial magnetic stimulation (TMS)	99 MD patients; Italy	[89]
Yes	Increased incidence of depression in hepatitis-C patients treated with interferon alfa-2b	139 hepatitis-C patients; Germany	[79]
Yes	Increased incidence of depression when combined with BDNF (G196A) SNP.	119 treatment-resistant MD patients, 392 controls; Finland	[85]
Yes	Decreased response to fluoxetine in female patients	222 MD patients; Taiwan	[113]
Yes	Higher frequency of medication non-remission	22 MD patients, 43 controls; USA	[114]
Yes	Decreased response to fluoxetine	224 MD patients; Taiwan	[115]
Yes	Higher frequency of citalopram non-remission when combined with SERT gene SNP (SLC6A4)	130 MD patients; Spain	[82]
Yes	Higher frequency of non-responders to medication	118 MD patients; Canada	[57]
Yes	Association with MD	129 MD patients, 134 controls; Canada	[34]
No	No difference in clinical response to antidepressants	206 MD patients; Belgium	[61]
No	No association with MD or anxiety	6445 Caucasians; Australia	[62]
No	No association with MD	86 MD patients, 395 controls; Finland	[63]
No	No association with short-term response to antidepressants	101 MD patients; Taiwan	[116]
No	No difference in clinical response to fluvoxamine	151 MD patients; Italy	[80]

Abbreviation: MD Major Depression.

Table 2. Studies of 5-HT$_{1A}$ promoter polymorphism in patients with schizophrenia, bipolar depression or panic disorder

Pathology	Effect?	Influence of rs6295	No. of patients, country	Ref.
Schizophrenia & psychosis	Yes	Lower performance on Theory of Mind task.	118 schizophrenia patients; Italy	[117]
	Yes	Impaired improvement in attention upon treatment with lurasidone or olanzapine.	30 schizophrenia patients; Japan	[97]
	Yes	Haplotype association of rs6295 with a 5-HT$_{1A}$ tagging SNP (rs878567) in psychosis	197 methamphetamine-induced psychosis patients, 337 controls; Japan	[118]
	Yes	Impaired negative symptom response to atypical antipsychotics.	1st cohort of 68 patients; 2nd cohort 130 patients; Germany	[86]
	Yes	Impaired negative symptom response to risperidone treatment.	130 schizophrenia patients; China	[96]
	Yes	Impaired negative and depressive symptom response to antipsychotics.	63 drug-naïve schizophrenia patients; Spain	[95]
	Yes	Association with schizophrenia	696 psychiatric patients, 107 controls; USA	[93]
	No	No association with schizophrenia (but association with BP)	1028 BP patients, 857 schizophrenic, 1810 controls; Japan	[94]
Bipolar Depression	Yes	Lower stress threshold prior to hospitalization	74 BP patients; Italy	[119]
	Yes	Association with BP (but not schizophrenia)	1028 BP patients, 857 schizophrenic, 1810 controls; Japan	[94]
	Yes	Decreased response to fluvoxamine	111 BP patients; Italy	[80]
Panic Disorder	Yes	Association of a 5-HT$_{1A}$ haplotype with panic disorder	107 PD patients and 125 controls; Brazil	[120]
	Yes	Higher panic symptom severity in patients without agoraphobia.	94 PD patients, 111 controls; South Korea	[69]
	Yes	Reduced response to SSRI treatment.	102 PD patients; Ukraine	[121]
	Yes	Decreased PFC activation in response to fearful stimuli, higher amygdala activation in response to happy faces	20 PD patients; Germany	[83]
	Yes	Association with panic disorder	696 psychiatric patients, 107 controls; USA	[93]
	Yes	Association with PD in patients with agoraphobia	134 PD patients, 134 controls; Germany	[68]

Abbreviations: PD Panic Disorder; BP Bipolar Depression. Some references are listed more than once under different pathologies.

Table 3. Studies of 5-HT_{1A} promoter polymorphism in suicide attempters and in patients with ADHD, alcohol dependence or eating disorder

Pathology	Effect?	Influence of rs6295	No. of patients, country	Ref.
Suicide	Yes	Fewer stressful life events preceding suicide.	323 suicide victims, 190 controls; Slovenia	[88]
	Yes	Higher frequency in suicide victims	102 suicide victims, 116 controls; Canada	[34]
	Yes	Higher frequency in suicidal attempters	65 suicide attempters, 63 controls; Poland	[122]
	No	No association with suicide frequency.	373 alcohol-related suicide victims; Slovenia	[123]
	No	No association with personality traits.	1st cohort: 111 suicide attempters, 289 controls; Germany. 2nd cohort: 64 mood disorder patients; Italy.	[124]
	No	No significant associations.	1st cohort: 167 suicide attempters, 92 suicide victims, 312 controls, Germany. 2nd cohort: 152 suicide attempters, 131 controls; Italy	[125]
	No	No significant associations.	181 suicidal depressed patients, 143 non-suicidal depressed patients, 176 healthy controls.	[126]
ADHD & attentional processes	Yes	Decreased susceptibility to ADHD	78 ADHD patients, 107 controls; South Korea	[71]
	Yes	Increased impulsiveness scores.	725 healthy subjects; Hungary	[127]
	Yes	Reduced attentional processes	72 healthy subjects; Germany	[128]
Alcohol dependenc e	Yes	Lower frequency of alcohol dependence; higher frequency of withdrawal symptoms	97 males with alcohol dependence, 76 male controls; South Korea	[90]
	No	No association	185 alcohol dependent patients; Germany	[129]
Eating disorder	Yes	Association with disordered eating symptoms	204 female subjects; South Korea	[130]

Abbreviation: ADHD Attention Deficit Hyperactivity Disorder.

CONCLUSION

One of the ongoing challenges of pharmacological intervention in schizophrenia is the issue of treatment resistance, which is observed in at up to a third of patients [110]. As discussed above, data from the pharmacogenomics studies of rs6295 suggest that antipsychotic treatment resistance is partly linked to the presence of the C-1019G polymorphism of the 5-HT_{1A} receptor promoter, at least concerning negative symptoms and cognitive deficits of schizophrenia. This raises the issue of identifying drugs that can remedy the 5-HT_{1A} receptor dysfunction elicited by this polymorphism and, it is hoped, overcome the resistance of patients to existing pharmacotherapy. Such considerations would represent a step towards a personalized medicine approach: patients would undergo a genomic screen prior to deciding the appropriate drug treatment. This may include the use of direct 5-HT_{1A} receptor agonists capable of re-establishing normal signaling at this target. In particular, it would be interesting to investigate "biased agonists" that exhibit preferential activation of cortical 5-HT_{1A} sites whilst avoiding activation of 5-HT_{1A} autoreceptors. Such compounds would be expected to attenuate mood and cognitive dysfunction without further impairing serotonergic neurotransmission. However, although such an approach is attractive, various questions remain to be clarified concerning the role of the rs6295, including its influence in different pathologies, ethnic groups and possible additive risk with other genetic polymorphisms, such as 5-HTTLPR. Nevertheless, it seems likely that pharmacogenomically-based personalized medicine will attract increasing interest and may lead to improved management of the debilitating negative symptoms and cognitive dysfunction of schizophrenia and other psychotic disorders.

REFERENCES

[1] Newman-Tancredi A, Kleven MS: Comparative pharmacology of antipsychotics possessing combined dopamine D(2) and serotonin 5-HT (1A) receptor properties. *Psychopharmacology* (2011).

[2] Meltzer HY, Li Z, Kaneda Y, Ichikawa J: Serotonin receptors: their key role in drugs to treat schizophrenia. *Prog Neuropsychopharmacol Biol Psychiatry* 27, 1159-72 (2003).

[3] Kapur S, Mamo D: Half a century of antipsychotics and still a central role for dopamine D2 receptors. *Prog Neuropsychopharmacol Biol Psychiatry* 27, 1081-90 (2003).

[4] Meltzer HY, Horiguchi M, Massey BW: The role of serotonin in the NMDA receptor antagonist models of psychosis and cognitive impairment. *Psychopharmacology (Berl)* (2011).

[5] Meltzer HY, Sumiyoshi T: Does stimulation of 5-HT(1A) receptors improve cognition in schizophrenia? *Behav Brain Res* 195, 98-102 (2008).

[6] Newman-Tancredi A: The importance of 5-HT1A receptor agonism in antipsychotic drug action: rationale and perspectives. *Curr Opin Investig Drugs* 11, 802-12 (2010).

[7] Prinssen EP, Colpaert FC, Koek W: 5-HT1A receptor activation and anti-cataleptic effects: high-efficacy agonists maximally inhibit haloperidol-induced catalepsy. *Eur J Pharmacol* 453, 217-21 (2002).

[8] Wadenberg ML, Ahlenius S: Antipsychotic-like profile of combined treatment with raclopride and 8-OH-DPAT in the rat: enhancement of antipsychotic-like effects without catalepsy. *J Neural Transm Gen Sect* 83, 43-53 (1991).

[9] Auclair AL, Kleven MS, Barret-Grevoz C, et al.: Differences among conventional, atypical and novel putative D2/5-HT1A antipsychotics on catalepsy-associated behaviour in cynomolgus monkeys. *Behav Brain Res* 203, 288-95 (2009).

[10] Yoshida K, Sugita T, Higuchi H, Hishikawa Y: Effect of tandospirone on tardive dyskinesia and parkinsonian symptoms. *Eur Psychiatry* 13, 421-2 (1998).

[11] Goff DC, Midha KK, Brotman AW, et al.: An open trial of buspirone added to neuroleptics in schizophrenic patients. *Journal of clinical psychopharmacology* 11, 193-7 (1991).

[12] Sumiyoshi T, Matsui M, Nohara S, et al.: Enhancement of cognitive performance in schizophrenia by addition of tandospirone to neuroleptic treatment. *The American journal of psychiatry* 158, 1722-5 (2001).

[13] Bardin L, Kleven MS, Barret-Grevoz C, Depoortere R, Newman-Tancredi A: Antipsychotic-like vs cataleptogenic actions in mice of novel antipsychotics having D2 antagonist and 5-HT1A agonist properties. *Neuropsychopharmacology* 31, 1869-79 (2006).

[14] Millan MJ: Improving the treatment of schizophrenia: focus on serotonin (5-HT)(1A) receptors. *J Pharmacol Exp Ther* 295, 853-61 (2000).

[15] Green AR: Neuropharmacology of 5-hydroxytryptamine. *Br J Pharmacol* 147 Suppl 1, S145-52 (2006).

[16] Celada P, Puig M, Amargos-Bosch M, Adell A, Artigas F: The therapeutic role of 5-HT1A and 5-HT2A receptors in depression. *J Psychiatry Neurosci* 29, 252-65 (2004).

[17] Ichikawa J, Ishii H, Bonaccorso S, et al.: 5-HT(2A) and D(2) receptor blockade increases cortical DA release via 5-HT(1A) receptor activation: a possible mechanism of atypical antipsychotic-induced cortical dopamine release. *J Neurochem* 76, 1521-31 (2001).

[18] Assie MB, Ravailhe V, Faucillon V, Newman-Tancredi A: Contrasting contribution of 5-hydroxytryptamine 1A receptor activation to neurochemical profile of novel antipsychotics: frontocortical dopamine and hippocampal serotonin release in rat brain. *J Pharmacol Exp Ther* 315, 265-72 (2005).

[19] Gobert A, Rivet JM, Cistarelli L, Melon C, Millan MJ: Buspirone modulates basal and fluoxetine-stimulated dialysate levels of dopamine, noradrenaline and serotonin in the frontal cortex of freely moving rats: activation of serotonin1A receptors and blockade of alpha2-adrenergic receptors underlie its actions. *Neuroscience* 93, 1251-62 (1999).

[20] Bortolozzi A, Masana M, Diaz-Mataix L, et al.: Dopamine release induced by atypical antipsychotics in prefrontal cortex requires 5-HT1A receptors but not 5-HT2A receptors. *Int J Neuropsychopharmacol*, 1-16 (2010).

[21] Sumiyoshi T, Bubenikova-Valesova V, Horacek J, Bert B: Serotonin1A receptors in the pathophysiology of schizophrenia: development of novel cognition-enhancing therapeutics. *Advances in therapy* 25, 1037-56 (2008).

[22] Sumiyoshi T, Matsui M, Yamashita I, et al.: The effect of tandospirone, a serotonin(1A) agonist, on memory function in schizophrenia. *Biological psychiatry* 49, 861-8 (2001).

[23] Meltzer HY, Sumiyoshi T: Does stimulation of 5-HT(1A) receptors improve cognition in schizophrenia? *Behavioural brain research* 195, 98-102 (2008).

[24] McCreary AC, Jones CA: Antipsychotic medication: the potential role of 5-HT(1A) receptor agonism. *Curr Pharm Des* 16, 516-21 (2010).

[25] Newman-Tancredi A, Chaput C, Verriele L, Millan MJ: Clozapine is a partial agonist at cloned, human serotonin 5-HT1A receptors. *Neuropharmacology* 35, 119-21 (1996).

[26] Bartoszyk GD, Roos C, Ziegler H: 5-HT1A receptors are not involved in clozapine's lack of cataleptogenic potential. *Neuropharmacology* 35, 1645-6 (1996).

[27] Bengtsson HJ, Kullberg A, Millan MJ, Hjorth S: The role of 5-HT1A autoreceptors and alpha1-adrenoceptors in the modulation of 5-HT release--III. Clozapine and the novel putative antipsychotic S 16924. *Neuropharmacology* 37, 349-56 (1998).

[28] Rollema H, Lu Y, Schmidt AW, Zorn SH: Clozapine increases dopamine release in prefrontal cortex by 5-HT1A receptor activation. *European journal of pharmacology* 338, R3-5 (1997).

[29] Millan MJ, Schreiber R, Dekeyne A, et al.: S 16924 ((R)-2-[1-[2-(2,3-dihydro-benzo[1,4] dioxin-5-yloxy)-ethyl]-pyrrolidin-3yl]-1-(4-fluoro-phenyl)-ethanone), a novel, potential antipsychotic with marked serotonin (5-HT)1A agonist properties: II. Functional profile in comparison to clozapine and haloperidol. *J Pharmacol Exp Ther* 286, 1356-73 (1998).

[30] Albert PR, Francois BL: Modifying 5-HT1A Receptor Gene Expression as a New Target for Antidepressant Therapy. *Frontiers in neuroscience* 4, 35 (2010).

[31] Albert PR, Le Francois B, Millar AM: Transcriptional dysregulation of 5-HT1A autoreceptors in mental illness. *Mol Brain* 4, 21 (2011).

[32] Le Francois B, Czesak M, Steubl D, Albert PR: Transcriptional regulation at a HTR1A polymorphism associated with mental illness. *Neuropharmacology* 55, 977-85 (2008).

[33] Wu S, Comings DE: A common C-1018G polymorphism in the human 5-HT1A receptor gene. *Psychiatric genetics* 9, 105-6 (1999).

[34] Lemonde S, Turecki G, Bakish D, et al.: Impaired repression at a 5-hydroxytryptamine 1A receptor gene polymorphism associated with major depression and suicide. *J Neurosci* 23, 8788-99 (2003).

[35] Lemonde S, Turecki G, Bakish D, et al.: Impaired repression at a 5-hydroxytryptamine 1A receptor gene polymorphism associated with major depression and suicide. *The Journal of neuroscience : the official journal of the Society for Neuroscience* 23, 8788-99 (2003).

[36] Czesak M, Lemonde S, Peterson EA, Rogaeva A, Albert PR: Cell-specific repressor or enhancer activities of Deaf-1 at a serotonin 1A receptor gene polymorphism. *J Neurosci* 26, 1864-71 (2006).

[37] Jacobsen KX, Vanderluit JL, Slack RS, Albert PR: HES1 regulates 5-HT1A receptor gene transcription at a functional polymorphism: essential role in developmental expression. *Mol Cell Neurosci* 38, 349-58 (2008).

[38] Szewczyk B, Albert PR, Burns AM, et al.: Gender-specific decrease in NUDR and 5-HT1A receptor proteins in the prefrontal cortex of subjects with major depressive disorder. *Int J Neuropsychopharmacol* 12, 155-68 (2009).

[39] Parsey RV, Oquendo MA, Ogden RT, et al.: Altered serotonin 1A binding in major depression: a [carbonyl-C-11]WAY100635 positron emission tomography study. *Biol Psychiatry* 59, 106-13 (2006).

[40] Sullivan GM, Ogden RT, Oquendo MA, et al.: Positron emission tomography quantification of serotonin-1A receptor binding in medication-free bipolar depression. *Biol Psychiatry* 66, 223-30 (2009).

[41] Parsey RV, Ogden RT, Miller JM, et al.: Higher serotonin 1A binding in a second major depression cohort: modeling and reference region considerations. *Biological psychiatry* 68, 170-8 (2010).

[42] David SP, Murthy NV, Rabiner EA, et al.: A functional genetic variation of the serotonin (5-HT) transporter affects 5-HT1A receptor binding in humans. *J Neurosci* 25, 2586-90 (2005).
[43] Iyo AH, Kieran N, Chandran A, et al.: Differential regulation of the serotonin 1 A transcriptional modulators five prime repressor element under dual repression-1 and nuclear-deformed epidermal autoregulatory factor by chronic stress. *Neuroscience* 163, 1119-27 (2009).
[44] Kieran N, Ou XM, Iyo AH: Chronic social defeat downregulates the 5-HT1A receptor but not Freud-1 or NUDR in the rat prefrontal cortex. *Neuroscience letters* 469, 380-4 (2010).
[45] Ou XM, Storring JM, Kushwaha N, Albert PR: Heterodimerization of mineralocorticoid and glucocorticoid receptors at a novel negative response element of the 5-HT1A receptor gene. *J Biol Chem* 276, 14299-307 (2001).
[46] Wissink S, Meijer O, Pearce D, van Der Burg B, van Der Saag PT: Regulation of the rat serotonin-1A receptor gene by corticosteroids. *The Journal of biological chemistry* 275, 1321-6 (2000).
[47] Kageyama R, Ohtsuka T, Hatakeyama J, Ohsawa R: Roles of bHLH genes in neural stem cell differentiation. *Exp Cell Res* 306, 343-8 (2005).
[48] Deng DR, Djalali S, Holtje M, et al.: Embryonic and postnatal development of the serotonergic raphe system and its target regions in 5-HT1A receptor deletion or overexpressing mouse mutants. *Neuroscience* 147, 388-402 (2007).
[49] Rumajogee P, Verge D, Hanoun N, et al.: Adaption of the serotoninergic neuronal phenotype in the absence of 5-HT autoreceptors or the 5-HT transporter: involvement of BDNF and cAMP. *Eur J Neurosci* 19, 937-44 (2004).
[50] Kushwaha N, Albert PR: Coupling of 5-HT1A autoreceptors to inhibition of mitogen-activated protein kinase activation via G beta gamma subunit signaling. *Eur J Neurosci* 21, 721-32 (2005).
[51] Goswami DB, May WL, Stockmeier CA, Austin MC: Transcriptional expression of serotonergic regulators in laser-captured microdissected dorsal raphe neurons of subjects with major depressive disorder: sex-specific differences. *Journal of neurochemistry* 112, 397-409 (2010).
[52] Pilot-Storck F, Chopin E, Rual JF, et al.: Interactome mapping of the phosphatidylinositol 3-kinase-mammalian target of rapamycin pathway identifies deformed epidermal autoregulatory factor-1 as a new glycogen synthase kinase-3 interactor. *Mol Cell Proteomics* 9, 1578-93 (2010).
[53] Carlson PJ, Bain E, Tinsley R, et al.: Serotonin-1A receptor binding in bipolar depression before and after mood stabilizer treatment. *Bipolar Disorders* 9 (Suppl 1), 26-27 (2007).
[54] Le Francois B, Czesak M, Millar AM, et al. Altered transcriptional regulation of 5-HT1A receptors by Deaf-1 in vivo: increase in autoreceptor levels and decrease in 5-HT levels. in *The neurobiology of depression: revisiting the serotonin hypothesis.*, Vol. 33 (eds. Descarries L, Albert PR & Benkelfat C) 22 (Groupe de recherche sur le système nerveux central, Montréal, Québec, 2011).
[55] Richardson-Jones JW, Craige CP, Guiard BP, et al.: 5-HT1A autoreceptor levels determine vulnerability to stress and response to antidepressants. *Neuron* 65, 40-52 (2010).

[56] Richardson-Jones JW, Craige CP, Nguyen TH, et al.: Serotonin-1A autoreceptors are necessary and sufficient for the normal formation of circuits underlying innate anxiety. *The Journal of neuroscience : the official journal of the Society for Neuroscience* 31, 6008-18 (2011).

[57] Lemonde S, Du L, Bakish D, Hrdina P, Albert PR: Association of the C(-1019)G 5-HT1A functional promoter polymorphism with antidepressant response. *Int J Neuropsychopharmacol* 7, 501-6 (2004).

[58] Savitz J, Lucki I, Drevets WC: 5-HT(1A) receptor function in major depressive disorder. *Prog Neurobiol* 88, 17-31 (2009).

[59] Albert PR, Francois BL: Modifying 5-HT1A Receptor Gene Expression as a New Target for Antidepressant Therapy. *Front Neurosci* 4, 35 (2010).

[60] Kishi T, Tsunoka T, Ikeda M, et al.: Serotonin 1A receptor gene and major depressive disorder: an association study and meta-analysis. *J Hum Genet* 54, 629-33 (2009).

[61] Noro M, Antonijevic I, Forray C, et al.: 5HT1A and 5HT2A receptor genes in treatment response phenotypes in major depressive disorder. *International clinical psychopharmacology* 25, 228-31 (2010).

[62] Chipman P, Jorm AF, Tan XY, Easteal S: No association between the serotonin-1A receptor gene single nucleotide polymorphism rs6295C/G and symptoms of anxiety or depression, and no interaction between the polymorphism and environmental stressors of childhood anxiety or recent stressful life events on anxiety or depression. *Psychiatric genetics* 20, 8-13 (2010).

[63] Illi A, Setala-Soikkeli E, Viikki M, et al.: 5-HTR1A, 5-HTR2A, 5-HTR6, TPH1 and TPH2 polymorphisms and major depression. *Neuroreport* 20, 1125-8 (2009).

[64] Kim HS, Sherman DK, Taylor SE, et al.: Culture, serotonin receptor polymorphism and locus of attention. *Soc Cogn Affect Neurosci* 5, 212-8 (2010).

[65] Lenze EJ, Shardell M, Ferrell RE, et al.: Association of serotonin-1A and 2A receptor promoter polymorphisms with depressive symptoms and functional recovery in elderly persons after hip fracture. *J Affect Disord* 111, 61-6 (2008).

[66] Lemonde S, Du L, Bakish D, Hrdina P, Albert PR: Association of the C(-1019)G 5-HT1A functional promoter polymorphism with antidepressant response. *The international journal of neuropsychopharmacology / official scientific journal of the Collegium Internationale Neuropsychopharmacologicum* 7, 501-6 (2004).

[67] Molina E, Cervilla J, Rivera M, et al.: Polymorphic variation at the serotonin 1-A receptor gene is associated with comorbid depression and generalized anxiety. *Psychiatric genetics* (2011).

[68] Rothe C, Gutknecht L, Freitag C, et al.: Association of a functional 1019C>G 5-HT1A receptor gene polymorphism with panic disorder with agoraphobia. *Int J Neuropsychopharmacol* 7, 189-92 (2004).

[69] Choi WS, Lee BH, Yang JC, Kim YK: Association Study between 5-HT1A Receptor Gene C(-1019)G Polymorphism and Panic Disorder in a Korean Population. *Psychiatry Investig* 7, 141-6 (2010).

[70] Dhingra V, Magnay JL, O'Brien PM, et al.: Serotonin receptor 1A C(-1019)G polymorphism associated with premenstrual dysphoric disorder. *Obstet Gynecol* 110, 788-92 (2007).

[71] Shim SH, Hwangbo Y, Kwon YJ, et al.: A case-control association study of serotonin 1A receptor gene and tryptophan hydroxylase 2 gene in attention deficit hyperactivity

disorder. *Progress in neuro-psychopharmacology & biological psychiatry* 34, 974-9 (2010).

[72] Zetzsche T, Preuss UW, Bondy B, et al.: 5-HT1A receptor gene C -1019 G polymorphism and amygdala volume in borderline personality disorder. *Genes Brain Behav* 7, 306-13 (2008).

[73] Ni X, Chan D, Chan K, McMain S, Kennedy JL: Serotonin genes and gene-gene interactions in borderline personality disorder in a matched case-control study. *Progress in neuro-psychopharmacology & biological psychiatry* 33, 128-33 (2009).

[74] Lothe A, Boni C, Costes N, et al.: Association between triallelic polymorphism of the serotonin transporter and [18F]MPPF binding potential at 5-HT1A receptors in healthy subjects. *Neuroimage* 47, 482-92 (2009).

[75] Karg K, Burmeister M, Shedden K, Sen S: The serotonin transporter promoter variant (5-HTTLPR), stress, and depression meta-analysis revisited: evidence of genetic moderation. *Archives of general psychiatry* 68, 444-54 (2011).

[76] Borg J, Henningsson S, Saijo T, et al.: Serotonin transporter genotype is associated with cognitive performance but not regional 5-HT1A receptor binding in humans. *Int J Neuropsychopharmacol* 12, 783-92 (2009).

[77] Anguelova M, Benkelfat C, Turecki G: A systematic review of association studies investigating genes coding for serotonin receptors and the serotonin transporter: II. Suicidal behavior. *Molecular psychiatry* 8, 646-53 (2003).

[78] David SP, Murthy NV, Rabiner EA, et al.: A functional genetic variation of the serotonin (5-HT) transporter affects 5-HT1A receptor binding in humans. *The Journal of neuroscience : the official journal of the Society for Neuroscience* 25, 2586-90 (2005).

[79] Kraus MR, Al-Taie O, Schafer A, et al.: Serotonin-1A receptor gene HTR1A variation predicts interferon-induced depression in chronic hepatitis C. *Gastroenterology* 132, 1279-86 (2007).

[80] Serretti A, Artioli P, Lorenzi C, et al.: The C(-1019)G polymorphism of the 5-HT1A gene promoter and antidepressant response in mood disorders: preliminary findings. *Int J Neuropsychopharmacol* 7, 453-60 (2004).

[81] Zhang K, Xu Q, Xu Y, et al.: The combined effects of the 5-HTTLPR and 5-HTR1A genes modulates the relationship between negative life events and major depressive disorder in a Chinese population. *Journal of affective disorders* 114, 224-31 (2009).

[82] Arias B, Catalan R, Gasto C, Gutierrez B, Fananas L: Evidence for a combined genetic effect of the 5-HT(1A) receptor and serotonin transporter genes in the clinical outcome of major depressive patients treated with citalopram. *Journal of psychopharmacology* 19, 166-72 (2005).

[83] Domschke K, Braun M, Ohrmann P, et al.: Association of the functional -1019C/G 5-HT1A polymorphism with prefrontal cortex and amygdala activation measured with 3 T fMRI in panic disorder. *The international journal of neuropsychopharmacology / official scientific journal of the Collegium Internationale Neuropsychopharmacologicum* 9, 349-55 (2006).

[84] Dannlowski U, Ohrmann P, Bauer J, et al.: Serotonergic genes modulate amygdala activity in major depression. *Genes, brain, and behavior* 6, 672-6 (2007).

[85] Anttila S, Huuhka K, Huuhka M, et al.: Interaction between 5-HT1A and BDNF genotypes increases the risk of treatment-resistant depression. *Journal of neural transmission* 114, 1065-8 (2007).

[86] Mossner R, Schuhmacher A, Kuhn KU, et al.: Functional serotonin 1A receptor variant influences treatment response to atypical antipsychotics in schizophrenia. *Pharmacogenet Genomics* 19, 91-4 (2009).

[87] Schmitz A, Kirsch P, Reuter M, et al.: The 5-HT1A C(-1019)G polymorphism, personality and electrodermal reactivity in a reward/punishment paradigm. *Int J Neuropsychopharmacol* 12, 383-92 (2009).

[88] Videtic A, Zupanc T, Pregelj P, et al.: Suicide, stress and serotonin receptor 1A promoter polymorphism -1019C>G in Slovenian suicide victims. *European archives of psychiatry and clinical neuroscience* 259, 234-8 (2009).

[89] Zanardi R, Magri L, Rossini D, et al.: Role of serotonergic gene polymorphisms on response to transcranial magnetic stimulation in depression. *European neuropsychopharmacology : the journal of the European College of Neuropsychopharmacology* 17, 651-7 (2007).

[90] Lee YS, Choi SW, Han DH, Kim DJ, Joe KH: Clinical manifestation of alcohol withdrawal symptoms related to genetic polymorphisms of two serotonin receptors and serotonin transporter. *Eur Addict Res* 15, 39-46 (2009).

[91] Parsey RV, Olvet DM, Oquendo MA, et al.: Higher 5-HT1A receptor binding potential during a major depressive episode predicts poor treatment response: preliminary data from a naturalistic study. *Neuropsychopharmacology : official publication of the American College of Neuropsychopharmacology* 31, 1745-9 (2006).

[92] Beste C, Heil M, Domschke K, Konrad C: The relevance of the functional 5-HT1A receptor polymorphism for attention and working memory processes during mental rotation of characters. *Neuropsychologia* 48, 1248-54 (2010).

[93] Huang YY, Battistuzzi C, Oquendo MA, et al.: Human 5-HT1A receptor C(-1019)G polymorphism and psychopathology. *Int J Neuropsychopharmacol* 7, 441-51 (2004).

[94] Kishi T, Okochi T, Tsunoka T, et al.: Serotonin 1A receptor gene, schizophrenia and bipolar disorder: an association study and meta-analysis. *Psychiatry research* 185, 20-6 (2011).

[95] Reynolds GP, Arranz B, Templeman LA, Fertuzinhos S, San L: Effect of 5-HT1A receptor gene polymorphism on negative and depressive symptom response to antipsychotic treatment of drug-naive psychotic patients. *Am J Psychiatry* 163, 1826-9 (2006).

[96] Wang L, Fang C, Zhang A, et al.: The --1019 C/G polymorphism of the 5-HT1A receptor gene is associated with negative symptom response to risperidone treatment in schizophrenia patients. *J Psychopharmacol* 22, 904-9 (2008).

[97] Sumiyoshi T, Tsunoda M, Higuchi Y, et al.: Serotonin-1A receptor gene polymorphism and the ability of antipsychotic drugs to improve attention in schizophrenia. *Adv Ther* 27, 307-13 (2010).

[98] Thomas P: Psychosocial and economic issues related to physical health in psychiatric illness. *European neuropsychopharmacology : the journal of the European College of Neuropsychopharmacology* 18 Suppl 2, S115-20 (2008).

[99] Patel A, Everitt B, Knapp M, et al.: Schizophrenia patients with cognitive deficits: factors associated with costs. *Schizophrenia bulletin* 32, 776-85 (2006).

[100] Nagai T, Murai R, Matsui K, et al.: Aripiprazole ameliorates phencyclidine-induced impairment of recognition memory through dopamine D1 and serotonin 5-HT1A receptors. *Psychopharmacology (Berl)* 202, 315-28 (2009).

[101] Bruins Slot LA, Kleven MS, Newman-Tancredi A: Effects of novel antipsychotics with mixed D2 antagonist/5-HT1A agonist properties on PCP-induced social interaction deficits in the rat. *Neuropharmacology* 49, 996-1006 (2005).

[102] Bortolozzi A, Diaz-Mataix L, Toth M, Celada P, Artigas F: In vivo actions of aripiprazole on serotonergic and dopaminergic systems in rodent brain. *Psychopharmacology (Berl)* 191, 745-58 (2007).

[103] Stahl SM, Sommer B, Allers KA: Multifunctional Pharmacology of Flibanserin: Possible Mechanism of Therapeutic Action in Hypoactive Sexual Desire Disorder. *J Sex Med* (2010).

[104] Newman-Tancredi A, Heusler P, Martel JC, et al.: Agonist and antagonist properties of antipsychotics at human dopamine D4.4 receptors: G-protein activation and K+ channel modulation in transfected cells. *Int J Neuropsychopharmacol* 11, 293-307 (2008).

[105] Newman-Tancredi A: Biased agonism at serotonin 5-HT1A receptors: preferential post-synaptic activity for improved therapy of CNS disorders. *Neuropsychiatry* 1, 149-164 (2011).

[106] Llado-Pelfort L, Assie MB, Newman-Tancredi A, Artigas F, Celada P: Preferential in vivo action of F15599, a novel 5-HT1A receptor agonist, at postsynaptic 5-HT1A receptors. *Br J Pharmacol* 160, 1929-40 (2010).

[107] Assie MB, Bardin L, Auclair AL, et al.: F15599, a highly selective post-synaptic 5-HT1A receptor agonist: in-vivo profile in behavioural models of antidepressant and serotonergic activity. *Int J Neuropsychopharmacol* 13, 1285-98 (2010).

[108] Depoortere R, Auclair AL, Bardin L, et al.: F15599, a preferential post-synaptic 5-HT1A receptor agonist: activity in models of cognition in comparison with reference 5-HT1A receptor agonists. *Eur Neuropsychopharmacol* 20, 641-54 (2010).

[109] Newman-Tancredi A, Martel JC, Assie MB, et al.: Signal transduction and functional selectivity of F15599, a preferential post-synaptic 5-HT1A receptor agonist. *Br J Pharmacol* 156, 338-53 (2009).

[110] McIlwain ME, Harrison J, Wheeler AJ, Russell BR: Pharmacotherapy for treatment-resistant schizophrenia. *Neuropsychiatric disease and treatment* 7, 135-49 (2011).

[111] Villafuerte SM, Vallabhaneni K, Sliwerska E, et al.: SSRI response in depression may be influenced by SNPs in HTR1B and HTR1A. *Psychiatr Genet* 19, 281-91 (2009).

[112] Wu Y, Xu Y, Sun Y, et al.: Association between the serotonin 1A receptor C(-1019)G polymorphism and major depressive disorder in the northern Han ethnic group in China. *Chin Med J (Engl)* 121, 874-6 (2008).

[113] Yu YW, Tsai SJ, Liou YJ, Hong CJ, Chen TJ: Association study of two serotonin 1A receptor gene polymorphisms and fluoxetine treatment response in Chinese major depressive disorders. *European neuropsychopharmacology : the journal of the European College of Neuropsychopharmacology* 16, 498-503 (2006).

[114] Parsey RV, Olvet DM, Oquendo MA, et al.: Higher 5-HT1A receptor binding potential during a major depressive episode predicts poor treatment response: preliminary data from a naturalistic study. *Neuropsychopharmacology* 31, 1745-9 (2006).

[115] Hong CJ, Chen TJ, Yu YW, Tsai SJ: Response to fluoxetine and serotonin 1A receptor (C-1019G) polymorphism in Taiwan Chinese major depressive disorder. *Pharmacogenomics J* 6, 27-33 (2006).

[116] Lin E, Chen PS, Chang HH, et al.: Interaction of serotonin-related genes affects short-term antidepressant response in major depressive disorder. *Progress in neuro-psychopharmacology & biological psychiatry* 33, 1167-72 (2009).

[117] Bosia M, Anselmetti S, Bechi M, et al.: Effect of 5-HT1A-receptor functional polymorphism on Theory of Mind performances in schizophrenia. *Psychiatry research* (2010).

[118] Kishi T, Tsunoka T, Ikeda M, et al.: Serotonin 1A receptor gene is associated with Japanese methamphetamine-induced psychosis patients. *Neuropharmacology* 58, 452-6 (2010).

[119] Benedetti F, Radaelli D, Poletti S, et al.: Association of the C(-1019)G 5-HT1A promoter polymorphism with exposure to stressors preceding hospitalization for bipolar depression. *Journal of affective disorders* (2011).

[120] Blaya C, Salum GA, Moorjani P, et al.: Panic disorder and serotonergic genes (SLC6A4, HTR1A and HTR2A): Association and interaction with childhood trauma and parenting. *Neuroscience letters* 485, 11-5 (2010).

[121] Yevtushenko OO, Oros MM, Reynolds GP: Early response to selective serotonin reuptake inhibitors in panic disorder is associated with a functional 5-HT1A receptor gene polymorphism. *J Affect Disord* 123, 308-11 (2010).

[122] Sawiniec J, Borkowski K, Ginalska G, Lewandowska-Stanek H: Association between 5-hydroxytryptamine 1A receptor gene polymorphism and suicidal behavior. *Przegl Lek* 64, 208-11 (2007).

[123] Zupanc T, Pregelj P, Tomori M, Komel R, Paska AV: No association between polymorphisms in four serotonin receptor genes, serotonin transporter gene and alcohol-related suicide. *Psychiatria Danubina* 22, 522-7 (2010).

[124] Serretti A, Calati R, Giegling I, et al.: Serotonin receptor HTR1A and HTR2C variants and personality traits in suicide attempters and controls. *J Psychiatr Res* 43, 519-25 (2009).

[125] Serretti A, Mandelli L, Giegling I, et al.: HTR2C and HTR1A gene variants in German and Italian suicide attempters and completers. *American journal of medical genetics. Part B, Neuropsychiatric genetics : the official publication of the International Society of Psychiatric Genetics* 144B, 291-9 (2007).

[126] Yoon HK, Kim YK: TPH2 -703G/T SNP may have important effect on susceptibility to suicidal behavior in major depression. *Progress in neuro-psychopharmacology & biological psychiatry* 33, 403-9 (2009).

[127] Benko A, Lazary J, Molnar E, et al.: Significant association between the C(-1019)G functional polymorphism of the HTR1A gene and impulsivity. *American journal of medical genetics. Part B, Neuropsychiatric genetics : the official publication of the International Society of Psychiatric Genetics* 153B, 592-9 (2010).

[128] Beste C, Domschke K, Kolev V, et al.: Functional 5-HT1a receptor polymorphism selectively modulates error-specific subprocesses of performance monitoring. *Hum Brain Mapp* 31, 621-30 (2010).

[129] Koller G, Bondy B, Preuss UW, Zill P, Soyka M: The C(-1019)G 5-HT1A promoter polymorphism and personality traits: no evidence for significant association in alcoholic patients. *Behav Brain Funct* 2, 7 (2006).
[130] Lim SW, Ha J, Shin DW, Woo HY, Kim KH: Associations between the serotonin-1A receptor C(-1019)G polymorphism and disordered eating symptoms in female adolescents. *J Neural Transm* 117, 773-9 (2010).

In: Schizophrenia Research: Recent Advances
Editor: Tomiki Sumiyoshi
ISBN: 978-1-62808-703-1

Chapter 16

Repetitive Transcranial Magnetic Stimulation: A New Option to Manage Negative Symptoms of Schizophrenia

Radovan Prikryl, Libor Ustohal and Hana Prikrylova Kucerova
CEITEC - Central European Institute of Technology,
Masaryk University Brno, Czech Republic
Department of Psychiatry Faculty of Medicine Masaryk University
and University Hospital Brno, Czech Republic

Abstract

Repetitive transcranial magnetic stimulation, which is used in psychiatry primarily for the treatment of the depressive disorder, isolated auditory hallucinations or obsessively compulsive disorder, represents a new therapeutic modality able to affect negative schizophrenia symptoms thanks to its unique ability to modulate neuronal activity of the cortical cerebral areas and neuronal circuits which are included into the pathophysiology of schizophrenia not only directly but also indirectly, by means of transsynaptic transfer. Theoretical substantiation of the repetitive transcranial magnetic stimulation efficacy in the event of negative schizophrenia symptoms lies in the fact that the high-frequency repetitive transcranial magnetic stimulation shows an activating impact on the neurons of the cerebral cortex. Negative correlation between the activity of the frontal cortex and severity of negative symptoms has been repeatedly demonstrated. Another, no less important fact consists in the effect of dopamine release from the mesolimbic and mesostriatal cerebral system by high-frequency stimulation of the frontal cortex. The mesolimbic brain structures play a key role in the pathogenesis of negative schizophrenic symptoms. Most of the studies have arrived at the conclusion that repetitive transcranial magnetic stimulation is an efficient method in the treatment of negative symptoms of schizophrenia. In our own study, whose objective was to show the impact of high frequency repetitive transcranial magnetic stimulation applied over the area of the left prefrontal cortex using the maximum stimulating intensity on the alleviation of the intensity of negative schizophrenia symptoms. Every patient was stimulated 15 times on workdays of three consecutive weeks. The real stimulation treatment led to a statistically significant decrease in the intensity of negative schizophrenia symptoms. The authors ascribe the rate of reduction of the negative symptoms intensity, which they consider clinically significant, to the number of 15 stimulation sessions, which was one of the highest number of stimulation sessions in the studies dealing with this issue. A valuable contribution for the assessment of rTMS application in the treatment of negative symptoms is brough about by meta-analyses. They have shown that the rate of effect is mild to moderate (d=0.43 to 0.68) based on the character of studies included into the statistic analysis. To sum it up, there will be higher probability of the repetitive transcranial magnetic stimulation effect on negative symptoms if 10 Hz stimulating frequency and a longer stimulation period in the extent at least three, ideally four to six weeks is used. Although rTMS represents a promising potential, especially for the augmenting treatment of negative symptoms resistant to antipsychotic drugs treatment, further studies are necessary for the verification of really clinically significant efficacy of rTMS in this clinical indication.

Keywords: Repetitive transcranial magnetic stimulation; treatment; negative symptoms; schizophrenia; neuromodulation; dopamine

INTRODUCTION

Repetitive transcranial magnetic stimulation (rTMS), which is used in psychiatry primarily for the treatment of the depressive disorder, isolated auditory hallucinations or obsessively compulsive disorder, represents a new therapeutic modality able to affect negative schizophrenia symptoms thanks to its unique ability to modulate neuronal activity of the cortical cerebral areas and neuronal circuits which are included into the pathophysiology of schizophrenia not only directly but also indirectly, by means of transsynaptic transfer (Klirova et al. 2008; Zaman et al. 2008; Anders et al. 2010; Havrankova et al. 2010).

THEORETICAL MECHANISMS UNDERLYING TREATMENT EFFECTS OF RTMS IN NEGATIVE SYMPTOMS OF SCHIZOPHRENIA

Hypofrontality is expected to be a functional correlate of negative symptoms (Kim et al. 2000; Lui et al. 2010). The promising results of rTMS in the depressive disorder, when just the area of the frontal cortex is stimulated, led to the hypothesis of using this method also in the treatment of schizophrenia. Theoretical substantiation of the rTMS efficacy in the event of negative schizophrenia symptoms lies in the fact that the high-frequency rTMS shows an activating impact on the neurons of the cerebral cortex (Post et al., 1997). Negative correlation between the activity of the frontal cortex and severity of negative symptoms has been repeatedly demonstrated. Another, no less important fact consists in the effect of dopamine release from the mesolimbic and mesostriatal cerebral system by high-frequency stimulation of the frontal cortex. The mesolimbic brain structures play a key role in the pathogenesis of negative schizophrenic symptoms like anhedonia or loss of interest (Heimer et al. 1997). By means of ^{11}C PET (positron emission tomography) Strafella has found out that high-frequency rTMS of the dorsolateral prefrontal cortex (PFC) induces release of the endogenous dopamine in the ipsilateral caudate nucleus in healthy volunteers (Strafella et al.,

2001). The high-frequency rTMS also causes down-regulation of serotonine 5-HT_2 receptors in the frontal cortex (Ben-Shachar et al 1999). The blockade of serotonine 5-HT_2 receptors leads to a compensatory relative increase in the dopamine concentration in the PFC and is associated with the remission of negative schizophrenia symptoms. These facts are the basis of the theoretical substantiation of the efficacy of rTMS on negative symptoms of schizophrenia. Any improvement in the negative symptoms after rTMS is probably caused by the activation of mesolimbic and mesostriatal dopaminergic systems (Strafella et al., 2001).

EFFICACY OF rTMS STUDIES IN THE TREATMENT OF NEGATIVE SYMPTOMS: OVERVIEW OF CURRENT STUDIES

The first two "pioneer" works which tried to treat schizophrenia symptoms by stimulation of prefrontal cortex were relatively small open studies. The first study assessing the rTMS effect on schizophrenia symptoms was the work of Geller (Geller et al., 1997). 10 patients have undergone low-frequency stimulation (0.03 Hz), each of them obtaining fifteen stimuli over the area of the right and left PFC in 30-second intervals. This has resulted in transient improvement of the mood in two patients. Feinsod treated 10 patients with schizophrenia in the open study using the low frequency stimulation of the right PFC in two one-minute daily stimulations for the period of 10 days. He managed to reach the reduction of anxiety and restlessness in 7 patients, however, he did not succeed in affecting other schizophrenia symptoms (Feinsod et al 1998).

The first double-blind study was the work of Klein from the year 1999, who based on his positive experience with the impact of low-frequency stimulation of the right PFC on the depressive symptomatology, tested the hypothesis whether the low-frequency rTMS applied over the area of the right PFC affects not only mood but also positive and negative schizophrenia symptoms. During the treatment, a slight improvement in the psychopathology occurred both in the placebo and in the rTMS treated group, however, no significant difference between the real and ineffective stimulation was found (Klein et al., 1999).

In the same year a pilot open study by Cohen et al. was published, trying to identify the impact of rTMS on the chronic negative symptoms. The study included 6 patients with schizophrenia with dominating negative symptoms. The left PFC was stimulated by 20 Hz frequency; the stimulation lasted 2 seconds and it was applied once in a minute for the total period of 20 minutes. Although a statistically significant decrease in the severity of negative symptoms was achieved, the clinical effect of this change was assessed as relatively low. During the stimulation also achieved was the improvement in all parameters of the applied neuropsychological tests, however, only the item of delayed visual memory reached the statistical significance. The authors explain this fact by the improvement of attention, especially the ability to keep attention. However, the neuronal activity of the PFC has not changed during the stimulation (Cohen et al., 1999).

In 2000, the results were published of the double-blind, placebo-controlled study including 7 schizophrenic patients in whose clinical condition the negative symptoms had been prevailing. The patients were stimulated by high-frequency (20 Hz) rTMS focused on the area of the left dorsolateral PFC. Although the real rTMS, when compared with placebo, led to the decrease in the intensity of negative schizophrenia symptoms, the results did not reach the statistic significance (Nahas et al., 2000).

In the same year, Rollnik published the work, whose objective was to assess the efficacy of rTMS in patients with schizophrenia in the conditions of the single-blinded, controlled study. The total of 12 patients with schizophrenia on a stabilized dose of antipsychotic drugs were included in the study. The left dorsolateral PFC was stimulated and each patient was applied 20 two-second stimulation trains within the period of twenty minutes (800 pulses in a single train, the total of 10 stimulations within the period of two weeks). The blinding in the placebo "sham" group consisted in the position of the stimulating coil (making a 45° angle with the head surface). The real rTMS led to a statistically significant reduction of the severity of schizophrenia symptoms. The fact that the intensity of schizophrenia symptoms had been reduced, leaving the symptoms of depression and anxiety unchanged, led the authors of the study to the conclusion that rTMS, applied over the PFC area of the dominant cerebral hemisphere, might show a specific antipsychotic effect (Rollnik et al., 2000).

Despite the positive conclusion of the Rollnik's study, the next study was published as late as in 2004. It was the double-blind study by Hajak et al. The priority of this work is the first use of an inefficient "sham" stimulating coil for placebo stimulation which led to the refinement of the methodological purity of the study and further reduced the possible placebo effect of rTMS. The sham stimulation coil actually gives out an equal acoustic accompaniment that may be heard by patients during the real stimulation, and therefore it is more difficult to distinguish between efficient and inefficient stimulation. The patients were treated by high-frequency (l0 Hz) stimulation over the left PFC area, using the stimulation intensity of 110 % of the MT (motor threshold) during 10 sessions. Each stimulation session included 1,000 impulses, divided into 20 five-second stimulation trains. Although in both groups the severity of psychopathology was reduced during the treatment, the reduction was more significant in the group of patients treated with real rTMS. The reduction of negative schizophrenia symptoms was not conditioned by the decrease in affective symptomatology. No significant change in the regional cerebral perfusion, related to the real/placebo stimulation, has been proved (Hajak et al., 2004).

In 2004, Holi published the double-blind, controlled study of rTMS, applied over the left PFC in the treatment of schizophrenia. The total of 22 patients with high intensity of schizophrenia symptoms were included in the study; the patients were randomized into two treatment arms, into the group of real or into the group of inefficient, i.e. placebo "sham" stimulation. The latter was reached by turning the stimulation figure-eight coil making a 90° angle with the head surface. The treatment included 10 stimulation sessions in the period of two weeks with the following stimulation parameters: twenty five-second trains followed by thirty-second intertrains, 10 Hz frequency and the intensity of stimulation of 100 % of the MT. Although in both compared groups there was a statistically significant decrease in the severity of symptoms, no statistically significant difference has been found between the real and inefficient rTMS. Based on the results the authors believe that the high-frequency rTMS over the left prefrontal cortex shows rather an unspecific therapeutic effect than the direct antipsychotic effect in patients with chronic schizophrenia (Holi et al., 2004).

Jin stimulated 27 patients with significant negative schizophrenic symptoms daily for the period of 2 weeks bilaterally over the area of the dorsolateral PFC, using various stimulation frequencies: 8-12 Hz (so-called alpha-frequency), 3 Hz, 20 Hz or inefficient "sham" stimulation. The theoretical basis of his work was the hypothesis that the cerebral alpha frequency (8-12

Hz), detected by electroencephalography (EEG), is associated with the occurrence and severity of negative schizophrenia symptoms. Actually, as it is known from the EEG studies, the patients with schizophrenia suffer from decreased alpha activity (both spectral power and coherence), not only in the rest conditions but also during sensory/cognitive stimulations (Stevens et al., 1982; Colombo et al. 1989; Hoffman et al., 1991). The results of the study confirmed the hypothesis to be tested, because rTMS with the "alpha" frequency (8-13 Hz) led to a more significant remission of negative symptoms (approximately by 29.6 %) in comparison with the remaining three treatment modalities (less than 9 %). In addition, changes in EEG during the stimulation with the alpha frequency predicated clinical improvement. According to the authors, the identified data prove that the higher the increase of power of alpha activity over the frontal lobe, the more considerable remission of negative schizophrenia symptoms (Jin et a1. 2005).

The effect of rTMS on negative schizophrenia symptoms and its relation to the electric activity of the brain was also the theme of the following open pilot study. The total of 10 patients with schizophrenia were included in the study. They were stimulated over the area of the left dorsolateral PFC for a period of 5 days. The stimulation frequency of 10 Hz was chosen; the stimulation session included 20 stimulating trains of 3.5 seconds, followed by 10-second intertrains. Slight improvement of negative and affective schizophrenia symptoms occurred after the treatment (reaching approximately 9 % in the case of negative symptoms and about 16 % in the case of affective ones; in both cases, however, reaching the statistic significance). The EEG analysis revealed the reduction of delta and beta activities frontotemporally on the right and, on the other hand, the increase of alpha activity, while temporally and parietooccipitally on the left the beta activity had been reduced. The authors suggest that despite the slight clinical improvement of negative symptoms the established changes of the EEG activity may be considered signs of improvement of negative schizophrenia symptoms after rTMS (Jandl et al., 2005).

Sachdev with his collaborators also treated four patients with the deficit syndrome of schizophrenia in the open study. They administered high-frequency (15 Hz) rTMS over the area of the left dorsolateral PFC during 20 sessions within the period of four weeks. A single stimulation session included 24 five-second stimulation trains. The stimulation treatment led to a statistically significant decrease in the severity of negative symptoms and improved general performance of the patients, persisting for the whole period of the subsequent one-month monitoring following the end of the stimulation (Sachdev et al.,2005).

Into his double-blind, fictitious stimulation-controlled, randomized study, Novak included 18 patients with the diagnosis of schizophrenia with prevailing negative symptoms. The patients were stimulated with high frequency (20 Hz) over the area of the left dorsolateral PFC for a period of two weeks. The placebo stimulation was reached by positioning the stimulating coil, making a 90° angle with the surface of the head, which ruled out the real stimulation. The intensity of stimulation was set to 90 % of the MT, a single stimulation session included 40 2.5-second stimulation trains with thirty-second intertrains. During the single stimulation the patients obtained 2,000 impulses, the total number of session was 10 within the period of two weeks. However, neither the clinically relevant effect of the high frequency rTMS in the treatment of negative symptoms of schizophrenia nor any impact on cognitive functions has been proved (Novak et al., 2006).

In 2007 the results were published of the double-blind study assessing the effect of high frequency rTMS on not only negative but also positive schizophrenia symptoms. The real treatment was characterised by the following stimulation parameters: 10Hz frequency, the left

PFC being the area of stimulation, the treatment consisting of 10 stimulation sessions with the length of the train of 4.9 s and that of the intertrain 30 s, repeated 20 times during a single 20-minute session, the intensity of the stimulation being defined to 110 % of the individual MT. The real stimulation treatment led to a significantly more substantial alleviation of the severity of negative symptoms compared to the placebo stimulation. The severity of positive symptoms remained equal regardless of the stimulation type (Goyal et al., 2007).

In the same year the work was also published whose aim was to assess not only the rTMS impact on negative schizophrenia symptoms but also to evaluate the effect of rTMS on mood, cognitive functions or quality of life (Mogg et al., 2007). The study was also enriched by a two-week monitoring after the end of the stimulation treatment. The real treatment was characterized by high-frequency 10Hz stimulation, pointed at the left PFC, with the intensity of 110 % of the individual MT. It included 10 sessions in the working days during two consecutive weeks. At each stimulation session 2,000 pulses were applied in 20 trains of 10 second duration with 50 second intertrains. In total 20,000 stimulation pulses were applied. The most important result of the study consisted in the finding that no statistically significant difference had been found between the impact of the real and of placebo rTMS on the negative schizophrenia symptoms. Since the age is considered one of the possible negative indicators of the rTMS treatment efficacy (Kozel et al., 2000), the effect of the age was taken into account in the final analysis, however, even in that case no significant efficacy of rTMS on negative symptoms was found. The same negative results were also found in relation to the quality of life, depression, anxiety or cognitive functions. However, there are certain limits of the study: small sample of patients and related risk of false negative results (Mogg et al., 2007).

Up to now published works are based on the main theoretical assumption that only the left PFC is included into the pathophysiology of negative schizophrenia symptoms (Klemm et al., 1996). Despite that the disturbed activation of the PFC related to negative schizophrenia symptoms is also shown in the right cerebral hemisphere (Wolkin et al., 1992) or bilaterally (Sabri et al., 1997). Therefore Fitzgerald proposed the study, in which he tried to verify the effect of the bilateral PFC stimulation for the treatment of negative schizophrenia symptoms (Fitzgerald et al., 2008). The stimulation frequency of 10 Hz was used; during a single stimulation session 20 trains of 5-second length were applied with intertrains lasting 25 seconds. In total 1,000 pulses were administered to each cerebral hemispheres. First the left and immediately after that the right PFC were stimulated. The results indicate that no statistically significant differences have been found between the real and placebo rTMSs both in the change of psychopathology and in cognitive functions (Fitzgerald et al., 2008).

In his work, Schneider verified the hypothesis that only high frequency stimulation of the PFC may be efficient in the reduction of negative symptoms. Therefore he proposed to form three investigation groups, each consisting of 17 patients; the first of them was to be treated by 10 Hz stimulation (1,000 pulses daily, the total of 20,000 pulses), the second using the 1 Hz stimulation (100 pulses daily, the total of 2,000 pulses) and the third using the placebo stimulation for the period of 4 weeks (20 stimulation sessions). The stimulation was targeted at the left PFC with the intensity of 110 % of the MT, the lengths of the train and intertrain being 5 seconds and 15 seconds, respectively. Placebo conditions were provided by the placebo "sham" coil. In the group treated by 10Hz rTMS a statistically significant decrease occurred in the severity of negative symptoms; such reduction did not occur in any other group. Also, if mutually compared, the high-frequency stimulated patients showed a statistically more significant reduction of negative symptoms then those of the two compared groups (Schneider et al., 2008).

Adequately significant influence of negative schizophrenia symptoms represents one of the basic prerequisites for successful schizophrenia treatment. Since the present pharmacotherapy has probably reached its limit in this area, there is a logical effort to use also other, non-pharmacological approaches. One of the most promising and in the clinical practice relatively long verified complement of the pharmacotherapy is rTMS. Most of the open studies have shown reduction in the negative symptoms upon the application of this method. However, there is a justified reproach regarding the additional placebo effect which is included in this method as such. Therefore, from the methodological point of view, double-blind, placebo stimulation controlled studies are more contributing. Although the conditions of the double-blinding are not optimal, the additional placebo effect is minimized if compared with the open studies. Most of those studies led to the conclusion that rTMS is an efficient method in the treatment of negative schizophrenia symptoms. However, there remains the problem of a low number of included patients, miscellaneous profile of negative symptoms, various stimulation parameters or absence of longer monitoring of the stimulation effect in most of the studies. Therefore, the valuable contribution for the assessment of rTMS application in the treatment of negative symptoms is brough about by meta-analyses. They have shown that the rate of effect is mild to moderate (d=0.43 to 0.68) based on the character of studies included into the statistic analysis. It can be summarized that a higher probability of rTMS efficacy on negative symptoms will be shown in case of 10 Hz stimulation frequency for a longer stimulation time to the extent of at least three, ideally four to six weeks.

Our Own Experience with the Application of rTMS in the Treatment of Negative Symptoms of Schizophrenia

In 2007 we designed our own study project with the aim to verify whether high–frequency rTMS applied above the area of the left prefrontal cortex including in total 15 stimulation sessions with maximum stimulation intensity is able to modify the negative symptoms of schizophrenia in the single-blinded, randomized study settings. The evaluated group included 22 patients (males) who were admitted to hospital due to schizophrenia at the Psychiatric clinic of the Faculty of Medicine of Masaryk University and Faculty Hospital in Brno, Czech Republic. Only those patients who fulfilled the criteria for schizophrenia (F20) according to the International Classification of Diseases, revision 10 (ICD-10) and diagnostic research criteria and who were stabilized long-term (for at least 6 weeks) on antipsychotics, who had significant negative symptoms without other psychiatric comorbidity such as mood, anxiety or personal disorders were included in the study. The diagnosis was verified by two independent experienced psychiatrists. The age of the enrolled patients ranged from 18 to 60 years. Patients who had a neurological disease (including epilepsy or abnormal EEG record), cardiovascular, cerebrovascular, endocrinal, systemic autoimmune disease, psychoactive drug abuse including alcohol or acute risk of suicide at screening or who had such condition in the past were not included in the study. Absence of psychoactive drug abuse was verified using the toxicology examination of urine for cannabis, amphetamines and opioids. Only those patients who signed an informed consent document and who had no contraindication for rTMS were included in the study. The study was approved by the local ethics committee and complies with the requirements of the Declaration of Helsinki.

The evaluated group was divided in two subgroups using a random number generator. The first subgroup (11 patients) received the real rTMS and the second subgroup (11 patients) received the sham rTMS. Both forms of rTMS treatment were performed on workdays, i.e. 5 times a week, until completion of 15 procedures. During the stimulation therapy the patients remained on their prescribed antipsychotic medication. The severity of psychopathological symptoms before and after the treatment was evaluated using the positive, negative and general symptoms scale (PANSS: Positive and Negative Syndrome Scale; SANS: Scale for the Assessment of Negative Symptoms; SAPS: Scale for the Assessment of Positive Symptoms), the Montgomery and Asberg Depression Scale (MADRS) and the Calgary depression scale for schizophrenia (CDSS): (MADRS: Montgomery-Āsberg Depression Rating Scale; CDSS: The Calgary Depression Scale for Schizophrenia) (Kay et al., 1987; Addington 1994; Filip 1997). Evaluation of the severity of the clinical status and performance of rTMS was mutually blinded. When the patients finished the treatment they were asked to estimate whether they were treated with the real or sham stimulation.

The rTMS treatment commenced with determination of the patient's motor threshold (MP) and localization of the site of stimulation. Motor threshold is determined using the electromyograph (EMG) in musculus abductor pollicis brevis l. dx. Determination of MP is defined as the lowest stimulation activity that causes at least 5 motor potentials with an amplitude at least 50 mV in 10 single impulses. The actual performance of rTMS is defined by the location of application (left dorsolateral prefrontal cortex), intensity of magnetic stimulation in % of MP (110% of MP), stimulation frequency (10 Hz), duration of impulse series (10 s), interval between sequences (30 s) and the total number of applied stimuli (1500). The clinical status and technical data of the application including temperature of the stimulation coil were observed over the whole application. The Magstim Super Rapid stimulation device was used for the rTMS, and EMG MedelecSynergy was used for evaluation of the motor threshold. The ineffectiveness of the sham rTMS was ensured by adjusting the location of the stimulation coil. It formed an angle of 90 degrees against the surface of the head, which was sufficient to prevent stimulation of the brain cortex. Blinding of patients was also ensured using a background sound that occurs during the real stimulation.

Concerning demographic results the real rTMS group included 11 patients (mean age 31.36 years; SD=8.43) with education defined by the number of years of compulsory education (mean 11.72 years; SD=0.91) and mean duration of disease (5.27 years; SD=5.87). All 11 patients stated they had been stimulated by real rTMS. The mean daily dose of antipsychotics was 217.73 mg (SD=216.92) of chlorpromazine equivalents. The sham rTMS group included 11 patients (mean age 36.46 years; SD=10.74) with education defined by the number of years of compulsory education (mean 12.46 years; SD=2.34) and mean duration of disease (8.18 years; SD=8.88). Only one patient assumed he had been treated with the sham rTMS while all other patients stated their stimulation had been real. The mean daily dose of antipsychotics was 247.73 mg (SD=164.11) of chlorpromazine equivalents. No statistically significant differences between the observed demographic data of the groups of patients who were treated with real or sham rTMS were found.

Concerning main clinical results statistically significant reduction of severity of the negative, common, affective and general symptoms of schizophrenia occurred in the real rTMS group which was indicated by reduction in the MADRS and CDSS scale, the PANSS general score including the negative and general subscales and the SANS scale. The rate of positive symptoms of schizophrenia was unchanged. A statistically significant reduction of severity of the common and general symptoms of schizophrenia occurred in the sham rTMS group, which was indicated by reduction in the PANSS general subscale and PANSS general score. The intensity of the negative symptoms of schizophrenia was statistically significantly reduced only in the SANS scale. However, it was unchanged in the PANSS subscale. The rate of affective and positive symptoms of schizophrenia was unchanged. However compared to the sham rTMS, the real rTMS caused a statistically significantly higher reduction of severity of the negative, affective and total symptoms of schizophrenia. On the contrary, no difference was found with respect to the positive and common symptoms of schizophrenia (Prikryl et al. 2007).

Although there is a lot of information about the efficacy of rTMS in the treatment of negative symptoms of schizophrenia, there is no study that would solve issue what time after successful rTMS treatment improvement of negative schizophrenic symptoms is enduring. It was a reason that we had performed a single case study with the aim to to assess influencing of negative schizophrenic symptoms using high frequency stimulation over the left dorsolateral prefrontal cortex within a simple blind randomised trial (sham and subsequent real rTMS) and following to consider the stability of potential improvement of negative symptoms in six months interval after rTMS therapy.

The study was carried out on a 42-year-old schizophrenic patient (paranoid subtype) with prominent negative symptoms. He had been suffering from schizophrenia for 72 months and taking clozapine 500 mg per day for two years. The patient signed an informed consent before inclusion into the trial.

The rTMS treatment was divided into two parts. He was treated with sham rTMS during the first three weeks and then with real rTMS during the following three weeks. Both forms of rTMS treatment were applied every working day, i.e. 5 times per week, up to the total number of 15 treatments. Severity of psychopathology was rated on PANSS, SANS, CDSS and MADRS before and after the sham and after the real rTMS therapy. The assessment of his clinical status and rTMS application was mutually blinded. The patient was blinded to the type of rTMS treatment, too. Then he was steadily monitoring in out patient setting. In period of six months after rTMS therapy the severity of psychopathology was rated again on PANSS, SANS, CDSS and MADRS. Pharmacological and psychosocial treatment was the same during all study.

The rTMS procedure proper was defined by the application locus (left dorsolateral prefrontal cortex), the intensity of magnetic stimulation (110% of motor threshold, the stimulation frequency (10 Hz), the duration of the pulse series (10 sec.), the intervals between individual sequences (30 sec.) and the total number of stimuli applied (1,500). The motor threshold was registered by an electromyograph to abductor pollicis brevis lat. dx. The motor threshold to be found is defined as the lowest stimulation activity to produce at least 5 motor potentials of amplitude 50 mV or greater per 10 individual impulses. The stimulation was performed using the Magstim Super Rapid device equipped with a focal figure 8-shaped coil that allowed continuous air cooling to prevent overheating during stimulation. Inefficacy of sham rTMS was achieved through stimulation coil position. To disable brain cortex stimulation sufficiently, the angle between the coil and the head surface was 90 degrees. In addition to that, the trial was blinded by preserving the sound produced during effective stimulation.

Concerning results basal score of total PANSS was 80, positive PANSS 13, negative PANSS 29, SANS 77, CDSS 0 and MADRS 12. The scores after sham stimulation and before real rTMS stimulation was 73 for total PANSS, 9 for positive PANSS, 30 for negative PANSS, 74 for SANS, 0 for CDSS and 9 for MADRS. The percentual changes of individual scales during sham rTMS were the following: a decrease over 9% in total PANSS, 31% in positive PANSS, 25% in MADRS, 4% in SANS, an increase over 3% in negative PANSS and no change in CDSS. The scores after real rTMS stimulation were 48 for total PANSS, 7 for positive PANSS, 18 for negative PANSS, 42 for SANS, 0 for CDSS and 3 for MADRS. The percentual changes of individual scales during real rTMS were following: a decrease over 35% in total PANSS, 23% in positive PANSS, 40% in negative PANSS, 67% in MADRS, 43% in SANS and no change in CDSS. In the end of the rTMS therapy, the patient was not able to identify which kind of rTMS treatment was effective and which not.

In period of six months after rTMS therapy the scores were 46 for total PANSS, 8 for positive PANSS, 17 for negative PANSS, 40 for SANS, 0 for CDSS and 4 for MADRS. The percentual changes of individual scales during six months after rTMS therapy (against scores after real rTMS) were as following: a decrease over 4% in total PANSS, 6% in negative PANSS, 5% in SANS, an increase over 14% in positive PANSS and 33% in MADRS, and no change in CDSS.

This small study presented data regarding to an effort to influence the negative symptoms of schizophrenia by high-frequency rTMS applied over the left dorsolateral prefrontal cortex and subsequently to evaluate the enduring of its potential therapeutic effect. Real rTMS led to a robust reduction of negative schizophrenic symptoms severity while no similar effect was observed in sham rTMS. A potential placebo effect was ruled out by performing sham stimulation before real rTMS. The observed alleviation of negative symptoms, a decrease of over 40% in negative PANSS and of over 43% in SANS, can also be considered as substantial from the clinical point of view.

The observed reduction in negative schizophrenic symptoms cannot be explained by the reduction of depressive symptoms as assessed on MADRS (decrease over 67%) alone. The MADRS score before real rTMS was 9. In trials dealing with treatment of depression, MADRS scores of 12 or less indicate good clinical response. Moreover the CDSS score, CDSS being a scale that distinguishes between depressive and negative schizophrenic symptoms, was zero before and after both sham and real rTMS treatment.

The patient was treated with antipsychotics on a long-term basis; the level of negative symptoms had remained constant and could not be influenced by pharmacotherapy to any greater degree. Thank to sham stimulation the therapeutic effect of rTMS would not be due to psychosocial or other enviromental factors like e.g. hospitalisation. The augmentation of rTMS led to a significant decrease of negative symptoms severity. A possible explanation for this result can be found in the potential of rTMS to influence the patophysiological basis of negative symptoms differently from antipsychotics.

The main contribution of our small study to the knowledge concerning possible treatment of negative symptoms of schizophrenia with rTMS can be seen in the fact that good therapeutic effect of rTMS has been lasting for at least six months after rTMS therapy. Medication and psychosocial conditions did not change during this period in any way. According to our information there is the first clinical experience that potential benefit of high frequency rTMS stimulation over left dorsolateral prefrontal cortex in the treatment of negative symptoms of schizophrenia can be lasting several weeks after the completion of rTMS therapy.

Certainly the results presented here should have been regarded in the light of the single case report study. The up to now very promising results must be verified in an adequately big population of patients within a double-blind randomised study design (Prikryl et al., 2007).

While the benefit of rTMS with regard to the negative symptoms of schizophrenia remains questionable (Freitas et al., 2009) there is a consensus regarding the potent therapeutic effect of rTMS in the treatment of isolated auditory hallucinations (Aleman et al., 2007; Freitas et al., 2009). However, only few studies refer to the benefit of rTMS in the treatment of delusions. The positive effects on delusions have only been occasionally reported (Pascual-Leone et al., 1996). According to a meta-analyses, low-frequency (1Hz) rTMS applied above the left temporoparietal cortex (TPC) is not suitable for treatment of delusions (Aleman et al., 2007; Freitas et al., 2009). Delusions, not like the auditory hallucinations, are associated with dysfunction of the orbitofrontal rather than temporoparietal cortex (Premkumar et al., 2008; Baas et al., 2008). Impaired gyrification of the orbitofrontal cortex, especially the lower volume of the medial orbital gyrus, is frequently found. They are associated with formal cognition disorders (Nakamura et al., 2007; 2008). Other findings originated from Diffusion Tensor Imaging (DTI) show a reduction of the white matter of the frontal cortex that correlates with impaired working memory (Schlösser et al., 2007). On the other hand, the parietal and cerebellar alterations of white matter cause delusions in the early stages of psychosis (Picard et al., 2007; Kyriakopoulos et al., 2008). All these findings show that other stimulation paradigms including the stimulation of sites other than the ones used in the previous studies need to be found for treatment of positive symptoms (e.g., delusions) of schizophrenia that go beyond isolated auditory hallucinations.

The stimulation parameters of the studies with rTMS differ mostly with regard to stimulation frequency, frequency of rTMS applications, stimulation intensity, or the overall number of stimulation impulses. There are relatively few studies involving stimulation of two brain regions. Simultaneous stimulation means that two brain regions are stimulated by rTMS at the same time using two stimulation doses. During sequential stimulation, we stimulate with one stimulation coil the first region followed by stimulation of the second region. This method of stimulation has been used in several rTMS studies focused on the treatment of depression and has yielded various results (Daskalakis et al., 2008). Only one study has been published regarding the treatment of schizophrenia using rTMS. However this work did not find any benefit of bilateral stimulation compared to unilateral stimulation of the left TPC in patients with resistant auditory hallucinations (Vercammen et al., 2009).

The human prefrontal cortex (PFC) is thought to be the brain structure responsible for control and integration of emotions, cognition, and the autoimmune nervous system. Common bilateral neuronal connections link the PFC with other cortical association areas such as the insula, limbic system, thalamus, and basal ganglia (Fuster et al., 1997; Langguth et al., 2007). The PFC also modulates the activity of dopaminergic neurons in the mesolimbic brain system by means of activation and inhibition pathways (Bertolino et al., 2000; Laruelle et al., 2003; Meyer-Lindenberg et al., 2002). Animal and human studies have shown that high-frequency rTMS applied over the PFC modulates the release of dopamine in the mesolimbic and mesostriatal system of the brain (Keck et al., 2002; Taber et al., 1995). The receptor, in vivo SPECT (single photon emission computed tomography) studies, has demonstrated a negative correlation between the density of benzodiazepine receptors and the positive symptoms of schizophrenia (Busatto et al., 1997). Due to the fact that the density of benzodiazepine receptors corresponds to the functional status of the type A subunit of the gamma butyric acid ($GABA_A$) inhibitory receptor, we can assume that the inhibitory system of the brain in schizophrenia is impaired. Because GABA neurons play a significant role in inhibition of brain interneurons, it is clear that schizophrenia is characterized by impairment of cortical inhibition. An imbalance of the fronto-temporal dopaminergic neurotransmitter system in the brain is considered to be a possible etiopathogenetic basis of schizophrenic symptoms (Prikryl et al., 2009). Therefore, we can theoretically assume that modulation of these pathways, using rTMS from two different stimulation sites, can produce more significant affects on these pathways and hence increase the therapeutic effects of rTMS on the basic symptoms of schizophrenia.

The case report was designed to investigate the influence of sequential fronto-temporal high frequency rTMS on schizophrenic symptoms in a single blind randomized design. To assess the impact of innovative stimulation paradigm on brain, the cortical silent period (CSP), which reflects a deficit of the cortical inhibition as an objective marker of reactivity, was also measured.

The study was carried out on a 35-year-old schizophrenic patient (paranoid subtype). He had been suffering from schizophrenia for 6 years and taking paliperidone 9 mg per day as monotherapy for the previous six months. The patient signed the informed consent before inclusion in the trial. The study was carried out in accordance with the Declaration of Helsinki; the study design was reviewed by the local ethics committee.

The rTMS treatment was divided into two parts. The patient was treated with sham rTMS during the first three weeks and then with actual rTMS during the next three weeks. Both rTMS treatments were applied 5 times per week (Monday through Friday), up to a total of 15 treatments per three weeks. The severity of the psychopathology was rated on the Positive and Negative Syndrome Scale (PANSS) before and after sham treatment and after actual rTMS treatment (Kay et al., 1987).

The actual rTMS procedure included two subsequent stimulations: a high-frequency rTMS above the left dorsolateral prefrontal cortex followed by a low-frequency rTMS above the left TPC with a 5 minutes delay between treatments. Both stimulation intensities were determined to be 110% of the individual motor threshold (MT). The stimulation parameters of high frequency rTMS were as follows: frequency: 10 Hz, duration of the pulse series: 10 s, interval between individual sequences: 30 s, total number of stimuli applied 1,500; the place of the stimulation: left dorsolateral prefrontal cortex (5 cm dorsally from the site of the motor cortex where the MT was registered). The stimulation parameters of low frequency rTMS were as follows: frequency: 0.9 Hz, duration of the pulse series: 20 minutes, total number of stimuli applied 1,080. Stimulation coil was placed over the left TPC defined as midway between the T3 and P3 EEG electrode sites in the international 10-20 system (Hoffmann et al., 2003).

The motor threshold was registered using an electromyograph attached to the abductor pollicis brevis lat. dx. The motor threshold was defined as the lowest stimulation activity to produce at least 5 motor potentials of amplitude 50 mV or greater per 10 individual impulses. Stimulation was performed using a Magstim Super Rapid TMS machine equipped with a focal figure 8-shaped coil, which allowed continuous air cooling to prevent overheating during stimulation. Inefficacy of the sham rTMS was achieved by maintaining an angle between the coil and the head surface of 90 degrees. In addition, stimulation was blinded by preserving the sound during both sham and active stimulation.

For the TMS measurements two magnetic stimulators (Magstim 200) were used and they were interconnected using a Bistim module (Magstim, Dyfed, UK) and a figure-eight stimulation coil with a diameter of 70 mm. The stimulation coil was placed on the surface of the patient's head in such a position relative to the motor cortex of the left brain hemisphere, so as it produced motor evoked potentials (MEP) with maximum peak to peak amplitude on the contralateral target muscle (musculus abductor digiti minimi). The optimal position of the stimulation coil was defined and fixed using recommended standards (Rossini and Rossi 1998). The stimulation coil attached to the scalp was directed occipitally with its holder and formed an angle of approximately 45 grades to the sagittal axis (i.e. approximately at a right angle to the central sulcus) (Brasil-Neto et al., 1992). With the stimulation coil in this position the induced electrical current expands in a anteromedial to posteriolateral direction approximately perpendicular to the direction of the central sulcus and preferentially activates the trans-synaptic corticospinal neurons (Werhahn et al., 1994). The induced cortical silent period was acquired using the application of single TMS pulses over the area of the motor cortex with an intensity of 1994 of the rest MT on the target muscle (musculus abductor digiti minimi) during willful weak tonic contraction. Duration of the CSP was defined as the time between the initiation of the MEP and return of willful EMG activity. This is called the absolute CSP and is concluded by any deviation of the EMG wave. (Wu et al., 2000). In total ten measurements were performed and then the CSP was acquired using automatic analysis performed by the EMG MedelecSynergy software.

Results demonstrated the effects of unipolar, left-sided, sequential fronto-temporal repetitive transcranial magnetic stimulation (rTMS) particularly on the positive but also on negative symptoms as well as the general symptoms of schizophrenia. A possible placebo effect was minimized by inclusion of a sham stimulation period, during which the patient was not informed about which type of rTMS therapy they were receiving. It is the first rTMS study which combines the two most widely used stimulation paradigms in the treatment of schizophrenia: (i) a high-frequency stimulation in the area of the left prefrontal cortex used especially in the treatment of negative symptoms of schizophrenia and (ii) a low-frequency stimulation of the left temporoparietal cortex which has proved to be effective in the treatment of isolated auditory hallucinations. A combination of both approaches may be provided promising clinical outcomes; probably based on enhanced modulation effects of rTMS on dopaminergic mesocortical and mesolimbic brain pathways.

The stimulation paradigm we chose caused a 50% reduction in positive subscale PANSS. In addition to the complete disappearance of the auditory hallucinations (P3) (improvement from to 6 to 1) there was also a reduction in delusions (P1) (improvement from 4 to 2) and suspicion (P6) (improvement from 4 to 2). Except for the full disappearance of the auditory hallucinations the sequential fronto-temporal stimulation also caused a reduction in the intensity of delusions and paranoia. While the effect of rTMS on auditory hallucinations is considered demonstrated, the positive effect on delusions has been reported only rarely (Pascual Leone 1996; 1996). The problem of effectiveness of rTMS on delusions may be due to the effects of rTMS on the dopaminergic system. It appears that the high-frequency rTMS antagonizes dopamine blockade by first generation antipsychotics in schizophrenia, which is evidenced by the fact that schizophrenic patients treated with first generation antipsychotics and by rTMS had a 50% reduction in the prolactin levels (Yu et al., 2002). Even if prolactin levels were not measured throughout stimulation therapy in our study, we may assume that the combination of high-frequency and low-frequency rTMS does not significantly interfere with dopamine blockade by antipsychotics. In addition, our patient was treated by paliperidone which is not a first-generation antipsychotic agent.

Except for positive symptoms, a considerable reduction in negative and general symptoms of schizophrenia occurred as well. This can be explained by activation of the PFC and mesolimbic dopaminergic pathways by high-frequency rTMS (Strafella et al., 2003. Based on functional imaging studies, we know that hypofrontality in schizophrenia is associated with negative symptoms and cognitive deficits (Hill et al., 2004; Weinberger et al. 2001). Moreover, the PFC plays an important role in modulation of the dopaminergic system of the brain by means of activation and inhibitory neuronal pathways (Bertolino et al., 2000; Laruelle et al., 2003; Peleman et al., 2009). Activation pathways from the PFC are mediated by direct and indirect glutamatergic projections into dopaminergic neurons. Inhibitory pathways are modulated by prefrontal glutamatergic efferent terminations on the GABA-ergic (gamma butyric acid) interneurons and striato-mesencephalic GABA neurons of the mid-brain. The dual modulation of the mesolimbic dopaminergic system by the PFC may be supported by studies which showed that the extracellular concentration of dopamine in the nucleus accumbens is increased or reduced by high-frequency or low-frequency stimulation of the PFC (Jackson et al., 2001).

A reduction in the severity of schizophrenic symptoms which occurred during rTMS therapy was associated with a prolongation of the CSP interval, which can be evaluated as an adjustment of cortical inhibition that is impaired in schizophrenia (Daskalakis et al., 2002). 2002). A reduced duration of the CSP is a marker of impaired cortical inhibition. The CSP duration is constantly found to be shortened in patients with schizophrenia, either without or with antipsychotics, compared to controls (Fitzgerald et al., 2002). The antipsychotic therapy extends the CSP and therefore causes an adjustment of abnormal cortical inhibition processes. (Daskalakis et al., 2002). A deficit of cortical inhibition in schizophrenia reflects the pathology of the cortical and subcortical brain areas. The abnormalities of the motor functions in schizophrenia are caused by the increased activity of the subcortical dopaminergic neurons which leads to disinhibition of cortical inhibitory neurotransmission (Walker et al., 1994). It is assumed that a reduced number of GABA-ergic interneurons in the prefrontal cortex, anterior cingulum, and hippocampus accounts for the deficit of inhibitory functions in schizophrenia (Benes et al., 1999). We speculate that the modulation of dopaminergic neurotransmission by rTMS affects the tone of not only dopaminergic but also associated GABA-ergic neurotransmission. This has been previously described in association with a reduction of auditory delusions together with a prolongation of the CSP (Langguth et al., 2006). The dynamic change of CSP during rTMS could be an objective marker of reactivity.

Modulation of the symptoms of schizophrenia, with the exception of the auditory hallucinations, by rTMS requires a new stimulation paradigm. Unipolar, left-sided, sequential fronto-temporal rTMS produce a significant reduction in all schizophrenia symptoms, especially the positive ones. A reduction in schizophrenic psychopathology was associated with prolongation of the CSP period, which can be assessed as an objective marker of reactivity. Since dual stimulation was well tolerated, it represents an alternative stimulation paradigm for treatment of schizophrenia. Complete verification will require a larger patient population sample, and preferably a double-blind study protocol. In conclusion unipolar, left side, sequential fronto-temporal rTMS caused alleviation of the symptoms of schizophrenia and was well tolerated. Therefore it may represent a new alternative therapy for schizophrenic patients (Prikryl et al., 2010)

META-ANALYSES OF THE rTMS STUDIES IN THE TREATMENT OF NEGATIVE SCHIZOPHRENIA SYMPTOMS

The efficacy of rTMS use in influencing the negative schizophrenia symptoms was, on the basis of so far published double blind studies also verified by means of two meta-analyses.

The first of them was published in 2009 (Freitas et al., 2009); in the area of assessment of rTMS efficacy on negative schizophrenia symptoms the total of 19 studies were analysed. The high frequency stimulation of the left PFC was used in 13 studies, 10 of them using the PANSS/SANS scale for the assessment of negative symptoms intensity changes. The statistical analysis finally included 8 studies because only in those studies average values and standard deviations had been available. The analysis indicated that the effect size corresponds to the value of 0.58, which represents mild to moderate effect of rTMS on the alleviation of negative schizophrenia symptoms. For comparison, the efficacy of rTMS in the treatment of isolated auditory hallucinations in the same meta-analysis was assessed as significantly higher (effect size 1.28). The results also indicate that the intensity of negative symptoms is considerably reduced if uncontrolled studies are included. However, if only controlled works are included in the analyses, the final therapeutic effect is lower. This reflects the presence of the placebo effect of rTMS, which is projected to the final result, especially in the open studies. The main conclusion of the meta-analysis therefore is that in patients treated by real stimulation there occurred only a statistically insignificant influence of the negative schizophrenia symptoms when compared to the placebo stimulation. Therefore, the hitherto used stimulation parameters do not seem to be sufficiently efficient. The explanation of the low effect of rTMS in this indication may also consist in the fact that the number of studies analysed was relatively low and, in addition, two works with positive results (Hajak et al., 2004; Jin et al., 2006) had been excluded due to insufficiently statistically supported data. Especially the Jin's study showed very promising results on the large population of patients, however, it was necessary to use the individualized alpha (8-13 Hz) frequency for successful treatment of negative schizophrenia symptoms.

The second meta-analysis published this year has concentrated only on verification of the rTMS efficacy in the treatment of negative schizophrenia symptoms (Dlabac-de Lange et al., 2010). Although 16 studies dealing with this theme had been found, due to methodological drawbacks or repeated publication of identical results only 9 of them were included in the final statistical analysis. Generally, the efficacy of rTMS was assessed on 213 patients (198 with schizophrenia and 15 with schizoaffective disorder). Upon the evaluation of the studies with any high-frequency stimulation of the left PFC, the effect of the treatment was low (d=0.43); when only the studies with 10 Hz frequency were included in the analysis, the effect of the treatment was moderate (d=0.63). In the event the studies without the presence of a stable antipsychotic medication during the course of stimulation had been excluded from the analysis, the effect of the treatment dropped to 0.34. The reason of such a decrease in the treatment effect consisted in the exclusion of the Goyal's study, since patients without medication had been included in the therapy and only during the course of the stimulation therapy antipsychotic drugs were started (Goyal et al., 2007). Another important conclusion of the meta-analysis is the finding that a longer stimulation therapy (three and more weeks) turned out to be more efficient than a shorter stimulation time (d=0.58 versus d=0.32).

CONCLUSIONS AND PERSPECTIVES FOR FUTURE RESEARCH

Future studies investigating rTMS efficacy on negative symptoms of schizophrenia should not only aim at the refinement of stimulation parameters with an effort to maximize the use of their potential; they should not only assess rTMS influence on the level of symptom reduction but should include functional potential changes or parameters in quality of life in the assessment. In the area of stimulation parameters, there is the possibility for application of a higher number of stimulation pulses during a single stimulation session, possibly two stimulation sessions in a single day. As known from rTMS studies in depression, twenty to thirty stimulation sessions show higher efficiency than half of that number (O'Reardon et al., 2007). Also, the possibilities of bifrontal stimulation have been only marginally investigated so far, not to mention the possibility of sequential stimulation of two brain areas (Prikryl 2010). To date, with the exception of the alpha activities change on the EEG, no changes in brain metabolism, in case of remission of the negative symptoms induced by rTMS stimulation, have been demonstrated, it is a question whether a statistical method, based on an analysis of the region of interest (e.g. frontal cortex), should be used for functional imaging instead of the commonly used voxel based analysis. The parameters such as quality of life, general functioning or change in cognitive functions have also been only minimally investigated. It is possible that any change in those parameters would be much more beneficial for patients than a mere reduction of the defined target symptoms. Future studies should also be aimed at the persistent effects of acute stimulation treatment with possible transfer of the patients to maintenance therapy, as in cases of electroconvulsive therapy.

Despite the promising results of some rTMS studies the potential of rTMS for the treatment of negative symptoms is currently relatively unclear. Large clinical studies are therefore needed, especially large multicentric studies like in depression rTMS studies (Cordes et al., 2009).

CONCLUSION

Schizophrenia is a serious disease, which can only partially be influenced by contemporary pharmacological treatment (Lieberman et al., 2005). Due to low adherence, a high degree of pharmacoresistance, associated with the progress of the disease, and deterioration of the socioeconomic status of patients, there is a logical pressure on augmenting treatments of negative symptoms, even if further large clinical studies are necessary to verify the natural benefit of this method for general clinical practice.

Dedication

This work was supported by a research plan of the Ministry of Education, Youth and Sports of the Czech Republic MSM0021622404 and grant IGA of the Ministry of Health of the Czech Republic No. 9890-4.

REFERENCES

[1] Aarre TF, Dahl AA, Hohansen JB, Kjoniksen I, Neckelmann D. Efficacy of repetitive transcranial magnetic stimulation in depression: a review of evidence. *Nordic Journal of Psychiatry* 2003; 57:227-232.

[2] Addington, D. et al., *Specificity of the Calgary Depression Scale for Schizophrenia Research*, 1994, 11, s. 239-244.

[3] Aleman, A., Sommer, I.E., Kahn, R.S., 2007. Efficacy of slow repetitive transcranial magnetic stimulation in the treatment of resistant auditory hallucinations in schizophrenia: a meta-analysis. *J. Clin. Psychiatry*. 68 (3), 416–421.

[4] Anders M, Dvorakova J, Rathova L, Havrankova P, Pelcova P, Vaneckova M, Jech R, Holcat M, Seidl Z, Raboch J. Efficacy of repetitive transcranial magnetic stimulation for the treatment of refractory chronic tinnitus: A randomized, placebo controlled study. *Neuroendocrinol Lett*. 31(2): 169-182.

[5] Baas, D., van't Wout, M., Aleman, A., Kahn, R.S., 2008. Social judgement in clinically stable patients with schizophrenia and healthy relatives: behavioural evidence of social brain dysfunction. *Psychol. Med*. 38 (5), 747–754.

[6] Benes FM (1999). Evidence for altered trisynaptic circuitry in schizophrenic hippocampus. *Biological Psychiatry* 46, 589-599.

[7] Ben-Shachar D, Gazawi H, Riboyad-Levin J, Klein E (1999). Chronic repetitive transcranial magnetic stimulation alters β-adrenergic and 5-HT_2 receptor characteristics in rat brain. *Brain Res*. 816: 78-83.

[8] Bertolino A, Breier A, Callicott JH, Adler C, Mattay VS, Shapiro M, Frank JA, Pickar D, Weinberger DR: The relationship between dorsolateral prefrontal neuronal N-acetylaspartate and evoked release of striatal dopamine in schizophrenia. *Neuropsychopharmacology* 2000; 22: 125–132.

[9] Brasil-Neto JP, Cohen LG, Panizza M, Nilsson J, Roth BJ, Hallett M (1992). Optimal focal transcranial magnetic activation of the human motor cortex: effects of coil orientation, shape of the induced current pulse, and stimulus intensity. *Journal of Clinical Neurophysiology* 9, 132-136.

[10] Bussato GF, Pilowsky LS, Costa DC et al (1997). Correlation between reduced in vivo benzodiazepine receptor binding and severity of psychotic symptoms in schizophrenia. *American Journal of Psychiatry* 154, 1398-1403.

[11] Cohen, E., Bernardo, M., Misana, J., Arrufat, F., J., Navarro, V., Valls, S. Repetitive transcranial magnetic stimulation in the treatment of chronic negative schizophrenia: a pilot study. *J Neurol Neurosurg Psychiatry*, 1999, 67, pp. 129-130.

[12] Colombo C, Gambini O, Macciardi F et al (1989). Alpha reactivity in schizophrenia and in schizophrenic spectrum disorders: demographic clinical and hemispheric assessment. *Int J Psychophysiol*. 7: 47–54.

[13] Couturier JL. Efficacy of rapid- rate repetitive transcranial magnetic stimulation in the treatment of depression: a systematic review and meta-analysis. *J Psychiatry Neurosci* 2005; 30:83-90.

[14] Daskalakis ZJ, Christensen BK, Chen R, Fitzgerald PB, Zipursky RB, Kapur S (2002). Evidence for impaired cortical inhibition in schizophrenia using transcranial magnetic stimulation. *Archives of General Psychiatry*, 59, 347-354.

[15] Daskalakis ZJ, Levinson AJ, Fitzgerald PB. Repetitive transcrabial magnetic stimulation for major depressive disorder: a review. *Canadian Journal of Psychiatry*, 2008, 53, 555-566

[16] Dell'osso B, Altamura AC. Augmentative transcranial magnetic stimulation (TMS) combined with brain navigation in drug-resistant rapid cycling bipolar depression: A case report of acute and maintenance efficacy. *World Journal of Biological Psychiatry,* 2008:1814-1412, first published on 13 November 2008

[17] Dlabac-de Lange JJ, Knegtering R, Aleman A (2010). Repetitive transcranial magnetic stimulation for negative symptoms of schizophrenia: review and meta-analysis. *J Clin Psychiatry* 71: 411-419.

[18] Feinsod, M., Kreanin, B., Chistyakov, A., Klein, E. Preliminary evidence for beneficial effect of low-frequency repetitive transcranial magnetic stimulation in patients with major depression and schizophrenia. *Depress Anxiety*, 1998, 7, pp. 65-68.

[19] Filip, V. et al. *Praktický manuál psychiatrických posuzovacích stupnic*. Psychiatrické centrum Praha, 1997

[20] Fitzgerald PB, Brown T, Daskalakis ZJ, Kulkarni J (2002). A transcranial magnetic stimulation study of inhibitory deficits in the motor cortex in patients with schizophrenia. *Psychiatry Research: Neuroimaging* 114, 11-22.

[21] Fitzgerald PB, Herciny S, Hoy K, McQueen S, Segrave R, Kulkarni J, Daskalakis ZJ (2008). A study of the effectiveness of bilateral transcranial magnetic stimulation in the treatment of the negative symptoms of schizophrenia. *Brain Stimulation*. 1: 27-32.

[22] Freitas C, Fregni F, Pascual-Leon A (2009). Meta-analysis of the effects of repetitive transcranial magnetic stimulation (rTMS) on negative and positive symptoms in schizophrenia. *Schizophrenia Research*. 108: 11–24.

[23] Fuster JM: *The Prefrontal Cortex*, ed 3. Philadelphia, Lippincott-Raven, 1997, pp 6–42.

[24] Geller, V., Grisaru, N., Abarbanel, J. M., Lemberg, T., Belmaker, R. H. Slow magnetic stimulation of prefrontal cortex in depression and schizophrenia. Prog. Neuropsychopharmacol. Biol. *Psychiatry*, 1997, 21, pp. 105-110.

[25] Gershon, A. A., Dannon, P. N., Grunhaus, L. Transcranial magnetic stimulation in the treatment of depression. *Am I Psychiatry*, 2003, 160, pp. 835-845.

[26] Goyal N, Nizamie SH, Desarkar P (2007). Efficacy of adjuvant high frequency repetitive transcranial magnetic stimulation on negative and positive symptoms of schizophrenia: preliminary results of a double blind sham-controlled study. *J. Neuropsychiatry. Clin. Neurosci*. 19: 464–467.

[27] Hajak, G., Marienhagen, J., Langguth, B., Werner, S., Binder, H., Eichhammer, P. High-frequency repetitive transcranial magnetic stimulation. in schizophrenia: a combined treatment and neuroimaging study. *Psychol Med*, 2004, 34, pp. 1157–1163.

[28] Havrankova P, Jech R, Walker N , Operto G, Tauchmanova J, Vymazal J, Dusek P, Hromcik M, Ruzicka E (2010). Repetitive TMS of the somatosensory cortex improves writer's cramp and enhances cortical activity. *Neuroendocrinol Lett*. 31(1): 73-86.

[29] Heimer L, Harlan RE, Alheid GF, Garcia MM, de Olmos J. Substantia innominata: a notion which impedes clinical-anatomical correlations in neuropsychiatric disorders. *Neuroscience* 1997; 76:957-1006.

[30] Hill K, Mann L, Laws KR, Stephenson CM, Nimmo-Smith I, McKenna PJ: Hypofrontality in schizophrenia: a meta-analysis of functional imaging studies. *Acta Psychiatr Scand* 2004; 110: 243–256.

[31] Hoffman R, Buchsbaum M, Escobar M, Makuch R, Neuchterlein K, Guich S (1991). EEG coherence of prefrontal areas in normal and schizophrenia males during perceptual activation. *J Neuropsychiatry Clin Neurosci*.3:169–175.

[32] Holi, M. M., Eronen, M., Toivonem, K., Toivonen, P., Marttunen, M., Naukkarinen, H. Left prefrontal repetitive transcranial magnetic stimulation in schizophrenia. *Schizophr Bull*, 30, 2004, pp. 429-34.

[33] Holtzheimer PE III, Russo J, Avery DH. A meta analysis of repetitive transcranial magnetic stimulation in the treatment depression. *Psychopharmacol Bull* 2001; 35:149-169.

[34] Jackson ME, Frost AS, Moghaddam B: Stimulation of prefrontal cortex at physiologically relevant frequencies inhibits dopamine release in the nucleus accumbens. *J Neurochem* 2001; 78: 920–923.

[35] Jandl, M., Bettner, R., Sack, A., Weber, B. Changes in negative symptoms and EEG in schizophrenic patients after repetitive Transcranial Magnetic Stimulation (rTMS): an open-label pilot study. *Journal of Neural Transmission*, 112, 2005, pp. 955.

[36] Jin Y, Potkin SG, Kemp AS, Huerta ST, Alva G, Thai TM, Carreon D, Bunney WE Jr (2006). Therapeutic effects of individualized frequency transcranial magnetic stimulation (rTMS) on the negative symptoms of schizophrenia. *Schizophr Bull*.32: 556–561.

[37] Karreman M, Moghaddam B. The prefrontal cortex regulates the basal release of dopamine in the limbic striatum: an effect mediated by ventral tegmental area. *J Neurochem* 1996;66:589-598.

[38] Kay, S.R., Fiszbein, A., Opler, L.A.: The positive and negative syndrome scale (PANSS) for schizophrenia. *Schizophr Bull.*, 13, 1987, pp. 261-276.

[39] Keck M, Welt T, Muller M, Erhardt A, Ohl F, Toschi N, Holsboer F, Sillaber I: Repetitive transcranial magnetic stimulation increases the release of dopamine in the mesolimbic and mesostriatal system. *Neuropharmacology* 2002; 43: 101.

[40] Kirkpatrick, B. Editor's Introduction: Theme Issue on Negative Symptoms. *Schizophr Bull*, 2006, 32, pp. 214-219.

[41] Kim AH, Reimers M, Maher B, Williamson V, McMichael O, McClay JL, van den oord EJ, Riley BP, Kendler KS, Vladimirov VI (2010). MicroRNA expression profiling in the prefrontal cortex of individuals affected with schizophrenia and bipolar disorder. *Schizophr Res*. 124(1-3): 183-191.

[42] Klirova M, Novak T, Kopecek M, Mohr P, Strunzova V (2008). Repetitive transcranial magnetic stimulation (rTMS) in major depressive episode during pregnancy. *Neuroendocrinol Lett* Vol 29 issue 1, 69-70.

[43] Klein, E., Kolsky, Y., Puyerovsky, M., Koren, D., Chistyakov, A., Feinsod, M. Right prefrontal slow repetitive transcranial magnetic stimulation in schizophrenia: a double blind sham-controlled pilot study. *Biol Psychiatry*, 1999, 46, pp. 1451-1454.

[44] Klemm E, Danos P, Grunwald F. et al (1996). Tempoval lobe dysfunction and correlation of regional cerebral blood flow abnormalities with psychopathology in schizophrenia and major depression – a study with single proton emission computed tomography. *Psychiatry Res*. 69: 1-10.

[45] Klirova M, Novak T, Kopecek M, Mohr P, Strunzova V (2008). Repetitive transcranial magnetic stimulation (rTMS) in major depressive episode during pregnancy. *Neuroendocrinol Lett*. 29(1): 69-70.

[46] Kozel FA, Nahas Z, deBrux C, Molloy M, Lorberbaum JP, Bohning D, Risch SC, George MS (2000). How coil-cortex distance relates to age, motor threshold, and antidepressant response to repetitive transcranial magnetic stimulation. *J. Neuropsychiatry Clin. Neurosci.* 12: 376–384.

[47] Kozel FA, George MS. Meta-analysis of left prefrontal repetitive transcranial magnetic stimulation (rTMS) to treat depression. *Journal of Psychiatric Practice* 2002; 8:270-275.

[48] Kyriakopoulos, M., Bargiotas, T., Barker, G.J., Frangou, S., 2008. Diffusion tensor imaging in schizophrenia. *Eur. Psychiatry*. 23 (4), 255–273.

[49] Langguth B, Eichhammer P, Kharraz A, Wiegand R, Hajak G. Repetitive transkranielle Magnetstimulation bei Schizophrenie. *Nervenheilkunde* 2003;22:1764-1768.

[50] Langguth B, Eichhammer P, Zowe M, Marienhagen J, Spiessl H, Hajak G (2006). Neuronavigated transcranial magnetic stimulation and auditory hallucinations in a schizophrenic patient : monitoring of neurobiological effects. *Schizophrenia Research* 84, 185–186.

[51] Langguth B, Wiegand R, Kharraz A, Landgrebe M, Marienhagen J, Fricks U, Kajak G, Eischhammer P (2007). Pre-treatment anterior cingulate activity as a predictor of antidepressant response to repetitive transcranial magnetic stimulation (rTMS). *Neuroendocrinol* Lett Vol 28 issue 5

[52] Laruelle M, Kegeles LS, Abi-Dargham *A: Glutamate, dopamine, and schizophrenia: from pathophysiology to treatment.* Ann NY Acad Sci 2003; 1003: 138–158.

[53] Lui S, Li T, Deng W, Jiang L, Wu O, Tang H, Yue O, Huang X, Chan RC, Collier DA, Meda SA, Pearlson G, Mechelli A, Sweeney JA, Gong Q (2010). Short-term Effects of Antipsychotic Treatment on Cerebral Function in Drug-Naive First-Episode Schizophrenia Revealed by "Resting State" Functional Magnetic Resonance Imaging. *Arch Gen Psychiatry*. 67:783-792.

[54] Martin JLR, Barbanoj MJ, Schlaepfer TE, Clos S, Perez V, Kulisevsky J et al. Transcranial magnetic stimulation for treating depression. *Cochrane Database of Systematic Reviews* 2004; 1.

[55] McNamara B, Ray JL, Arthurs OJ, Boniface S. Transcranial magnetic stimulation for depression and other psychiatric disorders. *Psychol Med* 2001; 31:1141-1146.

[56] Meyer-Lindenberg A, Miletich RS, Kohn PD, Esposito G, Carson RE, Quarantelli M, Weinberger DR, Berman KF: Reduced prefrontal activity predicts exaggerated striatal dopaminergic function in schizophrenia. *Nat Neurosci* 2002; 5: 267–271.

[57] Mogg A, Purvis R, Eranti S, Contell F, Taylor JP, Nicholson T, Brown RG, McLoughlin DM (2007). Repetitive transcranial magnetic stimulation for negative symptoms of schizophrenia: a randomized controlled pilot study. *Schizophr. Res.* 93: 221–228.

[58] Nahas Z, Teneback CC, Kozel A, Speer AM, DeBrux C, Molloy M, Stallings L, Spicer KM, Arana G, Bohning DE, Risch SC, George MS (2001). Brain effects of TMS delivered over prefrontal cortex in depressed adults: role of stimulation frequency and coil-cortex distance. *J Neuropsychiatry Clin Neurosci*. 13: 459-70.

[59] Nakamura, M., Nestor, P.G., McCarley, R.W., Levitt, J.J., Hsu, L., Kawashima, T., Niznikiewicz, M., Shenton, M.E., 2007. Altered orbitofrontal sulcogyral pattern in schizophrenia. *Brain* 130 (Pt 3), 693–707.

[60] Nakamura, M., Nestor, P.G., Levitt, J.J., Cohen, A.S., Kawashima, T., Shenton, M.E., McCarley, R.W., 2008. Orbitofrontal volume deficit in schizophrenia and thought disorder. *Brain* 131 (Pt 1), 180–195.

[61] Novak, T., Horacek, J., Mohr, P., Kopecek, M., Klirova, M., Rodriguez, M., Spaniel, F., Dockery, C., Hoschl, C. The double-blind sham-controlled study of high-frequency rTMS (20Hz) for negative symptoms in schizophrenia. Negative results. *Neuro Endocrinol Lett.* 2006, 25, pp. 209-213.

[62] Pascual-Leone A, Catala MD, Pascual-Leone A: Lateralized effect of rapid-rate transcranial magnetic stimulation of the prefrontal cortex on mood. *Neurology* 1996; 46: 499–502.

[63] Pascual-Leone A, Rubio B, Pallardo F, Catala MD: Rapid-rate transcranial magnetic stimulation of left dorsolateral prefrontal cortex in drug-resistant depression. *Lancet* 1996; 348: 233–237.

[64] Peleman K, Van Schuerbeek P, Luypaert R, Stadnik T, De Raedt R, De Mey J, Bossuyt A, Baeken C. Using 3D-MRI to localize the dorsolateral prefrontal cortex in TMS research. *World Journal of Biological Psychiatry*, 2009:1814-1412, first published on 26 January 2009

[65] Picard H., Amado I, Mouchet-Mages S, Olié JP, Krebs MO. The Role of the Cerebellum in Schizophrenia: an Update of Clinical, Cognitive, and Functional Evidences. *Schizophrenia Bulletin Advance Access* published online on June 11, 2007

[66] Post, R., M., Kimbrell, T. A., Frye, M. Implications of kindling and quenching for the possible frequency dependence of rTMS. *CNS Spectrums*, 1997, 2, pp. 54-60.

[67] Potkin, S.G., Alva, G., Fleming, K., Anand, R., Keator, D., Carreon, D., Doo, M., Jin, Y., Wu, J. C., Fallon, J. H. A PET study of the pathophysiology of negative symptoms in schizophrenia. *Am J Psychiatry*, 2002, 159, pp. 227-237.

[68] Premkumar, P., Kumari, V., Corr, P.J., Fannon, D., Sharma, T., 2008. Neuropsychological function-brain structure relationships and stage of illness: an investigation into chronic and first-episode schizophrenia. *Psychiatry. Res.* 162 (3), 195–204.

[69] Prikryl R, Kasparek T, Skotakova S, Ustohal L, Kucerova H, Ceskova E (2007). Treatment of negative symptoms of schizophrenia using repetitive transcranial magnetic stimulation in a double-blind, randomized controlled study. *Schizophr. Res.* 95: 151–157.

[70] Přikryl, R., Skotáková, S., Kašpárek, T., Češková, E., Kučerová, H., Pálenský, V. Six months alleviation from negative symptoms after repetitive transcranial magnetic stimulation (rTMS): a single case report study. *Psychiatrie* 2007; 11 (1): 21-23.

[71] Prikryl R, Ustohal L, Prikrylova Kucerova H, Ceskova E (2009). Paliperidon mediated modification of cortical inhibition. *Neuroendocrinol Lett* Vol 30, 275-420.

[72] Prikryl, R., Ustohal, L., Prikrylova Kucerova, H., Cermakova, I., Ceskova, E. Effect of sequential frontotemporal repetitive transcranial magnetic stimulation (rTMS) on schizophrenia. *Activitas Nervosa Superior Rediviva*, 2010, volume 52, No. 1, pp. 37-41

[73] Rollnik, J. D., Huber, T. J., Mogk, H., Siggelkow, S., Kropp, S., Dengler, R. High frequency repetitive transcranial magnetic stimulation (rTMS) of the dorsolateral prefrontal cortex in schizophrenic patients. *Neuroreport*, 2000, 11, pp. 4013-4015.

[74] Rossini PM, Rossi S (1998). Clinical applications of motor evoked potentials. *Electroencephalography and Clinical Neurophysiology* 106, 180-194.

[75] Sabri O, Erkwoh R, Schreckenberger M et al (1997). Regional cerebral blood flow and negative/positive symptoms in 24 drug-naive schizophrenics. *J Nucl Med.* 8: 181-188.

[76] Sachdev, P., Loo, C., Mitchell, P., Malhi, G. Transcranial magnetic stimulation for the deficit syndrome of schizophrenia: a pilot investigation. *Psychiatry Clin Neurosci.*, 2005, 59, pp. 354-7.

[77] Schlösser, R.G., Nenadic, I.,Wagner, G., Güllmar, D., von Consbruch, K., Köhler, S., Schultz, C.C., Koch, K., Fitzek, C., Matthews, P.M., Reichenbach, J.R., Sauer, H., 2007. White matter abnormalities and brain activation in schizophrenia: a combined DTI and fMRI study. *Schizophr. Res.* 89 (1–3), 1–11.

[78] Schneider AL, Schneider TL, Stark H (2008) Repetitive transcranial magnetic stimulation (rTMS) as an augmentation treatment for the negative symptoms of schizophrenia: A 4-week randomized placebo controlled study. *Brain Stimulation.* 1: 106–111.

[79] Stevens JR, Livermore A (1982). Telemetered EEG in schizophrenia: spectral analysis during abnormal behaviour episodes. *J Neurol Neurosurg Psychiatry.* 45:385–395.

[80] Strafella AP, Paus T, Barrett J, Dagher A (2001). Repetitive transcranial magnetic stimulation of the human prefrontal cortex induces dopamine release in the caudate nucleus. *J Neurosci.* 1: RC157.

[81] Strafella, A.P., Paus, T., Fraraccio, M., Dagher, A., 2003. Striatal dopamine release induced by repetitive transcranial magnetic stimulation of the human motor cortex. *Brain* 126, 2609-2615.

[82] Taber MT, Fibiger HC: Electrical stimulation of the prefrontal cortex increases dopamine release in the nucleus Accumbens of the rat: modulation by metabotropic glutamate receptors. *J Neurosci* 1995; 15: 3896–3904.

[83] Vercammen A, Knegtering H, Bruggeman R, Westenbroek HM, Jenner JA, Slooff CJ, Wunderink L, Aleman A. Effects of bilateral repetitive transcranial magnetic stimulation on treatment resistant auditory–verbal hallucinations in schizophrenia: A randomized controlled trial. *Schizophrenia Research* 2009, available on line

[84] Walker EF (1994). Developmentally moderated expressions of the neuropathology underlying schizophrenia. *Schizophrenia Bulletin* 20, 453-480.

[85] Weinberger DR, Egan MF, Bertolino A, Callicott JH, Mattay VS, Lipska BK, Berman KF, Goldberg TE: Prefrontal neurons and the genetics of schizophrenia. *Biol Psychiatry* 2001; 50: 825–844.

[86] Werhahn, KJ, Fong JK, Meyer BU, Priori A, Rothwell JC, Day BL, Thompson PD (1994). The effect of magnetic coil orientation on the latency of surface EMG and single motor unit responses in the first dorsal interosseus muscle. *Electroencephalography and Clinical Neurophysiology* 93, 138-146.

[87] Wolkin A, Sanfilipo M, Wolf AP et al (1992). Negative symptoms and hypofrontality in chronic schizophrenia. *Arch Gen Psychiatry*. 49: 959-965.

[88] Wu T, Sommer M, Tergau F, Paulus W (2000). Modification of the silent period by double transcranial magnetic stimulation. *Neurophysiology* 111, 1868-72.

[89] Yu HC, Liao KK, Chang TJ, Tsai SJ: Transcranial magnetic stimulation in schizophrenia. *Am J Psychiatry* 2002; 159: 494–495.

[90] Zaman R, Thind D, Kocmur M. Transcranial Magnetic Stimulation in Schizophrenia (2008). *Neuroendocrinol Lett* Vol 29 Supplement 1

INDEX

B

D

E

F

G

H

I

M

N

O

P

Q

R

S

T

X

Y

Z